Microsoft®

Microsoft System Center Configuration Manager 2007 Administrator's Companion

Steven D. Kaczmarek with the Microsoft System Center Configuration Manager team

PUBLISHED BY
Microsoft Press
A Division of Microsoft Corporation
One Microsoft Way
Redmond, Washington 98052-6399

Library of Congress Control Number: 2008920200

Printed and bound in the United States of America.

3 4 5 6 7 8 9 10 11 12 13 14 WCT 2 1 0

Distributed in Canada by H.B. Fenn and Company Ltd.

A CIP catalogue record for this book is available from the British Library.

Microsoft Press books are available through booksellers and distributors worldwide. For further information about international editions, contact your local Microsoft Corporation office or contact Microsoft Press International directly at fax (425) 936-7329. Visit our Web site at www.microsoft.com/mspress. Send comments to mspinput@microsoft.com.

Acquisitions Editor: Martin DelRe
Developmental Editor: Jenny Moss Benson
Project Editor: Melissa von Tschudi-Sutton
Editorial Production: Abshier House
Technical Reviewer: Greg Ramsey; Technical Review services provided by Content Master, a member of CM Group, Ltd.
Cover: Design by Tom Draper Design

Body Part No. X14-58149

I would like to dedicate this book to my parents, who proudly tell anyone who will listen that there is an author in the family. I am especially grateful to my partner, William, for his support and encouragement and to Scruffy, our Cairn terrier, who kept me from working too many continuous hours at my many computers by subtly reminding me of the importance of the occasional walk or wrestle. Finally, I want to call out the terrific writers who work with me in publishing all that great content about Configuration Manager and who continually impress me with their dedication to quality, their passion for you, our customers, and their incredible knowledge of and ability to navigate the often complicated synapses that is Configuration Manager.

Contents at a Glance

Part III
Site Database Management

Part IV
Appendixes

Table of Contents

Part I

Planning, Deploying, and Configuring

Part II
Managing Clients

Part III
Site Database Management

Part IV
Appendixes

Acknowledgments

Having authored and participated in the publication of several books in recent years, I can assert with conviction that the process takes the commitment of many people. This book was certainly no exception.

First and foremost, many thanks to the editorial team at Microsoft Press. Its dedication and hard work were outstanding in every respect. The editorial review process can be frustrating, but team members made the process comfortable for me, and I greatly appreciate their efforts, their comments, and their patience. In particular, thanks to Martin DelRe, my publisher, and to Melissa von Tschudi-Sutton and the excellent editorial team who made sure I dotted the i's and crossed the t's.

This book is intended to get the new administrator up and running and using the features quickly, and for the more experienced administrator as a quick reference for common tasks. Consequently, you'll notice that the book does not cover every nuance of this product. The Configuration Manager writing team whom I manage has already done a terrific job of documenting to that level of granularity in the Configuration Manager Documentation Library. Nevertheless, I realized early that I would reach the limits of my own expertise with this product quickly. So, I engaged five great additional writers from my team who are experts in their areas. I want to acknowledge them and their contributions to this book. Carol Bailey wrote Chapter 15, "Implementing Network Access Protection," and Chapter 16, "Managing Clients Across the Internet." Jeff Gilbert wrote Chapter 2, "Planning for and Deploying Configuration Manager Sites," and Chapter 5, "Upgrading to Configuration Manager." Rob Stack wrote Chapter 8, "Planning for and Installing Configuration Manager Clients," and Chapter 14, "Implementing Desired Configuration Management." Doug Eby, who also is architect of the Configuration Manager SuperFlow series, wrote Chapter 13, "Deploying Software Updates." Cathy Moya, my terrific project lead for Configuration Manager, wrote Chapter 20, "Configuration Manager 2007 Security."

One of our great partners in the community, Greg Ramsey, was our technical reviewer and did a superb job of keeping us on track and technically accurate. Thanks, Greg! Also, I'd like to acknowledge the particular assistance given by the following members of the Configuration Manager product team for their assistance in reviewing, researching, and gathering content. Thank you to Sangeetha Visweswaran, Development Lead, and Michael Wray, Software Development Engineer in Test, for your assistance with Chapter 15, and to Adam Meltzer, Software Development Engineer in Test, for your assistance with Chapter 16.

Finally, thanks to all of you—my customers, partners, and friends in the management community. Your support of our writing efforts has been invaluable.

Introduction

Microsoft has traditionally geared its development of Windows Server applications toward providing network administrators with tools that can facilitate the functionality and management of its Windows networks. For example, applications such as Microsoft Exchange 2007 and Microsoft SQL Server 2008 provide exceptional mail and database support through centralized management. Microsoft Systems Center Configuration Manager 2007 is just such a product. In this new release you have a superior product that provides centralized management and support for your install base of computers. Those of you who have grown up with Systems Management Server (SMS) 2003 and its plethora of tools, add-ons, and feature packs will be particularly impressed with the improvements made in this version, which enhances the functionality and scalability within large enterprise networks and the integration of features such as operating system deployment and mobile device management.

This book is designed to provide you with both a learning and practical guide to the administrative tasks you'll be performing with Configuration Manager. It is intended to get the new administrator up and running, and using the features quickly, and for the more experienced administrator as a quick reference for common tasks. Consequently, you'll notice that this book does not cover every nuance of this product. The Configuration Manager Writing Team at Microsoft has already done a terrific job of documenting to that level of granularity in the Configuration Manager Documentation Library. In fact, you'll find many references throughout the book that point you to the core documentation for more detailed information.

Part I: Planning, Deploying, and Configuring

Part I introduces the reader to Configuration Manager, outlining its features and functionality and comparing and contrasting it to the previous version, SMS 2003. This part also covers a wide range of topics specific to the installation and planning of a Configuration Manager site. Chapter 1, "Introducing System Center Configuration Manager 2007," presents an overview of Configuration Manager and identifies the new and updated features of the product, as well as an overview to navigating the Configuration Manager console. Chapter 2, "Planning for and Deploying Configuration Manager Sites," provides a detailed discussion of the installation process for a Configuration Manager primary site, including preinstallation requirements as well as postinstallation system modifications. You'll also learn how to navigate administrative functions using the Configuration Manager console, which uses the Microsoft Management Console (MMC) 3.0 format. In

Chapter 3, "Configuring Site Server Properties and Deploying Site Systems," you'll learn how to define and configure the Configuration Manager site and site systems. Chapter 4, "Implementing Multiple-Site Structures," suggests planning considerations for a multiple-site structure, including developing parent-child relationships among primary sites, creating secondary sites, and establishing Configuration Manager communication mechanisms between sites. Chapter 5, "Upgrading to Configuration Manager," shows you how to identify the decision points, and make the best choices, to plan your upgrade strategy and upgrade Configuration Manager successfully. Chapter 6, "Analysis and Troubleshooting Tools," introduces the reader to the various tools available in Configuration Manager that enable the administrator to monitor activity in the Configuration Manager site, track the flow of information, and analyze network and server performance. These tools are examined in more detail in subsequent chapters.

Part II: Managing Clients

Part II discusses three main areas of client system support through Configuration Manager: resource discovery, client installation, and remote control. Part II also discusses what is probably a Configuration Manager administrator's primary reason for purchasing Configuration Manager—the distribution of software and other packages to client systems through the network with little or no user intervention and the management of that software once it's installed.

Chapter 7, "Discovering Resources," and Chapter 8, "Planning for and Installing Configuration Manager Clients," describe the discovery and assignment process for Configuration Manager client systems. Before a client can be installed as a Configuration Manager client, it must be discovered and assigned to a Configuration Manager site. The various client setup methods are described, with the chapter focus being on the Client Push deployment method. Chapter 9, "Defining Collections," explains the concept of a collection in Configuration Manager and describes how collections are created and maintained.

Configuration Manager supports software inventory and hardware inventory, and the collection process for the Configuration Manager client is defined for both hardware and software inventory in Chapter 10, "Collecting Inventory." Chapter 11, "Distributing Software Packages," describes the package distribution process, including creating packages and programs, identifying package recipients through collections, and executing package commands at the client system. Chapter 12, "Deploying Operating Systems," discusses the operating system deployment feature of Configuration Manager—a tool for creating and managing images that can be deployed to computers managed by Configuration Manager 2007, and to unmanaged computers using bootable media such as a CD set, DVD, or USB. Chapter 13, "Deploying Software Updates," explains how you can use the software updates feature in Configuration Manager 2007 along with the Microsoft-recommended software updates management process to provide an effective system for updating software in your environment. Chapter 14, "Implementing Desired Configuration Management," introduces one of the key new features in Configuration Manager, desired configuration management. You'll learn how to configure this feature, download best practices configuration data, and how to evaluate your computers against this data. Chapter 15, "Implementing Network Access Protection," explores how you can use Configuration Manager's integration with Windows Network Access Protection (NAP) to help protect network assets, and extend central management of software updates with compliance enforcement. In Chapter 16, "Managing Clients Across the Internet," you'll learn how to use Configuration Manager to manage clients that are connected to your network through an Internet connection. In Chapter 17, "Managing Clients Remotely," you'll learn how to remotely monitor and troubleshoot a client system through the Configuration Manager console. Chapter 18, "Monitoring Software Usage with Software Metering," discusses how you can monitor and report on software usage on client systems.

Part III: Site Database Management

Part III covers a wide variety of topics related to the Configuration Manager database. Because the database itself must be maintained on a server running SQL Server 2005 Service Pack 2 or higher, this part approaches database management from two perspectives: management and reporting from within the Configuration Manager console, and maintenance and events related directly to SQL Server. In Chapter 19, "Extracting Information Using Queries and Reports," you'll learn how to query for and report on information kept in the database from within the Configuration Manager console. In Chapter 20, "Configuration Manager 2007 Security," you'll look at the new security mode provided with Configuration Manager, and explore how to make your Configuration Manager site secure. In Chapter 21, "Backing Up and Recovering the Site," you'll examine disaster recovery techniques. Chapter 22, "Maintaining the Configuration Manager Database through Microsoft SQL Server," covers SQL Server topics, including event triggers, SQL Server resources, and components used by Configuration Manager, maintenance and optimization techniques, and SQL Server backup and restore methods. This chapter isn't intended to be a primer for SQL Server; instead, it is designed to provide the SMS administrator with a basic understanding of SQL Server–related maintenance tasks.

Part IV: Appendixes

This book contains three appendixes. Appendix A, "Recommended Internet Sites," lists some of the Web sites that the author considers particularly useful for gathering additional information about or obtaining support for Configuration Manager and SQL Server 2005 Service Pack 2 or higher. Appendix B, "Backup Control File." contains the text for the backup control file used by the SMS Site Backup service when performing a site server backup scheduled through the SMS Administrator Console, as discussed in Chapter 21. Appendix C, "Understanding Windows Management Instrumentation," provides an overview of Windows Management Instrumentation.

How to Use This Book

Within the chapters, we've tried to make the material accessible and readable. You'll find descriptive passages, theoretical explanations, and step-by-step examples. We've also included a generous number of graphics that make it easy to follow the written instructions. The following reader's aids are common to all books in the Administrator's Companion series.

Real World   Title Starts Here

Everyone can benefit from the experiences of others. "Real World" sidebars contain elaboration on a theme or background based on the experiences of others who used this product during the beta testing period.

Note   Notes include tips, alternative ways to perform a task, or some information that needs to be highlighted.

More Info   Often there are excellent sources for additional information on key topics. We use these boxes to point you to a recommended resource.

Important   Boxes marked Important shouldn't be skipped. (That's why they're called Important.) Here you'll find security notes, cautions, and warnings to keep you and your network out of trouble.

Best Practices   Best Practices provide advice for best practices that this book's authors have gained from our own technical experience.

Security Alert   Nothing is more important than security when it comes to a computer network. Security elements should be carefully noted and acted on.

System Requirements

This book is designed to be used with the following software:

- System Center Configuration Manager 2007

- Microsoft SQL Server 2005 Service Pack 2 (or higher)

The following are the minimum system requirements to run the companion CD provided with this book:

- Microsoft Windows XP, with the latest service pack installed and the latest updates installed from Microsoft Update Service

- CD-ROM drive

- Internet connection

- Display monitor capable of 1024 x 768 resolution

- Microsoft Mouse or compatible pointing device

- Adobe Reader for viewing the eBook (Adobe Reader is available as a download at *http://www.adobe.com*)

About the Companion CD

The companion CD contains the fully searchable electronic version of this book and additional sample chapters from other titles that you might find useful. We've also included links to product TechCenter Web sites, tools, and Webcasts, and other useful information we found useful while we were writing this book.

This CD includes nine System Center Configuration Manager Feature Quizzes. These quizzes were developed by the System Center Configuration Manager 2007 User Assistance team to help you assess your understanding of the dependencies and requirements for key features of Configuration Manager. These quizzes are intended to raise your level of awareness of the some of the nuances of these features before you configure and use them. They can also be used to help train other Configuration Manager administrators within your organization.

Each quiz consists of 10 questions that can be answered Yes or No. Regardless of your answer, the quiz will display the correct information and include one or more links to the corresponding related content located in the Configuration Manager 2007 Documentation Library located on the Configuration Manager TechCenter (*http://technet.microsoft.com/configmgr/default.aspx*). These quizzes are published in downloadable format on the Microsoft Web site and can be found here: *http://www.microsoft.com/downloads/details.aspx?FamilyID=b9fb478a-ec98-47f2-b31e-57443a8ae88f&DisplayLang=en*. Periodically new quizzes will be added, and we encourage you to check the download site as well as the Configuration Manager Tech-Center for updates.

This CD also includes an audio excerpt from each chapter in .MP3 format. These excerpts were originally published on myITforum.com TV and are included here with permission from myITforum.com. myITforum.com, Inc. is the premier online destination for IT professionals responsible for managing their corporations' Microsoft Windows systems, especially for IT pros working with Microsoft Systems Management Server (SMS), System Center, Microsoft Operations Manager (MOM), Scripting, Windows Mobile, Group Policy (GPO), and Patching and Security. The centerpiece of myITforum.com, Inc. is a collection of member forums, e-mail lists, and technical articles where IT professionals actively exchange technical tips, share their expertise, and download utilities that help them better manage their Windows environments. myITforum.com, Inc. is owned and managed by Rod Trent, author of the best-selling books *Microsoft SMS Installer, Admin911: SMS*, and *IIS 5.0: A Beginner's Guide.* He has also written thousands of articles on topics related to the management of Microsoft Windows installations. Rod is a leading authority on Microsoft SMS and a regular speaker at the Microsoft Management Summit. Rod is also a member of a select group of Microsoft "Most Valuable Professionals" (MVPs), an honor accorded by Microsoft to "standouts in technical communities who share a passion for technology and the spirit of community."

Please visit *http://www.myitforum.com/aboutus/portfolio.asp* for a complete discussion of the value and benefits *myITforum.com* can bring to you and your organization.

Support

Every effort has been made to the accuracy of this book and companion CD content. Microsoft Press provides corrections to this book through the Web at *http://www.microsoft.com/mspress/support/search.aspx*

If you have comments, questions, or ideas regarding the book or companion CD content, please send them to Microsoft Press using either of the following methods:

E-mail: mspinput@microsoft.com

Postal mail:

Microsoft Press

Attn: *Microsoft System Center Configuration Manager 2007 Administrator's Companion* Editor

One Microsoft Way

Redmond, WA 98052-6399

Please note that product support is not offered through the preceding mail addresses. For support information, please visit the Microsoft Help and Support Web site at *http://support.microsoft.com.*

Part I
Planning, Deploying, and Configuring

Chapter 1
Introducing Microsoft System Center Configuration Manager 2007

Many computers

We will look after them now

Take the pain away

~ Rob Stack, Technical Writer, Configuration Manager

Welcome to Microsoft System Center Configuration Manager 2007, the newly engineered version of Microsoft System Management Server (SMS) 2003. The shorter name, Configuration Manager, is referred to throughout this book. This book gives you the insight and tools necessary to successfully plan for, deploy, and administer Configuration Manager. The fundamental components and features of Configuration Manager, such as distributing packages, collecting hardware and software inventory, distributing software updates, and remotely administering a computer, are explored, as well as new features such as deploying operating systems, managing desired configurations of users' computers, restricting noncompliant computers from accessing your network, and managing mobile devices. Planning and deployment procedures for site systems and clients are discussed, and the implementation of a Configuration Manager site hierarchy is examined. Relevant SMS 2003 migration and update readiness issues are also looked at, as well as disaster recovery and database maintenance recommendations.

As many of you know, Configuration Manager has gone through many generations and enhancements since its initial 1.0 release as Systems Management Server. Here's a brief history. Noting the shortcomings of the SMS 1.x family unabashedly reported to Microsoft by all of you SMS administrators, Microsoft released SMS 2.0. This was a complete renovation of the product that addressed many of the issues that SMS administrators raised. That version dropped some functionality (most notably the clunky Program Group Control), enhanced existing functionality (package distribution, inventory, and remote control), and added functionality (logon points, client access points, distribution points, and software metering). SMS 2003 further enhanced and refined the product, adding Active Directory support and integrating software update management. Configuration Manager represents the next generation of this product, integrating operating system deployment functionality, Windows Server Update Services, and desired computer configuration management among other features, and through sound planning and deployment, can very well help you to lower the total cost of ownership of computers in your organization.

To those of you who purchased the previous editions of this book, be assured that this isn't a repetition of the previous edition. To be sure, some features remain largely the same and so the content is refreshed only as needed. However, Microsoft has "touched" nearly every component in SMS 2003 as it generated Configuration Manager, so there is new material throughout. As always, there are new Configuration Manager administrators among you, so this chapter begins by introducing Configuration Manager and describing what this product is all about.

What Is System Center Configuration Manager 2007?

The computing industry has undergone many changes since the days of UNIVAC mainframes. In the early 1980s, the desktop computer as a viable business tool was relatively new. In fact, typical corporate discussions at the time centered around issues such as whether to purchase a desktop computer with a 10-MB hard drive at an additional cost of $1,700 because "users will just never need that much space."

Since that time, the desktop computer as a productivity tool has become a necessity in most organizations as well as in schools and at home. The need to provide processing power at the user's fingertips is a foregone conclusion. As a result, desktop computing has grown into a major industry and, consequently, a potentially huge administration headache. Desktop computer users can be territorial about their systems and the applications used. It's not unheard of to have an Information Technology (IT) group that supports a user running three different word-processing programs in several versions because that user is unwilling to risk converting the documents to a single word-processing version. On the other end of the spectrum, more businesses are taking advantage of tools like Configuration Manager, Microsoft Update, and Active Directory Group Policies to provide their users with a desktop that can not only be centrally maintained but also can't be modified at all by the user. Many businesses are now extending these tools and using other tools such as Systems Center Operations Manager (formerly Microsoft Operations Manager, or MOM) to support their server platforms as well. Both of these scenarios exemplify the fact that supporting multiple computers installed with a variety of program and server applications can be a challenge for even the best-equipped and best-funded IT support groups.

In addition to application support, IT groups often provide hardware support for their organization's users. This too can be a daunting prospect when the install base of computers is in the thousands or tens of thousands, deployed within different departmental, geographic, or international locations. It's not always practical—or even possible—to physically access every computer in an organization.

Many IT managers have acknowledged the need to provide standards for desktop computing and have begun to look for and to implement some kind of centralized desktop management system. IT support groups need to be able to respond actively and proactively to implement and update software on client systems and to respond to their users' requests for assistance as quickly, effectively, and consistently as possible. IT support groups should be able to perform as much user desktop management as possible while sitting at their own desktop computers. The key to effective remote desktop management is to provide a reliable set of remote management tools that enable an IT support group to be as effective as if they had actually laid hands on the user's desktop.

Configuration Manager is a powerful management product that offers a newly enriched set of desktop management features, with the capability of leveraging Active Directory. Configuration Manager, together with the other client management solutions that Microsoft offers, provides IT managers with perhaps their most effective set of centralized management tools to date. With Configuration Manager, you'll be able to remotely diagnose and troubleshoot desktop systems, install applications, and manage software.

In this major new release, the Configuration Manager product team has invested in four key development areas—security, simplicity, manageability, and operating system deployment—resulting in an end-to-end computer management solution.

What's Changed Since System Management Server 2003?

Configuration Manager offers new features, integration of external functionality, enhancements to existing features and functions, and improved security.

New Features

To support its commitment to enhancing computer manageability and security, the Configuration Management product team made a significant investment in developing and testing features that SMS customers had been asking for, and that they felt strongly would lead to a reduced total cost of ownership for many companies. These are alluded to earlier in this chapter. Configuration Manager has added the following new features:

- **Desired configuration management**   The ability to define granular computer configurations within your organization and compare and report compliance or non-compliance among your managed computers

- **Network Access Protection (NAP) for Configuration Manager**   The ability to leverage Windows Server NAP to identify and remediate managed clients using Configuration Management features such as software updates

- **Wake On LAN (WOL) support**   The ability to send a wake-up request to a Configuration Manager client that is in a sleep state to allow the running of a mandatory software update, software distribution advertisement, or task sequence

- **Internet-based computer management**   The ability to manage Configuration Manager 2007 clients when they are not connected to your company network but have a standard Internet connection

Integrated Features

Throughout the lifetime of SMS 2003, several feature packs and external wizards were developed and released. Recognizing the benefit to incorporating the most valuable of these into the product directly, the Configuration Manager product team invested in not only incorporating these into the core product, but also enhancing their functionality. The following external features have been integrated into Configuration Manager:

- **Operating system deployment**   The ability to create and manage images that can be deployed to computers managed by Configuration Manager 2007, and to unmanaged computers using bootable media such as CD set or DVD. The image, in a WIM format file, contains the desired version of a Microsoft Windows operating system and can also include any line-of-business applications that need to be installed on the computer. Also provides the ability to create and distribute task sequences—a series of one or more task steps that can be advertised to a Configuration Manager client—to customize image deployment and software distribution tasks.

- **Mobile device management**   The ability to manage Windows Mobile and Windows CE mobile devices similar to the way that Configuration Manager 2007 manages desktop computers, including hardware and software inventory, software distribution and updates, file collection, and Windows Mobile Settings.

- **Transfer Site Settings Wizard**   A wizard that facilitates the transfer of Configuration Manager site settings such as client agent properties, discovery configuration, package properties, and collection properties between Configuration Manager sites.

- **Manage Site Accounts tool**   A command-line interface that helps you update, create, verify, delete, and list user-defined Windows accounts for your Configuration Manager 2007 sites. It is called MSAC.exe and is located in <ConfigurationManager InstallDirectory>*AdminUI**bin*.

Enhanced Features

The following features, for a long time the mainstay of the core product, have undergone varying degrees of "plastic surgery." Wizards have been tightened up or eliminated in favor of simplified property pages, the "duh!" factor has been eliminated, or the feature simply has been brought into alignment with other server technologies. These features have all been enhanced:

- **Configuration Manager console**   As mentioned earlier in this chapter, the console has been reconfigured to group management tasks more intuitively, and facilitate finding tasks and features. It also displays information in three viewing areas: the console tree, for navigation; the results pane, for showing objects, charts, statistics, and other data related to the node you've selected in the console tree; and the actions pane, from which you can select actions related to the node you selected.

- **Collections**   The most notable change to collections is the addition of maintenance windows. A maintenance window lets you define a period of time within which changes can be made on the computers that are members of that collection.

- **Software updates**   Greatly enhanced from SMS 2003, software updates integrates closely with Windows Server Update Services (WSUS) 3.0, synchronizing with the WSUS database to retrieve the latest software updates from Microsoft Update, as well as custom published software updates. The Software Updates Client Agent is enabled by default, and updates are delivered to Configuration Manager clients by means of a deployment package rather than a software updates advertisement.

- **Remote tools**   Remote tools has been rehabbed to more effectively integrate with Remote Desktop and Remote Assistance. It includes a new remote tools agent, which uses the Microsoft RDP protocol supported on client computers running Windows XP and Windows 2003 Server and later. Windows 2000 clients use a modified version of the SMS 2003 Remote Tools agent. The Remote Reboot, Chat, File Transfer, Remote Execute, Ping, and Windows 98 Diagnostics utilities are no longer available in remote tools.

- **Backup and recovery**   Configuration Manager leverages the Volume Shadow Copy Service (VSS) available with Windows XP and Windows Server 2003 and later operating systems, providing the means to capture a stable backup image of your Configuration Manager site server, and store that image on the desired backup media.

Security and Site Modes

Configuration Manager has undergone significant enhancements in security as part of Microsoft's commitment to providing secure management environments. Configuration Manager security is discussed in detail in Chapter 20, "SCCM 2007 Security." As mentioned earlier, Configuration Manager gives you the ability to leverage the local system account and computer accounts to run services, connect between systems, and perform client-based functions, as well as the ability to leverage an existing Public Key Infrastructure (PKI) implementation to more fully secure site-to-site and site-to-client communications.

In addition, Configuration Manager now supports only one security mode, which functions the same as the SMS 2003 advanced security mode. Unlike SMS 2003, all site servers and site systems must belong to an Active Directory domain, and primary sites only support Windows Authentication for the Microsoft SQL Server site database. Configuration Manager offers two site modes: mixed and native. Mixed is intended for backward compatibility with Configuration Manager hierarchies that still support SMS 2003 sites or do not have PKI implemented. However, native mode is considered the more secure site mode and requires an existing PKI infrastructure.

And, of course, Configuration Manager has enhanced security in existing functions, and through new features, most notably with Network Access Protection.

Features and Functions of Configuration Manager

Configuration Manager offers centralized computer management in five primary areas:

- Inventory and resource management
- Diagnosis and troubleshooting

- Computer configuration management
- Site management
- Security

Inventory and Resource Management

Like its predecessor, Configuration Manager can collect and display resources deployed within your network. These resources include, of course, the workstations and servers that have been installed. You have the ability to discover and view your Windows domain users and groups, as well as any IP-addressable component connected to your local area network (LAN) or wide area network (WAN). Configuration Manager offers several configurable discovery methods, including four kinds of Active Directory discovery: Active Directory System Discovery, Active Directory User Discovery, Active Directory System Group Discovery, and Active Directory Security Group Discovery. Although not all discovered resources might be manageable, the administrator can display and view some basic properties. For example, a computer's discovery data includes its IP address, network card address (the Media Access Control [MAC] address), its computer name, and the domain of which it's a member. The process of discovering resources is discussed at length in Chapter 7, "Discovering Resources."

Note   The process of discovering a resource such as a computer doesn't automatically mean that Configuration Manager is installed on that computer. Nor does it mean that inventory is collected. Rather, it means that the "fact" of the resource being there is recorded along with some basic properties of that resource.

In addition to discovery data, Configuration Manager can collect hardware and software data from a Configuration Manager client. Two of the five client agents that can be installed on a Configuration Manager client computer are the Hardware Inventory Client Agent and the Software Inventory Client Agent. The Configuration Manager administrator enables and configures both and then installs them on a Configuration Manager client. Collected inventory is stored, viewed, and maintained in the Configuration Manager site database. This database is created and maintained on an SQL server. The Configuration Manager Administrator Console acts as a front end to this database and provides the Configuration Manager administrator with the tools to manage that data. For example, you view a Configuration Manager client's inventory through the Configuration Manager Administrator Console by selecting that client in an appropriate collection and executing a tool called the Resource Explorer. Configuration Manager also provides a number of pre-defined reports that can be viewed through the Configuration Manager console as well as through a Web report console.

When troubleshooting needs to be performed, it's not always possible, or even appropriate, that users have full knowledge of their hardware or software configuration. Having a Configuration Manager client's inventory readily available and up to date, however, provides an administrator with the computer configuration data needed to assist a user with a problem.

The Hardware Inventory Client Agent executes according to an administrator-defined frequency and collects system configuration such as hard drive space, processor type, RAM size, CD type, monitor type, and so on. In addition, you can configure the Hardware Inventory Client Agent to collect more granular information from Configuration Manager clients using the two template files included—SMS_DEF.MOF and Configuration.MOF—such as the installation date of the system's basic input/output system (BIOS), asset and serial number information, program group names, and printers installed. It does so by using the WMI service. WMI is Microsoft's implementation of Web-Based Enterprise Management (WBEM). (You can review the basics of WMI in Appendix C, "Understanding WBEM and WMI.") Briefly, WMI allows for more detailed system configuration data to be reported and stored on the workstation for use by management applications such as Configuration Manager. Once the Hardware Inventory Client Agent on a Configuration Manager client has collected the full inventory, only changes to the inventory on the client are reported in subsequent inventories. The hardware inventory process and configuration are discussed thoroughly in Chapter 10, "Collecting Inventory."

The Software Inventory Client Agent also executes according to an administrator-defined interval and essentially audits the Configuration Manager client for applications installed on its local hard drives. The Configuration Manager administrator can configure the Software Inventory Client Agent to audit other file types and report on specific files, as well as to collect copies of specific files. As with the Hardware Inventory Client Agent, the first time the Software Inventory Client Agent runs, a complete software audit or file collection takes place and the full inventory is gathered and reported. At each successive inventory interval, only changes to the audited files are reported. The software inventory collection and configuration process is discussed more completely in Chapter 10.

In 2006, Microsoft invested in a software product that can consolidate the software inventory collected by Configuration Manager and present this information in a more useable manner. This product, called Asset Intelligence, is included with Configuration Manager. When installed, it provides you with a set of reports that compares the software inventory against a master list of applications. Through a series of customizable reports, you can view the software installed on your managed clients by their "friendly" names, by class, and by suite. You learn more about this terrific feature in Chapter 10.

Diagnosis and Troubleshooting

Provided with Configuration Manager are several tools that can help the Configuration Manager administrator diagnose problems in the Configuration Manager site, problems with communications within and among sites, and problems with Configuration Manager client computers and troubleshoot those problems with little direct physical intervention. One of these tools is System Monitor.

System Monitor

When Configuration Manager is installed on a site server, it also adds several new objects that contain counters to the Windows 2000 Server and Windows Server 2003 Performance Monitor utility. These objects and their corresponding counters, along with the traditional Windows 2000 Server and Server 2003 objects and counters (Processor, Process, Memory, Logical Disk, Physical Disk, and so on) can assist the Configuration Manager administrator in performance-testing site systems and determining optimization alternatives. See Chapter 6, "Analysis and Troubleshooting Tools," for more information about working with Performance Monitor.

Remote Tools

Remote Tools has been perhaps the most appreciated feature of any Configuration Manager version. This utility enables the Configuration Manager administrator to gain keyboard and mouse control of a Configuration Manager client from the administrator's workstation. Through a video transfer screen, the administrator can "see" the user's desktop and diagnose and troubleshoot problems without having physical access to the remote client. As with the Hardware Inventory Client Agent and Software Inventory Client Agent, the amount of remote access that can be initiated is configured by the Configuration Manager administrator and rendered on the client by a Remote Tools Client Agent.

Remote Tools also includes remote diagnostic utilities specific to Windows NT 4.0 and later computers and other Windows operating systems that provide real-time access to system attributes such as interrupt usage, memory usage, services running, and device settings. You can also configure Remote Tools to manage the remote connection features of Windows XP Professional and later operating systems. This feature is discussed more thoroughly in Chapter 17, "Managing Clients Remotely."

Logs and Status Messages

All Configuration Manager services and processes create and update a wide variety of log files and generate detailed event status messages. These files and messages provide the Configuration Manager administrator with an extensive source of diagnostic data that's critical to the successful maintenance of the Configuration Manager site and also provide an ideal means to learn about the inner workings of Configuration Manager. Server-based log files aren't enabled by default to conserve server resources, but the Configuration Manager administrator can enable and configure them. Client-based log files are enabled by default and can be disabled through the client registry. You can view log files with any text editor.

Reports

Configuration Manager offers you the ability to create and manage meaningful reports directly through the Configuration Manager console. Features such as Asset Intelligence add to the robust set of reports available to the administrator. You learn more about reports and how to use them, including a feature called dashboards, in Chapter 19, "Extracting Information Using Queries and Reports."

Computer Configuration Management

One important way of reducing the total cost of owning and maintaining client computers is to minimize the amount of time an administrator needs to physically spend at a computer. When part of the administrator's job involves installing and upgrading software at a computer, applying software and security updates, installing or upgrading an operating system, or determining whether a computer is in compliance with company standards, the amount of time spent at each computer can be significant. Configuration Manager greatly enhances your ability to manage desktops remotely and reduce the total cost of computer ownership.

Through its package distribution feature, you can run programs on client computers to install and upgrade software, update files, execute tasks such as disk optimization routines, and modify configuration settings such as registry entries or INI files. Package distribution is discussed in detail in Part II, "Managing Clients."

The software updates feature integrates Windows Server Updates Services into the Configuration Manager infrastructure, allowing you a more seamless and efficient way to apply software and security updates in a timely fashion throughout your organization. Software updates are covered in detail in Chapter 13, "Deploying Software Updates."

Desired configuration management allows you to assess the compliance of computers with regard to a number of configurations, such as whether the correct Microsoft Windows operating system versions are installed and configured appropriately, whether all required applications are installed and configured correctly, whether optional applications are configured appropriately, and whether prohibited applications are installed. Additionally, you can check for compliance with software updates and security settings. A more detailed discussion of desired configuration management is provided in Chapter 14, "Implementing Desired Configuration Management."

Operating system deployment integrates the SMS 2003 Operating System Deployment Feature Pack into the product and provides you with a tool for creating operating system images for Windows operating systems such as Windows Vista that can be deployed to computers managed by Configuration Manager, and to unmanaged computers using bootable media such as CD set or DVD. This feature also provides a robust task-sequencing functionality that gives you more granular control over operating system deployment as well as other Configuration Manager tasks. You can read more about operating system deployment in Chapter 12, "Deploying Operating Systems."

Security

Configuration Manager gives you the ability to leverage the local system account and computer accounts to run services, connect between systems, and perform client-based functions. In addition, it offers the ability to leverage an existing PKI implementation to more fully secure site-to-client communications. A more detailed discussion of Configuration Manager security is provided in Chapter 20.

Configuration Manager also integrates Windows Network Access Protection services by using Configuration Manager to help bring computers determined to be outside defined security compliance parameters back into compliance. A more detailed discussion of the Network Access Protection feature is provided in Chapter 15, "Implementing Network Access Protection."

Key Elements of Configuration Manager

This section introduces and describes some of the key elements of Configuration Manager. These elements are referred to throughout the book and this introduction helps to set the context for later discussions.

At the highest level, you'll see the terms process and component frequently. The term *process* refers to a program that performs a specific Configuration Manager task. The term *component* refers to a computer running Configuration Manager software, in particular, server computers.

Configuration Manager Client

A *Configuration Manager client* is any computer that Configuration Manager manages. A Configuration Manager client can be a user's desktop or portable computer, workstation, mobile device, or a network server, including a Configuration Manager site server or site system. A Configuration Manager client can also be a computer running x86, x64, or IA64 processor platforms. Unlike SMS 2003, Configuration Manager offers only one client type. This client type is similar to the Advanced Client used by SMS 2003 and leverages Active Directory. Configuration Manager clients communicate with the site through the use of policies passed through management points and other Configuration Manager site systems. The following operating system platforms are supported by Configuration Manager clients:

- Windows 2000 Professional, Service Pack 4
- Windows XP Professional, Service Pack 2
- Windows Professional for 64-bit Systems
- Windows Vista, all editions
- Windows 2000 Server, Advanced Server, and Datacenter editions, Service Pack 4
- Windows Server 2003, all editions, Service Pack 1
- Windows Server 2003 R2 Standard and Enterprise editions
- Windows Server 2008

Configuration Manager Site

A *Configuration Manager site* defines the computers, users, groups, and other resources that Configuration Manager manages. Configuration Manager sites are defined by *site boundaries*. Site boundaries are defined by IP subnets, Active Directory sites IPv6 Prefix, or IP ranges. This means that you have a lot of flexibility as far as defining which resources you want to manage and allows Configuration Manager to scale more effi-ciently to your enterprise network. A Configuration Manager site consists of a Configura-tion Manager site server, Configuration Manager site systems, and Configuration Manager clients and resources. For those SMS 2003 administrators out there, the Config-uration Manager boundaries act like SMS 2003 roaming boundaries. There is no longer a separate site boundary setting.

Configuration Manager Site Server

The *Configuration Manager site server* is the Windows server on which Configuration Man-ager is installed and that manages the Configuration Manager site and all its component attributes and services. The Configuration Manager site server is the primary point of access between you and the Configuration Manager database. The site server can be either a primary or secondary site server (the distinctions are discussed later) and must be installed on a server running Windows Server 2003 (SP1 or later). If the Configuration Manager site server is a primary site, it also needs access to an SQL server running Microsoft SQL Server 2005, Service Pack 2. You can install a Configuration Manager site server on either a domain controller or a member server in a domain, but not on a stand-alone server.

Specific installation requirements for site servers are discussed in Chapter 2, "Planning for and Deploying Configuration Manager Sites."

Configuration Manager Site System

A *Configuration Manager site system* is a Windows server that performs one or more Configuration Manager roles for a Configuration Manager site. There are nine Configuration Manager site system roles:

- Management point
- Server locator point
- Distribution point
- Reporting point
- State migration point
- System Health Validator point
- PXE Server point
- Fallback status point
- Software update point

The first four look familiar to an SMS 2003 administrator as these "points" were around for SMS 2003. For the most part, they function the same as well. You'll also notice three new site system roles. Chapter 3, "Configuring Site Server Properties and Deploying Site Systems," covers all these roles in detail and also discusses additional server requirements necessary to support some new features and functionality of Configuration Manager. As with SMS 2003, you identify which servers should be Configuration Manager site systems within the Configuration Manager site, and assign various Configuration Manager roles or combinations of roles to those servers.

Note Configuration Manager no longer supports the Client Access Point role. This site system role existed to support the Legacy Client—computers running operating system platforms previously supported by SMS 2.0. Configuration Manager no longer supports Legacy Client computers.

Configuration Manager Console

A *Configuration Manager administrator* is the individual trusted with the implementation, maintenance, and support of a Configuration Manager site or specific objects in the Configuration Manager database. A *Configuration Manager console*, as shown in Figure 1-1, is the primary tool that a Configuration Manager administrator uses to maintain a Configuration Manager site. The Configuration Manager console can be installed on the following platforms:

- Windows XP Professional, Service Pack 2

- Windows Vista, all editions

- Windows Server 2003, all editions, Service Pack 1

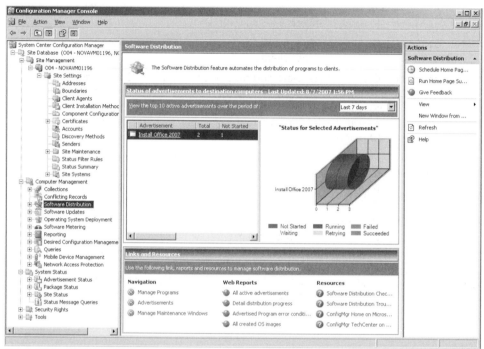

Figure 1-1 A representative Configuration Manager console displaying the different top-level objects that the Configuration Manager administrator can manage

The Configuration Manager Administrator Console is actually Microsoft Management Console 3.0 (MMC) (with .NET 2.0 installed) with the Configuration Manager Administrator snap-in added. The first thing a veteran SMS administrator notices is that instead of 12 top-level nodes in the console tree, there are 5 top-level Configuration Manager nodes in the Configuration Manager site database that can be administered. The console tree was redesigned to make it easier to find the Configuration Manager object that you want to administer. For example, in Figure 1-1, when you expand the Computer Management node in the console tree, you see the familiar SMS 2003 nodes, along with a couple of

new entries. The top-level nodes and the nodes under Computer Management are
described in Table 1-1.

Table 1-1   Configuration Manager Console Nodes

Node	Description
Site Management	Display the site hierarchy and contains site properties and site-wide component configurations, such as addresses, boundaries, client agents, installation methods, discovery methods, accounts, certificates, site systems, status filters, and summarizers.
Computer Management	Display components and features specific to the management of Configuration Manager clients.
Computer Management\ Collections	Create, delete, view, and modify predefined or Configuration Manager administrator–defined groupings of Configuration Manager resources, as well as view resource information, create advertisements, and initiate remote tools functions. Collections can consist of any Configuration Manager–discovered resources.
Computer Management\ Conflicting Records	Manage client records that Configuration Manager determines might be duplicate records (based on the hardware ID). You can merge duplicate records into one record, create a new record for the conflicting record, or create a new record and mark it blocked.
Computer Management\ Software Distribution	Display package and advertisements you create. A *package* is a set of files, programs, or commands that you want executed on a Configuration Manager client. Package programs are advertised to collections. Package files are stored in distribution points. An advertisement can be offered not only to Configuration Manager client computers, but also to any users or user groups that Configuration Manager has discovered.
Computer Management\ Software Metering	Monitor the usage of programs on Configuration Manager clients.
Computer Management\ Reporting	Create, modify, and run reports and dashboards.
Computer Management\ Queries	Provide a means of displaying database information based on a set of predefined criteria. Several queries are defined by default, and the Configuration Manager administrator can also create new queries.
Computer Management\ Software Updates	Maintain and distribute software and security updates to Configuration Manager clients.
Computer Management\ Network Access Protection	Leverage Windows Network Access Protection services using Configuration Manager to help bring computers determined to be outside defined security compliance parameters back into compliance.
Computer Management\ Operating System Deployment	Configure, maintain, and distribute operating system images to computers, as well as create task sequences to manage operating system deployment and other software distribution actions.

Table 1-1 Configuration Manager Console Nodes (Continued)

Node	Description
Computer Management\ Desired Configuration Management	Define granular computer configurations within your organization and compare and report compliance or noncompliance among your managed computers.
Computer Management\ Mobile Device Management	Manage Configuration Manager 2007 Windows Mobile and Windows CE mobile devices similar to the way that Configuration Manager 2007 manages desktop computers.
System Status	Equivalent in Configuration Manager to the Windows Event Viewer. Virtually every Configuration Manager service or process generates a robust set of status messages that outline the progress of that service or process. The information provided by the System *Status* object is the best place for a Configuration Manager administrator to begin troubleshooting.
Security Rights	Provide the capability to define and refine the level of access that users have when working with Configuration Manager objects. This gives you the ability to delegate specific tasks to specific groups of users.
Tools	Run the Configuration Manager Service Manager, for monitoring component and service status, stopping and starting Configuration Manager services and threads, and logging component and service activity.

One of the next things you notice when you look at the console is the new console layout. This layout is much more intuitive to use than previous consoles, although for veteran SMS administrators, this takes a little getting used to. You see that the screen is divided into three distinct areas. The left pane displays the traditional console tree and is where you do most of your navigation. As you select and highlight a node in the console tree, the middle, or results, pane displays information specific to that node. For example, if you highlight the Packages node, the results pane displays the packages that you have created and information about those packages. In Figure 1-1, the Software Updates node is highlighted. Notice the rich set of data that is displayed in the results pane. You can see the list of available software updates, a chart showing the breakdown of updates, and various ways to filter the data that is displayed. In addition, you are presented with reports and other links at the bottom of the pane that might be useful. The right pane, called the action pane, displays various actions or tasks that you can perform based on the node, or object in the results pane (like a specific package), that you have selected. Most of these actions can also be run by right-clicking the node in the console tree, or an object, such as a software update, in the results pane.

Veteran SMS administrators will be happy to learn that the Configuration Manager console now supports nested folders, drag and drop, and folder replication to child sites. The console and how to use and navigate it efficiently are covered in more detail in Chapter 2,

"Planning For and Deploying Configuration Manager Sites," and Chapter 7, "Discovering Resources," and, of course, as you tour the configuration and use of each feature.

Configuration Manager Site Hierarchy

A *Configuration Manager site hierarchy* resembles an organizational flowchart and exists whenever two or more Configuration Manager sites have been defined in a parent-child relationship. Configuration Manager site hierarchies provide a means of extending and scaling Configuration Manager support across a wide variety of organizational structures.

Parent and child sites are defined by their relationship within a Configuration Manager site hierarchy. A *parent site* is any site with at least one child site defined, and it has the ability to administer any child site below it in the Configuration Manager site hierarchy. A *child site* is any Configuration Manager site that has a parent defined. Child sites send discovery, inventory, and status information up to the parent site. Any Configuration Manager primary or secondary site can also be a child site. A Configuration Manager primary site can have a child site reporting to it, but a Configuration Manager secondary site can't.

A *Configuration Manager primary site* is a Configuration Manager site that has access to an SQL Server database. A Configuration Manager primary site can be directly administered through the Configuration Manager Administrator Console as well as by any Configuration Manager site above it in the Configuration Manager site hierarchy. A Configuration Manager primary site can also administer any child site below it in the site hierarchy. Configuration Manager primary sites can be children of other primary sites. They can also have child sites of their own. Configuration Manager primary sites can support all site system roles.

A *Configuration Manager secondary site* is a Configuration Manager site that doesn't have access to an SQL Server database. A Configuration Manager secondary site is always a child of a primary site and is administered solely through its parent or through another primary site above it in the Configuration Manager site hierarchy. A secondary site can't have child sites of its own nor can it support most site system roles. Site systems in a secondary site can be assigned the proxy management point role and distribution point role.

A *Configuration Manager central site* is a Configuration Manager primary site that resides at the top of the Configuration Manager site hierarchy. Inventory data, status messages, site control data, and discovery data roll from child to parent and are collected ultimately at the central site's Configuration Manager database. A Configuration Manager central site can administer any site below it in the Configuration Manager site hierarchy.

Figure 1-2 illustrates a simple Configuration Manager hierarchical model showing both primary and secondary sites as child sites of a central site. A Configuration Manager site system's roles don't all have to be enabled on the site server. Rather, these roles can be enabled on other servers in the domain.

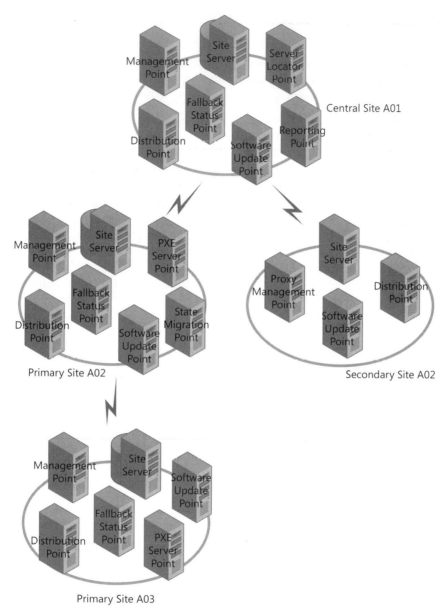

Figure 1-2   An example of a Configuration Manager hierarchical model

That's it for general terminology. All these components and terms are explored in more detail later in this book.

Summary

As you can see, Configuration Manager represents yet another significant advance from previous versions of SMS. It has a robust feature set that includes the ability to collect inventory information, distribute software applications, deploy software updates, and remotely manage clients. It offers increased functionality throughout its feature set along with improved client support and enhanced security, especially in the ability to leverage an existing certificate structure. It has incorporated and enhanced features that were previously available as add-ons, such as Operating System Deployment, and added new features to enhance client management and compliance such as desired configuration management and Network Access Protection. You have reviewed most of the enhancements and new features that you'll encounter when implementing and managing a Configuration Manager environment. You'll explore all of these more extensively as you progress through this book.

Chapter 2

Planning for and Deploying Configuration Manager Sites

This looks difficult.

I'll plan before I deploy,

To make it easy.

~ Jeff Gilbert, Technical Writer, Configuration Manager

Planning for Configuration Manager Sites

Installing Configuration Manager in a production environment without properly planning the deployment is not recommended. While great strides have been made to make Configuration Manager as simple to use as possible, it can still be a very complicated product and its deployment should be undertaken only after extensive planning.

Planning for Configuration Manager sites is broken down into two phases: preplanning and planning. In turn, each of the Configuration Manager planning phases is broken down into smaller sections that require specific attention during the planning process.

Preplanning Phase

The goal of the Configuration Manager preplanning phase is to document your current computing environment and identify which Configuration Manager features will be used to support your business and technical objectives. The Configuration Manager deployment is not directly focused on during the preplanning phase. Instead, this phase should be used to analyze and prepare your existing computing environment in preparation for Configuration Manager deployment.

During this phase, you should thoroughly examine and document your current computing environment and computer management objectives. After you identify the environment and objectives for installing Configuration Manager, you can create a test lab that represents your actual computing environment to begin deployment testing.

Examine and Document Your Current Computing Environment

As part of the preplanning phase, ensure that you have a thorough understanding of your computing environment. Documenting your computing environment will help you make decisions later during the planning phase of Configuration Manager deployment.

In general, the following preplanning information should be documented:

- **Organizational data** Create a high-level organization chart. This chart can be used to help assign Configuration Manager administration tasks and to develop a reporting structure for updating managers, users, and other Configuration Manager administrators about activities that may affect them.

- **Information Technology organization** Determine the IT support structure for your organization. Knowing about the administrators at both local and remote sites, and any local administrative policies affecting them, can help you decide whether or not to install a Configuration Manager site at their location.

- **Geographic profile** If your computing environment spans multiple time zones, it is important to know the time zone for each location. Also document any language differences for computer systems in use at all locations.

- **Active Directory** Document the logical and physical structure of your Active Directory environment. How domains and organizational units are configured, and which IP subnets have been assigned to what Active Directory sites, will be important information as you begin to plan your Configuration Manager sites.

- **Network topology** Create a high-level diagram of the network topology for your computing environment. Ensure that you identify the WAN/LAN architecture, the network bandwidth between locations, how heavily the links are used during different times of day, and the number of computers utilizing them. Knowing the

Active Directory sites, and the IP subnets assigned to them, for each location is also very important.

- **Server environment**   Document the location and function of the servers running core networking functions such as domain controllers, DNS servers, WINS servers, and IIS servers for each location that you will manage. Also take note of the operating systems and hardware that these servers are running on.

- **Client environment**   Determine the number of computers and the operating systems in use on the client computers in your environment. Any Group Policy objects affecting the clients or other administrative configurations should also be noted. How clients connect to your networking environment is also important to document. If users are connecting to the corporate network via VPN or from the Internet, you will need to plan to support them later.

- **Security**   Collect information about your organization's security policies. Document any account password policies, account rights policies, and any security lockdown policies in use.

More Info   To help document preplanning information, you can use the Configuration Manager preplanning worksheets located at *http://technet.microsoft.com /en-us/library/bb694080.aspx.*

Identify Business and Technical Needs

When preparing to deploy Configuration Manager, it is important to understand exactly what your business and technical needs are that have led you to consider deploying Configuration Manager in your environment. After defining these requirements, you can then map specific Configuration Manager features to them and begin the necessary planning to implement them.

When deciding which Configuration Manager features you will implement to support your goals, consider the amount of time it will take to implement them and what, if any, the impact will be on your project budget. For example, it may be necessary to hire additional administrators or purchase additional hardware or software licenses to support the features you use in your environment.

Create a Test Lab

Installing Configuration Manager in a production environment without first testing it on an isolated network can cause undesirable and potentially damaging results. The test lab should be a scaled-down representation of the production environment that will be managed by Configuration Manager. The test lab computers must use at least the minimum recommended configuration required for Configuration Manager client and site system role installations.

The test lab created should be used to perform tests throughout the planning process. Ensure that you use the test lab to test and verify the process of deploying Configuration Manager and installing Configuration Manager clients before beginning the pilot deployment in your production environment. After deploying Configuration Manager in your production environment, maintain the test lab for postdeployment and ongoing testing requirements.

Planning Phase

In the planning phase of Configuration Manager deployment, you plan the actual Configuration Manager hierarchy design and deployment strategy you will use. After the initial hierarchy design is completed, conduct a small pilot deployment to computers on your production network to verify your design and planning. As you perform these steps, test configuration variations and deployment scenarios in your test lab environment. Before beginning the deployment of Configuration Manager, consider the following:

Active Directory Planning

Knowing how Active Directory sites are configured (what subnets are assigned to each Active Directory site) is key to determining how you will assign Configuration Manager boundaries to sites. Also determine whether you will extend the Active Directory schema for Configuration Manager.

Checkpoints for Extending the Active Directory Schema for Configuration Manager

If you decide that you will need to extend the Active Directory schema for Configuration Manager you may need to build a strong case to the Active Directory administrators to get it done. Extending the Active Directory schema needs to be done only once per Active Directory forest, and once the schema is extended and the changes are replicated to all domain controllers, they are irreversible. Make sure that you review the online documentation about extending the schema and map the business requirements to the capabilities that Active Directory schema extensions provide.

It's best to extend the Active Directory schema before beginning Configuration Manager installation. If the Active Directory schema has been extended, the site server publishes site information at the end of Setup.

When extending the Active Directory schema for Configuration Manager, you need to create a container called System Management in the domain partition that the primary site server resides in, and then assign the site server's computer account full control permissions to the container *and all of its child objects* to allow the site server to publish site information to it. Do this for every domain that has a primary site server.

> **More Info**   For more information about deciding whether or not to extend the Active Directory schema for Configuration Manager, and how to do it properly, see "Decide If You Should Extend the Active Directory Schema" at *http: //technet.microsoft.com/en-us/library/bb694066.aspx* and "How to Extend the Active Directory Schema for Configuration Manager" at *http://technet.microsoft.com /en-us/library/bb633121.aspx.*

- **Discovery planning**   Determine how you will use the available Configuration Manager discovery methods to identify computer systems that you want to manage.

  > **More Info**   For more information about discovery methods, see Chapter 7, "Discovering Resources."

- **Client agent settings planning**   Determine the client agents that will be enabled and what their schedules should be.

- **Client installation method planning**   Determine how you will install the Configuration Manager client on discovered computer systems.

  > **More Info**   For more information about client installation and client agent planning, see Chapter 8, "Planning for and Installing Configuration Manager Clients."

- **Configuration Manager site planning**   Determine if you will have multiple Configuration Manager sites in your hierarchy. Will you need secondary sites to support clients located at remote sites over slow WAN connections? Are there computers that need to be managed over the Internet?

  > **More Info**   For more information about planning site structures, see Chapter 4, "Implementing Multiple Site Structures."

- **Configuration Manager site system planning**   Document the features that will be implemented, the business or technical goals that they support, and determine what site systems will be required to support them.

  > **More Info**   For more information about site system planning, see Chapter 3, "Configuring Site Server Properties and Deploying Site Systems."

■ **Backup and recovery planning**   It is important to plan how you will back up your hierarchy and develop a recovery plan in case of a site failure. Having a tested backup and recovery plan helps you to minimize the impact of a site failure should one occur.

> **More Info**   For more information about backup and recovery operations, see Chapter 21, "Backing Up and Recovering the Site."

■ **Security planning**   Configuration Manager is a powerful computer management technology and its use should be limited to authorized administrators only. If you will have multiple administrators for your Configuration Manager hierarchy, ensure that each has only the amount of access to enterprise systems as necessary.

> **More Info**   For more information about security planning, see Chapter 20, "Configuration Manager 2007 Security." More information about Configuration Manager security best practices can be found at *http://technet.microsoft.com/en-us/library/bb693588.aspx.*

Now that you have a pretty good idea of how you want to implement Configuration Manager to support your business and technical objectives, this is a good time to identify and coordinate with other administrators who will be involved in your deployment. For example, if you want to extend the schema, but your domain user account is not in the schema admins group, you will need to coordinate with someone with the necessary rights to extend the Active Directory schema and assign the appropriate permissions. As another example, if you will support Internet-based clients, you'll need to coordinate with the firewall administrators as well.

> **More Info**   For help in planning for Configuration Manager, you can use the Configuration Manager planning worksheets located at *http://technet.microsoft.com /en-us/library/bb694186.aspx.*

Site Mode Considerations

Configuration Manager sites can be configured to operate in one of two site modes: mixed mode and native mode. Site modes are used to configure client-to-server communication only, and provide no additional security benefits for site-to-site or server-to-server communication.

Configuration Manager site-to-site communication is secured by default using secure key exchange. Although you can disable this functionality on the Site Properties Advanced tab, it is not recommended to do so as this lowers the security of site-to-site communication. When sites communicate (site data replication or secondary site installation traffic), they verify the data being received by comparing the signature on the data to a public key for the sending site to verify that the data has been sent by a trusted site. If a receiving site does not already have the secure key for a sending site when data is received, it will attempt to retrieve the sending site's secure key from Active Directory Domain Services. If you have not extended the Active Directory schema, or sites are not publishing site information to Active Directory Domain Services, then you must manually exchange the site keys using the Preinst.exe tool. For more information about manually exchanging public keys between Configuration Manager sites, see "How to Manually Exchange Public Keys Between Sites" at *http://technet.microsoft.com/en-us/library/bb693690.aspx.*

More Info   To provide even stronger security for server-to-server communication, consider implementing IPsec. For more information about implementing IPsec for Configuration Manager sites, see "Implementing IPsec in Configuration Manager 2007" at *http://technet.microsoft.com/en-us/library/bb632851.aspx.*

Mixed Mode

Mixed mode is basically equivalent to SMS 2003 Advanced Security mode and is used to provide a supported site mode for environments without an existing public key infrastructure (PKI) and for backward compatibility with SMS 2003 sites and clients.

Although it is not as secure as native mode, consider using mixed mode when any of the following are true:

- The site will support SMS 2003 clients. Although an SMS 2003 client can be assigned to a mixed mode Configuration Manager site, Configuration Manager clients cannot be assigned to SMS 2003 sites.

- The site will support Windows 2000 Professional client computers. Windows 2000 Professional computers are not supported as native mode clients.

- The site has a parent site configured for mixed mode. Mixed mode sites can report to native mode sites, but native mode sites cannot be a child site of a mixed mode site.

- You have an existing PKI but have not yet installed the site server signing certificate on the site server. The site server signing certificate is required to be installed during Configuration Manager primary site installation.

More Info   Because mixed mode sites cannot use client certificates to authenticate clients, like native mode sites can using PKI, you must configure a client approval setting to allow clients to be fully managed by the site server. For more information about client approval, see "About Client Approval in Configuration Manager" at *http://technet.microsoft.com/en-us/library/bb694193.aspx.*

Native Mode

Native mode was introduced in Configuration Manager 2007 to provide a higher level of security between clients and servers than mixed mode provides as well as provide support for Internet-based clients.

Important   Native mode sites cannot be child sites of mixed mode sites, but mixed mode sites can be child sites of native mode sites. If you will support Internet-based clients or require native mode operations for any site in your hierarchy, ensure that the top-level, central site is configured to operate in native mode.

Before beginning the installation of a native mode Configuration Manager site, or migrating a mixed mode site to native mode operations, you must have all of the following configured:

- An existing Public Key Infrastructure (PKI).

- A site server signing certificate installed on the site server. The site server signing certificate is used to sign client policies.

- Web certificates installed, and IIS configured to use them, on the management point, site system distribution points (not server share or branch distribution points), software update point, and any proxy management point or state migration point site systems. The Web certificate on these site systems is used to encrypt data and authenticate the server to clients.

- Client authentication certificates on all Configuration Manager clients as well as the management point site system. The client authentication certificate is used to authenticate clients to site systems and monitor the health of the management point site system.

After installing a site in native mode, you will need to configure additional certificates if you plan to do the following:

- Support device clients

- Use the Operating System Deployment feature of Configuration Manager

- Use site systems configured to operate as part of a network load-balancing (NLB) cluster

There is no single method of deploying the required certificates for native mode sites. You'll need to create, install, and manage the certificates outside of Configuration Manager depending on your particular PKI deployment.

You can use any PKI that can support the certificates that native mode requires—it doesn't have to be Microsoft PKI, enterprise CA, or running on Enterprise Edition.

However, having all those things in place makes it a whole lot easier to manage the certificates. For example:

- A Microsoft Enterprise CA means that root certificates and intermediate certificates are automatically deployed to all computers in the forest.

- A Microsoft Enterprise CA makes auto enrollment and automatic renewal possible.

- The Enterprise Edition supports custom certificate templates, which makes specifying the site server signing certificate much easier.

More Info   For more information about deploying the required PKI certificates for native mode, see "Deploying the PKI Certificates Required for Native Mode" in the online documentation at *http://technet.microsoft.com/en-us/library /bb680312.aspx*.

Checkpoints for Planning Configuration Manager Installations

There are two main phases of planning required for Configuration Manager installations: preplanning and planning. The preplanning phase is used to document and verify your computing and network environment to aid you in planning for actual Configuration Manager deployment in the planning phase.

Be sure to identify areas that are outside of your normal administrative duties and responsibilities and coordinate with necessary administrators to ensure a smooth deployment.

Before beginning the deployment, ensure that you have a thorough understanding of Configuration Manager site modes and that you have prepared the environment for installation—especially if you will deploy a site operating in native mode.

Use the information collected during these planning phases to document a deployment plan and configure a test lab that represents your production environment to verify your deployment plan before beginning the pilot deployment or production deployment of Configuration Manager.

Preinstallation Requirements

After completing the preplanning and planning phases, and deciding which site mode you will use, you should be ready to begin the Configuration Manager deployment phase. Right? Wrong. Almost, though! Now that you have a pretty good idea about what you want to do with Configuration Manager, it's time to get down to the real details involved in preparing to deploy it.

More Info   Before beginning the installation process, ensure that your computing environment has been properly prepared. Begin by reviewing the Configuration Manager supported configuration and prerequisite documentation online at *http://technet.microsoft.com/en-us/library/bb680717.aspx* and *http://technet.microsoft.com/en-us/library/bb694113.aspx*, respectively.

After reviewing the Configuration Manager supported configurations documentation to determine the minimum supported hardware and general software requirements, you need to determine if the computers selected to host the basic Configuration Manager site systems are properly prepared for installation by ensuring that the necessary site system installation prerequisites have been installed.

General Site Server Prerequisites

There are a few general site server prerequisites required for computers chosen to host a Configuration Manager site system or site server role. Before beginning the setup process, ensure that these general site server prerequisites are met:

- Configuration Manager site systems must be members of a Windows 2000 or Windows 2003 Active Directory domain (installing a Configuration Manager site system on a domain controller server is possible, but not recommended).

- Primary site server computers must have the .NET Framework 2.0 installed (for hosting the Configuration Manager console).

- Internet Explorer 5.0 or later must be installed.

- Internet Information Services (IIS) 6.0 or later is required if the computer will be assigned any of the following site system roles:

    ❑ Management point (this role requires BITS server and WebDAV extensions).

    ❑ Reporting point (this role requires Active Server pages support).

    ❑ Software update point.

    ❑ Server locator point.

    ❑ Background Intelligent Transfer Service (BITS)-enabled distribution point. This role requires BITS server extensions and Web Distributed Authoring and Versioning (WebDAV) extensions. (IIS is not required for standard distribution point site systems.)

Note   Right now, you're only concerned with the core Configuration Manager site system roles (site server, SMS Provider computer, SQL Server, and management point) required for Setup. The remaining site system roles are discussed in Chapter 3, "Configuring Site Server Properties and Deploying Site Systems."

Site Database Server Prerequisites

Configuration Manager primary sites require an SQL Server 2005 (Service Pack 2 or later) database to store site information. Either SQL Server 2005 Standard or Enterprise Editions can be used to host the site database. However, it is not supported to use SQL Server 2005 Express Edition to host the site database.

> **Note**   Unlike previous versions of SMS, Configuration Manager allows you to install the site database using an SQL Server–named instance or even a clustered SQL Server virtual server instance name.

When installing SQL Server 2005 to host the site database, it is important to remember the following:

- The only SQL Server installation component required to host the site database is the SQL database service. However, if you only install the SQL database service component, you need to install the client components on another machine to access the database information natively through SQL Server 2005.

- Ensure that you document the collation settings used to install the SQL Server instance. For best results, each SQL Server instance installed later as part of the Configuration Manager hierarchy must use the same collation.

- Use the simple recovery mode to save hard disk space. The Configuration Manager backup and recovery solution makes snapshot backups only and tempdb files cannot be applied to the backup individually later.

SMS Provider Prerequisites

The SMS Provider is a WMI provider that is used by the Configuration Manager console and Resource Explorer to communicate securely with the site database. If you're going to create any custom tools or scripts to access the site database, you'll need to go through this provider as well.

> **More Info**   If the computer hosting the SMS Provider is offline, all Configuration Manager consoles for the site will not be able to communicate with the site database!

Because Configuration Manager 2007 allows you to install the SMS Provider on a computer other than the site server or site database server, check to ensure that the computer you identified to install the SMS Provider on meets the following prerequisites:

- The SMS Provider must be installed on a server-class computer in the same domain as the primary site server and SQL Server site database computers.

- The SMS Provider must be installed on a server-class computer using the same operating system language code page as the site server.

- The SMS Provider cannot be installed on a virtual SQL Server cluster instance or a computer hosting a virtual SQL Server cluster instance physical node.

- The SMS Provider cannot be installed on a computer already hosting the SMS Provider for a different site.

In previous versions of SMS, the installation location of the SMS Provider left very little installation footprint to worry about. In Configuration Manager 2007 installations, however, the SMS Provider installation can take up as much as 650 MB of hard disk space on the computer chosen to host this site role. The new disk space required is the result of the Windows Administration Installation Kit (Windows AIK) installation requirements to support the operating system deployment feature in Configuration Manager.

Configuration Manager Console Prerequisites

Before installing a remote Configuration Manager console, ensure that the computer that the Configuration Manager console will be installed on meets the following prerequisites:

- Windows XP Professional Service Pack 2 or later operating system

- Microsoft Management Console 3.0 is installed

- .NET Framework 2.0 is installed

Downloading Client Setup Prerequisites

During primary site or secondary site installation, the Configuration Manager Setup Wizard will prompt you to download the prerequisite components that must be installed on computers prior to running Configuration Manager client setup (CCMSetup.exe) on them to install the client. There are around 88 client prerequisite files (a little over 83 MB) that are required for Setup to continue. The first file to be downloaded is called ConfigMgr.Manifest.cab, which contains the .xml manifest file (ConfigMgr.manifest.xml) that lists the individual component files and from where they are to be downloaded. The files being downloaded include: Microsoft Remote Differential Compression Library (msrdcoob.exe in AMD64, IA64, and x86 versions), Windows Update Agent 3.0 (x86, x64, and IA64 versions), and BITS 2.0 and BITS 2.5 (in all supported client languages), and a WMI update for Windows 2000 computers. During the download process, you can see the files being downloaded, and from where they're being downloaded, by watching the ConfigMgrSetup.log log file. When you install a management point site system, the downloaded client installation prerequisite component files are transferred from the site server to the new management point to enable client installation processes to succeed.

There are two Setup Wizard pages used for downloading prerequisite client installation files: the Updated Prerequisite Components page and the Updated Prerequisite Component Path page.

The Updated Prerequisite Components page of the Configuration Manager Setup Wizard offers you two choices for obtaining client prerequisite files. You can either check for updates and download the newest prerequisite component files directly from Microsoft using the Internet, or if you have already downloaded the files to an alternate location, you can select the option to specify an alternate location to obtain the prerequisite component files, as shown in Figure 2-1.

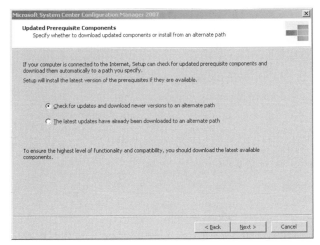

Figure 2-1   The Updated Prerequisite Components page

> **Note**   Even though you can use the same alternate source location for multiple Configuration Manager installations, if it has been a while since you downloaded them last, you should always download the latest available components in case the files have been updated since you last downloaded them.

The Updated Prerequisite Component Path page of the Configuration Manager Setup Wizard is used to specify the path to store or access the downloaded client installation prerequisite component files. If you chose to download the files from the Internet, the downloaded client installation prerequisite files are stored in the path specified. If you chose to specify an alternate location for the prerequisite files, type the path to where you have stored the downloaded files on this page, as shown in Figure 2-2.

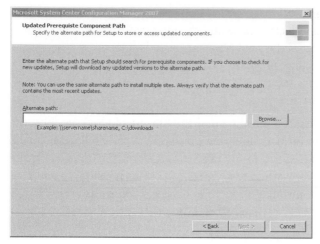

Figure 2-2   The Updated Prerequisite Component Path page

If your site server computer does not have Internet connectivity, you'll need to download the client installation prerequisite files and use the alternate location option. To download the files from a different computer, just start Configuration Manager Setup on a computer with Internet connectivity and use the following command: Setup/download <path to store files>. After the download has completed, ensure that the site server computer can access the downloaded prerequisite files and use the alternate location during site server installation. In some cases, you may need to store the downloaded files on a removable media to transfer to the site server computer itself.

Important   An additional step may be required in this process when performing secondary site push installations from a primary site because the secondary site installation wizard does not contain the client prerequisite component download pages.

When using installation media at the secondary site computer to install the secondary site using the secondary site installation wizard (the Install The Source Files From The Local Disk Or Removable Media At The Secondary Site Server option) create a subfolder called Redist under the SMSSetup directory in the installation source files and save the downloaded files there.

If you select the option to push the source files over the network to install the secondary site (the Copy Installation Source Files Over The Network From The Parent Site Server option), this step is not necessary.

Configuration Manager Setup Prerequisites

After verifying that the computers selected for hosting Configuration Manager site systems in your environment meet at least the minimum supported hardware requirements, you can begin the prerequisite checking process to ensure the software requirements are also met. To verify that required Configuration Manager Setup prerequisites are installed, you can use the Setup Prerequisite Checker utility.

The Setup Prerequisite Checker is automatically launched as part of the Configuration Manager Setup Wizard. It is used to verify that required installation prerequisite files have been installed. However, it is recommended to run the Setup Prerequisite Checker on systems as a planning tool before beginning the actual Configuration Manager Setup process to ensure a smooth and successful installation experience. This is especially true if you will be running an unattended setup (discussed later in this chapter).

You can launch the Setup Prerequisite Checker independently of Configuration Manager Setup from the installations splash screen (splash.hta) located in the root of the installation source files. To launch the Setup Prerequisite Checker from the installation splash screen, click Run The Prerequisite Checker, as shown in Figure 2-3.

Figure 2-3   The Configuration Manager Setup splash screen

Once started, the Setup Prerequisite Checker can be used to verify that required setup prerequisites are installed for both new setup and upgrade processes using the following options, as shown in Figure 2-4.

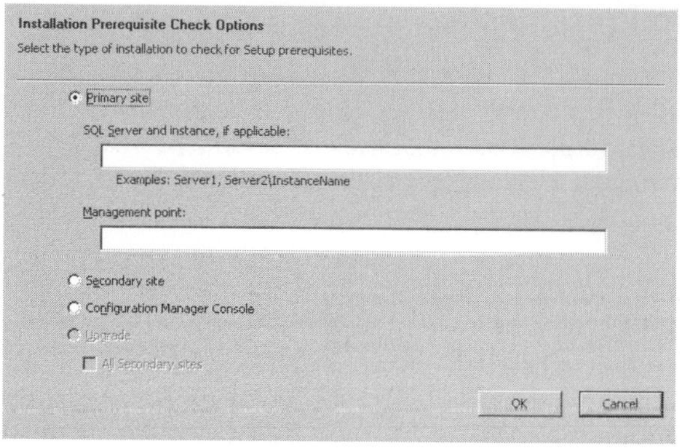

Figure 2-4   The Configuration Manager Setup Prerequisite Checker launched independently of Setup

- **Primary Site**   This option is used to verify that setup prerequisites are installed for new Configuration Manager primary site installations. When this option is selected, you must also provide the SQL Server name—and instance name if using a named instance of SQL Server—that will be used to host the site database. Optionally, if you want to install a management point site system during Setup, you can provide a computer name to verify management point installation requirements as well. Both of these site systems can be installed on the site server computer or be remote server computers to the site server itself.

- **Secondary Site**   This option is used to verify that setup prerequisites are installed for new secondary site installations.

- **Configuration Manager Console**   This option is used to verify that setup prerequisites are installed for new Configuration Manager console installations.

If SMS 2003 or previous versions of Configuration Manager components are already installed, the Setup Prerequisite Checker can be used with the following options to verify that all required Setup prerequisites are installed before beginning the upgrade process. (Upgrades are covered in Chapter 5, "Upgrading to Configuration Manager," but for now, here are the upgrade prerequisite options displayed.)

- **Upgrade**   This option is used to verify that setup prerequisites are installed for upgrading primary sites, secondary sites, and SMS 2003 administrator consoles or Configuration Manager consoles.

- **All Secondary Sites**   This option can be used to verify that upgrade prerequisites are installed on all secondary sites attached to a primary site being upgraded.

> **Note**   Even if you've run the Setup Prerequisite Checker outside of regular wizard-based Configuration Manager Setup, it will be run again during Setup to ensure that the required prerequisites are installed or configured properly. It is recommended to run the Setup Prerequisite Checker outside of Setup as a planning tool and to be sure that the actual installation will proceed successfully.

Configuration Manager Setup Options

There is more than one way to perform a Configuration Manager installation. You can use setup command-line options, the Configuration Manager Setup Wizard, or perform an unattended installation using a setup initialization file.

Before beginning any type of setup, ensure that you have properly prepared your environment for installation:

- Complete the necessary preplanning and planning steps.

- Review the supported configurations to ensure that you are using supported hardware and software.

- If you will extend the Active Directory schema for Configuration Manager, you can do so before or after installing a site, but it's recommended to do it beforehand.

- Review the installation prerequisites, and run the installation prerequisite checker to verify installation prerequisites are installed.

- If you will be deploying a native mode site, ensure that you have deployed the necessary PKI certificates required for successful site installation.

Configuration Manager Setup Command-Line Options

Configuration Manager Setup supports a number of command-line options that enable you to perform customized Configuration Manager installations and other actions. To see the supported setup command-line options, just navigate to setup.exe and use the following command to show the setup.exe command-line usage: setup /?. To use one of the supported setup command-line options, just navigate to the location of setup.exe (.\SMSSETUP\BIN\<i386, ia64, or x64 depending on your operating system>) and add the setup command-line option. For example, to install a site without starting Site Component Manager after the site is installed, use the following command:

SETUP /DONTSTARTSITECOMP

> **Note**   Capitalization of the setup command-line options is not important. They are capitalized here to help them stand out.

There are three main areas that the setup command-line options can help you with: checking for prerequisites, performing new installations, and preparing for or actually upgrading installations. Upgrades are covered in Chapter 5, but for now, here are some of the setup command-line options used to install new Configuration Manager installations:

- **/DOWNLOAD** This setup command-line option is used to download client prerequisite installation files without starting Configuration Manager Setup. When you use this command-line option, you must provide a path to save the downloaded files and run the command on a computer with an active Internet connection. Later, during actual site installation, you can specify this path as the alternate path to obtain the client prerequisite installation files. So, to save the client prerequisite files downloaded to C:\redist, your command line would look like: SETUP /DOWNLOAD c:\redist.

   Note It's also important to ensure that the site server will be able to access this location during site setup, so you should share out the folder so the site server can access it over the network later.

- **/TRACING:OFF** This setup command-line option disables logging of setup actions.

- **/NODISKCHECK** This setup command-line option disables verification of disk space requirement checking.

- **/DONTSTARTSITECOMP** This setup command-line option installs a site, but does not start the Site Component Manager (sitecomp) service. Using this command-line option causes the site to be inactive after installation has completed. The Site Component Manager service will be started automatically when the site server computer is restarted.

- **/NOUSERINPUT** This setup command-line option disables user input, but displays the Setup Wizard interface.

- **/NODEFAULTCOLL** This setup command-line option disables the creation of the default Configuration Manager default collections except for the All Systems collection.

- **/ALLCLIENTOPTIONSON** This setup command-line option enables all client agents.

- **/HIDDEN** Does not display the Setup Wizard interface. This command should be used with the /SCRIPT option (the /SCRIPT setup command-line option is used to perform unattended installations and is discussed later in this chapter).

   Note The setup command-line option /RESETSITE can be used after a site is installed to perform a site reset.

Using the Configuration Manager Setup Wizard

The Configuration Manager Setup Wizard is used to install new primary and secondary Configuration Manager sites as well as new Configuration Manager consoles.

More Info   The Configuration Manager Setup Wizard can also be used to perform upgrades, as you will see in Chapter 5.

Using the Configuration Manager Setup Wizard is a fairly straightforward process that won't be covered in too much detail here. Instead, the focus will be on the two installation settings options that you have for installing Configuration Manager sites: Custom Setup and Simple Setup. Later in the chapter, you'll walk through the various pages of the Setup Wizard that you see when installing primary or secondary sites and Configuration Manager consoles.

Configuration Manager Setup Wizard Installation Settings Options

When using the Configuration Manager Setup Wizard to install a primary site, there are two installation settings options available to you: Custom Settings and Simple Settings, as shown in Figure 2-5.

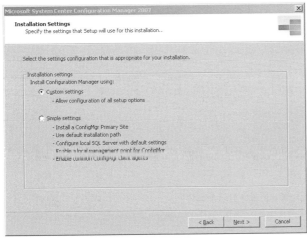

Figure 2-5   The Configuration Manager Setup Wizard Installation Settings page

Configuration Manager Simple Setup

The Simple Setup installation option installs a primary site in mixed mode, enables all of the common client agents (all except for NAP), enables all discovery methods except for network discovery, enables the client push installation method, and configures a single server to host all of the necessary site server roles for basic site operations. Simple Setup does not create boundaries for the site, cannot be used to install a secondary site, and requires SQL Server to be installed on the site system computer.

After successfully completing Simple Setup, the site server installed will host the following site system roles:

- Primary site server
- Site database server
- SMS Provider computer
- Management point
- Distribution point

Note   Because of the lack of customization available and limitations involved with using this setup option, Configuration Manager Simple Setup is generally recommended only for lab or evaluation purposes.

Configuration Manager Custom Setup

In most cases, you'll probably use the Custom Setup option for installing Configuration Manager sites. The Custom Setup option allows you to customize all of the setup options available for installing primary or secondary Configuration Manager sites as well as the option to install a Configuration Manager console.

By default, a distribution point site system role is installed on the site server computer and boundaries for the site are not created. However, when using the Custom Setup option to install Configuration Manager primary or secondary sites, you can configure the following:

- Whether to install the site in mixed mode or native mode. (If native mode is selected, you must also select a site server signing certificate.)
- A custom Configuration Manager 2007 installation directory.
- The Configuration Manager client agents to enable. (By default, all client agents are enabled except for the NAP client agent.)
- The SQL Server computer and instance name to use to host the site database. (The SQL Server computer can be a remote SQL Server computer or even an SQL Server cluster virtual instance name.)
- Where to install the SMS Provider components. (The SMS Provider components are required and can be installed on the site server, the site database server—unless it is a clustered SQL Server instance—or another computer.)
- Whether or not to install a local or remote management point site system.

- The ports that clients will use to communicate with Configuration Manager site systems. (http ports for mixed mode, https ports for native mode.)

Performing Unattended Configuration Manager Installations

New primary or secondary sites and Configuration Manager consoles can be installed using a custom setup initialization (.ini) file to answer the questions for which the Setup Wizard would normally prompt you during a wizard-based installation except that there are no default values. This is called performing an unattended or script-based installation.

To perform an unattended installation, create and use a setup initialization file. The setup initialization file is basically an answer file written in notepad.exe (or some other word processing program) with the .ini file extension that answers all of the Setup Wizard's questions so you don't have to use the wizard to answer them.

> **More Info**   For more information about Configuration Manager unattended installations, see "Unattended Setup Overview" at *http://technet.microsoft.com /en-us/library/bb693561.aspx*.

To instruct Setup to use a scripted installation file instead of prompting you for answers with the wizard pages, just use the setup command line /SCRIPT and then provide the location (full path) to the setup initialization file that you have previously created. You can also use the /HIDDEN setup command-line option to perform a completely unattended installation. All together, your setup command line would look similar to: SETUP /HIDDEN/SCRIPT *<full path to your .ini file>*.

> **Note**   Examples of how to do this for each of the installation options are described later in this chapter.

Installing Configuration Manager Primary Sites

There is more than one way to install a Configuration Manager primary site. The following sections describe how to install a Configuration Manager primary site in these ways:

- Attended installation using the Configuration Manager Setup Wizard
- Unattended installation using a custom setup initialization file (scripted setup)

Primary Site Installation Using the Configuration Manager Setup Wizard

The Configuration Manager Setup Wizard is used to perform an attended, wizard-based, primary site installation. This is the most common way to install a primary site, and you should be thoroughly familiar with these setup options before attempting to perform unattended installations.

You can start the Configuration Manager Setup Wizard from the splash screen (splash.hta) located in the root of the installation media or by starting setup.exe directly from the .\SMSSETUP\BIN\<i386, ia64, or x64 depending on your operating system> directory.

Configuration Manager Setup Wizard Pages for Installing Primary Sites

This section walks you through the installation of a primary site using the Configuration Manager Setup Wizard.

1. The first page of the Configuration Manager Setup Wizard displayed is the Welcome page, as shown in Figure 2-6. No action is necessary on this page except to click Next.

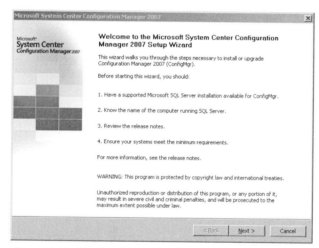

Figure 2-6   The Configuration Manager Setup Wizard Welcome page

Note   As soon as the Welcome page opens, Configuration Manager Setup goes to work. The ConfigMgrSetup.log (which records setup actions) and ConfigMgrPrereq.log (which records prerequisite checking) files are created in the root of the system drive and begin the process of logging the installation actions. Even at this point of the installation, the ConfigMgrPrereq.log has already checked for the existence of previous installations in the system registry and the ConfigMgrSetup.log records the Active Directory schema extensions check.

2. On the Available Setup Options page, shown in Figure 2-7, select the Install A Configuration Manager Site Server option.

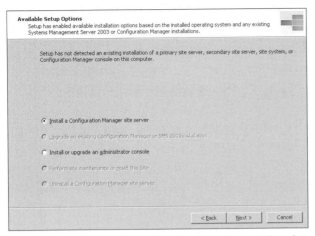

Figure 2-7   The Configuration Manager Setup Wizard Available Setup Options page

> **Note**   The available setup options enabled depend on the operating system of the computer that Setup is being run on and whether or not previous installations are discovered by Setup on the computer.

3. On the License Terms page, shown in Figure 2-8, you should read the license agreement terms and then agree with them to continue.

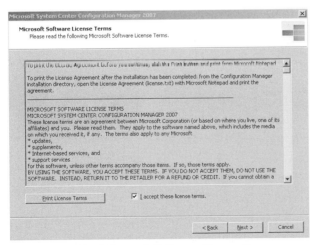

Figure 2-8   The Microsoft Software License Terms page

4. On the Installation Settings page, shown in Figure 2-9, choose whether to install the site using custom settings or simple settings, which were described earlier in this chapter. For this example, select Custom Settings (custom setup) to install a primary site.

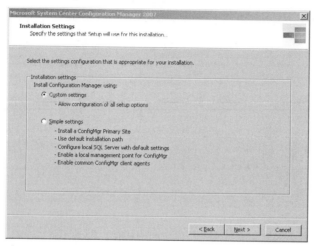

Figure 2-9   The Configuration Manager Setup Wizard Installation Settings page

5. On the Site Type page, shown in Figure 2-10, specify the type of site to install. You can choose to install a Primary Site or Secondary Site. Select the Primary Site option.

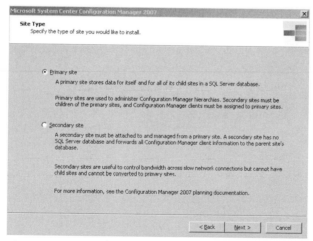

Figure 2-10   The Configuration Manager Setup Wizard Site Type page

6. On the Customer Experience Improvement Program Configuration page, as shown in Figure 2-11, you can choose a program participation selection. The Customer Experience Improvement Program (CEIP) is used to collect statistical information about your system's configuration, the performance of some components of Configuration Manager, and certain types of events generated by Configuration Manager. The data collected is not used to identify or contact you or your company.

    If you choose to participate in the program, a small summary file is automatically uploaded to Microsoft periodically containing collected information from the Configuration Manager console installation. CEIP settings are per user, per machine, and there is no site configuration which globally controls CEIP participation. If multiple administrators use the same Configuration Manager console installation, the default CEIP participation setting is based on the value selected when the console was installed. If one administrator changes the settings for the Configuration Manager console instance they use, it does not affect the other Configuration Manager console instances used by other administrators when they log on to the computer hosting the Configuration Manager console.

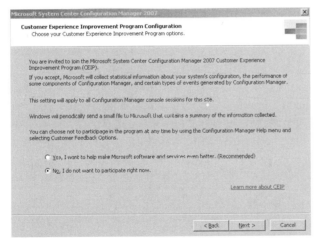

Figure 2-11   The Configuration Manager Setup Wizard Customer Experience Improvement Program Configuration page

---

Note   It is not necessary to participate in the program to install Configuration Manager. If you decide to participate in the program, you can discontinue participation later from within the Configuration Manager console.

7. On the Product Key page, shown in Figure 2-12, you must type a valid product installation key to enable Setup to continue.

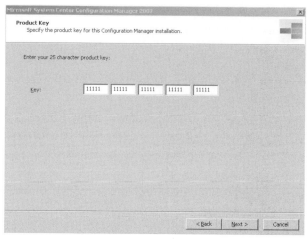

Figure 2-12   The Configuration Manager Setup Wizard Product Key page

8.   On the Destination Folder page, shown in Figure 2-13, you must specify the installation folder that will be used to install Configuration Manager installation files.

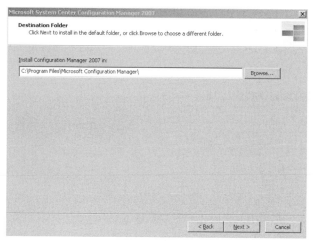

Figure 2-13   The Configuration Manager Setup Wizard Destination Folder page

9.   On the Site Settings page, shown in Figure 2-14, you must specify the site code and site description that will be used to identify this site in the hierarchy. Before assigning a site code, ensure that you have planned out your site naming conventions and are sure that the site code entered is the site code you want to use.

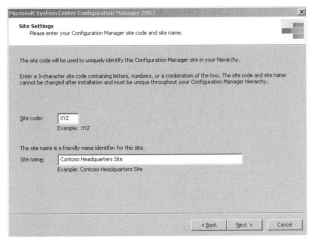

Figure 2-14   The Configuration Manager Setup Wizard Site Settings page

> **Important**   It is not supported to change either the site code or site description after the site is installed.

10. On the Site Mode page, shown in Figure 2-15, you select the site mode that the site will operate in after installation has completed—either native mode or mixed mode. For this example, mixed mode is selected.

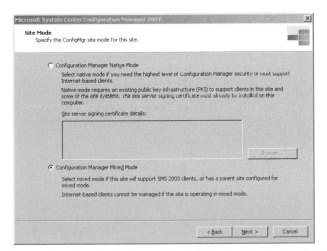

Figure 2-15   The Configuration Manager Setup Wizard Site Mode page

> **Important**   If you select native mode, you must also select a site server signing certificate on this page to continue.

11. On the Client Agent Selection page, shown in Figure 2-16, you can modify the client agents that will be enabled when the site installation has completed. By default, all client agents are enabled except for the Network Access Protection Client Agent.

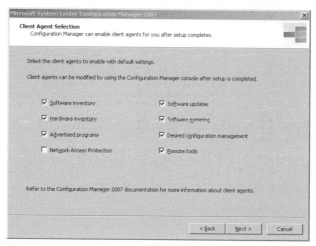

Figure 2-16   The Configuration Manager Setup Wizard Client Agent Selection page

12. On the Database Server page, shown in Figure 2-17, you must specify the Microsoft SQL Server computer that will be used to host the site database and what you will name the site database itself.

The site database SQL Server computer must be running at least SQL Server 2005 Service Pack 2. If SQL Server is installed on the site system computer itself, the site server's name will be shown in the SQL Server name data entry text box. You can overwrite this name if you prefer to install the site database on a different SQL server by entering the NetBIOS name of a remote SQL server or remote SQL Server instance name. If the SQL server is remote to the primary site server computer, the primary site server computer must have administrative rights to the SQL Server computer (the administrative rights are required to enable the site system to install necessary backup and recovery components later).

> **Note**   You can use the same SQL Server computer to host the site database for more than one Configuration Manager primary site. However, you can't install the SMS Provider on the SQL Server computer if it hosts the site database for more than one Configuration Manager site.

A suggested site database name is shown in the site database name data entry text box based on the site code you assigned the site earlier. You can change the site database name at this point if you prefer to call it something else. Using the suggested site database name on this page will enable Setup to create the site database for you using the SQL Server setup defaults. If you prefer to create the site database using nondefault SQL Server setup options, you can create an empty database yourself and specify it on this page for Setup to use during site installation.

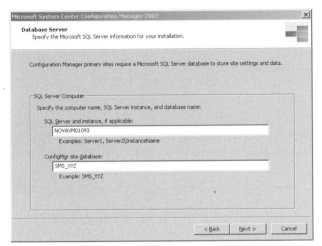

Figure 2-17   The Configuration Manager Setup Wizard Database Server page

> **Note**   If you have specified a remote SQL server to host the site database, at this point in the Setup Wizard the site server will try to connect to the remote SQL server to verify if the SQL Server instance specified is clustered and the version of SQL Server installed. If you see the following error when you click Next on this page of the Setup Wizard—*Could not connect or execute SQL query on a remote SQL server*—then you probably have the Windows Server firewall service enabled on the remote SQL Server computer.

13. On the SMS Provider Settings page, shown in Figure 2-18, you must specify the Net-BIOS name of the computer that will host the SMS Provider for the site. The SMS Provider can be installed on the site server, a remote SQL server (as long as it's not a clustered SQL Server instance or hosting the site database for multiple sites), or on a third, server class computer. By default, a suggested SMS Provider installation location (the local site server computer name) is shown in the data entry textbox on this page.

The SMS Provider is used to enable Configuration Manager consoles to connect to the site database and manipulate or view the data stored within it. It is very important to remember where the SMS Provider is installed and ensure that the computer is online as much as possible. (After the site has been installed, you can view the SMS Provider installation location on the site properties from within the Configuration Manager console connected to the site database.)

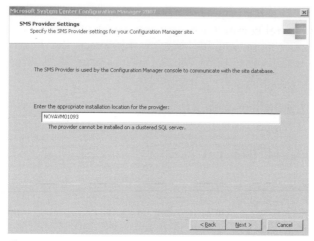

Figure 2-18   The Configuration Manager Setup Wizard SMS Provider Settings page

---

Important   If the SMS Provider computer is offline, all Configuration Manager consoles for the site will be unable to communicate with the site database!

---

14.   On the Management Point page, shown in Figure 2-19, you have the option to install a management point site system. By default, the name of the site server is shown in the data entry textbox. You can overwrite the suggested name with the NetBIOS name for a different server computer if you'd rather install the management point site system on a remote computer. If you would rather not install a management point right now, you can select the Do Not Install A Management Point option and install a management point after site installation has completed and before installing clients.

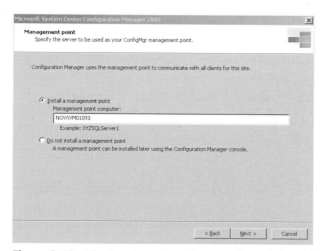

Figure 2-19   The Configuration Manager Setup Wizard Management Point page

15. On the Port Settings page, shown in Figure 2-20, you can specify the TCP port that will be used for client-to-server communication. You can either accept the default port or specify an alternate client communication port.

     If you are installing a site in mixed mode, only an http port (default mixed mode site port is 80) can be specified. Alternatively, if you are installing a site in native mode, only an https port (default native mode site port is 443) can be specified on this page.

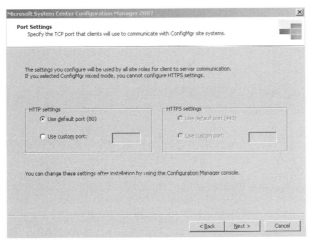

Figure 2-20   The Configuration Manager Setup Wizard Port Settings page

16. On the Updated Prerequisite Components page, shown in Figure 2 21, you are presented with two choices for obtaining client prerequisite files needed to install Configuration Manager clients later. You can either select Check For Updates And Download Newer Versions To An Alternate Path, or if you have already downloaded the files to an alternate location, you can select The Latest Options Have Already Been Downloaded To An Alternate Path.

17. On the Updated Prerequisite Component Path page, shown in Figure 2-22, you specify the path to store or access the downloaded client installation prerequisite component files. If you chose to download the files from the Internet, the downloaded client installation prerequisite files are stored in the path specified. If you chose to specify an alternate location for the prerequisite files, enter the path to where you have already stored the updated prerequisite files using the SETUP /DOWNLOAD command-line option discussed earlier.

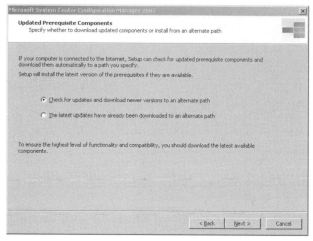

Figure 2-21   The Configuration Manager Setup Wizard Updated Prerequisite Components page

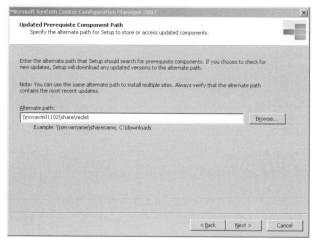

Figure 2-22   The Configuration Manager Setup Wizard Updated Prerequisite Component Path page

18. On the Settings Summary page, shown in Figure 2-23, review the installation actions that you have specified to ensure that they are correct. If they aren't, you can click back to the appropriate wizard page and make any necessary changes.

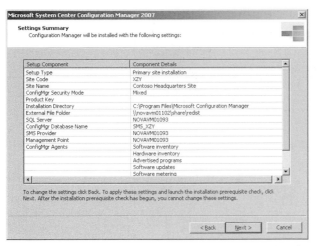

Figure 2-23   The Configuration Manager Setup Wizard Settings Summary page

> **Important**   Up until this point, Setup has made no changes to your
> server other than the addition of the ConfigMgrSetup.log and
> ConfigMgrPrereq.log log files. Once you click Next on the Prerequisite
> Check page, you will not have the option to return to previous wizard
> pages and Setup begins installing files.

19.   On the Installation Prerequisite Check page, the results of the installation prerequisite checker are displayed. This page verifies that site system prerequisites (as
opposed to the client installation prerequisite files downloaded earlier) are installed
and the site system is ready for installation. Review any messages in the results pane
to verify that all prerequisites have been met. If any of the required prerequisites have
not been met for Setup to continue, you may see something like Figure 2-24.

If this happens, don't feel bad. Each of the Setup prerequisites is well documented and
most can be quickly resolved. There is no need to exit Setup at this point, just select an
area off of the wizard on the server desktop and do what needs to be done to resolve the
prerequisite warning or error to allow Setup to continue, and then return to the prerequisite checker and rerun the Setup checks. If you are unsure about what a specific failure
is, double-click the prerequisite title and review the information displayed in the text box
area at the bottom of the prerequisite checker page.

> **More Info**   For more information about the Setup prerequisite checks, see
> "Setup Prerequisite Checks" at *http://technet.microsoft.com/en-us/library
> /bb680951.aspx.*

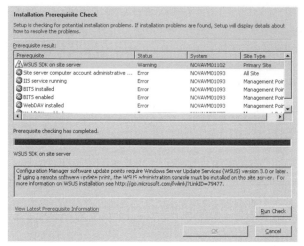

Figure 2-24   The Configuration Manager Setup Wizard Installation Prerequisite Check page with failures

The grayed out text at the bottom of the Prerequisite Check page displays information about how to resolve the prerequisite failures shown in Figure 2-24.

■ **WSUS SDK on site server** This prerequisite check verifies whether or not the WSUS 3.0 administrator console is installed on the site system computer. WSUS 3.0 (full installation) is required on all Configuration Manager software update points. The site server requires the WSUS 3.0 administrator console to be installed (even if the site server itself will not be used as a software update point for the site) to allow it to authorize and configure software update point components using the Configuration Manager console. If you need to install it, Windows Server Update Services 3.0 can be downloaded from *http://www.microsoft.com/downloads/details.aspx?familyid=E4A868D7-A820-46A0-B4DB-ED6AA4A336D9&displaylang=en.*

> **Note**   You won't actually use the WSUS administrator console to manage software update points for the site, but the installed components are leveraged by the site server's Configuration Manager console to allow it to configure remote WSUS installations on software update points.

■ **Site server computer account administrative rights** This rule can mean a couple of things. This usually means that either the user account being used to run Setup doesn't have required administrative rights on the site systems specified for component installation (site server, remote SQL server, or SMS Provider computer) or the site system computer account itself does not have administrative rights on the remote SQL Server computer. The site server computer account requires administrative rights on the remote SQL Server computer (and each physical node of clustered SQL Server instances if applicable) to install required Configuration Manager site backup and recovery component files.

- **IIS service running** This one is pretty self-explanatory. If Internet Information Services (IIS) is required, but not installed on site systems specified for installation, this error appears. Install IIS and rerun the prerequisite checker.

- **BITS installed** This check verifies that the Background Intelligent Transfer Service (BITS) Server Components are installed on computers specified to host site systems that require it (management points and BITS-enabled distribution points). To install BITS, just open the application server, locate Internet Information Services in the Add/Remove Windows Components of the Add or Remove Programs applet in Control Panel, and select the option to install BITS.

- **BITS enabled** This check goes hand-in-hand with the BITS installed check and just ensures that the service is actually running.

- **WebDAV installed** This check verifies that the Web-based Distributed Authoring and Versioning (WebDAV) components are installed on computers specified to host site systems that require it (management points and distribution points). To install WebDAV components, just open the application server, locate Internet Information Services, World Wide Web Publishing Service in the Add/Remove Windows Components of the Add or Remove Programs applet in Control Panel, and select the option to install WebDAV Publishing.

- **WebDAV enabled** This check just verifies if WebDAV is enabled. If you've enabled it in your IIS settings, you probably won't see this one again.

Note   Configuration Manager Setup can continue if only warnings are found, but it's not recommended to do so. The Setup prerequisite checks can usually quickly be resolved, and you never know when that warning might turn into a headache later that is hard to diagnose.

After all Setup prerequisite checks have completed successfully, you should see something similar to Figure 2-25, and Setup can now begin in earnest after you click Begin Installation.

Only prerequisite check warnings and errors are displayed in the results area of the prerequisite check page. To see all the checks that are being run against your server, review the ConfigMgrPrereq.log file in the root of the system drive and you should see something similar to Figure 2-26.

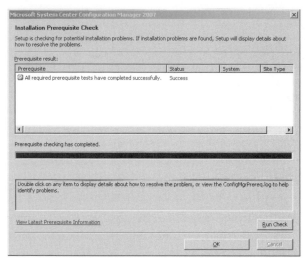

Figure 2-25   The Configuration Manager Setup Wizard Installation Prerequisite Check page with no failures

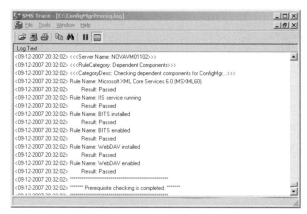

Figure 2-26   The Configuration Manager prerequisite log file (ConfigMgrPrereq.log)

On the Setup Action Status Monitoring page, shown in Figure 2-27, you can see the installation status as it progresses. If any of these steps fail, you can review the ConfigMgrSetup.log file located in the root of the system drive to see what happened.

Note   If you like to read log files to see what is going on behind the scenes you can watch the Site Component Manager log. After the Site Component Manager is displayed as completed on the Setup Action Status Monitoring page, you can review the Site Component Manager log (sitecomp.log), created in the Configuration Manager installation directory, to see when the Configuration Manager services are installed on the site system. Site Component Manager also publishes site and management point data to Active Directory at the end of Setup (if the Active Directory schema has been extended for Configuration Manager) and records the publication in the sitecomp.log.

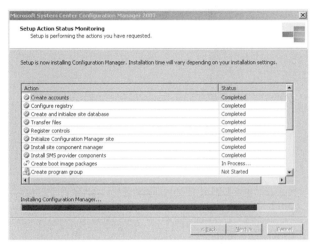

Figure 2-27   The Configuration Manager Setup Wizard Setup Action Status Monitoring page

Finally, the Completion page, shown in Figure 2-28, displays the installation completion status and offers you the option to open the Configuration Manager console after clicking Finish to close the wizard.

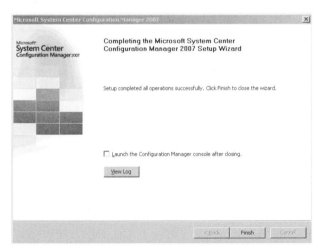

Figure 2-28   The Configuration Manager Setup Wizard Setup Completion page

Configuration Manager Primary Site Unattended Installation

You can also install Configuration Manager primary sites without using the Setup Wizard by using a setup initialization (.ini) file. For more information about unattended installations, see the section "Performing Unattended Configuration Manager Installations" earlier in this chapter.

Following is an example of a setup initialization file that can be used with Setup to perform an unattended installation of a primary site:

```
[Identification]
Action=InstallPrimarySite
[Options]
PrerequisiteComp=0 or 1 (1 = already downloaded. 0 = need to download)
PrerequisitePath=<path>
ProductID=[Product ID (with dashes)]
SiteCode=[Site Code]
SiteName=[Site Name]
SMSInstallDir=[Installation directory]
ManagementPoint=[management point server name (local or remote)]
SDKServer=[SMS Provider computer name]
[SQLConfigOptions]
SQLServerName=[SQL Server name]
CreateSQLDevice=[0 or 1 (0 for no, 1 for yes)]
DatabaseName=[SMS_<site code>]
```

Just fill in the values for the required fields in a new notepad.exe document and save it with an .ini file extension. Use the initialization file to perform an unattended installation using the /SCRIPT setup command-line option.

Installing Configuration Manager Secondary Sites

Generally, secondary sites are used in Configuration Manager hierarchies to support a smaller number of client computers than would warrant installation of a primary site, and the clients are usually located across a slow or WAN link from the primary site. Unlike primary sites, secondary sites do not require an additional Configuration Manager license or a dedicated installation of SQL Server. If you are considering installing a secondary site only to provide software distribution capabilities to remote clients, you should consider installing and using a branch distribution point at the remote location instead.

Note   Site-to-site communication between primary and secondary sites is compressed and controlled by site address connection properties.

The following sections describe how to install a Configuration Manager secondary site in the following ways:

- Using the Configuration Manager Installation Setup Wizard at the secondary site server computer

- Using the Configuration Manager console installed on a primary site to install a remote secondary site

Secondary Site Installation Using the Configuration Manager Setup Wizard

This section walks you through the installation of a secondary site using the Configuration Manager Setup Wizard. While similar to primary site setup, there are some differences when installing secondary sites using the Setup Wizard. Pictures for all of the Setup Wizard pages aren't shown this time, just the ones that are different from primary site installations using the Setup Wizard.

Installing a secondary site is not as complicated as installing a primary site. When installing secondary sites, the following pages are not present in the Setup Wizard:

- **Customer Experience Improvement Program page** Because the CEIP only tracks information retrieved from Configuration Manager console usage, this page is unnecessary for secondary sites that cannot have a Configuration Manager console connected to them.

- **Product Key page** Because a site server license is not required for secondary site installations, it is not necessary to enter a product key.

- **Site Mode page** Because secondary sites automatically inherit the Site mode of their parent site, this page is unnecessary.

- **Client Agents Selection page** Because secondary sites cannot have clients assigned to them, this page is unnecessary.

> **Note**   You can have a Configuration Manager client located within the boundaries assigned to secondary sites, but clients are always assigned to primary sites.

- **Database Server Information page** Because secondary sites do not require a separate site database, this page is unnecessary.

- **SMS Provider page** Because secondary sites cannot have a Configuration Manager console installed, there is no need for a dedicated SMS Provider computer for a secondary site. There is only one SMS Provider computer required for each primary site and all Configuration Manager consoles that will access information stored in the site database for the primary site.

- **Management Point page** While you can install a management point at a secondary site (called a proxy management point if it is set as the default management point for the secondary site), you are not given the option to install one during secondary site setup. You can install a management point for the secondary site from within the Configuration Manager console at the secondary site's primary, parent site later.

- **Ports page** Because secondary sites automatically inherit the client communication port settings in use at their parent site, this page is unnecessary.

When using the installation source files at a secondary site computer, there are a few things that you need to do on the primary site server as well. First, add the secondary site server's computer account to the SMS_SiteToSiteConnection_<site code> local group on the primary site server computer. This allows the secondary site server computer to connect to the primary site and exchange site information later. You also need to manually create a sender address on the primary site to the secondary site from within the Configuration Manager console installed at the primary site to enable it to communicate with the secondary site.

More Info   For more information about creating site addresses, see "How to Create Configuration Manager Site Addresses" at *http://technet.microsoft.com /en-us/library/bb680457.aspx*.

1. Once again, the first page of the Configuration Manager Setup Wizard displayed is the Welcome page. No action is necessary on this page except to click Next.

2. On the Available Setup Options page, select the Install A Configuration Manager Site Server option.

3. On the License Agreement page, you should read the license agreement terms and then agree with them to continue.

4. On the Installation Settings page, select whether to install the site using Custom Settings or Simple Settings. Select Custom Settings in order to install a secondary site.

5. On the Site Type page, specify the type of site to install. You can choose to install either a primary site or secondary site. Select the Secondary Site option.

6. On the Destination Folder page, specify the installation folder that will be used to install Configuration Manager installation files.

7. On the Site Settings page, specify the site code and site description that will be used to identify this secondary site in the hierarchy. Before assigning a site code, ensure that you have planned out your site naming conventions and are sure that the site code entered is the site code you want to use.

> **Important**   It is not supported to change either the site code or site description after the site is installed.

8. On the Parent Site Settings page, shown in Figure 2-29, specify the parent site information for this secondary site installation. Because secondary sites are always child sites of a primary, parent site, you cannot install a stand-alone secondary site.

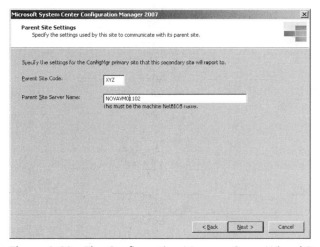

Figure 2-29   The Configuration Manager Setup Wizard Parent Site Settings page

9. On the Updated Prerequisite Components page, you are presented with the two choices for obtaining client prerequisite files needed to install Configuration Manager clients later. You can either check for updates and download the newest prerequisite component files directly from Microsoft using the Internet or, if you have already downloaded the files to an alternate location, you can select the option to specify an alternate location to obtain the prerequisite component files.

10. On the Updated Prerequisite Component Path page, you specify the path to store or access the downloaded client installation prerequisite component files. If you chose to download the files from the Internet, the downloaded client installation prerequisite files are stored in the path specified. If you chose to specify an alternate location for the prerequisite files, type the path to where you have already stored the updated prerequisite files using the SETUP /DOWNLOAD command-line option discussed earlier.

11. On the Settings Summary page, you should review the installation actions that you have specified to ensure that they are correct. If they aren't, you can click back to the appropriate Setup Wizard page and make any necessary changes.

12. On the Installation Prerequisite Check page, the results of the installation prerequisite checker are displayed. This page verifies that site system prerequisites (as opposed to the client installation prerequisite files downloaded earlier) are installed and the site system is ready for installation. Review any messages in the results pane to verify that all prerequisites have been met.

13. On the Setup Action Status Monitoring page, you can see the installation status as it progresses. If any of these steps fail, you can review the ConfigMgrSetup.log file located in the root of the system drive to see what happened.

14. The last page of the Configuration Manager Setup Wizard displayed when installing secondary sites is the Completion page, which displays the installation completion status. Unlike the Primary Site Installation Completion page, you are not offered the option to open the Configuration Manager console—secondary sites do not have Configuration Manager consoles and are managed by the Configuration Manager console installed on their primary, parent site.

After finishing the Setup Wizard, review the sender log (sender.log) on the secondary site server computer to ensure that the site is sending site information to the primary, parent site. After ensuring that there are no communication problems between the sites and the site information is being sent, review the despooler log file (despool.log) on the primary, parent site to ensure that it has received and is processing the secondary site information. The hierarchy manager log file (hman.log) on the primary site server will log actions taken to update the hierarchy structure of the sites, and site component manager (sitecomp.log) will publish secondary site information to Active Directory along with the primary site's information if the Active Directory schema has been extended for Configuration Manager and the site is configured to publish site information.

Note   Secure key exchange between sites is enabled by default in Configuration Manager sites. If sites are not configured to publish to Active Directory, you must manually exchange site public keys or the sites will not be able to communicate properly. For more information about manually exchanging site public keys, see "How to Manually Exchange Public Keys Between Sites" at *http://technet.microsoft.com/en-us/library/bb693690.aspx*.

Secondary Site Installation Using the Configuration Manager Console

You can install secondary sites using the Configuration Manager console connected to a primary site to perform a wizard-based installation. Make sure you do this on the primary site that will be the parent site for the secondary site as it will be connected as a child site to the site that the Configuration Manager console is connected to when the wizard is finished installing the secondary site.

Before attempting to install a secondary site, ensure that the Setup prerequisite checks have been run on the site system within the past seven days. If you're using the Configuration Manager console to install a new secondary site, ensure that you run the prerequisite checker against the secondary site server computer before beginning this process to ensure it is ready to begin the installation.

Important   Before attempting to install a secondary site, you must ensure that the Setup prerequisite checks have been run against the site server computer within the past seven days. If you're using the Configuration Manager console to install a new secondary site, ensure that you manually run the prerequisite checker against the secondary site server computer before beginning this process to ensure it is ready to begin the installation.

---

1. Start the Secondary Site Creation Wizard from within the Configuration Manager console by right-clicking on the primary site name and then clicking New Secondary Site, as shown in Figure 2-30.

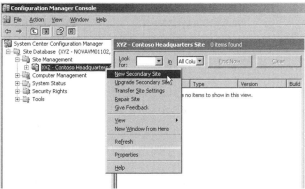

Figure 2-30   Starting the Secondary Site Creation Wizard from the Configuration Manager console

2. The first page of the Secondary Site Creation Wizard is the Welcome page, as shown in Figure 2-31. Read the Welcome page information and click Next.

3. The Site Identity page, shown in Figure 2-32, is used to specify the identification information for the new secondary site. Just as with primary site installations, you need to specify a unique three-digit, alphanumeric site code and a description.

Make sure you have this information planned out before getting to this page. It is not supported to change the site code or site description after the site is installed.

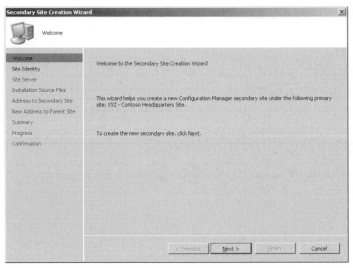

Figure 2-31   The Secondary Site Creation Wizard Welcome page

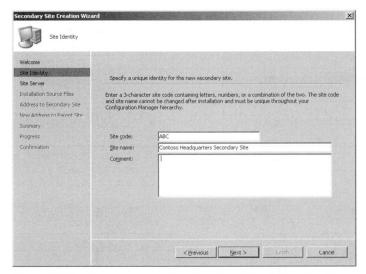

Figure 2-32   The Secondary Site Creation Wizard Site Identity page

Note   You can also type a comment for the site on this page, but it's not required and will not be displayed in the Configuration Manager console after the site is installed.

4. The Site Server page, shown in Figure 2-33, is used to specify the computer and installation directory for the new secondary site installation.

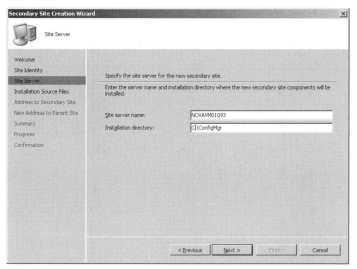

Figure 2-33   The Secondary Site Creation Wizard Site Server page

5. The Installation Source Files page, shown in Figure 2-34, is a very important page of the Secondary Site Creation Wizard. The options seem simple enough, but it is important to know exactly what it's asking you before deciding which option to use.

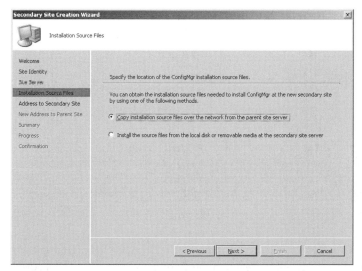

Figure 2-34   The Secondary Site Creation Wizard Installation Source Files page

The first option you have for obtaining source files for installing the secondary site is Copy Installation Source Files Over The Network From The Parent Site Server. This option will copy all of the source files required to install the secondary site server components over the network to the secondary site server computer. Depending on the network connection existing between the site server computers, this may not be such a good idea in all environments. If you have a fairly fast network connection between sites you probably won't have any problems with this option. However, because secondary sites are generally not installed where there is a fast connection between the primary, parent site and the secondary site, use this option only after carefully planning when to copy all of the files across the network. When you use this option, the primary site server will create a secondary site installation package and send it to the secondary site server computer. This is the bootstrap package, and you'll see it appear in the root of the installation drive on the secondary site server computer if you're watching closely. The bootstrap instructions copy all of the installation source files into a temporary directory on the secondary site server computer and run the installation from them for you. The primary site server watches the installation progress and waits for the bootstrap process to complete as the site is being installed (that process is discussed a little later in this section).

The second option on the Installation Source Files page of the Secondary Site Creation Wizard is Install The Source Files From The Local Disc Or Removable Media At The Secondary Site Server. Seems obvious enough, right? Problem is, you don't really get an option to say where those source files are when you use this option! *It's very important that the source files are located at the root of a drive on the secondary site server computer*. When Setup starts, it enumerates all of the drives on the secondary site server computer looking for the install.map to begin the installation. If you've tucked the files away in a subdirectory on the site server, Setup won't be able to find the install.map file and you will be unable to install the site. You need to copy the installation files to the root of one of the hard drives installed on the secondary site server computer so Setup can find them.

Important   In previous versions of SMS, you could just put the installation CD in the CD drive of the secondary site server computer and Setup could find them there. In Configuration Manager installations, however, you can't do this. This is because the Secondary Site Creation Wizard does not prompt you for the location of updated client prerequisite files, and you must provide them manually for Setup to succeed if you're using source files at the secondary site server computer. (When you do a secondary site "push" installation from the parent site, the prerequisite files are automatically copied over.) To get the files where they need to be, just create a subdirectory called Redist under the SMSSETUP directory in the installation source files at the secondary site computer and copy the client prerequisite files there. You can download them manually by running SETUP/DOWNLOAD <path to your redist directory> on the secondary site server computer before beginning the installation.

If you don't have the installation DVD handy at the secondary site server computer, and you don't want to copy all of the files over the network using the normal "push" secondary site server installation method or just a regular SMB file copy operation, you can take a few extra steps and add the secondary site server computer as a distribution point of the primary site server computer. Once the distribution point components are installed, you can then create a software distribution package containing the setup installation source files and assign it to the soon-to-be secondary site server distribution point. This will compress the installation files over the network and save you some bandwidth. After the installation files are present on the secondary site server computer, just copy them out of the distribution point share and uninstall the primary site's distribution point from the secondary site server computer before beginning the secondary site server installation. If you plan on installing a lot of secondary sites, this may actually save you some time downloading client prerequisite files and configuring the installation source files for each server.

6. The Address To Secondary Site page, shown in Figure 2-35, displays any existing sender addresses already configured to communicate with the new secondary site server computer. If one exists already, you can just select it and use the existing address to communicate with the secondary site.

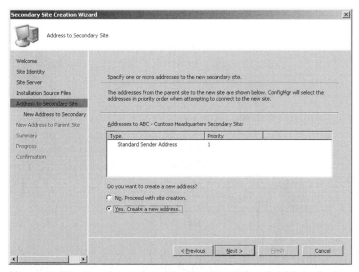

Figure 2-35 The Secondary Site Creation Wizard Address to Secondary Site page

7. The New Address To Secondary Site page, shown in Figure 2-36, is used to create a new sender address from the primary site to the secondary site computer if one doesn't already exist. Even if one does exist, you can still create a new one if you want to at this point. This is different from using the installation source files to run Setup at the secondary site server computer manually. If you don't use the wizard you have to create this address manually.

> **Note**   One of the options you can configure for the new address is the Site Connection Account properties. As you can see in Figure 2-36, a domain user account with administrative rights on the secondary site server computer is entered. If you do not use a domain user account for the site connection account, the primary site server's computer account will be used to connect to the secondary site server computer. If you do not want to put the primary site server's computer account in the local administrators group of the secondary site server computer, you can use this account to get around that requirement.

This address is created on the primary site server computer to allow it to communicate with the secondary site after it is installed. After installation, make sure that you review the address properties to ensure that they are set up to communicate across the network to your satisfaction.

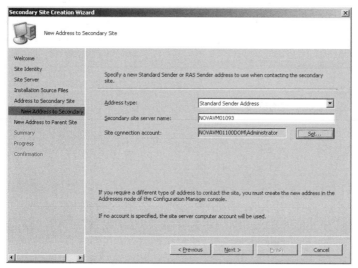

Figure 2-36   The Secondary Site Creation Wizard New Address to Secondary Site page

8. The New Address To Parent Site page, shown in Figure 2-37, is used to create a sender address from the new secondary site computer to the primary site server computer to enable site-to-site communication after the secondary site is installed.

After the site is installed, review the settings for this sender address in the secondary site server's node in the Configuration Manager console to ensure that the address is set up to communicate according to the schedule and network usage priority like you want it to.

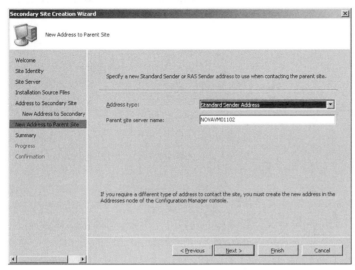

Figure 2-37 The Secondary Site Creation Wizard New Address to Parent Site page

9. The Summary page, shown in Figure 2-38, displays the installation settings you have specified up to this point in the wizard. Review the information displayed to ensure that it is correct. If not, you can click back and change any of the installation settings as needed.

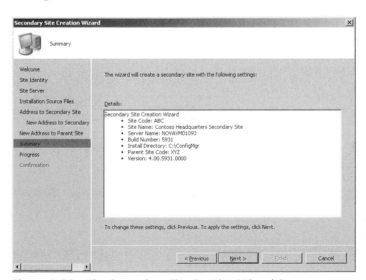

Figure 2-38 The Secondary Site Creation Wizard Summary page

10. The Progress page is displayed after you click Next on the Summary page while the secondary site server bootstrap installation file instructions are created on the primary site server. It's generally a pretty quick page in the wizard (so quick no screen shot is provided!) and overall not very interesting. If something does go wrong during the bootstrap creation process, it appears on the next page of the wizard.

11. The Completion page, shown in Figure 2-39, displays the details of the wizard actions you have performed. The installation settings sent to the secondary site server computer for installation are displayed and the bootstrap process is already underway. Click Close to exit the wizard.

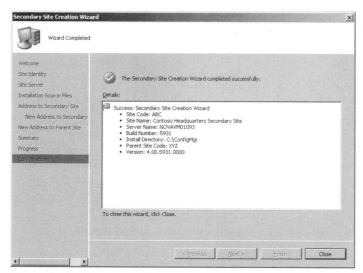

Figure 2-39   The Secondary Site Creation Wizard Completion page

To view the installation actions set into motion by the Secondary Site Creation Wizard, you can watch the drives and some logs on the computers involved to see the installation taking place. In a nutshell, here's what happens in the background, and how to see it:

- After you close the wizard, Hierarchy Manager on the primary site server creates a secondary site installation request and sends it to the secondary site server computer using the sender you created. Hierarchy Manager also adds the secondary site server computer to the SMS_SiteToSiteConnection <site code> local group on the primary site server for you. You can see all of this taking place by reviewing the hman.log file on the primary site server computer.

Note If you're installing a secondary site using Setup.exe locally on the secondary site server computer (not using the wizard), you have to do this manually.

- Next, review the sender.log file on the primary site server to see it copying over the bootstrap installation files.

- When the installation begins, you can review the ConfigMgrSetup.log file on the secondary site server computer to monitor the installation of the secondary site server components.

- When installation is completed, the secondary site server computer sends site data to the parent site to complete the installation. You can review the sender.log on the secondary site server computer to check that the data is sent, and the despool.log file on the primary site server to ensure that the data is received and processed properly.

Note   If the secondary site installation status stays at Pending for an extremely long time in the Configuration Manager console (it may take some time anyway if your secondary site is across a WAN) or if you see anything out of the ordinary in the despool.log on the primary site server computer when it receives site data from the secondary site (saying something about not being able to find a public key for the site), you may have a public key exchange problem on your hands. Remember that secure key exchange between sites is enabled by default in Configuration Manager sites. If sites are not configured to publish to Active Directory, you must manually exchange site public keys or the sites will not be able to communicate properly. For more information about manually exchanging site public keys, see "How to Manually Exchange Public Keys between Sites" at *http://technet.microsoft.com/en-us/library/bb693690.aspx.*

- At this point, if all has gone well, in a few minutes you should see the secondary site installed in the Configuration Manager console, and you can now manage the secondary site, as shown in Figure 2-40.

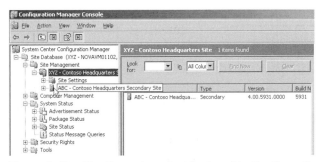

Figure 2-40   The Secondary site displayed in Configuration Manager console

Secondary Site Unattended Installation

You can also install Configuration Manager secondary sites without using the Setup Wizard by using a setup initialization (.ini) file at the secondary site server computer itself.

For more information about unattended installations, see the section "Performing Unattended Configuration Manager Installations" earlier in this chapter.

The following is an example of a setup initialization file that can be used with Setup to perform an unattended installation of a secondary site:

```
[Identification]
Action=InstallSecondarySite
[Options]
PrerequisiteComp=0 or 1 (1 = already downloaded. 0 = need to download)
PrerequisitePath=<path>
SiteCode=[Site Code]
SiteName=[Site Name]
SMSInstallDir=[Installation directory]
AddressType=MS_LAN
ParentSiteCode_[Parent Site's Site Code]
ParentSiteServer=[Parent Site's Server Name]
```

Just fill in the values for the required fields in a new notepad.exe document and then save it with an .ini file extension. Use the initialization file to perform an unattended installation using the /SCRIPT setup command-line option.

Installing Configuration Manager Consoles

Configuration Manager consoles are used to manage Configuration Manager sites and connect to the site database for a site by way of the SMS Provider computer. You can manage primary sites and all of their child sites using the Configuration Manager console.

The Configuration Manager console is a snap-in for the MMC 3.0 and provides you the ability to centrally manage your Configuration Manager site hierarchy as well as decentralize the administration duties to other administrators.

To decentralize administrative duties, you must create custom Configuration Manager consoles to delegate specific tasks and abilities to other administrators as well by adjusting the security rights on console objects to those administrators. When they open their Configuration Manager console and connect to the site database, the SMS Provider will only allow them to perform the actions you have specifically given them the rights to perform.

Configuration Manager Console Installation Using the Configuration Manager Setup Wizard

Although a Configuration Manager console is installed by default on the primary site server computer, you might want to install one on a different computer like your workstation or the workstations of other administrators or help desk personnel. The easy way to do this is to use the Configuration Manager Setup Wizard.

As always, ensure that the computer on which you are attempting to install the Configuration Manager console is supported to host that role. Also, ensure that no other site systems (either SMS 2003 or Configuration Manager) are installed on the system chosen for console installation.

Note   You've already seen most of these pages so only new ones required for Configuration Manager console installations are shown here.

---

1. The first page of the Configuration Manager Setup Wizard displayed is the Welcome page. No action is necessary on this page except to click Next.

2. On the Available Setup Options page, select the Install Or Upgrade An Administrator Console option.

3. On the License Agreement page, you should read the license agreement terms and then agree with them to continue.

4. On the Customer Experience Improvement Program Configuration page, you can choose a program participation selection. The Customer Experience Improvement Program (CEIP) is used to collect statistical information about your system's configuration, the performance of some components of Configuration Manager, and certain types of events generated by Configuration Manager. The data collected is not used to identify or contact you or your company.

   If you choose to participate in the program, a small summary file is automatically uploaded to Microsoft periodically containing collected information from the Configuration Manager console installation. CEIP settings are per user, per machine, and there is no site configuration which globally controls CEIP participation. If multiple administrators use the same Configuration Manager console installation, the default CEIP participation setting is based on the value selected when the console was installed. If one administrator changes the settings for the Configuration Manager console instance they use, it does not affect the other Configuration Manager console instances used by other administrators when they log on to the computer hosting the Configuration Manager console.

5. On the Destination Folder page, specify the installation folder that will be used to install Configuration Manager console installation files.

6. On the Site Server page, specify the primary site server that this Configuration Manager console will connect to, as shown in Figure 2-41.

7. On the Settings Summary page, review the installation actions that you have specified to ensure that they are correct. If they aren't, you can click back to the appropriate Setup Wizard page and make any necessary changes.

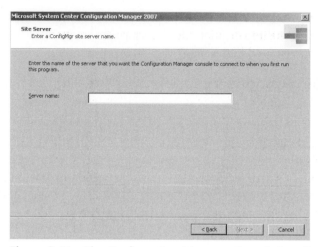

Figure 2-41   The Configuration Manager Console Installation Site Server page

8. On the Installation Prerequisite Check page, the results of the installation prerequisite checker are displayed. This page verifies that site system prerequisites are installed and the site system is ready for installation. Review any messages in the Results pane to verify that all prerequisites have been met.

9. On the Setup Action Status Monitoring page, you can see the installation status as it progresses. If any of these steps fails, you can review the ConfigMgrSetup.log file located in the root of the system drive to see what happened.

10. The last page of the Configuration Manager Setup Wizard displayed when installing Configuration Manager consoles is the Completion page, which displays the installation completion status. You are also offered the option to open the Configuration Manager console after installation is complete.

Configuration Manager Console Unattended Installation

Just like primary and secondary sites, you can also install Configuration Manager consoles without using the Setup Wizard by using a setup initialization (.ini) file. For more information about unattended installations, see the section "Performing Unattended Configuration Manager Installations" earlier in this chapter.

The following is an example of a setup initialization file that can be used with Setup to perform an unattended installation of a Configuration Manager console:

```
[Identification]
Action=InstallAdminUI
[Options]
SMSInstallDir=<Installation directory>
ParentSiteServer=<Primary Site the console will connect to>
SDKServer=<SMS Provider computer name>
```

Just fill in the values for the required fields in a new notepad.exe document and then save it with an .ini file extension. Use the initialization file to perform an unattended installation using the /SCRIPT setup command-line option.

Checkpoints for Installing Configuration Manager Sites and Consoles

Before beginning any type of Configuration Manager installation, ensure that you have reviewed the supported configurations and prerequisite documentation online.

You can use the Configuration Manager Setup Wizard, setup command-line options, and scripted installation methods to perform Configuration Manager installations. Secondary sites can also be installed by starting the Secondary Site Installation Wizard from within the primary site's Configuration Manager console. Understanding the benefits of each installation method and the individual requirements for each type of installation will help you better plan for deployment of your sites and consoles.

Navigating the Configuration Manager Console

The Configuration Manager console is divided into a few different panes. Each pane is used for a different purpose in helping you administer your site(s). The different parts are shown in Figure 2-42.

- **Console tree**   The console tree of the Configuration Manager console is displayed on the far left pane and contains all of the nodes you will use to manage the Configuration Manager sites managed by the console.

- **Details pane**   The details pane—sometimes called the results pane—is the central section of the Configuration Manager console where information about the currently selected console tree node is displayed.

- **Links And Resources**   Depending on the console tree node you have selected, you may see a smaller section displayed at the bottom of the details pane that shows you various feature-related links or other information resources. These are commonly displayed when you select a feature node for the features that have home pages displayed in the details pane.

- **Actions pane**   The Actions pane is displayed on the far right of the Configuration Manager console and provides shortcuts to actions that you can take based on the console tree node currently selected.

The first time you open the Configuration Manager console, you will see something similar to Figure 2-42. If the computer hosting the Configuration Manager console does not have an active Internet connection, a message indicating that the home page cannot be displayed appears. If the computer hosting the Configuration Manager console does have an Internet connection, the Configuration Manager console's home page appears, which displays information about what to do next now that you've successfully installed your site or console.

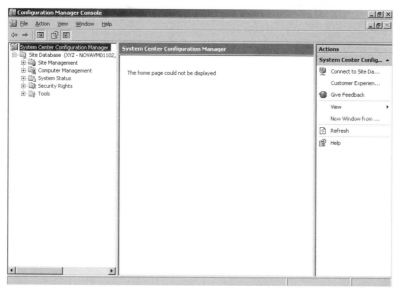

Figure 2-42   The Configuration Manager console

Looking at the Configuration Manager console, you can see that there are many nodes in the console tree with multiple nodes beneath each. Each of these nodes is quickly explained here as well as what they are used for next.

The top-level site node is displayed when you select the site that the Configuration Manager console is directly connected to. Expanding this node allows you to view and configure all of the site settings for the site and any child sites.

The Site Management node, shown in Figure 2-43, is where all of the configuration and management of the site, site systems, and client agents are performed. What each of the subnodes of the site management node are used for is discussed in the section "Modifying the Installation."

The Computer Management node, shown in Figure 2-44, is used to perform management tasks directly relating to clients. In this node of the console tree you configure client collections and Configuration Manager features that directly affect the clients and how you manage them.

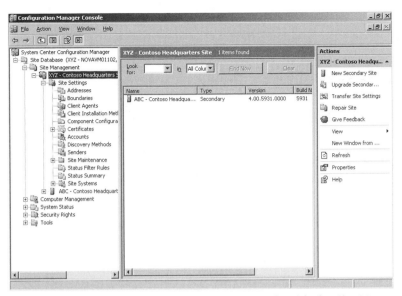

Figure 2-43 The Configuration Manager console with the Site Management node expanded

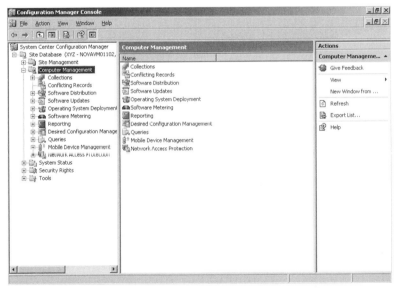

Figure 2-44 The Configuration Manager console with the Computer Management node expanded

The System Status node, shown in Figure 2-45, is used to view the status of the software distribution advertisements created by the site, the status of package distribution to distribution points, the site component and site system status for the site and any of its child sites, and where you can run status message queries.

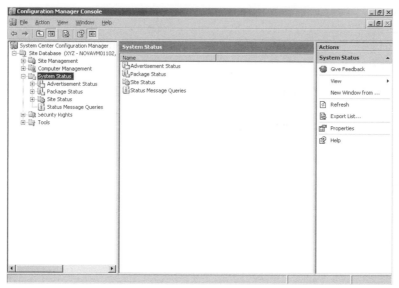

Figure 2-45   The Configuration Manager console with the System Status node expanded

The Security Rights node, shown in Figure 2-46, is used to view and assign security rights to the various Configuration Management console nodes to the users defined for the site. This node is used when adding users and assigning permissions to Configuration Manager console objects.

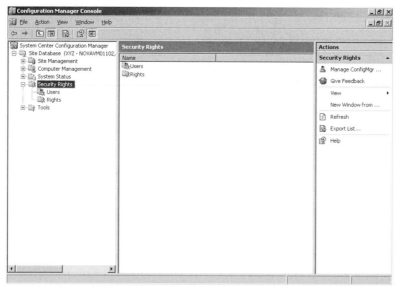

Figure 2-46   The Configuration Manager console with the Security Rights node expanded

The Tools node, shown in Figure 2-47, is used to start the ConfigMgr Service Manager tool. This tool is used to query the status of the site systems and site components installed on them, to verify their current status, and to configure individual logging options for each component.

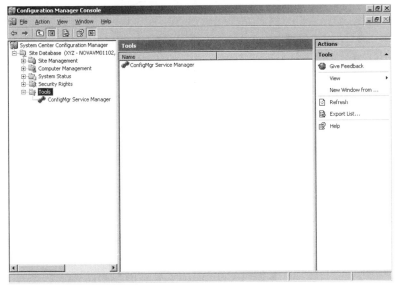

Figure 2-47   The Configuration Manager console with the Tools node expanded

Modifying the Installation

After installing sites, there are some additional post-setup considerations to be aware of. Not every detail of modifying the installation is explained here because the choices you make after installation are dependant on what you want to accomplish and how you have installed your site(s). However, the most important aspects of modifying the installation that you will probably run into are covered.

> **Note**   All of these installation settings are found under the Site Management node of the Configuration Manager console for your site.

Address Properties

You won't have any addresses configured for your site unless you have installed child sites (either primary or secondary) or your primary site is a child site of another primary site. If you have installed a secondary site, recently attached your primary site to another primary site as a child site, or are preparing to install a secondary site remotely using the Configuration Manager Setup Wizard (in this last case, you'll need to create a new address), you should review the settings for the site sender addresses in the Configuration Manager console. After you double-click the address to be reviewed, the main things to look at are the General, Schedule, and Rates Limits tabs of the address properties:

- **Address Properties General tab**   The General tab contains the basic information about the sender address. On this tab you can see the site code and site server that this address is configured to contact, this addresses priority relative to other addresses to the same site (a value of 1 is the highest priority), and the site connection account configured to access the remote site server. The information is basically static and for informational purposes only, but you can reconfigure the site address account on this tab if you need to. By default, the site server's computer account is used to connect to the remote site server, but you can configure the site address to use a domain user account if you prefer.

> **Note**   The General tab of the site Address Properties contains different options and information depending on the type of sender the address is configured for. The previous information is for the standard, LAN sender.

- **Address Properties Schedule tab**   The Schedule tab is used to define the site-to-site communication schedule that this address will use. You can configure how the network is used between sites depending on the priority of the traffic being sent as well as by the day and time period selected using the date/time picker control on this tab.

- **Address Properties Rates Limits tab**   The Rates Limits tab is used to set the maximum site-to-site data communication rates by the hour for the times that you have made the address available to the site server using the Schedule tab. After the site server has determined that the site address is available for use, it will check the rate limits imposed on it to see how much data it can send to the remote site. You can specify unlimited use, Pulse mode, or a maximum data transfer rate by hour.

> **Important**   Unless you have unlimited bandwidth between sites, you definitely want to take a look at the Address Properties. By default, Configuration Manager sender addresses are configured to transmit all priorities of site data as needed 24 hours a day, seven days a week!

> **More Info**   For more information about Configuration Manager addresses and senders, see "Configuration Manager Site to Site Communications" at *http://technet.microsoft.com/en-us/library/bb694289.aspx*.

Boundaries

By default, Configuration Manager sites (both primary and secondary) do not have a default boundary defined during site installation. If you are going to manage clients using the site, you'll need to configure boundaries to properly assign clients. Configuration Manager boundaries can be configured from IP Subnets, AD Sites, IPv6 prefixes, IP address ranges, or any combination of these. You'll also be able to define the speed of the boundary as either fast or slow. The speed of the boundary is taken into consideration during software distribution actions.

> **More Info**   For more information about boundaries, see "Planning Configuration Manager Boundaries" at *http://technet.microsoft.com/en-us/library/bb632910.aspx*.

Client Agents

You have the opportunity to enable client agents during primary site setup, but you'll also need to check the individual client agent settings and schedules (where applicable) to ensure that they're configured to support your computer management needs.

> **More Info**   For more information about client agents, see "Client Agents Properties" at *http://technet.microsoft.com/en-us/library/bb694053.aspx*.

Client Installation Methods

The Client Installation Methods node is where you configure the client installation methods available to you from within the Configuration Manager console. Neither the client push installation method or the software update point client installation method is enabled by default. So if you're going to use one of these methods to install clients, you'll need to configure at least one of these methods after primary site installation.

> **More Info**   For more information about installing Configuration Manager clients, see "Overview of Configuration Manager Client Deployment" at *http://technet.microsoft.com/en-us/library/bb633063.aspx*.

Component Configuration

The Component Configuration node is where you configure the main components of the site. If you're going to be supporting intranet-based clients, you'll definitely need to configure the default management point site component as one of your first tasks after opening the Configuration Manager console for the first time. This node is also used to configure software distribution, software update point, status reporting, and the System Health Validator components.

> **More Info**   For more information about configuring these components, see "Component Configuration Properties" at *http://technet.microsoft.com /en-us/library/bb680790.aspx*.

Discovery Methods

The Discovery Methods node is used to configure the various computer discovery methods available to you. It is not necessary to enable all of the discovery methods, but if you use the client push installation method, you'll need to enable at least one.

> **More Info**   For more information about Configuration Manager discovery methods, see "Discovery Methods Properties" at *http://technet.microsoft.com /en-us/library/bb680867.aspx*.

Site Maintenance

The Site Maintenance node is used to configure the site database server maintenance tasks. There are built-in tasks and you can also create your own custom SQL Server commands here. In addition to the tasks in this node, there are other recommended daily, weekly, and periodic maintenance tasks that should be performed to maintain a healthy Configuration Manager site.

> **More Info**   For more information about performing site maintenance, see "Overview of Site Maintenance" at *http://technet.microsoft.com/en-us/library /bb632386.aspx*, and "Configuring Site Maintenance" at *http://technet.microsoft.com /en-us/library/bb680757.aspx*.

Checkpoints for Navigating the Configuration Manager Console

When you first open the Configuration Manager console, the initial display will be different if the computer the console is installed on has an active Internet connection or no Internet connectivity.

When you close the Configuration Manager console, the location in the console where you were is saved; when you reopen the console, it opens at the same node selected when you last closed it.

Become familiar with the different parts of the Configuration Manager console and understand what each of the different areas is used for.

It is important to perform site adjustments and modifications to the default values using the Configuration Manager console after installing Configuration Manager primary sites. Ensure that you understand and configure the client agents, site features, and site maintenance requirements before beginning client deployment actions.

Removing Configuration Manager Installations

At some point, it may become necessary to undo all of the work you've done installing Configuration Manager sites or Configuration Manager consoles. The following sections walk you through the steps required to do the following:

- Uninstall primary sites
- Uninstall secondary sites
- Uninstall Configuration Manager consoles

Uninstalling Primary Sites

To uninstall a Configuration Manager primary site, you use the Configuration Manager Setup Wizard. You can either start the wizard straight from the installation source files, or you can use the Add or Remove Programs applet in the Control Panel by selecting the installation to uninstall.

Important   To avoid orphaning clients or child sites of the site to be uninstalled, if applicable, you need to ensure that any child sites have been reattached to other sites and any assigned clients have been reconfigured to be managed by a different primary site. Site migrations are covered in Chapter 5.

1. The first page is the Welcome page. Click Next.

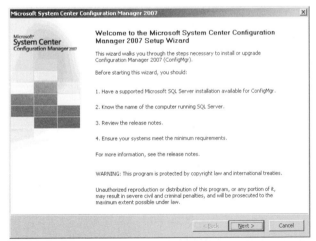

Figure 2-48   The Configuration Manager Setup Wizard Welcome Page

2. On the next page, the Available Setup Options page, as shown in Figure 2-49, select the Uninstall A Configuration Manager Site Server option.

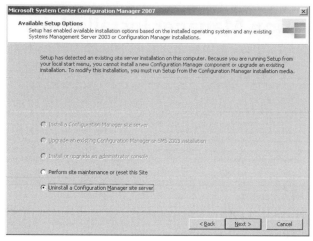

Figure 2-49   The Configuration Manager Setup Wizard Available Setup Options page

3. Click Yes in the uninstall confirmation box that appears to confirm that you really want to uninstall this primary site, as shown in Figure 2-50.

Figure 2-50   The uninstall confirmation box

4. Review the uninstallation as it progresses on the Setup Action Status Monitoring page, shown in Figure 2 51, and click Next when it has finished.

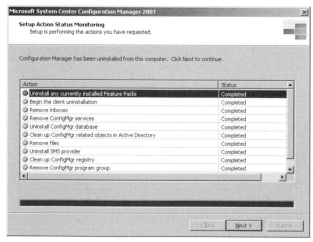

Figure 2-51   The Configuration Manager Setup Wizard Setup Action Status Monitoring page

5. To complete the uninstallation process, review the completion status on the Completion page, as shown in Figure 2-52, and click Finish to close the wizard.

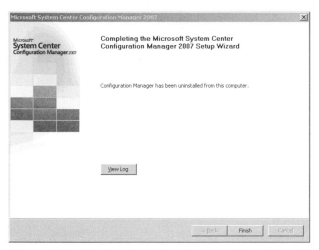

Figure 2-52   The Configuration Manager Setup Wizard Completion page

6. Last, review the ConfigMgrSetup.log file on the primary site server computer to ensure that the site has completed the uninstallation process.

Uninstalling Secondary Sites

Uninstalling secondary sites can be done either by running Configuration Manager Setup or using the Delete Secondary Site Wizard from within the Configuration Manager console managing the secondary site's parent site.

Uninstalling secondary sites using Configuration Manager Setup is basically exactly like uninstalling primary sites using that method, so the focus in this section is on the Delete Secondary Site Wizard.

1. To start the wizard, right-click the secondary site name in the primary site server's Configuration Manager console and click Delete, as shown in Figure 2-53.

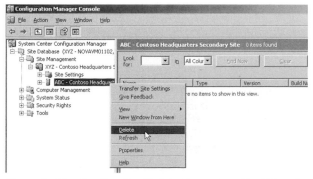

Figure 2-53   Starting the Delete Secondary Site Wizard

2. On the Welcome page of the wizard, shown in Figure 2-54, confirm that the correct secondary site has been selected to be uninstalled and click Next.

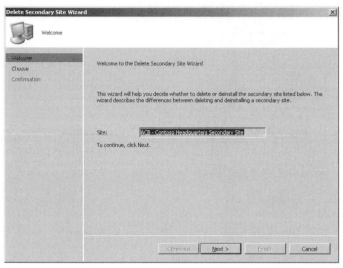

Figure 2-54   The Delete Secondary Site Wizard Welcome page

3. On the next page of the wizard, shown in Figure 2-55, select the Deinstall The Site option.

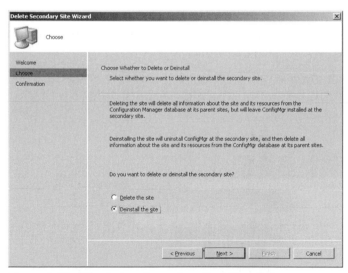

Figure 2-55   The Delete Secondary Site Wizard Choose page

4. On the Confirmation page, shown in Figure 2-56, review the information displayed and confirm the decision to uninstall the secondary site.

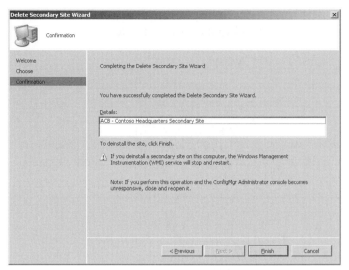

Figure 2-56   The Delete Secondary Site Wizard Confirmation page

Uninstalling Configuration Manager Consoles

To uninstall unwanted Configuration Manager consoles, start the Configuration Manager Setup Wizard from the installation source files or the Add or Remove Programs Control Panel applet.

1. The first page displayed is the Welcome page. Click Next.

2. The next page of the Setup Wizard is the Setup Options page. On this page, select the Uninstall Configuration Manager console option.

3. When prompted, click Yes to confirm your decision to uninstall the Configuration Manager console.

4. On the Setup Action Status Monitoring page of the wizard, review actions being taken to uninstall the Configuration Manager console.

5. On the Completion page, click Finish to close the wizard.

6. After closing the wizard, you can review the ConfigMgrSetup.log file to verify the uninstallation as it progresses.

Note   If you prefer to do it using a setup command line to perform an unattended deinstallation, you can use the following: SETUP /DEINSTALL /NOUSERINPUT. You can also use the SETUP /DEINSTALL /NOUSERINPUT to uninstall primary and secondary sites, but if you do, there are a lot of files still left behind and the site deletion is not propogated up the hierarchy. For that reason, you really shouldn't use this command on anything but Configuration Manager console installations.

Checkpoints for Removing Configuration Manager Installations

You can uninstall Configuration Manager sites and consoles using the Configuration Manager Setup Wizard or by using setup command-line options. Using the Add or Remove Programs applet in Control Panel to begin the uninstallation automatically launches Setup Wizard. Be sure to verify that all site installation files and directories are removed when you use the setup command-line option /DEINSTALL to perform unattended deinstallations.

When uninstalling Configuration Manager primary sites, ensure that the sites do not have any child sites attached to them that may become orphaned after the site is uninstalled.

Summary

This chapter explored the steps necessary to properly plan for and deploy Configuration Manager primary sites, secondary sites, and Configuration Manager consoles in your network environment. You looked at a variety of methods that you can use to perform Configuration Manager installations. At the other end of the spectrum, how to properly uninstall Configuration Manager should the need arise was also discussed.

Before beginning any type of Configuration Manager installation, ensure that you have properly planned for it by completing the necessary planning phases. Use the steps outlined in the preplanning and planning phases before beginning the actual deployment phase of Configuration Manager deployment to ensure a smooth and successful deployment. Without properly planning and conducting the necessary coordination with other server and service administrators, deploying Configuration Manager can be both a daunting and unpredictable task. Configuration Manager is a powerful management server technology and shouldn't be deployed without careful planning and consideration given to how you will secure it afterward.

Because of the new site systems, features, and functions introduced with Configuration Manager, it requires many more prerequisites than previous versions of SMS—for both site systems and clients. Review the supported configurations and installation prerequisites to ensure that the hardware and network environments are ready for Configuration Manager installation. Using the tools provided by Configuration Manager to download and check for the necessary prerequisites is paramount to successful installations. The Setup Prerequisite Checker (launched from the Setup splash screen) should be used as a planning tool and not just considered another part of site setup. Keeping a current copy of the client prerequisite files handy by using the Setup /download <path to store files> command should be one of the first things that you do after determining your deployment requirements.

The two setup types offered for Configuration Manager Setup are Simple Setup and Custom Setup. In most cases, performing Configuration Manager Setup using the Simple Settings option should only be used in lab or proof-of-concept type environments. Simple Setup can only be used to install primary sites. Custom Setup allows far greater customization and control over the final Configuration Manager installation and should be used to perform production environment installations. Custom Setup is also the only setup option that allows you to install a secondary site.

Knowing the differences between the site modes available for Configuration Manager installations—native mode and mixed mode—is also very important, and one of the earliest decisions that you will need to make when installing Configuration Manager sites. While native mode requires a PKI infrastructure to be in place, it also provides for a higher level of client-to-server communication and other types of client support (Internet-based) that mixed mode does not.

Configuration Manager Setup offers you the ability to install primary sites, secondary sites, and Configuration Manager consoles as well as the ability to uninstall them. Knowing the values and purposes of each is important to understand to ensure that you perform the correct installation. Primary sites require an SQL Server database to store site information and require a Configuration Manager license to install. Secondary sites do not require a license, and can only be child sites of primary sites. Secondary sites are generally used to support clients that are located across slow or WAN network connections from the primary site and help reduce the amount of network traffic sent across the wire (site-to-site communication is compressed). If you're planning on installing a secondary site to support only software distribution, using a remote branch distribution point could be a better option and require less administrative overhead. Consider the amount of clients at the remote location and how much network traffic they will generate when you are deciding whether or not to install a secondary site. Configuration Manager consoles are used to manage and administer your sites. They can be secured to allow lower-level administrators to perform only specific tasks through security restrictions enforced by the SMS Provider computer.

After you have decided to begin the installation process, you can either use an attended wizard-based installation or use a setup initialization file to perform unattended installations. You can also use the setup command-line options to perform customized installations or perform various tasks as needed. Be conscious of the requirements and limitations of each of these methods—especially when installing secondary sites, as described in this chapter.

You can view the progress of Configuration Manager installations or deinstallations of sites and consoles by reviewing the log files used during setup operations: ConfigMgr-Prereq.log, ConfigMgrSetup.log, and ComponentSetup.log. The ConfigMgrPrereq.log file records prerequisite check actions and can be used to verify that all prerequisite checks have either succeeded or failed. The ConfigMgrSetup.log file records actions that Setup takes during installations and the steps taken when uninstalling Configuration Manager sites and consoles. The ComponentSetup.log file records the installation of site components during primary or secondary site installations.

Chapter 3
Configuring Site Server Properties and Site Systems

The SQL server

If configured for cluster

Can have no provider.

Jeffrey Gilbert, Technical Writer, Configuration Manager

Now that you have successfully installed your System Center Configuration Manager primary site server, the next step in your deployment strategy is to begin configuring your site. This configuration might consist of two parts. Certainly, you need to configure the single Configuration Manager site. This means identifying which components should be enabled, what the Configuration Manager site boundaries should be, and what additional servers should be enabled as component or site systems for the site. You might also need to establish a Configuration Manager site hierarchy for your organization. This means, among other things, identifying parent-child relationships, establishing a reporting and administration path, configuring communication mechanisms, and identifying primary and secondary sites.

This chapter concentrates on the first part of the configuration process—that is, configuring the single Configuration Manager site, including setting site boundaries, monitoring status and flow, and identifying site systems. In Chapter 4, "Implementing Multiple Site Structures," you learn how to implement a site hierarchy.

Defining and Configuring the Configuration Manager Site

The first step in configuring your new Configuration Manager site is to identify which clients should become members of the site. Configuration Manager determines which clients should be assigned to the site according to the site boundaries you configure. You can only assign Configuration Manager clients to one site. Configuration Manager site boundaries are defined by Internet Protocol (IP) subnet, Active Directory site, IPv6 prefix, or IP address range. A subnet is a segment of a network whose members share the same network address and is distinguished from other subnets by a subnet number and subnet mask. An Active Directory directory service site defines a physical relationship among domain controllers based on their IP subnets and represents a unit of optimum network performance for Active Directory replication and authentication. An IPv6 prefix is the first fixed 48 bits of an IPv6 address and is used to identify the IPv6 subnet. An IP address range is used to identify computers assigned with IP addresses within the specified range as Configuration Manager clients. When an IP address range is used to specify a Configuration Manager boundary, the IP range used for client assignment includes the starting address and ending address specified.

> **More Info**   For a detailed discussion about IP addresses and IPv6, see "TCP/IP Fundamentals for Microsoft Windows" published through Microsoft TechNet at *http://www.microsoft.com/technet/network/evaluate/technol/tcpipfund/tcpipfund.mspx*. For a more thorough examination of the purpose and configuration of Active Directory sites, please attend Microsoft Certified Course 6043, *Implementing Active Directory Domain Services in Windows Server 2008*, or read *Introducing Windows Server 2008*, published by Microsoft Press. For detailed information about planning for and deploying your Configuration Manager server infrastructure, see "Planning and Deploying the Server Infrastructure for Configuration Manager 2007" in the Configuration Manager Documentation Library.

Don't confuse site assignment with the discovery process. Configuration Manager uses any of several configurable discovery processes to "look for" and record an instance of a resource. A resource might be a client computer. However, it might also be a user; a global group; an Active Directory user, group, or system; or an IP-addressable device such as a switch or a network printer. Discovering a resource doesn't make it a Configuration Manager client. A client computer can't become a Configuration Manager client until it is assigned to a Configuration Manager site based on the boundary with which it's associated. After it is assigned, it can be installed with the Configuration Manager client software. To sum up, the Configuration Manager site server can discover clients as a site resource, but not necessarily install them. Likewise, it can install them as Configuration Manager clients, but not discover them. But in all cases, a client must be assigned to a Configuration Manager site before it can be installed. The discovery process is explored in detail in Chapter 7, "Discovering Resources."

Site systems, on the other hand, do not need to be located within the boundaries of the site with which they're associated unless, of course, they will also become clients of that site. In some cases, site system roles can be shared across sites or Configuration Manager clients can reference site systems that are members of another Configuration Manager site in the site hierarchy.

Systems Management Server (SMS) 2003 supports two kinds of boundaries: local boundaries and roaming boundaries. The main difference between the two has to do with the kind of Configuration Manager client support provided: Standard Client or Advanced Client. However, Configuration Manager supports only one kind of client and no longer distinguishes between site boundaries and roaming boundaries. Configuration Manager boundaries are similar to SMS 2003 roaming boundaries.

Roaming is the ability to move a Configuration Manager client from the designated boundaries of a Configuration Manager site to within the assigned boundaries of another Configuration Manager site or to a network location not defined as a boundary for a Configuration Manager 2007 site at all. Configuration Manager clients are able to communicate with site systems that are members of another site in the Configuration Manager 2007 hierarchy when they roam.

Boundaries are used to assign Configuration Manager clients to the Configuration Manager site based on their IP subnet, IPv6 prefix, the IP address range they belong to, or an Active Directory site association. Using Active Directory sites to define site assignment provides you with the easiest way to assign new clients that join the network regardless of their IP information.

For example, if you use only IP subnets, every time a new client or set of clients joins the network, in addition to associating them with an appropriate Active Directory site, you must ensure that the IP subnets of those clients are represented in the site boundary for the appropriate site. However, if you define the site boundary based on Active Directory sites, you need only associate the new clients with the appropriate Active Directory site. The Configuration Manager site will already "know" that the Configuration Manager client should be assigned to it.

When you configure the boundaries for a site, all the client agent settings that you define are applied to all the clients assigned to that site when the Configuration Manager software is installed on new clients or when the client policy is updated on existing clients. In other words, agent and component settings are sitewide settings and apply equally to all members of the site. If different sets of clients require different client components, you might need to create a separate site for those clients. For example, if 100 out of 1000 clients require Software Metering to be enabled and the remaining clients do not, you need to segment these clients into their own subnet, create a Configuration Manager site for that subnet, assign those 100 clients to that site, and enable Software Metering for that site. There are ways to get around this limitation, of course—both supported and unsupported. Nevertheless, your goal as an administrator should not be "getting around" a product's boundaries. This is one of the reasons a well-conceived deployment strategy is extremely valuable to you as you construct your Configuration Manager site hierarchy.

To set the boundary for your Configuration Manager site, follow these steps:

1. Open the Configuration Manager console.

2. Under System Center Configuration Manager, expand the Site Database node, and then expand the Site Management node to display the site node (in the form, sitecode - sitename). Expand the site node to display the Site Settings node.

3. Expand the Site Settings node, and select Boundaries, as shown in Figure 3-1. The default boundary for the site along with any other boundaries that have been configured are displayed in the results pane.

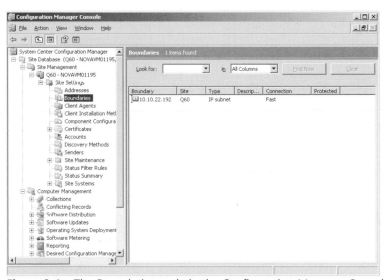

Figure 3-1   The Boundaries node in the Configuration Manager Console

4. Right-click the Boundaries node and choose New Boundary from the context menu to display the New Site Boundary dialog box, as shown in Figure 3-2. (You can double-click on any existing boundary to display a similar dialog box and edit the existing settings.)

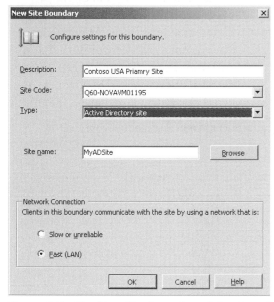

Figure 3-2   The New Site Boundary dialog box displaying settings for an Active Directory site boundary

5. Select the type of boundary you want to configure, and provide the IP or Active Directory information requested. In this scenario, you are adding an Active Directory site as a boundary, so you browse for and type the Active Directory site name.

6. Click OK or Apply to save your changes.

Real World   Site Boundaries and Subnet Masks

When you use IP subnets to determine site assignment, Configuration Manager checks the client's discovery record to see whether the client's IP address falls within the IP boundaries set by the Configuration Manager administrator. It does so by checking the client's subnet mask. (The subnet mask determines the subnet address for that segment of the network.) Checking the client's subnet mask is significant because most companies don't use a subnet mask of 255.255.0.0 or something similar to define their network segments. In fact, they likely will use a mask such as

255.255.248.0 to segment the network into different subnets for organizational reasons, network routing considerations, security, localization of resources, and so on.

Using a subnet mask such as 255.255.0.0 makes it easy to identify the subnet address. With this particular mask, every number in the third and fourth octets constitutes a host device address. Every number in the first and second octets constitutes a different IP subnet address. For example, consider these two IP addresses: 172.16.20.50 and 172.16.10.50. Using subnet mask 255.255.0.0, it's easy to see that they're both in the same subnet. If you set the Configuration Manager site boundary to 172.16.0.0, you'll be sure to discover and assign both clients.

Now take the same two IP addresses, but use subnet mask 255.255.248.0 instead. This subnet mask places each client address into a different subnet. If your site boundary is 172.16.8.0, it will discover and assign clients whose IP addresses fall within the range 172.16.8.1 through 172.16.15.254. Thus the client with address 172.16.10.50 would be assigned and the client with address 172.16.20.50 would not. To include the latter client, you need to add its subnet address—172.16.16.0—to the site boundaries.

You might need to refresh your IP addressing skills to fully appreciate the significance of subnet masking and Configuration Manager. But rest assured, the subnet mask does make a difference.

Now consider using Active Directory sites as your Configuration Manager site boundary. Without going into a lengthy discussion about Active Directory sites, suffice it to say that they also depend in part on subnet objects. These subnet objects consist of both subnet addresses and masks. This makes it easier to associate computer objects with a particular Active Directory site and so makes it easier for the Configuration Manager administrator to assign those clients to a Configuration Manager site.

Configuring Site Properties

In Configuration Manager, you can configure several other site properties in addition to site boundaries, including site accounts and security. In this section, you learn how to configure these properties.

To display the site properties for a Configuration Manager site, follow these steps:

1. Open the Configuration Manager console.

2. Under System Center Configuration Manager, expand the Site Database node, and then expand the Site Management node to display the site node (in the form, site-code - sitename).

3. Right-click the site node and choose Properties from the context menu. Or, high-light the site node, and from the Action menu choose Properties to display the Properties dialog box for the site, as shown in Figure 3-3. Start with the General tab.

Figure 3-3   The General tab of the site Properties dialog box

The General Tab

The General tab displays some descriptive information about your site server. For example, in Figure 3-3 you can see that the site server is a primary site. You can identify its version and build numbers, the server name, the Configuration Manager installation directory, and the current security mode. You can also see whether this site participates in a site hierarchy as a child site to another site. Because in Figure 3-3 the Parent Site label is set to "None," you can conclude that this site is either a stand-alone site, because it has no parent site, or that it might be the central or topmost site in a Configuration Manager site hierarchy. You use the Set Parent Site button to identify the parent site that this site should communicate with in a Configuration Manager site hierarchy. Creating parent-child relationships is discussed in Chapter 4.

Descriptive comments always add value to objects in Configuration Manager, as they help provide additional information that might otherwise not be available. In this case, you can use the Comment text box to indicate the name of the company (Contoso Corporation), its site hierarchy role (Primary Site), and its location (Corporate Headquarters).

The Wake On LAN Tab

Wake On LAN support is a new feature of Configuration Manager. Wake On LAN can send wake-up transmissions prior to the configured deadline for a software update deployment or at the configured schedule of a mandatory advertisement (which can be for software distribution or a task sequence). Computers must have a network card installed and configured to support this feature.

To configure Wake On LAN, complete the following steps:

1. Click the Wake On LAN tab in the site Properties dialog box, as shown in Figure 3-4.

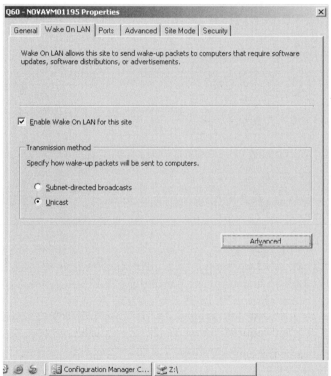

Figure 3-4   The Wake On LAN tab of the site Properties dialog box

2. To enable Wake On LAN support for the site, select the Enable Wake On LAN For This Site option.

3. Select which transmission method—Subnet-directed broadcasts or Unicast—the site will use to send wake-up packets to computers. Subnet-directed broadcasts uses the media access control (MAC) address and IP subnet of the client as reported in the most recent Configuration Manager hardware inventory to broadcast the wake-up packet to all computers on that subnet. Unicast uses the MAC address to construct the wake-up packet and the IP address of the client as reported in the most recent hardware inventory to route to the client's subnet, and then send the packet directly to the client.

4. Click Advanced to set additional Wake On LAN properties shown in Figure 3-5, including the number of retry attempts, the maximum number of wake-up packets to send, the number of transmission threads to use, and a transmission offset value, then click OK.

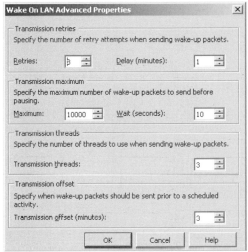

Figure 3-5   The Wake On LAN Advanced Properties dialog box

5. Click OK or Apply to save your changes.

The Ports Tab

The settings on this tab let you configure which ports Configuration Manager should use in your environment to support client requests through HTTP or HTTPS and Wake On LAN.

To configure ports, complete the following steps:

1. Click the Ports tab in the site Properties dialog box, as shown in Figure 3-6.

2. The Active Ports window displays the services used by the ports, the assigned ports, and a description of each port. Note that one HTTP and one HTTPS port are

enabled by default, along with Wake On LAN, and set to the default ports of 80, 443, and 9, respectively. You must have at least one HTTP and HTTPS port enabled. Enable services by selecting the check box of the service.

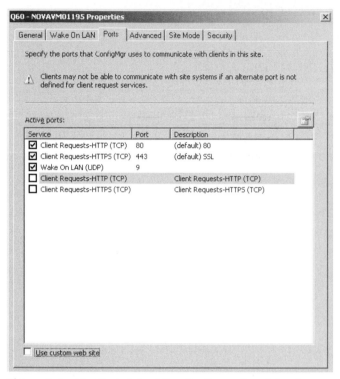

Figure 3-6   The Ports tab of the site Properties dialog box

3. Modify the properties of a service by selecting the service and clicking the Properties button above and to the right of the Active ports window to display the Port Detail dialog box, as shown in Figure 3-7. Here you can change the port number to be used by Configuration Manager and the description of the port. Click OK when you're done.

4. Click OK or Apply to save your changes.

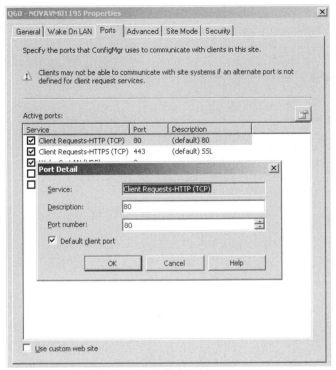

Figure 3-7   The Port Detail dialog box

The Advanced Tab

You can configure how Configuration Manager should handle conflicts resulting from the detection of duplicate hardware IDs, how to publish the site, and whether to require secure key exchange between sites.

To configure options of the Advanced tab, follow these steps:

1. Click the Advanced tab in the site Properties dialog box, as shown in Figure 3-8.

2. In the Conflicting Records section of the dialog box, specify how Configuration Manager should handle computer records with duplicate hardware IDs by selecting either Automatically Create New Client Records For Duplicate Hardware IDs or Manually Resolve Conflicting Records.

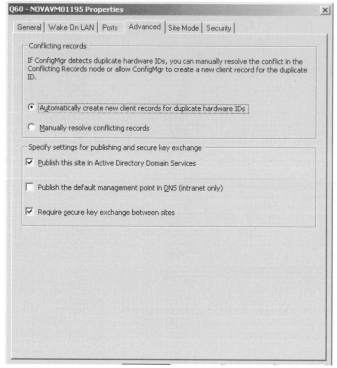

Figure 3-8   The Advanced tab in the site Properties dialog box

3. Select the Publish This Site In Active Directory Domain Services option to have Configuration Manager publish site information directly to Active Directory. This is the default option and required if you are running Configuration Manager in native mode. If the site server is also a management point, you can select Publish The Default Management Point In DNS as a Service Location (SRV) record.

4. Select Require Secure Key Exchange Between Sites to ensure that communication is allowed between this site and its child sites only when keys can be securely exchanged between the two sites.

5. Click OK or Apply to save your changes.

The Site Mode Tab

The Site Mode tab allows you to define which of the two security modes Configuration Manager will use: mixed mode, similar to Advanced Security in SMS 2003; or native mode, which is more advanced and the more secure operating mode. You must choose which mode you want to use when you run setup, but you can migrate to native mode from mixed mode using the Site mode setting on this tab. Refer to Chapter 20, "Config-uration Manager 2007 Security," for a more detailed discussion about mixed mode and native mode. In brief, however, choose native mode if:

- You require the highest security controls using industry-standard protocols.

- You require Internet-based client management.

Choose mixed mode if:

- You do not have the supporting Public Key Infrastructure (PKI).

- You have not installed the specific certificates required by Configuration Manager 2007.

- The site contains SMS 2003 clients.

- The site contains clients running Windows 2000 Professional or Windows 2000 Server .

- The parent site is configured for mixed mode.

- Site systems running Internet Information Services (IIS) are not dedicated to Con-figuration Manager, and you cannot configure a custom Web site.

- You must use WINS as the means by which clients can find their default manage-ment point.

- You do not want the site's secondary sites to be automatically migrated to native mode.

If your site is configured to run in mixed mode, you can modify the options displayed in Figure 3-9.

The default Approval setting for mixed mode is the Automatically Approve Computers In Trusted Domains option. Clients must be approved before they can receive policies that might contain sensitive data. However, you could choose the Manually Approve Each Computer option or the Automatically Approve All Computers option. The latter option is not recommended as it is the least secure. Select This Site Contains Only ConfigMgr 2007 Clients if you are not supporting any SMS 2003 clients in the site. You can include an additional level of security by selecting the Encrypt Data Before Sending To Manage-ment Point option.

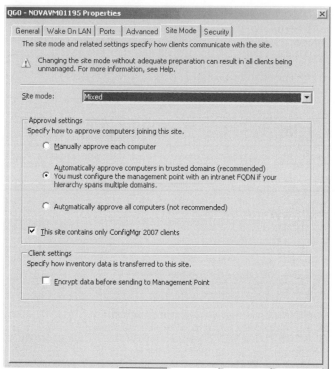

Figure 3-9   The Site Mode tab of the site Properties dialog box displaying mixed mode options

If your site is configured to run in native mode, you can modify the options displayed in Figure 3-10.

You can specify the signing certificate to use for the site by either browsing for it in the site server's certificate store or entering the thumbprint for the certificate. You can also click Specify Root CA Certificates to import exported root certification authority certificates for clients assigned to the site and that might be required for operating deployment clients to complete installation.

The settings in the Client settings published to Active Directory specify those native mode site settings that are published to Active Directory and automatically used with client push installations. The Enable CRL Checking On Clients option specifies whether Configuration Manager clients should use a certificate revocation list (CRL) before using the PKI certificates required by native mode. It is enabled by default. Select the Allow HTTP Communication For Roaming And Site Assignment option to enable a native mode client to use HTTP to communicate with a management point in a site running mixed node. The Certificate Store field specifies the location of the client certificate used in

Native mode, and the Certificate selection criteria lets you specify a selection criteria to use if there is more than one valid certificate in the certificate store. You can select:

- Check Only Certificate Purpose (the default)
- Subject Or Alt Contains (type the string in the text box below this field)
- Subject Or Alt Includes Attributes (type the string in the text box below this field)

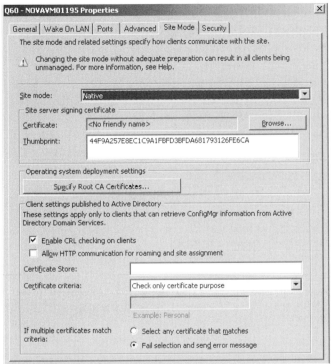

Figure 3-10 The Site Mode tab of the site Properties dialog box displaying native mode options

---

The Security Tab

The Security tab, shown in Figure 3-11, displays the current security rights for the *Site Properties* object. Every object in the Configuration Manager database has both class and instance security that can be applied. Applying security to Configuration Manager objects is similar to creating an access control list (ACL) for Windows files, folders, or shares. To set object class security rights, click the yellow star button in the Class Security Rights frame to display the Object Class Security Rights Properties dialog box. You can specify permissions such as Administer, Create, or Delete by selecting the boxes in the Permissions list. To set object instance security rights, click the yellow star button in the Instance Security Rights frame and follow the same procedure for setting the class security rights.

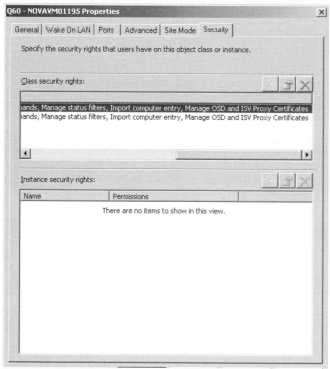

Figure 3-11   The Security tab of the site Properties dialog box, showing the two default accounts granted permissions to manage the *Site Properties* class of object

Class versus Instance Security Rights

Class security rights indicate the access granted to all objects of this type. In the example displayed in Figure 3-11, the class security rights apply not only to this specific site, but also to any other site that might enter into a parent-child relationship with this site.

Instance security rights (not displayed in Figure 3-11) indicate the access granted to that specific instance of the object. In this example, the instance security rights apply only to this particular site.

As another example, consider the *Collections* object. The class security rights indicate which users and groups have been granted specific permissions for working with *all* collections. Each individual collection, however, has an instance security right that identifies which users or groups have been granted specific permissions to that *one* collection. You can view and modify the instance security rights for a specific instance of an object by clicking the Security tab of that object's properties dialog box.

By default, the administrative-level account that was used to perform the Configuration Manager site server installation as well as the local system account (NT Authority\System) are granted full class security rights for all Configuration Manager objects in the database. The list of permissions that are granted, or that can be granted, vary from object to object. Full permissions to the Site Properties class include Administer, Create, Delegate, Delete, Import computer entry, Manage OSD and ISV Proxy Certificates, Manage SQL Commands, Manage Status Filters, Meter, Modify, and Read. Full permissions to the Collections class include Administer, Advertise, Create, Delegate, Delete, Delete Resource, Modify, Modify collection setting, Modify Resource, Read, Read Resource, Use Remote Tools, and View Collected Files.

So, permissions granted to a user for a class of object apply to all objects of that class. Permissions granted to a user for a specific object in a class (an "instance") apply to that object alone. If a user is a member of two or more groups, each with different permissions, permissions are cumulative for the user; that is, the least restrictive of the permissions apply. For example, if the user is a member of a group called FINHELP that has the read permission assigned to it and a member of a group called FINMGRS that has full permissions assigned to it, the user's permissions are full permissions. The least restrictive permission prevails. However, permissions at the instance level of an object will override the class permissions granted. For example, suppose you want a specific help desk group named FINHELP to be able to initiate remote tools sessions only with the clients in the Finance collection. You would grant FINHELP no permission to the Collection class, but full permission to the Finance collection. This not only restricts members of FIN-HELP to only the Finance collection, but also their Configuration Manager consoles would display only the Finance collection. As you can see, class and instance security give the Configuration Manager administrator quite granular control over securing objects in the Configuration Manager database.

Site Settings

Typically, you think of Configuration Manager site settings and component attributes such as client agent settings, site addresses, site systems and their roles, and so on, as properties of the site, and rightly so, because these settings are indeed specific to each site. However, as you've seen, these other settings aren't part of the Site Properties dialog box for a Configuration Manager site. The Configuration Manager Site Properties dialog box might better be thought of as relating to the site object properties rather than to settings and attributes of components within that site. You've already looked at one of these—the Boundaries node—which lets you specify and configure boundaries for the site.

To access the component settings, expand the Site node in the console tree and then expand the Site Settings node. Under the Site Settings node, you'll find Configuration Manager component settings, as discussed previously, and as shown in Figure 3-1. Each of these site settings is discussed in detail in later chapters as their roles become significant to a particular action or feature. For example, Chapter 4 looks at the Addresses node and Chapter 7 looks at the Discovery Methods node. Remember, though, that these site settings are integral and unique to each specific Configuration Manager site and can rightly be termed properties of the site.

The Site Configuration Process Flow

Different Configuration Manager services and processes carry out different tasks depending on the site property or site setting you enable or configure. However, there is still one basic process flow that takes place when any site setting changes. The change is requested by you and posted to the Configuration Manager database, then the change is carried out by the appropriate Configuration Manager site server component processes, and the database is updated with the change. This process is explored more closely in the following sections.

Site settings are stored in the site control file. This file is named Sitectrl.ct0 and is maintained in the <InstallationFolder>\Inboxes\Sitectrl.box directory on the site server. This file is a text file that you can view using any text editor. The beginning of a representative site control file is displayed in Figure 3-12. The file is quite complete and detailed. It's the single most significant file for the site, apart from the database itself, because it contains every site setting parameter.

Figure 3-12   An example of some of the site properties contained in the site control file, showing the site code and site name (Q60 and Contoso Corp – Primary Site), the site server platform (X86), the installation directory (C:\SMS), and the site server name and domain (Contoso1 and ContosoCorpDOM)

The site control file can be modified either through a change initiated by the Configuration Manager administrator or through a change initiated by a Configuration Manager component. Figure 3-13 outlines the process flow for initiating and carrying out a change to the site control file. The Configuration Manager SQL Monitor service and the Hierarchy Manager and Site Control Manager threads are the three Configuration Manager components responsible for maintaining and updating the site control file.

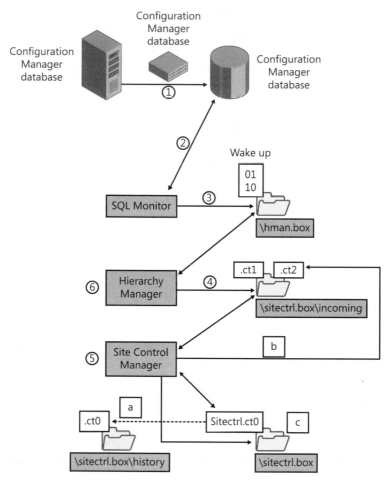

Figure 3-13   The process flow for carrying out changes to the site control file in a Configuration Manager site

This process is broken down into the following steps:

- When the Configuration Manager administrator makes a change to a site setting through the Configuration Manager Administrator's Console, the Configuration Manager Provider directs that request to the Configuration Manager database through Windows Management Instrumentation (WMI). It matches the change against the current database settings (called the site control image) and then creates a delta site control image that contains the changes to be made.

- An SQL-stored procedure (one of over 200) is triggered, which wakes up the Configuration Manager SQL Monitor Service.

- The Configuration Manager SQL Monitor, in turn, writes a wake-up file to Hierarchy Manager's inbox, <InstallationFolder>\Inboxes\Hman.box. This filename is in the form sitecode.ssu or sitecode.scu, where sitecode is the three-character code you assigned to the site during setup.

- The Hierarchy Manager component on the site server monitors Hman.box for any new files. When the wake-up file is written to that folder, the Hierarchy Manager thread accesses the database and looks for any proposed changes to the site settings. If a delta image exists in the database, Hierarchy Manager creates a delta site control file with the extension .ct1 and writes this file to Site Control Manager's inbox, <InstallationFolder>\Inboxes\Sitectrl.box\Incoming.

- The Site Control Manager component on the site server monitors Sitectrl.box\Incoming for any new files. When the .ct1 file is written, the Site Control Manager thread wakes up, reads the .ct1 file, and performs three actions:

  ❑ It copies the current Sitectrl.ct0 file to the <InstallationFolder>ns\Sitectrl.box\History folder. Configuration Manager retains the last 100 site control files. As you'll discover, these files can multiply quickly.

  ❑ It merges the changes into the current site control file and creates a .ct2 file in Hierarchy Manager's inbox, <InstallationFolder>\Inboxes\Hman.box.

  ❑ It creates a new Sitectrl.ct0 file in the <InstallationFolder>\Sitectrl.box directory.

- Hierarchy Manager wakes up when the .ct2 file is written to its inbox and updates the Configuration Manager database with the new site control data.

Note   Hierarchy Manager and Site Control Manager wake up whenever a file is written to their respective inboxes on the site server. However, they also have wake-up cycles. Hierarchy Manager will wake up every 60 minutes by default, and Site Control Manager will wake up once a day at midnight by default to generate a heartbeat site control file for Hierarchy Manager.

Site Control Filenames

As you monitor the Hierarchy Manager and Site Control Manager inboxes, you'll see the .ct1 and .ct2 files created. You'll also notice the rather strange filenames that are assigned to these files. When the files are created, they're assigned randomly generated filenames. This is done to ensure uniqueness and to provide security. By scanning the status messages that are generated, or the log files, for Hierarchy Manager and Site Control Manager, you can follow the creation of these files as they move from inbox to inbox.

The history copy of the site control file that Site Control Manager writes to the <InstallationFolder>\Inboxes\Sitectrl.box\History folder, however, has a definite naming convention. Here each site control history file is named *.ct0, where * represents the site control file serial number in hexadecimal format. Thus, site control file 9 would be saved with the filename 00000009.ct0, and site control file 10 would be saved with the filename 0000000A.ct0.

The site control file's serial number is simply its sequential order in relation to other site control files. The site control file created during setup is serial number 0. The next one representing a change in site settings would be serial number 1, and so on. The serial number is recorded in the sixth line of the site control file, which can be read using any text editor.

This is not the whole story, of course. When you initiate a change, you might be asking Configuration Manager to enable a component, schedule a task, or initiate discovery or installation. Other Configuration Manager components also monitor the Sitectrl.ct0 file for changes, or the SQL Monitor Service might write a wake-up file directly to the appropriate component's inbox. When Site Control Manager generates the new site control file or SQL Monitor writes a wake-up file to an inbox, these other components wake up, read the file(s) for changes that pertain to that component, and then carry out the change. These same components might themselves create .ct1 files to update the site control file with changes that have been carried out.

As you can see, the Site Control Manager process is very much event driven, meaning that services and threads wake up when a change is detected rather than waiting a predetermined period of time before waking up and checking for any activity that needs to take place.

More Info   Throughout this book, you explore process flows relating to specific processes such as package distribution and client installation. You look at the highlights of these process flows—those elements that most facilitate troubleshooting. However, many of these process flows are far more complex. For a thorough treatment of various Configuration Manager process flows, refer to the flowcharts included with the Configuration Manager Documentation Library.

Monitoring Status and Flow

Configuration Manager offers an excellent set of tools for monitoring the status and flow of the Site Control Manager process: site status messages and site component log files. Together, these tools provide you the means not only to effectively troubleshoot a Configuration Manager process but also to learn the process and become familiar with the way Configuration Manager components interact with, and react to, one another.

Status Messages

Each of the Configuration Manager components responsible for carrying out the Site Control Manager process generates a set of status messages specific to this process. To view these status messages, expand the System Status node in the Configuration Manager console, expand Site Status, and then expand your site. Click Component Status to view a list of status messages for all the components, as shown in Figure 3-14. You'll find entries for Hierarchy Manager and Site Control Manager listed here.

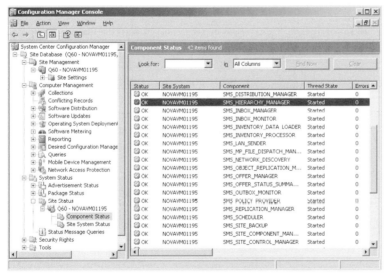

Figure 3-14 The Site Component Status window, listing the general status level for all the Configuration Manager components

To view all the detailed status messages generated for a component, right-click the component, choose Show Messages from the context menu, and then choose All. Configuration Manager displays the rich set of detailed messages that that component has generated during a predefined period by default since midnight that day. Figures 3-15 and 3-16 show the messages generated by Hierarchy Manager and Site Control Manager, with the content of one message displayed. You can view message content by double-clicking the message or by positioning your cursor on the description area of each message to open a pop-up window. Viewing and configuring status messages are discussed in detail in Chapter 6, "Analysis and Troubleshooting Tools."

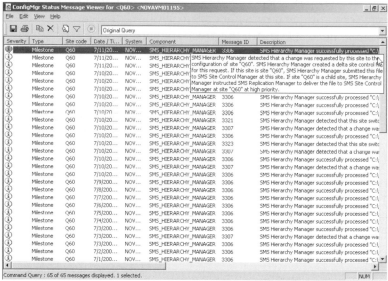

Figure 3-15   Status messages generated by Hierarchy Manager. Message IDs 3306 and 3307 (displayed) are specific to the Site Control Manager process.

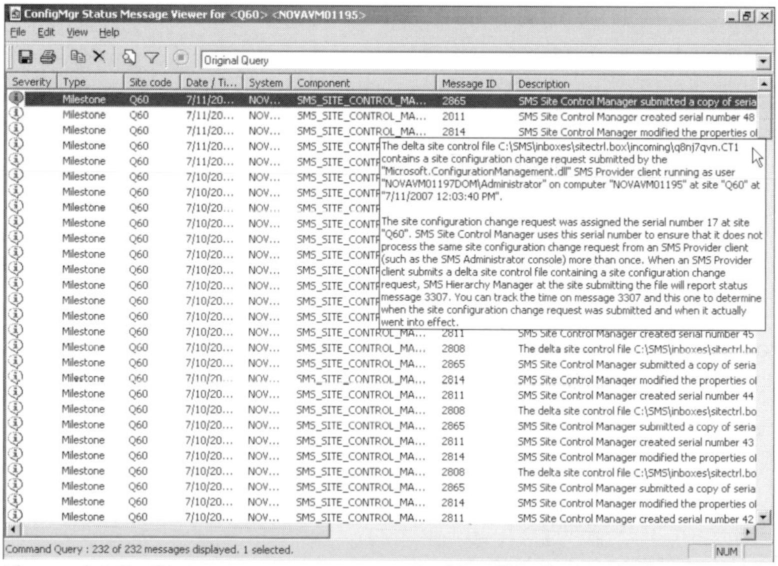

Figure 3-16   Status messages generated by Site Control Manager. Message IDs 2807, 2811, 2814 (displayed), and 2865 are specific to the Site Control Manager process.

Log Files

In addition to status messages, you can configure each component to create and maintain log files. Logging is enabled for several Configuration Manager components by default. Keep in mind, however, that logging component activity requires an additional expense of resources on the site server. Depending on the Configuration Manager features you install and the components you enable and configure, Configuration Manager could generate 40 or more log files.

Needless to say, it's not always practical, or even necessary, to enable logging for every Configuration Manager component. Logging is intended primarily as a troubleshooting tool. However, you would do well to practice using logging in a test environment to learn how the Configuration Manager components interact with one another. Logging is certainly not the most exciting activity you can engage in, but nevertheless this exercise is enlightening from a Configuration Manager perspective.

Enabling Configuration Manager Log Files

You enable and disable Configuration Manager component log files through the Configuration Manager Service Manager tool launched in the Configuration Manager console. Follow these steps to enable Configuration Manager component log files:

1. Expand the Tools node in the Configuration Manager console.

2. Right-click ConfigMgr Service Manager, choose All Tasks from the context menu, and then choose Start ConfigMgr Service Manager. Configuration Manager launches the ConfigMgr Service Manager console. Notice that it makes its own connection to the Configuration Manager database.

3. Expand the site node and highlight Components, as shown in Figure 3-17.

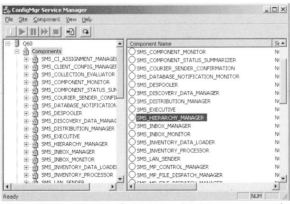

Figure 3-17   The ConfigMgr Service Manager console

4. Right-click the component for which you want to enable logging—for example, SMS_Hierarchy_Manager—and then choose Logging from the context menu to display the ConfigMgr Component Logging Control dialog box, as shown in Figure 3-18.

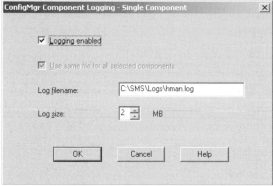

Figure 3-18   The ConfigMgr Component Logging Control dialog box for single components

5. Select the Logging Enabled check box. Note the location and name of the log file that is created. Modify this entry only if you need to. Note also the default log size of 2 MB. This setting ensures that the log doesn't compromise disk storage space. Again, you can modify this entry (in MB) if you need to.

6. Click OK and then close the ConfigMgr Service Manager console.

Note   When the log file reaches its maximum log size, that file is renamed with an .lo_ extension and a new file is started. This is done so that you can see the last set of log file entries. For example, when hman.log reaches its maximum size of 2 MB, it is renamed as hman.lo_, and a new hman.log file is created. With over 40 components each saving potentially a total of 4 MB of log data, you can see how server disk space can quickly be consumed.

Real World   Enabling Logging for Multiple Components

Obviously, there's much more to Configuration Manager Service Manager, which you look at more closely in Chapter 6. However, one feature that's definitely applicable here is the ability to enable logging for multiple Configuration Manager components at one time.

You can enable logging for multiple components at one time by holding down the Ctrl key and clicking the components you want to log, just like selecting multiple files in Windows Explorer. You can enable logging for all components by clicking the Component menu in the Configuration Manager Service Manager console and then choosing Select All or by right-clicking a component and choosing Select All from the context menu. With all the components selected, you can either right-click any one of them and choose Logging from the context menu or click the Component menu once again, choose Logging, and then enable logging as described earlier.

When you enable logging for multiple Configuration Manager components in this way, the Use Same File For All Selected Components option is selectable in the ConfigMgr Component Logging Control dialog box, as shown in Figure 3-19.

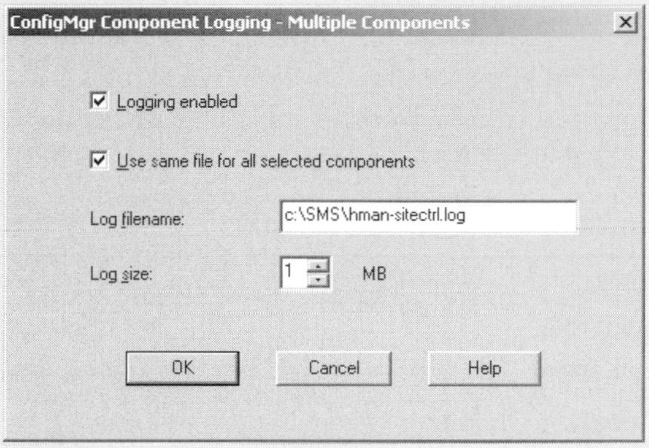

Figure 3-19   The ConfigMgr Component Logging Control dialog box for multiple components

Selecting this option causes the components that you select to write their logging data to a single file. With more than two or three components, this log file can become confusing and somewhat unwieldy. Nevertheless, for something like the site configuration change process, in which two Configuration Manager threads are involved, this file can provide a single source of tracking information. Before you select this option, though, write down the name and location of the original file so that you can revert back to single log files if you need to. The tool does not have a facility for doing this for you. For example, in Figure 3-19, I used the names of the log files for the two components I was tracking as the basis for the new log file name. This way, I can revert each back to a single file using the original file name if I need to.

Log files are text files that are written, by default, to the <InstallationFolder>\Logs folder. You can save these files anywhere you want when you enable logging, but unless you have disk resource concerns, why make changes? You can view log files using any text editor or using the Configuration Manager Trace utility included as part of the Configuration

Manager Toolkit available for download from the Configuration Manager product site at *http://www.microsoft.com/smserver/default.mspx.* The advantage of using Configuration Manager Trace is that it displays one or more log files in real time—that is, while they're being updated. A text editor will display the file only as it appears up to that point in time. For details on how to use Configuration Manager Trace effectively, refer to Chapter 6.

Defining and Configuring Site Systems

New site systems for the Configuration Manager site are defined as site settings for the site. As such, you could consider these site systems to be properties of the site as well. In this section, you review the site systems that you can define and examine how each becomes a site system for your Configuration Manager site. The various site roles that you can assign to a Configuration Manager site system and the specific features they are related to are listed in Table 3-1.

Table 3-1   Site System Roles and Features They Are Associated With

Site system role	Related feature
Site server	Basic site system role
Database server	Basic site system role
Branch distribution point	Software distribution, Operating System Deployment
Device management point	Device management
Distribution point	Software distribution, Operating System Deployment
Fallback status point	Basic site system role, device management
Management point	Basic site system role
PXE service point	Operating system deployment
Reporting point	Basic site system role
Server locator point	Basic site system role
Software update point	Software updates
State migration point	Operating system deployment
System health validator point	Configuration Manager network access protection

Each of these roles is supported to a greater or lesser extent depending on the operating system platform the site system is using. Chapter 2, "Planning for and Deploying Configuration Manager Sites," describes the server requirements for the Configuration Manager Site Server and Configuration Manager SQL Server in detail. As with Configuration Manager Site Server, you can assign the site system roles to any server that is a member of a

Windows 2000 Server or the Windows Server 2003 Active Directory domain. Table 3-2 outlines additional requirements for specific site system roles.

Table 3-2   Additional Requirements for Site System Roles

Site system role	Requirement
Device management point	If you intend to use a server as a management point for devices, you must have Internet Information Services (IIS) installed and enabled, as well as BITS, and Web-Based Distributed Authoring and Versioning (WebDAV).
Distribution point	If you intend to use the Background Intelligent Transfer Service (BITS) to throttle network bandwidth when downloading packages, both the site server and the distribution point must have Internet Information Services (IIS) installed and enabled, as well as BITS, and Web-Based Distributed Authoring and Versioning (WebDAV).
Management point	If you intend to use a server as a management point, you must have Internet Information Services (IIS) installed and enabled, as well as BITS, and Web-Based Distributed Authoring and Versioning (WebDAV).
PXE service point	This role must be installed on a Windows server that has Windows Deployment Services (WDS) installed. Windows Server 2008 includes WDS. However, if the server is running Windows Server 2003 Service Pack 1, you must first install Remote Installation Services (RIS), and then the Windows Automated Installation Kit (Windows AIK). If the server is running Windows Server 2003 Service Pack 2 you can skip Windows AIK, and install WDS using Add/Remove Programs.
Reporting point	If you intend to use a server as a reporting point, you must install and enable IIS as well as Active Server Pages. Any server or client that will use the Report Viewer component must have Internet Explorer 5.01 with Service Pack 2 or later installed, and the server will need Office Web Components to use graphs in the reports.
Server locator point	If you intend to use a server as a server locator point, you must install and enable IIS.
Software update point	You must install and configure Windows Server Update Services (WSUS) 3.0 on the site system server before you assign the software update point site role or the software update point component installation will fail.
System health validator point	If you intend to use Configuration Manager Network Access Protection, this role must be installed on the Windows Server 2008 server configured with the Network Policy Server (NPS) role.

You've already looked closely at installing and configuring the site server and the site database server (the SQL server). Now focus on the other site system roles. The Configuration Manager administrator generally assigns site system roles. The Configuration

Manager administrator can assign all the site system roles mentioned so far to any server that meets the requirements already outlined.

You must be sure that the proposed site system meets the requirements outlined in Table 3-2. In addition, check for space and partition requirements as outlined in the relevant sections later in this chapter for each site system role. For example, disk space is arguably the most significant consideration when assigning the distribution point role to a server. Also, clients must be able to access site systems such as distribution points and management points in order to access advertisements, client component files and configuration updates, to write discovery and inventory data, and to read and execute package scripts. In large part, Configuration Manager assigns the appropriate level of permissions, but this doesn't totally absolve you from checking and testing permissions and access.

Site System Connection Accounts

The number, type, and purpose of Configuration Manager accounts are discussed in detail in Chapter 20. However, because the discussion here is about site systems, it's appropriate to speak about the accounts used by Configuration Manager to facilitate communications between the site server and its site systems. Consequently, a brief discussion follows about Configuration Manager accounts as they relate to site systems.

Configuration Manager uses some account types to facilitate communications between the site server and its site systems. Site servers need to connect to site systems to transfer information such as advertised programs, package information, client component option updates, and so on. Site systems, on the other hand, need to connect to site servers to transfer information that they've collected, such as client inventory data and discovery information.

The following accounts facilitate communications between the Configuration Manager site server and a site system.

- **Computer account <computername$>**   The computer account is used to facilitate most Configuration Manager computer-to-computer communications, providing a highly secure method of accessing resources on site systems. With respect to site systems, the computer account of the site server is used to:
    - Communicate with child and parent sites
    - Install secondary sites when initiated from the Configuration Manager console
    - Install remote site systems
    - Retrieve data from site systems

The computer account of the site system is used to:

❑ Provide access to the site database for management points, reporting points, server locator points, PXE service points, and state migration points.

❑ Push data back to the site server from management points, device management points, PXE service points, state migration points, System Health Validator points, software update points, and fallback status points. In this case, the site system computer account of each site system must be a member of the Site System to Site Server Connection group

■ **Site system installation**   The site system installation account can be used to install and configure site systems if you would rather not use the site server's computer account to do so. If the site system is located in a remote, untrusted forest, you must configure this account. This is created in Windows and specified for each site system through the Configuration Manager console. The account must have Administrator rights on the site system that it will communicate with. This account must also have Access This Computer From The Network enabled in the security policy on the site system.

■ **Site System To Site Server Connection (SMS_SiteSystemToSiteServerConnection_sitecode)**   The Site System To Site Server Connection group gives site systems the ability to connect to the site server to read and write resources such as advertised programs and inventory. Its members should be only the site system *computer* accounts that require this level of access. Configuration Manager automatically adds the computer accounts for the following site systems to this group:

❑ Management points

❑ Fallback status points

❑ PXE service points

❑ Software update points

❑ State migration points

❑ System Health Validator points

■ **Database connection accounts**   By default, Configuration Manager uses the computer account of the site system to connect to the site database. However, you can configure alternate accounts to use for management points, PXE service points, and server locator points. If a management point needs to access a site database in a different domain than the site server is in, or if a PXE service point needs to access a site database in a remote, untrusted forest, then you must create this account for that site system.

This account is created and maintained in Windows by the administrator and specified for each site system through the Configuration Manager console. For a management point, this account must be manually added to the smsdbrole_MP role in the site database. For a PXE service point, this account must be manually added to the smsdbrole_PSP role in the site database. For a server locator point, this account must be manually added to the smsdbrole_SLP role in the site database.

More Info   For a detailed discussion about accounts and account management in Configuration Manager, see "Security and Privacy" in the Configuration Manager Documentation Library.

Assigning Site System Roles

Now that you have identified the servers that will become site servers and created any necessary connection accounts, you must tell Configuration Manager that the server should be considered a site system. To do so, follow these general steps:

1. In the Configuration Manager console, navigate to the Site Settings folder and expand it.

2. Select the Site Systems folder. Initially, the only entry you see in the results pane is the site server itself.

3. Add a new site system by right-clicking the Site Systems folder and choosing New from the context menu to display the two site system options listed: Server and Server Share. Choose either Server or Server Share.

   Choosing Server launches the New Site System Server Wizard, as shown in Figure 3-20. On the general page, type the name of the Windows server that you want to make a site system. In addition, you can type a fully qualified domain name (FQDN), as well as the FQDN for an Internet-facing server that will act as a connection point for Internet-based clients. By default, Configuration Manager uses the computer account of the site server to install and configure the site system, but if you create an alternative account in Windows, you can specify that account instead. The Enable This Site System As A Protected Site System option lets you prevent clients from accessing the site system unless they are located within the configured protected boundaries of the site system. If a site system is configured as a protected site system and no boundaries are specified, clients are unable to access the site system. This option applies only to site systems that are configured as distribution points and state migration points. When you're finished, click Next.

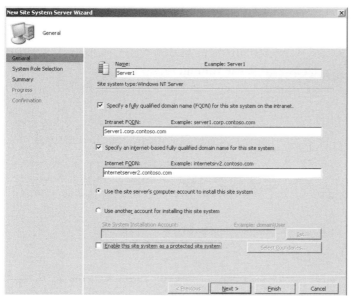

Figure 3-20   The New Site System Server Wizard General page for a new site system server

Choosing Server Share will display a slightly different Site System Properties window, as shown in Figure 3-21. Click Set and type the name of the server and share (which you have already created) that you want to define as the site system. Click the tab for the site system role you want to assign to the server and make the appropriate option choices. Notice that only the distribution point role can be assigned to a share.

Planning   It's not necessary that you assign a site system role immediately. You might choose to wait until you complete your assessment as to the best number and placement of site system servers. This is particularly useful when you plan a phased rollout of your site.

The main difference between the Server and Server Share options is that by creating a share first and defining it as the site system, you can direct where Configuration Manager creates and writes the support files for the distribution point roles. However, if you use Server Share, Configuration Manager does not create a discovery record for that site system.

Note   If you need a discovery record for the site system created as a Server Share, create the site system as both a Server Share and Server. Simply assign the desired roles to the Server Share site system entry; don't assign any site system roles to the Server site system entry.

4. Click Next to display the System Role Selection page, as shown in Figure 3-22. Select the site system role or roles you want to assign to the server, then click Next to continue.

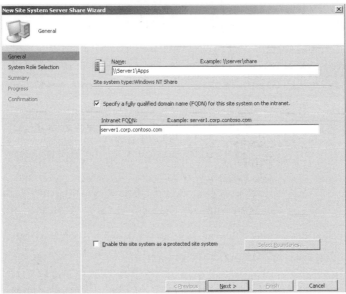

Figure 3-21   The New Site System Server Wizard General page for a server share

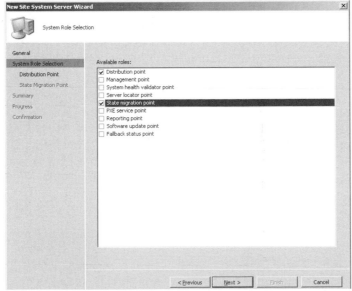

Figure 3-22   The New Site System Server Wizard System Role Selection page

5. Click Next to display pages requesting any additional parameters or settings related to the roles you select. These specific settings are discussed in more detail in the chapters for which the site system roles are relevant. Figure 3-23 shows the Distribution Point page as an example.

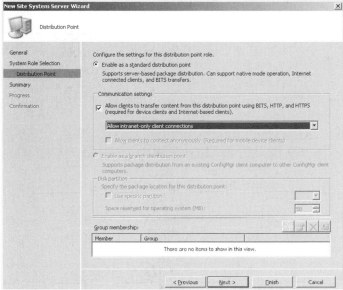

Figure 3-23 The New Site System Server Wizard Distribution Point page

6. After completing these pages, click Next to review your settings, and then click Next again to start the installation process.

7. Click Close to complete the wizard.

The next few sections explore the basic site system roles—distribution point, management point, reporting point, server locator point, and fallback status point—and the options that are available when you assign that role to a server. The other site system roles are addressed within the context of the feature they support.

Distribution Points

The distribution point is a Configuration Manager site system that stores the package files, programs, and scripts necessary for a package to execute successfully at a Configuration Manager client computer. When the site server is installed, it becomes a distribution point by default. However, you might want to assign other site systems as distribution points and remove this role from the site server to reduce its resource requirements and improve its performance as well as to load balance the potentially significant network traffic generated by clients downloading package source files.

BITS-Enabled Distribution Points

Configuration Manager clients can take advantage of Background Intelligent Transfer Service (BITS), which was first supported in Systems Management Server 2003. BITS is a service that can be enabled on distribution points that serve Configuration Manager clients. It's used to help control the amount of bandwidth used by a Configuration Manager client during download, as well as to insure that the Configuration Manager client doesn't necessarily have to wait a lengthy period for a package while, say, being connected to the network through a slow or unreliable connection. BITS provides a checkpoint restart of a package. If the download of package files is interrupted, the connection is lost accidentally or because the user needs to disconnect, the download can continue from the point it was interrupted when a new connection is established rather than starting over from the beginning.

Important   The checkpoint restart will restart the download with the last file that was being accessed at the time the connection was lost. If this was the 10th file out of 20, the download restarts with the 10th file when the connection is reestablished. However, if your package consists of a single executable file, such as an .exe or .msi file, the download restarts at the beginning, because that was the file that was interrupted.

The Configuration Manager client remains assigned to its original site. However, when the Configuration Manager client needs to retrieve an advertised package, it can download or run the package from a local distribution point, rather than from its assigned site. Remember this when you choose remote servers to be distribution points.

To protect your Configuration Manager clients from excessive bandwidth consumption, enable BITS on your distribution points that serve Configuration Manager clients. This provides an efficient file transfer mechanism through client-sensitive bandwidth throttling. It also provides checkpoint restart download of packages, which allows files to be transferred to the client in a throttled manner.

Protected Distribution Points

The protected distribution point is designed to protect network links to distribution points from unwanted traffic. The Configuration Manager administrator specifies which roaming boundaries or site boundaries Configuration Manager clients must be in to use the protected distribution point. Any clients outside those boundaries are unable to download or run packages from that distribution point.

To restrict access to a distribution point that's across a slow or unreliable network link, plan to enable it as a protected distribution point. This is beneficial at remote locations where a small number of Configuration Manager clients and a distribution point are connected to the primary site by a WAN. For example, consider configuring a protected distribution point on secondary site servers that are connected to their parent primary site by a WAN link.

Branch Distribution Points

Configuration Manager introduces a new site server role called the branch distribution point. This role allows small office locations to host packages on workstation computers without requiring another primary or secondary site to be installed at that location. This is particularly useful for offices with fewer than 10 workstations, where maintaining a separate server for a Configuration Manager site might not be practical.

Branch distribution points function in much the same way as standard distribution points, but have the advantage of providing greater control over network traffic, which is necessary for branch offices that may have limited network bandwidth availability. Branch distribution points not only let you manually copy packages onto the host computer, but also let you configure settings for scheduling and throttling network traffic and enabling BITS to help minimize network impact. Also, you have the option to allow on-demand package distribution, in which packages are only downloaded to the branch distribution point when specifically requested by a client computer. Branch distribution points are discussed in more detail in Chapter 16, "Managing Clients Across the Internet."

To configure the distribution point role, follow these steps:

1. Follow the steps for installing a new site server role listed earlier, or double-click an existing site server listed in the results pane and select New Role.

2. On the System Role Selection page, select Distribution Point and click Next.

3. On the Distribution Point page, shown in Figure 3-24, enter the appropriate settings and parameters. The Enable As A Standard Distribution Point option is selected by default. If you want to take advantage of the benefits of using BITS communication, select the Allow Clients To Transfer Content From This Distribution Point Using BITS, HTTP, or HTTPS option. You can specify what kinds of Configuration Manager clients to apply this setting to by selecting it from the drop-down list. The types available depend on the kinds of clients you enable support for—for example, Internet-based clients. Select the Enable As A Branch Distribution Point option if you intend to use the computer as a branch distribution point in a small remote office scenario. Select the Use Specific Partition option to specify a particular partition to use to host the SMSPKG<driveletter>$ package directory.

4. Distribution point groups let you group your distribution points into more manageable units. Packages can then be targeted to a distribution point group rather than

to individual distribution points. If you want to make this distribution point a member of a distribution point group, in the Group Membership section, click the yellow star button on the right to display the Distribution Point Group dialog box, as shown in Figure 3-25.

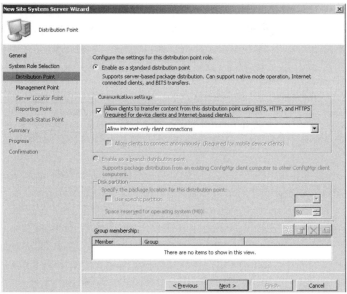

Figure 3-24   The New Site System Server Wizard Distribution Point page

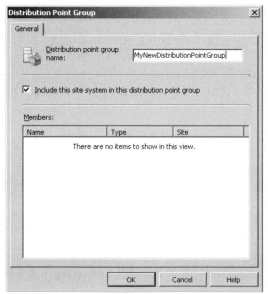

Figure 3-25   The Distribution Point Group dialog box

5. Type the name of the distribution point group you want to create. If you want the site system you selected to be included in the group you're creating, select the Include This Site System In This Distribution Point Group check box. Then click OK.

6. Click OK again to save this setting.

7. Complete any other system role pages, click Next to review your settings, then Next again to start the installation process.

8. Click Close to complete the wizard.

If you want to remove the distribution point role from the site server, right-click the site server and follow the same procedures as you did to assign a management point role to the site system; however, clear the Distribution Point check box when you're in the System Role Selection page.

When you enable the new distribution point, you have initiated a change to the site control information for the site. A new site control file will be created according to the process described in the section "The Site Configuration Process Flow" earlier in this chapter. However, no Configuration Manager components are installed on the distribution point.

The distribution point is not written to until a package is actually distributed. At that time, the Distribution Manager thread on the site server checks the distribution point for the partition with the most free space. On that partition, it creates a shared folder named SMSPkgx$, where x is the drive letter of the partition. The share is a hidden share—a change from earlier versions of Configuration Manager. Then the Distribution Manager component on the site server copies the package and program files to a subfolder beneath SMSPkgx$. If in the course of copying packages to the distribution point, you begin to run low on disk space, the Distribution Manager finds the next partition with the most free space and creates another shared SMSPkgx$ folder there. You encounter the Distribution Manager again in Chapter 16.

Note Distribution points cannot be shared among Configuration Manager sites. Configuraiton manager does not support having one server assigned as a distribution point for more than one Configuration Manager site.

Management Points

The management point is a Configuration Manager site system that functions as the main exchange point between Configuration Manager clients and the Configuration Manager site server. Components of Configuration Manager clients such as the Remote Tools and

Hardware Inventory Agent are configured and enabled through a client policy obtained from a management point as are advertisement information and other client instructions. Inventory, status, and discovery information that's collected on a client is written to a management point. When a client receives an advertisement for a program, it also includes a list of distribution points at which the client can find the package files.

If you install Configuration Manager using the Custom Setup option, the site server doesn't become a management point by default. This is a role that you assign to it or other site systems. Several factors might influence the placement and number of management points that you decide to implement. Generally, you choose one server to be the default management point for that site, and that management point supports all your Configuration Manager clients. However, you might choose to have additional management points for network load balancing or backup purposes in case the default server is down or unavailable, especially if you have large numbers of Configuration Manager clients that need to be supported.

When you configure the management point role, you'll notice reference to an SQL database. Again, because typically you'll have one management point implemented, it uses the data in the Configuration Manager site database. However, if you do need to implement additional management points, you might choose to off-load some of the SQL Server resource requirements for the management point from the Configuration Manager site database to a replicated copy of the site database, perhaps installed on the management point itself.

To configure the management point role, follow these steps:

1. Follow the steps for installing a new site server role listed earlier, or double-click an existing site server listed in the results pane and select New Role.

2. On the System Role Selection page, select Management Point and click Next.

3. On the Management Point page, shown in Figure 3-26, enter the appropriate settings and parameters. If you want to use the management point to support devices such as smart phones, select the Allow Devices To Use This Management Point option. You can specify what kinds of Configuration Manager clients to connect to the management point by selecting a type from the Allow Client Connections dropdown list. The types available depend on the kinds of clients you enable support for—for example, Internet-based clients.

    The Use The Site Database option is selected by default. Keep it selected if the management point should access the Configuration Manager site database for reading and writing client data. Select the Use A Database Replica option and supply the requested information if the management point should access a database other than the Configuration Manager site database—for example, if you have replicated the Configuration Manager site database to another SQL server for load balancing or failover. By default, Configuration Manager uses the computer account of the management point site server to connect to the site database. If you configure another account to use, select the Use Another Account option and click Set to enter the account name.

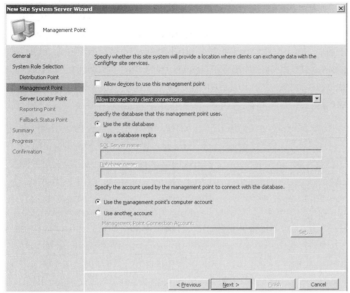

Figure 3-26   The New Site System Server Wizard Management Point page

4. Complete any other system role pages, click Next to review your settings, then Next again to start the installation process

5. Click Close to complete the wizard.

If you want to remove the management point role from the site server, right-click the site server and follow the same procedures as you did to assign a management point role to the site system; however, clear the Management Point check box when you're in the System Role Selection page.

As with other site systems, when you enable a new management point, you have initiated a change to the site control information for the site. A new site control file is created according to the process described in the section "The Site Configuration Process Flow" earlier in this chapter. Recall that during that process, after the new site control file is generated, other components wake up and read the file to determine whether they need to perform any tasks. As with other site systems, Site Component Manager is responsible for the setup of a management point.

The Configuration Manager Agent Host (Ccmexec.exe) loads and starts and is used to provide change and configuration management services. Two directories are created on the new management point. The folder %Systemroot%\System32\CCM is created and is the location for the agent support files. The folder CCM is created on the NTFS partition with the most free space and acts as the "clearinghouse" for data provided to the client and received from the client.

Management Point Component Configuration

In addition to assigning the management point role to a site system, you also have the option of configuring the default settings for the management point role function. You can do this through the Management Point Component configuration properties by completing the following steps:

1. In the Configuration Manager console, navigate to the Site Settings folder and expand it.

2. Highlight the Component Configuration folder to display the list of Configuration Manager components that you can configure in the results pane.

    Right-click the entry Management Point Component and choose Properties from the context menu to display the Management Point Properties dialog box, as shown in Figure 3-27. If there is to be no default management point, select the None option. If you want to name a default management point for the site, select the Management Point option and select the name of the site system that will function as the default management point. Every site must have one default management point specified. If you want the management point to be a Network Load Balancing (NLB) virtual cluster rather than a physical server, select the Network Load Balancing Cluster Virtual Server option and enter the cluster server's virtual IPV4 or IPV6 address. Also, in the Private DNS text box specify the FQDN name of the NLB cluster on the intranet if the NLB management points accept client connections on the intranet. This is a requirement for native mode sites. If you have configured support for Internet-based clients, then in the Public DNS text box, specify the FQDN name of the NLB cluster on the Internet if the NLB management points accept client connections from the Internet.

3. Click OK to save these settings.

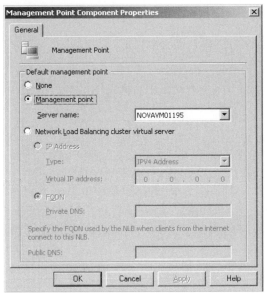

Figure 3-27   The Management Point Component Properties dialog box

The site control information is updated to reflect your component configuration choices.

Proxy Management Points

Configuration Manager clients located at a secondary site and reporting to a management point at a parent primary site across a WAN link might have an effect on the available bandwidth of the WAN link between the secondary site and its parent primary site. Significant network traffic can be produced when client status and hardware or software inventory data is sent to the parent primary site. Because Configuration Manager clients can be assigned only to a primary site, network traffic generated by client policy requests also reduces the available bandwidth between the two sites.

Installing a proxy management point at the secondary site can significantly reduce the effect on available network bandwidth created by Configuration Manager clients located within that site's roaming boundaries or site boundaries. Configuration Manager clients send inventory data, software metering data, and status data to the proxy management point. The proxy management point uses the site's sender functionality to transfer the data to the parent primary site. By using the sender's bandwidth control functionality, you can specify when the data is sent to the primary site. The proxy management point also caches some client policy information. Configuration Manager clients obtain this client policy information from the proxy management point, rather than from the management point at the primary site.

Component Server

Any site system that runs the SMS Executive service is considered a component server. A type of component server that you might define in your site would support the site server by running senders. *Senders* are communication routines used by one site server to contact another site server in a site hierarchy to transfer information. For example, a child site will send inventory data, discovery data, status messages, and site control information to its parent through a sender. A parent site will send package information, advertisements, collections, and configuration data to its child sites through a sender.

When a sender is installed on another Windows server, the SMS Executive and all required support files for that sender are copied to the server and the server becomes a component server—a site system for that Configuration Manager site. The best example of using a component server effectively in a production environment is when a Remote Access Service (RAS) server connection is required or is available as an alternative connection mechanism between two sites. It would probably not be practical or advisable to install the Configuration Manager site server on the RAS server. The combined resource requirement would no doubt result in reduced performance. So with RAS on one server and Configuration Manager on another, you could install the RAS server with a Configuration Manager RAS sender, making it a component server for the Configuration Manager site. Outside of this scenario, the network traffic that might be generated between the site server and the component server (depending on the size and number of packages, advertisements, and so on) might counterbalance any benefit derived from having the additional sender capability. Senders are discussed more closely in Chapter 4.

Reporting Points

A reporting point is a site server that stores the report files used for the Web-based reporting feature in Configuration Manager. Because a reporting point can communicate only with the local site database, this role can be used only within primary sites. In a large site hierarchy, you might consider placing reporting points at each site in hierarchy for access by specific users within those sites, or higher up in the hierarchy so that information about several sites can be reported about several sites.

To configure the management point role, follow these steps:

1. Follow the steps for installing a new site server role listed earlier, or double-click an existing site server listed in the results pane and select New Role.

2. On the System Role Selection page, select Reporting Point and click Next.

On the Reporting Point page, shown in Figure 3-28, enter the appropriate settings and parameters. The Report Folder text box displays the name of the folder created on this site system where the report information will be stored. Recall that IIS must be installed and enabled on the site system to support the reporting point role. Configuration Manager creates the folder under \Inetpub\wwwroot beneath the site server root. The name of the folder is also used as the name of the virtual directory, as displayed in IIS. The URL text box displays the Uniform Resource Locator (URL) used to access reports as determined by the Report Folder name. In the Transfer Protocol section, you can specify whether the Configuration Manager console should open the Report Viewer Web page using HTTP or HTTPS, and the port number to use. HTTP with port 80 is specified as the default. Modify these values as appropriate for your environment.

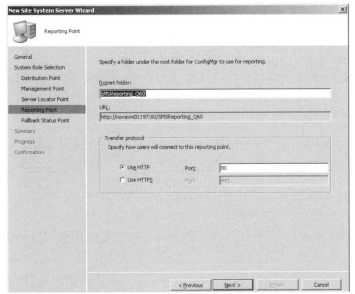

Figure 3-28 The New Site System Server Wizard Reporting Point page

3. Complete any other system role pages, click Next to review your settings, then click Next again to start the installation process.

4. Click Close to complete the wizard.

If you want to remove the reporting point role from the site server, right-click the site server and follow the same procedures as you did to assign a reporting point role to the site system; however, clear the Reporting Point check box when you're in the System Role Selection page.

As with other site systems, when you enable a new reporting point, you have initiated a change to the site control information for the site. A new site control file is created according to the process described in the section "The Site Configuration Process Flow" earlier in this chapter. Recall that during that process, after the new site control file is generated, other components wake up and read the file to determine whether they need to perform any tasks. As with other site systems, Site Component Manager is responsible for the setup of a reporting point. The Configuration Manager Reporting Point Service is loaded and started, and the Report Folder is created under the IIS folder structure.

Server Locator Points

A server locator point is used to implement a client installation point for Configuration Manager clients when using a logon script to initiate client installation or to provide auto-assignment of Configuration Manager clients to a site when the Active Directory schema has not yet been extended. Like the reporting point, a server locator point communicates directly with the local site database and is in contact only with the sites beneath it in the Configuration Manager site hierarchy. Consequently, this role can't be assigned to site systems in a secondary site. Server locator points support the client installation process by locating a management point to which the client can connect to receive component installation files.

Typically, you install the server locator point at the central site. If the server locator point creates too much load at the central Configuration Manager site database, you have the option to use a replicated SQL Server database for that site. If there are excessive client requests, causing excessive traffic on a single server locator point, you can set up multiple server locator points at the central site, but this is not generally recommended.

To configure the server locator point role, follow these steps:

1. Follow the steps for installing a new site server role listed earlier, or double-click an existing site server listed in the results pane and select New Role.

2. On the System Role Selection page, select Server Locator Point and click Next.

3. On the Server Locator Point page, shown in Figure 3-29, enter the appropriate settings and parameters. Select the Use The Site Database option, which is enabled by default, if the server locator point should access the Configuration Manager site database for reading and writing data. Select the Use A Database Replica option and supply the requested information if the server locator point should access a database other than the Configuration Manager site database—for example, if you have replicated the Configuration Manager site database to another SQL server for load balancing or failover. By default, Configuration Manager uses the computer account of the server locator point site server to connect to the site database. If you configure another account to use, select the Use Another Account option and click Set to enter the account name.

4. Complete any other system role pages, click Next to review your settings, then click Next again to start the installation process.

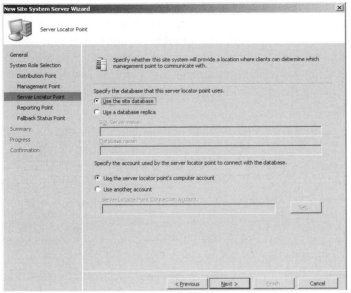

Figure 3-29   The New Site System Server Wizard Server Locator Point page

5.   Click Close to complete the wizard.

If you want to remove the server locator point role from the site server, right-click the site server and follow the same procedures as you did to assign a management point role to the site system; however, clear the Server Locator Point check box when you're in the System Role Selection page.

As with other site systems, when you enable a new server locator point, you have identified a change to the site control information for the site. A new site control file is created according to the process described in the section "The Site Configuration Process Flow" earlier in this chapter. Recall that during that process, after the new site control file is generated, other components wake up and read the file to determine whether they need to perform any tasks. As with other site systems, Site Component Manager is responsible for the setup of a server locator point. The SMS Server Locator Point service loads and starts, and an SMS_SLP support virtual directory is created under the IIS default Web site structure. This virtual directory points to \sms\bin\i386\SMS_SLP.

Fallback Status Points

A fallback status point in Configuration Manager 2007 is an optional but recommended site system role that is used to help administrators monitor client deployment and identify any problems encountered during installation or assignment. It is also used to help identify clients that are unmanaged because they have problems communicating with their management point, which is particularly relevant for when the site is operating in native mode.

The fallback status point receives state messages from Configuration Manager clients and then relays these back to the site. The state message system allows client computers to send short messages to the fallback status point or to the management point that indicate changes of state—for example, success or failure. These changes of state are then made available to the administrator through a number of Configuration Manager reports. Fallback status reports are discussed in more detail in Chapter 8, "Planning for and Installing Configuration Manager Clients."

To configure the fallback status point role, follow these steps:

1. Follow the steps for installing a new site server role listed earlier, or double-click an existing site server listed in the results pane and select New Role

2. On the System Role Selection page, select Fallback Status Point and click Next.

3. On the Fallback Status Point page, shown in Figure 3-30, enter the appropriate settings and parameters. You can specify what kinds of Configuration Manager clients the fallback status report point can receive status data from by selecting a type from the Allowed Client Connections drop-down list. The types available depend on the kinds of clients you have enabled support for—for example, Internet-based clients. If necessary, you can also change the default number of state messages that the fallback status point can send to the site server within the specified throttle interval, as well as the default throttle interval to control bandwidth usage or server processing resources on the site server.

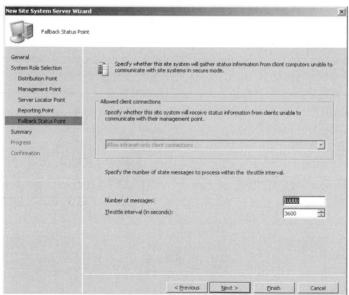

Figure 3-30   The New Site System Server Wizard Fallback Status Point page

4. Complete any other system role pages, click Next to review your settings, then click Next again to start the installation process.

5. Click Close to complete the wizard.

If you want to remove the fallback status point role from the site server, right-click the site server and follow the same procedures you did to assign a management point role to the site system; however, clear the Fallback Status Point check box when you're in the System Role Selection page.

As with other site systems, when you enable a new server locator point, you have initiated a change to the site control information for the site. A new site control file is created according to the process described in the section "The Site Configuration Process Flow" earlier in this chapter. Recall that during that process, after the new site control file is generated, other components wake up and read the file to determine whether they need to perform any tasks. As with other site systems, Site Component Manager is responsible for the setup of a fallback status point.

Checkpoints

If you've been reading carefully, you'll have encountered several notes and cautions describing situations that, if not considered, can result in strange and unusual things happening in your site. These administrative lapses might be called "gotchas" because of the sneaky way they have of jumping up to get you. Following is a recap of the most significant gotchas.

Planning and Identifying Site Systems

First and foremost, be sure that your deployment strategy identifies which servers will serve as site systems, how many servers you might need, and which roles they will play. Your answers will depend on the size of your site; the number of clients, packages, advertisements, and so on involved; and the current state of your network and network traffic. The soundest approach is to test, track, and analyze. Use the tools available to learn how your site server and site systems will perform under different conditions.

The Performance console's System Monitor is an ideal Windows tool to assist you with this analysis on Windows servers. Use Network Monitor to track and analyze traffic generated between the site server and its site systems. Identify, wherever possible, those times when site traffic might take advantage of lighter traffic loads. As you delve more deeply into Configuration Manager processes, such as inventory collection and package distribution, you'll learn how to identify and analyze network traffic.

Disk Space

The amount of disk space required for each type of site system varies. Be sure that the site systems you have in mind have adequate disk space to carry out their function and store their data. Management points, for example, need space to store inventory data, discovery data, and status messages from clients, as well as package information, advertisements, site lists, and client configuration files. Of course, the number of clients you manage and the number of packages and advertisements that you generate affect the disk space requirements, but this quantity can—with some effort and resource analysis—be determined.

Distribution points require as much disk space as each package you store. Again, with some calculation effort and planning, you can determine this number. The space required by a reporting point depends on the number of reports that you have configured and the location of the reporting point within the hierarchy. Server locator points probably require the least amount of additional space because their primary function is to direct a client to an appropriate management point.

Summary

This chapter explored how to configure site server properties such as the site boundaries, roaming boundaries, and site accounts. You explored the site configuration process flow and identified three main Configuration Manager components involved in most site property changes: Configuration Manager Hierarchy Manager, Configuration Manager Site Component Manager, and Configuration Manager Site Control Manager.

This chapter also covered how to identify and configure site systems for your Configuration Manager site. The site server could, of course, be assigned all site system roles, and in many environments this might be appropriate. However, other concerns might lead you to assign one or more site system roles to other servers in your site. These concerns, as you have seen, include performance limitations of the site server, the number and location of your clients and users, network infrastructure, and network traffic patterns. Now that you understand how to manage systems within your site, you can explore in Chapter 4 the process of joining different Configuration Manager sites into an enterprise-wide site hierarchy.

Chapter 4

Implementing Multiple-Site Structures

Centralized network

Manage software from afar

All your apps are mine.

~ Author unknown

For most large organizations, maintaining a single Configuration Manager site to manage all network resources isn't practical. In an organization whose network infrastructure consists of subnets that still communicate through slower WAN connections, routers, and so on, implementing multiple Configuration Manager sites might well prove to be the stronger strategy.

With that in mind, this chapter examines the strategies and processes involved in designing and implementing a site hierarchy for your organization. The concepts of parent-child relationships and creating secondary sites are explored, and you look at methods of communicating between sites. You also examine the factors that affect your site structure strategy, such as network performance, domain model, number and location of clients, and the client components you want to install. Begin with the basic building block of the Configuration Manager site structure—the parent-child relationship.

Defining Parent-Child Relationships

Parent and child sites are defined by their relationship within a Configuration Manager site hierarchy. Related terms and concepts are explained in Chapter 1, "Introducing System Center Configuration Manager 2007." These are reviewed first and then explored in more detail. A *parent site* is any site with at least one child site defined; the parent site has the ability to administer any child sites below it in the Configuration Manager hierarchy. A *child site* is any Configuration Manager site that has a parent defined.

A Configuration Manager *primary site* has three main distinguishing characteristics:

- A primary site is a Configuration Manager site that has access to a Microsoft SQL Server database.

- A primary site can be administered through the Configuration Manager console as well as by any Configuration Manager primary sites above it in the site hierarchy. A primary site can also administer any child sites below it in the site hierarchy.

- A primary site can be a child of other primary sites, and it can have child sites of its own.

The requirement that a primary site has access to a SQL Server database might translate into an additional investment in hardware and software for each Configuration Manager site, site server, or both. On the other hand, because a primary site can be both a parent and a child site, it's relatively easy to restructure your site hierarchy if all your sites are primary sites, as seen in the section "Implementing a Parent-Child Relationship Between Primary Sites" later in this chapter.

A Configuration Manager *secondary site* is also distinguished by three main characteristics:

- A secondary site doesn't have access to an SQL Server database.

- A secondary site is always a child of a primary site and is administered solely through its parent or through another primary site above it in the Configuration Manager site hierarchy.

- A secondary site can't have child sites of its own.

Because a secondary site doesn't require access to an SQL Server database, it might not command the same investment in hardware and software as a primary site. However, a secondary site can be administered only through its parent site or through another primary site above it in the site hierarchy. If a Configuration Manager administrator on the same local subnet as the secondary site wants to administer the site, that Configuration Manager administrator first needs to connect to the site database for the secondary site's parent site. If the SQL database for the parent site is accessed across a WAN link, response might be slow or inefficient. On the other hand, if no local Configuration Manager administrator is available, a remote Configuration Manager administrator can rather easily manage the secondary site in the same manner.

Important   To switch primary and secondary site roles, you must first uninstall and then reinstall Configuration Manager.

A *central site* is a Configuration Manager primary site that resides at the top of the Configuration Manager hierarchy. Database information rolls from child to parent and is collected ultimately at the central site's Configuration Manager database. A central site can administer any site below it in the Configuration Manager hierarchy and can send information down to its child sites.

Child sites send inventory data, discovery data, site control data, and status messages to their immediate parent sites. A child site never sends information directly to its "grandparent" site. Parent sites, in turn, send information about collections, package definitions, advertisements, and site control files to their child sites. Although child sites send data only to their immediate parent, a parent site can send information to any child below it in the Configuration Manager site hierarchy, provided it has an address for that site. Addresses are discussed later in this chapter.

Because child sites send inventory data to their parent sites, database storage space becomes a greater concern at the parent sites at each successive layer up in the hierarchy. In the hierarchy shown in Figure 4-1, site A04 reports its inventory data to site A03. Site A03's database needs to be large enough to accommodate its own information plus the information coming from site A04. Similarly, site A03 reports its inventory data to site A01. Because site A01 is also the central site, it receives information from all sites below it in the hierarchy. Site A01's database, therefore, needs to be large enough to accommodate its own information plus that of all sites below it in the hierarchy.

> **Note** Try to keep your site hierarchy as flat as possible. A flatter hierarchy requires information to flow through fewer layers (sites) before reaching the central site. Child site information is reported to the central site more quickly and efficiently. In addition, the simpler the hierarchy, the less concern you'll have about database space requirements at parent sites at each level of the hierarchy.

Installing a Secondary Site

In Chapter 2, "Planning for and Deploying Configuration Manager Sites," you learned how to install a Configuration Manager primary site. This section explores the process of installing a Configuration Manager secondary site. Recall that a secondary site can be a child of only a specific primary site, and it is managed only through that primary site or through any site above it in the site hierarchy. Because of this, it's most appropriate to think of the Configuration Manager secondary site as being a property of a primary site.

You can initiate a Configuration Manager secondary site installation through the Configuration Manager console. However, you can also install it directly from the Configuration Manager CD. The setup program gives you the option of installing a secondary site. You might choose this option if you need to install the secondary site but don't yet have a

WAN connection available to the primary site, or if the existing WAN connection is "network traffic challenged" and you want to avoid the additional traffic involved in performing the installation from the primary site server. Also, when installing a secondary site from CD, you can choose which Configuration Manager components you want to install on the secondary site server much like the custom installation reviewed in Chapter 2. When you install the secondary site from the parent site, all Configuration Manager components are installed on the secondary site server.

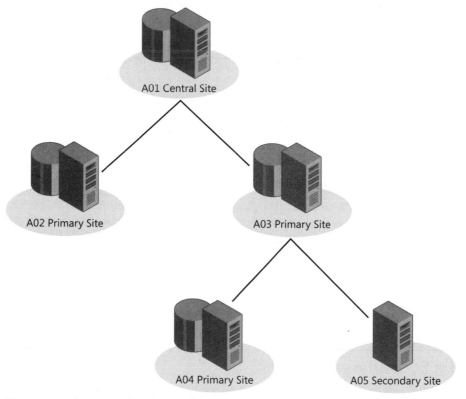

Figure 4-1   An example of a Configuration Manager site hierarchy

---

Note   When using the secondary site installation wizard from the primary site server's console, you have to run the Configuration Manager Prereq Checker manually on the secondary site computer. However, if there are multiple secondary sites to check, the Configuration Manager Prereq Checker will fail after the first secondary site in the series fails.

A better option is to manually run the Configuration Manager Prereq Checker on the secondary site server computer itself or use Configuration Manager Setup directly at the secondary site computer to install it.

Important   You must have run the Configuration Manager Prereq Checker successfully within the last seven days of starting the secondary site installation in
order for the installation to proceed successfully. You can run the Prereq Checker
from the splash screen of the Configuration Manager installation CD.

Installing the Secondary Site from Its Parent Primary Site

Follow these steps to install a Configuration Manager secondary site server from a primary site:

1. In the Configuration Manager console, navigate to the site entry folder (this should
   fall directly below the Site Hierarchy folder), right-click it, and choose New Secondary Site from the context menu to run the Secondary Site Creation Wizard. The
   Welcome page is shown in Figure 4-2.

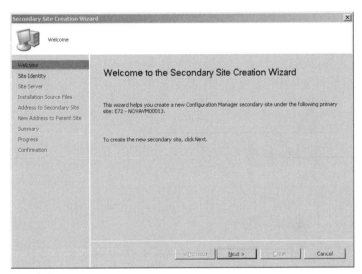

Figure 4-2   The Welcome page of the Secondary Site Creation Wizard

2. Click Next to display the Site Identity page, as shown in Figure 4-3. Type a
   three-character site code, a descriptive name for the site, and optionally a
   descriptive comment.

   Important   Do not use three-character site codes that are also Windows
   NT reserved words as these can cause the creation of the Configuration
   Manager folder on the site server to fail. For more information, see
   Microsoft Knowledge Base article 182420 located at
   http://support.microsoft.com/kb/182420.

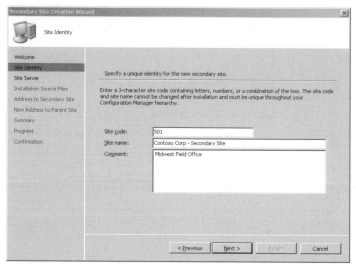

Figure 4-3   The Site Identity page

3. Click Next to display the Site Server page, as shown in Figure 4-4. Type the NetBIOS name of the site server and the installation directory.

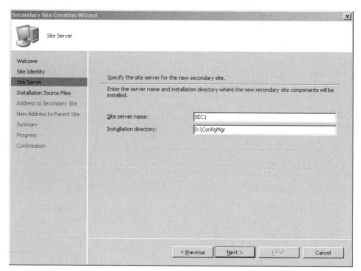

Figure 4-4   The Site Server page

Note   Be sure to type the server name correctly. The Secondary Site installation process doesn't verify that the server actually exists.

4. Click Next to display the Installation Source Files page, as shown in Figure 4-5. This page lets you specify where the source files for installing the secondary site reside. If you select the Copy Installation Source Files Over The Network From The Parent Site Server option, Setup obtains the installation files from the primary site server and copies them across the network to the target secondary site. This option, of course, generates a fair amount of network traffic. If you select the Install The Source Files From The Local Disk Or Removable Media At The Secondary Site Server option, Setup looks for the installation files on the local (secondary site) server. This option assumes, of course, that you have inserted the Configuration Manager CD into the CD drive on the target secondary site server, have copied the Configuration Manager source files to a local drive on the target server, or mapped a drive to a shared folder that contains the Configuration Manager source files.

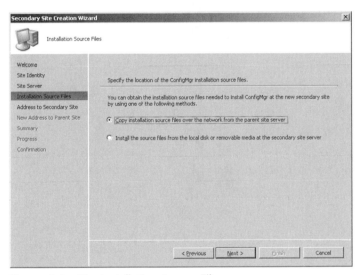

Figure 4-5   The Installation Source Files page

5. Click Next to display the Address To Secondary Site page, as shown in Figure 4-6. If you have already created one or more addresses to the target secondary site—for example, using the Standard Sender (through LAN or WAN connections) or the Asynchronous RAS Sender (through dial-up)—these are listed in the Addresses To list. If you haven't created an address to the secondary site or if you want to create a new address, select the Yes. Create A New Address option and go on to step 6. Otherwise, select the No. Proceed With Site Creation option to use the existing address and proceed to step 7. If there is no existing address to select, you must create a new address.

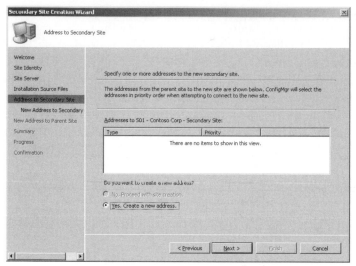

Figure 4-6   The Address To Secondary Site page

Important   By default, Configuration Manager uses the primary site server's computer account when connecting to the secondary site. However, you can also specify a Windows domain user account by clicking the Set button. If you choose the latter, be sure to make the account a member of the Domain Admins global group in the secondary site's Microsoft Windows domain, if not in the same domain. Also, be sure that the account is a member of the local Administrators group on the secondary site server itself—either explicitly or by virtue of its being a member of the Domain Admins global group—and that it has the Log On As A Service user right on the secondary site server. If any of these prerequisites is missing, the installation process will fail—miserably!

---

6. If you select Yes in the preceding step, clicking Next takes you to the New Address To Secondary Site page, as shown in Figure 4-7. Here you must select a sender address type and confirm the secondary site server name.

Note   When you create an address using Setup, you have only the options Standard Sender Address and Asynchronous RAS Sender Address in the Address Type drop-down list. If you choose to use an RAS sender, the RAS service must be installed on the server you'll use for the secondary site server or on another server accessible to the proposed secondary site server. If you need any other sender type, you must create the address through the Configuration Manager console before beginning the secondary site installation process.

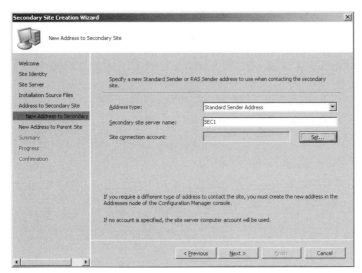

Figure 4-7   The New Address To Secondary Site page

7. Click Next to display the New Address To Parent Site page, as shown in Figure 4-8. Specify a sender address type and confirm the primary site server name. Because the secondary and primary site servers must be in the same Active Directory forest, Configuration Manager uses the secondary site server's computer account as shown in Figure 4-8, and you won't be able to reference any other account.

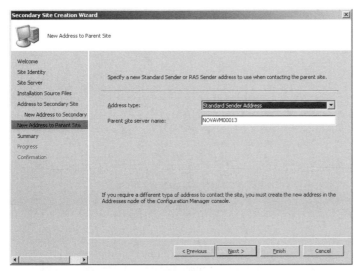

Figure 4-8   The New Address To Parent Site page

8. Click Next to display the Summary page. Review the information on this page to ensure it accurately reflects your choices and then click Next. A progress page

appears. When finished, Configuration Manager displays the Confirmation page that specifies whether the installation was successful or not.

Installing the Secondary Site Locally from the Configuration Manager CD

Follow these steps to install a Configuration Manager secondary site server from the Configuration Manager CD:

1. Insert the Configuration Manager CD into the server drive, or click Autorun in the root of the installation files directory.

2. Click Configuration Manager 2007 to display the setup wizard's Welcome page, as you did when you installed the primary site.

3. Click Next until the Configuration Manager Site Type page appears and then select Secondary Site.

4. On the Destination Folder page, enter a custom installation directory, or click Next to use the default directory location.

5. On the Configuration Manager Site Information page, type the three-character site code you'll assign to the secondary site server and a unique descriptive name for the site.

6. Click Next to display the Configuration Manager Parent Site Settings page. Type the site code and server name of the parent primary site and select the network connection type that the secondary site will use to connect to that parent site. Your connection choices include Local Area Network, the default, Asynchronous RAS link, ISDN RAS link, X.25 RAS link, and SNA Over RAS link.

   Important   You still need to create a valid address at the primary site server that identifies connection parameters that allow the primary site to connect back to the secondary site server. The steps for creating an address are discussed in the section "Creating an Address" later in this chapter.

7. Click Next to display the Summary page, review your selections, and then click Next to begin the installation process. You can click the Back button from this page or any previous page to go back and modify your entries.

   Note   When you apply a service pack to your Configuration Manager sites, secondary sites aren't automatically upgraded when the parent site is upgraded. To upgrade your secondary site server, first upgrade its parent primary site. When you right-click the secondary site object in the Configuration Manager console for the primary site, you have an option to upgrade the site. When you select this option, an upgrade wizard walks you through the upgrade process.

The Secondary Site Installation Process Flow

The process of installing a secondary site from the Configuration Manager CD is relatively straightforward. Setup simply creates the subdirectory structure, loads services and components as necessary, and connects to the parent site to complete the parent-child relationship. This process is similar to the primary site server installation. However, installing a secondary site from a primary site server involves Configuration Manager primary site server components, network traffic, and installation routines installed and run on the secondary site server. This section provides a basic overview of that process.

When you initiate the installation of a secondary site through the Configuration Manager console, you are, in effect, changing the primary site's properties, and the site configuration process flow described in Chapter 3, "Configuring Site Server Properties and Deploying Site Systems," starts. Hierarchy Manager queries the sites table and site control file in the Configuration Manager site database. From this information, it determines that a secondary site installation process needs to be initiated and generates a request to do so in the Scheduler's inbox (<installationfolder>\Inboxes\Schedule.box). The Scheduler, in turn, creates the package and instruction files that support the installation and that need to be sent to the secondary site server and creates a send request file for the sender that connects to the secondary site server. The sender is the same connection mechanism you selected when you initiated the setup process.

The sender connects to and copies the package and instruction files to the secondary site server and loads a bootstrap service that creates the Configuration Manager folder structure, starts the setup process, and loads and starts the Site Component Manager. Site Component Manager completes the installation and configuration of Configuration Manager components, loads and starts the Configuration Manager Executive service, and generates a new site control file. Finally, the connection back to the parent site is configured, and the Replication Manager sends the new secondary server site control information back to the parent site through the Scheduler and sender at the secondary site.

You can follow the flow of this process by monitoring the status messages and log files (if enabled) on the primary site server for Hierarchy Manager, Site Control Manager, Discovery Data Manager, the Scheduler, and the appropriate sender, such as the Standard Sender.

Differences in Installation Between Primary and Secondary Sites

The Configuration Manager secondary site server is installed much like the Configuration Manager primary site server. Setup builds the Configuration Manager directory structure, including the component support files and inboxes, and installs the secondary site server as a Configuration Manager client. Setup installs the secondary site as a site system with the distribution point role by default and doesn't enable any discovery, installation methods, or client agents until the Configuration Manager administrator does so through the Configuration Manager console. The Executive, Site Component Manager, and Site Backup components are loaded; the Executive and Component Manager are started; and the Configuration Manager, Network Access Layer (NAL), and other Configuration Manager service keys are added to the Windows server registry. The same shares are created on the secondary site server as on the primary site server.

However, the secondary site server is fully administered through a parent site, as shown in Figure 4-9. Thus, no Systems Management Server program group is created, and no Configuration Manager console is installed by default. The Configuration Manager SQL Monitor service isn't installed, nor are any references to SQL Server or SQL Server triggers placed in the Windows server registry. Also missing from the Configuration Manager directory structure are folders or files, or both, that reference Configuration Manager components and options that aren't applicable to the secondary site, such as the product compliance database.

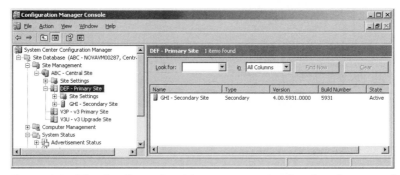

Figure 4-9   The Configuration Manager console, showing the secondary site

Because the secondary site is administered through its parent site, site property changes take place across the network, generating some network traffic. This network traffic generally includes writing the change to the site control file on the secondary site server or writing a file to a component inbox on the secondary site server. The secondary site server will experience performance similar to the primary site server, and you should plan your hardware investment for a secondary site server in much the same way as you would for a primary site server. Because you don't have the added overhead of SQL Server database access, the resource requirements for the secondary site server aren't as high as for a primary site server. Nevertheless, you'll sell yourself, your organization, and the secondary site short if you don't include the same planning and testing strategies when implementing the secondary site as you do when implementing a primary site.

When viewing the site properties of the secondary site through the parent site's Configuration Manager console, you'll notice that any site tasks related to the presence of a database are missing. For example, consider the folder Site Settings\Site Maintenance. For a primary site, you can schedule SQL commands and enable and configure a variety of database tasks, such as backing up the database and setting aging intervals for discovery data and inventory records. For a secondary site, you can schedule only a site backup.

Additionally, the only other site system role supported by a secondary site is management point (in this scenario, called a proxy management point). As you can see in Figure 4-10, if you assign this role, you must specify whether to use the parent site's database or some database on another server.

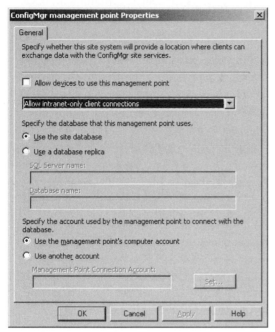

Figure 4-10   The Site Systems Properties dialog box for the management point role for a secondary site site system

> **Note**   You can use the Transfer Site Settings Wizard, discussed later in this chapter, to transfer site settings from a Configuration Manager site to the secondary site.

Uninstalling a Secondary Site

Although there might be several reasons for wanting to remove a secondary site, keep one main consideration in mind—the relationship between the secondary site and its parent. Because the secondary site can't exist without a parent site, it's more closely related to its parent than two primary sites would be in a parent-child relationship. For example, if you want to move the secondary site from one parent to another, you must completely uninstall the secondary site first and then reinstall it for the new parent.

The process for uninstalling a secondary site is similar to that for uninstalling a primary site, as described in Chapter 2. You can initiate an uninstall by running setup from the Configuration Manager source CD, navigating to the Setup Options page, and selecting

Remove Configuration Manager. You can also initiate the uninstall process through the Configuration Manager console. Start the Configuration Manager console for the parent site of the secondary site that you want to remove. Right-click the secondary site entry in the console and choose Delete from the action menu. This starts the Delete Secondary Site Wizard. When you click Next, the setup process displays the Delete Or Uninstall page.

With Configuration Manager, you have the option to completely remove the secondary site installation (the Uninstall This Site option on this page) or to simply remove all references to the secondary site from its parent while leaving the server installation intact (the Delete This Site option). Select the Delete This Site option if, for example, the secondary site server is no longer functioning or no longer exists. In that case the Uninstall This Site option won't work because the secondary site server isn't able to respond to commands to uninstall. Only error messages would be generated at the parent, and the uninstall would fail from the parent's point of view. However, the Delete This Site option bypasses the uninstall portion of the process and simply removes the reference of the secondary site from the parent site. Of course, you might still need to do some cleanup on the secondary site server.

When the removal process is complete and you refresh the parent site console, the secondary site entry is no longer present. You then can proceed to perform your server cleanup tasks for cleaning up an uninstalled primary site, as described in Chapter 2.

Implementing a Parent-Child Relationship Between Primary Sites

When you install a Configuration Manager secondary site, it becomes a child of the primary site from which it's installed, and, voila, you have a parent-child relationship. As discussed, however, primary sites can also enter into parent-child relationships. Two main requirements must be met to successfully implement a parent-child relationship between two primary sites: each site must have an address to the other site, and the child must identify its parent.

Creating an Address

An address in Configuration Manager is yet another site setting—that is, a property of the site. A site server needs to know which other site servers it needs to communicate with—for sending package information, inventory data, status messages, and site control information—and how to establish that communication.

Both the parent and the child need an address to each other. The child sends inventory data, status messages, discovery data, and site control information to its immediate parent. The parent site sends package, collection, advertisement, and site control information to its child. A parent site can also send this information to any other site below it in the hierarchy. It does so by routing the information through its child sites or by configuring an address directly to the other site.

This flow of information is illustrated in Figure 4-11. Sites A04 and A05 report data directly to their parent, site A03. Site A03, in turn, reports its data (which includes the data from sites A04 and A05) directly to its parent, central site A01, as will site A02. Sites A04 and A05 need an address to site A03, and sites A02 and A03 need an address to site A01. Similarly, site A01 needs an address to sites A02 and A03, and site A03 needs an address to sites A04 and A05. Site A01 can administer any site below it in the hierarchy. It can send package and advertisement information to sites A04 and A05 by routing that information through site A03, for which it has an address. However, if the Configuration Manager administrator configures an address in site A01 for site A04, site A01 could send information directly to site A04.

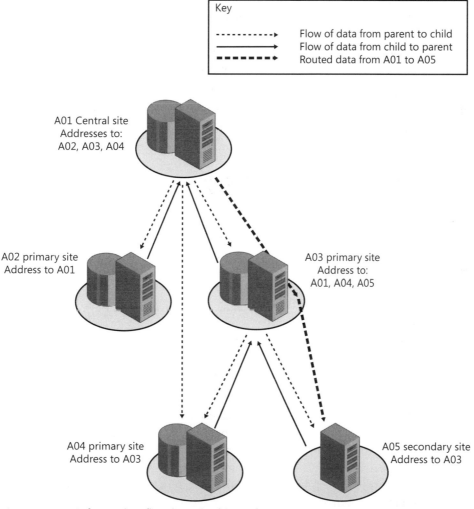

Figure 4-11   Information flow in a site hierarchy

A Configuration Manager site delivers information to another site by connecting to that site using a communication mechanism called a *sender*. The five available senders are Standard Sender (regular LAN/WAN connection), Asynchronous RAS Sender, ISDN RAS Sender, X.25 RAS Sender, and SNA RAS Sender. These senders, along with a sixth sender named Courier Sender, are discussed in detail in the section "Communicating Through Senders" later in this chapter.

These senders connect to a default share point on the target site named SMS_Site. This shared folder references the <Installationfolder>\Inboxes\Despoolr.box\Receive directory and is created automatically during the installation of a primary or secondary site server. By default, Configuration Manager uses the site server computer accounts to connect to this share.

Creating an Address to Another Site

To create an address to another site, follow these steps:

1. In the Configuration Manager console, navigate to the Site Settings folder and expand it.

2. Right-click the Addresses folder and choose New from the context menu. A list of sender address types is displayed, as shown in Figure 4-12.

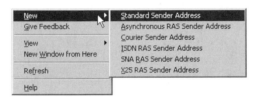

Figure 4-12   Displaying a list of sender address types

3. Choose the sender address type you need to display its New Address Wizard. Fill in the General page for each sender type as follows:

   ❑ In the New Standard Sender Address Wizard General page, shown in Figure 4-13, select the site from the Destination Site Code drop-down list for the target site. In the Destination Access frame, type the name of the destination site's server. Click Set to specify the name and password of the account on the target site that has at least Change permission for the SMS_Site share on the target site.

   ❑ In the New Asynchronous RAS Sender Address Wizard General page, shown in Figure 4-14, select the site from the Destination Site Code drop-down list for the target site. In the RAS Access frame, type the RAS phone book entry that references dial-up information for accessing the target site. Click Set to specify the dial-up access account and phone number to be used when dialing in to the target site. In the Destination Access frame, type the name of the target site's server and the domain of which it is a member. Click Set to specify the name and password of the account on the target site that has at least Change permission for the SMS_Site share on the target site. If you're running in advanced security mode, this account is displayed as Local System, and you won't be able to change it.

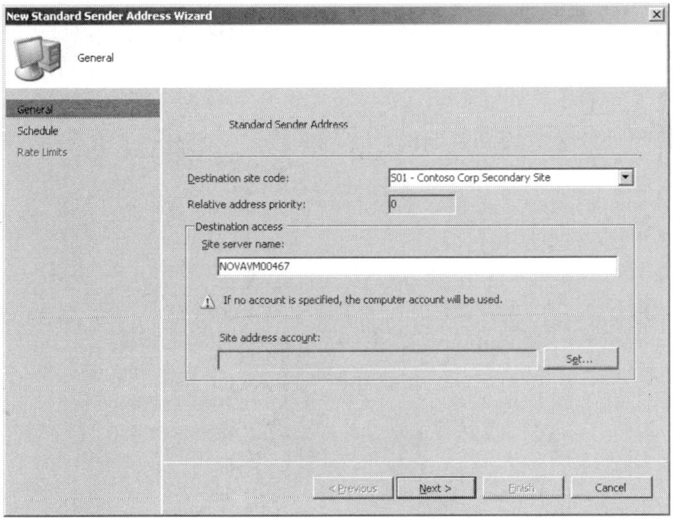

Figure 4-13 The New Standard Sender Address Wizard General page

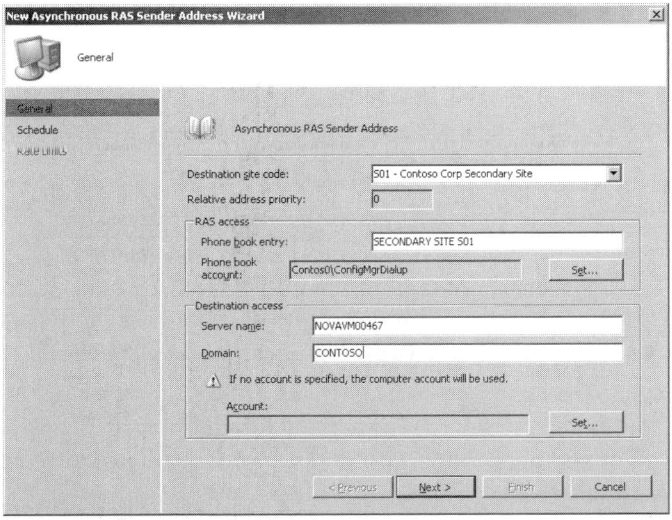

Figure 4-14 The New Asynchronous RAS Sender Address Wizard General page

❑ In the New ISDN RAS Sender Address Wizard General page, shown in Figure 4-15, select the site from the Destination Site Code drop-down list for the target site. In the RAS Access frame, type the RAS phone book entry that references dial-up information for accessing the target site. Click Set to specify the dial-up access account and phone number to be used when dialing in to the target site. In the Destination Access frame, type the name of the target site's site server and the domain of which it is a member. Click Set to specify the name and password of the account on the target site that has at least Change permission for the Configuration Manager_Site share on the target site. If you're running in advanced security mode, this account is displayed as Local System, and you won't be able to change it.

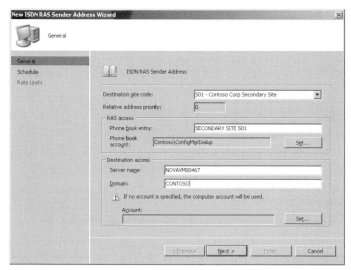

Figure 4-15   The New ISDN RAS Sender Address Wizard General page

❑ In the New X.25 RAS Sender Address Wizard General page, shown in Figure 4-16, select the site from the Destination Site Code drop-down list for the target site. In the RAS Access frame, type the RAS phone book entry that references dial-up information for accessing the target site. Click Set to specify the dial-up access account and phone number to be used when dialing in to the target site. In the Destination Access frame, type the name of the target site's site server and the domain of which it is a member. Click Set to specify the name and password of the account on the target site that has at least Change permission for the Configuration Manager_Site share on the target site. If you're running in advanced security mode, this account is displayed as Local System, and you won't be able to change it.

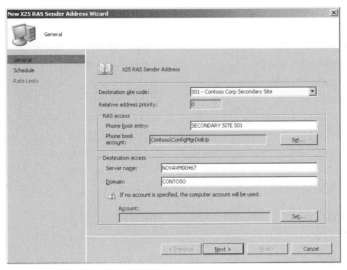

Figure 4-16   The New X.25 RAS Sender Address Wizard General page

❑   In the New SNA RAS Sender Address Wizard General page, shown in Figure 4-17, select the site from the Destination Site Code drop-down list for the target site. In the RAS Access frame, type the RAS phone book entry that references dial-up information for accessing the target site. Click Set to specify the dial-up access account and phone number to be used when dialing in to the target site. In the Destination Access frame, type the name of the target site's site server and the domain of which it is a member. Click Set to specify the name and password of the account on the target site that has at least Change permission for the Configuration Manager_Site share on the target site. If you're running in advanced security mode, this account is displayed as Local System, and you won't be able to change it.

❑   For details on how to create a Courier Sender address, refer to the section "Courier Sender."

4.   Click Next to display the Schedule page, as shown in Figure 4-18. This page is the same for all sender types. As you can see, by default the sender is available for all priority send requests at all times. Select the time period you want to modify by highlighting it using the mouse. In the Availability list, select the appropriate option: Open For All Priorities, Allow Medium And High Priority, Allow High Priority Only, Closed. The priority of a send request such as a package is set when the package is created. Choose Closed for periods when you don't want the sender to send anything, such as during regular backup times. If there are multiple addresses to a target site, Configuration Manager automatically chooses the next sender in order of

priority (based on the Relative Address Priority setting in the General tab) if the current sender is unavailable for some reason. Select the Unavailable To Substitute For Inoperative Addresses check box to prevent this sender from being used as an alternative sender (used when a higher-priority sender is in use or unavailable).

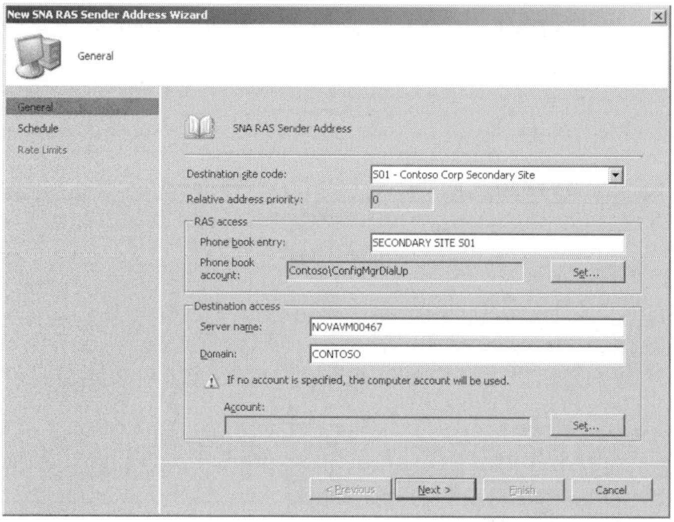

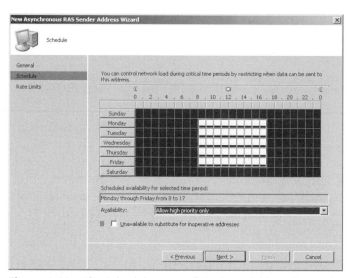

Figure 4-17   The New SNA RAS Sender Address Wizard General page

Figure 4-18   The Schedule page of the New Address Properties dialog box

5. Click Next to display the Rate Limits page, as shown in Figure 4-19. This page is the same for all sender types. Notice that by default Configuration Manager can use as much bandwidth as it wants when transferring data to the target site. Select the Limited To Specified Maximum Transfer Rates By Hour option and highlight the period of time you want to modify using the mouse. In the Rate Limit For Selected Time Period frame, select a preferred bandwidth percentage from the drop-down list. Another option on this page is Pulse Mode. You can use Pulse Mode to limit the amount of data sent between sites by specifying the size of the data blocks sent as well as a time delay between each data block.

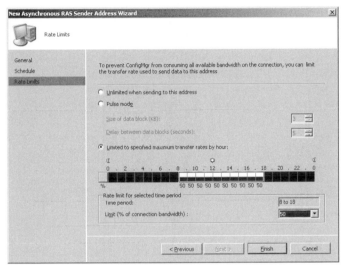

Figure 4-19   The Rate Limits page

6. Click OK to create the address.

If multiple addresses exist for a target site, the order of priority in which Configuration Manager uses them to connect to the target site is the order in which the addresses are created. This is known as the *relative address priority*—that is, the priority of one address relative to another. You can change the relative priority of an address by navigating to the Site Settings\Addresses node in the Configuration Manager console, right-clicking one of the addresses in the details pane, and choosing either Increment Priority or Decrement Priority from the context menu. If you have only one address listed, the priority options are dimmed.

Multiple addresses to the same target site provide Configuration Manager with alternative ways of connecting to a site and transferring data if one sender is busy or unavailable.

You can install only one sender of each type within a given site. For example, you can't install two Standard Senders on the same site server or on two different servers, but you can install the Standard Sender once and the Asynchronous RAS sender once within the same site.

Real World   Alternate Senders to a Target Site

A more likely scenario is this: You use the Standard Sender on your site server to connect to a target site. Another server in the domain is already being used as an RAS server. An RAS server also exists in the target site server's domain. To provide an alternative means of connecting to the target site and transferring data, you can install the Configuration Manager Asynchronous RAS Sender on the RAS server and create an Asynchronous Sender Address to the target site. Now Configuration Manager can use the Standard Sender, the Asynchronous RAS Sender, or both, to connect to the target site and transfer data.

You'll want to closely monitor the traffic generated between the site server and the RAS server—which, in this case, is functioning as a component server for the Configuration Manager site. Assuming that both servers are on the same subnet, the traffic shouldn't be significant. Nevertheless, you don't want to find yourself in a situation where the benefit you gain in improved sending performance to the target site is negated by excess traffic or degraded network performance between the site server and the RAS server.

Identifying the Parent Site

Before you identify a site's parent, you must create an address to that parent site. The child site will use that address to connect to the parent and transfer its site control information—including the fact that the parent now has a new child site. You can then set the parent site by following these steps:

1. In the Configuration Manager console, navigate to the site entry, right-click it, and choose Properties from the context menu.

2. The site's Properties dialog box appears, as shown in Figure 4-20. In the General tab, click Set Parent Site.

Figure 4-20   The General tab of the site's Properties dialog box

3. In the Set Parent Site dialog box, shown in Figure 4-21, select the Report To Parent
    Site option, type the three-character site code of the parent site, and click OK to
    return to the Site Properties dialog box.

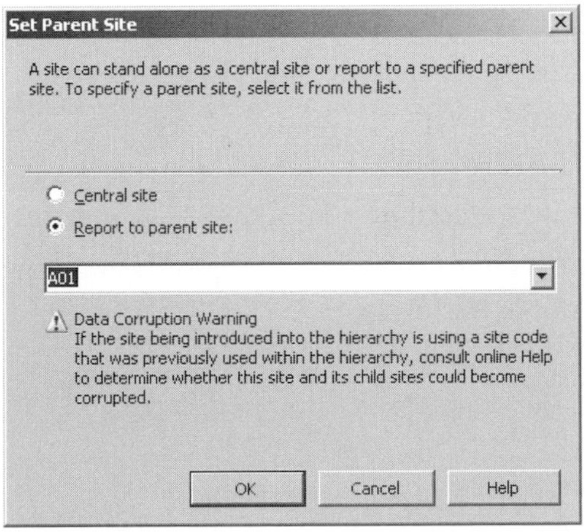

Figure 4-21   The Set Parent Site dialog box

4. Click OK again to set the parent site, which starts the site configuration change process.

The site configuration change process includes not only updating the child site with the new parent site information but also sending data to the parent site and updating the parent site's database and site control information. This process shouldn't take more than a few minutes, but factors such as the resource capabilities of both the child and parent sites, available bandwidth, and other database activity will affect the length of time it takes for the parent-child relationship to be established and "recognized" by both parent and child. When you first create the address entry for the parent or the child, the site entry should include the site code and should indicate that the site name is unknown. After the relationship is established and site control data transferred, this information is updated to reflect the actual site name of the addressed site.

You can follow the flow of the site configuration change process and the transfer of information that takes place by monitoring the status messages that the Configuration Manager components record at each point in the process. For a detailed explanation on how to view status messages, refer back to the section "Status Messages" in Chapter 3. Table 4-1 lists the Configuration Manager components and the status messages that relate to this process.

Table 4-1   Status Messages Generated During the Establishment of a Parent-Child Relationship

Configuration Manager component	Status message codes	Description
Discovery Data Manager	2603, 2607	Transferring discovery data to the parent site
	2611, 2634	Updating child discovery data (at the parent site)
Inventory Data Loader	2708, 2709, 2711, 2713	Transferring inventory data to the parent site
Replication Manager	4000	Creating jobs to send data to parent site
Hierarchy Manager	3306, 3307	Processing site control files (at the parent site)

You can also monitor the log files associated with the appropriate Configuration Manager components for information regarding the flow of this process if you have enabled logging for those components. These log files can be found in the directory <Installationfolder>\Logs and include Hman.log (Hierarchy Manager), Sched.log (Scheduler), Sender.log (Sender), DDM.log (Discovery Data Manager), or Replmgr.log (Replication Manager), depending on which components you have enabled logging for. These log files are text based and can be viewed using any text editor such as Notepad.

Implementing Site Hierarchies

In Chapter 2, you learned about the importance of developing a viable deployment strategy for Configuration Manager. A significant part of that design process should include determining the kind of site hierarchy—if any—that you need to implement for your organization. A Configuration Manager site hierarchy exists whenever two or more Configuration Manager sites are defined in a parent-child relationship; its structure resembles an organizational flowchart. Site hierarchies provide a means of extending and scaling Configuration Manager support across a wide variety of organizational structures. Figure 4-22 shows what the completed Configuration Manager hierarchy looks like when viewed through the Configuration Manager console from the central site server. As you can see, the central site has the ability to view and manage any site below it in the hierarchy.

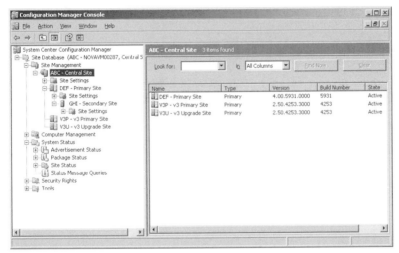

Figure 4-22 Configuration Manager hierarchy viewed through the Configuration Manager console

Configuration Manager sites, as you have seen, are identified by the boundaries that you assign. Clients are assigned to a Configuration Manager site based on either Internet Protocol (IP) subnet or Active Directory directory service site boundaries. As such, a multinational organization with locations in different countries could be managed by one large Configuration Manager site or by individual Configuration Manager sites in each location connected to a central site. Figure 4-23 illustrates an example hierarchy. Contoso Ltd. has a corporate office in Chicago and regional offices in New York, London, and Tokyo. Each office has its own IP subnet. The single Configuration Manager site, located in Chicago, could manage all Contoso locations because it includes all the IP subnets in its boundaries.

Contoso Domain

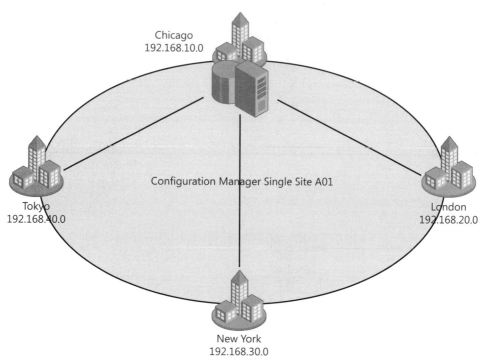

Figure 4-23   The Contoso site hierarchy, with one Configuration Manager site

In contrast, Figure 4-24 shows the same organization, but this time with individual Configuration Manager sites in each region, each reporting back to a central site located at Contoso headquarters in Chicago.

Many factors and circumstances can affect your site structure strategy. Each must be considered carefully before implementing the hierarchy. These factors are likely to include, but are certainly not limited to, the following:

- Network performance
- Configuration Manager client components
- Location and number of clients
- International site considerations
- Administrative model of the organization
- Active Directory domain model

Contoso Domain

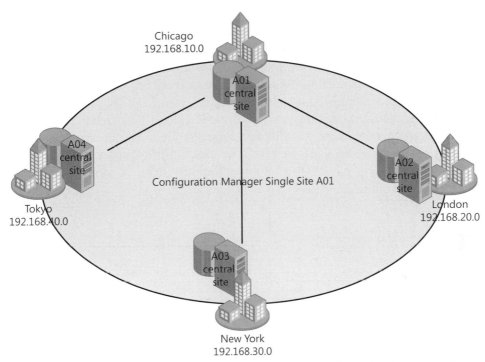

Figure 4-24   The Contoso site hierarchy, with multiple Configuration Manager sites

The following sections look at each of these factors in detail.

Network Performance

Network performance issues are no doubt the single most significant factor in determining what your site structure should look like. Varying amounts of network traffic are generated among Configuration Manager site servers, Configuration Manager site systems, and Configuration Manager clients. Site servers communicate package, advertisement, and site configuration data to their site systems. The amount of traffic that's generated depends on the nature of the data being sent. For example, a site that distributes three packages a day with an average size of 50 MB to 10 distribution points is generating 500 MB of network traffic three times a day. This traffic could be significant on an already crowded network infrastructure. Or suppose that hardware inventory files representing only changes that have occurred are collected from a group of 32-bit Configuration Manager clients. If inventory is collected once a week from 5000 clients, the amount of traffic generated is probably not going to be significant. Even at 100 KB per client—the average size of a full default inventory file—this traffic would total 500 MB once a week and would largely be randomized.

Network traffic concerns are particularly significant when Configuration Manager traffic must cross WAN connections. You might ask yourself whether the existing WAN connections are well-connected and efficient enough to handle the traffic generated between the proposed Configuration Manager site systems or whether it would make more sense to create an additional Configuration Manager site at the other end of a WAN connection. Return to the Contoso example. Suppose that you need to send a 50 MB package from the site server in Chicago to 10 distribution points in New York, as illustrated in Figure 4-25. This transaction generates about 500 MB of package distribution traffic across the WAN connection between Chicago and New York because Configuration Manager must deliver the entire package to each distribution point individually within the same site—and generally uncompressed.

Contoso Domain

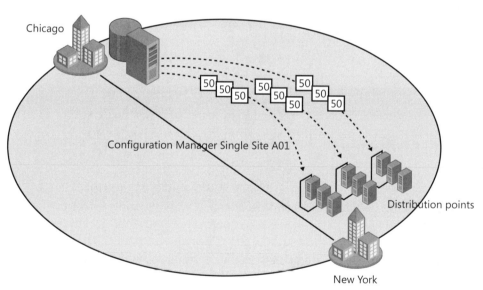

Figure 4-25   A package distributed from a site server to multiple distribution points in a remote location

On the other hand, Configuration Manager sends packages from one site to distribution points in another site by sending the package to the target site once and letting the target site distribute the package to its local distribution points. Furthermore, it generally sends the package to the target site in a compressed format. As illustrated in Figure 4-26, the amount of WAN traffic generated for the same package scenario is considerably less—only about 25 MB as opposed to around 500 MB. Your site deployment strategy should already have assessed and predicted how you'll use Configuration Manager and the amount of data that you'll generate within the site. Armed with this information, consider its effect on the current network traffic patterns and volumes, especially across WAN links, when deciding whether to implement one large Configuration Manager site or several Configuration Manager sites participating in a site hierarchy.

Contoso Domain

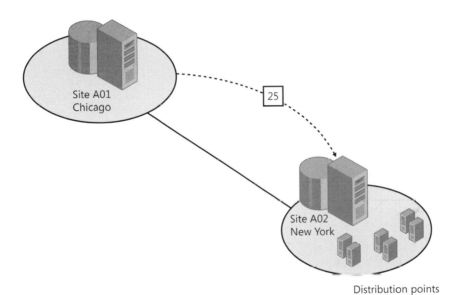

Distribution points

Figure 4-26   A package distributed from one site to distribution points in another Configuration Manager site

> **More Info**   The scenarios suggested here aren't exhaustive. Configuration Manager introduces new server roles and additional server properties, such as proxy management points and protected distribution points, both of which affect network traffic and server performance in their own ways. For a more detailed discussion of factors that can affect network traffic and server performance, refer to the Configuration Manager 2007 Documentation Library and search on Performance Planning.

Note   Microsoft recommends implementing a single Configuration Manager site across WAN links only if the WAN links are fast and reliable and can handle network traffic within acceptable thresholds (as identified by you, of course).

Real World   Branch Distribution Points

One of the new site system roles introduced with Configuration Manager is the branch distribution point. While not intended to replace a distribution point, branch distribution points are an option to consider when you need the efficiency of distributing packages to a small office with limited bandwidth, but do not have the infrastructure to support a secondary site at that location. As shown in Figure 4-27, instead of installing and managing a secondary site at the remote location, you can use the branch distribution point and gain similar efficiencies of network traffic and bandwidth uses.

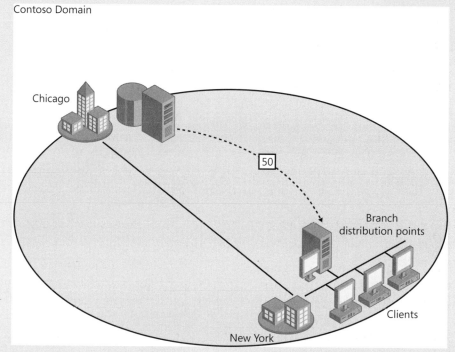

Figure 4-27   A package distributed from one site to a branch distribution point in a remote location

A branch distribution point can be installed on a server computer or a workstation. Note that when installed on a workstation, it is held to the limitations of the operating system running on the workstation computer. For example, a Windows XP computer used as a branch distribution point is limited to 10 or less simultaneous client connections.

Branch distribution points use Background Intelligent Transfer Service (BITS) to manage network traffic and transfer rates when downloading packages. In the case of an interruption or failed download, BITS uses a checkpoint restart to restart the download at the point it was interrupted.

Because the branch distribution point is essentially a "regular" distribution point, all the other considerations about setting up and managing distribution points discussed in Chapter 3 apply. This includes space and security considerations.

Client Components

Client component settings within a given Configuration Manager site apply to all the clients assigned to that site—they are sitewide settings. As such, there are no means of installing certain components on one set of clients and other components on another set. For that matter, there are no means of enabling one set of attributes for a component for some clients and a different set of attributes for the same component for other clients.

The most frequent example of this situation concerns the Remote Tools component. If Remote Tools is enabled as a client agent for the Configuration Manager site, all Configuration Manager clients are enabled with Remote Tools. If the Do Not Ask For Permission configuration option is disabled for the Remote Tools Client Agent, permission is required on all clients before a Remote Tools session can be established. In other words, if your site has 1000 clients and 100 don't require Remote Tools, or if 100 don't require permission to establish a Remote Tools session, you can't accommodate those clients. They must all either have Remote Tools installed or not. They must all either require permission or not. Chapter 17, "Managing Clients Remotely," discusses the Remote Tools Client Agent and its configuration options in more detail.

One solution is to create one Configuration Manager site for those clients that require Remote Tools (or that require permission to establish a Remote Tools session) and another Configuration Manager site for those clients that don't require Remote Tools (or that don't require permission to establish a Remote Tools session) and to enable Remote Tools appropriately. The same reasoning applies to all the client component options.

Location and Number of Clients

Another factor that might affect the structure of your Configuration Manager site hierarchy is the number and location of Configuration Manager clients and resources. Each

Configuration Manager primary site can potentially handle 100,000 or more assigned clients, with a supported maximum of 200,000 assigned clients for each Configuration Manager hierarchy. But if you think this gives you license to create one large site and be done with it, go back and read the section "Network Performance" earlier in this chapter.

The true number of clients that any one Configuration Manager site server can manage will be dictated more realistically by the server hardware—how powerful it is—as well as by the number of Configuration Manager features and options you enable on that server. The minimum hardware requirements for a Configuration Manager site server are a 750 MHz Pentium processor, 256 MB of RAM, and a recommended 2 GB of hard drive space (5 GB if you intend to use Operating System Deployment). Say that you have two site servers with this configuration. Suppose you install and enable Hardware Inventory on one server and install all options and enable all client components on the other. The resource requirements for the latter site server obviously surpass those of the former server. It follows logically, then, that the second site server might manage fewer Configuration Manager clients than the first site server.

Location of clients can also be a factor, as it is with network performance. Your site server can easily manage 100,000 assigned Configuration Manager clients or more. However, their location in the network might suggest the creation of multiple Configuration Manager sites depending on the Configuration Manager features you implement, the amount of network traffic generated, the efficiency of your WAN link, and the number of clients that need to be managed. For example, suppose you have three regional locations. If these are relatively small offices—say, 10 to 20 clients—with a modest WAN link between them and the corporate Configuration Manager site server, you might create a single Configuration Manager site, perhaps placing a distribution point in each local subnet. On the other hand, if these regional locations have 100 or more clients, you might begin to weigh the possibility of creating separate Configuration Manager sites in each location and linking them together into a site hierarchy—depending, of course, on what features (such as package distribution) you enable, the size of packages, the frequency of advertisements, and so on.

International Site Considerations

Just as Windows supports a wide variety of language versions in its operating system, so too does Configuration Manager support a wide variety of language versions for both the site server and Configuration Manager clients. Configuration Manager site servers support the following languages:

- Chinese (simplified and traditional)
- English
- French
- German
- Japanese
- Korean

Each of these site server languages supports clients in its language, as well as English-language clients, with the exception of French, which doesn't support English-language clients. Note also that English is the default language for the server-side user interfaces for Chinese and Korean site servers, but you can choose to display the local language characters. The client-side user interfaces have been localized to the local language.

In addition to English, Configuration Manager clients are available in 21 additional language versions:

- Chinese (simplified and traditional)
- Czech
- Danish
- Dutch
- Finnish
- French
- German
- Greek
- Hungarian
- Italian
- Japanese
- Korean
- Norwegian
- Polish
- Portuguese-Brazilian
- Portuguese-Portugal
- Russian
- Spanish
- Swedish
- Turkish

For the most part, you can create a site hierarchy with any combination of language versions. Keep in mind, however, that some data that's recorded in one language version is transferred between sites in that language version. For example, site code, collection, package, and advertisement names and Management Information Files (MIFs) are always transferred in the language version in which they are created. This untranslated information can cause a problem if the parent and child site servers are using different language code pages. If they use the same code pages, data is passed on and displayed correctly. If not, the names might appear corrupted.

Default collection names are defined at each site; however, in a parent-child relationship, the default collection names from the parent site overwrite those of the child sites. Again, if both sites use the same code page to view the default collection names, the names appear correctly. If the child site is using a different code page, the default collection names might be corrupted.

If the site servers are using different code pages, you have a couple of options. You could use all ASCII characters or a combination of ASCII and the language characters either in the Name or Comment field of collections, advertisements, packages, and programs properties to provide easier identification. You could also use a separate Windows computer running the Configuration Manager console with the appropriate code page enabled. Also, be aware that extended and double-byte character names aren't supported in domain and site server names. When your sites represent a mix of languages, use ASCII characters when naming domains and site servers.

More Info   The Configuration Manager 2007 Documentation Library discusses language considerations; consult these references for more specific information. If language versions are a concern within your organization, you should also periodically review the Microsoft Knowledge Base articles published for Configuration Manager for references to specific issues you might be encountering (see *http://support.microsoft.com*).

Planning   If you have installed an International Client Pack (ICP) for your Configuration Manager site and plan to upgrade to a Configuration Manager service pack, be sure to upgrade your ICP with the service pack version as well. If you don't, the ICP files will be overwritten and only English language clients will be supported. Also, in order to correctly process and display characters in the appropriate language in the Configuration Manager console on a Windows 2003 or higher computer, the Locale Regional Options setting on that computer, located on the Control Panel, must be set to match the language of the data you want to view or input.

Administrative Model

The structure of your organization's Information Services (IS) support (as well as company policies) no doubt influence your Configuration Manager site structure. Whether or not a proposed Configuration Manager site has a designated Configuration Manager administrator locally might determine, for example, whether you install a primary or a secondary site at that location. The size and location of the administrative staff might also determine the number of child sites in the hierarchy, as well as its depth.

This is a good opportunity to make a recommendation regarding Configuration Manager administrative staff. The reality of many corporate environments is that a small number of persons manage large numbers of computers and networks and typically fulfill many roles: database administrator, network administrator, mail server administrator, and so on. The role of the Configuration Manager administrator is just as significant and time consuming. As you've already seen, implementing Configuration Manager is far from trivial. A successful installation requires a significant amount of planning and testing.

The ongoing management of Configuration Manager clients and resources, troubleshooting, and maintenance are no less trivial. Therefore, you could recommend that many Configuration Manager tasks be delegated to other support personnel. For example, resource administrators in specific departments might be given the ability to create and distribute packages to users and clients within their departments. Nevertheless, these are administrative tasks, and they make up only a small percentage of the overall management of a Configuration Manager site or a Configuration Manager site hierarchy.

Active Directory Domain Model

Certainly the Active Directory site structure that you use within your organization will have a significant impact on the look of your Configuration Manager hierarchical structure because you can use Active Directory site names to define Configuration Manager site boundaries. Similarly, the domain model that supports your organization also influences your Configuration Manager hierarchical structure. You might, from an administrative point of view, decide to simply let your Configuration Manager structure reflect your Active Directory site structure or domain model. If your organization spends a great deal of thought and planning when implementing its Active Directory site structure and domain model, and it's well organized and optimized, then following that model for your Configuration Manager site hierarchy makes the most sense. However, if your current Active Directory site structure and domain model is less than optimal, you might want to consider cleaning it up before you implement your Configuration Manager site hierarchy or choose not to base your Configuration Manager hierarchy or your site boundaries on your Active Directory structures.

If you implement Configuration Manager in a multiple-domain environment, especially in a mixed-mode environment (Active Directory and Windows NT domains), and you run Configuration Manager in standard security mode, remember that Configuration Manager still requires the use of the Configuration Manager Service account and several internal accounts to connect between sites and site systems within a site. When multiple domains are involved, and you want to reference in one domain a Configuration Manager account such as the Configuration Manager Service account from another domain, you need to understand if and how trust relationships are implemented between those domains or create duplicate accounts that Windows can use through pass-through authentication, or both. Refer to your Windows documentation for more detail on the authentication process and how it can affect your Configuration Manager sites. Also, refer to the topic "Configuration Manager Multiple Site Planning and Deployment" in the Configuration Manager Documentation Library for a more detailed discussion of domain-specific issues.

Communicating Through Senders

As you've seen, Configuration Manager uses a sender to connect to another site and transfer information to that site. A sender is a highly reliable and fault-tolerant communication mechanism that transfers data in 256 KB blocks, making it more efficient than dragging and dropping or using an XCOPY command. Senders can communicate using the standard LAN/WAN connection that exists between two sites, or they can use one of four RAS Sender types: Asynchronous RAS Sender, ISDN RAS Sender, X.25 RAS Sender, and SNA RAS Sender. There is also a Courier Sender type that enables you to create and send package information to another Configuration Manager site if you have a slow or unreliable (therefore not well-connected) link between a site and its parent. However, one of the other sender types must still be installed and available for regular inter-site communication.

Sender Process Flow

Three main Configuration Manager components are involved in sending data from one site to another: Replication Manager, Scheduler, and a sender. With the exception of the Courier Sender, the sender component wakes up when it receives a send request file in its outbox. The process begins earlier than that, however, as illustrated in Figure 4-28. When a request to send data is made, a Configuration Manager component creates a replication file and places the file in Replication Manager's inbox. When the parent-child relationship is established, for example, the Inventory Data Loader places an .mif file in Replication Manager's inbox (<Installationfolder>\Inboxes\Replmgr.box\Outbound) so that it can send the child site's inventory data to the parent site. As another example, when a package is identified for distribution to another site, Distribution Manager places a replication object file (.rpl or .rpt) in Replication Manager's inbox.

Replication Manager will in turn bundle the data if necessary and then create information files for the Scheduler. The Scheduler creates packages, the instructions needed for sending the data in question, and a send request file (.SRQ) for the sender. The package and instruction files are placed in the <Installationfolder>\Inboxes\Schedule.box\Tosend directory. The send request file is an instruction file for the sender that contains information such as the priority of the request, the site code and preferred address of the target site, a job identifier, the location of the sender's outbox, the location and names of the package and instruction files, action codes, and routing information if a direct address to the target site doesn't exist. This file is written to the preferred sender's outbox (<Installationfolder>\Inboxes\Schedule.box\Outboxes\sender, where sender is the sender type, such as LAN, RASAsynch, RASISDN, and so on).

When this file is written, the sender wakes up and reads the send request file. It also checks to see whether the address properties have placed any restrictions on when requests of this priority can be sent and whether any bandwidth limits have been set. The sender then changes the extension of the send request file to .srs and writes status information to the file, including when the sending process starts, when it ends, and how much data is transferred at any point in time.

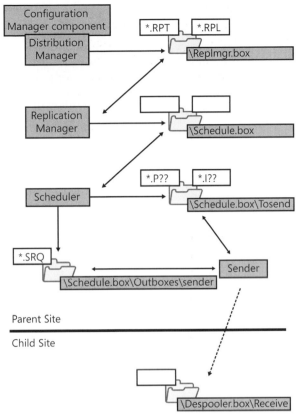

Figure 4-28 The sender process flow, showing the flow of information among Configuration Manager components

> **Note** The Total Bytes To Send and Bytes Left To Send values in the send request file serve an important fault-tolerance role. If the sending process is interrupted for any reason—for example, if a send request of higher priority is created—the sender knows how to pick up where it left off.

The sender connects to the target site's SMS_Site share—the <Installationfolder>\Inboxes \Despoolr.box\Receive directory—where the Despooler component completes the processing of information at the target site. If the sender discovers an error while transferring the data, it writes an error status to the .srs file. When the data is completely transferred, the send request file is updated to Completed status and is then deleted.

Defining a Sender

When the Configuration Manager site server is first installed, Setup creates the Standard Sender and Courier Sender by default. The Configuration Manager administrator can then choose to install additional senders as necessary. As mentioned, only one sender of each type can be installed on the same server. However, you can install the same sender type on multiple servers. These servers become Configuration Manager component servers when you install a sender on them.

There is nothing special involved in adding a Standard Sender on a Configuration Manager component server. The only requirement is that you have an existing LAN or WAN connection between the Standard Sender component server and the target site server. Then, of course, you must configure an additional address to the target site using the new Standard Sender.

The other four sender types are RAS senders: Asynchronous RAS Sender, ISDN RAS Sender, X.25 RAS Sender, and SNA RAS Sender. Enabling the use of one or more of these sender types assumes that you have already established an RAS server at each site installed with the appropriate hardware and software support—that is, a modem, ISDN, X.25, or SNA connection. It's not necessary, or even desirable, that the site server itself be installed as an RAS server; it's only necessary that the site server for each site have access and connectivity to an RAS server (appropriately configured) on their local networks.

Senders on Other Servers

When you install a Configuration Manager sender on another server, such as the Asynchronous RAS Sender on an RAS server, that server becomes a Configuration Manager component server. The Configuration Manager Executive, support files, and directories for the sender are all installed on that server. Because the sender doesn't reside on the site server, it won't wake up when a send request file is created. Instead, the sender wakes up on a 5-minute polling cycle.

This polling cycle requires some additional resources on the sender's server. Also, network traffic is generated between the site server and the sender server to transfer send request, package, and instruction data. The ultimate effect on the network's and sender server's performance depend on the amount of usage the sender experiences and, of course, the current usage of the server itself. Alternative senders provide a means for the Scheduler to improve sending performance from one site to another. The Configuration Manager administrator needs to determine the significance of any trade-off between having an alternative sending mechanism and the network and server performance hits that might occur.

The immediate benefit to your Configuration Manager site when you install additional senders on other servers is that the site then has one or more alternative ways to send data to a target site—assuming that you create addresses to those sites referencing each available sender. Data can be sent using an alternative sender when the primary sender is unavailable. Data can also be sent concurrently to the same site or to different sites using all available senders. Again, the trade-off is in the area of network traffic and network performance. As always, be sure to monitor network usage to be sure that you gain the most out of your senders' configuration.

You add new senders to the site through the Configuration Manager console as a site setting. To establish a new sender, follow these steps:

1. In the Configuration Manager console, navigate to the Site Settings folder and highlight the *Senders* node. One sender is displayed in the details pane—the Standard Sender installed by default. (Please note that the Courier Sender isn't displayed. Although the Courier Sender is installed by default, it can't be modified. For details, refer to the section "Courier Sender" later in this chapter.)

2. Right-click Senders and choose New from the context menu to display the five sender type options, as shown in Figure 4-29. Select the type of sender you want to establish.

Figure 4-29   The list of sender type options

> **Note**   Because all the sender types display a similar series of Property dialog boxes, only the pages for the Asynchronous RAS Sender are shown here.

3. On the General tab of the sender's Properties dialog box, shown in Figure 4-30, type the name of the server on which you want to create the sender—in this case, the name of the RAS server.

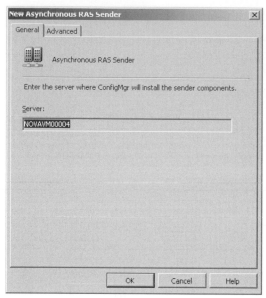

Figure 4-30   The General tab of the sender's Properties dialog box

4. Click the Advanced tab, as shown in Figure 4-31, and type values for the Maximum Concurrent Sendings and Retry Settings options.

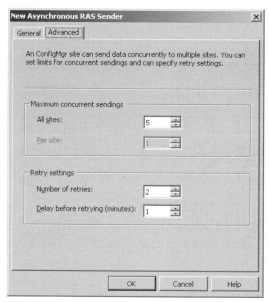

Figure 4-31   The Advanced tab of the sender's Properties dialog box

Maximum Concurrent Sendings represents the number of concurrent transmissions that can be made to all sites through this sender or to any single site (Per Site). The Per Site setting is set to 1 and disabled for RAS senders by default. The Retry Settings options consist of the number of retries to attempt if a connection fails and the number of minutes to wait between retries (Delay Before Retrying). Your choices for these options depend primarily on the kind of network connection you have between the sites. For example, if you have a well-connected network connection and the amount of bandwidth used is low, you might increase the Maximum Concurrent Sendings value and decrease the Retry Settings options.

5. Click OK to begin the site configuration process.

Establishing a new sender initiates the same site configuration change process seen in earlier examples. Part of this process includes creating an outbox for the sender in the <Installationfolder>\Inboxes\Schedule.box\Outboxes directory. If the sender is installed on another server, the process includes installing the Configuration Manager Executive on the sender server (making it a component server), installing the sender support files and the sender's support directory, and then updating the site server's site control file appropriately. Status messages for the new sender include a notice of successful installation, as shown in Figure 4-32. Of course, you can also follow the process by checking status messages and logs for Hierarchy Manager, Site Control Manager, and Site Component Manager.

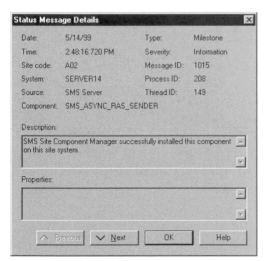

Figure 4-32   Status message indicating that the Asynchronous RAS Sender has been successfully installed on the component server

Courier Sender

As mentioned, the Courier Sender enables you to create and send package information to another Configuration Manager site through non-network channels, such as regular postal service or a package delivery service if you have a slow or unreliable link between a site and its parent. It can also be used to send packages that are so large that an existing address might not provide adequate performance levels. It's not, however, meant to be used as a consistent alternative to existing network communication mechanisms, nor can it be used to transmit data packages generated internally by Configuration Manager.

As with other senders, to use the Courier Sender as an alternative means of sending packages, you must create an address to the target site using the Courier Sender as the sender type, as shown in Figure 4-33. How to create an address to the target site using other sender types is discussed in the section "Creating an Address to Another Site" earlier in this chapter. Similarly, in the Configuration Manager console, navigate to the Site Settings folder and expand it. Right-click the Addresses node and choose New and then Courier Sender Address from the context menu, which brings you to the New Courier Sender Address Wizard shown in Figure 4-33.

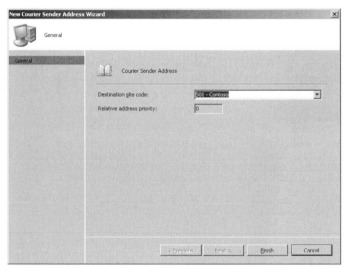

Figure 4-33   The General page of the New Courier Sender Address Wizard

When you create the package, you can also identify the Courier Sender as the preferred sender type for that package, as shown in Figure 4-34. (For details on creating packages, please refer to Chapter 11, "Distributing Software Packages.")

You also need to identify the target site as a distribution point for the package. Please refer back to Chapter 3 for details.

Note   If you have more than one address to a target site and you want to send a package using the Courier Sender, choose Courier Sender as the preferred sender type when you create the package.

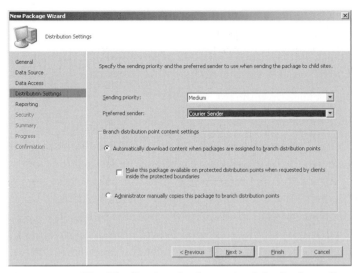

Figure 4-34   The Distribution Settings tab of the Package Properties dialog box

When you use the Courier Sender as the sending mechanism to transfer a package, the package files are compressed into a single package (.pck) and placed in the <Installationfolder>\Smspkg directory. A send request file is also created and placed in the Courier Sender's outbox. Because no automatic connection needs to be made to the target site, you must next launch Courier Sender Manager from the Systems Management Server program group. To create outgoing parcels, follow these steps:

1. In Courier Sender Manager, choose Create Outgoing Parcel from the File menu.

2. Select your package from the list and click Next.

3. In the Parcel Properties section, type the name of the package, a tracking name, the method you're using to send the parcel (for example, UPS or Federal Express), and a descriptive comment. Click Next.

4. Type the path where you want to save the parcel. The default is Configuration Manager\Inboxes\Coursend.box\Out. Click Next.

5. Click Finish to create the parcel (.pcl) file.

You can now copy this parcel to some other medium, such as CD-ROM, and then send it using some non-network method, such as the U.S. Postal Service. The Configuration Manager administrator at the target site in turn copies this parcel to a directory on the target site server. (The default used by Courier Sender Manager is Configuration Manager\Inboxes\Coursend.box\In.) The Configuration Manager administrator then launches Courier Sender Manager on the target site server, essentially reversing the sending process by following these steps:

1. In Courier Sender Manager, choose Receive Incoming Parcel from the File menu to display the Courier Sender Wizard's Receive An Incoming Parcel page.

2. Click Browse, select the package from the list, and click Open.

3. Click Next and then Finish to complete the package receiving process.

Courier Sender Manager processes this parcel as though a package had been sent using one of the other senders. If necessary, an SMSPkgx$ directory is created (where x stands for the drive letter), and the package files are uncompressed and copied to a subfolder below the directory. When the process is complete, you can check the parcel's status by choosing Parcel Status from the Courier Sender Manager's File menu at the sending site. Because the nature of Courier Sender is that the package is sent by some non-network method, parcel status is also updated by a non-network method—that is, you need to manually update the status.

When you first create the parcel, the parcel status is displayed as "created." After you send the parcel to the target site, you can change the status to either "sent" or "confirmed." After you change the status to "sent," your only other option can be "confirmed," which you might select, for example, when the administrator from the target site notifies you that the parcel was received and processed.

Change the status of a parcel by following these steps:

1. In the Courier Sender Manager, right-click the parcel whose status you want to change and select Properties from the Action menu.

2. In the Parcel Properties dialog box, click Change Status.

3. In the Change Status dialog box, select the option that reflects the parcel's new status.

Note   For more information about using and troubleshooting the courier sender process, see the online help available when you launch the Courier Sender Manager.

Summary

In this chapter, you explored how to implement multiple site structures. Various factors influencing your choice of site hierarchy were introduced and discussed. You also examined the concept of parent-child relationships in Configuration Manager, and you learned how to establish that relationship through addresses and senders. You also learned how to install a secondary site and the site configuration process involved. Last, you looked at defining and implementing Configuration Manager senders and traced the sending process. Chapter 5, "Upgrading to Configuration Manager," outlines several considerations for you to keep in mind when migrating to Configuration Manager from Systems Management Server 2003.

Chapter 5

Upgrading to Configuration Manager

All things must change now,

a new version has arrived.

Today I upgrade.

~ Jeff Gilbert, Technical Writer, Configuration Manager

Upgrading to System Center Configuration Manager 2007 requires just as much—and maybe even more—preplanning and testing of your proposed plan as the deployment of new Configuration Manager sites. During the upgrade process, you will need to consider the effects of your upgrade actions on existing client computers, site systems, and the network environment.

Before beginning the actual setup process to upgrade existing sites and site systems to Configuration Manager, there are many decisions you must make. The information contained in this chapter can help you identify the decision points and make the best choices to plan your upgrade strategy and deploy Configuration Manager successfully.

Planning the Site Structure

Just as you need to plan for new installations of Configuration Manager, you must also plan before upgrading SMS 2003 sites. When planning to upgrade to Configuration Manager, your goal should be to complete the upgrade process successfully and efficiently with minimal interruption to your users and the network.

The first step in the upgrade process is to define the goals of the upgrade process and the results you hope to achieve by upgrading SMS 2003 sites to Configuration Manager. Use the defined goals to create an upgrade plan to guide you throughout the upgrade process.

Configuration Manager deployment preplanning and planning worksheets also can be used to help create an upgrade plan after you define the business and technical goals of the upgrade process.

More Info   For more information about the preplanning and planning phases of Configuration Manager deployment, see Chapter 2, "Planning for and Deploying Configuration Manager Sites."

After determining your business and technical objectives, you must next analyze and document your existing SMS 2003 site infrastructure; ensure that you have a detailed understanding of Configuration Manager features, and the new client management capabilities each feature provides; and determine how you will implement any of the required prerequisite technologies required by Configuration Manager and its features. You should also decide whether you will maintain the same site structure or modify it during the hierarchy upgrade process. For example, if one of your upgrade goals is to consolidate sites and reduce the amount of secondary sites in use, the new Configuration Manager branch distribution point site system role can be used to replace secondary sites installed only for software distribution purposes and supporting a small number of clients.

Maintaining Mixed Sites within the Same Site Structure

During your upgrade planning, you may decide not to upgrade one or more existing SMS 2003 sites. The two main considerations you should consider when deciding if you will maintain a mixed hierarchy of SMS 2003 and Configuration Manager sites are:

- Site version considerations
- Site administration considerations

Site Version Considerations

If you determine that you will maintain some sites in your hierarchy at the SMS 2003 level when planning your new site infrastructure, consider the following:

- Configuration Manager sites are not supported, and will not function correctly, as child sites of SMS 2003 sites, and there can be no SMS 2003 Legacy Clients in a Configuration Manager site hierarchy. However, because SMS 2003 sites *can* be child sites of Configuration Manager sites, if you need to support an SMS 2003 site in your hierarchy for any reason, you must attach it to a Configuration Manager parent site as a child site during the upgrade process.

- Configuration Manager sites operating in native mode cannot be child sites of Configuration Manager sites operating in mixed mode. If you plan to support Internet-based clients in your upgraded site hierarchy, they must be assigned to a native mode site. Because native mode sites cannot be child sites of mixed mode sites, you could plan to have a native mode central site and child primary sites in different modes. For example, you could have a native mode central site with a native mode child site supporting Internet-based clients and a mixed mode child site supporting intranet-based clients.

- Configuration Manager clients *cannot* be assigned to an SMS 2003 site. This is because Configuration Manager clients require specific policy versions and capabilities to function properly. During client installation and assignment, the client installation software queries the server locator point site system or site capability information in Active Directory to determine the site's version and capabilities. If you attempt to assign a Configuration Manager client to an SMS 2003 site, client assignment will fail and the computer will be unmanaged.

- SMS 2003 clients *can* be assigned to a Configuration Manager site. It is supported for SMS 2003 clients to be assigned to Configuration Manager sites to allow the SMS 2003 client to be upgraded to the Configuration Manager client. If you have any SMS 2003 clients that cannot be upgraded to the Configuration Manager client software, you can have them assigned to the Configuration Manager site, but these clients will not be able to take advantage of all the Configuration Manager features that the newer client version will.

> **Important**   If you will have any SMS 2003 clients assigned to a Configuration Manager site, ensure that you do not select the This Site Contains Only Configmgr 2007 Clients option in the Site Properties, Site Mode tab of mixed mode sites. Selecting this option will configure some client policy settings created by the site server to be modified so that only Configuration Manager clients can process them.

Site Administration Considerations

If you will implement a mixed-site environment, there are things you should know and plan for when deciding how you will administer your site infrastructure. For example, when viewing the site hierarchy from a Configuration Manager console with SMS 2003 child sites, you can see the top-level node of an SMS 2003 primary site (and the top-level node of any of the child sites directly underneath it), but the site(s) cannot be managed using the Configuration Manager console, as shown in Figure 5-1.

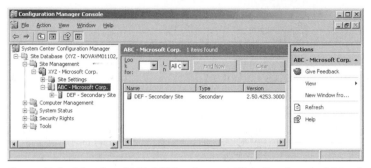

Figure 5-1   Viewing SMS 2003 primary child sites from within the Configuration Manager console

To manage SMS 2003 primary sites installed as child sites of a Configuration Manager primary site, you must install a remote SMS 2003 Administrator console or manage the SMS 2003 child site directly from the SMS 2003 primary site's Administrator console.

Unlike SMS 2003 primary sites, SMS 2003 secondary sites that are directly attached beneath the Configuration Manager primary site in the hierarchy can be managed from within the Configuration Manager console. After the SMS 2003 primary child site in Figure 5-1 (ABC) is upgraded to Configuration Manager, you can view its secondary site's (DEF) properties and manage it from within the Configuration Manager console either from the parent site (ABC) or, as shown in Figure 5-2, from the central site (XYZ) Configuration Manager console.

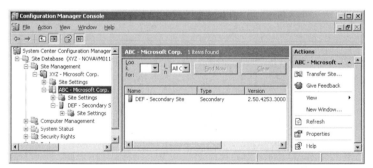

Figure 5-2   Viewing a Configuration Manager primary site's SMS 2003 secondary child site from within the Configuration Manager console

Upgrading to Configuration Manager 2007

All site hierarchy upgrades must begin with the central site and continue in a top-down upgrade process. After upgrading the central site, you should next upgrade any child primary sites and secondary sites. After a site has been upgraded from SMS 2003 to Configuration Manager, you can then begin upgrading clients assigned to the site.

Note   You can't upgrade SMS 2003 clients before upgrading their assigned site first because Configuration Manager clients cannot be assigned to SMS 2003 sites.

Real World   Upgrading from an Evaluation Copy

Unlike SMS 2003, Configuration Manager allows you to upgrade the free 120-day evaluation version software to the fully licensed version. This capability allows you to set up and evaluate Configuration Manager without purchasing an actual Configuration Manager software license. To upgrade an evaluation version Configuration Manager primary site installation, you must completely rerun Configuration Manager Setup to upgrade the primary site installation using a valid product installation key corresponding to your purchased license.

The evaluation version of Configuration Manager cannot be used to upgrade an existing SMS 2003 primary site installation because the SMS 2003 software was not designed to allow upgrades to, or from, evaluation version software.

You can download the 120-day evaluation version of Configuration Manager 2007 at *http://www.microsoft.com/downloads /details.aspx?FamilyID=23945ee2-bd1e-4bd8-a5fa-3e846fd8bd49&DisplayLang=en.*

Preparing to Upgrade

Before beginning the upgrade process, ensure that the site is capable of upgrading smoothly. If a site upgrade fails, you could end up with a nonfunctioning site and unmanaged clients.

More Info   Before beginning the upgrade process, ensure that your computing environment is capable of being upgraded successfully to Configuration Manager. Begin by reviewing the Configuration Manager–supported configuration and prerequisite documentation online at *http://technet.microsoft.com/en-us/library /bb680717.aspx* and *http://technet.microsoft.com/en-us/library/bb694113.aspx*, respectively.

When preparing to upgrade an existing SMS 2003 site, consider the following:

- SMS 2003 sites to be upgraded must be configured to use SMS 2003 Advanced Security.

- Because SMS 2003 Legacy Clients are not supported in Configuration Manager site hierarchies, all clients in the site to be upgraded must be SMS 2003 Advanced Clients.

- If you have configured the site database to use SQL replication, you must disable replication before beginning the upgrade process.

- Uninstall all SMS 2003 Feature Packs except for the Inventory Tool for Microsoft Updates (ITMU).

- Any default Configuration Manager collections not present in SMS 2003 sites will be created. The only SMS 2003 default collection that will be overwritten with Configuration Manager default query values is the All Systems collection.

- If you have made hardware inventory customizations to the SMS 2003 SMS_def.mof file, make a backup copy of this file before beginning the upgrade process. After the upgrade is completed, you can add any customized data classes to the Configuration Manager configuration.mof file and custom reporting classes to the Configuration Manager SMS_def.mof file.

Note   You should not modify the configuration.mof or SMS_def.mof files in the Configuration Manager installation source files before upgrading an SMS 2003 site. Configuration Manager Setup verifies existing installation configurations and modifies the information to be inventoried during installation. Modifying the default .mof files in the installation media may cause the upgrade to be unsuccessful.

More Info   For more information about upgrade considerations, see "Considerations for Upgrading Sites" at *http://technet.microsoft.com/en-us/library /bb680667.aspx*.

Many Configuration Manager site system prerequisites have changed from those required for SMS 2003 site systems. For example, Web-based Distributed Authoring and Versioning (WebDAV) was not a requirement for management points in SMS 2003, but it is for Configuration Manager management points.

When upgrading to Configuration Manager 2007 from SMS 2003, it is important that you first verify that all site systems meet any new prerequisite requirements using the Setup Prerequisite Checker.

In addition to site systems, Configuration Manager client installation also requires updated prerequisite component files to be available on the management point site system. The updated client prerequisite component files can be downloaded during primary site installation or before starting Setup by using the /download Setup command-line option.

Setup Prerequisite Checker

The Setup Prerequisite Checker is used to verify that required installation prerequisites have been met for new Configuration Manager site system installations or upgrades from SMS 2003 SP2 or later.

To use the Setup Prerequisite Checker to verify installation prerequisites for upgrading SMS 2003 site systems, you can either run the Configuration Manager Setup Wizard and allow the prerequisite checks to occur as part of Setup, or use the link on the Setup splash screen (splash.hta) to launch the Setup Prerequisite Checker without starting the full Setup Wizard.

Just as when you are installing new installations of Configuration Manager, it is recommended to use the stand-alone Setup Prerequisite Checker to verify that installation prerequisites are installed before starting the actual Setup Wizard. The prerequisite checking process at the end of the Configuration Manager Setup Wizard should be a final verification that you are ready to begin the upgrade process.

> **Note**   Using the Setup Prerequisite Checker to verify installed prerequisites for installations is discussed in Chapter 2.

If SMS 2003 or previous versions of Configuration Manager components are already installed, the Setup Prerequisite Checker can be used with the following options to verify that all required Setup prerequisites are installed before beginning the upgrade process:

- **Upgrade**   This option is used to verify that setup prerequisites are installed for upgrading primary sites, secondary sites, and SMS 2003 Administrator consoles or Configuration Manager consoles.

- **All Secondary Sites**   When this option is used when running the Setup Prerequisite Checker from an SMS 2003 primary site, you can verify that the upgrade prerequisites are installed on all secondary sites attached to a primary site being upgraded. When you use this option, all secondary sites are checked for prerequisites one after another.

> **Note**   If a secondary site fails the prerequisite checking process, all successive secondary sites checked will also fail. After one secondary site fails the prerequisite checking process, you'll need to verify which site failed, remediate any failures, and then rerun the prerequisite checker on all secondary sites. To see the results of the prerequisite checking process, review the ConfigMgrPrereq.log file at the root of the installation drive.

Client Prerequisite Component Downloader

Just as in new Configuration Manager installations, updated client prerequisite component files should be downloaded—or an alternate location for Setup to find them specified—when the Configuration Manager Setup Wizard is run. The Setup Wizard pages for downloading updated client prerequisite component files are the same when upgrading as they are when installing new sites.

If the site server being upgraded does not have Internet access, you must download the updated client prerequisite installation files from a different computer with Internet access using the /download Setup command-line option and save them in a location where the site server can access them during site installation.

> **More Info**   For more information about the updated client prerequisite component download and path pages of the Configuration Manager Setup Wizard, see Chapter 2.

Upgrading Primary Sites

When upgrading primary sites, there are two methods that can be used. Each method has pros and cons to consider when deciding the best method to use when upgrading your specific environment. The two upgrade methods that can be used to upgrade SMS 2003 primary sites to Configuration Manager are the in-place upgrade method and the side-by-side upgrade method.

In-Place Upgrade Method

An in-place upgrade is the easiest way to upgrade an SMS 2003 primary site to Configuration Manager and offers the following benefits over the side-by-side upgrade method:

- Generally easier to do and requires less planning

- Better suited for when you do not want to modify any server hardware currently in use in your SMS 2003 site installations

- Does not require the purchase of new hardware

- Does not require site boundary changes between sites

- Does not require clients to be reassigned to new sites

If you're going to do an in-place upgrade of an SMS 2003 primary site, you'll need to verify that the site database will successfully upgrade before starting the Configuration Manager Setup Wizard to upgrade the site.

> **Important**   Before beginning the site database upgrade test, ensure that SQL replication is not configured for the site database before backing it up in preparation for the test. If the site database was configured for SQL replication before backing it up, the database upgrade test will fail.

To verify that the site database upgrade will be successful, run the following command on a backup copy of the site database: Setup /testdbupgrade *<site database name>*. Make sure you don't run this command on the actual site database because after this test is run, the database will be incompatible with previous versions of SMS.

To view the results of the site database upgrade test, you can review the ConfigMgrPre-req.log and ConfigMgrSetup.log log files located at the root of the system drive. If the test is successful, you can be assured that the site database will upgrade successfully. If the test fails, you'll need to make any necessary changes required for the upgrade to succeed before upgrading the site.

More Info   For more information about the /testdbupgrade command, see "How to Test the Site Database Upgrade Process" at *http://technet.microsoft.com /en-us/library/bb693648.aspx*.

To perform an in-place upgrade to Configuration Manager, follow these steps:

1. Start the Configuration Manager Upgrade Wizard on the primary site server to be upgraded. On the Welcome page of the Setup Wizard, click Next, as shown in Figure 5-3.

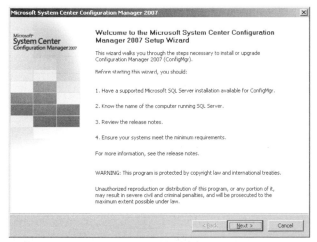

Figure 5-3   Configuration Manager Setup Wizard Welcome page

2. On the Available Setup Options page, select the Upgrade An Existing Configuration Manager Or SMS 2003 Installation option, as shown in Figure 5-4.

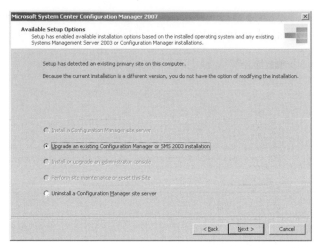

Figure 5-4   Configuration Manager Setup Wizard Available Setup Options page

Note   This option includes the ability to upgrade an existing Configuration Manager installation because you can upgrade the 120-day evaluation version installation of Configuration Manager to the full version as well as existing SMS 2003 installations.

3. On the Microsoft Software License Terms page, review the license agreement terms, select the I Accept These License Terms option, and click Next, as shown in Figure 5-5.

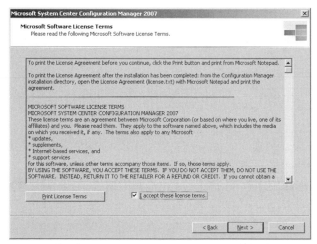

Figure 5-5   Configuration Manager Setup Wizard Microsoft Software License Terms page

4. On the Customer Experience Improvement Program Configuration page, review the program participation options, select an option, and click Next, as shown in Figure 5-6.

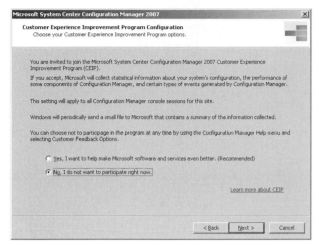

Figure 5-6 Configuration Manager Setup Wizard Customer Experience Improvement Program Configuration page

5. On the Product Key page, type a valid installation product key, and click Next, as shown in Figure 5-7.

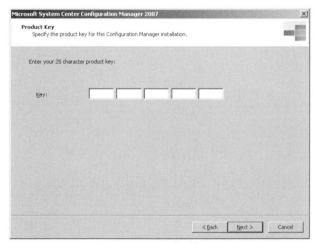

Figure 5-7 Configuration Manager Setup Wizard Product Key page

6. On the Updated Prerequisite Components page, you are presented with the two choices for obtaining client prerequisite files needed to upgrade SMS 2003 clients to the Configuration Manager client version. You can either check for updates and download the newest prerequisite component files directly from Microsoft using

the Internet, or, if you have already downloaded the files to an alternate location, you can select the option to specify an alternate location to obtain the prerequisite component files, as shown in Figure 5-8

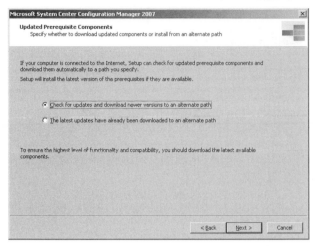

Figure 5-8   Configuration Manager Setup Wizard Updated Prerequisite Components page

7. On the Updated Prerequisite Component Path page, you specify the path to store or access the downloaded client installation prerequisite component files. If you chose to download the files from the Internet, the downloaded client installation prerequisite files are stored in the path specified. If you chose to specify an alternate location for the prerequisite files, type the path to where you have already stored the updated prerequisite files, as shown in Figure 5-9.

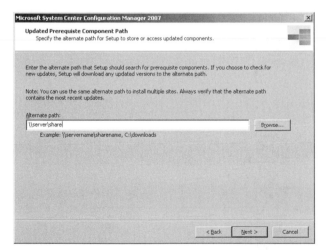

Figure 5-9   Configuration Manager Setup Wizard Updated Prerequisite Components Path page

8. On the Settings Summary page, review the settings you have selected for the upgrade and click Next, as shown in Figure 5-10.

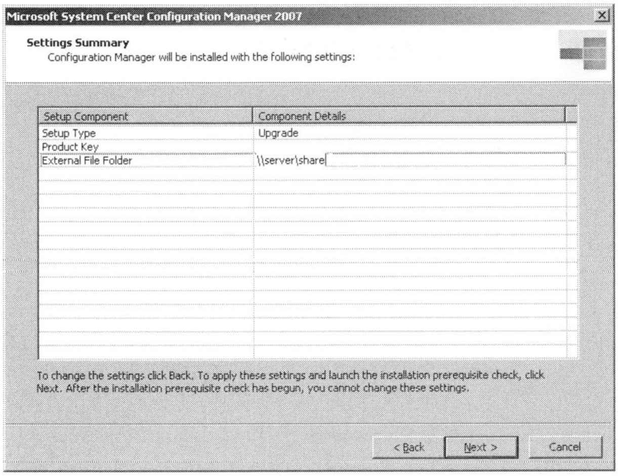

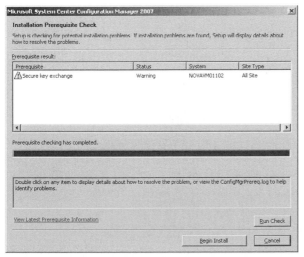

Figure 5-10 Configuration Manager Setup Wizard Settings Summary page

9. On the Installation Prerequisite Check page, review the results of the installation prerequisite checks to ensure that there are no errors that would prevent you from continuing with the upgrade process. If an error or warning appears, you can resolve the prerequisite issue and return to the Prerequisite Check page and click Run Test to retest the server for upgrade prerequisites. If no prerequisite check errors are found, or you want to continue despite any displayed warnings, click Begin Install to begin the in-place upgrade process, as shown in Figure 5-11.

Figure 5-11 Configuration Manager Setup Wizard Installation Prerequisite Check page

10. On the Setup Action Status Monitoring page, review the upgrade installation status as the site is being upgraded to determine the current upgrade action status. After the site has been upgraded, click Next, as shown in Figure 5-12.

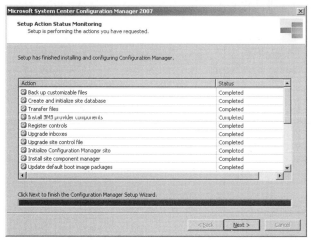

Figure 5-12   Configuration Manager Setup Wizard Setup Action Status Monitoring page

11. The Setup Wizard completion page is displayed after the site upgrade process has finished. To review the ConfigMgrSetup.log log file created during the upgrade process, click View Log. You can also select the Launch Configuration Manager Console After Closing option by clicking Finish, as shown in Figure 5-13.

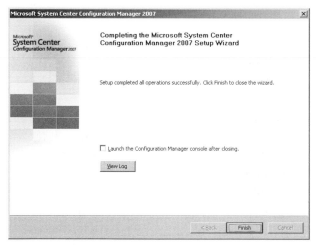

Figure 5-13   Configuration Manager Setup Wizard completion page

Side-by-Side Upgrade Method

Side-by-side upgrades to Configuration Manager require a new installation of Configuration Manager on hardware not in use by your existing SMS 2003 site infrastructure and require much more planning and administrative action to complete the upgrade process than in-place upgrades require.

More Info   For more information about performing new installations of Configuration Manager primary sites, see Chapter 2.

While side-by-side upgrades require some additional planning and administrative action, they offer the following benefits:

- They are better suited to upgrade sites when new hardware will be used.

- They make it easier to revise the existing SMS 2003 site hierarchy.

- They allow you to rearrange sites and reassign clients within the site hierarchy.

Note   You don't have to use the same upgrade method on every one of your SMS 2003 sites. Based on your upgrade plan, you may decide to use the in-place upgrade method on some sites and the side-by-side upgrade method on others. For example, you may decide to use the in-place upgrade method on your central site and the side-by-side upgrade method to consolidate multiple child primary sites. Remember, however, that regardless of the method you choose to upgrade your site, you must always begin with the central site.

When deciding to perform a side-by-side upgrade of SMS 2003 to Configuration Manager, ensure that you consider and plan for the following:

- **Site boundaries**   Be sure that you don't have the same site boundaries assigned to multiple sites. As you install a new Configuration Manager site, migrate the site boundaries over to the newly installed site only after removing them from the pre-existing SMS 2003 site.

- **Site systems**   You don't want any of the clients that have been reassigned to the Configuration Manager site contacting SMS 2003 site systems still in operation after you reassign them. If you won't need the SMS 2003 site systems anymore, uninstall them and ensure that the site system information is removed from Active Directory and, if applicable, WINS or DNS.

- **Replicated objects**   Because custom collections and software distribution objects are replicated down the hierarchy, if you want to retain those objects you must perform an in-place upgrade of an existing SMS 2003 primary site and attach the newly installed Configuration Manager site as a child site to allow the objects to replicate down. After all objects have successfully replicated down, you can break the connection and decommission the upgraded site if it is no longer needed.

> **Note**   Because the site codes will be different, replicated collection and software distribution objects will have IDs different from objects created by the new Configuration Manager 2007 site, but will continue to function correctly.

- **Historical data**   If you only have one site, but want to keep the client historical data for your existing site, consider making the existing SMS 2003 site a child site of the newly installed Configuration Manager site. This will allow client historical data to flow up the hierarchy and be retained after the SMS 2003 site has been decommissioned or clients have been reassigned to the new Configuration Manager site.

- **Upgrading cients**   One of your major goals when performing a side-by-side upgrade should be to maintain all existing clients in a managed state. If you will be reassigning boundaries early in the upgrade process, ensure that you enable a discovery method at the new site and configure the client push installation method on the site. If you do not move site boundaries to the new site early in the process, you could still enable a discovery method at the new site and use the client push installation wizard at the new site to both upgrade and reassign clients to the new site. After all clients have been upgraded and reassigned using this method, you could move the site boundaries over to the newly installed primary site.

Upgrading Secondary Sites

When upgrading secondary sites, there are two methods that can be used. Just like the primary site upgrade methods, each method has pros and cons to consider when deciding how you will upgrade your specific environment. You can upgrade secondary sites either by using the Configuration Manager console or the Configuration Manager Setup Wizard.

> **Note**   You cannot upgrade a secondary site to a primary site. To change a secondary site to a primary site, you must uninstall the secondary site and install a new primary site. Also, existing SMS 2003 secondary sites will not be upgraded automatically to Configuration Manager 2007 secondary sites when their parent primary site is upgraded. You must manually upgrade each secondary site. During the upgrade process, it is not possible to change a secondary site's parent site. To change a secondary site's parent site, you must uninstall and reinstall the secondary site.

Upgrading Secondary Sites Using the Configuration Manager Console

After upgrading the parent primary site that a secondary site is attached to, you can use the Configuration Manager console at the parent site to upgrade the secondary site using the Upgrade Secondary Site Wizard. To start the Upgrade Secondary Site Wizard, right-click the primary site name and select Upgrade Secondary Site. During the secondary site upgrade process, the hman.log and sender.log log files on the primary site server computer can be used to monitor the upgrade package file creation, compression, and deployment to the secondary site server computer. At the secondary site server computer, the SMS_BOOTSTRAP.log and ConfigMgrSetup.log log files can be used to monitor the upgrade processes directly.

Important   Before you use the Upgrade Secondary Site Wizard to upgrade a secondary site, ensure that you have run the prerequisite checker on the secondary site server computer successfully (with no errors) within the past seven days. When the upgrade begins, it will check the prerequisite checker registry key entry on the secondary site server computer; if it contains data older than seven days, or any errors, the upgrade will fail.

To upgrade a secondary site, follow these steps:

1. After clicking Upgrade Secondary Site, the Upgrade Secondary Site Wizard Welcome page is displayed, as shown in Figure 5-14.

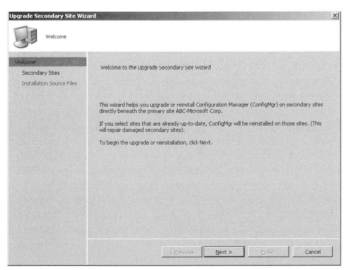

Figure 5-14   Upgrade Secondary Site Wizard Welcome page

2. On the Secondary Sites page, select one or more secondary sites to upgrade, as shown in Figure 5-15.

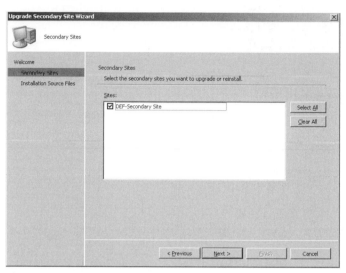

Figure 5-15   Upgrade Secondary Site Wizard Secondary Sites page

3. On the Installation Source Files page, select an option to specify how the secondary site installation source files will be accessed by the secondary site server computer, as shown in Figure 5-16. Be sure that you consider the network bandwidth that will be used to transfer the source files to the secondary site server computer if you select the option to Copy Installation Source Files Over The Network From The Parent Site Server. Clicking Finish on this page closes the Upgrade Secondary Site Wizard and begins the secondary site upgrade process.

Important   If you select the option to upgrade the secondary site using installation source files at the secondary site server computer, the installation source files must be located at the root of a disk drive or Setup will not find the files and the upgrade will fail. Also, when using this option, you must manually create a client installation prerequisite component file directory named Redist under the SMSSETUP directory of the installation source files and prepopulate it with the updated client prerequisite component files—downloaded previously using the /download Setup command line option—before beginning the upgrade process.

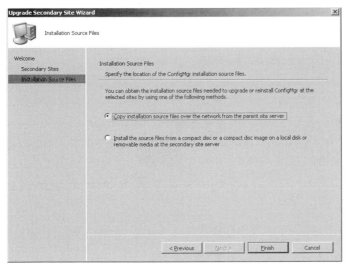

Figure 5-16   The Upgrade Secondary Site Wizard Installation Source Files page

Upgrading Secondary Sites Using Configuration Manager Setup

The second option for upgrading SMS 2003 secondary sites to Configuration Manager 2007 is to run the Setup Wizard directly at the secondary site server computer itself. Because you've already seen all of the Setup Wizard pages, those pages with their descriptions are not included here.

To upgrade a secondary site using Configuration Manager Setup, follow these steps:

1. To begin the secondary site upgrade process, start the Configuration Manager Upgrade Wizard on the secondary site server to be upgraded. On the Welcome page of the Setup Wizard, click Next.

2. On the Available Setup Options page, select the Upgrade An Existing Configuration Manager Or SMS 2003 Installation option.

3. On the Microsoft Software License Agreement page, read the license agreement terms, agree with them, and click Next to continue.

4. On the Updated Prerequisite Components page, you are presented with the two choices for obtaining client prerequisite files needed to install Configuration Manager clients later. You can either check for updates and download the newest prerequisite component files directly from Microsoft using the Internet, or, if you have already downloaded the files to an alternate location, you can select the option to specify an alternate location to obtain the prerequisite component files.

5. On the Updated Prerequisite Component Path page, specify the path to store or access the downloaded client installation prerequisite component files. If you chose to download the files from the Internet, the downloaded client installation prerequisite files are stored in the path specified. If you chose to specify an alternate location for the prerequisite files, type the path to where you have already stored the updated prerequisite files using the SETUP /DOWNLOAD command-line option.

6. On the Settings Summary page, review the installation actions that you have specified to ensure that they are correct. If they aren't, you can click back to the appropriate Setup Wizard page and make any necessary changes.

7. On the Installation Prerequisite Check page, the results of the installation prerequisite checker are displayed. This page verifies that site system prerequisites (as opposed to the client installation prerequisite files downloaded earlier) are installed and the site system is ready for installation. Review any messages in the results pane to verify that all prerequisites have been met.

8. On the Setup Action Status Monitoring page, you can see the installation status as it progresses. If any of these steps fails, you can review the ConfigMgrSetup.log file located in the root of the system drive to see what happened.

9. The last page of the Configuration Manager Setup Wizard displayed when installing secondary sites is the completion page, which displays the installation completion status.

Upgrading Administrator Consoles

After the site to which an SMS 2003 Administrator console is connected, it will no longer be able to connect to the upgraded site database. However, if you still have SMS 2003 sites in the hierarchy, you can use the Database Connection Wizard to attach the SMS 2003 Administrator console to a different SMS 2003 site database. To allow for this, when you upgrade an SMS 2003 Administrator console using the Setup Wizard, the console itself isn't really upgraded. A new Configuration Manager console is installed side-by-side with the existing SMS 2003 Administrator console. If you will no longer need the SMS 2003 Administrator console, uninstall it before installing the new Configuration Manager console. After the Configuration Manager console is installed, the only way to uninstall the SMS 2003 Administrator console is to uninstall both consoles—there is an option to uninstall only the Configuration Manager console in Add or Remove Programs in Control Panel. If you do choose to install the Configuration Manager console side-by-side with the SMS 2003 Administrator console, you'll need to use the Database Connection Wizard to attach the Configuration Manager console to the appropriate site database after installation has completed. Another option that can be used to upgrade an SMS 2003 Administrator console is the /upgrade Setup command line option. When the /upgrade Setup command-line option is used to upgrade an SMS 2003 Administrator console to the Configuration Manager console, the SMS 2003 Administrator console is uninstalled during the upgrade process.

More Info   For more information about the database connection wizard, see "Connect to Site Database Wizard" at *http://technet.microsoft.com/en-us/library /bb632612.aspx.*

To upgrade an SMS 2003 Administrator console to a Configuration Manager console using the Setup Wizard, the following pages are displayed. Because these wizard pages have already been shown previously, only descriptions of the pages you will see when upgrading an SMS 2003 Administrator console are included in the following steps.

1. Start the Configuration Manager Setup Wizard on the computer that the SMS 2003 Administrator console is installed on and select the Install Or Upgrade An Administrator Console option.

2. On the Microsoft Software License Agreement page, read the license agreement terms, agree with them, and click Next to continue.

3. On the Customer Experience Improvement Program Configuration page, review the program participation options, select an option, and click Next.

4. On the Settings Summary page, review the settings you have selected for the upgrade and click Next.

5. On the Installation Prerequisite Check page, review the results of the installation prerequisite checks to ensure that there are no errors that would prevent you from continuing with the upgrade process and click Begin Install.

6. On the Setup Action Status Monitoring page, review the upgrade installation status as the console is being upgraded to determine the current upgrade action status and click Next.

7. The Setup Wizard completion page is displayed after the Administrator console upgrade process has finished. To review the ConfigMgrSetup.log log file created during the upgrade process, click View Log. You can also select the Launch Configuration Manager Console After Closing option before clicking Finish to close the Setup Wizard.

Post-Upgrade Tasks

After upgrading SMS 2003 primary or secondary sites to Configuration Manager, check the site for general health and ensure that it is configured properly to support your business and technical objectives of upgrading to Configuration Manager.

The first thing to do after upgrading a primary or secondary site is to review the site system and site component status in the Configuration Manager console. Because site systems are uninstalled and reinstalled when they are upgraded, you may see some temporary initialization errors for some upgraded site systems. If the errors do not clear up within a reasonable amount of time, investigate to ensure that the upgrade has completed successfully for those site systems.

After verifying that the site has upgraded successfully, you can begin configuring the site for operation. Verify that the proper client agents are enabled and that they are scheduled properly. Assign any new site system roles you need to, and configure the site maintenance tasks, discovery methods, client installation methods, and boundaries.

> **Note** After upgrading an SMS 2003 site with site boundaries configured, the existing site boundaries cannot be modified. To change any of the preexisting SMS 2003 site boundaries, you'll need to delete them and re-create them as Configuration Manager boundaries.

After verifying that the site has upgraded successfully, you can begin reconfiguring the site hierarchy, upgrading child sites, SMS 2003 Administrator consoles, and clients as necessary using a top-down approach.

Summary

This chapter explored the procedures required to upgrade existing SMS 2003 primary sites, secondary sites, and Administrator consoles to Configuration Manager 2007.

All hierarchy upgrades must begin with the central site. Configuration Manager sites cannot be attached as child sites to SMS 2003 sites, and Configuration Manager clients cannot be assigned to SMS 2003 primary sites.

There are two methods that can be used to upgrade SMS 2003 primary sites to Configuration Manager: the in-place upgrade method and the side-by-side upgrade method. The in-place upgrade method is easier to do than the side-by-side upgrade method, but if you want to reconfigure your hierarchy or install Configuration Manager sites on new hardware, you'll want to use the side-by-side upgrade method.

There are two methods that can be used to upgrade SMS 2003 secondary sites to Configuration Manager: using the Upgrade Secondary Site Wizard from within the parent primary site's Configuration Manager console, or by using the Configuration Manager Setup Wizard. Before using the Upgrade Secondary Site Wizard from within the Configuration Manager console, ensure that the Setup Prerequisite Checker has run against the secondary site server computer successfully within the past seven days. If you will use installation source files at the secondary site server computer, you must copy the client installation prerequisite component files, downloaded during primary site setup or by using the /download Setup command line option, to a subdirectory of the SMSSETUP directory named Redist before beginning the secondary site upgrade process.

SMS 2003 Administrator consoles cannot be used to manage a Configuration Manager site and Configuration Manager consoles cannot be used to manage an SMS 2003 primary site. When upgrading an SMS 2003 Administrator console using the Setup Wizard, the existing console is not uninstalled, which allows you to manage additional SMS 2003 primary sites in your hierarchy. If you do not need to have a side-by-side installation of the SMS 2003 Administrator console with the Configuration Manager console, you can use the /upgrade Setup command line option to upgrade the SMS 2003 Administrator console or uninstall the SMS 2003 Administrator console before beginning the upgrade process using the Setup Wizard. After upgrading an SMS 2003 Administrator console to the Configuration Manager console using the Setup Wizard, there is no option to uninstall only the SMS 2003 Administrator console in Add or Remove Programs.

After upgrading an SMS 2003 Administrator console using the Setup Wizard, neither the SMS 2003 Administrator console or the new Configuration Manager console will be connected to a site database until you run the Site Database Connection Wizard to connect the console to the applicable site database.

After upgrading SMS 2003 primary sites or secondary sites to Configuration Manager, ensure that the site was upgraded successfully and it is configured to support your computer management needs before continuing to upgrade the remainder of your site hierarchy and clients.

Chapter 6
Analysis and Troubleshooting Tools

What has happened here?

My status just turned red!

Must now read the logs.

~ *Steve Kaczmarek, Content Manager, Configuration Manager*

In the preceding chapters, you viewed log files and status messages as a way of interpreting and troubleshooting process flows and component activity in your Microsoft System Center Configuration Manager 2007 site. In this chapter, you spend a little more time exploring the uses of these tools and look at some additional tools that will help you maintain your site. In particular, you learn how to view status messages, use status summarizers, filter status messages, report status to other Configuration Manager components, and use queries to customize the status messages displayed. You also learn how to use Configuration Manager Service Manager to start, stop, and monitor the status of the components as well as to enable logging.

Working with Status Messages

Virtually every Configuration Manager component and service generates status messages as it goes about its business. These messages aren't the sometimes vague or unhelpful variety you might have come to dread in the Windows Event Viewer. On the contrary, Configuration Manager status messages are rich with details. In the event of error messages, the details often offer potential reasons for the error and suggest possible remedies.

Status messages represent the flow of process activity for each site system and client. They're automatically consolidated and filtered for display using status summarizers and status filters (discussed in detail in the sections "Understanding Status Summarizers" and "Filtering Status Messages" later in this chapter). As you see throughout this book, these status messages provide your first, and often best, insight into how a process or task works and what to do in the case of a problem.

There are three levels of severity for status messages in Configuration Manager: informational, warning, and error. *Informational messages* are just that—informational. They simply record the fact of an event occurring, such as a service or component starting, the successful completion of a task, and so on. *Warning messages* are of concern, but they aren't necessarily fatal to the site server's operation. They generally indicate potential problems, such as low disk space, a component that failed or that is retrying a task, or a file that is corrupted. *Error messages* are usually of great concern, as they indicate problems that could harm the Configuration Manager site. These require the attention of the Configuration Manager administrator for resolution. Error messages include authentication problems, the complete failure of a service or component to complete a task, database access problems, and so on.

Every status message that's generated falls into one of three message type categories: milestone, detail, and audit. *Milestone message types* usually relate to the start or completion of a task. For example, a successful completion generates a milestone informational message, whereas an unsuccessful task generates a milestone warning or error message. *Detail message types* generally refer to the steps in a process and make sense only in the context of the status message process flow. Again, these might be informational, warning, or error messages, depending on the severity of the process steps being reported. *Audit message types* refer to objects being added, deleted, or modified in some way, usually by the Configuration Manager administrator—for example, assigning a site system role or modifying a collection membership.

> **Note**   Status messages sometimes stand alone and can be readily interpreted from the detail message. In many cases, however, a status message makes sense only in the context of a process flow. It's always a good idea, therefore, to look not only for a specific message reference, but also at the status messages preceding and following the reference to gain further insight into the specific message. Throughout this book, when process flows are explored, review the status messages for *all* the Configuration Manager components and services involved in that process flow to develop a well-rounded understanding of the process.

You can view status messages through the System Status node in the Configuration Manager console, as shown in Figure 6-1. From this node, you can view the advertisement status, the package status, and the component and site system status for the Configuration Manager site, and you can execute status message queries. Status messages for advertisements and packages are discussed as you get to those topics in Chapter 11, "Distributing Software Packages."

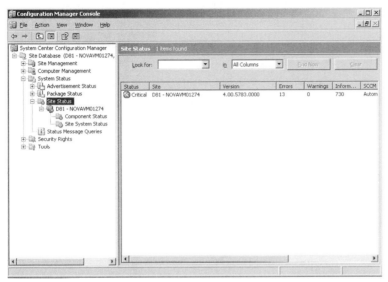

Figure 6-1   The expanded System Status folder in the Configuration Manager console

Viewing Site Status Messages

Site status messages fall into two categories: component status and site system status. If all is well with your site, you should see a green check mark (an OK indicator) in front of each folder, as you do for the Site System Status folder in Figure 6-1. If any problems have been detected, this check mark might change to an "x" in a red circle (an Error indicator), as seen for the Component Status folder in Figure 6-1, based on default thresholds, or the thresholds you set. (For a detailed discussion of thresholds, see the section "Status Message Thresholds" later in this chapter.) The icons for OK, Warning, or Error help you to determine which components need attention.

> **Note**   Critical error status messages are displayed directly on the Site Status folder home page, as shown in Figure 6-1, to help you quickly identify situations that could adversely affect your site.

Always begin troubleshooting by viewing the summary information. First, select Component Status in the Configuration Manager console to display a list of all Configuration Manager components and services and a summary of their current status, as shown in

Figure 6-2. In the Component Status window, you can see at a glance the component status; the site system on which the component is running; the component name; its current state; the number of error, warning, and informational messages that have been generated; how the component wakes up (type); when a scheduled component next runs; the last time the component woke up; and the last time a message was written. In this case, you can see that while most components are running properly, the component SMS_Site_SQL_Backup has been elevated to Critical status, and the component MS_MP_Control_Manager has been elevated to Warning status.

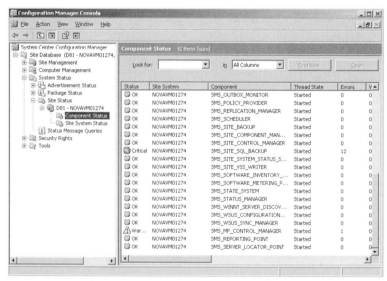

Figure 6-2   The Component Status window in the Configuration Manager console

---

Note   Click the Show/Hide Console Tree icon (fourth from the right on the toolbar at the top of the Configuration Manager console) to hide the console tree so that you can more easily view the Component Status window.

Click the Site System Status folder to display a list of all the site systems identified for the site and their summary status by site system role, as shown in Figure 6-3. In the Site System Status window, you can view the site system status, the site system name, the role that has been assigned to the site, the location of the storage object (partition and folder or database), total and free storage space, free space represented as a percentage of the total, and whether the system has been down. In this case, all site systems are running properly.

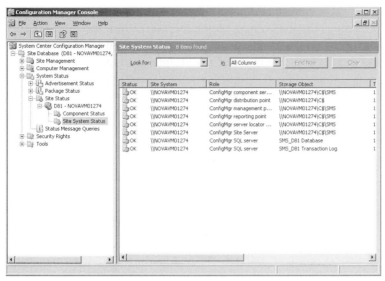

Figure 6-3   The Site System Status window

The detailed information behind each summary entry in the Component Status window pertains specifically to that component. However, the detailed messages behind each summary entry in the Site System Status window reference messages from any number of Configuration Manager components and services that are running on, or affect, that particular site system.

You examined how to view status messages in Chapter 3, "Configuring Site Server Properties and Deploying Site Systems;" you can review it here. To view the detailed messages for a specific component in the Component Status window, for example, for the SMS_Site_SQL_Backup component in Figure 6-2 that indicates a critical status, follow these steps:

1.   Right-click the component's summary entry and choose Show Messages from the context menu to display a list of message types, as shown in Figure 6-4.

Figure 6-4   Displaying a list of message type options

2. The All option displays all messages collected for this entry, Errors displays only error messages, Warnings displays only warning messages, and Info displays only info messages. For this example, choose Error. The Status Message Viewer appears, as shown in Figure 6-5.

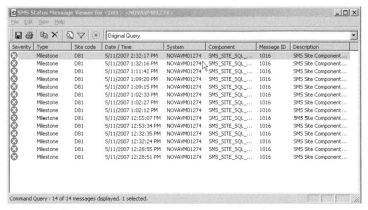

Figure 6-5   The Status Message Viewer

3. To view a detailed description of the message, position the mouse pointer over the Description field to display a pop-up window, as shown in Figure 6-6.

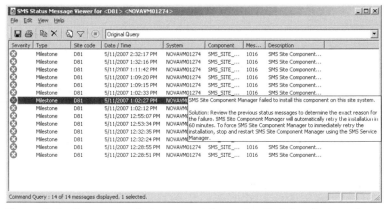

Figure 6-6   A pop-up window containing a detailed description of a status message

Alternatively, you can double-click the message to display the Status Message Details dialog box, as shown in Figure 6-7. This dialog box provides you with more specific details about the message. It also provides buttons to enable you to view the previous and the following messages. For this example, click OK to close the dialog box.

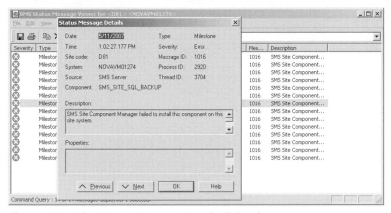

Figure 6-7   The Status Message Details dialog box

4. Close the Status Message Viewer when you finish reviewing the message details.

To view the detailed messages for a specific site system in the Site System Status window, follow these steps:

1. Right-click the summary entry for a site system and choose Show Messages from the context menu to display a list of message types.

2. Choose All to display all messages collected for this entry, choose Errors to display only error messages, choose Warnings to display only warning messages, or choose Info to display only informational messages.

3. After you choose an option, the Set Viewing Period dialog box appears, as shown in Figure 6-8. Select the Specify Date And Time option to display only messages generated after the date and time you enter. Select the Select Date And Time option to display messages generated within a more generic time period from 1 hour ago to 1 year ago.

4. Click OK to display the Status Message Viewer, as shown in Figure 6-9. You can also click Skip if you prefer not to limit the scope of the messages displayed.

5. View the detailed description for each message either by positioning your mouse pointer on the message's Description field to display a pop-up window or by double-clicking the message to display the Status Message Details dialog box.

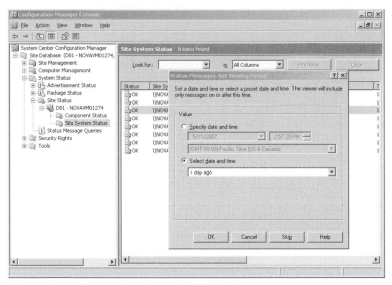

Figure 6-8 The Set Viewing Period dialog box

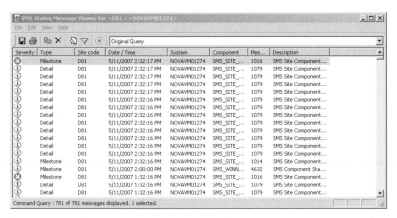

Figure 6-9 The Status Message Viewer for a Site System Status window summary entry

6. Close the Status Message Viewer when you finish reviewing the message details.

This section discussed how to view status messages in the Status Message Viewer. You continue to explore how to utilize this viewer in the next section.

Setting Status Message Viewer Options

When Configuration Manager components or services generate status messages, they're written to the site database. The Status Message Viewer uses the ConfigMgr Provider to query the database for the detailed messages when you use the technique described in the preceding section.

As shown in Figure 6-9, the Status Message Viewer for the site system status displays all the Configuration Manager components that are running on that site system or that affect it in any way. These messages are the same as those displayed for each component in the Component Status window. For example, the highlighted SMS_Site_SQL_Backup message in Figure 6-9 is the same as the message highlighted in Figure 6-6.

Regardless of whether you're viewing component status or site system status, the Status Message Viewer always displays the following information:

- **Severity** Specifies whether the message category is info, warning, or error

- **Type** Specifies whether the message type is milestone, detail, or audit

- **Site Code** Specifies the three-character site code of the site for which the message was generated

- **Date / Time** Specifies the time and date stamp indicating when the message was generated

- **System** Specifies the server name of the site system for which the message was generated

- **Component** Specifies the name of the Configuration Manager component or service that generated the message

- **Message ID** Specifies the numeric code related to the task performed by the Configuration Manager component or service that generated the message

- **Description** Provides a detailed description of the message

The Status Message Viewer provides many features that can facilitate your analysis of messages. Begin with some of the graphical user interface (GUI) features. You can change the sort order of each column simply by clicking the column header. Each column has three sort options: click once to sort from lowest to highest, click again to sort from highest to lowest, and click once again to return to the default column order. You can, of course, resize the columns by clicking the border between each column heading and dragging to make the column wider or narrower. You can also move the columns to customize the display simply by dragging and dropping a column header to a new position.

By right-clicking any message entry to display its context menu, you can copy it, delete it, or display its Status Message Details window. You can also set a filter for the Status Message Viewer or refresh all the messages from this menu. You can select multiple messages for copying, deleting, and printing by using the Windows Explorer Ctrl+click method.

The Status Message Viewer also provides a variety of options and features that are enabled through the menus on its menu bar. Because most of these settings are self-evident, you look here only at those that are unique or of particular interest to the Configuration Manager administrator—in particular, the options in the Status Viewer Options dialog box and the Filter Status Messages window.

The Status Viewer Options Dialog Box

Start by looking at the Status Viewer Options dialog box. Begin by displaying the Status Message Viewer for a component or site system. Choose Options from the View menu to display the Status Viewer Options dialog box, as shown in Figure 6-10. The General tab is shown by default.

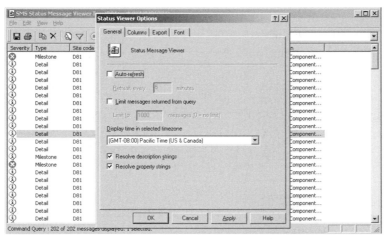

Figure 6-10   The Status Viewer Options dialog box

The General Tab

The Status Message Viewer doesn't refresh the interface with new messages by default unless you tell it to—for example, by pressing F5. The General tab lets you enable auto-refresh and specify a refresh interval. However, having the viewer automatically refresh itself will incur additional resource cost, so don't select this option unless you intend to leave the viewer open for a long time—perhaps to follow the flow of a task or the generation of messages. You can also limit the number of messages collected and displayed.

The Status Message Viewer displays messages stamped with the local time and date. The General tab lets you specify different time zones if you want to see when a message was generated on a site or site system in a different geographic location.

Most status messages are generated based on generic text strings in which variables have been inserted to customize the detail to a specific component, time, and so on. For example, message ID 4611 for the SMS Component Status Summarizer contains the text:

```
MS Component Status Summarizer reset the status of component %1, running on computer
%2, to OK.
```

This message always reads the same, except that the percent values are replaced with a specific Configuration Manager component value and server value. Displayed in the Status Message Viewer for SMS Site Component Manager on site server SQL1, this message would read:

```
SMS Component Status Summarizer reset the status of component "SMS Site Component
Manager", running on computer "SQL1", to OK.
```

If you clear the Resolve Description Strings and Resolve Property Strings check boxes in the General tab, the status messages resolve more quickly but leave empty quotation marks in the variable positions, rendering the messages not especially helpful to the Configuration Manager administrator.

The Columns Tab

The Columns tab of the Status Viewer Options dialog box, shown in Figure 6-11, enables you to customize the information displayed in the Status Message Viewer by adding columns to view thread and process IDs or by removing columns that might not be of interest.

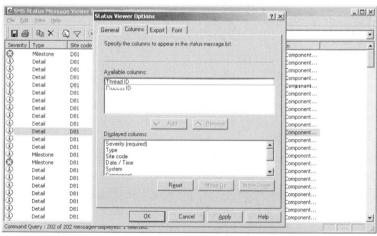

Figure 6-11   The Columns tab of the Status Viewer Options dialog box

The Export Tab

By default, status messages are deleted after seven days, but you can adjust this setting to suit your needs. Because some components can generate a multitude of messages, you might decide to delete messages more frequently to better manage database space. If you need to save or copy status messages to file for future reference and analysis or to print them out, the Export tab of the Status View Options dialog box, shown in Figure 6-12, provides options for doing so.

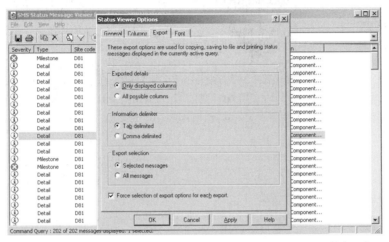

Figure 6-12   The Export tab of the Status Viewer Options dialog box

The Exported Details frame lets you specify whether to include all possible data about a status message or only the data associated with the displayed columns. Under Information Delimiter, you can identify whether columns should be exported as tab delimited or comma delimited. This option is helpful if you expect to import this data into some other reporting or analysis tool such as Microsoft Excel or Microsoft Access. The Export Selection frame lets you specify whether to export only messages that you select in the viewer or all messages. By default, every time you choose to copy, print, or save a message, this Export tab is displayed, allowing you to modify the options before continuing. If you want the same options to apply to every copy, print, or save operation, clear the Force Selection Of Export Options For Each Export check box.

The Font Tab

The Font tab, shown in Figure 6-13, enables you to set the typeface, style, and size of the font that will be used to display messages in the Status Message Viewer. Be careful to choose something readable. A decorative font might look pretty at first, but if you scrutinize messages for long periods of time, a poorly chosen font can give you a headache.

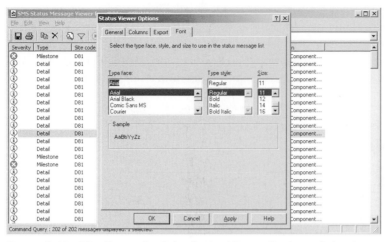

Figure 6-13   The Font tab of the Status Viewer Options dialog box

Filter Options

Another neat feature of the Status Message Viewer is the set of filter options that let you customize which messages are displayed in the Status Message Viewer. If you've used the filter options in the Windows Event Viewer, these filter options will be familiar. To set the filter options, choose Filter from the View menu to display the Filter Status Messages dialog box, as shown in Figure 6-14, or click the Filter icon from the toolbar (the one that looks like a funnel).

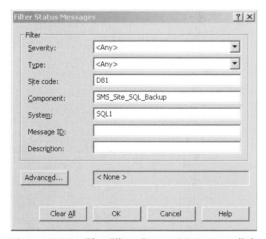

Figure 6-14   The Filter Status Messages dialog box

You can filter messages based on any status message detail. Figure 6-14 shows a filter that displays error messages of any type (milestone, detail, and audit) for site D81 and generated by the component SMS Site SQL Backup on site system SQL1. Click Advanced to display the Advanced Filter Options dialog box, where you can also specify filtering based on Process ID and Thread ID, message properties, and a range of time.

Real World   Using Queries to Customize the Status Message Viewer

The status messages that are displayed for a particular component, site system, package, advertisement, and so on are built based on a Configuration Manager query for that status message object. By default, the reference "Original Query" is listed in the drop-down list on the Status Message Viewer toolbar, as you see in Figure 6-9. To view the Original Query's criteria, choose Query Information from the View menu to display the Query Information dialog box, as shown in Figure 6-15.

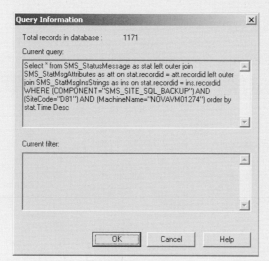

Figure 6-15   The Query Information dialog box

The Original Query usually shows all messages for a specific component on a specific site system. However, many predefined queries are available that you can run against any status message object; you look at some of these predefined queries later in this section. You can display and compile the status messages based on a query by selecting the query you want from the drop-down list of queries on the Status Message Viewer toolbar. For example, Site Component Manager status messages might include messages generated on several site systems in your site as well as on child sites. Perhaps you need to see only the status messages for your site or for a specific site system. Status message queries are available from the drop-down query list for both of these situations: All Status Messages From A Specific Component At A Specific Site and All Status Messages From A Specific Component On A Specific System, as shown in Figure 6-16.

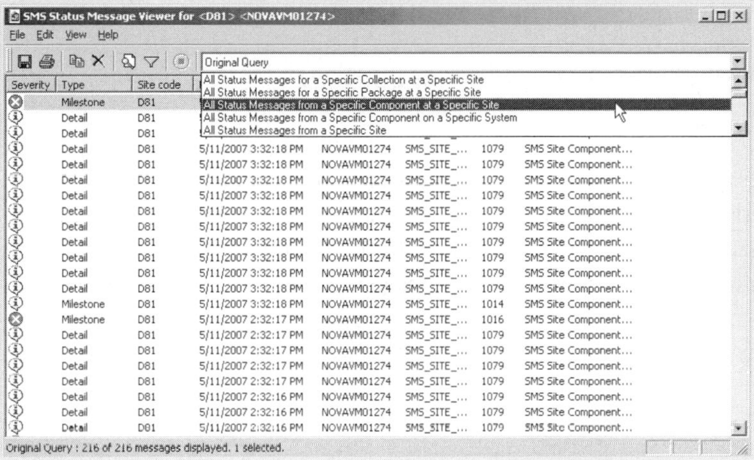

Figure 6-16   Status Message Viewer showing drop-down query list

To resolve these queries, from the drop-down query list, select one of these queries to display its corresponding query resolving window, specify the prompted values, and then click OK to execute the query. The Status Message Viewer screen is refreshed accordingly.

Understanding Status Summarizers

You can configure status messages in a variety of ways. For the most part, the default configuration of the status message system serves the average site quite well and generates a sufficient number of messages to facilitate reporting and troubleshooting. However, you might need to modify or enhance the reporting of status messages. One way to control the way messages are displayed in the Configuration Manager console is by using status summarizers.

Status summarizers provide a mechanism to consolidate the copious amounts of data generated by status messages into a succinct view of the status of a component, a server, a package, or an advertisement. In the Component Status window (shown in Figure 6-2), for example, you're presented with a single entry for each component that indicates the component's status (OK, Warning, or Error), its state (Started or Stopped), and the number of error, warning, and info messages that have been generated. Remember that behind each of these entry summaries can be a host of detailed messages. The following sections explore some techniques for modifying how the status summarizers consolidate and display the data you see in the Configuration Manager console.

Display Interval

The status messages that are displayed are filtered first by a display interval. By default, only status messages generated since midnight are displayed. This limitation doesn't mean that all previous status messages have been deleted. On the contrary, all status messages are written to the Configuration Manager database by default (you learn more about the status message reporting process in the section "Status Message Process Flow" later in this chapter). The length of time that status messages are retained in the database is determined by the Status Message Filter Rules. By default, audit messages are retained for 180 days, and other messages are retained for 30 days. The display interval merely facilitates your view of recent messages. You can modify the display interval for status summaries displayed in the Component Status folder and the Advertisement Status folder. Because summaries displayed in the Site System Status folder and the Package Status folder are based solely on state, you can't modify the display interval for these status messages.

To modify the display interval, right-click the Component Status folder or the Advertisement Status folder and choose Display Interval from the context menu to display a list of interval options, as shown in Figure 6-17.

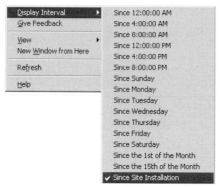

Figure 6-17   Displaying the list of display interval options

Select the interval option that best suits your viewing needs. Be aware that choosing an interval such as Since Site Installation is likely to net you a significant number of messages to scroll through when you choose Show All Messages from the context menu.

Strictly speaking, the display interval is not so much an attribute of the status summarizer mechanism as it's a way to facilitate your view of the status messages kept in the database. You can also view package status based on display interval; package and advertisement status are discussed in detail in Chapter 11.

Status Message Thresholds

A *status message threshold* is a limit that defines when the status summary for a component or site system should indicate OK, Warning, or Critical status. This threshold is set by determining the number of actual OK, Warning, and Critical messages that have been generated for each component or site system. When a predetermined number of messages has been collected, the status changes from OK to Warning or from Warning to Critical.

For example, consider the Status Threshold Properties dialog box shown in Figure 6-18, which you can display by right-clicking a status summary entry in the Component Status window and choosing Properties. The Status Message Threshold settings indicate that if one error type status message is generated for SMS Site Component Manager, the status summarizer will change the component's status from OK to Warning. If five error type status messages are generated, the component's status changes from Warning to Critical. Similarly, if 2000 informational type status messages are generated for SMS Site Component Manager, the status summarizer changes the status of SMS Site Component Manager from OK to Warning, and if 5000 informational type status messages are generated, the status changes from Warning to Critical.

Figure 6-18   The Status Threshold Properties dialog box, showing the default number of status message thresholds

Status thresholds for site system status are calculated similarly, but are based on available free space in the Configuration Manager site system database. Figure 6-19 shows the Free Space Thresholds Properties dialog box, which you can access by right-clicking any status summary entry in the Site System Status window and choosing Properties. Notice that the free space thresholds for all site systems generate a warning status message if free space falls below 102 MB (102,400 KB) and a critical status message if free space falls below 51 MB (51,200 KB).

Figure 6-19   The Free Space Thresholds Properties dialog box for the Site System Status

Other thresholds are specific to the databases based on a percentage of the database size. You learn how to modify these values or add new threshold values in the next section.

Configuring Status Summarizers

You can configure three status summarizer components: Component Status Summarizer, Site System Status Summarizer, and Advertisement Status Summarizer. To access these status summarizers, in the Configuration Manager console expand the site's Site Settings folder and then expand the Status Summarizers folder. You look at the specific property settings for each of these status summarizers in the following sections.

Component Status Summarizer

To configure the Component Status Summarizer, follow these steps:

1. Navigate to the Status Summary node in the Configuration Manager console (Site Database\<your site>\Site Settings\Status Summary).

2. Right-click Component Status Summarizer in the details pane of the Status Summary node and choose Properties from the context menu to display the Component Status Summarizer Properties dialog box, as shown in Figure 6-20.

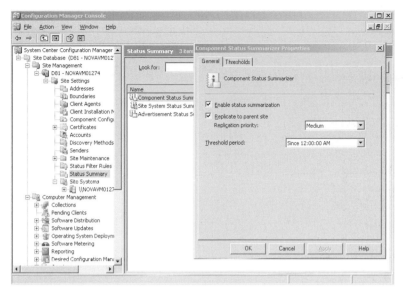

Figure 6-20   The General tab of the Component Status Summarizer Properties dialog box

Notice that the Enable Status Summarization and Replicate To Parent Site options are selected by default. If you want to disable component status summarization, clear the Enable Status Summarization option. If you do, however, the status message system won't be of much help to you as you'll no longer be tracking the activity of Configuration Manager components.

If you don't want to send status information to administrators in a parent site, clear the Replicate To Parent Site option. You might choose to do so if all site troubleshooting occurs at your site or your parent site administrators don't want to receive status information from your site, or both. If you're replicating status messages to a parent site, you can set the replication priority for those messages. The default, as you see in Figure 6-20, is Medium. You might choose Low as a replication priority if you've set address options limiting the priority of intersite communications (refer to Chapter 4) and you want to control when status messages are sent to the parent. This dialog box also gives you another place to modify the display interval, here called the threshold period.

3. Click the Thresholds tab to configure summary thresholds for each component, as shown in Figure 6-21.

4. Select the Message Type you want to set the threshold for—Informational, Warning, or Error—from the drop-down list and then double-click the component whose thresholds you want to change to display the Status Threshold Properties dialog box.

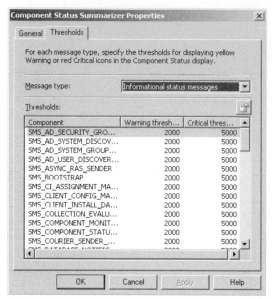

Figure 6-21 The Thresholds tab of the Component Status Summarizer Properties dialog box

The default status message thresholds differ for each message type. Figure 6-22 shows the default settings for informational status messages for the SMS Hierarchy Manager.

Note By default, the thresholds are the same for all components.

Figure 6-22 The default status message thresholds for informational status messages

Figure 6-23 shows the default settings for warning status messages.

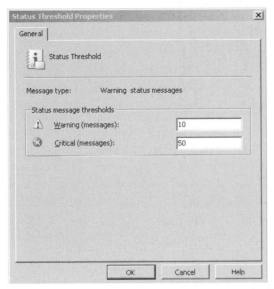

Figure 6-23   The default status message thresholds for warning status messages

Figure 6-24 shows the default settings for error status messages.

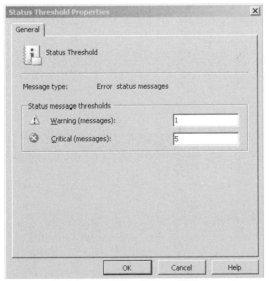

Figure 6-24   The default status message thresholds for error status messages

5. Specify the number of warning and error messages that need to be generated (the threshold) before the Component Status Summarizer changes the summary status from OK to Warning or to Critical.

6. Click OK to close the Status Threshold Properties dialog box and then click OK in the Component Status Summarizer Properties dialog box to save your modifications.

Site System Status Summarizer

To configure the Site System Status Summarizer, follow these steps:

1. Right-click Site System Status Summarizer in the details pane of the Status Summary node and choose Properties from context menu to display the Site System Status Summarizer Properties dialog box, as shown in Figure 6-25.

    Notice that the Enable Status Summarization and Replicate To Parent Site options are selected by default. If you want to disable site system status summarization, clear the Enable Status Summarization option. If you do, however, the status message system won't be of much help to you as far as tracking site system thresholds. However, you'll still be collecting component status. You might decide that tracking component status is enough, and because, let's say, you have resource concerns on the site server, you might choose to turn off site system status summarization to conserve resources.

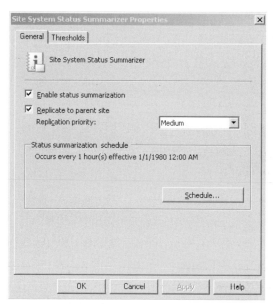

Figure 6-25   The General tab of the Site System Status Summarizer Properties dialog box

If you don't want to send status information to administrators in a parent site, clear the Replicate To Parent Site option. You might choose to do so if all site troubleshooting occurs at your site or your parent site administrators don't want to receive status information from your site, or both. If you replicate status messages to a parent site, you can set the replication priority for those messages. The default, as you see in Figure 6-25, is Medium. You might choose Low as a replication priority if you set address options limiting the priority of intersite communications (refer to Chapter 4) and you want to control when status messages are sent to the parent.

Click Schedule to display the Schedule dialog box, where you can specify a schedule for when and how often site system status summarization takes place.

2. Click the Thresholds tab to configure space thresholds for each database and for each site system, as shown in Figure 6-26.

    Configuration Manager has already set general default values for site systems. You can modify these settings by typing new values in the Warning or Critical text boxes. Configuration Manager has also defined specific threshold values for the Configuration Manager database. If you need to change these values, double-click the entry to display the Free Space Threshold Properties dialog box, where you can specify the values you prefer. Then click OK to close the dialog box.

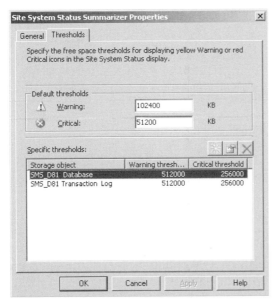

Figure 6-26 The Thresholds tab of the Site System Status Summarizer Properties dialog box

3. To add a specific site server to monitor its status, click the New button (the yellow star) in the Specific Thresholds frame to display the Free Space Threshold Properties dialog box, as shown in Figure 6-27.

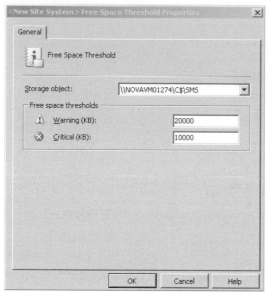

Figure 6-27 The Free Space Threshold Properties dialog box

Select the site system to monitor from the Storage Object drop-down list, type the desired amount of free space thresholds to monitor for in the Warning and Critical text boxes, and click OK.

4. Click OK again to save your changes.

Advertisement Status Summarizer

To configure the Advertisement Status Summarizer, follow these steps:

1. Right-click Advertisement Status Summarizer in the details pane of the Status Summary node and choose Properties from the context menu to display the Advertisement Status Summarizer Properties dialog box, as shown in Figure 6-28.

   Notice that the Enable Status Summarization and Replicate To Parent Site options are selected by default. If you want to disable site advertisement status summarization, clear the Enable Status Summarization option. If you do, the status message system no longer tracks advertisement status. If you manage a lot of packages at this site, disabling this option effectively robs you of the ability to follow the progress of a package advertisement to a target collection.

   As with Component and Site System status, if you don't want to send status information about advertisements to administrators in a parent site, clear the Replicate To Parent Site option. You might choose to do so if all package maintenance occurs at your site or your parent site administrators don't want to receive information about advertisements from your site, or both. If you're replicating status messages to a parent site, you can set the replication priority for those messages. The default, as you see in Figure 6-28, is Medium. You might choose Low as a replication priority if you set address options limiting the priority of intersite communications (refer to Chapter 4) and you want to control when status messages are sent to the parent.

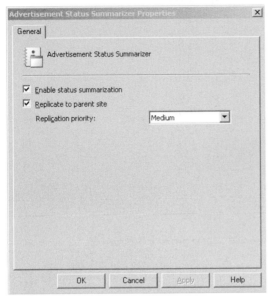

Figure 6-28   The General tab of the Advertisement Status Summarizer Properties dialog box

2.   Click OK to save your modifications.

Status summarizers help you define how component, system, and advertisement status is displayed to the Configuration Manager administrator based on their message type, OK, Warning, and Critical. The next section shows you how to further refine which status messages are captured and displayed in the Status Message Viewer.

Filtering Status Messages

Configuration Manager components and site systems generate a constant stream of status messages. Most of these messages will prove to be extremely helpful in resolving issues or troubleshooting problems you might be having with your Configuration Manager site. Some messages, however, might simply be flooding the Status Message Viewer with interesting but not particularly useful information, or too much information, or not the kind of information you're looking for.

There are several ways to filter status messages and display just the status information of interest. You looked at one technique in the section "Setting Status Message Viewer

Options" earlier in this chapter. You can also accomplish status filtering in a more global fashion by modifying the status reporting properties or by defining status filter rules.

Configuring Status Reporting Properties

One way to define how status reports are generated is to configure the Status Reporting component. To configure the Status Reporting component properties, follow these steps:

1. In the Configuration Manager console, navigate to and expand the Site Settings node, and then select Component Configuration.

2. In the details pane, right-click Status Reporting and choose Properties from the context menu to display the Status Reporting Properties dialog box, as shown in Figure 6-29.

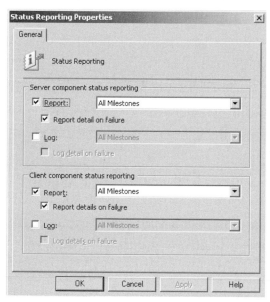

Figure 6-29   The Status Reporting Properties dialog box

By default, reporting is enabled for both the site server and the client components for the following types of messages:

■ All milestones

■ All milestones and all details

■ Error and warning milestones

■ Error milestones

By selecting the appropriate message types from the drop-down lists, you can control how much data is reported. For example, to show only milestone messages that are errors or warnings, select Error And Warning Milestones from the drop-down list in the Server Component Status Reporting frame of the dialog box.

Caution   The default settings for message reporting are considered appropriate for most Configuration Manager sites. Enabling too many messages or filtering out too much information can make the status message system less effective as a problem-solving tool.

The Report Detail On Failure option is also selected by default. This powerful feature ensures that when a failure occurs or an error is reported, the affected component reports details as to the nature of the failure as well as possible causes and remedies. You will probably not want to disable this feature—unless, of course, you can troubleshoot without knowing the details of a problem.

You can also enable logging for the same message types to the Windows Event Log and include failure details in the log by selecting those options.

Status Filter Rules

The second way to globally affect how status messages are reported is by using status filter rules. Configuration Manager creates 15 status filter rules of its own to control how status messages are reported and viewed, as shown in Figure 6-30. In the Configuration Manager console, expand the Site Settings node, then select the Status Filter Rules node to display these status filter rules. These default filter rules are used to control how many, and which, status messages are reported and displayed in the Status Message Viewer.

When a Configuration Manager component generates a status message, the SMS Status Manager tests the message against these status filter rules to determine how that message should be handled. The SMS Status Manager then performs one or more of the following actions:

- Writes the message to the Configuration Manager database
- Writes the message to the Windows Event Log
- Replicates the message to the parent site
- Sends the message to a status summarizer
- Executes a program

Most of the default status filter rules generate a system message that's displayed on the site server using a NET SEND command. You should not fool around with any of these default status filter rules. Each has been created for a reason, and they're all significantly useful. But you might find that you want to create additional filter rules. You can customize status filter rules to discard certain types of messages that you don't want or don't need to see, to replicate certain types of messages to a parent site at a higher priority than others or not replicate certain messages at all, and to execute a program based on a message type.

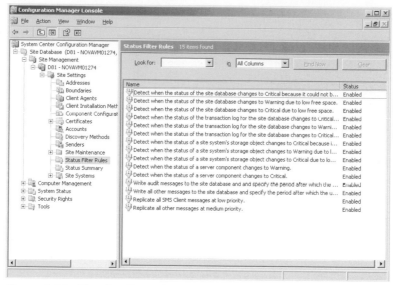

Figure 6-30   The Configuration Manager default status filter rules

Begin by deciding just what messages you need to see and what messages you don't need to see. For example, if your site participates in a parent-child relationship but is fully administered within the site—that is, no administration occurs at the parent site—it might be unnecessary to replicate any status messages to the parent site. Eliminating this replication would certainly decrease the amount of network traffic generated between the parent site and your site.

> **Note**   Do not modify existing status filters or define any new filter rules until you're fully comfortable with and knowledgeable about the status message system. If you make a change without knowing its full effect, you could render the status message system useless to you as a troubleshooting tool.

Follow these steps to create a new status filter rule:

1. In the Configuration Manager console, navigate to and expand the Site Settings node.

2. Right-click Status Filter Rules and choose New Status Filter Rule from the context menu to run the New Status Filter Rule Wizard, as shown in Figure 6-31.

3. On the General page, type a descriptive name for your filter.

> **Note**   The status filter name should adequately explain the function and purpose of the status filter rule you're creating. Use the default filter names as a guideline for creating your own.

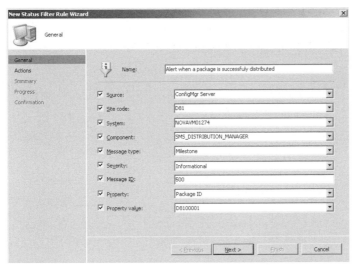

Figure 6-31   The General page of the New Status Filter Rule Wizard

You can narrow your filter criteria further by selecting any combination of options available in the General tab. These options are described in Table 6-1.

Table 6-1   Status Filter Rule Options

Filter option	Description
Source	The source of the status message: Configuration Manager Server, Configuration Manager Client, or ConfigMgr Provider
Site Code	The site code corresponding to the source of the status message
System	The name of the Configuration Manager client or server that generates the status message
Component	The name of the Configuration Manager component that generates the status message
Message Type	The status message type: Milestone, Detail, or Audit
Message Severity	The message severity: Informational, Warning, or Error
Message ID	The specific status message ID you're reporting on—for example, an ID of 500 generally relates to a component starting up
Property	The name of a specific property, such as Advertisement ID, Collection ID, Package ID, Policy Assignment ID, or Policy ID, that might be present in some status messages you want to report on
Property Value	A specific property attribute for the property name you specified, such as Advertisement ID, Collection ID, Package ID, Policy Assignment ID, or Policy ID, that might be present in some status messages you want to report on

4. Click Next to open the Actions page, as shown in Figure 6-32, and specify what Status Manager should do when the message criteria defined in the General tab are met.

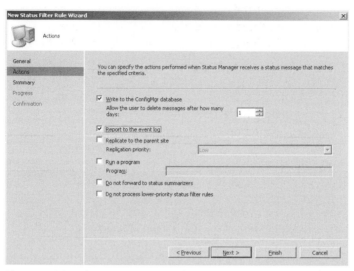

Figure 6-32   The Actions page of the New Status Filter Rule Wizard

In this example, Status Manager is instructed to write the message to the Configuration Manager database as well as to the Windows Event Log. By default, the message is also forwarded to the appropriate status summarizer to be included in the Status Message Viewer. Other actions available to you are described in Table 6-2.

Table 6-2   Status Filter Action Options

Action option	Description
Write To The Configuration Manager Database	Includes the status message as a record in the Configuration Manager database. By default, messages are kept in the database for one day and then deleted, unless this value is modified.
Report To The Event Log	Writes the status message to the Windows Event Viewer application log.
Replicate To The Parent Site	Sends a copy of the status message to the site's parent.
Run A Program	Directs Configuration Manager to execute the command entered in the Program text box when the status message is generated.
Do Not Forward To Status Summarizers	Prevents the status message from being handled by any status summarizer. This means that it might not be included in determining warning or error thresholds in the status viewer.
Do Not Process Lower Priority Status Filter Rules	Effectively ends any further processing of this status message. This means that it won't be evaluated by any additional filter rules.

5. Click Next to review your choices, click Next to create the new status filter rule, and then click Close to close the wizard.

The new status filter rule is added at the end of the list of existing rules. However, the actual order in which the rules are listed is determined by their relative priority. Status messages are passed through all the filters if you don't select the Do Not Process Lower-Priority Status Filter Rules check box for a filter in the Actions tab. If you select this option for a filter, the message won't pass through any filters below this one in the filter list. You can change the order of filter processing by right-clicking a filter, choosing All Tasks from the context menu, and then choosing Increment Priority to move the filter up in the list or Decrement Priority to move the filter down in the list.

Note   The Run A Program option in the Actions tab can be a useful alert tool if you're using a Windows-compatible paging application or some other notification tool that can be executed through a command line. For example, you can type the command-line sequence for executing a page to notify you when a specific status message is generated.

Using Status Filter Rules

After you become comfortable with the status message system and the way in which the various Configuration Manager components work and interact, you might want to filter out simple informational messages, such as messages generated when a component starts or wakes up, that can add communication or administrative overhead to your network. Here is a sample filter rule for discarding status messages from a component that's flooding the network. Follow the steps outlined earlier to define this simple filter. On the General page of the New Status Filter Rule Wizard, type a name in the form "Discard message *xyz* from component *abc* on server *123*." For example, let's say that you want to exclude startup messages for Site Control Manager that are generated on the system D81. The status filter rule name might be "Discard startup messages for the Site Control Manager generated on server D81". Fill in the property fields, as shown in Figure 6-33.

In the Actions tab, select the Do Not Forward To Status Summarizers check box. This setting ensures that the message is disregarded and that it won't be displayed in the Status Message Viewer. Depending on where this new rule sits in relation to the other rules, you might also want to select the Do Not Process Lower-Priority Status Filter Rules check box to prevent any subsequent filters from picking this message up and possibly writing it to the database or displaying it in the Status Message Viewer.

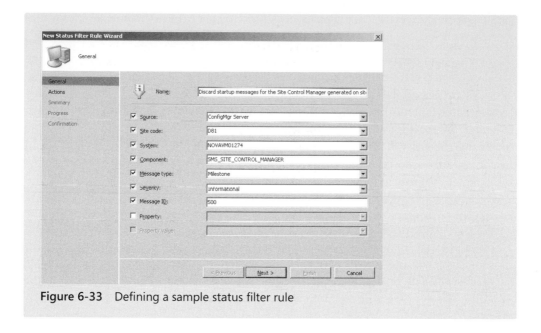

Figure 6-33   Defining a sample status filter rule

Working with Status Message Queries

You already know how to effectively use the Status Message Viewer to customize status messages and troubleshoot components and site systems. The Status Message Viewer displays messages on a per-component or per-system basis. Sometimes, however, you might need to see all messages of a specific type generated across all the site systems or from several components.

Configuration Manager includes over 60 status message queries as a means of accomplishing just that. These queries are listed in the Status Message Queries window, as shown in Figure 6-34. In the Configuration Manager console, navigate to the System Status node and expand it, then select the Status Message Queries node to display the status message queries in the details pane. As an example, the query highlighted in Figure 6-34 will generate a list of all Configuration Manager clients on which the Hardware Inventory Client Agent reported some problem when trying to generate the Management Information Format (MIF) file needed to report the client's hardware information to the site database. Running a query of this type is certainly easier than scanning for the error status message for every client reporting messages to the Component Status Summarizer.

Note   Use the Look For field in the details pane to help narrow down the list of queries to choose from. In this example, typing "hardware inventory" in the Look For field and then clicking Find Now narrows the list to five status message queries, including the one specified in the example.

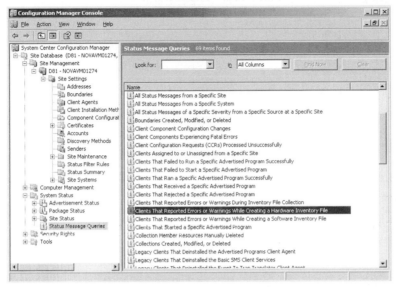

Figure 6-34   The Status Message Queries window

Most of these default queries are prompted—meaning that you must provide information such as a site code, the server name, and so on. To execute a status message query, right-click the query in the Status Message Queries window and choose Show Messages from the context menu. Any values that need to be resolved are listed, and you must enter the information or values requested.

You can also create your own status message queries. To do so, follow these steps:

1. Right-click Status Message Queries and choose New Status Message Query from the context menu to run the New Status Message Query Wizard shown in Figure 6-35.

2. Type a descriptive name for your query and a comment that further explains the query's purpose.

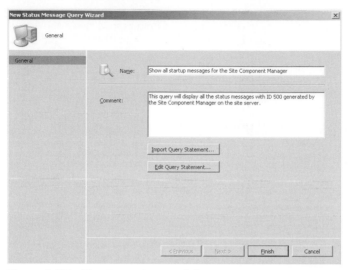

Figure 6-35   The General page of the New Status Message Query Wizard

3. Click Import Query Statement to display the Browse Query dialog box that lists all the available status message queries, as shown in Figure 6-36. Select the query you want to import into your new query and click OK.

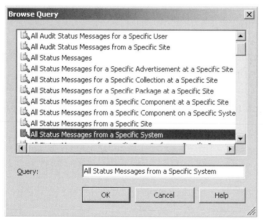

Figure 6-36   The Browse Query dialog box

4. Click Edit Query Statement to display the Query Statement Properties dialog box. In this dialog box, you can modify the properties of the query you imported in step 3. If you did not import an existing query, then you can create your own new query here.

    By default, a status message query displays only status messages in its results list; thus all the options in the General tab are unavailable, as shown in Figure 6-37.

Figure 6-37   The General tab of the Query Statement Properties dialog box

5. Click the Criteria tab to create or modify the query statement. Any existing query statements are displayed in the Criteria list, as seen in Figure 6-38.

Figure 6-38   The Criteria tab of the Query Statement Properties dialog box

6. Click the New button (yellow star) to add a new criteria statement or highlight an existing criteria statement and click the Edit button (hand holding paper) to display the Criterion Properties dialog box, as shown in Figure 6-39.

Figure 6-39   The Criterion Properties dialog box

7. Select the criterion type (in most cases, this will be Simple Value) from the drop-down list and specify the attribute class and the attribute by clicking Select to display the Select Attribute dialog box shown in Figure 6-40. The attributes describe a Configuration Manager object type and are grouped into one or more attribute classes. In this example, the attribute class Status Message consists of attributes that include component, machine name, severity, and site code, any of which can be used to qualify the results of the query. Select an appropriate Attribute Class and Attribute and click OK to go back to the Criterion Properties dialog box. Next, specify an operator by choosing one from the drop-down list. Click Value to display all the values related to the attribute you selected that have been recorded in the Configuration Manager database. Click OK.

8. To add criteria to your query, repeat steps 6 and 7 for each additional criteria statement. When you finish, click OK twice to save your query.

The new status message query is now available in the Status Message Queries window. Figure 6-41 shows the results of running your sample query by right-clicking the sample query and choosing Show Messages from the context menu. Notice that the result of the query is to display the message "This Component Started" for every component on the site server.

Figure 6-40   The Select Attribute dialog box

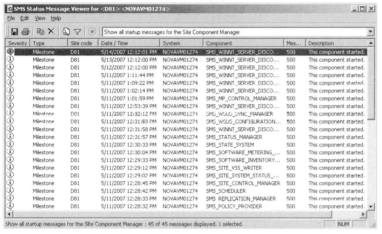

Figure 6-41   The results of running a sample status message query

More Info   You find a complete discussion about creating and maintaining queries for Configuration Manager in Chapter 19, "Extracting Information Using Queries and Reports."

Status Message Process Flow

Now that you've examined the different tools for handling status messages, look at the status message process flow. Nearly every Configuration Manager service and component generates status messages. Not only does the site server itself generate messages, as one would expect, but the components and services running on site systems (management points, client access points, and so on) and agents running on Configuration Manager clients also generate status messages. The status message system in Configuration Manager has the capacity to generate a multitude of messages; however, as you've seen, status summarizers and filters keep these messages to a manageable level by default. Nevertheless, status message reporting can add to your existing network traffic bandwidth issues.

Reporting Status on Site Servers and Site Systems

Status messages generated on the site server are processed within the site server itself and then updated to the Configuration Manager database. If the Configuration Manager database resides on the same server, no additional network traffic is generated. However, status messages that Configuration Manager services and components generate on site systems are copied to the site server so that they can be updated to the Configuration Manager database. Figure 6-42 depicts the process flow for status messages generated on the site server and site systems.

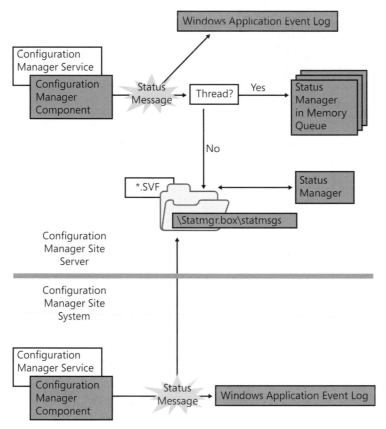

Figure 6-42 Status message process flow for status messages generated on the site server and site systems

As mentioned in the section "Configuring Status Reporting Properties," several options are available to the Configuration Manager administrator when configuring status message reporting. Remember that one option enables the Configuration Manager administrator to specify whether to convert the status message to a Windows event. When a Configuration Manager service or thread generates a status message, that service or thread checks its properties to see whether this option has been set. If it has, the status message is first converted to a Windows event and written to the Windows Application Event Log. If no other reporting options have been configured, the process stops here. If other reporting options have been configured, the status message must be handed off to the Status Manager component on the site server. If the server on which the status message was generated is the site server, the status message is placed either in the In Memory Queue if a thread component generated the message or in the inbox (<Installation-Path>SMS\Inboxes\Statmgr.box\Statmsgs) as an .svf file if a service component generated the message.

If the server on which the status message was generated is a site system, the status message is copied to Status Manager's inbox on the site server. If for some reason the component is unable to copy the status message to the site server, it stores the status message(s) in the %Systemroot%\System32\Smsmsgs subdirectory on the site system and retries until it can successfully copy the status message to the inbox on the site server.

Reporting Status from Clients

As you've seen, Configuration Manager components and agents residing on Configuration Manager clients also generate status messages, and these messages also must be reported back to the site server for updating to the Configuration Manager database.

Status information is collected not only from Configuration Manager client components and agents, but also as the result of application installations in the form of status MIF files. For example, both the package program created through the Configuration Manager console and the packages compiled through the Systems Management Server 2007 SMS Installer tool have the ability to generate status MIF files upon the execution of the program or package.

When a status message is generated on the Configuration Manager client by a Configuration Manager client component, its properties are checked by that component to determine whether the message needs to be converted to a Windows event. If so, and if the Configuration Manager client is also a Windows 2000 client or higher, the status message is written to the Windows Application Event Log. Next, the status message and status MIF files are written to an .svf file and stored in the %Systemroot% or in the %Temp% or %TMP% directory. The client passes this file up to the management point. From there, the file is moved to the inbox on the site server.

> **Note**   Each client component generates a log file in the %windir%\System32 \Ccm\logs directory on the client computer by default. Check these log files to determine whether the .svf file was created during troubleshooting of status message generation. Additionally, in the log file of the component that should have generated the status message, look for a line that begins with "**STATMSG**" on or around the time that the status message should have been generated. If it doesn't exist, or if the next line begins with the text **CserverStatusReporter**, the component might have had trouble generating and reporting the status message.

Reporting Status to the Configuration Manager Database

After the status message is written to its in-memory queue or to its inbox, Status Manager wakes up and reads the status message or .svf file. It evaluates the message against the status filter rules established by Configuration Manager during setup or modified by the Configuration Manager administrator. As already discussed, a status message can be handled in one of five ways, as shown in Figure 6-43.

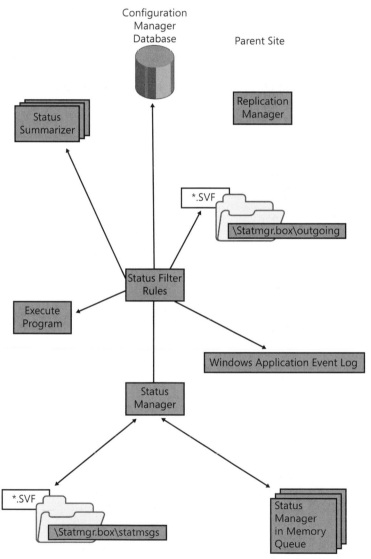

Figure 6-43   Using status filter rules to handle the disposition of a status message

The status message could be written to the Configuration Manager database or discarded. If the Status Manager has not already done so, the status message could be converted to a Windows event and written to the Windows event log. The status message could be handed to a status summarizer to be condensed for viewing through the Configuration Manager console. If a parent site exists, the message could be sent to the parent site for inclusion in its Configuration Manager database or viewing through its Configuration Manager console. The Configuration Manager administrator could also configure a program to be executed upon receipt of a status message. This program might be a system pop-up notification on the Configuration Manager administrator's desktop, the execution of a batch file, or a notification using paging software.

As you can see, the status messaging system in Configuration Manager is quite robust and is capable of inundating you with information about your site server, site systems, and clients. Fortunately, you can control which status messages are reported and how these messages are handled, and you can tailor their generation to fit your specific reporting needs.

Using Configuration Manager Service Manager

Status messages will be, and should be, your first stop when you're trying to understand a Configuration Manager process or to troubleshoot a problem on your site. However, in addition to status messages, you can also study the log files that each component can generate. Log files provide an even greater level of detail in describing how a Configuration Manager component is functioning, especially in relation to other components.

As discussed in Chapter 3, log files aren't enabled in Configuration Manager by default in order to conserve server resources. After all, there are more than 45 Configuration Manager components and services that can generate log files. In addition, each log file can hold up to 2 MB of data before archiving that data to an archive log. Altogether, if all component logs and archive logs are full, the server would require over 180 MB worth of storage space just for these files.

On the other hand, while log files are not enabled by default on the site server, they are enabled on Configuration Manager clients by default like they were in SMS 2003. This is because there are considerably fewer client components to monitor. It's also done so that the Configuration Manager administrator doesn't have to visit a client to enable logging. Each client log file defaults to 256 KB in size. You also explored using Configuration Manager Service Manager to enable Configuration Manager log files through the Configuration Manager console in Chapter 3.

Configuration Manager Service Manager is also used to monitor the status of components. Unlike the Status Message Viewer, Configuration Manager Service Manager provides an at-a-glance view of Configuration Manager components and services running on the site server and on each site system.

To monitor the status of components using the Configuration Manager Service Manager, follow these steps:

1. Navigate to the Tools node in the Configuration Manager console.

2. Right-click ConfigMgr Service Manager in the details pane, and choose Start ConfigMgr Service Manager from the context menu to display the ConfigMgr Service Manager window, as shown in Figure 6-44.

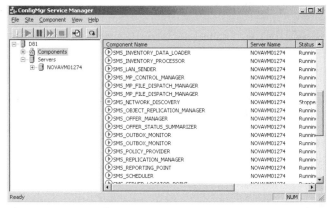

Figure 6-44   Configuration Manager Service Manager, displaying a list of components and services running on the site server

3. Select and expand Components to display a list of components, then select a specific component to view its status.

4. Select and expand Servers to display a list of servers running one or more Configuration Manager components, then select a server to see the list of components installed on that server.

5. Select a component, then choose Component\Query from the menu to display the status of that component.

6. Alternatively, choose Component\Select All to select all the components, then Component\Query to display the status of all the components.

As shown in Figure 6-44, you can see the status of each component represented both as an icon preceding each entry and in the Status field, the server the component is running on, the last time the component was polled, and the component type. The icon preceding each entry appears only after you query each component for its current status by right-clicking it and choosing Query from the context menu. Using the same technique, you can also stop, pause, and resume component activity.

Note If you want to stop all the SMS Executive threads, stop SMS_SITE
_COMPONENT_MANAGER first and then stop SMS_EXECUTIVE using Configuration Manager Service Manager, because the Site Component Manager might
attempt to restart the SMS Executive if it's stopped. The Windows Services administrative tool also enables you to stop these services; however, using Configuration Manager Service Manager is the preferred method.

Note Just because a Configuration Manager component is listed as stopped
doesn't necessarily mean that there's a problem with the service. Some services,
such as SMS_Network Discovery, highlighted in Figure 6-44, run on a predetermined or administrator-defined schedule. It's important to familiarize yourself
with viewing status messages and log files so that you can determine whether a
component problem exists.

Using Windows System Monitor with Configuration Manager

Generally, Windows System Monitor tends to be an underappreciated utility. This is
because administrators really haven't taken the time to learn how to use it effectively.
With a product such as Configuration Manager, which requires a significant amount of
resources to function efficiently, System Monitor can be one of the most effective tools at
your disposal to identify server resource usage and load. This discussion is approached,
therefore, with two objectives: to reintroduce you to the System Monitor tool and ensure
that you understand how to navigate it, and to identify some System Monitor objects and
counters that can be of specific use when monitoring resource usage and load on your
site systems.

Using System Monitor

Perhaps one of the more important tasks involved in troubleshooting problems on
your server, whether it's any Microsoft Windows server or a Configuration Manager site
system, is to spot potential problem sources and develop and analyze trends before the
problems materialize. Two basic steps are involved in achieving this kind of analysis-
baseline creation and real-time tracking. Always create a baseline chart or log of so-
called "normal" activity on your server. In your case, this should include the objects
and counters specific to Configuration Manager server activity. When you analyze performance, you can create real-time charts using the same objects and counters as you
use for your baseline chart and then compare it to the baseline to determine how server
performance is affected.

Here are some basic suggestions on how to create and use System Monitor charts. When referring to a System Monitor object and one of its counters, the following syntax is used: *Object:Counter*. For example, the *Processor* object has several counters that you can chart, one of which is the *% Processor Time*. This object and counter set is referred to as *Processor:% Processor Time*.

More than 20 different System Monitor objects come with Windows by default. These facilitate the monitoring of basic system resources such as memory, processor, disk, and network. In fact, these are the four areas that you'll want to monitor on any given Windows server, especially your Configuration Manager servers. In addition to these, other objects with their corresponding counters are added when other applications are installed, for example, Configuration Manager or Microsoft SQL Server. These represent additional items to monitor that can give you more information about what might be causing a specific resource situation.

Note   Monitoring objects alone with no other object data against which to reference is an exercise in futility for the administrator because you can't obtain any useful or specific information. For example, if the *Processor: % Processor Time* value is consistently higher than 80 percent, you might conclude that the processor is overutilized. However, you have no information as to what might be overutilizing the processor. Add the *Process: % Processor Time* object for suspected processes, and you now have connected data upon which to begin your analysis.

Baselines are also important in determining when a given system is being "resource-challenged." It should seem obvious, but bears repeating, that unless you know what "normal" resource utilization is like on any given system, you can't begin to analyze problems or bottlenecks, develop trends, or implement load balancing across systems. Start by creating a chart.

Creating a System Monitor Chart

To create a system monitor chart, complete the following steps:

1. Start the Performance console from the Administrative Tools group, and then select the System Monitor node.

2. Click the Add button (the plus sign) from the chart window toolbar to display the Add Counters dialog box, as shown in Figure 6-45.

3. Confirm the system you're monitoring in the Select Counters From Computer drop-down list or choose Use Local Computer Counters if you're monitoring the local computer.

Figure 6-45   Add Counters dialog box

Note   Because running System Monitor on a Windows server requires additional resources in and of itself, it's recommended that you remotely monitor your systems from your workstation rather than at the actual system in question.

---

4. Select the Object, Counter, and an appropriate Instance if necessary, and then click Add. If you're unsure of a counter's purpose or function, select it and click Explain to display a brief description at the bottom of the dialog box.

5. Repeat step 4 for each object:counter combination you want to track. Then click Close.

6. Specify the desired color, scale, width, and style for your chart lines by selecting an object:counter in the legend at the bottom of the graph, right-clicking it, and choosing Properties to display the System Monitor Properties dialog box, as shown in Figure 6-46.

Figure 6-47 shows a representative chart. Three objects are being monitored: *Processor: % Processor Time, Process: % Processor Time* for the SMS Executive instance (smsexec), and *Memory: Pages/sec*. After the chart is created, switch back to Configuration Manager Administrator Console and the Collection memberships are updated. You can see on the chart at what point this is done by the peaks recorded for each object.

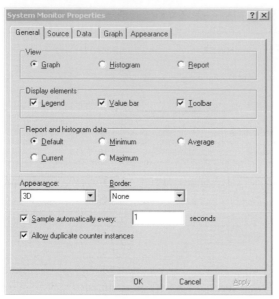

Figure 6-46   System Monitor Properties dialog box

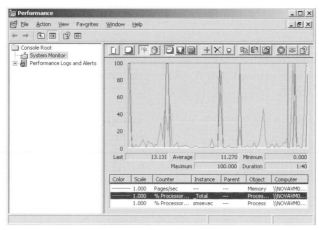

Figure 6-47   A simple chart that monitors three object:counter values

> **Note**   As more objects are monitored in a chart, the busier the chart becomes. You can facilitate the reading of chart lines by turning on a highlight feature. With the chart open, press Ctrl+H. Now when you select a line on the chart, it displays with a heavy white highlight making it easier to read. Press Ctrl+H again to turn off the highlight feature.

Configuration Manager performance, like most Windows systems, tends to revolve around a specific set of system resources that you can monitor and analyze with the help of System Monitor. These resources include processor usage, disk I/O, physical memory, and network. Table 6-3 outlines the more useful objects and counters to use when tracking and analyzing Configuration Manager Site System server performance using System Monitor.

These and other System Monitor objects and counters are meant to be used together to determine overall system performance as well as to narrow down problem processes and potential resource bottlenecks.

It's significant to note that you can't perform effective problem or trend analysis of a system if you don't have statistics relating to so-called normal performance of that system. To get this data, you should create and save chart information during periods of normal and peak performance. This gives you the baseline data you need to begin with. You can create these baselines by saving them as System Monitor logs.

Table 6-3   System Monitor Objects

Object:Counter	Description	Instance	Threshold suggestions
Memory:Committed Bytes	This represents the amount of virtual memory that has been committed for use for paging RAM.	N/A	This value should be less than the amount of physical RAM. The higher the value, the more likely that the system is experiencing a high level of paging and thrashing.
Memory:Page Reads/sec	This represents the frequency that data had to be read from the page file back into RAM to resolve page faults.	N/A	A value less than 5 generally represents acceptable performance. Values over 5 might indicate a need for more RAM.
Network Interface: Packets Received/second	This represents the total number of network packets received on this network interface.	Each network card	This value should remain relatively consistent and reflect average network traffic being generated. Prolonged increases in this number might indicate that a process or server on the network segment is generating additional traffic and using potentially more bandwidth.
Network Interface: Total Bytes Received/second	Represents the number of bytes received per second on this network interface.	Each network card	This value should remain relatively consistent and reflect average network traffic being generated. Prolonged increases in this value may indicate that a process or server on the network segment is generating additional traffic and using potentially more bandwidth.

Table 6-3   System Monitor Objects (Continued)

Object:Counter	Description	Instance	Threshold suggestions
Physical Disk:% Disk Time	This represents the amount of time the disk is engaged in servicing read/ write requests.	Each physical disk	Levels less than or equal to 80 percent generally represent acceptable system performance.
Physical Disk: Current Disk Queue Length	This represents the number of read/write requests currently waiting to be processed on the physical disk.	Each physical disk	Subtract from this value the number of spindles on the disks. For example, a redundant array of independent disks (RAID) device would have two or more spindles. The resulting value should be less than 2.
Process:% Processor Time	This represents the percentage of time spent by the processor(s) executing threads for the process selected.	_Total, or for each process currently running	Use with Processor:% Processor Time to determine which Configuration Manager process in particular is utilizing processor time, and to what extent.
Processor:% Processor Time	This represents the percentage of time spent by the processor or processors executing nonidle threads.	_Total, or each installed processor	Levels less than or equal to 80 percent generally represent acceptable system performance.
SQL Server:Cache Manager:Cache Hit Ratio	This represents how often SQL Server requests could be resolved from the SQL Server cache rather than having to query the database directly.	N/A	This value should be high, 98 percent or greater, which indicates efficient and responsive processing of SQL queries.
System:Processor Queue Length	This represents the number of threads waiting to be processed.	N/A	There should generally be no more than two requests waiting to be processed. Use this object while also monitoring *the SMS Executive Thread States*.
Thread:Context Switches/sec	This represents the number of context switches between threads, such as one thread requesting information from another or yielding to a higher priority thread.	_Total/ _Total	The lower the value, the better.

Creating a System Monitor Log

To create a System Monitor log, follow these steps:

1. Start the Performance console from the Administrative Tools group.

2. Expand Performance Logs And Alerts in the console tree and select Counter Logs.

3. Right-click Counter Logs and choose New Log Settings to display the New Log Settings dialog box, as shown in Figure 6-48.

Figure 6-48   The New Log Settings dialog box

4. Type a name for your log file, and click OK to display the log settings dialog box, as shown in Figure 6-49.

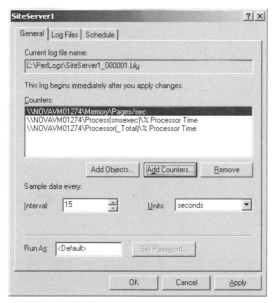

Figure 6-49   The log properties dialog box for the SiteServer1 log

5. Click Add Objects to add objects and Add Counters to add counters to the log just as you did in the section "Creating a System Monitor Chart" earlier in this chapter.

6. In the Log Files tab shown in Figure 6-50, click Configure to enter a location to store the log file, a file name, and size limit for the file.

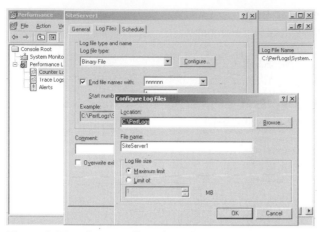

Figure 6-50   The Log Files tab settings

7. Use the settings in the Schedule tab, shown in Figure 6-51, to determine when System Monitor should begin to write information to the log, when it should stop, and whether another log file or command option should run.

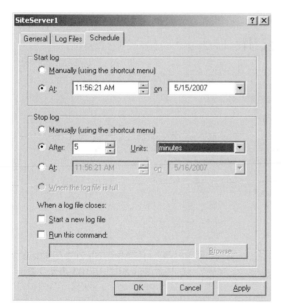

Figure 6-51   The Schedule Tab settings

8. Click OK to schedule the log.

Viewing a Log File

After the log runs, you can view the associated data in the performance window by selecting System Monitor in the console tree and clicking the View Log File Data button (the disk drive icon). Navigate to the location of the log file you created, select it, and choose Open to display the collected data in a static chart, as shown in Figure 6-52.

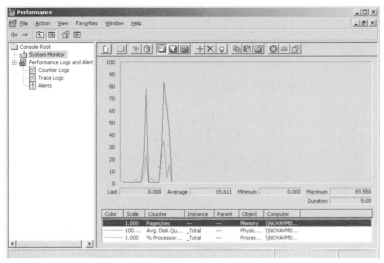

Figure 6-52   Static chart from a log file

Configuration Manager Specific Objects and Counters

When Configuration Manager is installed, setup adds a set of Configuration Manager–specific objects and counters to System Monitor. You can use these to assess performance levels of your Configuration Manager site system. Table 6-4 outlines these objects and some of their more useful counters for you.

Table 6-4   Configuration Manager–Specific System Monitor Counters

Object	Counter	Description
SMS Discovery Data Manager	Total DDRs Processed	The total number of Discovery Data Records (DDRs) processed by the Discovery Data Manager during the current session. This number should generally be high.
SMS Executive Thread States	Running Thread Count	When using the _Total instance, this indicates the total number of Configuration Manager threads currently running. By scrolling through the instances, you can assess thread count on a thread-by-thread basis. You can also monitor sleeping threads blocked by *Yield()* and yielding threads ready to run but not allowed due to a need to limit running threads.
SMS Inbox	File Current Count	This displays the current number of files residing in the inbox you select as an instance.

Table 6-4   **Configuration Manager–Specific System Monitor Counters (Continued)**

Object	Counter	Description
SMS In-Memory Queues	*Total Objects Dequeued*	This represents the total number of objects added to the queue by a specific component since the component last started. You can monitor numbers for each component by selecting it in the instance list.
SMS Inventory Data Loader	*Total MIFs Processed*	This represents the total number of inventory records processed by the Inventory Data Loader during the current session. You can also monitor the number of Management Information Format (MIF) files processed per minute and the number of bad MIF files processed.
SMS MP DAL	*Connections Created*	This represents the total number of connections created by the management point to the Configuration Manager database.
SMS MP Ddr Mgr	*Total Reports*	This represents the total number of Discovery Data Manager reports processed by the management point.
SMS MP Get Auth	*MPCERT Requests*	This represents the total number of MPCERT authentication requests received by the management point.
SMS MP Get Policy	*Requests/second*	This represents the number of policy requests made to the management point per second.
SMS MP Get SDM Package	*Total Requests*	This represents the total number of SDM package requests received by the management point.
SMS MP Hinv Mgr	*Total Reports*	This represents the total number of hardware inventory reports processed by the management point.
SMS MP Hinv Retry Mgr	*Failed Reports*	This represents the total number of hardware inventory reports that failed to process due to problems like insufficient disk space or memory.
SMS MP Location Ngr	*DP Requests/second*	This represents the number of requests for the location of packages on a distribution point received by the management point per second.
SMS MP Policy Mgr	*PA Requests/second*	This represents the number of policy assignment requests received by the management point per second.
SMS MP Registration	*Total Processed Requests*	This represents the total number of registration requests received by the management point.

Table 6-4   Configuration Manager–Specific System Monitor Counters (Continued)

Object	Counter	Description
SMS MP Relay Mgr	Total Reports/second	This represents the total number of reports processed by the management point per second.
SMS MP SINV CollFile Mgr	Number of Files	This represents the number of collected files received by the management point through software inventory.
SMS MP Sinv Mgr	Total Reports	This represents the total number of software inventory reports processed by the management point.
SMS MP State Message	Messages/second	This represents the number of client state messages processed by the management point per second.
SMS MP Status Mgr	Total Events/second	This represents the total number of status messages processed by the management point per second.
SMS Outbox	File Current Count	This displays the current number of files residing in the outbox you select as an instance.
SMS Scheduler	Number of Jobs	This represents the number of jobs the Scheduler component needs to process.
SMS Server Availability	Total Requests	This represents the total number of requests made by the Configuration Manager site system you select as an instance.
SMS Software Inventory Processor	Total SINVs Processed	This represents the total number of software inventory records processed by the Software Inventory Processor during the current session. You can also monitor the number of software inventory records processed per minute and the number of bad records processed.
SMS Software Metering Processor	Total SWM Usage Records Processed	This represents the total number of software metering usage records processed at the site since the Software Metering Processor last started.
SMS Standard Sender	Sending Thread Count	This represents the number of threads currently sending to a destination. You can monitor the total number or monitor on a site-by-site basis by selecting the appropriate instance.
	Average Bytes/second	This represents the average throughput of the sender. This number, generally, should be high. You can also monitor total bytes attempted, failed, and sent to establish baselines for the sender.

Table 6-4   Configuration Manager–Specific System Monitor Counters (Continued)

Object	Counter	Description
SMS State System	*Total Message Records Processed*	This represents the total number of state messages processed by the site server.
SMS Status Messages	*Processed/second*	This represents the number of status messages that the Status Message Manager has processed per second. Depending on the instance selected, you can monitor the total number of status messages processed or break it down between those processed from the In Memory Queue and from the Status Manager's Inbox.

Some of these objects are informational, providing additional data for you to help you understand how a component is working. They can all by and large assist you in establishing how resources are being utilized on your Configuration Manager servers. Remember, the idea here is to use these Configuration Manager–specific objects and counters along with the traditional objects and counters used to monitor processor, memory, disk, and network performance to establish a baseline of normal activity on your Configuration Manager servers and then use that baseline to help you determine when performance is outside the norm and when it becomes unacceptable.

> **More Info**   System Monitor contains additional features and options. For a more complete discussion of System Monitor, refer to the online Help files included with Windows. Also, see the topic "Configuration Manager Site Capacity Planning" in the *Configuration Manager Documentation Library* included as part of the Configuration Manager documentation for a more thorough discussion of performance-related issues to consider when planning your Configuration Manager site.

Summary

In this chapter, you learned about two of the most useful troubleshooting and learning tools you have at your disposal through Configuration Manager: status messages and log files. Although status messages provide you with most of the information you need to successfully monitor and troubleshoot Configuration Manager component activity, the log files, when enabled, give you that extra level of granularity that can so often provide the elusive bit of data needed to pull all the pieces of a puzzle together.

In addition, you explored the use of System Monitor to help track the performance of your site systems. In the next two chapters, you explore the process of discovering resources in the Configuration Manager site, and in particular, finding and installing Configuration Manager clients.

Part II
Managing Clients

Chapter 7
Discovering Resources

Where are they? You ask,

Oh, these systems must be found!

I say, here they are.

~ Jeff Gilbert, Technical Writer, Configuration Manager

Now that your Microsoft System Center Configuration Manager site has been implemented, and monitoring, analysis, and troubleshooting tools are ready and at your disposal, it's time to begin adding resources and clients to your site. After all, you can't use any of the neat features you've learned about—package delivery, desired configuration management, software updates, and Network Access Protection—unless you identify and install System Center Configuration Manager clients. In Part II, you learn about discovery methods and client installation and look at the following client management options:

- Operating system deployment

- Desired configuration management

- Network Access Protection

- Internet-based client management

- Inventory collection

- Remote tools

The installation process, as you see in Chapter 8, "Planning for and Installing Configuration Manager Clients," consists of discovering a client, assigning it to a Configuration Manager site, and then installing Configuration Manager client components on that computer. In this chapter, you look specifically at the resource discovery methods and process, and Discovery Data Manager.

Understanding Discovery

In talking about the Configuration Manager database, you're generally referring to the population of client computers in the environment that you want to manage. These clients are probably the most significant resources that you deal with in Configuration Manager sites on a day-to-day basis.

In addition to discovering client computers, you can also discover other resources and add them to the Configuration Manager database. These other resources include user accounts and global groups from a Windows domain account database, other site systems, routers, hubs, switches, network printers, and any other Internet Protocol (IP)–addressable devices on the network, including mainframe computers or UNIX workstations. Configuration Manager can also discover Active Directory objects such as users, groups, and computers.

Of course, you won't be able to send a package of TrueType fonts to a network printer that Configuration Manager discovers—not yet, anyway. But you can know that the printer is there and make it part of the database of information about the network. And you do have the ability to advertise programs not only to clients, but also to users and groups.

When a Configuration Manager discovery method discovers a resource, a record is created for it and included in the Configuration Manager database. This record is called a discovery data record (DDR), and the DDR file generated by the discovery method has a .ddr extension. The information that is "discovered" varies depending on the resource, but it might include such data as the NetBIOS name of a computer, IP address and IP subnet of a computer or device, user name, Configuration Manager globally unique identifier (GUID), operating system, Media Access Control (MAC) address, Windows account domain, and so on.

The six methods that you can use to discover resources are:

- Network Discovery
- Heartbeat Discovery
- Active Directory System Discovery
- Active Directory User Discovery
- Active Directory System Group Discovery
- Active Directory Security Group Discovery

These discovery methods are configurable by the Configuration Manager administrator. Configuration Manager also creates DDRs for site server and site system computers when you assign a site system role to that computer. This method of discovery is automatic and not configurable.

> **Note**   Configuration Manager does not install Configuration Manager client
> software on a site server or site system unless you also enable the Client Push
> Installation method described in Chapter 8, "Planning for and Installing Configu-
> ration Manager Clients."

When a DDR is created, Configuration Manager assigns that resource a GUID to distinguish it from other resources in the database. Depending on the discovery method chosen, discovery records are periodically regenerated to keep the discovery data up to date
in the database and to verify that the resource is still a valid resource within the site.

Recall that when you install Configuration Manager using the Custom Setup option, the
only discovery methods that are enabled are Heartbeat Discovery, which is set to run on
an existing Configuration Manager client once a week, and the automatic site system and
inventory discovery mentioned earlier. Therefore, the Configuration Manager administrator must determine which methods to use and how to configure them. When Configuration Manager is installed using the Express Setup option, however, all discovery
methods are enabled by default except for Network Discovery.

> **Note**   Chapter 2, "Planning for and Deploying Configuration Manager Sites" shows
> the Configuration Manager features and components that are installed or enabled dur-
> ing Express and Custom Setup and their main default values.

Examining Resource Discovery Methods

In this section, you examine the individual discovery methods. You learn how to configure each discovery method if applicable, the mechanics involved in carrying out the discovery process, the network traffic generated, and the elements you might need to
troubleshoot when you work with each discovery method.

> **More Info**   For a detailed discussion of planning issues to consider when
> choosing a discovery method, see the online help included with Configuration
> Manager when you install it, or the online Configuration Manager Documentation
> Library located at: *http://technet.microsoft.com/en-us/library/bb735860.aspx*.

Network Discovery

The Network Discovery method is designed to provide the Configuration Manager administrator with the means of discovering any network resources that are IP addressable,
which means that you can discover not only computers, but also printers, routers, bridges,

and so on. The discovery that takes place using this method can be far reaching. You can discover these resources on the local subnet in which the site server resides, or you can discover resources throughout your enterprise network using Dynamic Host Configuration Protocol (DHCP), Simple Network Management Protocol (SNMP), and other mechanisms. Resources discovered using this method are automatically added to the All Systems collection, which is viewable through the Configuration Manager console.

By default, network discovery discovers the network topology, but it also can be configured to discover the following information as part of the discovery record:

- Configuration Manager GUID
- NetBIOS name
- IP addresses
- IP subnets
- Internetwork Packet Exchange (IPX) addresses
- IPX network numbers
- Last logon user domain
- Last logon user name
- MAC addresses
- Name
- Resource domain
- User domain
- Operating system name and version
- Resource ID
- Configuration Manager assigned sites
- SNMP community name
- System roles

This discovery method can be useful in a variety of contexts. It can be used, for example, to find computers that could become Configuration Manager clients. When a computer is discovered, its IP address and subnet mask are included in the discovery record. This information can help you identify where your potential Configuration Manager clients are located and how they are distributed among the subnets, enabling you to formulate a more specific plan for locating and implementing your Configuration Manager sites, site servers, and site systems.

You can also use this information to plan the best client installation method for implementing Configuration Manager on those computers. For example, if you plan to use the Client Push Installation method, which is described in Chapter 8, you need to first discover the clients. You can use Network Discovery to create the DDRs for clients that will be installed using the Client Push Installation method.

Enabling Network Discovery

Like the other discovery methods, Network Discovery is enabled through the Configuration Manager Administrator Console. To enable Network Discovery, follow these steps:

1. Expand the site's Site Settings node and select the Discovery Methods node. The list of available discovery methods is displayed in the results pane.

2. Right-click Network Discovery and choose Properties from the context menu to display the Network Discovery Properties dialog box, as shown in Figure 7-1.

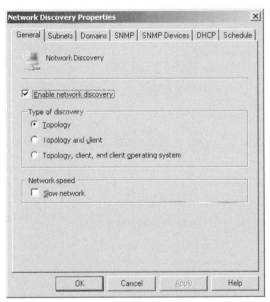

Figure 7-1 The Network Discovery Properties dialog box

3. On the General tab, select the Enable Network Discovery check box.

4. Specify the type of discovery you want. Selecting the Topology option causes Network Discovery to discover IP-addressable resources such as subnets and routers using SNMP. (You can also configure options in the Subnets, SNMP, SNMP Devices, and DHCP tabs, as you see shortly.) The Topology And Client option additionally discovers computers and resources such as printers and gateways using SNMP,

DHCP, and the Windows browser. Topology, Client, And Client Operating System also picks up the computer's operating system name and version using SNMP, DHCP, Windows browser, and Windows Networking calls.

5. Select the Slow Network check box for networks with speeds less than 64 Kbps. This option causes Network Discovery to decrease the number of outstanding SNMP sessions it generates by doubling SNMP time-outs.

6. Click the Subnets tab, shown in Figure 7-2. Here you can add, enable, and disable the subnets you want Network Discovery to search. By default, Network Discovery searches the local subnet in which the site server is a member. If you want to ignore that subnet, clear the Search Local Subnets check box.

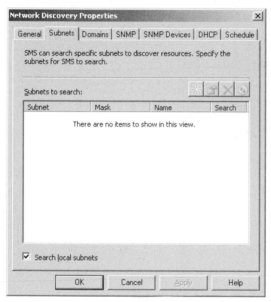

Figure 7-2   The Subnets tab

Network Discovery displays the subnets it discovered during each previous search. As it discovers the subnets, it marks them with a lock to indicate that they can't be modified or deleted—in fact, subnets discovered by Network Discovery, unlike those you add yourself, can't be modified or deleted once they've been discovered. However, you can enable or disable those subnets that you want Network Discovery to search on subsequent cycles.

7. To add subnets to the list, click the New button to display the New Subnet Assignment dialog box, as shown in Figure 7-3. Provide the appropriate subnet address and subnet mask, and click OK.

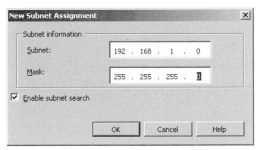

Figure 7-3   The New Subnet Assignment dialog box

8. If you select a discovery type other than Topology in the General tab, click the Domains tab, shown in Figure 7-4, and type the name of the Windows domain that you want to search for resources.

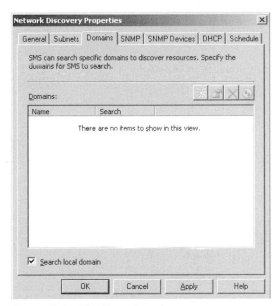

Figure 7-4   The Domains tab

By default, the local Windows domain to which the site server belongs is searched. If you want to ignore that domain, clear the Search Local Domain check box.

Note   Network Discovery can find any computer that you can find using Network Neighborhood to browse the network. Once it finds a computer, it still must obtain its IP address and will use one of the other methods (DHCP, SNMP, and so on) to do so. Network Discovery pings each computer to determine whether it's active, finds its subnet mask, and generates a DDR for it.

9.   To add Windows domains to the list, click the New button to display the Domain Properties dialog box, as shown in Figure 7-5. Type the appropriate domain name. The domain must be accessible through the network. By default, the Enable Domain Search check box is selected. This option enables Network Discovery in the domain. Click OK to close the dialog box.

Figure 7-5   The Domain Properties dialog box

10.   Click the SNMP tab, as shown in Figure 7-6, and specify the SNMP community you want Network Discovery to search.

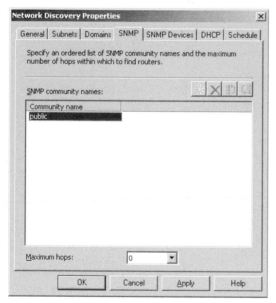

Figure 7-6   The SNMP tab

11.   To add SNMP communities, click the New button to display the New SNMP Community Name dialog box, as shown in Figure 7-7. Type the appropriate community name and click OK to return to the SNMP tab. If you type multiple communities, you can specify the order in which you want them to be searched by using the two Order buttons.

Figure 7-7   The New SNMP Community Name dialog box

Note   It's not necessary to have the SNMP Service installed on the site server performing Network Discovery. This discovery method uses its own SNMP stack to make requests and discover data.

12. Network Discovery attempts to access the local router to obtain IP addresses and data from the device. If the Maximum Hops value is set to 0, Network Discovery searches only the default gateway. You can set this value as high as 10. Each successive increment extends discovery to another set of routers. For example, setting Maximum Hops to 1 enables Network Discovery to search the default gateway and any routers connected to it.

13. Click the SNMP Devices tab (a companion to the SNMP tab), as shown in Figure 7-8.

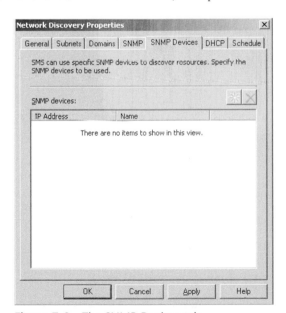

Figure 7-8   The SNMP Devices tab

On this tab you can identify specific SNMP devices that you want to discover by clicking the New button and supplying the IP address or name of the device. The SNMP devices can include routers, hubs, and token-ring media access units.

14. Click the DHCP tab, shown in Figure 7-9, and identify which Microsoft DHCP servers you want Network Discovery to query for a list of IP addresses leased to computers.

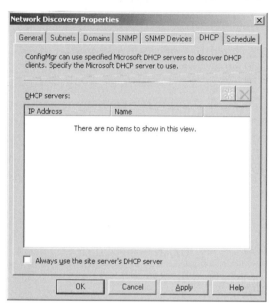

Figure 7-9   The DHCP tab

If the site server is itself a DHCP client, Network Discovery automatically queries the site server's DHCP server. If you want to ignore that DHCP, clear the Use Local DHCP Servers check box.

15. To add Microsoft DHCP servers to the list, click the New button and provide the appropriate subnet addresses or server names.

16. Click the Schedule tab, shown in Figure 7-10, and identify the frequency at which you want Network Discovery to run.

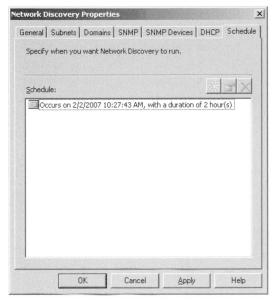

Figure 7-10   The Schedule tab

17. To add a new schedule, click the New button to display the Custom Schedule dialog box, as shown in Figure 7-11.

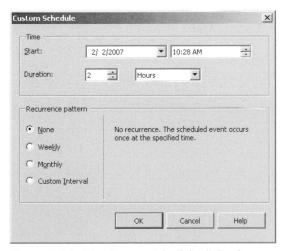

Figure 7-11   The Custom Schedule dialog box

18. To modify a schedule's properties, highlight the schedule and click the Properties button (the hand holding a piece of paper) to display the same Custom Schedule dialog box.

In the Schedule dialog box, type the time you want discovery to begin. You can also specify a recurrence pattern. Selecting None directs Network Discovery to search only one time for resources. You might select this option as a first pass to find all subnets, for example. The other options direct Network Discovery to perform subsequent searches according to your specified schedule. Duration indicates the period of time Network Discovery has to complete its search for resources. On a local subnet, two hours might be sufficient. However, if you perform a search of an enterprise network across several router hops with several thousand potential resources, you might need to increase this number so that Network Discovery has enough time to complete its search. If Network Discovery runs out of time, it logs a message to that effect in the netdisc.log file, and completes DDRs only for the part of the search that is complete.

19. Click OK to save your settings and initiate the Network Discovery process.

Network Discovery Process

The discovery process itself is once again fairly straightforward. Depending on the discovery options you enabled, Network Discovery attempts to search for subnets, routers, computers, and other devices. It needs to retrieve an IP address and subnet mask for each resource in order to generate a DDR for it. Network Discovery uses the information it receives from DHCP servers and SNMP to communicate directly with a device, such as a router, and then uses the router's ipNetToMedia table and Router Interface table to obtain subnet masks. It also uses Routing Information Protocol (RIP), SNMP, and Open Shortest Path First (OSPF) protocol multicast addresses to discover routers.

Network Discovery uses Windows Management Instrumentation (WMI) to store discovered resource information and generates DDRs based on this information. When Network Discovery generates a DDR, it writes the DDR to Discovery Data Manager's inbox (<InstallationPath>\SMS\Inboxes\Ddm.box). Discovery Data Manager, in turn, adds the record to the Configuration Manager database.

Network Discovery is capable of discovering literally thousands of devices on your network, and in doing so, it can generate a fair amount of network traffic. For this reason, your choice of schedule is significant. If you need to find large numbers of devices, you might opt to schedule Network Discovery to run during quiet periods on the network. And as suggested earlier, you might also need to increase the Duration value (shown in Figure 7-11) to accommodate processing of larger numbers of resources. Like the other discovery methods, Network Discovery generates status messages that you can view through the Configuration Manager Administrator Console. Message IDs in the 13xx range relate specifically to the discovery of resources. Also, if you enabled logging for Network Discovery, more detailed information is written to the Netdisc.log file.

Checkpoints for Using Network Discovery

Verify that you've identified not only the correct subnet address to search, but also the correct subnet mask. Network Discovery is more concerned with the subnet mask when retrieving device IP address information.

Look in the All Systems collection to see the discovered system resources. System resources include any IP-addressable device. Network Discovery also discovers logical networks and subnets. To view these resources, create a query to display the logical networks and subnets that are discovered. Refer to Chapter 19, "Extracting Information Using Queries and Reports," for more information about creating queries in Configuration Manager.

Heartbeat Discovery

Heartbeat Discovery is designed to keep DDRs up to date. This discovery method is significant because it ensures that resource records won't accidentally be aged out of the Configuration Manager database.

Heartbeat Discovery is installed as part of the Configuration Manager client installation and is used to keep existing DDRs up to date rather than to create new DDRs. By default, Heartbeat Discovery runs once a week but is configurable. The client refresh cycle runs once every 25 hours and is not configurable. The DDR created by Heartbeat Discovery is pushed when the client refresh cycle runs. So keep in mind that even if you configure Heartbeat Discovery to run less than 25 hours—say, every 2 hours—the updated DDR(s) will be pushed on the next client refresh cycle, which might be as long as 25 hours.

Enabling Heartbeat Discovery

Heartbeat Discovery is enabled by default and generates DDRs from each client every seven days. If you disable Heartbeat Discovery, you need to have enabled some other discovery method to keep the DDR information up to date. Furthermore, Heartbeat Discovery is active only on computers that have already been installed as Configuration Manager clients.

To configure Heartbeat Discovery, follow these steps:

1. In the Configuration Manager Administrator Console, expand the site's Site Settings node, and select the Discovery Methods node.

2. Right-click Heartbeat Discovery and choose Properties from the context menu to display the Heartbeat Discovery Properties dialog box, as shown in Figure 7-12.

    If you want to disable Heartbeat Discovery, clear the Enable Heartbeat Discovery check box.

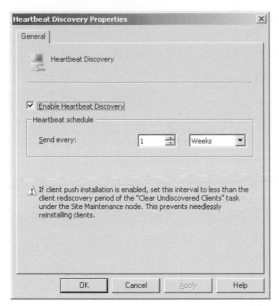

Figure 7-12   The Heartbeat Discovery Properties dialog box

3.   Specify the frequency at which you want Heartbeat Discovery to generate DDRs.

4.   Click OK to implement your schedule.

Checkpoints for Using Heartbeat Discovery

The only potential problem here is ensuring that Heartbeat Discovery has in fact been enabled and not disabled by accident. Also, be sure that the schedule you create causes the DDRs to be generated frequently enough that the DDR isn't accidentally deleted from the Configuration Manager database.

When Configuration Manager 2007 client software is installed on a computer, the client record in the site database is flagged with an installed status. The client record in the database maintains the installed status even if the Configuration Manager 2007 client software is later uninstalled. The Clear Install Flag site maintenance task clears the installed flag on the client record in the site database if the client is not rediscovered by Heartbeat Discovery. When the client is rediscovered, it is reinstalled.

The client rediscovery period is set to 21 days by default in the properties of the Client Install Flag maintenance task. If you set Heartbeat Discovery to be greater than the client rediscovery period, when the Client Install Flag maintenance task runs, it will think that the client has not been rediscovered by Heartbeat Discovery and will clear the installed flag, causing the client to be reinstalled when it is rediscovered.

Consequently, be sure that you do not set the Heartbeat Discovery schedule to be greater than the client rediscovery period. Otherwise, you might be needlessly reinstalling the client on computers that are already perfectly valid clients.

Active Directory Discovery Methods

There are four Active Directory discovery methods: Active Directory User Discovery, Active Directory Security Group Discovery, Active Directory System Discovery, and Active Directory System Group Discovery. Each of the Active Directory discovery methods polls the closest Active Directory domain controller.

These methods are configurable by the Configuration Manager administrator. The objects returned reflect those objects contained in Active Directory when the discovery method last ran. Therefore, don't consider this method to be dynamic.

Active Directory User Discovery includes the following information about the user account:

- User name
- Unique user name (which includes the domain name)
- Domain (Active Directory)
- User container name

Active Directory Security Group Discovery includes the following information about the security group account:

- Security group name
- Domain (Active Directory)
- Group container name

Active Directory System Discovery includes the following information about the system account:

- Computer name
- Active Directory container name
- Active Directory site name
- IP address
- MAC address
- SMS assigned site
- SMS Unique Identifier (GUID)

Active Directory System Group Discovery includes the following information about the system group account:

- Organizational unit
- Global groups
- Universal groups
- Nested groups
- Nonsecurity groups

Enabling and Configuring an Active Directory Discovery Method

To configure the Active Directory User Discovery, Active Directory Security Group Discovery, Active Directory System Discovery, and Active Directory System Group Discovery methods, follow these steps:

1. In the Configuration Manager Administrator Console, navigate to the site's Site Settings node, expand it, and select the Discovery Methods node.

2. Right-click the appropriate Active Directory discovery method in the results pane. The procedures for each method are essentially the same, so in this example Active Directory System Discovery is selected. Choose Properties from the context menu to display the Active Directory System Discovery Properties dialog box, as shown in Figure 7-13.

3. In the General tab, select the Enable Active Directory System Discovery check box.

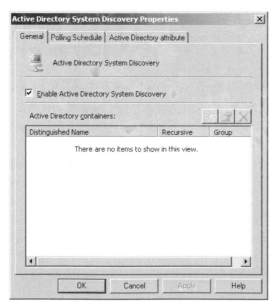

Figure 7-13   The Active Directory System Discovery Properties dialog box

4. Click the New button in the Active Directory Containers frame of the Properties dialog box to specify the location in Active Directory that Configuration Manager should search for the container. The New Active Directory Container dialog box appears, as shown in Figure 7-14. Select Local Domain, Local Forest, or type a Custom LDAP Or GC Query in the Path text box. Select the Search option you prefer. Recursive, which is enabled by default, determines whether or not child containers should be searched. Include Groups, when enabled, specifies that the search should include objects within groups.

Figure 7-14   The New Active Directory Container dialog box

5. Click the Polling Schedule tab, as shown in Figure 7-15. Notice that you can choose to have Configuration Manager run the discovery method as soon as possible by selecting the Run Discovery As Soon As Possible option, or set a specific time for discovery to run.

6. To set a specific time for discovery to run, click Schedule to display the Schedule dialog box. Define the frequency with which the discovery method should run and click OK. If you want the discovery method to begin as soon as possible after you finish configuring it, select the Run Discovery As Soon As Possible option.

7. The Active Directory System Discovery and Active Directory User Discovery methods include a third tab called Active Directory Attribute, shown in Figure 7-16. This tab lists the Active Directory attributes that are discovered by the discovery method by default. You can add additional attributes to discover by clicking the New button and typing the attribute, and you can delete any attribute in the list by selecting it and clicking the Delete button.

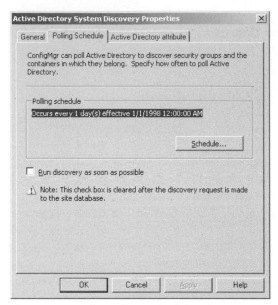

Figure 7-15   The Polling Schedule tab

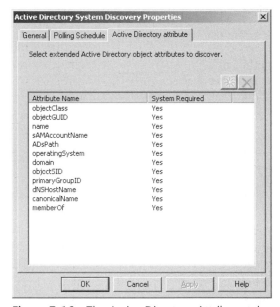

Figure 7-16   The Active Directory Attribute tab

8.   Click OK to begin the discovery process.

Like the other discovery methods that poll for information, the four Active Directory discovery methods can generate a significant amount of network traffic. Therefore, be cautious with the polling schedule you configure so you are not discovering resources during periods of peak network usage.

Real World   Packages for Discovered Users or User Groups

The beauty of Configuration Manager in the context of package distribution is that you can also advertise programs to collections that contain users or security groups discovered from Active Directory. This gives the Configuration Manager administrator an alternative target for certain packages. For example, suppose you have a budget spreadsheet that must be distributed and available to all finance department users, regardless of which computer they're logged into. If you discover those users through Configuration Manager or discover a Windows global group named Finance that contains these users, you can create a Configuration Manager collection with those users or that group as its members. You can then create a package that contains the spreadsheet and advertise it to your user or group collection. Whenever a member of that collection checks for advertisements on whatever Configuration Manager client the member happens to log in on, that spreadsheet is made available. Furthermore, if the collection gains any new members, those users (or group members) automatically receive all advertisements targeted to that collection.

Checkpoints for Using an Active Directory Discovery Method

When the Configuration Manager site server is in the same Active Directory domain, Configuration Manager must have at least read access to the containers that you specify when you configure each discovery method. If the site server is in a different Active Directory domain from the domain that you're polling, Configuration Manager must be at least a domain user in that domain. Other than that, check that the scheduling options and Active Directory locations are configured correctly.

Discovery Data Manager

The most prominent and common Configuration Manager site server component in the discovery process is Discovery Data Manager. Its role is to process DDRs written to its inbox on the site server (<InstallationPath>\SMS\inboxes\ddm.box) and to create site assignment rules based on the site boundaries as specified in the site control file. It also forwards the site assignment rules to secondary sites and creates Client Configuration Manager requests for discovered Windows clients if Client Push Installation is enabled. (*Site assignment rules* are the list of subnets, IP ranges, and Active Directory sites that define the site boundaries to determine whether discovered computers are assigned to Configuration Manager sites. See Chapter 8 for details.) Discovery Data Manager also forwards discovery information through Replication Manager to the parent site, if one exists.

Because it's a site server component, Discovery Data Manager generates status messages and writes more detailed information to its log file ((<InstallationPath>\SMS \Logs\Ddm.log) if logging is enabled for this component. Look for status message IDs in the 26xx range for specific information related to the processing of DDRs.

Summary

This chapter explored the first step in populating the Configuration Manager database and installing Configuration Manager clients—discovering resources. A variety of discovery methods were looked at that you can use to carry out the discovery process. In Chapter 8, you examine the various client installation methods available to the Configuration Manager administrator.

Chapter 8

Configuration Manager Client Installation

Deploy the Client!

Many options to choose from

It will be managed

~Rob Stack, Technical Writer, Configuration Manager

Introduction

In Chapter 7, "Discovering Resources," you learned how to discover resources and add them to the Microsoft System Center Configuration Manager site database. To manage a computer, however, you must make that computer a Configuration Manager client by installing the Configuration Manager client components. This chapter focuses on the client installation and assignment process. You'll begin by exploring the concept of site assignment, and then look at the available client installation methods and the installation and assignment flow, learn methods for managing clients, and finally how to run reports detailing the status of clients in your site.

If you are currently administering a Systems Management Server (SMS) 2003 site, it's recommended that you review the topic "What's New in Client Deployment for Configuration Manager" (*http://technet.microsoft.com/en-us/library/bb693939.aspx*) in the Configuration Manager Documentation Library to familiarize yourself with the many new or changed features of client installation in Configuration Manager 2007.

Planning for Client Installation

Before a computer can be managed by Configuration Manager, you must assign it to a Configuration Manager site. Although site assignment occurs after the client has been installed, it is important to plan for site assignment before you begin to install clients.

Configuration Manager clients can be installed and automatically assigned to sites when the computer resource is within the boundaries defined for a Configuration Manager site. However, when you install clients that are outside the boundaries defined for a Configuration Manager site, these clients must be manually assigned to a site, by specifying the site code of the required site. Clients that are not successfully assigned to a site will remain unmanaged. This means that these clients cannot receive policy and will be unable to install software distributions, software updates, run task sequences, and so forth. These clients must be manually assigned to a site, or site boundaries must be reconfigured to include the client's network location.

Understanding and Configuring Boundaries

Boundaries are a critical component of your Configuration Manager 2007 infrastructure. Boundaries are used not just with automatic site assignment, but also to define client behavior when running advertisements and software update deployments. For example, the default behavior of a software distribution advertisement for a client that is not within the configured boundaries of the site is to not install the software. Boundaries also define whether clients are within the administrative scope of a secondary site, which enables clients to locate distribution points closest to them, and a proxy management point in the secondary site.

Because boundaries are such a critical component of the Configuration Manager infrastructure, it is important to plan and configure boundaries for each site before you start to install clients in the hierarchy. Boundary configuration affects not just assignment, but ongoing management of Configuration Manager clients.

Configuration Manager boundaries have the following characteristics, some of which have changed from SMS 2003:

■ Boundaries can be defined by IP address, range of IP addresses, IP subnet, Active Directory site, and IPv6 prefix. To help you decide which configuration to use, see "Choose Configuration Manager Boundaries" (*http://technet.microsoft.com/en-us/library /bb633084.aspx*) in the Configuration Manager Documentation Library.

■ Boundaries are published to Active Directory Domain Services and retrieved from the site database by server locator points.

■ Whereas SMS 2003 had site and roaming boundaries, Configuration Manager has just boundaries that are defined for the site.

■ Whereas SMS 2003 referred to boundaries as being local or remote, Configuration Manager boundaries are defined as having fast and reliable networks or slow and unreliable networks. This configuration controls whether clients install software over slow networks.

■ Whereas the installation of a primary site in SMS 2003 automatically created a boundary for the site server's local subnet, no boundaries are automatically configured when you install Configuration Manager 2007.

■ A client's network location by IP address or Active Directory site must be uniquely identifiable as belonging to a boundary within a single Configuration Manager site. Boundaries that overlap between sites cause nondeterministic client behavior and are unsupported by Microsoft for this reason. The Configuration Manager console will not prevent you from creating overlapping boundaries, but unlike SMS 2003, Configuration Manager lets you view all configured boundaries using the Boundaries node, so that you can visually check that they do not overlap. For more information, see "How to View Configuration Manager Boundaries" (*http://technet.microsoft.com/en-us/library/bb694074.aspx*) in the Configuration Manager Documentation Library.

■ Be aware that some computers might have more than one IP address, for example a LAN network card and a wireless network card or dial-up modem. Make sure that all addresses are defined in boundaries. During site assignment, the network card that is bound first is used for matching the client's network address to a boundary.

You specify boundaries for each site using the Configuration Manager console. In this example, you'll configure boundaries based on IP subnet by following these steps:

1. Expand the Site Settings node, right-click the Boundaries node, and then click New Boundary to open the New Site Boundary dialog box, as shown in Figure 8-1.

2. In the Description field, type a descriptive name for the new boundary.

3. From the Site Code drop-down list, select the Configuration Manager site to which this boundary will belong.

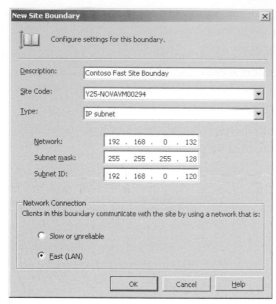

Figure 8-1   The New Site Boundary dialog box

4. From the Type drop-down list, select the type of boundary you want to configure for the specified site. For this example, select IP Subnet.

5. In the Network field, you can optionally specify an IP address within the new boundary that will be used in conjunction with the subnet mask to calculate the subnet ID.

6. In the Subnet Mask field, you can optionally specify a subnet mask that will be used in conjunction with the value entered in the Network field to calculate the subnet ID.

7. If you have typed values for Network, and Subnet Mask, then the Subnet ID field will be automatically completed for you. If you have not entered values, you must manually specify the Subnet ID in this field.

8. Under Network Connection, select whether clients in this boundary will communicate with the Configuration Manager site using a fast or a slow connection. An example of a fast connection is a wired LAN network connection; an example of a slow connection is a dial-up modem connection.

9. Click OK to save this boundary and close the New Site Boundary dialog box.

Understanding and Configuring Client Approval

When a Configuration Manager site is operating in mixed mode, client computers are not authenticated before they are allowed to join a site. Client approval is new in Configuration Manager and provides additional security to prevent unauthorized clients from receiving sensitive data from the site.

Client approval is not necessary in native mode sites, because the Public Key Infrastructure (PKI) certificates authenticate clients to the management point and other site systems.

You configure client approval from the Configuration Manager console. In this example, you'll configure client approval to automatically approve computers that are in trusted domains (the recommended setting):

1. Expand the Site Management node, right-click the site name, click Properties.

2. In the Site Mode tab of the Site Properties dialog box, as shown in Figure 8-2, select the This Site Contains Only ConfigMgr 2007 Clients check box if the site does not have SMS 2003 clients. This option provides stronger client communication security settings for Configuration Manager clients that are incompatible with SMS 2003 clients.

3. Select the Automatically Approve Computers In Trusted Domains (recommended) option.

4. Click OK to close the Site Properties dialog box.

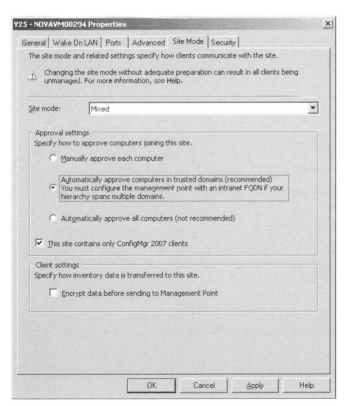

Figure 8-2   The Site Properties dialog box

If a computer is not approved, this status will be displayed in the Collections node of the Configuration Manager console. You can manually approve a client by right-clicking the client and then clicking Approve.

Choosing Client Installation Methods

There are a number of client installation methods you can use to deploy the Configuration Manager client, each with its own advantages and disadvantages. You should carefully plan which method (or methods) best suits your organization. The following client installation methods are available:

- Client Push Installation
- Software update point based installation
- Group Policy installation
- Manual installation
- Logon script installation
- Software distribution installation
- Installation using computer imaging

You can find further details on each of these installation methods later in this chapter. Refer to the topic "Determine the Configuration Manager Client Installation Method to Use" (*http://technet.microsoft.com/en-us/library/bb694166.aspx*) in the Configuration Manager Documentation Library for detailed information about choosing the best client installation method for your organization.

Choosing Client Agents to Enable

All Configuration Manager clients receive a core set of components when the client is installed. Additionally, client agents are installed for Configuration Manager features, which are then enabled and configured through client policy from the clients' assigned site. Configure the client agents in the Configuration Manager console before installing the clients, so that clients are immediately configured for their site features upon successful client installation and site assignment. If you enable or reconfigure a client agent after assignment, the configuration will not take affect until the client downloads its client policy. Clients automatically download their policy by default every 60 minutes, and client policy retrieval can also be manually initiated from the client, using the Actions tab and Machine Policy Retrieval & Evaluation Cycle option.

There are 10 client agents:

- Hardware Inventory Client Agent (enabled by default, but can be disabled during setup)

- Software Inventory Client Agent (enabled by default, but can be disabled during setup)

- Advertised Programs Client Agent (enabled by default, but can be disabled during setup)

- Computer Client Agent (this is always enabled and cannot be disabled)

- Desired Configuration Management Client Agent (enabled by default, but can be disabled during setup)

- Mobile Device Client Agent (not enabled by default, but can be enabled during setup)

- Remote Tools Client Agent (enabled by default, but can be disabled during setup)

- Network Access Protection Client Agent (not enabled by default, and should not be enabled until the site has successfully published to Active Directory Domain Services)

- Software Metering Client Agent (enabled by default, but can be disabled during setup)

- Software Updates Client Agent (enabled by default, but can be disabled during setup)

The procedure for enabling and configuring each client agent is covered in the chapters for each feature.

Preparing for Client Deployment

Before you begin deploying the Configuration Manager client on computers in your network, carefully review the installation prerequisites. Some important installation prerequisites are described in the following sections. A full list of client and server prerequisites can be found in the topic "Prerequisites for Configuration Manager Client Deployment" (*http://technet.microsoft.com/en-us/library/bb680537.aspx*) in the Configuration Manager Documentation Library.

Client Prerequisites for Client Deployment

Perhaps the most important client prerequisite is that the Configuration Manager client requires at least Windows 2000 Professional Service Pack 4 to be installed on computers on which you want to install the client for a mixed mode site. If a client is going to be managed in a native mode site, the computer operating system must be Windows XP SP2 or higher.

Other required prerequisites will be automatically downloaded when the client is installed.

Real World   Updating BITS on Computers

One of the prerequisites that computers require before installing the Configuration Manager client is Microsoft Background Intelligent Transfer Service (BITS), version 2.5 or higher. The client installation process automatically downloads and installs BITS client components if they are needed, but this frequently results in the client installation requiring a restart to complete. Without the restart, clients will not function correctly. To avoid this restart requirement after client installation, predeploy BITS version 2.5 client components on computers in your organization before deploying the Configuration Manager client.

Server Prerequisites for Client Deployment

In addition to the client prerequisites, make sure that one or more of the following Configuration Manager site systems are in place in preparation for managing clients:

Management Point

By default, computers install the Configuration Manager client by obtaining client installation source files and prerequisite component files from the default management point over HTTP (mixed mode) or HTTPS (native mode). Clients installed manually can be configured to use an alternative source location for the client files, such as the site server or a manually created source folder on the network.

Using the default source location of the management point makes sense for most client installations because management point site systems are also required to send client policies and to receive client information. If a management point site system is not installed, client computers cannot be managed. However, scenarios in which specifying an alternative source location are appropriate include when the management point is over a slow WAN link from the client, and when installing a client on the Internet for Internet-based client management. More information about Internet-based client management can be found in Chapter 16, "Managing Clients Across the Internet."

Server Locator Point

Client computers require a server locator point if they cannot locate site information in Active Directory Domain Services. In this scenario, a server locator point is used to automatically assign clients to a site, must be used to verify site compatibility to complete site assignment, and can be used to locate management points if clients cannot find their site's default management point using DNS publishing.

If you have extended the Active Directory schema for Configuration Manager 2007, all sites in your hierarchy are publishing to Active Directory Domain Services, and all clients belong to the same Active Directory forest as the site servers, you do not need a server locator point.

However, if you have not extended the Active Directory schema for Configuration Manager 2007, or if you have workgroup clients or clients from another Active Directory forest, you must install a server locator point and ensure that clients can connect to it.

Fallback Status Point

The fallback status point is a new site system role in Configuration Manager 2007 that receives state messages sent by clients. It is an optional but recommended site role that helps you to manage clients. For example, the fallback status point allows computers that cannot connect to a management point to send state messages to the fallback status point, which are then relayed to the site database. Configuration Manager has a number of built-in reports that leverage the fallback status point to give you centralized and detailed information about the status of client deployments in your site. Using a fallback status point will provide useful reports to identify client installation progress and investigate client installation failures. Other reports that use the fallback status point identify client communication problems, which is particularly useful when the client is managed in a native mode site and certificate issues prevent the client from communicating with its assigned management point.

Installing and Configuring the Fallback Status Point

The fallback status point is a Configuration Manager site system role that requires Internet Information Services (IIS). The fallback status point always communicates with clients using HTTP, which uses unauthenticated connections and sends data in clear text, even when the site is in native mode. To minimize the security risks associated with this configuration, install the fallback status point on a dedicated server and do not install other site system roles on the same server.

To install and configure a fallback status point, follow these steps:

1. In the Configuration Manager console, expand the Site Systems node and then click Site Systems

2. Right-click the server on which you wish to install the fallback status point, and then click New Roles.

> **Note**   If the required server does not appear in the list, right-click the Site Systems node, click New, and then click Server. In the first page of the New Site System Server Wizard, type the name of the server you want to use and then follow the rest of these instructions.

3. On the General page of the New Site Role Wizard, as shown in Figure 8-3, optionally specify the intranet fully qualified domain name and the required Internet fully qualified domain name for the fallback status point site system if the site system will accept connections from Internet-based clients. If the site server's computer account cannot be used to install and configure the site system, specify the installation account and credentials to use. Click Next to continue.

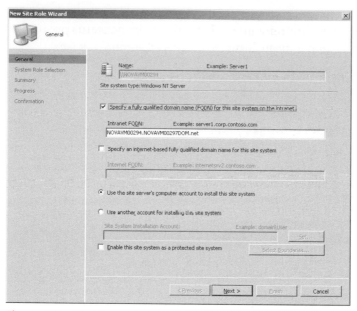

Figure 8-3   The General page of the New Site Role Wizard

4. On the System Role Selection page of the New Site Role Wizard, as shown in Figure 8-4, select Fallback Status Point and click Next.

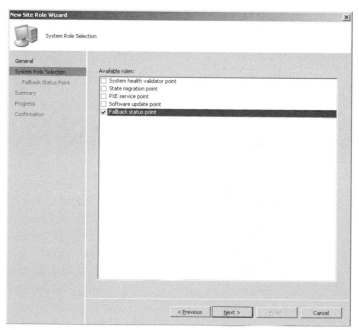

Figure 8-4   The System Role Selection page of the New Site Role Wizard

5. On the Fallback Status Point page of the New Site Role Wizard, as shown in Figure 8-5, configure throttling intervals for this fallback status point. If you are unsure what these values mean, leave them as the default. Click Next.

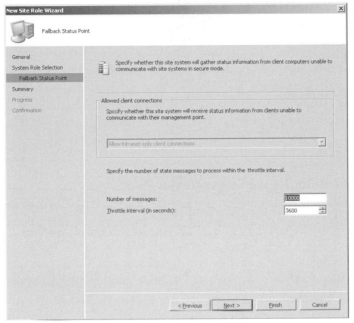

Figure 8-5 The Fallback Status Point page of the New Site Role Wizard

6. Review the Summary page of the New Site Role Wizard and click Next.

7. After the Progress page disappears, review the Wizard Completed page, and then click Close to close the New Site Role Wizard.

Real World Configuring the Fallback Status Point Throttle Interval

Fallback status point throttling allows you to limit the number of state messages that are sent to the site server for a specified period of time. By default, the fallback status point can send 10,000 state messages every 3600 seconds. If more state messages are received than the throttling intervals allow, state messages will backlog on the fallback status point until they can be sent to the site server. This might result in an unacceptable delay before client deployment reports are available to view. In some scenarios, such as a client deployment to many thousands of computers, high numbers of state messages will be sent to the fallback status point, and to accommodate them, you can temporarily increase the throttle values to allow more state messages to be passed to the site server in a shorter amount of time. Plan carefully before changing these values because too many state messages that are sent to the site server at once might consume too much network bandwidth between the fallback status point and the site server and also require more processing power than the site server can sustain.

For more information, refer to the following topics in the Configuration Manager Documentation Library: "Determine If You Need to Configure Throttle Settings for the Fallback Status Point" (*http://technet.microsoft.com/en-us/library/bb680587.aspx*) and "Troubleshooting State Message Backlogs" (*http://technet.microsoft.com/en-us/library/bb932207.aspx*).

How to Configure Clients to Use the Fallback Status Point

Although you can install multiple fallback status points in a site, clients can only ever use one fallback status point. There are three methods of assigning the fallback status point to a client computer.

- If a fallback status point site system role is installed in a site, and you are using Client Push Installation, the site's first installed fallback status point will be automatically assigned during client installation.

- If a fallback status point site system role is installed in a site and the site is publishing to Active Directory Domain Services, running CCMSetup.exe with no command-line properties will initiate a search for the site's first installed fallback status point in Active Directory Domain Services. If the client belongs to the same Active Directory forest as the site server, the site's first installed fallback status point will be automatically assigned during client installation.

- If you are installing clients manually using CCMSetup.exe, specifying the client.msi property *FSP= <server>* will directly assign a fallback status point to a client.

Installing Clients Using Client Push Installation

In this section, you'll learn how to configure Client Push Installation and how to use the Client Push Wizard to deploy clients to discovered computers in your organization. Before you use the procedures in this section, you should have read Chapter 7 and configured a suitable discovery method for your Configuration Manager site.

Preparing for Client Push Installation

Before pushing the client installation software to computers in your site, you must enable and configure the Client Push Installation method using the Configuration Manager console. Follow these steps to enable and configure Client Push Installation:

1. In the Configuration Manager console, navigate to the Client Installation Methods node under Site Hierarchy.

2. Right-click Client Push Installation and select Properties from the context menu to display the Client Push Installation Properties dialog box, as shown in Figure 8-6.

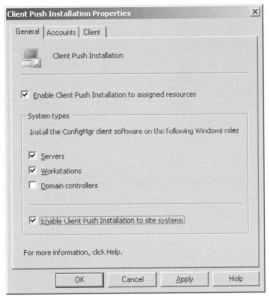

Figure 8-6   The General tab of the Client Push Installation Properties dialog box

3. In the General tab, select the Enable Client Push Installation To Assigned Resources option. Select the system types to which Configuration Manager should push the client software. Finally, select the Enable Client Push Installation To Site Systems option if you want site systems to automatically receive the Configuration Manager client software.

4. In the Accounts tab, shown in Figure 8-7, use the New button to specify one or more accounts for Configuration Manager to use when connecting to the computer to install the client software. Configuration Manager will consecutively try each account until it finds an account with administrator rights on the computer. If no accounts are entered in this tab, or if none of the entered accounts has administrator

rights on the computer, Configuration Manager will attempt to connect to the computer using the site server's computer account.

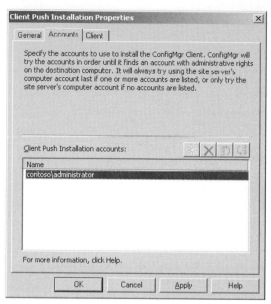

Figure 8-7   The Accounts tab of the Client Push Installation Properties dialog box

5. In the Client tab, shown in Figure 8-8, enter any custom client.msi installation properties that you want Configuration Manager to use when installing the client into the Installation Properties text box. For example, type **SMSCACHESIZE=1000** if you want the client temporary program download folder (cache) to be 1000 MB in size, rather than the default size of 5120 MB. SMS 2003 administrators might notice that whereas they were used to seeing SMSSITECODE=AUTO in this installation text box, and changing the value with the specific site's site code, Configuration Manager automatically populates the site code for you.

> **Important**   A full list of client installation properties can be found in the topic "About Configuration Manager Client Installation Properties" (*http://technet.microsoft.com/en-us/library/bb680980.aspx*) in the Configuration Manager Documentation Library. Note that you can specify only properties for client.msi in this tab; you cannot specify properties for CCMSetup.exe.

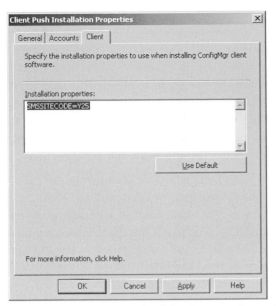

Figure 8-8   The Client tab of the Client Push Installation Properties dialog box

6. Click Apply, and then click OK.

At this point, you'll take a small diversion to investigate an interesting new feature in Configuration Manager 2007. If you have specified additional client installation properties in the Client tab of the Client Push Installation Properties dialog box and also extended the Active Directory schema for Configuration Manager 2007, these installation properties will publish to Active Directory Domain Services. This means that whenever any client installation runs without any installation properties, the properties specified in this tab will be used for the client installation.

A number of other client installation properties are also published to Active Directory Domain Services. These are listed in the topic "About Configuration Manager Client Installation Properties Published to Active Directory Domain Services" (*http://technet.microsoft.com /en-us/library/bb633205.aspx*) in the Configuration Manager Documentation Library.

> **Note**   If you supply any client installation properties when you install clients manually using CCMSetup.exe, installation properties published to Active Directory Domain Services will not be used.

To get back on course, you now need to consider Configuration Manager discovery. This is covered in detail in Chapter 7. Client Push Installation can install the client only to discovered resources. The following procedure assumes that you have run a discovery method on your site and can see a list of computer resources in the Configuration Manager console. If these computer resources display Yes in the Assigned column in the results pane, it means that their discovered network location falls within a configured boundary in the Configuration Manager hierarchy, and automatic site assignment will succeed. If, however, you have computer resources displaying No in the Assigned column, site Client Push Installation will not succeed for the specified computer, and you must reconfigure your boundaries to include the network location of the computer, or use another installation method that does not use automatic site assignment.

Because you have enabled the Client Push Installation method for the site, you might already have some or all of your computers that are now Configuration Manager clients. These appear in the results pane with Yes for the Client column, and their site code in the Assigned column. If so, congratulations! If not, you might just need to wait a while for the client to be installed. Depending on the number of computers you are attempting to install using the Client Push Installation method and how busy the site server is it might take a while before clients are installed. If a client doesn't install on a targeted computer in a few minutes, that computer might be offline or otherwise unavailable. In this scenario, the site server automatically attempts to install the client once every hour for up to 168 hours (one week).

However, sometimes, you might want to speed things along a bit and manually initiate a Client Push Installation to discovered computer resources using the Client Push Installation Wizard instead of the site Client Push Installation method. The Client Push Installation Wizard also allows you to install the Configuration Manager client, using the same client installation account configured for the Client Push Installation method, when the selected computer resource does not fall within one of the configured boundaries, and it appears as an unassigned computer resource.

Using the Client Push Installation Wizard

To install the Configuration Manager client using the Client Push Installation Wizard, follow these steps:

1. In the Configuration Manager console, navigate to the Collections node and expand it.

2. Right-click either a collection, or a computer resource in a collection, and then select Install Client to launch the Client Push Installation Wizard.

3. On the Installation Options page shown in Figure 8-9, specify whether the client software should be installed on domain controllers if the target resource is a domain controller, whether the client should be installed only on computer

resources that are assigned to the site, whether the client should also be installed to any subcollections of a selected collection, and whether the client should always be installed, even if the client is already installed on a targeted computer.

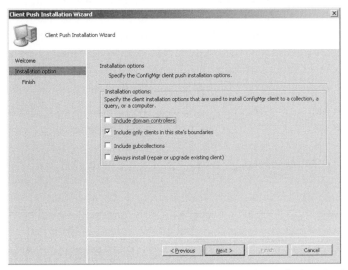

Figure 8-9   The Client Push Installation Wizard Installation Options page

4. To complete the Client Push Installation Wizard, click Next. Review the installation settings and click Finish to close the wizard.

For more information about installing clients using Client Push, refer to the topic "How to Install Configuration Manager Clients Using Client Push" (*http://technet.microsoft.com /en-us/library/bb632380.aspx*) in the Configuration Manager Documentation Library.

Overview of Other Available Client Installation Methods

In addition to the Client Push Installation method, there are six other client installation methods available in Configuration Manager 2007. Full details about how to use these installation methods are described in the Configuration Manager Documentation Library. An overview of each installation method follows.

Software Update Point Based Installation

Software update point based client installation is a new client installation method in Configuration Manager 2007 that leverages an existing WSUS 3.0 software updates infrastructure to install client software, similar to installing software updates. This method can be used to upgrade an existing client or to install the client on a new computer. It does not require the computer to be discovered before the client can be installed. If the target computer does not already have the Configuration Manager client installed, use Group Policy to specify the source software update point from which the computer will download the client installation software. Advantages of using this method include automatic reinstallation if the client is uninstalled, and installation does not require administrative rights to run. For detailed information about installing the client using this method, see the topic "How to Install Configuration Manager Clients Using Software Update Point Based Installation" (*http://technet.microsoft.com/en-us/library/bb633194.aspx*) in the Configuration Manager Documentation Library.

Group Policy Installation

You can install the Configuration Manager 2007 client with Group Policy by using a custom Microsoft Installer (MSI) version of CCMSetup named CCMSetup.msi, supplied with Configuration Manager 2007. Using Group Policy, CCMSetup.msi can be assigned to computers in your Active Directory forest to install or upgrade the Configuration Manager client software. Computers do not need to be discovered by Configuration Manager before they can be installed using this method. For detailed information about installing the client using this method, see "How to Install Configuration Manager Clients Using Group Policy"(*http://technet.microsoft.com/en-us/library/bb633010.aspx*) in the Configuration Manager Documentation Library.

Manual Installation

As with SMS 2003, you can install the client manually by running the client setup program on the command line. However, the manual installation procedure is different in Configuration Manager 2007 than SMS 2003, because you can no longer run the executable file, client.msi. Instead, use the CCMSetup.exe file to manually install the Configuration Manager client.

To run CCMSetup.exe, you must be an administrator on the target computer. This method might be useful when you are troubleshooting a failed client installation and don't have immediate access to the site server, or you are installing a client on a computer image, or you are installing a client in a workgroup. CCMSetup.exe provides a myriad of installation properties you can use to customize the client installation. A complete list of these properties can be found in the topic "About Configuration Manager Client Installation Properties" (*http://technet.microsoft.com/en-us/library/bb680980.aspx*) in the Configuration Manager Documentation Library. For detailed information about installing the client manually, see "How to Install Configuration Manager Clients Manually" (*http://technet.microsoft.com/en-us/library/bb693546.aspx*) in the Configuration Manager Documentation Library.

You must use manual installation if you are installing clients that are in a workgroup, on the Internet, or belong to a different Active Directory forest than their site server's forest.

Logon Script Installation

This installation method allows you to initiate a client installation from a logon script and is actually identical to manual client installation. Because a manual installation requires local administrative rights to run, ensure that the login script runs with administrator rights on the target computer.

A useful installation property when you are using logon script installation is /logon. When this installation property is specified, client installation will not run if CCM-Setup.exe finds an existing client Configuration Manager 2007 or SMS 2003 client on the computer. This prevents the client from repeatedly installing each time the user logs on.

For more information about installing clients using logon scripts, see "How to Install Configuration Manager Clients Using Logon Scripts" (*http://technet.microsoft.com/en-us/library/bb633072.aspx*) in the Configuration Manager Documentation Library.

Software Distribution Upgrade Installation

By virtue of the fact that you are using Configuration Manager software distribution to install the client, you cannot install new clients using this installation method; it is suitable only for upgrading a client. Configuration Manager includes a package definition file that makes packaging the client an easy task.

Full instructions about how to install clients using the software distribution upgrade installation method can be found in the topic "How to Upgrade Clients Using Software Distribution in Configuration Manager" (*http://technet.microsoft.com/en-us/library/bb632690.aspx*) in the Configuration Manager Documentation Library.

Installation using Computer Imaging

Another way to install the Configuration Manager client is to install it onto a computer from which you capture an image. You then can use this image to build computers in your enterprise. To utilize this method, remove any Configuration Manager information that is specific to the computer, such as the assigned site code and any certificates that are stored in the computer. When the image is applied to computers, the client will be installed, but it is unmanaged until it becomes assigned to a Configuration Manager site.

Full instructions about how to install clients using computer imaging can be found in the topic "How to Install Configuration Manager Clients Using Computer Imaging" (*http://technet.microsoft.com/en-us/library/bb694095.aspx*) in the Configuration Manager Documentation Library.

> **Note**   Some client installation methods (including software update point based installation and Group Policy installation) do not allow you to include client installation properties in the installation command line. If the Active Directory schema has been extended for Configuration Manager 2007, the client installation properties detailed in the Configuration Manager Documentation Library topic "About Configuration Manager Client Installation Properties Published to Active Directory Domain Services" (*http://technet.microsoft.com/en-us/library/bb633205.aspx*) will be applied automatically when the client is installed. If the Active Directory schema is not extended for Configuration Manager 2007, or if you want to use installation properties that are not automatically published to Active Directory Domain Services, you can provision computers with client installation properties before the client is installed. For information about this procedure, see "How to Provision Configuration Manager Client Installation Properties using Group Policy" (*http://technet.microsoft.com/en-us/library/bb632469.aspx*) in the Configuration Manager Documentation Library.

Real World   Firewall Settings for the Configuration Manager Client

Windows operating systems from Windows XP SP2 and later include the Windows Firewall that helps to block suspicious or unwanted connections to computers. In addition, many third-party firewalls are available that might be installed on computers in your organization. Most firewalls will, by default, block some of the programs and ports that Configuration Manager clients need to operate correctly. To make sure that firewalls and intervening network devices are configured correctly and will not prevent client installation from succeeding, review the topic "Firewall Settings for Configuration Manager Clients" (*http://technet.microsoft.com/en-us/library/bb694088.aspx*) in the Configuration Manager Documentation Library before deploying clients.

Understanding the Client Deployment Process

In this section, you take a more detailed look at the process involved in client installation and assignment from when an administrator (or one of the client installation methods) kicks off CCMSetup.exe to install the Configuration Manager client to when it becomes managed by a Configuration Manager site.

The Client Installation Process

The first thing that the client installation process (CCMSetup) needs is a location from which to download the necessary client prerequisites and installation files to proceed with installation. By default in Configuration Manager 2007, these files are downloaded from a management point. You can specify the management point to use with the CCMSetup installation property */mp:<Computer Name>,* or if you have extended the Active Directory schema for Configuration Manager 2007, CCMSetup will automatically search Active Directory Domain Services for a management point. If the Active Directory schema is not extended, CCMSetup will search WINS (unless you have used the SMSDIRECTORYLOOKUP=NOWINS installation property) for a management point, or a server locator point that can be used to find a management point. If you do not want to download the files from a management point, you can still use the same method as in SMS 2003 to download the files from a network share and specify */source:<Path>* as a CCMSetup installation property. Finally, if no management point can be found, CCMSetup will search the folder from which it was run for the required installation files. If CCMSetup.exe cannot find a source from which to download the client prerequisites and installation files, client installation will fail.

After CCMSetup has connected to a source location for the client prerequisites and installation files, it will check whether the correct version of Background Intelligent Transfer Service (BITS) is installed on the target computer. If it is not, this is downloaded and installed first. Remember, BITS often requires the computer to be restarted before installation completes, so it might be a good idea to make sure that the client version of BITS is up to date on target computers before proceeding with client deployments.

After BITS is installed and running on the target computer, any other client prerequisites that are needed are downloaded and installed. These client prerequisites are listed in the topic "Prerequisites for Configuration Manager Client Deployment" (*http://technet.microsoft.com /en-us/library/bb680537.aspx*) in the Configuration Manager Documentation Library.

After the necessary client prerequisites are on the target computer, CCMSetup downloads client.msi and runs it to install the Configuration Manager client.

Of course, this is not the whole story. When the client is first installed, it is initially unmanaged. To be able to manage the client and use its features, move on to client assignment.

The Client Assignment Process

Client assignment is the process of attaching a client computer to a Configuration Manager site so that it can be managed by that site. This process involves four steps:

- Site assignment
- Site compatibility check

- Locating the default management point
- Locating site mode settings

In this section, you will look at these four steps in detail.

Site Assignment

Until a Configuration Manager client is assigned to a site, it will not be managed. It is possible to install the client without assigning it to a site, but it will not perform any of its functions until it is assigned to a site. You can assign a client to a site either automatically (using boundary information), or manually.

After clients are assigned to a site, they remain assigned to the same site unless an administrator manually changes their site assignment. This holds true even if clients move ("roam") from one site to another. In this scenario, although the clients' network location changes and they might connect to site systems in the new site, their site assignment remains the same.

There are two methods you can use to assign client computers to a Configuration Manager site: manual or automatic.

Manual Site Assignment

You can manually assign a client to a site by explicitly specifying the site code as a CCMSetup installation property. Use the client.msi installation property *SMSSITECODE=< site code>* to specify the site you want to manage the client.

When CCMSetup runs client.msi, a check is performed to determine whether the specified site exists by searching Active Directory Domain Services (if the schema is extended) or by querying a server locator point. If the specified site code cannot be found, assignment fails (although the client remains installed).

You can also use the Advanced tab from Configuration Manager in the client's Control Panel to manually enter the site code for the client.

Automatic Site Assignment

If you have specified the client.msi installation property *SMSSITECODE=AUTO*, the client will try to find its own site to assign to, using boundary information. The client does this by comparing its network location (for example, IP address or Active Directory site) against the boundaries configured for each site in the hierarchy. If the client's network location is within the boundaries of a site, the client is assigned automatically to that site. The exception to this is when a client falls within the boundaries of a secondary site. In this case, the client is assigned to the parent site of the secondary site.

If you have extended the Active Directory schema for Configuration Manager 2007, and the client is a member of the same forest, the client first looks in Active Directory Domain

Services for a site to which to assign. If the client cannot find a site in Active Directory Domain Services, it then looks for a server locator point from which to find its site.

If you have not extended the Active Directory schema for Configuration Manager 2007, make sure that a server locator point is either specified as part of the client installation properties or that clients can locate it using WINS. If you have extended the Active Directory schema for SMS 2003 but not for Configuration Manager 2007, clients can find a server locator point in Active Directory Domain Services. See the topic "Configuration Manager and Service Location (Site Information and Management Points)" (*http://technet.microsoft.com/en-us/library/bb632435.aspx*) in the Configuration Manager Documentation Library for more information about how clients find a server locator point.

If the client cannot find a site configured with boundaries that match its own network location, the client will retry every 10 minutes until it is able to assign to a site.

If any of the following scenarios apply, you cannot use automatic site assignment; you must manually assign the client:

- The client is already assigned to a site.

- The client is an Internet-based client.

- The client will locate the site's default management point using DNS publishing.

- The client's IP address does not fall within one of the configured boundaries for a site in the Configuration Manager hierarchy.

Additionally, if the client has more than one IP address (for example, multiple network cards) or if the client might be roaming in the hierarchy during site assignment, manual site assignment will be more reliable than automatic site assignment.

Site Compatibility Check

Before site assignment completes, further checks must be made to ensure that the client will work correctly in its assigned Configuration Manager site. The following checks are performed:

- Is this Configuration Manager 2007 client assigned to an SMS 2003 site?

- Is this client running Windows 2000 and being assigned to a native mode site?

If either of these checks fails, the site compatibility check will fail.

For these checks to be made, the client must be able to locate site information from either Active Directory Domain Services or a server locator point.

If the site compatibility checks fail, or fail to complete, site assignment will fail, and the client will remain unmanaged until the site compatibility check is successful.

Note   If the client is in native mode and configured to use an Internet-based management point, no site compatibility check is performed when you assign it to its native mode site. In this scenario, be certain that you are assigning the client to the correct site.

Locating the Default Management Point

After the client is successfully assigned to a site, it then must locate that site's default management point so that it can download its client policy. Or, if it assigned when on the Internet, it connects to its specified Internet-based management point. When the client has downloaded client policy from its assigned site's management point, the client is then a managed client.

Client computers locate their site's default management point using the following mechanisms in the order specified:

Active Directory Domain Services

When the Active Directory schema is extended for Configuration Manager 2007 and all sites in the Configuration Manager hierarchy are configured to publish to Active Directory Domain Services, the default management point for each site is published to Active Directory.

In this scenario, Configuration Manager clients that belong to the same Active Directory forest as the management point automatically find their default management point through Active Directory publishing using an LDAP query to a global catalog server, and they will not use the other mechanisms to find their default management point. However, if this fails (for example, because of unreliable network connectivity) clients will automatically try the next method.

If the Active Directory schema has not been extended for Configuration Manager 2007, management points cannot be published to Active Directory Domain Services, and clients must have an alternative mechanism to locate their default management point.

Additionally, if you have clients that are not in the same Active Directory forest as the site servers (such as workgroup clients or clients from other Active Directory forests), these clients will not be able to locate the management points published to Active Directory Domain Services and must use one of the following alternative mechanisms to locate their default management points.

DNS

For a client computer to find its site's default management point in DNS, two conditions must be met:

- The DNS zone that contains the management point entry (SRV record) must contain a host record for the computer assigned with the management point role. This record can be entered manually, or it can be automatically entered if the site is configured to automatically publish the default management point in DNS. Details about this can be found in the topics "How to Automatically Publish the Default Management Point to DNS" (*http://technet.microsoft.com/en-us/library/bb681063.aspx*) and "How to Manually Publish the Default Management Point to DNS" (*http://technet.microsoft.com/en-us/library/bb632936.aspx*) in the Configuration Manager Documentation Library.

■ Clients must be configured with a DNS suffix for site assignment. Details of this configuration can be found in the topic "How to Configure Configuration Manager Clients to Find their Management Point using DNS Publishing" (*http://technet.microsoft.com/en-us/library/bb633030.aspx*) in the Configuration Manager Documentation Library.

DNS is the preferred method by which clients locate their default management point if they cannot locate it using Active Directory Domain Services, and so is suitable for the following clients:

■ Workgroup clients and clients from another forest

■ All clients if the Active Directory schema is not extended for Configuration Manager 2007 and the site is not publishing to Active Directory Domain Services

Server Locator Point

If clients cannot locate management points through Active Directory Domain Services or DNS, they next attempt to locate their default management point by contacting a server locator point.

If you have assigned a server locator point role to a site system in the Configuration Manager hierarchy, the server locator point is capable of querying the site database to identify management point site systems for client computers. Because the server locator point accesses the site database for the site it is installed in, server locator points can identify management points only when they are in the same site as the server locator point, or lower in the same branch of the hierarchy.

Server locator points can be assigned to clients by NetBIOS name or IP address using the CCMSetup property SMSSLP. If a server locator point is not directly assigned to clients, clients can locate it using WINS if the client has not been installed with the SMSDIRECTORYLOOKUP=NOWINS installation property.

WINS

When a site system computer assigned to the management point role is configured to use WINS through its TCP/IP configuration, it automatically publishes the management point to WINS, which clients can use if all other mechanisms to locate their site's default management point have failed.

However, if the site is operating in native mode, clients cannot use WINS to locate management points.

Note   Because WINS does not provide a secure method of storing management point information, a CCMSetup command-line property can be used to prevent clients from using WINS for locating management points, even in mixed mode. More information about this SMSDIRECTORYLOOKUP property can be found in the topic "About Configuration Manager Client Installation Properties" (*http://technet.microsoft.com/en-us/library/bb680980.aspx*) in the Configuration Manager Documentation Library.

Locating Site Mode and Related Settings

By this point, your client should now be assigned to a site and be communicating with that site's default management point. There is one more check the client needs to make before it is fully deployed.

The site mode check examines the site to which the client is assigned to find out whether it is in mixed mode or native mode.

If the Active Directory schema is extended for Configuration Manager 2007, the client will attempt to find this information from Active Directory Domain Services. If the client is in the wrong communication mode for its assigned site, for example, a mixed mode client is assigned to a native mode site, the client's communication mode will be automatically changed to match its assigned site's site mode. At this point, additional settings will also be applied to the client if the site is in native mode, such as whether the client checks the certificate revocation list and what to do if more than one valid certificate is available on the client.

If the Active Directory schema is not extended for Configuration Manager 2007, or if the client cannot contact Active Directory Domain Services, the client must obtain site information from a server locator point, which cannot automatically reconfigure site mode settings on the client. In this scenario, you must reinstall the client to configure the required site mode and related settings. To do this, you can reinstall the client manually using the native mode CCMSetup option, or use Client Push Installation so that the client automatically inherits the site configuration. Until the client is configured for the correct communication mode, it cannot connect to the site's default management point. For more information about installation properties to configure the client's communication mode and native mode settings, see the topic "About Configuration Manager Client Installation Properties" (*http://technet.microsoft.com/en-us/library/bb680980.aspx*) in the Configuration Manager Documentation Library.

Managing the Configuration Manager Client

In this section, you'll look at some of the methods you can use to manage clients in your Configuration Manager hierarchy.

Removing the Configuration Manager Client

On occasions, you might want to remove the Configuration Manager client. In SMS 2003, this was accomplished by using the Ccmclean utility. However, in Configuration Manager 2007, Ccmclean is no longer supported; instead, client removal has been incorporated into the client install program CCMSetup.exe. To remove the client, enter the following from a command prompt on the client computer:

CCMSeup.exe /uninstall

> **Note**   By default, CCMSetup.exe is stored on the client computer in the %windir%\system32\ccmsetup folder.

If you want to uninstall the client from many computers, consider creating a package using Configuration Manager software distribution that will distribute this command to targeted computers. Note that the uninstall routine is completely silent, with no user notification. Use the log file CCMSetup.log in the %windir%\system32\ccmsetup folder on the client computer to verify that the client has been removed successfully.

> **Important**   Many of the client installation methods will automatically reinstall the client if it is removed. If you have a business requirement that the client should not be installed on specific computers, refer to the topic "How to Prevent the Configuration Manager Client Software from Being Installed on Specific Computers" (*http://technet.microsoft.com/en-us/library/bb693996.aspx*) in the Configuration Manager Documentation Library.

Understanding the Configuration Manager Client in Control Panel

When the Configuration Manager client is installed, a number of new elements are installed to the Windows Control Panel that allow administrators or users of the computer to install, update, or repair components on the client. The main element is a new icon called Configuration Manager, as shown in Figure 8-10. This is the icon that was previously called Systems Management in SMS 2003. Depending on which client agents are enabled, other programs might be added to the Control Panel including Program Download Monitor, Run Advertised Programs, and Remote Control.

Figure 8-10   The Control Panel showing Configuration Manager components

The Configuration Manager Icon

Use the Configuration Manager icon to install, update, and repair Configuration Manager components installed on the client. Double-click this icon in the Control Panel to display the Configuration Manager Properties dialog box. Depending on which features of Configuration Manager are installed, this dialog box will contain up to seven tabs:

- General
- Components
- Actions
- Advanced
- Updates
- Configurations
- Internet

General Tab

The General tab, shown in Figure 8-11, displays a list of the client's properties. This is a subset of the discovery data reported to the Configuration Manager site and includes the client's IP address and subnet, MAC address, operating system, domain or workgroup membership, and site communication mode. This can be a useful overview to determine whether a client has the correct settings.

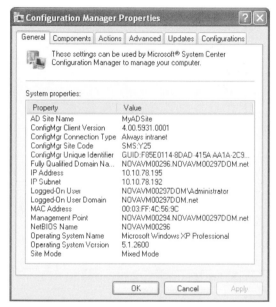

Figure 8-11   The General tab of the Configuration Manager Properties dialog box

Components Tab

The Components tab, shown in Figure 8-12, displays a list of the Configuration Manager client components currently available on the client together with their version and current status. Background services such as ConfigMgr Client Core Components are displayed as Installed. Remember that all client agents are installed on the computer regardless of whether they have been enabled in the Configuration Manager console. The client agents will display a status of Disabled if you haven't yet configured and enabled the agent for the site (or if you have enabled it but the client hasn't yet downloaded its client policy to obtain the new setting) and Enabled if the agent has been enabled.

If you suspect that any client components are not functioning correctly, you can reinstall that component by selecting it and clicking Repair.

Actions Tab

The Actions tab, shown in Figure 8-13, displays a list of procedures to run that are related to the various components that are installed and enabled on the Configuration Manager client. If, for example, you want the client to get the latest client policy outside the interval configured by the site administrator, select Machine Policy Retrieval & Evaluation Cycle in the Actions list, and click Initiate Action.

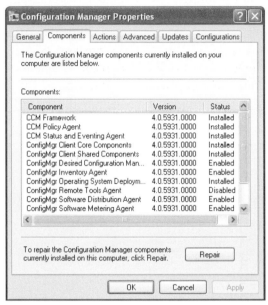

Figure 8-12   The Components tab of the Configuration Manager Properties dialog box

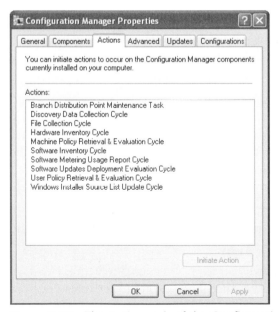

Figure 8-13   The Actions tab of the Configuration Manager Properties dialog box

Advanced Tab

The Advanced tab, shown in Figure 8-14, allows a user with administrative rights to change some of the client's settings. The ConfigMgr Site section of this tab displays the current site to which the client is assigned. Either type a new site code to manually assign the client to a site, or click Discover, which results in automatic site assignment with the client searching for a site to assign to, comparing its network location with configured boundaries. You can also remove the site assignment by deleting the site code value. If you do this, however, the client becomes unmanaged and discovery records, inventory data, and status messages will not be generated, and the client cannot download client policy until you assign the client to a new site.

The Advanced tab is also where you must specify the DNS suffix of the site's default management point if the client will find its site's default management point using DNS publishing.

In the Temporary Program Download Folder section, you can modify the folder location where the client caches downloaded advertised programs. You can also manage the size of this folder and delete its contents. The client automatically deletes older files from this folder when the disk space limit is reached.

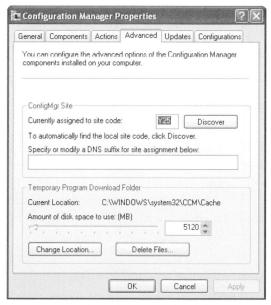

Figure 8-14   The Advanced tab of the Configuration Manager Properties dialog box

Updates Tab

The Updates tab, shown in Figure 8-15, allows you to specify a regular schedule for when you want this client to install software updates. If you do not specify a schedule, software updates will be installed at the deadline date and time specified by the software updates administrator. You can specify both the day and the time when software updates will be installed, or you can specify Every Day. These settings are disregarded, however, if a mandatory software update deadline is reached. In this case, the updates will be installed to client computers regardless of the settings in this tab.

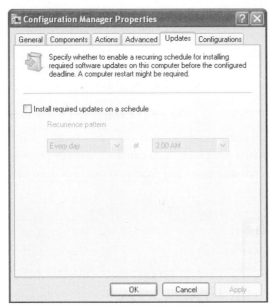

Figure 8-15   The Updates tab of the Configuration Manager Properties dialog box

Configurations Tab

The Configurations tab, shown in Figure 8-16, is displayed only if the desired configuration management client agent is enabled. This tab displays a list of the configuration baselines that have been assigned to this computer and provides options to immediately evaluate these configuration baselines and display compliance reports. For details about desired configuration management in Configuration Manager 2007, see Chapter 14, "Implementing Desired Configuration Management."

Internet Tab

The Internet tab, shown in Figure 8-17, is displayed only if the client is communicating in native mode. This tab allows you to specify information that the client needs to communicate with an Internet-based management point. For more information about Internet-based clients, see Chapter 16, "Managing Clients Across the Internet."

Figure 8-16   The Configurations tab of the Configuration Manager Properties dialog box

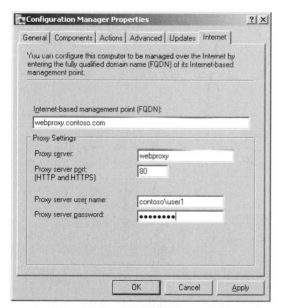

Figure 8-17   The Internet tab of the Configuration Manager Properties dialog box

Using Client Deployment Reports

Configuration Manager 2007 includes many reports that can help you to monitor and manage clients. These reports are found under the Reports node of the Configuration Manager console and have the category of SMS Site – Client Information.

Many of these reports display data collected from computers using state messages. To use these reports, a fallback status point must be defined for the site from which you are running the report, and a fallback status point must be assigned to client computers. There is no native viewer for state messages; these messages can only be viewed through reports or by inspecting Configuration Manager log files.

For a complete list of the available client reports, see "About Reports for Configuration Manager Clients" (*http://technet.microsoft.com/en-us/library/bb633154.aspx*) in the Configuration Manager Documentation Library.

Checkpoints for Client Deployment

- Be sure that an appropriate client installation method or methods have been selected, enabled, and correctly configured. Review all your clients (servers and workstations) to determine whether your selected installation method is appropriate for all your clients. For example, the logon script initiated installation method might not be appropriate for installing the Configuration Manager client on servers if administrators rarely or never log on locally to them.

- Confirm the boundary configuration to ensure that auto-site assignment will succeed.

- If your installation method requires local administrative rights on the target machine, ensure that this condition can be met.

- Review the topic "About Reports for Configuration Manager Clients" (*http://technet.microsoft.com/en-us/library/bb633154.aspx*) in the Configuration Manager Documentation Library and be aware which reports require a fallback status point.

- Remember that if you have not extended the Active Directory Schema for Configuration Manager 2007, clients will need to contact a server locator point to complete site assignment, even if you manually assign them to a site.

Summary

In this chapter, you explored some of the new features of Configuration Manager client deployment and learned about the different installation methods available to you. You examined the installation and assignment process in detail and discovered some of the reporting options you have available to help you troubleshoot when things go wrong. You also discovered how you can remove the Configuration Manager client, should the need arise.

In the next chapter, you'll learn how to organize your clients into more easily managed collections of computers.

Chapter 9
Defining Collections

So much stuff to send

Target using collections

Except for Vista

~Steve Kaczmarek, Content Publishing Manager

The creation and use of collections is fundamental to many client management processes in Configuration Manager. So, before you begin to examine the package distribution process in earnest, you'll learn about collections. In this chapter, you'll learn how to define, create, and update collections, how collections are handled in a Configuration Manager site hierarchy, and how to troubleshoot potential problems.

Defining Collections

Although the focus here is on the use of collections in the package distribution process, collections have many other uses. Collections are groups of Configuration Manager resources and can consist not only of computers, but also of Microsoft Windows users and user groups, as well as any resources discovered through the Network Discovery method or the Active Directory directory service discovery methods, as discussed in Chapter 7, "Discovering Resources." Package programs can be advertised to collections that consist of users, user groups, or computers. Computer collections, however, are the starting point for performing many client management tasks. For example, you can initiate Remote Tools, view inventory information through Resource Explorer, and view Event Viewer and diagnostic information for each client by selecting the client through a collection.

Important   Collections represent discovered resources. The computer resources that are discovered and displayed in a collection might not actually be installed as Configuration Manager clients. If a client hasn't been installed and the appropriate client component hasn't been enabled, you won't be able to initiate a Remote Tools session, collect inventory, and so on, even though the discovery data record (DDR) exists.

You know that if a computer is discovered but not installed as a Configuration Manager client, that computer can't be the recipient of an advertisement because the Advertised Programs Client Agent is a Configuration Manager client component. On the other hand, a discovered Windows *user* obviously can't be installed as a Configuration Manager client because there's no equivalent user installation method. However, a discovered user can be the recipient of an advertisement when that user is logged on at a Configuration Manager client. For example, suppose that a company's auditing department has developed a spreadsheet that its auditors use when auditing other departments. If Configuration Manager discovers the auditors' user accounts, those user accounts can be grouped into a collection called *Auditors*. The audit spreadsheet then can be advertised to the *Auditors* collection and would subsequently be available to auditors at whatever Configuration Manager client they log on to, in whatever department they're visiting.

In many ways, collections are similar to Windows global groups. You use Windows groups to organize users into easily managed units. Groups are used to assign access permissions to Windows resources such as printers, folders, files, and shares. When a new user joins a group, that user automatically inherits all the permissions assigned to that group.

The same concept applies to Configuration Manager collections. You use collections to organize your Configuration Manager–discovered resources into manageable units. For example, suppose you've installed 1000 clients as Configuration Manager clients. These clients appear as part of the All Systems collection in the Configuration Manager console. If each of these clients belongs to a different business unit or department within your organization and you need to send these computers packages based on their affiliation with their business unit or department, you could create a collection for each business unit or department and add each client to the appropriate collection. Your clients are now grouped into manageable units to which you can easily target packages.

Collections can contain subcollections to give the Configuration Manager administrator more flexibility (or more headaches, depending on your point of view). Subcollections work in much the same way as nested groups in Windows. Actions performed on a main collection can also be performed on its subcollections. The most common use for subcollections is in connection with advertisements. Package programs are advertised to collections, but you can also configure an advertisement to target a collection's subcollections as well.

Subcollections are not considered to be *members* of the collection that contains them. Think of subcollections more as a convenient way to link different collections so that they can be treated as one unit. Membership rules are unique for each subcollection and don't affect any other collection. The next section looks at collection membership.

Collection Membership

Collection membership rules can be either direct or query-based. *Direct membership* is a manual membership method, meaning that you define which resources are to be members of the collection. You're also responsible for maintaining the collection over time. If, for example, computers are added or removed from the business group or department, you'll need to add or remove those computers from their corresponding collections.

Query-based membership, on the other hand, is more dynamic in nature. You define the rules by which the collection membership is established, and then Configuration Manager keeps the collection up to date by periodically rerunning the query. For example, suppose your company standard for naming computers is to include a business unit or departmental code—for example, all computers in the finance department are named FIN203-PCx, where x is a value that's incremented each time a new computer name is needed. You could create a collection named Finance whose membership rule is based on a query that searches the database for all computers whose names begin with FIN203. Configuration Manager would automatically populate the collections with the appropriate computers. If computers are added or removed from the finance department, the collection would be updated automatically when the collection query was next executed.

As you can see, query-based collections are generally more practical and efficient than those based on direct membership rules.

Real World   Automating Collections and Packages

Let's build on our query-based collection example, in which all computers in the finance department are named FIN203-PCx and a Finance collection has been created whose membership rule is based on a query that searches the database for all computers whose names begin with FIN203. Because package programs are always advertised to collections, all members of the Finance collection would receive any advertisement to that collection. If computers are added or removed from the finance department, the next time the Finance collection is (automatically) updated, this change is reflected to the collection, and any new computers that were added to the collection will receive advertisements made to the collection. Similarly, if a computer is removed from the Finance collection, that computer no longer receives any advertisements made to the collection.

This process makes it easier for the Configuration Manager administrator to automate some client management tasks, such as updating a proprietary application.

Suppose your advertisement is to update a local fee structure file on each client in the finance department once a month. You already have the Finance collection, so all you need to do is create a recurring advertisement (you learn how to do this in Chapter 11, "Distributing Software Packages,") that copies a new update file to the clients on a specified day of each month.

Working together, the advertisement and the collection ensure that all computers in the finance department receive the update file once a month. If new computers are added to the finance department, the next time the collection is automatically updated they will automatically receive the same advertisement for the update file that every other member of the Finance collection receives. Similarly, if a computer is moved to another department, the next time the collection is automatically updated that computer will no longer receive advertisements for the updated file. The only administrative task that you need to worry about is obtaining the updated fee structure file once a month and making it available to the advertised package.

Predefined Collections

As mentioned, collections represent discovered resources that haven't necessarily been installed as Configuration Manager clients. For example, Windows users and user groups can be discovered as resources for a Configuration Manager site and the discovered users and user groups are automatically made members of the All Users and All User Groups collections—two examples of predefined collections.

Collections are used to group resources into more easily managed units. When you install Configuration Manager, 16 default collections are created. These default collections are described in Table 9-1.

Table 9-1   Default Collections Created During Configuration Manager Site Server Installation

Collection	Description
All Active Directory Security Groups	Displays all security groups discovered through the Active Directory Security Group Discovery method
All Desktops and Servers	Displays all discovered desktop and server computers, including notebook computers.
All Systems	Displays all computers and Internet Protocol (IP)-addressable resources discovered through any discovery method except Active Directory User Discovery
All User Groups	Displays all user groups discovered through the Active Directory User Discovery method

Table 9-1   Default Collections Created During Configuration Manager Site
Server Installation (Continued)

Collection	Description
All Users	Displays all users discovered through the Active Directory User Discovery method
All Windows 2000 Professional Systems	Displays all discovered computers running the Windows 2000 Professional operating system
All Windows 2000 Server Systems	Displays all discovered computers running the Windows 2000 Server family operating system
All Windows Mobile Devices	Displays all discovered Windows mobile devices
All Windows Mobile Pocket PC 2003 Devices	Displays all discovered Windows mobile devices running the Windows Mobile Pocket PC 2003 operating system
All Windows Mobile Pocket PC 5.0 Devices	Displays all discovered Windows mobile devices running the Windows Mobile Pocket PC 5.0 operating system
All Windows Mobile Smartphone 2003 Devices	Displays all discovered Windows mobile devices running the Windows Mobile Smartphone 2003 operating system
All Windows Mobile Smartphone 5.0 Devices	Displays all discovered Windows mobile devices running the Windows Mobile Smartphone 5.0 operating system
All Windows Server 2003 Systems	Displays all discovered computers running the Windows Server 2003 family operating system
All Windows Server Systems	Displays all discovered computer systems running the Windows 2000 family, Windows Server 2003 family, or Windows Server 2008 family of operating systems
All Windows Workstation or Professional Systems	Displays all discovered computers running the Windows 2000 Professional, Windows XP Professional, Windows Vista Business, or Windows Vista Enterprise operating systems
All Windows XP Systems	Displays all discovered computers running the Windows XP operating system

As you can see, these default collections are primarily designed to group resources by operating system. The collections can be used as targets for receiving advertisements. They're
updated once a day by default, but you can change that frequency by clicking the Schedule
button in the Membership Rules tab in the collection's Properties window, as you'll see in
the section "Creating a Query-Based Collection" later in this chapter. Note that you can manage the default collections only from the central site. You can't modify them from child sites.

Creating Collections

The default collections provide some basic resource groupings, but these won't always be
the best way to manage your resources, especially when it comes to advertising package

programs to Configuration Manager clients. Instead, you can create your own collections, grouping together your resources in as many logical units as makes sense within your Configuration Manager site or site hierarchy.

Part of creating a collection involves defining the collection membership using membership rules. Recall that a collection's membership rules can be either direct—a manual method that requires more maintenance—or query-based, which provides greater flexibility and less maintenance. In this section, you'll learn how to create collections with both types of membership rules.

Creating a Direct Membership Collection

To create a direct membership collection, follow these steps:

1. Navigate to the Collections folder in the Configuration Manager console.

2. Right-click the Collections folder, and choose New Collection from the context menu to run the New Collection Wizard, as shown in Figure 9-1.

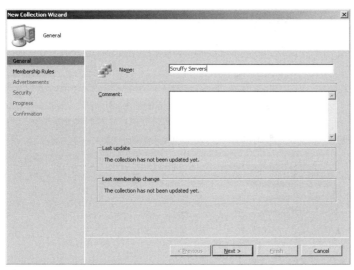

Figure 9-1   The New Collection Wizard

3. On the General page, type a descriptive unique name for your collection along with a descriptive comment if you want, and then click Next.

4. On the Membership Rules page, click the Direct Membership button (the computer) to launch the Create Direct Membership Rule Wizard. Figure 9-2 shows the Create Direct Membership Rule Wizard Welcome page.

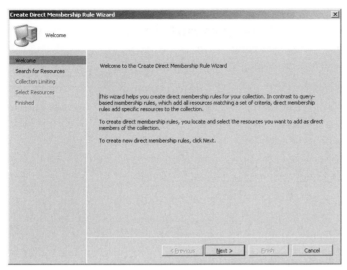

Figure 9-2   The Create Direct Membership Rule Wizard Welcome page

5. Click Next to display the Search For Resources page, as shown in Figure 9-3. Select the resource class for the resource you want to add to the collection. In the Resource Class drop-down list, the User Group Resource and User Resource options let you add members discovered by the Active Directory User Discovery methods. The System Resource option relates to discovered computers. For this example, System Resource is selected.

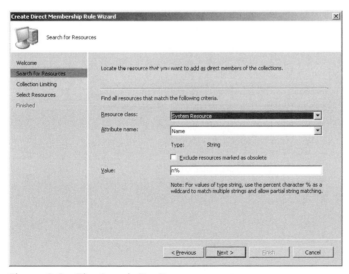

Figure 9-3   The Search For Resources page

6. Select the resource attribute on which you'll base your membership choice. Attributes include resource name, resource ID, IP information, domain information, and so on. The attributes listed reflect the discovery data collected for that class of resource. For this example, specify Name.
7. Enter the appropriate attribute value to look for when selecting members for this group. The % sign is a wildcard character, and you can use upper or lower case characters—case is not sensitive. In this case, you're looking for all computers whose name begins with the letter "N."
8. Click Next to display the Collection Limiting page, as shown in Figure 9-4. From this page you specify which existing collection to use to look for the resources you identified. You can leave the field blank if you have sufficient permissions to search the entire Configuration Manager database. Otherwise, you must type the name (or select Browse to select the name) of a collection that you have permissions to view.

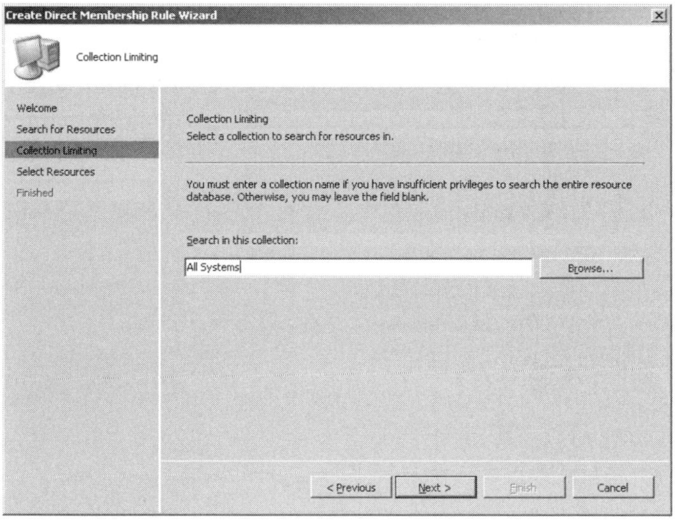

Figure 9-4 The Collection Limiting page

9. Click Next to display the Select Resources page, as shown in Figure 9-5. This page shows a list of the resources that match your membership criteria—in this case, a list of all the computer names that begin with the letter N. Select the resources you want to include in the collection.

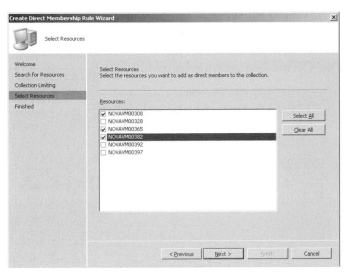

Figure 9-5   The Select Resources page

10. Click Next to display the Completing The Create Direct Membership Rule Wizard page, as shown in Figure 9-6. You can also click Previous to review or change your settings. Review your choices, and then click Finish.

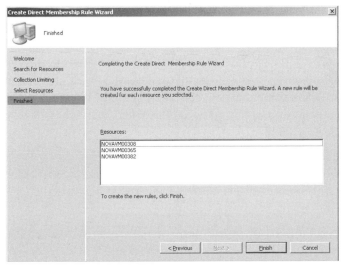

Figure 9-6   The Completing The Create Direct Membership Rule Wizard page

The resources you selected will now appear in the Membership Rules page of the New Collection Wizard, as shown in Figure 9-7.

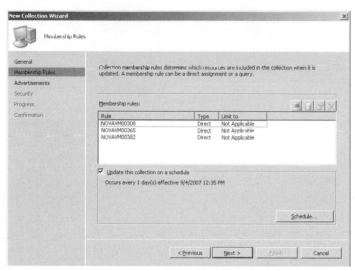

Figure 9-7   The Membership Rules page of the New Collection Wizard

11. In step 8, you specified a collection to use to look for resources you identified. On the Membership Rules page, you can select the Update This Collection On A Schedule check box to have the Collection Evaluator browse the collection you specified on a schedule you configure to see whether the resource still exists. If the resource is no longer a member of the specified collection, it is removed from this new collection. *Collection Evaluator* is the Configuration Manager thread component that performs collection management tasks such as updating or refreshing collection data. By default, the collection will be updated once a day. Click Schedule to modify the collections' update schedule.

12. Click Next to display the Advertisements page of the New Collection Wizard, as shown in Figure 9-8. The Advertisements page lists all advertisements that have targeted clients that are members of that collection, as well as advertisements for collections of which this might be a subcollection.

13. Click Next to display the Security page of the New Collection Wizard, as shown in Figure 9-9. The Security tab lets you specify who can access this collection—and collections in general—and to what extent they can administer the collections. Security is discussed in detail in Chapter 20, "Configuration Manager 2007 Security."

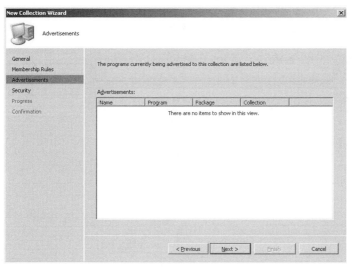

Figure 9-8   The Advertisements page of the New Collection Wizard

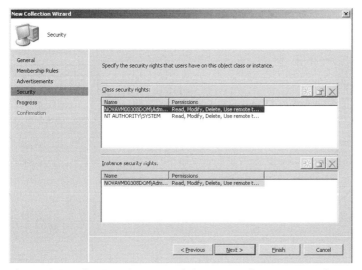

Figure 9-9   The Security page of the New Collection Wizard

14. Click Next to finish and create the collection. Then click Close on the Confirmation page.

Creating a Query-Based Collection

To create a query-based collection, follow these steps:

1. Navigate to the Collections folder in the Configuration Manager console.

2. Right-click the Collections folder and choose New Collection from the context menu to run the New Collection Wizard, as shown in Figure 9-1.

3. On the General page, type a descriptive unique name for your collection along with a descriptive comment if you want, and then click Next.

4. On the Membership Rules page, click the Query Rules button (the database icon) to display the Query Membership Rule Properties dialog box. Figure 9-10 shows the Query Rule Properties dialog box.

Figure 9-10   The Query Rule Properties dialog box

5. On the General tab, type a name for your query or click Import Query Statement to choose from a list of existing Configuration Manager queries.

6. Select the resource class for a set of related objects you want to add to the collection. The Systems Resource option is selected by default. In the Collection Limiting frame, select Limit To Collection if you want to narrow the query

to a specific collection's membership. Click Browse to select from a list of existing collections.

7. Click Edit Query Statement to display the Query Statement Properties dialog box, as shown in Figure 9-11.

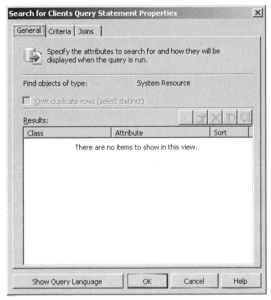

Figure 9-11   The Query Statement Properties dialog box

8. On the General tab, you'll notice that you don't have the ability to create or modify a Query Results list. This is because the query is being used to populate a collection membership instead of displaying resource attributes.

9. Click the Criteria tab, as shown in Figure 9-12, where you can define how to populate the collection.

10. Click the New button (the yellow star) to display the Criterion Properties dialog box, as shown in Figure 9-13.

11. Select the criterion type. The available choices are Null Value, Simple Value, Attribute Reference, Subselected Values, and List Of Values. (See Chapter 19, "Extracting Information Using Queries and Reports," for a description of each criterion type.)

12. Click Select to define the attribute class and attribute on which you're basing the query.

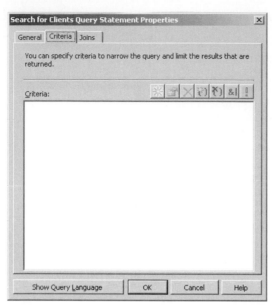

Figure 9-12   The Query Statement Properties dialog box Criteria tab

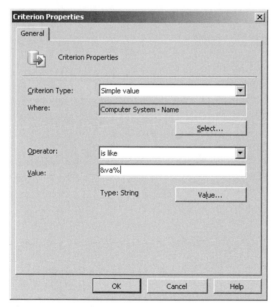

Figure 9-13   The Criterion Properties dialog box

13. Select an operator and enter a value appropriate to the attribute class and attribute you defined, or click Value to make your selection from a list of values recorded in the Configuration Manager database. When you finish, click OK.

> **Important**   String values require an exact value entry. If you want to use a wildcard character, use the operator Is Like or Is Not Like and then use the percent sign (%), as shown in Figure 9-11, or one of the other wildcard characters described in Chapter 19.

14. Repeat steps 10 through 13 to add additional selection criteria.

> **Note**   As mentioned, a collection can be mixed—that is, it can contain computers, users, and groups. It can also consist of a mix of direct and query-based membership rules.

15. Click OK to return to the Query Statement Properties dialog box. Click OK again to return to the New Collection Wizard Membership Rules page.

16. On the Membership Rules page, selecting the Update This Collection On A Schedule check box sets the frequency with which Collection Evaluator will browse the collection you specified to see whether the resource still exists. If the resource is no longer a member of the specified collection, it is removed from this new collection. *Collection Evaluator* is the Configuration Manager thread component that performs collection management tasks such as updating or refreshing collection data. By default, the collection is updated once a day. Click Schedule to modify the collections update schedule.

17. Click Next to display the Advertisements page of the New Collection Wizard, as shown in Figure 9-8 previously. The Advertisements page lists all advertisements that have targeted clients that are members of that collection, as well as advertisements for collections of which this might be a subcollection.

18. Click Next to display the Security page of the New Collections Wizard, as shown in Figure 9-9 previously. The Security tab lets you specify who can access this collection—and collections in general—and to what extent they can administer the collections. Security is discussed in detail in Chapter 20.

19. Click Next to finish and create the collection.

As with direct membership collections, the Advertisements tab of the Collection Properties dialog box lists all advertisements that have targeted that collection.

Creating Subcollections

When a collection has one or more subcollections associated with it, any actions (such as advertisements) performed on the collection can also be performed on the subcollection. However, each subcollection is still its own collection and as such is governed by its own membership rules. Placing them as subcollections within a new collection provides a way to link different collections rather than a method of nesting collections.

Suppose a particular business unit can be further subdivided into smaller units. Management Information Services (MIS), for example, might be divided into various support areas—say, PC Support, Network Support, and Server Support. Say that you create a collection for each of these groups—MIS, PC Support, Network Support, and Server Support. The last three collections could become subcollections of the MIS collection. This reclassification enables you to advertise packages to the MIS collection, which includes the members of the three subcollections. If you don't need to hit all the collections, you can opt not to when you create the advertisement. And you still have the ability to advertise to each collection directly.

Configuration Manager supports two kinds of subcollections: dependent and linked. A dependent subcollection is a new collection that you create under an existing collection. If you delete the "parent" collection, you will also delete the dependent subcollection so long as you have not also linked the subcollection to another collection. A linked subcollection is an existing collection or subcollection that you link to another existing collection. In this scenario, if you delete a collection, the linked subcollections are not deleted if they still exist as an independent collection, or as the subcollection of another collection.

To create a new (dependent) subcollection, follow these steps:

1. Navigate to the Collections folder in the Configuration Manager console and expand it.

2. Right-click the collection or subcollection that you want to associate with a subcollection, choose New from the Context menu, and then choose Collection to run the New Collection Wizard. Follow the steps as described earlier for creating either a direct membership or query-based collection.

To create a linked collection, follow these steps:

1. Navigate to the Collections folder in the Configuration Manager console and expand it.

2. Right-click the collection or subcollection that you want to associate with a subcollection, choose New from the Context menu, and then choose Link To Collection to display the Browse Collection dialog box, as shown in Figure 9-14.

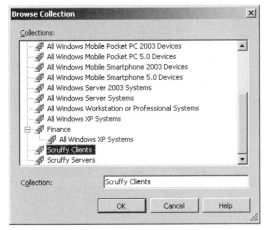

Figure 9-14   The Browse Collection dialog box

3. The Browse Collection dialog box contains a list of all the available collections. Select the collection you want to add as a subcollection, and then click OK.

You can easily view which collections have subcollections and what those subcollections are by expanding the collection entries in the Configuration Manager console.

Unlinking Subcollections

"Unlinking" a subcollection is basically the same as deleting it. If you need to unlink a subcollection to reorganize your collection structure, follow these steps:

1. Navigate to the Collections folder, expand it, and select the subcollection you want to delete.

2. Right-click the subcollection and then choose Delete from the context menu to initiate the Delete Collection Wizard, as shown in Figure 9-15.

3. Verify the subcollection name, and then click Next to display the Delete Collection Instance page, as shown in Figure 9-16.

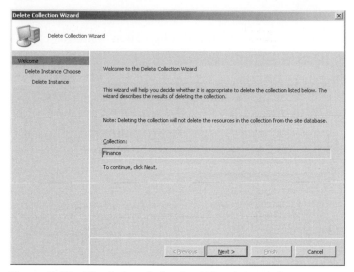

Figure 9-15   The Delete Collection Wizard General page

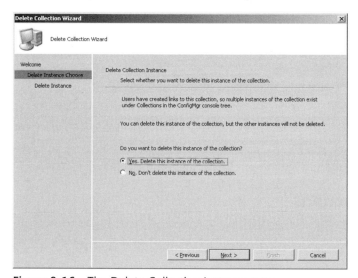

Figure 9-16   The Delete Collection Instance page

4. Select Yes. Delete This Instance Of The Collection. Note that you'll be deleting only this instance of the collection. You won't delete any other instance of the same collection that appears elsewhere in the Collections folder.

5. Click Next, and then click Finish. The Collections folder is refreshed, and the sub-collection is no longer displayed or linked.

More Info   Running the Delete Collection Wizard is described in more detail in the section "Deleting a Collection."

Now that you've created and deleted collections and subcollections, take a look at how you can keep them up to date through Configuration Manager.

Updating Collections

As you've seen, collections that are based on direct membership rules need to be maintained by the Configuration Manager administrator because they're manually created and defined. Collections that are based on queries, however, can be updated automatically based on the schedule that you define. The Configuration Manager component responsible for carrying out this updating task is Collection Evaluator.

Collection Evaluator executes the query and updates the collection whenever the scheduled interval occurs or when the Configuration Manager administrator forces an update through the Configuration Manager console. When the Configuration Manager administrator forces an update or modifies a collection, creates a new collection, or deletes an existing collection, SQL Monitor notifies Collection Evaluator of the event.

Forcing an Update

Collection Evaluator executes a collection's query and updates the collection membership according to whatever schedule you define. However, sometimes you might need or want to update the collection membership outside of that schedule. The Configuration Manager administrator can force Collection Evaluator to update all the collections or any individual collection at any point in time.

Updating All Collections

To update all the collections at once, follow these steps:

1. Navigate to the Collections folder in the Configuration Manager console and expand it.

2. Right-click the Collections folder and choose Update Collection Membership from the context menu.

3. A message box appears confirming the update of all collections. Click OK. This update might take some time to complete depending on the number of collections, network traffic if the Configuration Manager database is on another computer, and so on.

4. When the update is complete, all the collections in the Configuration Manager console will show an hourglass alongside the collection icon in the Configuration Manager console, as shown in Figure 9-17. The hourglass indicates that the collections are updated, but that the Configuration Manager console window needs to be refreshed.

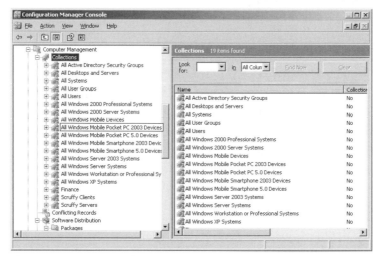

Figure 9-17   The Configuration Manager console with updated collections before being refreshed

5. To refresh the Configuration Manager console window, right-click the Collections folder again and choose Refresh from the context menu. The collections now display their updated memberships.

Updating an Individual Collection

To update an individual collection, follow these steps:

1. Navigate to the Collections folder in the Configuration Manager console and expand it.

2. Right-click the collection you want to update and choose Update Collection Membership from the context menu.

3. As shown in Figure 9-18, a message box appears confirming the update of this collection and giving you the option of simultaneously updating the collection's subcollections. If you want the subcollections updated as well, select the Update Subcollection Membership check box. Click OK to begin the update.

Figure 9-18   Message box confirming the collection update

4. When the update is complete, the collection in the Configuration Manager console will show an hourglass icon alongside the collection entry. This indicates that the collection is updated but that you still need to refresh the Configuration Manager console.

5. To refresh the Configuration Manager console window, right-click the collection again and choose Refresh from the context menu. The collection displays its updated membership.

Deleting a Collection

That which the Configuration Manager administrator gives, the Configuration Manager administrator can take away. This, of course, is true of collections. While you maintain collections, you might need to reorganize your collection structure by creating new collections and deleting existing ones. Deleting a collection can have consequences other than just removing that collection. When you delete a collection, you also perform the following actions:

- Any advertisements that have targeted *only* this collection are also deleted. (If an advertisement is also targeting another collection, it won't be affected.)

- Any desired configuration management configuration baselines that have targeted *only* this collection will no longer be applied to members of that collection. (If a configuration baseline is also targeting another collection, it won't be affected.)

- When you create a query, you can limit its scope by associating it with a particular collection. When the collection is deleted, the query's scope is no longer limited.

- Any collections whose membership rules (queries) are limited to the collection that's being deleted will still process the rule but will display no resources.

■ Through the object class or instance security (discussed in Chapter 20) you can identify which Configuration Manager administrators have the ability to view the membership of each collection. After you remove a collection, the administrators you identified will no longer be able to view that collection's resources if the resources aren't in other collections that the administrators can view.

Note   If the collection you're deleting has a subcollection linked to it, that sub-collection is also deleted unless the subcollection itself has its own subcollections. If the latter is true, when you delete the top-level collection, the subcollection isn't deleted and will still exist in the collection tree.

Fortunately, when you delete a collection, the Delete Collection Wizard warns you of these effects and shows you what properties of the collection might be affected.

Important   When you right-click a collection, you have an option called Delete Special. Be careful when using this option. It bypasses the Delete Collection Wizard and simply deletes all the resources not only from the collection, but also from the Configuration Manager database along with the resources' discovery and inventory information. Consequently, you could inadvertently delete resources from the Configuration Manager database that you did not intend to.

Follow these steps to delete a collection:

1. Navigate to the Collections folder in the Configuration Manager console and expand it.

2. Right-click the collection you want to delete and choose Delete from the context menu. The Delete Collection Wizard General page is displayed, as shown previously in Figure 9-15. Verify the name of the collection to be deleted.

3. Click Next to display the Effects Of Deleting This Collection page, as shown in Figure 9-19. This page warns you about the effects of deleting a collection and lets you choose whether to display details about the effects.

4. Select the Yes option to view individual pages describing what will be affected by the deletion. Select the No option to proceed with the deletion.

   If you select the No option, proceed to step 13, where you would simply delete the collection. For this example, select Yes.

5. Click Next to display the Subcollections page, as shown in Figure 9-20. This page displays a list of this collection's subcollections. Note the warning that deleting this collection also deletes the subcollections.

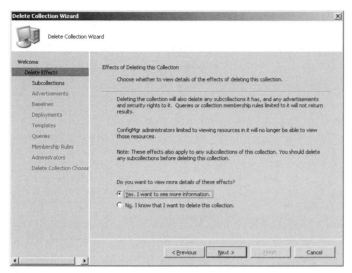

Figure 9-19   The Effects Of Deleting This Collection page

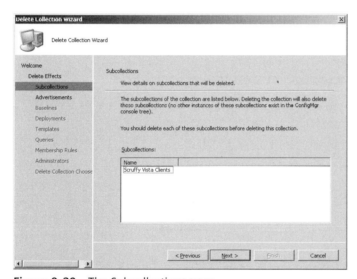

Figure 9-20   The Subcollections page

6. Click Next to display the Advertisements page, as shown in Figure 9-21, which displays a list of all the advertisements that have targeted this collection. Again, note the warning that deleting this collection also deletes the advertisements (if they're not also targeted to another collection).

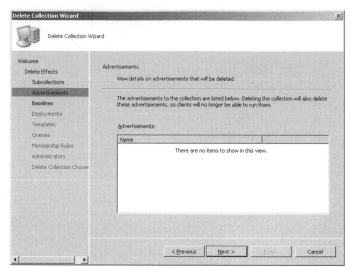

Figure 9-21   The Advertisements page

7. Click Next to display the Baselines page, as shown in Figure 9-22, which lists any configuration baselines you configured using a desired configuration management that has been associated with this collection. A similar warning message is provided.

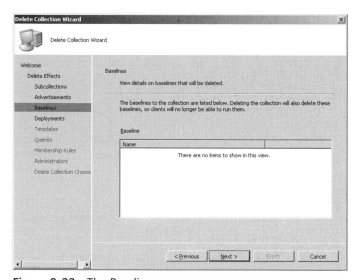

Figure 9-22   The Baselines page

8. Click Next to display the Deployments page, as shown in Figure 9-23, which lists any operating system deployments that have been associated with this collection. A similar warning message is provided.

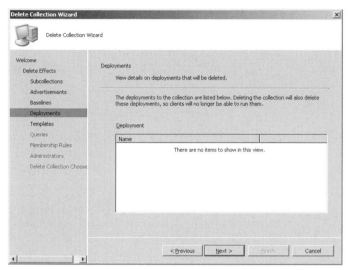

Figure 9-23 The Deployments page

9. Click Next to display the Templates page, as shown in Figure 9-24, which lists any templates that have been associated with this collection. A similar warning message is provided.

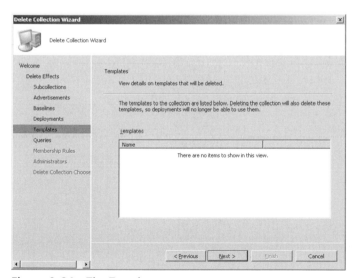

Figure 9-24 The Templates page

10. Click Next to display the Queries page, as shown in Figure 9-25, which lists any queries that have been associated with this collection. A similar warning message is provided.

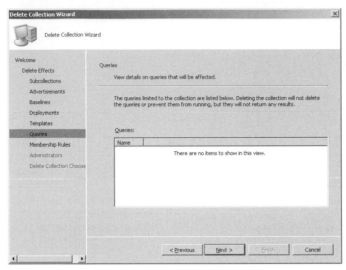

Figure 9-25   The Queries page

11. Click Next to display the Collection Membership Rules page, as shown in Figure 9-26. This page displays a list of collections whose membership rules are limited to this collection and warns of possible effects.

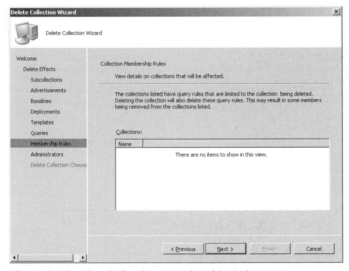

Figure 9-26   The Collection Membership Rules page

12. Click Next to display the Administrators page, as shown in Figure 9-27, which lists the administrators who have permissions to view resources in this collection and the effect that the deletion might have on them.

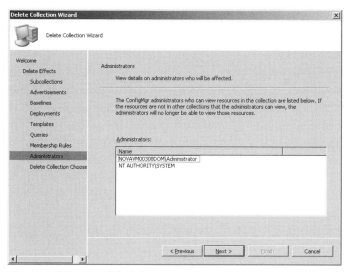

Figure 9-27   The Administrators page

13. Click Next to display the Choose Whether To Delete This Collection page, as shown in Figure 9-28. This final confirmation page asks whether you want to proceed with the deletion. Click Next and Finish to continue and delete the collection.

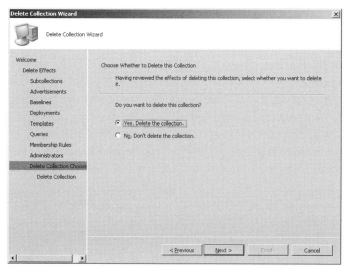

Figure 9-28   The Choose Whether To Delete This Collection page

In this section, you've seen Configuration Manager administrators update and maintain collections and subcollections. Next, you'll see how you can define maintenance windows for your collections.

Assigning a Maintenance Window to a Collection

Configuration Manager has added a new configuration option for collections called the maintenance window. Also known as a service window, a maintenance window lets you define a specific period of time within which changes can be made to clients that are members of that collection. For example, if you have a set of computers that should only receive software updates and other advertisements between midnight and 3:00 A.M. each day, you could create a collection that includes those computers as members; then configure a maintenance window that only allows changes between midnight and 3:00 A.M. each day. Maintenance windows are not intended to be the primary method for scheduling updates to client computers. In fact, Microsoft recommends that if you need to use a maintenance window for a set of computers, you should create a separate collection for those computers. A maintenance window cannot be longer than any given 24-hour period. If you need a longer maintenance window, create multiple windows for the collection.

Configuration Manager determines whether a client can be changed by comparing the Maximum allowed run-time setting for an advertised program and the Advertised Programs Client Agent countdown duration against the next scheduled maintenance window to determine whether there is enough time to run the program. If the time left in the maintenance window is greater than or equal to the Maximum Run Time value plus the agent's countdown, then the program will be allowed to run.

For example, say that an advertised program has a Maximum Run Time value of 30 minutes, with a 5-minute countdown. That's a total of 35 minutes required for that program to start and run. If that program is advertised to a collection with a defined maintenance window of 60 minutes, then 60 ≥ 35, and the program will run. Now let's say a second program with a Maximum Run Time of 25 minutes and a countdown of 5 minutes (for a total of 30 minutes) is advertised to the same collection to run at the same time. Because the first program requires 35 minutes, there are now 25 minutes left in the maintenance window for that collection. That's not enough time for the second program to start and run, so the second program waits until the next available maintenance window.

Important   If the Maximum Run Time value is set to Unknown, the collection will not evaluate the advertised program against the maintenance window, and the program will be allowed to start and run regardless of how much time is available in the maintenance window.

If a client is a member of two or more collections that have maintenance windows defined, it is subject to each of those maintenance windows. If each window is defined as a separate time and they do not overlap, they function as described earlier. However, if one or more of the maintenance windows overlap, the client's effective maintenance window is the sum of the overlapping windows. For example, say that client A is a member of collections B and C. Collection B has a maintenance window that begins at 3:00 P.M. and lasts for 60 minutes (until 4:00 P.M.). Collection C has a maintenance Window that begins at 3:30 and lasts for 90 minutes (until 5:00 P.M.). There is a 30-minute overlap as you see. So, client A's effective maintenance window is 3:00 to 5:00, or 120 minutes.

Maintenance windows are not enforced for the following Configuration Manager features and actions:

- Wake On LAN configurations
- Advertisements or operating system deployments configured to override a maintenance window
- Configuration Manager policy downloads
- Inventory collection and other data reporting
- Evaluation of configuration baselines

To configure a maintenance window for a collection, follow these steps:

1. Navigate to the Collections folder in the Configuration Manager console and expand it.

2. Right-click the collection you want to configure and choose Modify Collection Settings from the context menu. Click the Maintenance Windows tab, as shown in Figure 9-29.

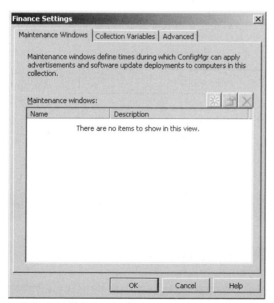

Figure 9-29   The Modify Collection Settings Maintenance Windows tab

3. Click the New icon to display the <new> Schedule dialog box for the maintenance window, as shown in Figure 9-30. Type a name for the maintenance window, and specify the schedule for the window in the Time section, including a recurrence pattern if desired. Select the UTC option if you want the maintenance window evaluated based on Coordinated Universal Time rather than local time. Select the This Schedule Applies Only To Operating System Deployment Task Sequences option if you want to limit the window specifically to those task sequences.

Figure 9-30   The <new> Scheduled dialog box for a maintenance window

4. Click OK to save the maintenance window.

Real World   Assigning Policy Polling Intervals

In previous versions of Systems Management Server, you were unable to have different policy polling intervals for specific groups of client computers in your site. Like other site settings, the policy interval you set for the Configuration Manager Computer Client Agent is a site-wide setting applied to all clients managed by that site. The default value is 60 minutes.

However, Configuration Manager now allows you to override the site-wide policy polling value for a specific group of client computers. Along with maintenance windows, you can also specify a policy polling interval for the computers that are members of a given collection. The value you set for the collection will be applied to all computers that are members of that collection, overriding the site-wide setting. For example, this can be extremely useful when you want or need to have a frequent polling cycle for the majority of the clients managed by a site, but because of network bandwidth or other performance reasons, would like to lengthen that polling cycle for computers in a particular location or department.

1. Create a collection for those computers.

2. Right-click that collection and select Modify Collection Settings to display the Settings dialog box as shown in Figure 9-29.

3. On the Advanced tab, select the option Enable Collection Specific Policy Polling Interval and specify a value in minutes.

4. Click OK to save the setting.

The value you set will be propagated and applied to the members of that collection. Notice that you can override the site-wide setting for client restart countdown and client restart settings on the Advanced tab as well.

Collection Evaluator Update Process Flow

Collection Evaluator assigns resources to collections according to the most recent data about the resources. Collection Evaluator waits for a file change notification from SQL Monitor before the update process starts. As shown in Figure 9-31, SQL Monitor writes a wake-up file to Collection Evaluator's inbox (<installationfolder>\Inboxes\Colleval.box). SQL Monitor writes an update collection (.udc) file when the update is forced or a collection is modified, an add collection (.adc) file when a new collection is created, and a delete collection (.dc) file when a collection is deleted. SQL Monitor—like so many other components in Configuration Manager—is driven by SQL trigger events that cause the component ultimately to wake up and perform its task. Collection Evaluator then executes the query and updates the membership results in the Configuration Manager database.

If the Configuration Manager site has child sites, Collection Evaluator also creates a .psd file that contains the collection definition and membership. It writes this file to Replication Manager's inbox (<installationfolder>\Inboxes\Replmgr.box) so that the file can be scheduled and copied to Collection Evaluator's inbox on the child site. If the child site is a secondary site, the file is rewritten to disk as a .clf file and contains only the collection memberships. If the child site is a primary site, the collection will be processed in much the same fashion as described in the beginning of this section.

When a child site changes its parent site affiliation, Collection Evaluator is responsible for removing any collections that the parent created (and are therefore locked at the child site). When the child site joins the new parent site, the collections created at the parent site are passed down to the child site, and Collection Evaluator locks them and keeps them updated.

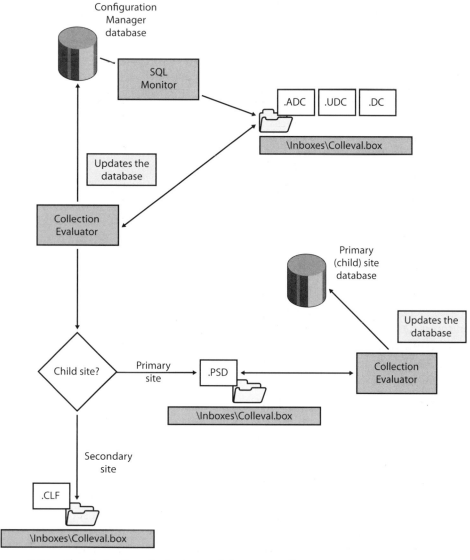

Figure 9-31   The Collection Evaluator update process flow

Status Messages

As with all Configuration Manager components, Collection Evaluator generates status messages as it processes collections and subcollections, as well as a log file if you've enabled logging for this component. The Status Message Viewer window, as shown in Figure 9-32, displays typical status messages generated by Collection Evaluator. Notice that this component's message IDs lie within the 25xx range. For example, message ID 2516 indicates that Collection Evaluator was notified that a new collection was added (by the Configuration Manager administrator, of course). The .adc file is a wake-up file written by SQL Monitor.

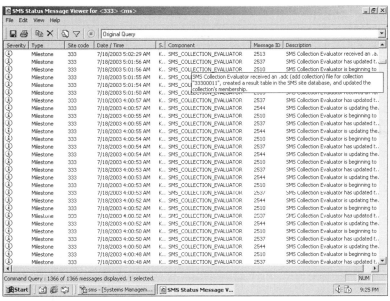

Figure 9-32   Status messages generated by Collection Evaluator as it processes Configuration Manager collections

The pairing of messages 2539 and 2510 indicates when the membership rules for a collection were processed and when the collection was updated. A 2508 message indicates that Collection Evaluator is set to replicate the site's collections and subcollections to child sites.

In addition to these status messages, Collection Evaluator writes its thread activity to a log file named Colleval.log if you enabled logging for this component. Figure 9-33 displays log entries as viewed using Microsoft Notepad. As you can see, there's really nothing remarkable here, except that you can view on a per-thread basis when Collection Evaluator processes each collection, updates or deletes wake-up files, and so on.

Figure 9-33   Log entries generated by Collection Evaluator during normal processing

Collections and the Configuration Manager Site Hierarchy

Because the manner in which collections are handled within a Configuration Manager site hierarchy can be confusing, take a brief look at this topic. Collection definitions created at a parent site will be propagated to that parent's child primary sites. However, the configurations of these collections will be locked to the child site's Configuration Manager administrator. A small lock icon appears next to these collections in the Configuration Manager console showing that the collections are locked and can't be modified. The lock feature is by design. Collections created at the parent site can be modified only at the parent site. Child sites that receive these collections will evaluate them and populate them based on their Configuration Manager database if they're also primary sites. You can delete all the members of a locked collection by right-clicking the locked collection and choosing Delete Special from the context menu. However, if the deleted members are still valid at the parent site, they will reappear the next time the collection is evaluated and updated.

Child sites can have their own collections. These collections are fully manageable by the child site's Configuration Manager administrator and are not forwarded back up to the parent site. They will be propagated to their child sites and, of course, will be locked at the child sites.

Because secondary child sites don't maintain a Configuration Manager database of their own, their collections will be created and maintained at their parent sites. The secondary child sites will receive only the list of collection members that belong to their secondary site.

> **Note**   If a collection hasn't been updated for a week, Configuration Manager will automatically send the entire collection from a primary site to its child sites to synchronize the collections.

Checkpoints

There's not much danger lurking as far as collections are concerned. Any potential problems lie mostly in the setup of the collection. For example, remember that the most useful collections are those based on queries. Query-based membership rules allow the collection to be updated on a regular schedule that you define, ensuring that the collection will be kept up to date. However, this regular updating won't take place unless you enable that option in the Membership Rules tab of the Collection Properties window. Because this option isn't enabled by default, it can be easily missed.

Another "gotcha" comes through the Configuration Manager console. To view the members in a collection, you expand the Collections folder and select the collection entry. Remember that the collection members are not updated in the console automatically. After Collection Evaluator reevaluates the collections' memberships, you still need to refresh the console by right-clicking the Collections folder and choosing Refresh from the context menu. And if you force an update to one or all of the collections, you still need to refresh the console—an update does not also refresh.

Summary

In this chapter, you've seen how much easier the life of the Configuration Manager administrator can become when the appropriate collections have been created, updated, and evaluated. Good collections, like properly configured Windows groups, can facilitate other Configuration Manager management activities, such as accessing clients for remote control, targeting clients for package distribution, troubleshooting remote clients, and so on. Chapter 11 will build on this management theme when you begin your examination of the package distribution capabilities of Configuration Manager. But first, you'll explore how Configuration Manager collects and manages hardware and software inventory for its clients in Chapter 10, "Collecting Inventory."

Chapter 10
Collecting Inventory

All hardware, software

Can easily be found here

SMS_def.mof

~ *Jeff Gilbert, Technical Writer, Configuration Manager*

The collection of hardware and software inventory from Microsoft Systems Center Configuration Manager 2007 clients is certainly one of the more popular client options that Configuration Manager administrators can enable for their Configuration Manager sites. Inventory collection offers the obvious advantage of reporting to a central database certain specific pieces of information that can be of interest or use to the Configuration Manager administrator. Data such as disk space, memory, processor type, NIC, operating system, IP address, and installed software applications can be reported to the Configuration Manager database. You might then use that information to identify which clients need an upgrade or a patch for a particular piece of software or an upgrade to Windows Vista, for example, or to identify which clients have the hardware requirements to support a program installation or an upgrade.

In this chapter, you explore the inventory collection process for hardware and software, including how to enable hardware inventory and software inventory, how to view inventory, and how to customize hardware inventory. As in previous chapters, you also look at the log files and status messages that are generated throughout the inventory collection process and discuss how to interpret them.

Hardware Inventory

The Hardware Inventory Client Agent collects a broad assortment of hardware properties from the client. When you think of hardware inventory, most of us, especially those familiar with earlier versions of Configuration Manager, think of the basic data: disk information such as space used and space available; memory, video, processor, and operating system data; and MAC, IP, and subnet addresses. To be sure, some of this hardware information sounds a lot like the discovery data stored in the discovery data records (DDRs) you looked at in Chapter 7, "Discovering Resources." However, hardware inventory is *nothing* like discovery data.

In fact, a great deal more hardware information is collected than just these basics. The hardware inventory process is designed to query the Windows Management Instrumentation (WMI) to obtain its data. Windows Management itself can expose a vast amount of information about the client, obtaining information from various providers, including the WIN32 subsystem of Windows, the registry, the computer's basic input/output system (BIOS), and so on. WMI is updated with Configuration Manager–specific classes as part of the Configuration Manager client installation.

Configuration Manager uses an inventory collection file to determine how much information is collected from WMI reporting classes and by default queries for approximately 1,500 different hardware properties. The inventory collection file is a Managed Object Format (MOF) file and is named SMS_def.mof. The master version of this file is stored on the Configuration Manager site server. The amount of data reported about each of the basic hardware components is considerable and can actually be extended further. For example, you could report on program groups created on the client, network printer connections, or account information such as the user's full name or security ID (SID). This extension is done by modifying the SMS_def.mof file to include additional WMI reporting classes. There is more discussion about this file later in this chapter.

You can also add information to the inventory data normally collected. For example, you could add asset-related information, contact names, and so on. You accomplish this reporting through the creation of text files known as Management Information Format (MIF) files that you present to Configuration Manager as an update to the database record for a specific Configuration Manager client. In addition, Configuration Manager now includes a new file called configuration.mof. This file allows you to add additional data classes to the hardware inventory collected by Configuration Manager.

Best Practices   As a best practice, Microsoft recommends that you modify the configuration.mof file when you need to add new data class information to clients for inventory collection, and the SMS_def.mof file when you need to add new reporting class information.

If information isn't available directly through the Hardware Inventory Client Agent, you can update client records with your own manually generated data—or even create whole new classes of object types, such as "multimedia equipment." After hardware inventory is collected at the client, it's passed on to the management point. The management point, in turn, forwards the hardware inventory to the site server. Hardware inventory is ultimately stored in the Configuration Manager site database, so it's important to draw a distinction between primary and secondary site servers. As you saw in Chapter 4, "Implementing Multiple-Site Structures," the main difference between a primary and a secondary site server is that a primary site server maintains access to an SQL Server database.

In a secondary site, the Configuration Manager client passes its inventory to the management point of the parent site to which it is assigned, unless a proxy management point has been installed at the secondary site in which case the client passes its inventory to the proxy management server, and the secondary site passes it on to the primary site server. Inventory is propagated up the Configuration Manager site hierarchy to the central site.

Enabling Hardware Inventory

Begin by getting the Hardware Inventory Client Agent enabled on your Configuration Manager clients. Then you'll explore how inventory is actually collected. Like all client agents, the Hardware Inventory Client Agent is installed but not enabled on Configuration Manager clients by default. You can enable the Hardware Inventory Client Agent through the Configuration Manager Administrator Console. When you enable the Hardware Inventory Client Agent, you're making a change to the site properties, and the site's site control file (Sitectrl.ct0) is updated as a result (as described in Chapter 3, "Configuring Site Server Properties and Deploying Site Systems"). The agent configuration information is incorporated into a client policy that is stored on the management point and propagated to the client the next time the client machine policy is refreshed.

To enable and configure the Hardware Inventory Client Agent, follow these steps:

1. Under Site Settings, navigate to and select the Client Agents node.

2. Right-click Hardware Inventory Client Agent in the results pane and choose Properties from the context menu to display the Hardware Inventory Client Agent Properties dialog box, as shown in Figure 10-1.

3. Select the Enable Hardware Inventory On Clients check box.

4. The default inventory collection schedule on the client is once a week. With the Simple Schedule option, you can specify inventory collection to run once every 1 to 59 minutes, 1 to 23 hours, or 1 to 31 days. Or you can select Custom Schedule and click Customize to display the Custom Schedule dialog box, as shown in Figure 10-2. Here you can designate a more specific start time and recurrence pattern. When you finish, click OK.

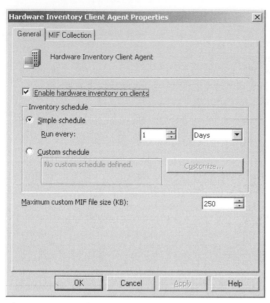

Figure 10-1   The Hardware Inventory Client Agent Properties dialog box

5. You can modify the default value for the Maximum Custom MIF File Size if you anticipate using custom MIFs larger than 250 KB to append data to the inventory data being collected.

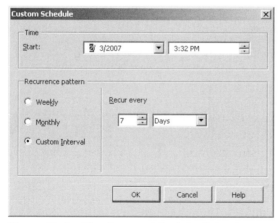

Figure 10-2   The Custom Schedule dialog box

6. Use the options in the MIF Collection tab shown in Figure 10-3 to identify whether to collect custom MIF files (IDMIF and NOIDMIF) from the Configuration Manager client.

Important   In order for a custom MIF to be successfully collected as part of hardware inventory, the file must be located in the correct folder on the client. IDMIF files must be stored in the Windows\System32\CCM \Inventory\idmifs folder. NOIDMIF files should be located in the Windows \System32\CCM\Inventory\noidmifs folder. You learn the difference between these MIF file types later in this chapter.

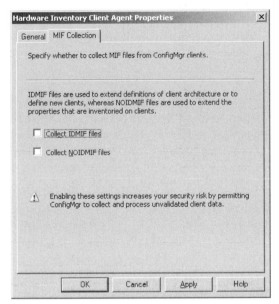

Figure 10-3   The Hardware Inventory Client Agent Properties dialog box MIF Collection tab

7. Click OK again to begin the site update process.

The SMS_def.mof and configuration.mof files contain the instructions for what data are collected from Configuration Manager clients when hardware inventory is run. These files are stored on the site server in the folder <InstallationPath> SMS\\inboxes\clifiles.src\hinv. Information from these files along with the agent configuration information is incorporated into a client policy that is stored on the management point.

The next time the Configuration Manager client machine policy is refreshed – usually when the client restarts, or at the next client update interval (every 25 hours), the client obtains the updated client policy information and the agent is enabled and configured appropriately. At this time, the SMS_def.mof and configuration.mof file information is compiled into the WMI layer on the client, the hardware inventory log files are updated, and the agent is started. Ten minutes after the Hardware Inventory Client Agent starts, the first complete inventory is collected from the client as specified by MOF files through WMI and is then copied to the management point.

Client Requirements and Inventory Frequency

A complete default inventory generates a hardware information file about 200 KB in size. A copy is stored on the client as part of the WMI Common Information Model (CIM) repository. The initial inventory is also passed to the management point and then to the site server. Subsequent inventory files generally report only changes to hardware inventory, however, so you can expect a corresponding amount of network traffic associated with the installation (one time), with the first complete inventory (one time), and with subsequent delta inventories (according to your schedule). The *delta inventory* is an inventory cycle that creates a delta inventory file containing the information that has changed since the previous inventory.

The schedule you specify should reflect the frequency with which you need to collect or update your clients' inventory records. If your clients have fairly standard hardware installations and don't make, or aren't allowed to make, substantial changes on their own, you could collect inventory less frequently—say, once a week or even once a month.

However, if your client computers are volatile regarding hardware changes, you might need to report changes to the inventory more frequently—perhaps once a day or once every 12 hours. The more frequent the inventory, the more potential network traffic is generated. The Hardware Inventory Client Agent reports inventory regardless of whether a user is actually logged on to the client. If the client isn't currently connected to the network, the agent still runs and stores the collected data on the client until the next time the client can connect.

Note   The Hardware Inventory Client Agent can be forced to run through Configuration Management in the Control Panel. Double-click the Configuration Management icon to display the Configuration Management Properties dialog box, and click the Actions tab. Select the Hardware Inventory Cycle in the Actions tab and click Initiate Action.

Important   Inventory stored in the Configuration Manager database is historical in nature, meaning that it's only as accurate as the last time you collected the inventory record. If your clients are volatile, as described earlier, and you rely on the inventory to identify clients' available disk space for installation applications, you might require an inventory schedule that's more frequent.

Hardware Inventory Collection Process Flow

The hardware inventory collection process will now be explored in more detail. Recall that the Hardware Inventory Client Agent uses WMI to obtain hardware inventory data about various classes of objects designated in the SMS_def.mof and configuration.mof files. When the Hardware Inventory Client Agent is scheduled to run, it queries the CIM Object Manager component of WMI for the object properties it needs to report on. The CIM Object Manager, in turn, retrieves the current information from the appropriate object providers, such as WIN32, and then passes the data to the Hardware Inventory Client Agent.

The first time the Hardware Inventory Client Agent runs—approximately 10 minutes after it is enabled—a complete inventory is collected and its history is maintained in the CIM repository on each client. Each subsequent inventory generates a delta file only, detailing only those inventory properties that have changed since the last interval.

If MIF file collection is configured for the agent, the agent looks for any MIF files that reside in the Windows\System32\CCM\Inventory\Noidmifs or Windows\System32\CCM\Inventory\idmifs folders on the Configuration Manager client. Refer to the section "MIF Files" later in this chapter for details about MIF files. If the client deems the MIF file to be valid, it's included as part of the inventory file. If not, a Badmifs subfolder is created under the Noidmifs or Idmifs folder, depending on the MIF type, and the invalid file is moved there.

> **Note**   The Badmifs folder is created only if a bad NOIDMIF or IDMIF is detected. By default, the maximum MIF file size is set to 250 KB, although you can change this value through the Hardware Inventory Client Agent properties described earlier. A NOIDMIF or an IDMIF is considered bad if it exceeds the maximum size or if it can't be parsed successfully because of syntax errors or because, in the case of IDMIFs, it's being used to update the system architecture for an existing client record.

The MIF data is appended to the inventory data already collected and a temporary inventory file is created on the client. The client sends the inventory file to the SMS_CCM\Inventory folder on the management point. The MIF files are placed in the SMS_CCM\Inventory\idmifs and SMS_CCM\Inventory\noidmifs folders as appropriate.

> **Note**   Once the inventory file is copied to the management point, the temporary inventory files are deleted. This process generally happens in a matter of seconds, so you might not see the files unless you're watching closely.

The Configuration Manager Management Point File Dispatch Manager on the management point in turn moves the file to the Inventory Processor's inbox (the <InstallationPath> SMS\Inboxes\Inventry.box folder) on the site server. If the site server is a primary site server, the Inventory Processor adds a binary header to the .nhm file, renames it with the extension .mif, and moves it to the Inventory Data Loader's inbox (the <InstallationPath> SMS\Inboxes\Dataldr.box folder). The Inventory Data Loader then reads the .mif file, parses the data, and writes it to the Configuration Manager database on the server running SQL. If a parent site exists, the Inventory Data Loader forwards the .mif file to the Replication Manager, which forwards it to the Inventory Data Loader's inbox on the parent site server.

If the site server is a secondary site server, the Replication Manager forwards the .mif file to the parent primary site server's Inventory Data Loader inbox, where it's processed as described earlier.

Hardware Resynchronization

Occasionally, the Inventory Data Loader might determine that the inventory data it receives is somehow "bad" or out of sync with the Configuration Manager database. In these instances, a resynchronization (resync) is triggered automatically. *Resync* is a corrective process that can cause the client agent to ignore the history file and collect a complete hardware inventory. Specific events that trigger hardware inventory resync include the following:

- The inventory delta contains updates for a database record that doesn't exist.
- The inventory delta itself contains bad or corrupted data.
- The client has attached to a new Configuration Manager site.
- The client has upgraded from SMS 2003 to Configuration Manager.

Note   Resync doesn't change the hardware inventory schedule—the next inventory cycle will start at the scheduled time.

When a resync is triggered for a Configuration Manager client, the Inventory Data Loader purges any Noidmif data that was received from the client. The Policy Provider on the site server creates a resync policy and sends it to the management point. At the next policy refresh period on the Advanced Client, the resync request is received, and a full hardware inventory is run.

Status Messages and Log Files for Hardware Inventory

Status messages and log files are generated throughout the inventory installation and collection process. Begin with the log files. Unlike log files generated on the site server, client logs are enabled by default and written automatically to the Windows\System32\Ccm\logs folder on each client. Monitor the Policyagent.log file for updates received by the client, which would include enabling Inventory Agent on the client and configuring hardware inventory collection. Monitor the InventoryAgent.log file, a portion of which is shown in Figure 10-5, for collection of inventory data.

You can view status messages regarding inventory activity on a client by running a status message query through the Configuration Manager Administrator Console. To do so, follow these steps:

1. Navigate to the System Status node, expand it, and select the Status Message Queries node.

2. In the results pane, right-click the query All Status Messages From A Specific System and choose Show Messages from the context menu to display the All Status Messages From A Specific System properties page, as shown in Figure 10-4.

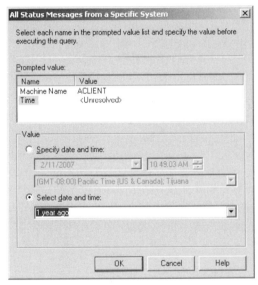

Figure 10-4   The All Status Messages From A Specific System properties page

3. In the Prompted Value list, select Machine Name. Click Specify and type the name of the client computer you want to report on or select Load Existing to have Configuration Manager query the Configuration Manager database and compile a list of all client names it has recorded.

Note   This process can take a while for large databases.

---

4. Select Time in the Prompted Value list. The options in the Value frame will change. Either specify a starting date and time from which you want to see status messages or select Select Date And Time to enter a range of hours (1, 2, 6, or 12 hours ago), days (1 or 2 days ago), weeks (1 or 2 weeks ago), months (1, 3, or 6 months ago) or 1 year ago.

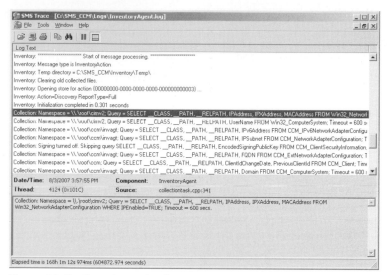

Figure 10-5   Sample entries for InventoryAgent.log in SMS Trace

5.   Click OK. The Configuration Manager Status Message Viewer displays all the status messages recorded for that client during the period specified in the Status Message Viewer window.

Look for message IDs of 10500, indicating that inventory has been successfully collected; or 10505, indicating that the inventory schema (SMS_def.mof) has been updated. To view status messages for clients based on their collection membership, run the status message query All Status Messages For A Specific Collection At A Specific Site. Of course, you could create your own status message query as well. Refer back to Chapter 6, "Analysis and Troubleshooting Tools," for more information on how to create status message queries.

On the site server, monitor the status messages of Inventory Data Loader. Look for messages in the 27*xx* range identifying successful processing of MIFs. Monitor the status messages for Inventory Processor for resynchronization and monitor status messages for Replication Manager for forwarding of MIF files to a parent site.

You can also use the Configuration Manager Report Viewer to view status information related to the inventory process. To launch the Configuration Manager Report Viewer, follow these steps:

1.   Navigate to the Computer Management\Reporting node in the Configuration Manager Administrator console.

2.   Right-click the Reports node. From the context menu, select Run, then the name of the reporting point site system (if there's more than one) to display the Configuration Manager Report Viewer, as shown in Figure 10-6.

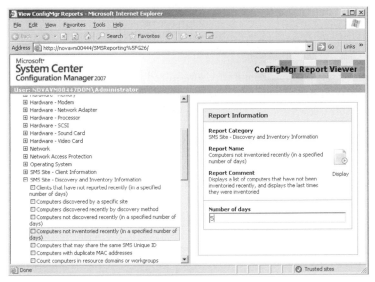

Figure 10-6   The Configuration Manager Report Viewer

3. Expand SMS Site-Discovery and Inventory Information and select an appropriate report. In Figure 10-6, Computers Not Inventoried Recently is selected. Type whatever prompted information is required and then click Display. The results are displayed in a results window, as shown in Figure 10-7.

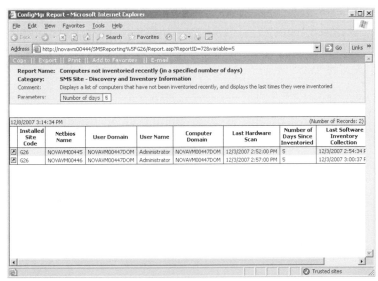

Figure 10-7   The results window for a report run through the Configuration Manager Report Viewer

Alternatively, you could use the new results pane to also find and run the report:

1. Navigate to the Computer Management\Reporting\Reports node in the Configuration Manager Administrator console.

2. Select the report you want to run from the list in the results pane.

3. Right-click on the report and select Run from the context menu, or click Run in the Actions pane.

4. Type whatever prompted information is required and then click Display. The results are displayed in a results window.

    - OR -

5. Navigate to the Computer Management\Reporting\Reports node in the Configuration Manager Administrator console.

6. To filter the number of reports listed, in the results pane in the Look For field, type **Inventory**, and in the In field, type **Category**, and then click Find Now. Figure 10-8 shows the filtered list of reports.

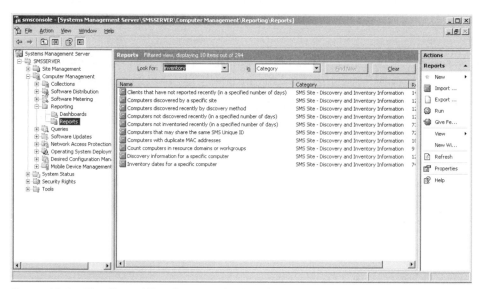

Figure 10-8   The filtered list of reports displayed in the results pane

7. Select the report you want to run from the list in the results pane.

8. Right-click the report and select Run from the context menu, or in the Actions pane, click Run.

9. Type whatever prompted information is required and then click Display. The results are displayed in a results window.

Viewing Hardware Inventory

You view hardware inventory through the Configuration Manager Administrator Console. To do that, follow these steps:

1. Navigate to the Computer Management\Collections node and expand it.

2. Select the collection that contains the client or clients whose inventory you want to view.

3. Right-click the appropriate client entry in the results pane, choose Start from the context menu, and then choose Resource Explorer.

4. In the Resource Explorer window, expand Hardware to view a list of object classes for which properties have been collected, as shown in Figure 10-9. Select each object to view its instances and properties. The Resource Explorer window lists properties horizontally across the viewing screen, requiring you to scroll across to see all the properties.

Note   If you double-click the entry in the viewing pane, you can view the same properties listed in a vertical column, which can be much easier to read. This can be particularly useful when comparing properties in the Hardware History section of the Resource Explorer.

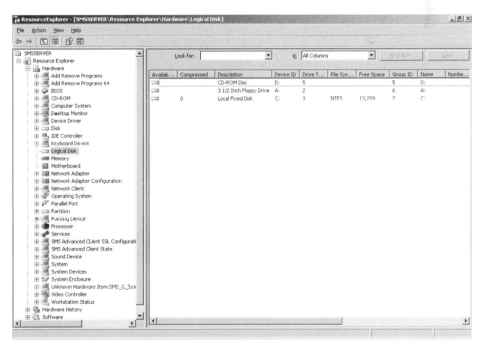

Figure 10-9   The Resource Explorer window, with Logical Disk selected

5. Expand Hardware History to view information collected from previous inventories such as Add Remove Programs History, Logical Disk History, Services History, and Operating System History, as shown in Figure 10-10.

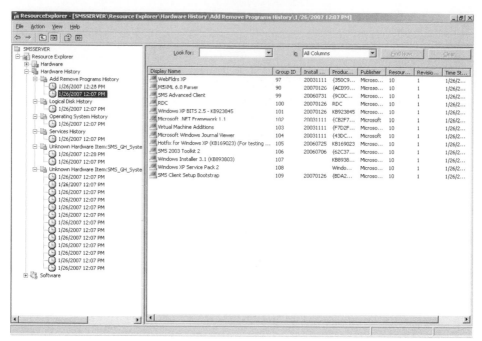

Figure 10-10   The Resource Explorer window, with Hardware History expanded

Note   You can use the Web reporting feature of Configuration Manager to view inventory as well. Web reports are discussed in more detail in Chapter 18, "Monitoring Software Usage with Software Metering."

Note   You can use Hardware History to develop resource usage trends for your clients—for example, to track how much disk storage is utilized over a period of time or whether paging might be excessive due to a lack of RAM.

The entries listed under Hardware in the Resource Explorer window represent the object classes identified through the SMS_def.mof, configuration.mof, and any MIF files that were created to be appended to or modify the client's inventory record. As you can see, it's quite a thorough list.

Customizing Hardware Inventory

There are two ways to customize the inventory that you collect from a client or add to the database as a new class of object: You can modify the default SMS_def.mof or configuration.mof file, or you can create custom MIF files. Either method requires some planning and testing on the part of you, the Configuration Manager administrator. As you've seen, the default SMS_def.mof and configuration.mof files collect a large amount of data. Modifying the file could result in larger amounts of data to track, more network traffic when sending the data to the management points and site server, and so on. Adding an MIF file can also result in additional inventory data being reported.

SMS_def.mof and configuration.mof

You can consider the SMS_def.mof and configuration.mof files as templates that define for Windows Management on Configuration Manager clients which inventory objects, or hardware classes, should be queried and how much data should be collected for each. These files are stored and maintained in the <InstallationPath> SMS\Inboxes\clifiles.src\hinv folder on the site server. As mentioned earlier, they are used to create an inventory rules policy that's propagated to each client through the management point.

You can modify the class and property settings contained in these files or add new classes and properties by opening the file with any text editor, such as Microsoft Notepad. Figure 10-11 shows a portion of the SMS_def.mof file as displayed using Notepad. Each class and property includes a flag named SMS_Report. When this flag is set to True, the property is collected as part of inventory. In Figure 10-11, you can see that the SMS_Report flag for the class SMS_LogicalDisk is set to True and that the values for the properties Availability, Description, DeviceID, DriveType, FileSystem, and FreeSpace are collected from the client. Figure 10-12 displays a list of the Class Qualifiers and their descriptions as outlined in the SMS_def.mof file.

Figure 10-11   Sample of SMS_def.mof file displayed using Notepad

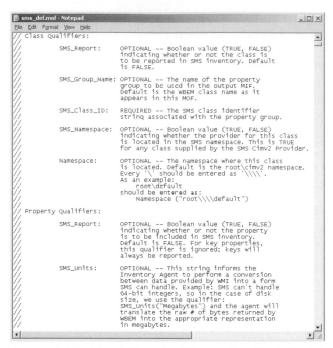

Figure 10-12   List of Class Qualifiers as listed in SMS_def.mof file

If you want to prevent a class or property from collecting inventory data, set the SMS_Report flag to False. If you want to enable a class or property to collect data for inventory, set the flag to True.

Figure 10-13 shows a portion of the configuration.mof file as displayed using Notepad. While you can modify the SMS_def.mof file to extend inventory classes, Microsoft recommends that you modify the configuration.mof file to extend inventory to collect data such as registry classes (for which many of you undoubtedly extended the SMS_def.mof file in the past). In Figure 10-13, you can see the general format for defining registry classes as applied to Add Remove Programs.

Real World   Customizing SMS_def.mof to Collect RAM Chip Information

Here's an example of how you can customize the SMS_def.mof file to collect and report physical RAM chip information from Configuration Manager client computers. This customization reports the number of RAM chips installed on the computer as well as chip properties such as the type of chip. This information can be especially useful when trying to determine whether a computer meets memory requirements for things like an upgrade to Windows Vista, or just to help you know what kind of RAM to buy, and what memory slots are open and available on the computer's motherboard.

```
[SMS_Report (TRUE),
SMS_Group_Name ("Physical Memory"),
SMS_Class_ID   ("Microsoft|Physical_Memory|1.0")]

class Win32_PhysicalMemory : SMS_Class_Template
{
[SMS_Report (TRUE)] string BankLabel;
[SMS_Report (TRUE), SMS_Units("Megabytes")]  uint64 Capacity;
[SMS_Report (TRUE)] string Caption;
[SMS_Report (TRUE)] string DeviceLocator[];
[SMS_Report (TRUE)] uint16 FormFactor;
[SMS_Report (TRUE)] string Manufacturer;
[SMS_Report (TRUE)] uint16 MemoryType;
[SMS_Report (TRUE)] uint32 PositionInRow;
[SMS_Report (TRUE)] uint32 Speed;
[SMS_Report (TRUE),Key] string    Tag;
[SMS_Report (TRUE),Key] string    CreationClassName;
};
```

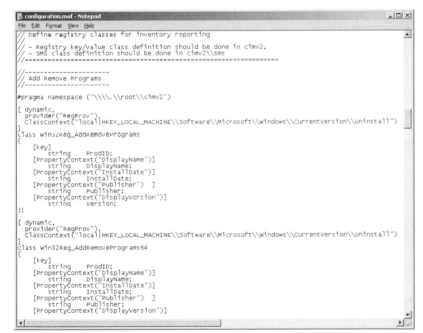

Figure 10-13   Sample configuration.mof file displayed using Notepad

MIF Files

Another way to modify hardware inventory is through the creation of MIF files. MIF files
modify the database by creating architectures, object classes, and attributes. Architectures
define entire new classes of objects, whereas object classes and attributes are generally
added to existing architectures.

You can create two types of MIF files: NOIDMIFs and IDMIFs. NOIDMIFs are used to modify or append object classes and properties to existing client inventory records—hence the term "no id." You're not creating a new architecture; you're simply appending to an existing architecture—namely, System Resources. You could use a NOIDMIF to add a client system's asset number, information about peripheral devices attached to the computer, or even the department name or code to the existing client record.

IDMIFs, on the other hand, are used to create new architectures of object classes and attributes. For example, suppose you want to report on all the multimedia equipment you have in your organization. Through an IDMIF, you can create a new architecture (say, Multimedia Equipment) with its own object classes—(perhaps *Audio, Video, CD, Tape,* or *PC Conferencing*), each of which would have one or more attributes (*Model, Manufacturer, Asset number, Cost,* and so on). You can also use IDMIFs to update existing architectures—for example, to add stand-alone computers to the database or to associate an architecture with existing computer records for the purpose of creating queries and collections that can be linked to unique properties.

> **More Info**   Although it would be nice to present examples showing how each of these types of MIFs can be used and explain their basic structure, there is no need to reinvent the wheel here with an in-depth explanation of MIF usage and interaction. You can find a greater level of detail, along with a detailed discussion of MOF files, in the Configuration Manager Documentation Library, which is included when you install Configuration Manager. The most current version of this file can be viewed and downloaded from the Configuration Manager TechCenter at *http://technet.microsoft.com/en-us/library/bb680651.aspx*. It is also recommended that you read the *Start to Finish Guide to MOF Editing* by Jeff Gilbert, one of the technical writers on the Configuration Manager writing team. While written for SMS 2003, the information provided there largely applies to Configuration Manager as well. This e-book is available through the SMS Expert Web site at *www.smsexpert.com*. You can find several useful editing tools and scripts on this site as well.

The basic structure of IDMIFs and NOIDMIFs is essentially the same. Because they're text files, you can create them using any text editor. Actually, most third-party add-ons for Configuration Manager are capable of generating MIF files that update the database with various kinds of information. SMS Installer can notify the site server about the successful or failed installation of an application through a status MIF file. The MIF file format is an industry standard format. If you've created any kind of scripts or batch files in the past, you'll find it easy to create an MIF file. Start with the NOIDMIF.

Creating a NOIDMIF

NOIDMIFs are perhaps the most commonly used MIF files because they add to existing computer records and they're the easiest to create. Figure 10-14 shows a sample of a NOIDMIF designed to add the client computer's department name and department code to its existing hardware record in the Configuration Manager database.

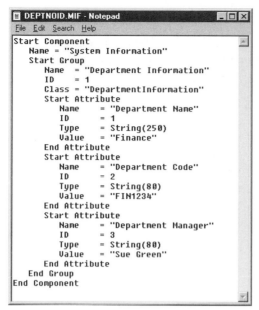

Figure 10-14   A sample NOIDMIF file

NOIDMIFs always begin with Start Component and a general component name. The next step is to create an object class. You do this by adding the Start Group statement, a Name describing the group, an ID, and a class. The *Name* attribute is the string displayed in the Resource Explorer that refers to this class. The *ID* attribute represents this group in relation to any other group in this MIF. For example, if you add another group, you give it an ID of 2, and so on—the number is unique. The *Class* attribute is used by Configuration Manager internally for processing the group information.

Next, list each attribute that you're adding for this object. In this case, you're adding three attributes: *Department Name, Department Code,* and *Department Manager.* Each attribute entry begins with Start Attribute and ends with End Attribute. For each attribute you must provide at a minimum *Name, ID, Type,* and *Value* settings. These attributes are fairly self-explanatory. *Name* is a descriptive attribute name. *ID* represents the attribute in relation to other attributes. *Type* indicates whether the value is a text string, a number, or a list, and gives the value's length when appropriate. *Value,* of course, is the current value you assign to the attribute. End the MIF file with End Group and End Component statements.

Save the NOIDMIF with a descriptive file name and the .mif extension. Place the file in the Windows\System32\CCM\Inventory\noidmif folder on each client you want to update. You can do this using Configuration Manager's package distribution process, which is discussed in Chapter 11, "Distributing Software Packages." At the next hardware inventory cycle, the MIF file will be read, evaluated for syntax, and added to the client's inventory file, as described in the section "Hardware Inventory Collection Process Flow" earlier in this chapter, and then updated to the client's Configuration Manager database record. You can then view it through Resource Explorer, where it is listed along with the other classes that are collected.

Important   Be sure that the MIF file you create using a text editor is saved with the .mif extension. Text editors such as Notepad append a .txt extension. It's easy to miss this, and if you do, you'll spend an inordinate amount of time trying to figure out why the MIF file isn't working.

Creating an IDMIF

As mentioned, the basic structure of an IDMIF is similar to that of a NOIDMIF. The main difference comes at the beginning of an IDMIF file, as you can see in the example shown in Figure 10-15.

IDMIFs require that you include the following two statements at the top of the MIF:

- **//Architecture**   Identifies the name of the new architecture (object class) you're creating

- **//UniqueID**   Defines a single unique value that identifies this specific instance of the architecture in the database

```
//Architecture<MediaEquip>
//UniqueID<awesome101>

Start Component
        Name = "Video Equipment"
        Start Group
            Name = "MediaEquip"
            ID = 1
            Class = "MediaEquip"
            Key = 1
                Start Attribute
                    Name = "corp"
                    ID = 1
                    Access = READ-ONLY
                    Storage = Specific
                    Type = String(20)
                    Value = "Awesome"
                End Attribute
        End Group

        Start Group
            Name = "Video1"
            ID = 2
            Class = "VideoEquip"
            Key = 1
                Start Attribute
                    Name = "Unit1"
                    ID = 1
                    Access = READ-ONLY
                    Storage = Specific
                    Type = String(20)
                    Value = "101"
                End Attribute
                Start Attribute
                    Name = "Model"
```

Figure 10-15   A sample IDMIF file

IDMIFs also require that you include a top-level group that has the same name as the architecture and that has at least one attribute defined. Also, if a class has more than one instance within an architecture, you must have defined at least one key attribute to avoid overwriting previous instances with subsequent information. A key value is simply one of the group attributes. As with NOIDMIFs, you must save the file with an .mif extension. You can place the file in the Windows\System32\CCM\Inventory\idmif folder on any Configuration Manager client.

Viewing an IDMIF

Unlike NOIDMIFs, which are associated with specific clients, IDMIFs generally add new object classes to the database. Therefore, you can't view this information through Resource Explorer. Instead, you must create a query to extract and view the relevant data from the Configuration Manager database. For details on creating queries, refer to Chapter 19, "Extracting Information Using Queries and Reports."

As mentioned, NOIDMIFs are generally associated with individual client records, and, as such, they must be placed in the Windows\System32\CCM\Inventory\noidmif folder on each client. Of course, you can use Configuration Manager package distribution to accomplish this. IDMIFs can also be placed in the Idmifs folder on the Configuration Manager client. However, because IDMIFs generally aren't associated with any one client, you can place an IDMIF in the Idmifs folder on any one Configuration Manager client. For that matter, you could also place the IDMIF in the <InstallationPath> SMS\Inboxes\Inventry.box folder on the site server. The result is the same.

Software Inventory

Configuration Manager offers greatly enhanced software inventory capabilities. Like its hardware counterpart, the Software Inventory Client Agent runs automatically on the client according to a schedule you create and collects information according to options you select. Similar to the Hardware Inventory Client Agent, the Software Inventory Client Agent queries the WMI for installed .exe information from the root/ccm/invagt/filesystemfile namespace. It then writes the information to the filesystemfile.log file on the management point indicating how many .exe files were found and what was not inventoried.

The Software Inventory Client Agent collects application information that includes the following data:

- File name, version, and size
- Manufacturer name
- Product name, version, and language
- Data and time of file creation (presumably at installation)

The Software Inventory Client Agent can also collect copies of specific files.

As with hardware inventory, inventory collected at the client is passed on to the management point. The management point, in turn, forwards the information to the site server. Software inventory is ultimately stored in the Configuration Manager database, so it's again important to draw a distinction between primary and secondary site servers. Recall that the main difference between a primary and a secondary site server is that a primary site server maintains access to an SQL Server database.

As with hardware inventory, you can enable the Software Inventory Client Agent for the clients on a secondary site. As a matter of fact, the configuration settings for the Software Inventory Client Agent even can be different from the secondary site's parent site. The client passes its inventory to the management point of the parent site, unless a proxy management point is installed at the secondary site.

Enabling Software Inventory

To begin, enable and install the Software Inventory Client Agent on your Configuration Manager clients. Then explore how inventory is actually collected. To enable the Software Inventory Agent through the Configuration Manager Administrator Console, follow these steps:

1. Under Site Settings, navigate to and select the Client Agents node.

2. In the results pane, right-click Software Inventory Client Agent and choose Properties from the context menu to display the Software Inventory Client Agent Properties dialog box, as shown in Figure 10-16.

Figure 10-16   The Software Inventory Client Agent Properties dialog box

3. Select the Enable Software Inventory On Clients check box.

4. The default inventory collection schedule on the client is once a week. With the Simple Schedule option, you can specify inventory collection to run once every 1 to 59 minutes, 1 to 23 hours, or 1 to 31 days. Or you can select Custom Schedule and click Customize to display the Custom Schedule dialog box, as shown in Figure 10-2, earlier in this chapter. Here you can designate a more specific start time and recurrence pattern. When you finish, click OK.

5. Click the Inventory Collection tab, as shown in Figure 10-17.

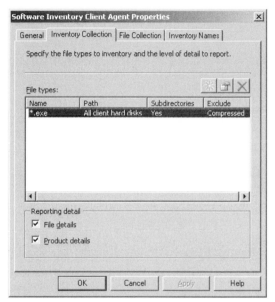

Figure 10-17   The Software Inventory Client Agent Properties dialog box Inventory Collection tab

6. Notice that the default files that the agent will scan for are those with an .exe extension. You can click the New button (the yellow star) to display the Inventoried File Properties dialog box, as shown in Figure 10-18. Here you can identify the file or files to inventory using wildcards and specific paths and choose whether to exclude encrypted or compressed files from the inventory scan. This example is asking that file and/or product details be collected about any files with the .mif extension.

7. On the Inventory Collection tab, select the appropriate options under Reporting Detail. These two options can tailor how data is collected and represented to you.

    The File Details option reports information that the agent can determine for all files that match the criteria, including unknown files. Unknown files include those for which the header information contains no product information—for example, some game files. File details include the file name, location, and size.

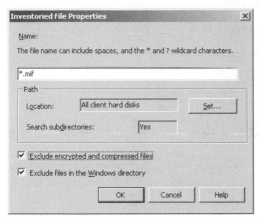

Figure 10-18   The Inventoried File Properties dialog box

The Product Details option reports information that the agent can read from the file header of all files that match the criteria. Product details include company name, product name, version, and language.

You must select at least one of the two options to enable Configuration Manager to report information on inventoried files. By default, both options are enabled.

8. Click the File Collection tab, as shown in Figure 10-19, if you also want to collect a copy of specific files from each client. The Maximum Traffic Per Client value displayed at the bottom of this tab is informational and represents the estimated amount of traffic that the specified files might generate based on the file size and, assuming a so-called fast, reliable network connection between the client and the management point.

9. To add the name of a specific file, click the New button to display the Collected File Properties dialog box, similar to the Inventoried Files dialog box, as shown in Figure 10-18. Here you can identify the file or files to inventory using wildcards and specific paths and choose whether to exclude encrypted or compressed files from the inventory scan and the maximum file size. Click OK to return to the File Collection tab. Using the Collected File Properties dialog box, the file widget.txt is added to be collected by software inventory that you see in Figure 10-19.

10. Click the Inventory Names tab, as shown in Figure 10-20, to standardize the names of the companies or products that are displayed when you view software inventory information. Sometimes, as companies update their software applications or create new versions, the developers include variations on the company's or the product's name in the header information included in the program executable. Of course,

when you view the software inventory, the products are sorted and displayed according to each variation of the company or product name. This can make it difficult for you to find all versions of the product.

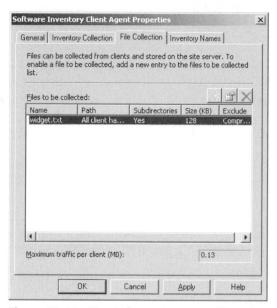

Figure 10-19   The Software Inventory Client Agent Properties dialog box File Collection tab

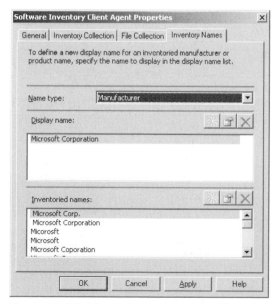

Figure 10-20   The Software Inventory Client Agent Properties dialog box Inventory Names tab

This example shown in Figure 10-20 lists several variations of the company name for Microsoft—Microsoft Corp., Microsoft Corporation, Micorosft, and so on—that will be displayed as Microsoft Corporation when viewing software inventory information.

11. Select which name type you want to standardize; your choices are Product and Manufacturer. In the Display Name section, click New to display the Display Name Properties dialog box. Type the name you want to be displayed on the product information screen and then click OK to return to the Inventory Names tab. In the Inventoried Names section, click New to display the Inventoried Name Properties dialog box. Type the names that have been inventoried by the Software Inventory Client Agent that you want standardized to the display name you typed in the Display Name section, and then click OK to return to the Inventory Names tab.

12. Click OK to begin the site update process.

Collected files are stored on the site server in the <InstallationPath> SMS\Inboxes\sinv.box\FileCol folder. If the file changes at all on the client, the Software Inventory Client Agent will collect it again at the next cycle. By default, Configuration Manager retains the last five copies of the files that were collected. Think about that. If you collected 1 MB per file and 5 collected copies per client, for 1000 clients, you would require 5 GB of storage space just for your collected files. Not pretty! Obviously, you wouldn't use this as an alternative backup process. However, you can use it to look for files that should *not* be on a client, like a game executable. The number of such collected files ought to be significantly smaller. By default all collected files are kept in the database for 90 days before they're aged out, although you can modify this setting by changing the Delete Aged Collected Files site maintenance task in the Configuration Manager console. For more information about modifying site maintenance tasks, see Chapter 22, "Maintaining the Configuration Manager Database through SQL Server."

Note   To modify the number of copies of collected files maintained at the site server, you need to modify the following registry entry: HKEY_LOCAL_MACHINE \Software\Microsoft\SMS\Components\SMS_Software_Inventory_Processor. Look for the value Maximum Collected Files and change it as desired.

When you enable the Software Inventory Client Agent, you're making a change to the site properties, and the site's site control file (Sitectrl.ct0) is updated as a result (as described in Chapter 3). The agent configuration information is incorporated into a client policy that is stored on the management point.

The next time the Configuration Manager client restarts or at the next client update interval every 25 hours the client obtains the updated client policy information and the agent is enabled and configured appropriately. At this time, the SMS_def.mof and configuration.mof file information is compiled into the WMI layer on the client, the hardware inventory log files are updated, and the agent starts.

Thirty minutes after the Software Inventory Client Agent starts, the first complete inventory is collected from the client as specified by the inventory and collected files options you specified.

Client Requirements and Inventory Frequency

The size of the software inventory file that's generated depends on what you told the agent to scan for, how much data it found, and whether you chose to collect files. Software inventory history is maintained on each client. The initial inventory is also passed to the management point and then to the site server. Like hardware inventory, subsequent software inventory cycles generally report only changes to the inventory. Therefore, you can expect a corresponding amount of network traffic associated with the installation (one time), with the first complete inventory (one time), and with subsequent delta inventories (according to your schedule).

As with hardware inventory, the schedule you choose should reflect the frequency with which you need to collect or update your clients' inventory record. If your clients have fairly standard software installations and don't make or aren't allowed to make substantial changes on their own, you could collect inventory less frequently—say, once a month.

If your client computers keep changing in terms of software installations, updates, and uninstalls, you might need to report changes to the inventory more frequently—perhaps once a week or once a day. The more frequent the inventory is collected, the more potential network traffic is generated. Like the Hardware Inventory Client Agent, the Software Inventory Client Agent continues to run and reports inventory if the computer is turned on, regardless of whether a user is actually logged onto the client.

Note   You can force the Software Inventory Client Agent to run through Systems Management in the Control Panel. Double-click the Systems Management icon to display the Systems Management Properties dialog box, and click the Actions tab. Select the Software Inventory Cycle in the Actions tab, and click Initiate Action.

Software Inventory Collection Process Flow

The first time inventory collection runs—30 minutes after enabling the Software Inventory Client Agent—a complete software inventory is collected and its history is maintained on the client. Depending on the applications installed, and whether you've chosen to also collect files, this first inventory can be rather large. Each subsequent inventory generates a delta file containing the details for only those inventory properties that have changed since the last interval. When a complete inventory file is generated, the agent writes a temporary file with an .sic (software inventory complete) extension to the Windows\System32\Ccm\Inventory\temp folder until it's moved to the management point.

Note   After the inventory file is moved to the management point, the temporary files are deleted.

The Configuration Manager Management Point File Dispatch Manager on the management point in turn moves the file to the Software Inventory Processor's inbox (the <InstallationPath> SMS\inboxes\sinv.box folder) on the site server. If the site server is a primary site server, the Software Inventory Processor writes the data to the Configuration Manager database on the server running SQL. If the file is deemed corrupt, it's written to the <InstallationPath> SMS\Inboxes\sinv.box\Badsinv folder. If a parent site exists, or if the site receiving the software inventory is a secondary site, the Software Inventory Processor forwards the file to the Replication Manager, which forwards the file to the Software Inventory Processor inbox on the parent site server. Collected files are removed from the inventory file and written to the <InstallationPath> SMS\Inboxes\sinv.box\FileCol\ID folder. Files collected from Configuration Manager clients are stored in a separate ID folder for each client. The ID folder name represents the resource ID assigned to the client when the client was discovered.

Note   You can find each client's resource ID by viewing its discovery data in the Collections folder in the Configuration Manager Administrator Console or by creating a query to display the resource IDs for all the clients.

Software Resynchronization

Occasionally, the Software Inventory Processor might determine that the inventory data it receives is somehow bad or out of sync with the Configuration Manager database. In these circumstances, a resync is triggered automatically. The following events can trigger a software inventory resync:

- The inventory delta contains updates for a database record that doesn't exist.
- The inventory delta itself contains bad or corrupted data.
- The client has attached to a new Configuration Manager site.
- The client has upgraded from SMS 2003 to Configuration Manager.

When one of these events triggers a resync, the rest of the process proceeds much like the hardware resynchronization process discussed earlier. The difference, of course, is that the Software Inventory Processor on the site server creates the resync request.

Status Messages and Log Files for Software Inventory

As you've seen, status messages and log files are generated throughout the inventory installation and collection process. As you did for hardware inventory, you begin here with the log files. As you know, client logs are enabled by default and are written automatically to the Windows\System32\Ccm\logs folder on Configuration Manager clients. Monitor the PolicyAgent.log file for updates received by the client, which includes enabling the Inventory Agent on the client and configuring hardware inventory collection. Monitor the InventoryAgent.log file, a portion of which was shown earlier in Figure 10-5, for collection of inventory data.

As with hardware inventory, you can view status messages regarding inventory activity on a client by running a status message query through the Configuration Manager Administrator Console using the process described earlier. A message with ID 10600 indicates that inventory has been successfully collected; 10605 indicates that a file has been collected; 10204 from the Client Component Information Manager (CCIM) reports that the Software Inventory Client Agent was successfully installed.

On the site server, monitor the status messages of the Software Inventory Processor. Look for messages in the 37xx range, which identify successful processing of MIF files. Also monitor status messages for the Replication Manager for forwarding of MIF files to a parent site.

As with hardware inventory, you can also use the Configuration Manager Report Viewer to view status information related to the inventory process.

Viewing Software Inventory

You can view software inventory through the Configuration Manager console as well as through Web reports in much the same way as you view hardware inventory. The procedure using the console is described here:

1. Navigate to the Computer Management\Collections node and expand it.

2. Select the collection that contains the client or clients whose inventory you want to view.

3. Right-click the appropriate client entry in the results pane, choose Start from the context menu, and then choose Resource Explorer.

4. In the Resource Explorer window, expand Software to view a list of collected files and software, as shown in Figure 10-21.

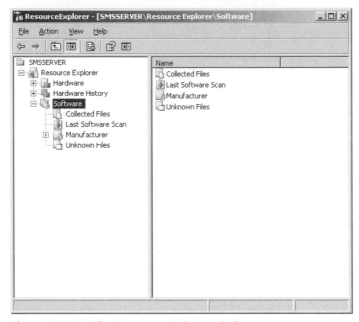

Figure 10-21   The Resource Explorer window

5. Select Collected Files to view a list of files collected from the client. You can double-click each file to open and review the contents of the collected file.

Important   Don't open an executable or other program file this way unless you know what the result might be. Running an unknown file could cause your computer (or site server, if you are performing this action there) to crash.

---

6. Select Last Software Scan to determine the last time the agent ran.

7. Select and expand Manufacturer to see a list of inventoried files sorted by manufacturer, as shown in Figure 10-22. Expand each manufacturer to see the list of applications associated with that manufacturer. Select each application to see a list of files associated with that application, including the file name, description, file size, file version, and file location. In Figure 10-22, you can see the list of Configuration Manager (reflected as Systems Management Server:4.00) files installed on this client.

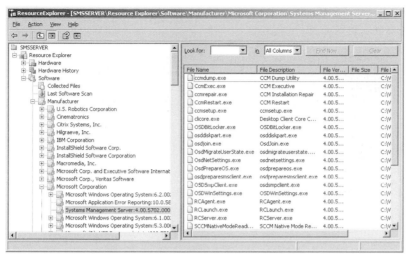

Figure 10-22   Software inventory sorted by manufacturer

8. Select Unknown Files to view a list of files that the inventory process could not associate with a manufacturer, as shown in Figure 10-23. These are generally files that do not include manufacturer information coded in the header data of the file.

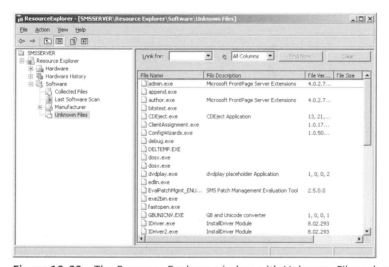

Figure 10-23   The Resource Explorer window with Unknown Files selected

Asset Intelligence

With Systems Management Server 2003 Service Pack 3, Microsoft introduced Asset Intelligence. The result of an acquisition, Asset Intelligence combines a data store of over 2,000 known software applications with the Configuration Manager database. The Asset Intelligence data store presents installation information about software applications in a far more friendly way than the Configuration Manager Resource Explorer. It compares the manufacturer files against its data store, and merges the data into a single application entry. For example, when Configuration Manager collects inventory about Microsoft Word, it collects and sorts files under the manufacturer Microsoft, and the software application Microsoft Word. However, any file that has references to Microsoft Word in the header data of the file appear in this list—.exe files, .dll files, and so on. And, you have no way of knowing how many instances of Word might be installed, or what versions might be installed.

Asset Intelligence Reports

Asset Intelligence provides more "intelligent" reporting about these software applications through a series of reports added to the Configuration Manager reports. Software products are grouped by family (communications, corporate, personal, and so on) and category—human resources and accounting within corporate, or games and DVD players within personal. In addition to software information, Asset Intelligence can also report on hardware information and license data. Many reports provide drill-down capabilities to subreports that provide a greater level of detail. Most software and hardware reports eventually drill into a Computer Details report. You can find detailed information about viewing all Configuration Manager reports in Chapter 19.

Asset Intelligence reports are divided into three categories:

- Software Asset Management reports
- Hardware Asset Management reports
- License Management reports

Twelve *Software Asset Management* reports provide information about software applications installed on Configuration Manager clients. For example, you can run the Computers With A Specified Software Product report to find all the Configuration Manager clients that have Microsoft Word installed. You can run the Installed Software On A Specific Computer report to find out what software applications have been installed on a specified client.

Thirteen *Hardware Asset Management* reports provide information about hardware devices installed on Configuration Manager clients, and to the extent that the information is available through the computer BIOS, these reports can provide asset tag information as well. For example, you can run the Computers Within An Age Range report to display all the clients that have a CPU that was manufactured within a specified date range. You can run the Computers With A Specified USB Device report to display all clients that are connected to a particular USB device. You can run the Hardware That Is Not Ready For A Software Upgrade report to list the clients that do not meet the minimum hard drive, memory, processor, or operating system requirements to upgrade to or install a specified software application.

Ten *License Management* reports provide Microsoft license information about software applications such as volume or site licenses, stand-alone licenses, or licenses obtained through sales channels. You can use these reports to identify when clients are running software applications that are not within accepted company license channels. For example, you can run the License Information On A Specified Computer report to display the Windows Vista volume licensing information on a specific client. You can run the Count Of Licenses By License Status report to display the clients that are reporting an unlicensed, licensed, out-of-box grace, or out-of-box tolerance/expired grace period status. Most License Management reports require that the Windows Vista Key Management Service (KMS) be installed to successfully run the report.

The *Microsoft License Ledger* report, found under the License Management reports has particular significance, because this is the main Microsoft license compliance reporting mechanism. This report is intended to be used in conjunction with the Microsoft License Statement for a software application and facilitate the analysis of license usage and compliance within your organization.

Summary

Well, that's it for the inventory collection process. As you can see, Configuration Manager can report on a lot of stuff—both hardware-related and software-related. Using the SMS_def.mof and configuration.mof files, and customized NOIDMIF and IDMIF files, you can append data to the existing client architecture and add new architectures, object classes, and attributes to the database. You can view inventory through Resource Explorer, and you can further refine what you see through the use of queries.

The Asset Intelligence reports facilitate viewing and assessing software application data, giving you a clearer picture of the applications installed on your clients and a better way to manage software license compliance within your organization.

Because the inventory process is fairly straightforward, this chapter didn't include a "Check-points" section. You can easily spot and correct any problems you might encounter by monitoring the log files and status messages. You're more likely to encounter issues as you work with MOF Manager and create custom MIF files, and, in that regard, there are no better resources than the *System Center Configuration Manager Documentation Library* included and installed with the product, and available online through the Microsoft Configuration Manager TechCenterWeb site (http://technet.microsoft.com/en-us/configmgr/default.aspx).

Chapter 17, "Managing Clients Remotely," continues your exploration of client management tools as you look at Remote Tools.

Chapter 11
Distributing Software Packages

New apps transform you
As spring calls forth pink blossoms:
Software Distribution
~ Author Unknown

One of the primary features of System Center Configuration Manager 2007 is its ability to distribute packages to, and run programs on, Configuration Manager client computers. This process consists of three main elements:

- Creating and distributing the package
- Advertising a package program to a collection
- Receiving the advertisement and executing the program on a client

The package distribution process is the focus of this chapter. First, some terms are defined and just what Configuration Manager does throughout the distribution process is outlined. Then you'll explore the administrative tasks involved in the creation of packages and advertisements. Finally, you learn how to monitor status messages and log files for the appropriate Configuration Manager components involved and how to test the package and its programs to ensure that they execute properly on the target clients.

Defining Package Distribution

Somehow, Configuration Manager administrators and users often misunderstand or mislabel the package distribution process. It's important to remember that Configuration Manager is fundamentally a package delivery tool. Basically, Configuration Manager is designed to make a package that you create available to a specified target or targets. The key here is that you are responsible for creating the package. You're also responsible for ensuring that the package will execute as intended when it reaches its target. Configuration Manager will get it there for you, but Configuration Manager won't correct errors for you—nor should you expect it to.

Look at it this way: suppose you send a bicycle to your nephew. You box up the parts carefully, including instructions on how to assemble it, go to your nearest package delivery service office, fill out the appropriate forms, pay the appropriate fees, and hand over the box. The responsibility of the package delivery service now is to get the box containing the bicycle to your nephew's house within the time frame you specified and paid for. When the package arrives at your nephew's house, he opens the package, reads the instructions, and assembles the bicycle. The extent to which your nephew is successful depends on how accurate and easy to understand the instructions are.

Configuration Manager works in much the same way. You, the Configuration Manager administrator, are responsible for creating the package and ensuring that all the appropriate pieces are assembled: source files, scripts, executables, command switches, and so on. You identify where the package must go and who should receive it. Configuration Manager carries out your instructions and even "opens" the package when it arrives at the target. However, the package's ability to execute—or the user's ability to use the application, for that matter—isn't Configuration Manager's responsibility.

Understanding Package Distribution Terminology

This description of the basic package distribution process uses some terms with which you're probably familiar. Take a moment here to review these terms in more detail.

A Configuration Manager *package* generally represents a software application that needs to be installed on a Configuration Manager client computer. However, a package might also contain update programs or software patches, single files such as a virus update file, or no files at all—just a command to execute a program already resident on the client. You need to identify to Configuration Manager exactly what the package consists of.

Every package must contain at least one program. A Configuration Manager *program* identifies what should occur on the client when the package is received. Perhaps a setup routine is executed, or a virus scan is performed, or a file is copied to a particular directory. Perhaps the user needs to supply information such as the program directory, or perhaps no user intervention is required at all. A package may have several programs associated with it, allowing the application to be run in a variety of ways on different clients. Consider a Microsoft Office installation. You can choose to perform one of several types of software installation, including Typical, Custom, or Laptop installation. If this software were a Configuration Manager package—and it could be—you would have to include a program for each of these installation methods if you intended to use them. Once again, you must define the program to Configuration Manager and include any and all appropriate references to script files or command switches. The program also defines the platform and environment within which the package can run. For example, can the package run on any platform or only on Microsoft Windows XP computers with Service Pack 2 installed? Can the program be executed by any user, or can it run only in an administrator context?

Some applications include predefined scripts called package definition files that can be used with Configuration Manager. Package definition files contain all the package and program information required for Configuration Manager to successfully distribute the package and, usually, to deploy it. Package definition files are often included with the application's source file, or they can be obtained from the developer. You can also create package definition files using various tools and utilities from Microsoft. Package definition files are covered later in this chapter in the section "Creating a Package from a Definition File."

An *advertisement* makes the program and package available to a specified collection. Recall from Chapter 9, "Defining Collections," that collections can contain not only Configuration Manager client computers but also Windows users and groups. This means that a program can be advertised to clients as well as to users and groups. So before you create the advertisement, you need to create the appropriate collections.

Advertisements are often used to schedule when a program runs and to specify whether the user can reschedule the program. Advertisements can also be configured to recur— that is, to make a program available on a recurring basis. For example, if you distribute an application update file on a monthly basis, you might create an application update package and program and then an advertisement that makes the application update file available on a monthly basis.

The Advertised Programs Client Agent is installed on the Configuration Manager client when you first install the client and assign it to a site. As with other client agents, this agent is optional, and the Configuration Manager administrator must configure and enable it. The Advertised Programs Client Agent's job is to monitor for available advertised programs that target the client or the user at the client. When an advertisement is found and the program is ready to be run, the agent connects to an available distribution point—as defined in the package details—to execute the program. If the program runs an existing file on the client, the agent executes the program appropriately.

Two Configuration Manager site systems, management points and distribution points, in addition to the site server, are involved in the package distribution process. The management point is always the point of interchange between the site server and Configuration Manager clients. In this exchange, package detail information and advertisements are copied as a policy to the management point for propagation to the client. The actual source files that constitute the package are copied to distribution points. Before you can distribute any packages, you need to have an assigned management point and at least one distribution point. Remember that the site server becomes a distribution point by default when you install Configuration Manager. Remember, too, that you can have only one management point defined per site. (The role of site systems and how they're assigned is discussed in Chapter 3, "Configuring Site Server Properties and Deploying Site Systems.")

Preparing for Package Distribution

As you can see from the previous section, many components are involved in package distribution. Before continuing the discussion of package distribution, look at the following list of actions required for the distribution process:

- Define your distribution points for the package.
- Create appropriate collections.
- Gather all source files, setup routines, scripts, and so on, needed for the package.
- Create the Configuration Manager package.
- Define at least one program for the package.
- Distribute the package to the distribution points.
- Advertise the programs to one or more collections.
- Execute the advertised program on the client.

After reviewing these elements of the distribution process, you'll have a solid foundation on which to build. The following sections of this chapter cover how to configure various components for package distribution.

Creating Packages for Distribution

Now you can delve into the package distribution process in more detail, beginning with package creation itself. This section explores the package creation process, including identifying distribution points and creating programs.

Gathering Source Files

If your package involves the accessing of source files, such as performing a software installation, you must define a location for the source files. The location can be a shared folder on the site server or on a remote server, including a CD-ROM drive. The most important characteristic of the source file location is that it must be accessible to the Configuration Manager site server using the site server's computer account. If your program involves using a script file or files, be sure to include them as part of your source files as well or the program will fail.

Creating a Package from Scratch

As in all things Configuration Manager, you begin in the Configuration Manager console. You can create a package either from scratch—one for which you provide all the configuration details—or from a package definition file that already contains all the package details. This section looks at creating a package from scratch.

To create a package from the ground up, follow these steps:

1. Navigate to the Computer Management\Software Distribution\Packages folder, right-click it, choose New from the context menu, and then choose Package to run the New Package Wizard, as shown in Figure 11-1.

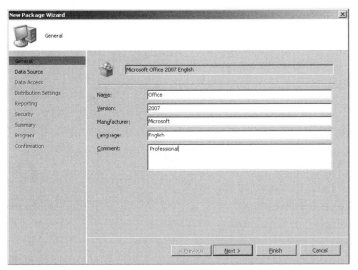

Figure 11-1   The New Package Wizard General page

2. On the General page, type the name of the package, its version, its publisher, its language, and a descriptive comment if desired. The only required value here is Name. Notice that the full package name is displayed in the text box at the top of the screen.

3. Click Next to display the Data Source page, as shown in Figure 11-2. This page lets you define details concerning the source files for the package. If the package contains source files—even a single file—select the This Package Contains Source Files check box to enable the options in the Source Directory frame.

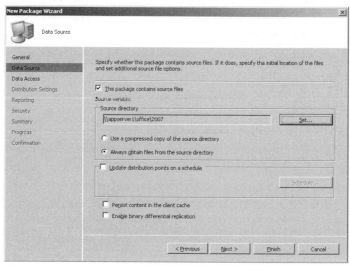

Figure 11-2   The Data Source page

4. Click Set to display the Set Source Directory dialog box, as shown in Figure 11-3. In this dialog box, you define the location of the source files. The location can be either a local drive path on the site server or a Universal Naming Convention (UNC) path to a remote share. Type the location or click Browse to look for the directory. Then click OK to return to the Data Source tab.

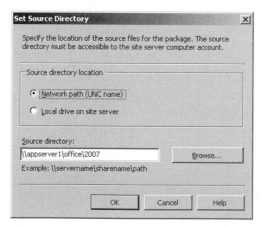

Figure 11-3   The Set Source Directory dialog box

If your source files aren't likely to change or are on a removable medium such as a CD-ROM, or if the source path is likely to change, select the Use A Compressed Copy Of The Source Directory option. This option causes Configuration Manager to create and store a compressed version of the source files on the site server. When the package needs to be sent to a new distribution point or updated on existing distribution points, Configuration Manager will access the compressed files, uncompress them, and send them to the distribution points.

If your source files are likely to change periodically—for example, if they include a monthly update file—select Always Obtain Files From The Source Directory. Selecting this option also allows you to select the Update Distribution Points On A Schedule check box. Setting an update schedule ensures that as the source files change, the distribution points will be updated regularly.

Select the option Persist Content In The Client Cache if you want the package content to remain cached on the target client computer indefinitely. By default, the client cache is adjusted as new programs become available for download. Older programs can be deleted to make room for new programs. Selecting this option might prevent programs from being downloaded to the client computer, especially if there is not enough available space left in the cache.

The Enable Binary Differential Replication option allows binary delta comparison for source files that have changed for this package. This means that if a source file changes, only the parts of the file that have changed are distributed rather than the entire file. This can result in performance and bandwidth savings.

5. Click Next to display the Data Access page, as shown in Figure 11-4. The Data Access page defines how Configuration Manager will store the package source files on distribution points. The default setting is Access The Distribution Folder Through Common ConfigMgr Package Share. With this setting, Configuration Manager will define a shared folder on the distribution points and place the source files in a folder in that share. If you create a new distribution point, the share will always be SMSPKGx$, where x represents the drive with the most free disk space. This share is a hidden share to keep prying eyes from browsing for it. When Configuration Manager runs out of disk space, it finds the next drive with the most free space and creates an additional SMSPKGx$ directory and share there.

    If you prefer to create your own folder organization and access shares, you may do so first and then reference the share by selecting the Share The Distribution Folder option and typing the UNC path to the share. This value can be a share or a share and a path, but whatever value you enter must be unique among all packages. Also, the share and path must already exist on every distribution point that you target. If you type only a share name (in the form *server**appshare*), any file or subfolders created within the share will be deleted and re-created whenever the package is updated or refreshed. If you type a share that includes a path (*server**appshare**word*), only the down-level folder will be deleted and re-created.

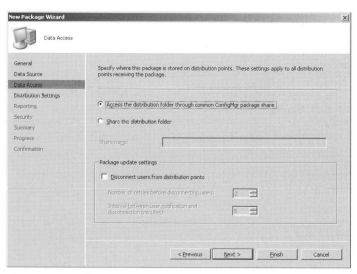

Figure 11-4   The Data Access page

Select Disconnect Users From Distribution Points to do just that. If you want to ensure that no users are connected to the package folder on the distribution points when files are being refreshed or updated, this option will cause Configuration Manager to inform users that they will be disconnected. Users will be disconnected after the time period you specify in the User Grace Period text box. The default value is 5 minutes, but you can specify from 0 to 59 minutes. The Number Of Retries Before Disconnecting Users option indicates how many times Configuration Manager will attempt to refresh the distribution points before disconnecting users. This value can range from 0 to 99.

6. Click Next to display the Distribution Settings page, as shown in Figure 11-5. On this page, you identify the sending priority and preferred sender to use when sending this package to distribution points in a child site. If you have no child sites, these settings will have no effect. (Refer to Chapter 4, "Implementing Multiple-Site Structures," for a discussion of parent-child relationships and the role of the sender in transferring information between sites in the hierarchy.)

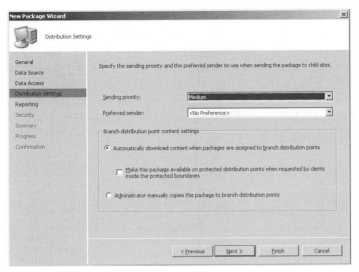

Figure 11-5   The Distribution Settings page

7. There are two main options available in the Branch Distribution Point Content Settings section. Branch distribution points are discussed in more detail later in this chapter. The Automatically Download Content When Packages Are Assigned To Branch Distribution Points option is selected by default and ensures that the package content (source files, and so on) are copied to any branch distribution points you specify. With this default option selected, you can also enable the Make This Package Available On Protected Distribution Points When Requested By Clients Inside The Protected Boundaries option. That's a long option name! What it means, essentially, is you can configure boundaries that a client must be in to use a protected distribution point. Clients outside the boundaries are unable to download or run packages from the protected distribution point. If a client is in the designated boundaries and can access a branch distribution point that has not already been designated as a distribution point for the package, selecting this option ensures that the package will be downloaded to the branch distribution point for that client to access.

    Because a branch distribution point might be a desktop computer in a remote location, you might prefer to manually copy the source files to that computer; for example, after business hours. In this case, select the Administrator Manually Copies This Package To Branch Distribution Points option.

8. Click Next to display the Reporting page, as shown in Figure 11-6. This page lets you identify how Configuration Manager reports installation status Management

Information Format (MIF) files from the client when the package is run. Select Use Package Properties For Status MIF Matching to simply use the values you supplied on the General page to identify status MIF files generated during installation. Or select Use These Fields For Status MIF Matching and fill in the fields if you want to specify different values for reporting purposes.

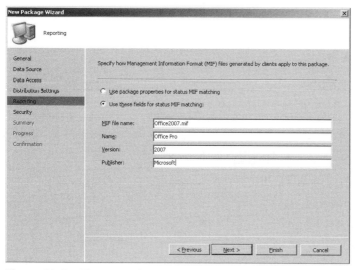

Figure 11-6   The Reporting page

9. Click Next to display the Security tab to set class and instance security rights for the package. This type of security is discussed in Chapter 20, "Configuration Manager 2007 Security."

10. Click Next to view and review details on the Summary page, and then click Next again to begin the package creation process. Click Close on the Confirmation page to close the wizard.

You haven't quite finished creating this package. If you expand the new package entry you just created in the Configuration Manager console, as in the example shown in Figure 11-7, you'll see that three areas of configuration remain. The first area, defining access accounts, allows you to further secure who has access to the distribution source files. The other two areas are absolutely essential to the successful distribution of the package: defining distribution points, without which the client has no access to the source files; and defining programs, which specifies how to install or run the source files. Configure the access account first.

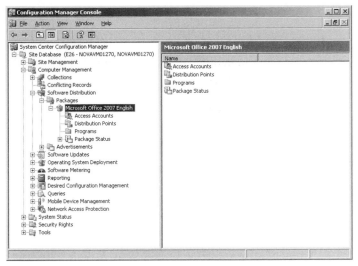

Figure 11-7   A sample expanded package entry

Defining Access Accounts

By default, when Configuration Manager creates the SMSPKGx$ share, it grants Read access to the local Users group and Full Control to the Administrators group. The default Users and Administrators entries map to the local Users and Administrators groups for Windows distribution points. These accounts are known as generic access accounts.

Because the default share is a hidden share, the only way a client should know that a package is available to it is through the package distribution process. In other words, the client agent will see an advertisement for that package that targets a collection of which the client is a member. Bear in mind that users will be users, and it's possible that they will find the hidden share, navigate to a package folder, and execute any programs they find there. This could also happen if you create your own shares.

There are a couple of ways to deal with this little breach of security. One is for you to evaluate the share (or NT file system [NTFS]) security for the Configuration Manager shares or for the package folders within the share. This is a time-consuming and potentially destructive process if you happen to lock out Configuration Manager from accessing the share. The other solution is to define access accounts for the package through the Configuration Manager console. When you define an access account, you also define the level of access or permission for the specified user or group. This is much like creating access control lists (ACLs) in Windows.

To define an access account, follow these steps:

1. Navigate to the Packages folder, find your package entry, and expand it.

2. Right-click Access Accounts, choose New from the context menu, and then choose the type of access account you want to create.

3. The two types of access accounts are listed here:

   ❑ **Windows User Access Account**   Defines a Windows user or group account and the level of permission allowed for that account.

   ❑ **Generic Access Account**   Defines additional or replacement user, guest, or administrator accounts and the level of permission to all for those accounts. This account type maps to an operating system-specific account.

   Select the appropriate option to display the New Generic Access Account Properties dialog box or Windows Access Account Properties dialog box. The New Windows User Access Account properties dialog box is shown in Figure 11-8.

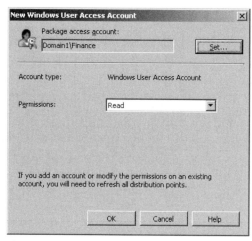

Figure 11-8   The New Windows User Access Account properties dialog box

4. Click Set to specify the account information as follows:

   ❑ For a Windows user account, the Windows User Account dialog box will appear, as shown in Figure 11-9. Type the user or group account in \Domain\user format and select User or Group.

Figure 11-9   The Windows User Account dialog box

❏   For a Generic account, the Generic Account dialog box will appear, as shown in Figure 11-10. Select the account type.

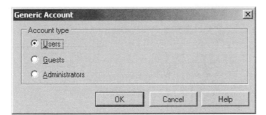

Figure 11-10   The Generic Account dialog box

5.   Click OK to return to the Access Account Properties dialog box. Select the appropriate level of permissions from the Permissions drop-down list. For most applications, Read permission is sufficient. However, if the program requires any kind of writing back to the source directory, you need to assign at least Change permission.

6.   Click OK to create the account.

Defining Distribution Points

An essential configuration detail for any package that contains source files is identifying the distribution points on which the package can be found. You should have already assigned the distribution point role to one or more site systems in your Configuration Manager site, as well as at any child sites. You now need to tell Configuration Manager which of those distribution points will host the package.

Note   If you're distributing the package to a child site, even if the Configuration Manager administrator for that site will ultimately distribute the package to its clients, you still must identify at least one distribution point at that child site when you create the package.

To define distribution points, follow these steps:

1. Navigate to the Packages folder, find your package entry, and expand it.

2. Right-click Distribution Points, and choose New Distribution Points from the context menu to run the New Distribution Points Wizard, as shown in Figure 11-11.

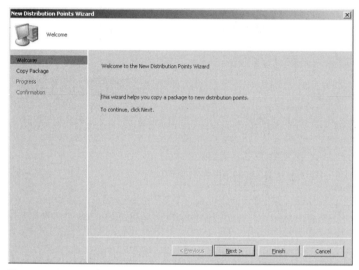

Figure 11-11   The New Distribution Points Wizard Welcome page

3. Click Next to display the Copy Package page, as shown in Figure 11-12. This page shows a list of available distribution points. Scroll through the list and select the distribution points you want.

4. Click Select Group to open the Browse Distribution Point Group dialog box, as shown in Figure 11-13. Here you can view a list of distribution point groups and their member site systems. If you select one of the distribution point groups and click OK, all the site systems that are members of that group will be selected in the Copy Package page.

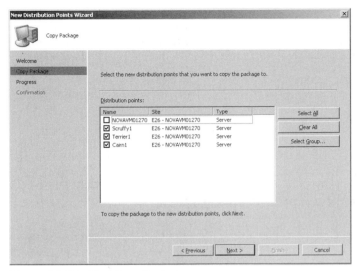

Figure 11-12   The Copy Package page

Figure 11-13   The Browse Distribution Point Group dialog box

5. Click Next to add the distribution points you selected to the package details, and then click Close to exit the wizard.

After you add a distribution point to the package, that distribution point no longer appears in the list of available distribution points if you run the New Distribution Points Wizard again. The wizard displays only distribution points that are available. If you need to remove a distribution point from the package, select it, right-click it, and choose Delete from the context menu. When you delete a distribution point, you also delete the package source directory on that distribution point.

It's often desirable to group distribution points so that packages can be distributed to them as a block rather than having to name the distribution points individually. Distribution point groups are defined through the site settings of your site—in the same place that you assign the distribution point role.

To define a distribution point group, follow these steps:

1. In the Configuration Manager console, navigate to the Site Settings\Site Systems folder and expand it.

2. In the left pane, select the site system assigned with the distribution point role that you want to add to a distribution group.

3. In the Details pane, right-click the distribution point role and choose Properties from the context menu to display the ConfigMgr Distribution Point Properties dialog box, as shown in Figure 11-14.

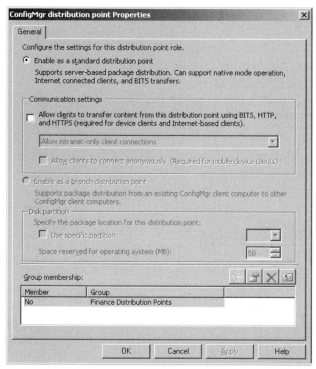

Figure 11-14   The ConfigMgr Distribution Point Properties dialog box

4. To add a new distribution point group, in the Group Membership section click the New button (the yellow star) to display the Distribution Point Group dialog box, as shown in Figure 11-15. Type the name of the group and indicate whether this site system is to be a member of the distribution point group. Then click OK to return to the ConfigMgr Distribution Point Properties dialog box.

Figure 11-15   The Distribution Point Group dialog box

5. Repeat steps 2 through 4 to select the next site system you want to include in the distribution point group. Notice that any distribution point groups you have created are listed in the ConfigMgr Distribution Point Properties dialog box for each site system, as shown in Figure 11-16.

6. Select the distribution point group that this site system should be a member of and click the Properties button (the hand holding a piece of paper) to display the Distribution Point Group Properties dialog box, as shown in Figure 11-17. Select the Include This Site System In This Distribution Point Group check box and then click OK to return to the Distribution Point tab. The site system now shows that it's a member of the distribution point group, as shown in Figure 11-18. Click OK again.

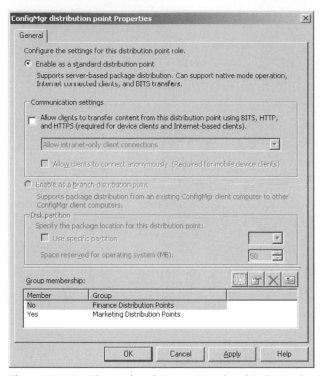

Figure 11-16   The updated Group Membership list in the ConfigMgr Distribution Point Properties dialog box

Figure 11-17   The updated Distribution Point Group dialog box

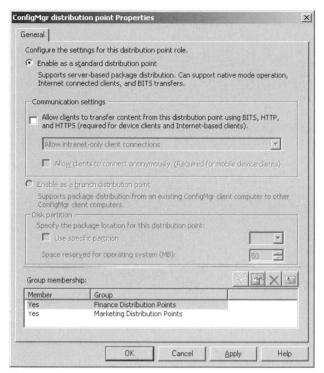

Figure 11-18   The updated ConfigMgr Distribution Point Properties dialog box

7. Repeat step 5 for every site system that needs to be a member of a distribution point group.

If you need to remove a site system from a distribution point group, simply repeat this procedure, but clear the Include This Site System In This Distribution Point Group check box. If you need to remove a distribution point group altogether, select any site system and open its ConfigMgr Distribution Point Properties, as described earlier. Select the distribution point group in the Group Membership list and click the Delete button (the red X).

Creating Programs

Finally, it's necessary to create at least one program for each package. This program specifies how the package is to be executed at the client. Many packages can have more than one program associated with them. For example, a package might have different installation methods such as Custom, Typical, Unattended, and Manual. This is where you really have to know your package. The command-line information you provide here will either make or break the package when it's run on the client. You can create programs for managed devices as well as managed computers.

To create a program, follow these steps:

1. Navigate to the Packages folder, find your package entry, and expand it.

2. Right-click Programs, choose New from the context menu, and then choose Program to display the General page of the New Program Wizard, as shown in Figure 11-19.

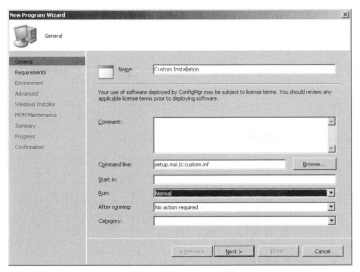

Figure 11-19   The General page of the New Program Wizard

3. On the General page, type a descriptive name for the program—for example, Custom Installation or Unattended Installation. Type additional descriptive information in the Comment text box.

   In the Command Line text box, type the command that should be executed at the client. For example, this could be a Setup.exe file, a batch file, or an .msi file; however, you must include any and all command-line arguments required for successful execution. For example, if you run the Setup program, which uses a script file called Custom.inf, and the Setup program invokes this script file through a "/c" command-line switch, you must type the full command as it references the script: `setup.msi /c:custom.inf.`

   In the Start In text box, type the name and path of the directory in which you want the program to start. This field is optional, and by default the distribution folder on the distribution point is used.

From the Run drop-down list, select an option—Normal, Minimized, Maximized, or Hidden—to specify how the program will be displayed to the user. Hidden means that nothing will be displayed; this option is best used with fully unattended, or silent, installations.

From the After Running drop-down list, select an option—No Action Required, ConfigMgr Restarts Computer, Program Restarts Computer, or ConfigMgr Logs User Off—to specify what action, if any, will be performed after the program completes.

4. Click Next to display the Requirements page, as shown in Figure 11-20. This page lets you specify descriptive elements regarding the program's estimated size and installation run time. More importantly, it allows you to identify on which operating system platforms the program can run. This enables you to filter out those clients on whose platform the program can't run.

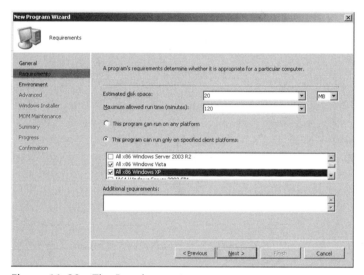

Figure 11-20   The Requirements page

5. Click Next to display the Environment page, as shown in Figure 11-21. In this tab, user interaction and drive mode requirements are defined. First, specify when the program can run. The drop-down list options are Only When A User Is Logged On, which might apply particularly when user interaction is required; Whether Or Not A User Is Logged On; and Only When No User Is Logged On. If either of these last two options is selected, the Run With User's Rights Under Run Mode option is automatically disabled because no user interaction is implied as required and there is no gurantee that a user will be logged on at the time when this program is run.

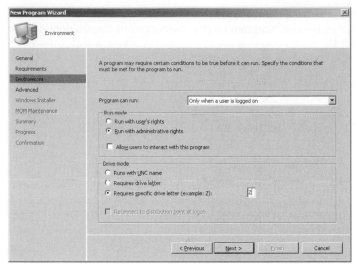

Figure 11-21   The Environment page

If the program requires the user to click even a single OK button, you must select Only When A User Is Logged On from the Program Can Run drop-down list. If the program must be run in the local administrative security context, select the Run With Administrative Rights option in the Run Mode frame. If you select this option, you can also select the Allow Users To Interact With This Program option if the user must enter information while the program runs. Clear this option only if the program is fully scripted (automated). You can also select Allow Users To Interact With This Program if you selected Whether Or Not A User Is Logged On, and user interaction is required, or allowed.

Important   Selecting Allow Users To Interact With This Program with the Run With Administrative Rights option allows any connected user to interact with the program in an administrative security context. This could provide an opportunity for a security breach on that client. Select this option only if absolutely necessary for the successful execution of the program.

In the Drive Mode frame, select the option that best fits the program. As you have no doubt experienced, although most programs understand UNC paths, some do not and require a drive letter mapping. If you need to have the client reconnect to the distribution point each time the user logs on, select the Reconnect To Distribution Point At Logon check box. This option could be useful if the application needs to write information back to the distribution folder on the distribution point, retrieve startup files, and so on.

6. Click Next to display the Advanced page, as shown in Figure 11-22, which provides several additional options. If you need to run another program before this one—for example, to install a service pack or a patch, select the Run Another Program First check box and then select the appropriate package and program. This assumes, of course, that you have already created the other package and program. In this example, you won't need to advertise the other program separately.

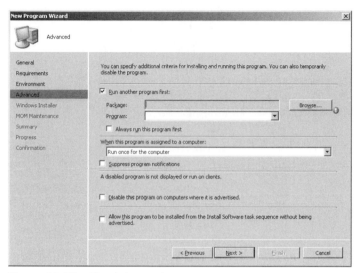

Figure 11-22   The Advanced page

If you've assigned a program to run on a computer, you can either execute it once for the computer or once for every user who logs on to the computer by choosing one of two run-time options in the When This Program Is Assigned To A Computer section. Select Run Once For The Computer, the default, to execute the program once for use by all users on the computer. Select Run Once For Every User Who Logs On to execute the program once for each user when the user logs on. Note that this option is only available if you select Only When A User Is Logged On on the Environment page. Use the Suppress Program Notifications check box to turn off notification and countdown icons and messages for this program.

To temporarily disable the program from being run—even if it has been assigned a specific time—select the Disable This Program On Clients Where It Is Advertised check box. This option can be handy if you need to update files, test an installation, and so on.

Finally, if you are using a task sequence to run this program—for example, as part of an operating system deployment—select Allow This Program To Be Installed From

The Install Software Task Sequence Without Being Advertised. The Install Software task sequence referenced in this option is a task sequence step that allows you to specify a package and program to run as part of a task sequence. Task sequences are discussed in more detail in Chapter 12, "Deploying Operating Systems."

7. Click Next to display the Windows Installer page, as shown in Figure 11-23, to specify Windows Installer product information to enable Configuration Manager to manage the location of source files for Windows Installer-based programs. This feature is useful for determining the location of source files when Windows Installer needs to initiate a repair. Click Import to locate and select the Windows Installer package associated with the program and populate the Windows Installer Product Code and Windows Installer File fields.

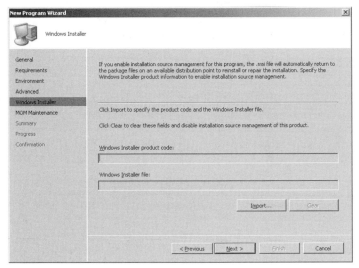

Figure 11-23   The Windows Installer page

8. Click Next to display the MOM Maintenance Mode page, as shown in Figure 11-24. If you are using System Center Operations Manager (or Microsoft Operations Manager) to monitor activity on your servers and clients, it is possible that when the program runs, it could trigger an Operations Manager rule. This might be intentional, but it could also be a false alarm for the Operations Manager administrator. For example, a system restart after a software installation might be misinterpreted as a problem for that computer. To minimize the effects of this scenario, select Disable Operations Manager Alerts While This Program Runs. Additionally, you can notify the Operations Manager administrator if the program fails by selecting Generate Operations Manager Alert If This Program Fails.

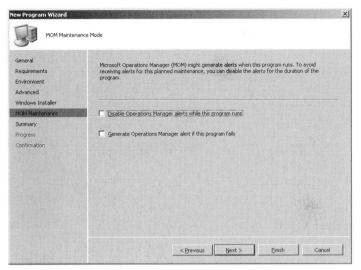

Figure 11-24   The MOM Maintenance Mode page

9.   Click Next to review and confirm your settings, click Next again to create the program, and then click Close to exit the wizard.

To create a program for a managed mobile device, follow these steps:

1.   Navigate to the Packages folder, find your package entry, and expand it.

2.   Right-click Programs, choose New from the context menu, and then choose Program For Device to display the General page of the New Program For Device Properties Wizard, as shown in Figure 11-25.

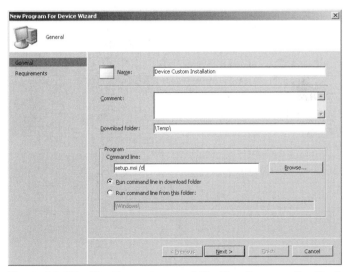

Figure 11-25   The General page of the New Program For Device Wizard

3. On the General page, type a descriptive name for the program. Type additional descriptive information in the Comment text box.

    Specify the download folder on the mobile device that the program should be downloaded to if other than the default \Temp\. In the Command Line text box, type or browse for the command that should be executed at the client. Select Run Command Line In Download Folder if the command should run in the folder you specified, or select Run Command Line From This Folder and enter the appropriate folder.

4. Click Next to display the Requirements page, as shown in Figure 11-26. This page lets you specify descriptive elements regarding the program's estimated size and any additional requirements. From the Download Program drop-down list, you can choose to download the program Any Time, Only Over A Fast Network, or Only When The Device Is Docked.

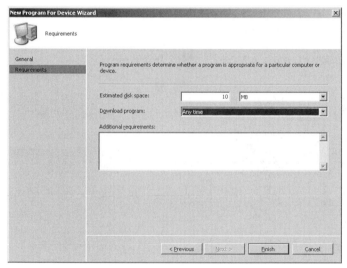

Figure 11-26   The Requirements page

5. Click Finish to create the program and exit the wizard.

If you later decide to delete a program, right-click the program in the Configuration Manager console and choose Delete from the context menu to activate the Delete Program Wizard. This wizard walks you through the process and helps you decide whether to delete the program. Deleting a program produces a ripple effect for other Configuration Manager components. Any advertisements of the program will also be deleted and will no longer be made available to the client. The wizard displays all the affected advertisements and prompts you once more to confirm the deletion.

In Chapter 9, you examined the advantages of using collections whose membership rules are query-based when advertising programs. When a new member joins the collection, it automatically receives any advertisements made to that collection. In general, you should leave programs advertised until they're no longer needed or until they should be retired.

Creating a Package from a Definition File

You've seen what's involved in creating a package from the ground up. Now you can see how much simpler the process becomes when you're creating a package from a package definition file.

To create a package from a predefined definition file, follow these steps:

1. Navigate to the Packages folder, right-click it, choose New from the context menu, and then choose Package From Definition. This initiates the Create Package From Definition Wizard, as shown in Figure 11-27.

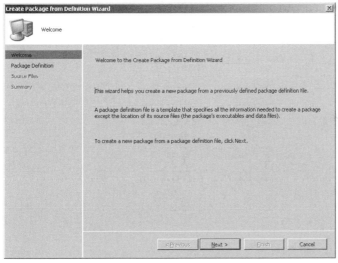

Figure 11-27   The Create Package From Definition Wizard Welcome page

2. Click Next to display the Package Definition page, as shown in Figure 11-28. Select one of the definitions included with Configuration Manager from the Package Definition list or click Browse to search for a Configuration Manager–compatible .sms or .pdf file or for a Windows Installer (.msi) package file.

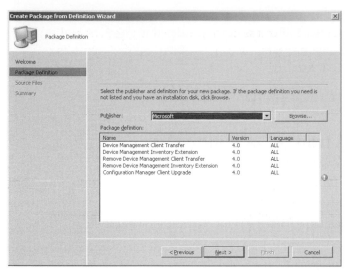

Figure 11-28   The Package Definition page

3. Click Next to display the Source Files page, as shown in Figure 11-29. Here you specify how Configuration Manager should manage source files.

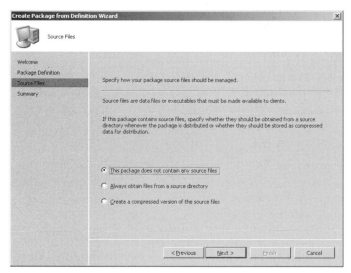

Figure 11-29   The Source Files page

4. If you select This Package Does Not Contain Any Source Files and click Next, you'll proceed directly to step 5. If you select one of the other options and click Next, the Source Directory page appears, as shown in Figure 11-30. On this page, identify either the network or local drive location of the source files and click Next.

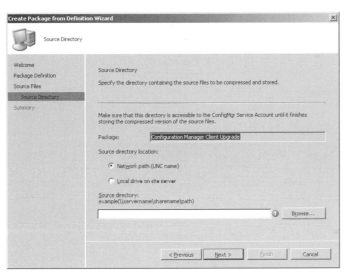

Figure 11-30   The Source Directory page

5. The Summary page is displayed. Review your choices and then click Finish.

Right-clicking the package you just created in the Configuration Manager console will display the package's Properties dialog box. The result will be the creation of a package with the essential package details filled in and the appropriate programs created with their essential details specified in the General, Data Source, and, sometimes, the Reporting tabs of the package's Properties dialog box. The Data Access and Distribution Settings tabs are left with the default values. Figures 11-31 through 11-36 will give you an idea of the type of information generated by the package definition file used in the example. Of course, although Configuration Manager or any other application developer provides the package definition file itself, you'll still need to obtain a copy of the source files for the application.

The General tab of the package's Properties dialog box, shown in Figure 11-31, contains the package detail information.

The settings in the Data Source tab, as shown in Figure 11-32, are based on the parameters you defined using the Create Package From Definition Wizard.

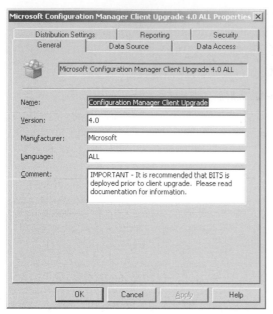

Figure 11-31   The General tab of the package's Properties dialog box

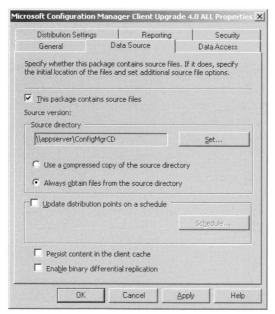

Figure 11-32   The Data Source tab of the package's Properties dialog box

The package definition file is designed to generate all appropriate programs for the application package. The package definition file used in this example created one program, Advanced Client Silent Upgrade, as shown in Figure 11-33.

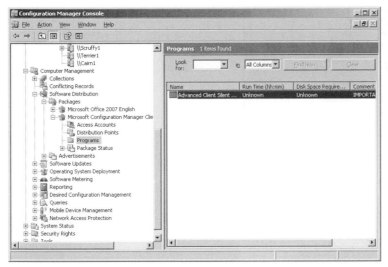

Figure 11-33   The Configuration Manager console showing the program generated by the package definition file

Right-clicking the Advanced Client Silent Upgrade program in the Details pane and selecting Properties displays the General tab of that program's Properties dialog box, as shown in Figure 11-34. Notice that the program definition file supplied the appropriate command-line executable file and switches.

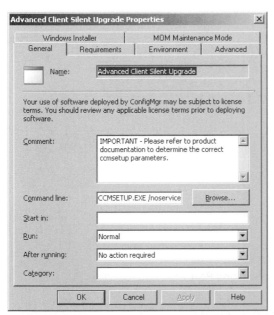

Figure 11-34   The General tab of the Advanced Client Silent Upgrade Properties dialog box

The Requirements tab, as shown in Figure 11-35, displays the platform specification as provided by the package definition file.

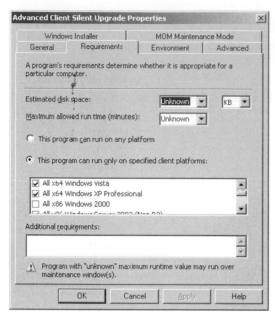

Figure 11-35   The Requirements tab of the Advanced Client Silent Upgrade Properties dialog box

Because this program requires administrative level access at the client, the package definition file configured that option in the Environment tab, as shown in Figure 11-36.

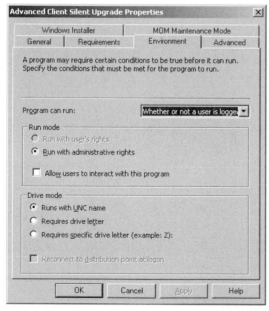

Figure 11-36   The Environment tab of the Advanced Client Silent Upgrade Properties dialog box

In general, the package definition file provides package details for the General and Data Source tabs of the package's Properties dialog box, which should make sense. Distribution settings, for example, define how a package is sent from one site to another, and only the Configuration Manager administrator for each site can modify those settings. On the other hand, the package definition file will usually provide most of the property settings in the programs' Properties dialog boxes. The exceptions are the options in the Advanced, MOM Maintenance Mode, and Windows Installer tabs. The package definition file typically doesn't provide any property settings for these tabs. Again, it's up to you to decide whether to run another program first, temporarily disable the advertisement, or whether it's necessary to provide Windows Installer path and file information.

Package Distribution Process Flow

The process behind the creation and distribution of a package is fairly straightforward. You begin, as always, with the Configuration Manager administrator defining the package, distribution points, and programs. The Configuration Manager Provider writes this information to the Configuration Manager database. This action triggers SQL Monitor to write a package notification wake-up file to Distribution Manager's inbox (\SMS\Inboxes\Distmgr.box). The wake up file takes the form of a site code and package ID as the filename with a .pkn extension. For example, a package notification file for site A01 might be named A0100003.pkn.

The Distribution Manager component wakes up and processes the package based on the package details you provided. Distribution Manager performs the following general tasks:

- Compresses the source files, if necessary
- Copies the package source directory to the specified distribution points
- Creates various instruction files for clients that are copied to management points
- Creates replication files for sending the package to child sites

If you specified that a compressed version of the files should be used, Distribution Manager compresses the files and stores them either in the location specified when the Software Distribution component was configured (this process is discussed in the next section) or by default in the SMSPKG folder created on the drive on which Configuration Manager was installed on the site server, with the same filename and the extension .pkg.

Distribution Manager then copies the source file directory to the SMSPKGx$ folder created on each specified distribution point within the site. If the package files were compressed, Distribution Manager uncompresses them first.

Distribution Manager generates three files and writes them to the\SMS\Inboxes\Pkginfo .box folder on the site server. These files (with filenames as described earlier) are:

- **.PKG**   Package program detail information
- **.NAL**   Location of distribution points
- **.ICO**   Icon file information

These files serve as instruction files for the client after it receives an advertisement. These files are part of the policy the client receives when it is targeted with an advertisement. At this point, the process stops unless the package needs to be sent to a child site.

If the package needs to be sent to a child site, Distribution Manager writes a package replication file (.rpt) to Replication Manager's inbox (\SMS\Inboxes\Replmgr.box\Outbound). If a compressed copy of the package source directory doesn't already exist, Distribution Manager also compresses the source directory into a temporary directory on the site server and then moves the file to the SMSPKG folder (on the Configuration Manager installation drive on the site server or the drive you specified when configuring the Software Distribution component).

Now Replication Manager takes over and begins the sending process. This process is discussed in detail in Chapter 4, so you'll look at only the highlights here. Replication Manager creates a minijob for the Scheduler and places it in the Scheduler's inbox (\SMS\Inboxes\Schedule.box). The Scheduler creates the package and instruction files needed for sending the data in question, as well as a send request file for the sender. The package and instruction files are placed in the \SMS\Inboxes\Schedule.box\Tosend directory. The send request file is written to the preferred sender's outbox (\SMS\Inboxes \Schedule.box\Outboxes\sender, where *sender* is the sender folder, such as LAN, RASAsynch, RASISDN, and so on). Recall that both the sending priority and the preferred sender are identified in the Package Properties dialog box.

When the send request file is written, the sender wakes up and reads the file. It also examines whether the address properties have placed any restrictions on when requests of this priority can be sent and whether there are any bandwidth limits. It then changes the extension of the send request file to .srs and writes status information to it.

The sender connects to the target site's Configuration Manager_SITE share—the \SMS\Inboxes\Despoolr.box\Receive directory—where the Despooler component on the target site completes processing of the information at the target site. When the data has been completely transferred, the send request file is updated to a status of "completed" and the file is deleted. Distribution Manager on the target site will carry out any necessary tasks. For example, if you identified distribution points at the target site, the

Despooler will decompress the package and pass it to Distribution Manager, which processes the package for those distribution points.

Configuring the Software Distribution Component

You can configure additional settings for the package distribution process if the Configuration Manager defaults aren't appropriate within your environment.

To access these settings, in the Configuration Manager console, navigate to the Component Configuration folder under Site Settings and select it. In the Details pane, right-click Software Distribution and select Properties to display the Software Distribution Properties dialog box, as shown in Figure 11-37.

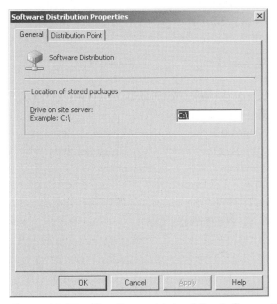

Figure 11-37   The General tab of the Software Distribution Properties dialog box

The only option you can configure on the General tab is the Location Of Stored Packages. This option lets you specify on which drive Configuration Manager should create the compressed package folder (SMSPKG).

Configuration Manager 2007 supports multithreaded communications to distribution points. This means that it can distribute package files concurrently to multiple distribution points. This is an enhancement from previous versions of Systems Management Server. Figure 11-38 displays the distribution setting options you can configure.

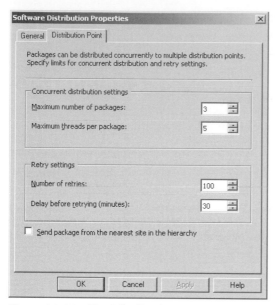

Figure 11-38   The Distribution Point tab of the Software Distribution Properties dialog box

On the Distribution Point tab, you can identify the Maximum Number Of Packages that you can send concurrently to distribution points, as well as the Maximum Threads Per Package to use when sending the packages. You can also configure Retry Settings, which are fairly self-explanatory.

Distributing Software from a Resource

In addition to the methods described earlier in this chapter for creating and distributing a package and an advertisement, Configuration Manager includes an alternative tool that lets you initiate software distribution from a collection, a resource in a collection, a package, a program, or an advertisement. This wizard walks you through each step in the process of creating or identifying a package and program, defining a distribution point, creating or identifying a collection or resource to a target, and creating an advertisement.

To run the wizard, follow these steps:

> **Note**   These steps vary slightly depending on where you start the wizard.

1. Right-click any collection, resource, package, program, or advertisement in the Configuration Manager console Details pane, choose Distribute from the context menu, and then choose Software to launch the appropriate wizard. In Figure 11-39,

the wizard is launched by right-clicking a computer in a collection, so the wizard name is Distribute Software To Resource Wizard. The wizard steps vary slightly depending on where you launch it, but the following steps are representative of what you will find.

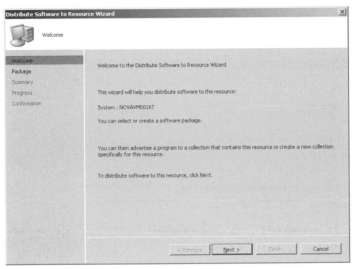

Figure 11-39   The Distribute Software To Resource Wizard Welcome page

2. Click Next to display the Package page, as shown in Figure 11-40. Here you can create a new package and program from scratch or from a definition file, or you can select an existing package by clicking Browse and selecting your package.

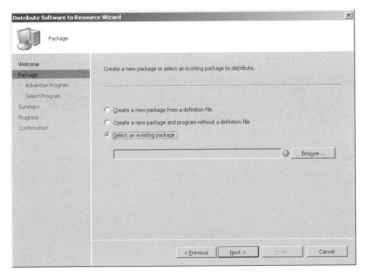

Figure 11-40   The Package page

3. Click Next. The next few Distribute Software To Resource Wizard pages will vary depending on whether you're creating a new program from scratch or from a package definition or by selecting an existing program. If you selected and specified an existing package, the Distribution Points page is displayed, as shown in Figure 11-41. Select the distribution point that should receive the package source files. Click Next to select the appropriate program to advertise and then click Next again to view existing advertisements or to create a new advertisement.

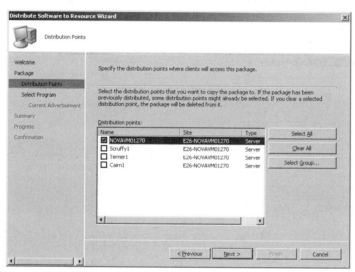

Figure 11-41   The Distribution Points page

If you selected Create A New Package From A Definition, you're presented with pages asking you to select the package definition file and define the source file directory and other configuration settings similar to those when you run the Create Package From Definition Wizard.

If you selected Create A New Package And Program, the wizard prompts you for a package name and identification, the location of source files (if there are any), the program name and command line, whether user input is required or administrative rights are needed, and other configuration settings similar to those when you run the New Package Wizard.

4. All three options give you the choice of creating an advertisement for the program, and the next few pages of the wizard prompt for advertisement properties. The next section describes advertisements in detail. If you choose to create

a new advertisement, the wizard displays the Advertisement Target page first, as shown in Figure 11-42. The program and resource you selected are already specified. You can either select an existing collection to advertise the program to, or create a new collection.

> **Note**   If you choose to create a new collection, you'll be presented with two additional wizard pages that let you specify the collection name and create a collection membership rule. Refer to Chapter 9 for more information about collections and collection membership.

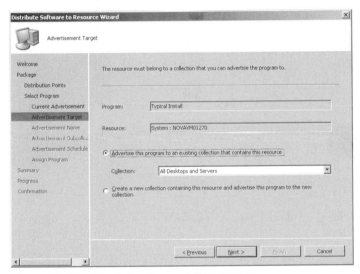

Figure 11-42   The Advertisement Target page

5. Click Next to display the Advertisement Name page shown in Figure 11-43. On the Advertisement Name page, type a descriptive name and comment for the advertisement. The wizard will devise a default name based on the package and program name.

6. Click Next to display the Advertisement Subcollection page, as shown in Figure 11-44. Here you can specify whether to advertise to the collection's subcollections if any exist.

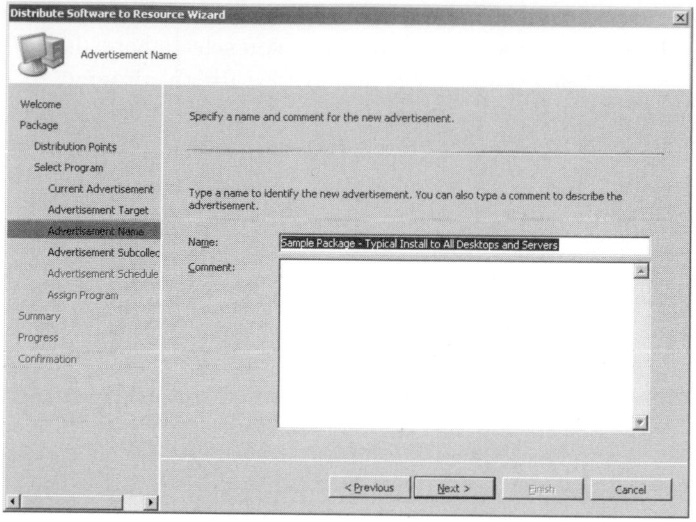

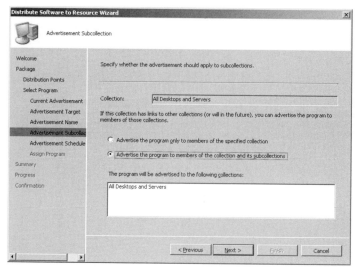

Figure 11-43   The Advertisement Name page

Figure 11-44   The Advertisement Subcollection page

7. Click Next to display the Advertisement Schedule page, as shown in Figure 11-45. This page lets you specify when the advertisement should be offered and whether it expires.

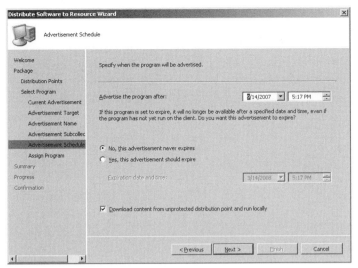

Figure 11-45   The Advertisement Schedule page

8. Click Next to display the Assign Program page, as shown in Figure 11-46. Here you can specify an assigned time if necessary.

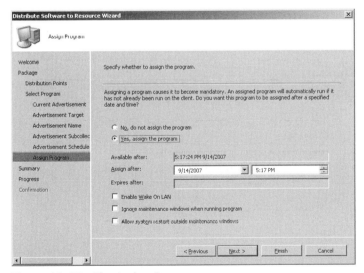

Figure 11-46   The Assign Program page

9. Click Next to display the Summary page, where you can review the settings you specified through the wizard. If you are satisfied with your settings, click Next to begin the package distribution and advertisement processes and then click Close to exit the wizard.

The Distribute Software Wizard doesn't present you with all possible options available for packages, programs, and advertisements. For example, you can't create a recurring advertisement using this wizard. However, the wizard does provide a fine method for generating packages, programs, collections, and advertisements with all the typical settings needed.

Note   In case you were wondering, you can now press Ctrl+click to select more than one client at a time in a collection. This is a convenient way to target a group of two or three computers that are part of a larger membership without creating a separate collection for them. The wizard creates the collection for you.

Creating an Advertisement

After you create your packages and programs, the next step is to create an advertisement. Remember, before you configure an advertisement, you must have identified and created the collections to which you'll advertise the programs. Programs are always advertised to collections—even if it's a collection of one.

To create an advertisement, follow these steps:

1. In the Configuration Manager console, navigate to the Software Distribution\Advertisements folder, right-click it, choose New from the context menu, and then choose Advertisement to display the New Advertisement Wizard, as shown in Figure 11-47. You can also choose to create an Advertisement For Device.

2. On the General page, type a descriptive name for the advertisement. Type a descriptive comment to add more detail. Select the package and program to advertise from their respective list boxes. Type the collection name or browse for it by clicking Browse. If the collection has subcollections and you want to include them in the advertisement, select the Include Members Of Subcollections option.

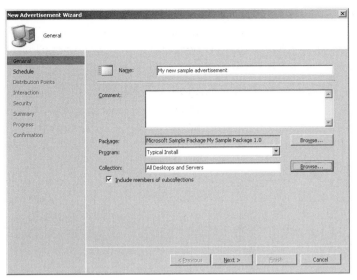

Figure 11-47   The New Advertisement Wizard General page

3. Click Next to display the Schedule page, as shown in Figure 11-48. Begin by select-
    ing the start time and date for the advertisement. This setting represents the time at
    which the program is advertised and made available for the client to run. By default,
    the advertisement will be made available at a specific hour in each time zone—for
    example, at 3:00 in New York, Chicago, and London.. If you want the advertisement
    to be made available in all time zones at the same time, meaning that if the adver-
    tisement start time is 3:00 in New York, it's made available in New York at 3:00, in
    Chicago at 2:00, in London at 8:00, and so on, select the UTC option. UTC stands
    for Coordinated Universal Time.

    If the advertisement will be available for only a specific period of time, select the
    Advertisement Expires option, select an expiration date, and select UTC if desired.

    You can also configure the advertisement to run at a specific time. This is known as
    a mandatory assignment. To configure this option, click New (the yellow star but-
    ton) in the Mandatory Assignments section of the Schedule page to display the
    Assignment Schedule dialog box, as shown in Figure 11-49. Here you can assign a
    mandatory time and date for the advertised program to run. If the program is not
    run by this time and date, the Advertised Programs Client Agent on the client will
    execute it.

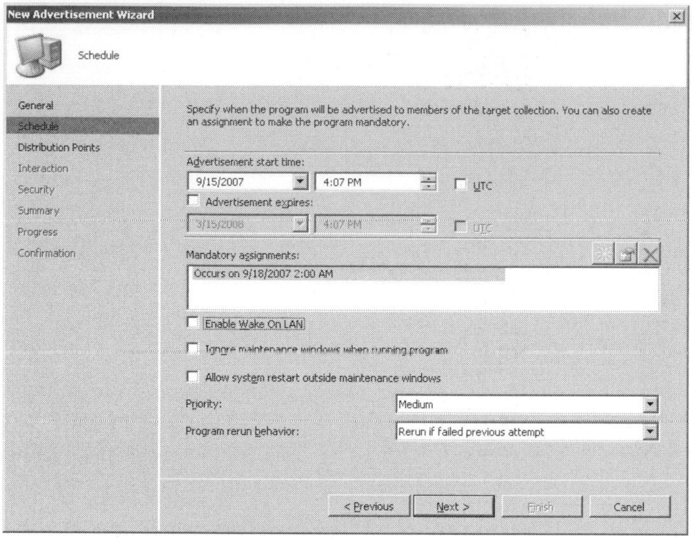

Figure 11-48   The Schedule page

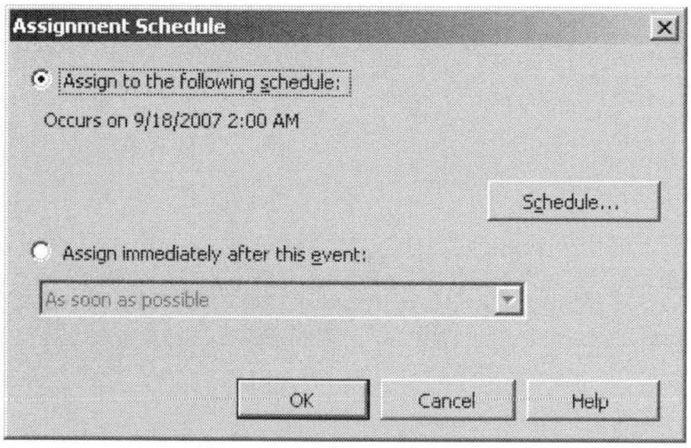

Figure 11-49   The Assignment Schedule dialog box

If you select Assign To The Following Schedule and click Schedule, the Custom Schedule dialog box appears, as shown in Figure 11-50. In this dialog box, you can specify exactly when you want to run the advertised program. You can also set a recurrence interval for advertisements such as monthly file updates.

If you select the Assign Immediately After This Event option in the Assignment Schedule dialog box, you can choose to have the advertised program execute As Soon As Possible—meaning as soon as the program reaches the client and all program requirements (correct platform, user logged on, administrator access, and so on) are met; at Logoff—the next time a user logs off the client; or at Logon—the next time a user logs on to the client.

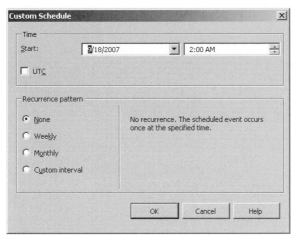

Figure 11-50   The Custom Schedule dialog box

Click OK to return to the Schedule tab. If you configure a mandatory assignment, three additional options become available. Select Enable Wake On LAN to have the advertised program wake up the client computer at the assigned time to run the program. The computer must be configured with a network card that supports Wake On LAN functionality. Select Ignore Maintenance Windows When Running Program to have the advertised program ignore any maintenance windows that might be configured for the collection to which you are targeting the advertisement. You might choose this option if the program must be installed immediately. Select Allow System Restart Outside Maintenance Windows to let the program initiate a computer restart to complete (if the program is configured to do so) outside a configured maintenance window.

Finally, specify a priority for Configuration Manager to use when sending this advertisement to a child site and select a Program Rerun Behavior. Program Rerun Behavior defines how and whether the advertisement should be rerun if you scheduled a recurring mandatory assignment. There are four selections in the Program Rerun Behavior drop-down list. Select Rerun If Failed Previous Attempt to have the advertisement run the program again at the assigned time only if the previous attempt failed. Select Rerun If Succeeded On Previous Attempt to have the advertisement run the program again at the assigned time only if the previous attempt was successful. Select Never Rerun Advertised Program to stop the program from running again at the next assigned time. Select Always Rerun Program to ensure that the program runs again at the next assigned time regardless of whether the previous attempt was successful or not.

4.   Click Next to display the Distribution Points page, as shown in Figure 11-51. These options determine how a program should run when a client attempts to access a distribution point within a Configuration Manager boundary that is considered "fast"

or "slow\unreliable." These options generally map to how a client accesses a network when connected locally or remotely, or when roaming within the hierarchy.

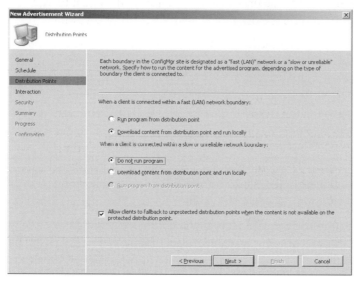

Figure 11-51   The Distribution Points page

In the When A Client Is Connected Within A Fast (LAN) Network Boundary section, the default option is Download Content From Distribution Point And Run Locally. This option ensures that the entire package is downloaded to the client before the program is executed. If the distribution point supports Background Intelligent Transfer Service (BITS) and the computer becomes disconnected from the distribution point before the files are downloaded, the download picks up where it left off when the computer reestablishes a connection. You can also choose Run Program From Distribution Point. This means that the program is run from the distribution point. However, if the computer loses its connection to the distribution point while the program is running, and the distribution point does not support BITS, the program will fail.

In the When A Client Is Connected Within A Slow Or Unreliable Network Boundary section, the default option is Do Not Run Program. By default, packages aren't run if the distribution point is not local. Because Configuration Manager clients can roam to the boundaries of other Configuration Manager sites in the hierarchy, there might not be a local distribution point available that has the package. If the package is located on a distribution point in the client's assigned site, the distribution point is considered remote. Choose the Download Content From Distribution Point And Run Locally option if this package needs to be run on the client and the package is large or the network link to the remote site is slow. The Run Program From Distribution Point option is unavailable when the client is connected to a slow or unreliable network (but it's there anyhow).

Finally, select the Allow Clients To Fallback To Unprotected Distribution Points option to allow the Advertised Programs Client Agent to contact a distribution point that might be outside the protected boundaries of the client to locate the program if the program does not exist on a protected distribution point.

5. Click Next to display the Interaction page, as shown in Figure 11-52. The options on this page define how the user can interact with the program and how the user is notified, and are fairly self-explanatory. If you have configured the program to run at an assigned time, the Allow Users To Run The Program Independently Of Assignments option lets the user override the assignment. This is useful if you want to give a user the ability to reschedule when a program runs, or run it earlier than assigned. If you select this option, you can also select Display Reminders According To The Client Agent Reminder Intervals to let the user know that the program has not yet been run. Select Use Custom Countdown Notification Length (Minutes) to configure a countdown interval for an assigned program. This is useful for giving users notice that a program is about to run, so they can save their work or give you a nervous phone call.

> **Important**   Regardless of the countdown time you set, the program will run at the mandatory time you configure. For example, if you configure the mandatory time as 8:00 P.M., with a countdown of 60 minutes, and the client receives the advertisement at 7:45 P.M., the program will run at 8:00 and not wait for the 60-minute countdown to finish.

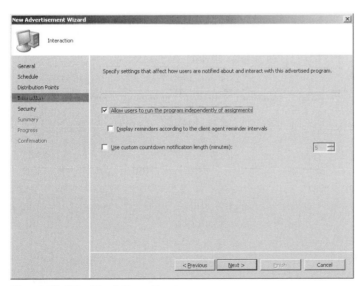

Figure 11-52   The Interaction page

6. Click Next to display the standard Security page, where you can configure and assign permissions for this advertisement.

7. Click Next to review the details of the advertisement, and then click Next to create it. Click Close to exit the wizard.

Note If you haven't yet identified a distribution point for the package, you'll be notified of that fact when you click OK. Also, if you haven't yet enabled the Advertised Programs Client Agent for the clients, you'll be given the option to do so.

Real World   Recurring Assignments

As we've seen, you can specify a recurring schedule for your advertisement. This setting can be useful for programs that need to be executed on a regular basis. Let's return to our application update file example. Suppose you've created a package that distributes an update file for a proprietary application once a month. On the 14th of every month, you obtain a new update file and replace the old file in the package source file directory with the new file. You also configure the package to refresh its distribution points once a month, say on the 15th.

When you create the advertisement, give it an assigned recurring schedule. Set it to run on the 16th, maybe at 11:00 P.M. Now all you have to do is remember to update the source file directory once a month. The package and advertisement process will take care of the rest.

If there is a local script that must be run to add the new update file, you could also create a package that executes that script on the client. Again, you could assign a recurring advertisement to run the script at regular intervals. Here's another twist on this scenario: let's say that you want the script to run immediately after the new update file is installed. You've seen that when you create a program, you have an advanced option to run another program first. You would then create a program that executes the script but first copies the update file. Then create a recurring advertisement that runs that program once a month at the appropriate time.

You can use recurring advertisements to handle a variety of events. For example, use them to perform disk maintenance tasks such as monthly defragmentation or optimization routines. With a little creativity and imagination, you can automate many such tasks and make your job as a system administrator more productive.

Configuring the Client Agent

Of course, life would not be complete if you didn't have a client component to configure, and you do. In order for the client to receive any advertisements you're targeting to it, you must configure the Advertised Programs Client Agent and have it enabled on each client. As with other client agents, you can find this agent in the Client Agents folder under Site Settings in the Configuration Manager console.

Recall that all client agents are installed with the Configuration Manager client software, so the agent components already exist on the client. After you enable and configure the agent, the Advertised Programs Client Agent will be enabled on the client at the client's next policy refresh (once every hour or at the next computer startup).

To configure the Advertised Programs Client Agent, follow these steps:

1. Navigate to the Client Agents folder, select Advertised Programs Client Agent in the Details pane, right-click it, and choose Properties from the context menu to display the Advertised Programs Client Agent Properties dialog box, as shown in Figure 11-53.

Figure 11-53   The Advertised Programs Client Agent Properties dialog box

2. On the General tab, select the Enable Software Distribution To Clients check box. Select the Allow User Targeted Advertisement Requests option to ensure that the agent will find and run programs that you target to users as well as computers.

Advertised programs are listed on Configuration Manager clients in Add Or Remove Programs in Control Panel (Programs and Features in Windows Vista) as well as in the Run Advertised Programs application on Configuration Manager clients. When a new advertisement is available, the new program notification icon is displayed on the task bar by default.

In the Client Setting section, select the New Program Notification Icon Opens Add Or Remove Programs option to have the notification icon open Add Or Remove Programs (Programs and Features in Windows Vista) to display new advertisements. If you leave this option cleared, the notification icon will open Run Advertised Programs.

3. Click the Notification tab, as shown in Figure 11-54. This tab provides several options for defining how the client is notified of an advertisement.

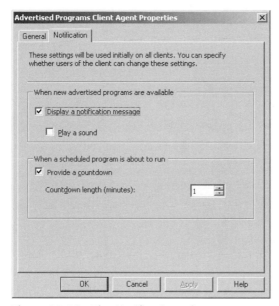

Figure 11-54   The Notification tab

4. The options in the Notification tab are fairly self-explanatory. Select the options that fit your needs and then click OK to save the configuration and begin the site update process.

If you don't select any options in this tab, the client agent will check for an advertisement but will never notify the user that an advertisement has been received. The user would have to periodically run the Run Advertised Programs application from Control Panel to find and run advertisements. If the advertised program had a mandatory assignment, it would simply run, again without notification to the user. In general, it's not a good idea to not notify the user when an advertisement has been received. Notifying the user can prevent unfortunate occurrences such as the user logging off or shutting down before the program finishes running.

When the client agent is enabled at the client, two new icons will be added to the Control Panel on each client—Run Advertised Programs and Program Download Monitor.

Running Advertised Programs on Clients

Once an hour, by default, the client agent checks the management point for new advertisements targeting that client. Advertised programs always appear in both Add Or Remove Programs (Programs and Features in Windows Vista), as shown in Figure 11-55, and in the Run Advertised Programs application.

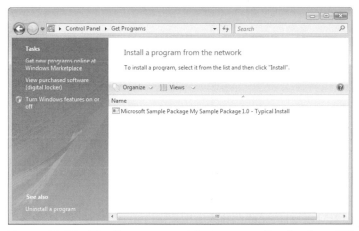

Figure 11-55   The Programs and Features application from Windows Vista showing the advertised program in the Install A Program From The Network window

Take a look at the software distribution-related Control Panel programs installed on the Configuration Manager client.

Run Advertised Programs

The Run Advertised Programs application is installed on Configuration Manager clients and is used to display available advertisements, select advertisements to run, and view the properties of advertisements. However, if an advertisement is assigned a mandatory run time, it is not displayed, and users will not have the option to run it independently of its assigned schedule. When accessed through the Control Panel, Run Advertised Programs causes the Advertised Programs Client Agent to check the management point for new advertisements. When an advertised program is available for the client, the New

Advertised Programs Are Available icon appears on the taskbar (if you enabled this type of notification). You can also launch Run Advertised Programs through the New Advertised Programs Are Available icon (unless you configured this option to always launch Add Or Remove Programs through the agent properties as discussed earlier).

To launch Run Advertised Programs, follow these steps:

1. Click the Run Advertised Programs icon in the Control Panel, double-click the New Advertised Programs Are Available icon on the taskbar (if that option was enabled), or right-click the New Advertised Programs Are Available icon and choose Run Advertised Programs Wizard from the context menu. The Run Advertised Programs dialog box appears, as shown in Figure 11-56.

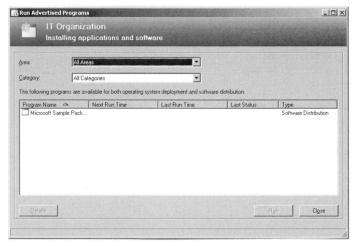

Figure 11-56   The Run Advertised Programs dialog box

2. Select a program from the Program Name list and click Details to display that program's properties. Properties include any special categories the administrator assigned the program to, general comments in the General tab, and Advanced tab options.

3. Select a program from the Program Name list and click Run to execute the program. If the program requires the package to be downloaded first, the Program Download Required message box is displayed, as shown in Figure 11-57. Here you can view the package's properties and choose to have the program run automatically when the download finishes. Click Download to begin the download or click Cancel to stop.

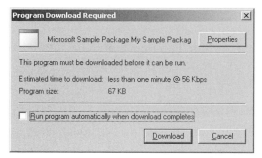

Figure 11-57   The Program Download Required message box

4. If you click Download in step 3, the Program Download Status dialog box appears, as shown in Figure 11-58. Again, you can view the program's properties, choose to have the program run automatically when the download finishes, cancel the download, or hide the dialog box.

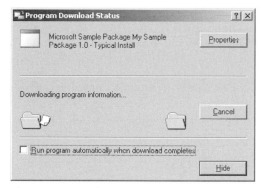

Figure 11-58   The Program Download Status dialog box

Program Download Monitor

The Program Download Monitor is installed on Configuration Manager clients and provides information about programs that are pending to run on the client. When you launch the Program Download Monitor from the Control Panel (or from the taskbar), it displays advertised programs that need to be downloaded or are downloading, as shown in Figure 11-59. You can use Program Download Monitor to show status of a download, to cancel downloads, and to specify that a program start automatically after the download completes by highlighting the program in the Program list and selecting the appropriate option from the Download menu.

Figure 11-59   The Program Download Monitor

Managing the Configuration Manager Client Download Cache

When you configure the advertisement properties, you can specify whether the package should be downloaded to the Configuration Manager client before it runs (see Figure 11-51). If so, it's stored in the Configuration Manager client download cache. The cache can become too full to accommodate the download of any additional packages. When a package is downloaded and placed into cache, the client agent locks it. The package is unlocked after 24 hours have passed since the program was run, or 30 days have passed and the program hasn't run. After the package is unlocked, it can't be locked again unless it's removed from cache and downloaded again.

When a package needs to be downloaded and the cache is too full, Configuration Manager checks the other cached packages to see whether it can delete any or all of the oldest packages to free up enough space to accommodate the new package. If it can, it does so and downloads the package. If it can't, as might be the case if a package is locked, the package isn't downloaded.

Users with administrative credentials on the client can manage this download cache. They can change the size of the cache and its location, as well as delete the contents of the cache. As the Configuration Manager administrator, you can manage the client download cache by following these steps:

1. Open the Configuration Manager application in Control Panel and click the Advanced tab, as shown in Figure 11-60. You manage the client download cache settings in the Temporary Program Download Folder frame.

2. Click Configure Settings to enable the setting options. Enter the Amount Of Disk Space To Use value or use the slide bar to set the amount.

3. Click Change Location to modify the disk location for the download cache folder.

4. Click Delete Files to delete the entire contents of the download cache.

5. Click OK to save your settings.

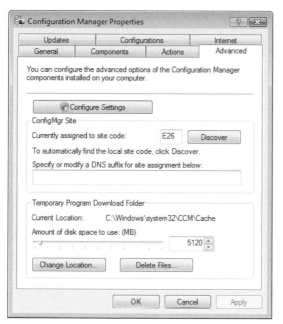

Figure 11-60 The Configuration Manager application Advanced tab

---

Note If you installed the Configuration Manager client using the command-line option DISABLECACHEOPT=True, you are unable to modify the local cache settings through the Configuration Manager program in Control Panel. You will need to use a script to modify the settings.

Advertised Programs Process Flow

The advertisement and its associated files are generated in a process even more straightforward than the package distribution process. Just as with the package distribution process, when the advertisement is created and written to the Configuration Manager database, an SQL trigger causes the Configuration Manager SQL Monitor service to write a wake-up file (.ofn) to Offer Manager's inbox (\SMS\Inboxes\Offermgr.box).

The Offer Manager component generates instruction files for the Advertised Programs Client Agent and writes these to the \SMS\Inboxes\Offerinf.box directory on the site server. These instruction files consist of an offer file (with a name similar to that of the package but with an .ofr extension), which is the actual advertisement; an installation file (.ins) that references the advertisement ID and the collection ID it's targeting; and up to three lookup files (.lkp), depending on the collection membership. These lookup files act as filters to determine whether the client (*sitecode*systm.lkp), the user (*sitecode*usr.lkp), or the user group (*sitecode*usrgrp.lkp) should receive the advertisement. At this time, Offer Manager also evaluates the collection membership to determine which lookup files to create. The Configuration Manager Policy Provider copies the advertisement information to the management point as a client machine policy.

On the Configuration Manager client, the Configuration Manager Agent Host (CCMexec.exe) is responsible for retrieving client policy updates from the management point and providing the Advertised Programs Client Agent with advertised program and package information. It's also responsible for forwarding status information back to the management point.

Monitoring Status

Both the package distribution process and the advertised programs process generate status messages. You can monitor status in the same place you have monitored other Configuration Manager functions—the System Status folder in the Configuration Manager console. You can also expand the Component Status folder and view the messages for Distribution Manager and Offer Manager.

You've probably noticed two other folders in the Configuration Manager console: Package Status and Advertisement Status, located under System Status. A Package Status folder also exists under each package entry you created. These folders pertain specifically to packages and advertisements and are more useful for monitoring their status. As with Component Status, both Package Status and Advertisement Status have status summarizers, which consolidate status messages generated by the Configuration Manager components involved in the package and advertisement processes.

In Figure 11-61, the Advertisement Status and Package Status folders have been expanded to demonstrate the information they summarize. Package status detail is summarized at two levels—by site and by distribution point. Advertisement status detail is summarized by site. At each level, you can view the detailed messages that were generated for that particular package or advertisement by right-clicking an entry in the Details pane, choosing Show Messages from the context menu, and then choosing All. After you specify a view data and time range, the Status Message Viewer displays the messages related to the package or advertisement.

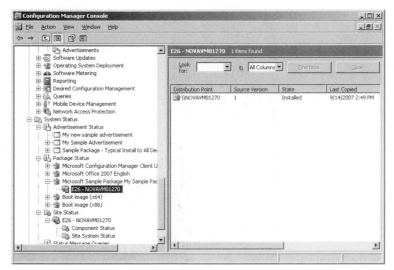

Figure 11-61   The expanded Advertisement Status and Package Status folders

The summary information displayed when a site entry is selected, as in Figure 11-61, shows when the package was copied to the distribution point and last refreshed. The summary information displayed when a specific package is selected, as in Figure 11-62, shows at a glance how many clients installed the package, how many failed, and how many are retrying.

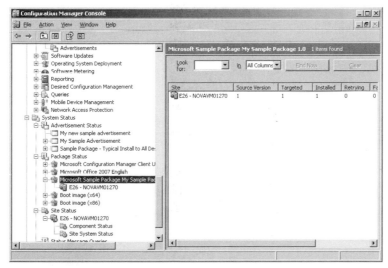

Figure 11-62   Sample summary information displayed when a package is selected in the Configuration Manager console

Figure 11-63 shows the status messages generated at the site level for a package.

Figure 11-64 shows the detailed messages for a specific distribution point in the site.

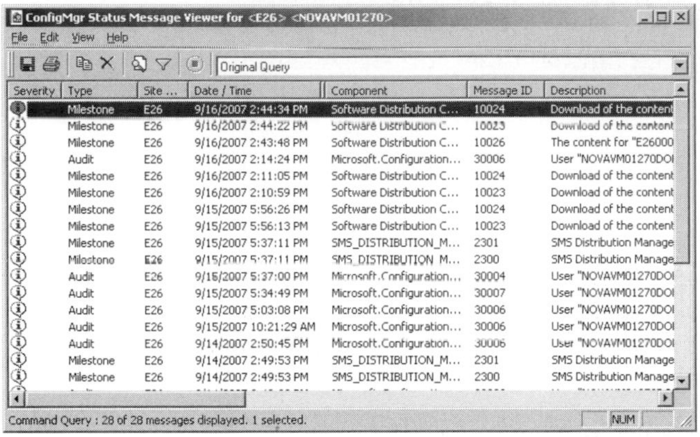

Figure 11-63   Status messages for a package generated at the site level

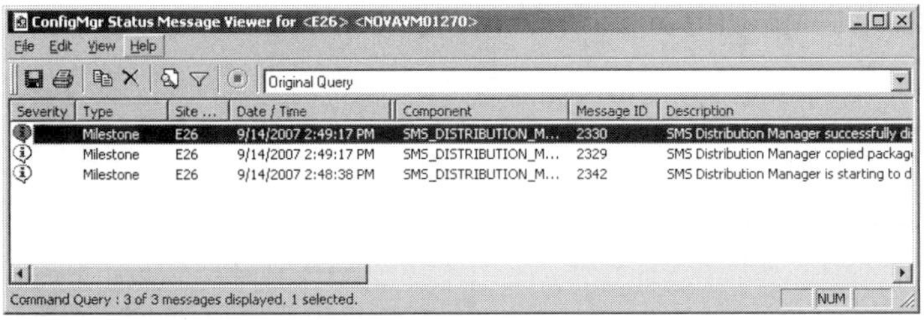

Figure 11-64   Status messages for a specific distribution point in a site

Notice the difference in messages summarized for each. Messages for the distribution point are specific to that distribution point. Messages in the 23xx range refer to Distribution Manager tasks.

Figure 11-65 shows the summary information displayed in the Configuration Manager console when you select an advertisement. This summary information includes success and failure status generated by the program as it runs on the targeted clients.

Figure 11-66 shows some of the detailed messages generated for an advertisement associated with one of the package's programs. Messages generated by the Offer Manager component fall within the 39xx range. The messages generated by the Software Distribution agent that you see in Figure 11-66 came from the client. The complete message text (under Description) tells you when the advertisement was received, when the program started, and when the program completed.

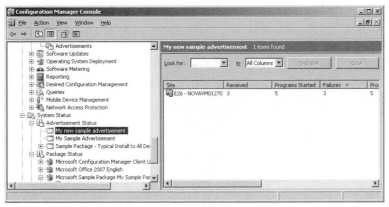

Figure 11-65   Advertisement summary showing program run statistics on the targeted clients

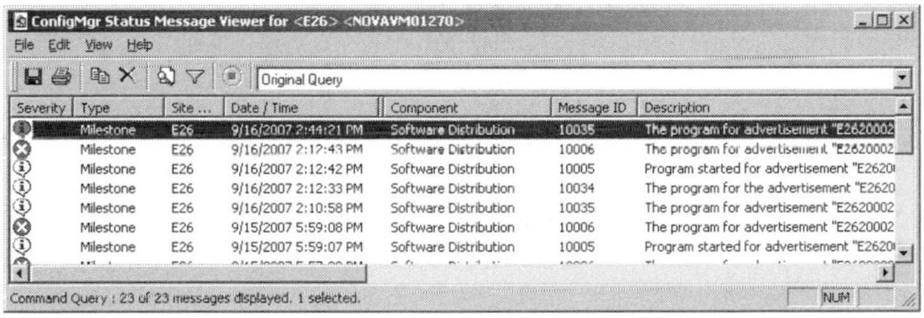

Figure 11-66   Detailed messages generated for an advertisement associated with one of the package's programs

When a program executes at the client and a status MIF is generated, you can determine whether the program completed, how the program ran, and, if it failed, what caused the problem. It should be no surprise, therefore, that you can determine not only whether a program ran, but also how it ran, whether it was successful, and, if it was unsuccessful, why it failed, as shown in Figure 11-66. The degree to which a program can generate this information depends on whether the program generates a status MIF for Configuration Manager reporting and the exit codes that are generated. Configuration Manager interprets any nonzero exit code as an error or a failure. For example, a Setup.bat file might simply execute an XCOPY of a file to a directory on the client. Even though the XCOPY command is successful, the exit code that it generates is interpreted as an error. Nevertheless, the detailed message is still far more useful and informative.

As always, you can also view the log files associated with the Distribution Manager and Offer Manager—Distmgr.log and Offermgr.log. These logs will provide thread activity details, but they're more useful for determining why a source file couldn't be copied to a distribution point or why a program couldn't be advertised—in other words, to troubleshoot the package distribution and advertised program processes. For monitoring the package distribution and program execution process, the Status Viewer will be more than sufficient and probably more efficient.

Working with Branch Distribution Points

A new feature of Configuration Manager is the branch distribution point. This site system role is meant to facilitate software distribution to smaller or remote offices. With previous versions of Systems Management Server, the best way to manage bandwidth and connectivity issues related to software distribution to smaller or remote offices where WAN connectivity might have been an issue was to install a secondary site server in that location. You could then take advantage of the bandwidth controls available when communicating between sites to also manage software distribution.

The branch distribution point is a fine alternative to installing a secondary site server if the primary reason you need the secondary site server is to distribute software. For all practical purposes, the branch distribution point functions like a standard distribution point. However, it depends on the availability of a BITS-enabled standard distribution point from which it receives its content—otherwise, it will not function.

Like the standard distribution point, a branch distribution point can use BITS to manage network bandwidth usage and to provide a local checkpoint restart if the package download is interrupted. Branch distribution points also provide an option that downloads a package from the standard distribution point to the branch distribution point only when requested by a client. This can help manage not only network bandwidth but local storage on the branch distribution point.

The branch distribution point can be a high-end desktop-class computer, or a server-class computer. The same considerations regarding performance, storage, and network usage apply here as to the standard distribution point. However, local usage is another consideration. If the branch distribution point is a high-end desktop-class computer, then you are subject to the shared connectivity limitations associated with a desktop computer—mainly that you are limited to 10 concurrent shared connections. Also, if that computer doubles as a user's workstation, that user's desktop performance will likely be affected by client requests for packages.

Creating a Branch Distribution Point

You assign the branch distribution point role in much the same way as you assign a standard distribution point role, which is described in Chapter 3. To assign the branch distribution point role, follow these steps:

1. In the Configuration Manager console, navigate to the Site Settings folder and expand it.

2. Add a new site system by right-clicking the Site Systems folder and choosing New from the context menu. Choose either Server or Server Share from the site system options that appear.

3. Choosing Server launches the New Site System Server Wizard, which is described in detail in Chapter 3. On the General page, type the name of the Configuration Manager client that you want to make a site system. Be sure to type a fully qualified domain name (FQDN) for the client, as shown in Figure 11-67.

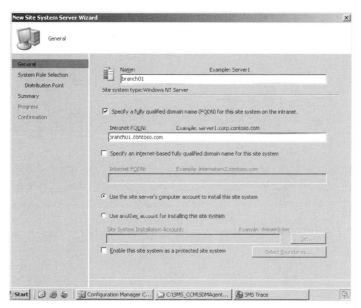

Figure 11-67 The New Site System Server Wizard General page for a new site system server

4. Click Next to display the System Site Role page. Select Distribution Point from the Available Roles list.

5. Click Next to display the Distribution Point page. Select the Enable As A Branch Distribution Point option, as shown in Figure 11-68. Optionally, you can choose to specify a local partition to use for storing package content as well as the amount of disk space to reserve for use by the local operating system.

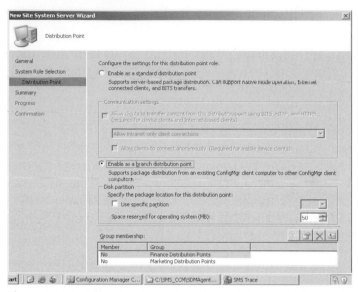

Figure 11-68   The New Site System Server Wizard Distribution Point page for a new branch distribution point

6. Click Next to review your choices, click Next again to create the role, and then click Close to exit the wizard.

Managing Branch Distribution Points

After you have deployed a branch distribution point, distributing packages is pretty much the same as described in this chapter. One thing you can do differently on a branch distribution point is prestaging a package. It might happen that you have a large package that you do not want to distribute to the branch distribution point over the network because of usage and performance concerns. In this case, you have the option of prestaging the package on the branch distribution point.

Recall that a branch distribution point depends on the availability of a standard distribution point to receive its content. You'll need to have already distributed the package you want to prestage to a standard distribution point and assigned the branch distribution point role before proceeding.

To prestage a package on a branch distribution point, follow these steps:

1. If the SMSPKGx$ folder and share (where *x* represents the drive letter) do not already exist on the branch distribution point, create them.

2. On the standard distribution point, locate the package folder and its contents and copy them to the SMSPKGx$ folder you created on the branch distribution point.

3. On the branch distribution point, run the Configuration Manager application in Control Panel.

4. On the Actions tab, select the Branch Distribution Point Maintenance Task option, and then click Initiate Action. This causes the branch distribution point to synchronize with the standard distribution point as having received the package.

Checkpoints

As you've seen, the process flows for package distribution and advertised programs are quite straightforward. Outside of normal network traffic issues that might interfere with the copying of source files to a distribution point or the copying of policy updates to a management point, not much can go wrong. The amount of network traffic generated by updating management points with package and advertisement information is relatively small, as the files involved are generally no more than 1 KB to 2 KB in size.

The real traffic comes with the copying or refreshing of source files to the distribution points. Remember that distribution points receive their files in an uncompressed format. That 200-MB application is generating 200 MB worth of network traffic when the source files are copied to the distribution point, and this traffic increases proportionally to the number of distribution points you're targeting, and whether you are targeting multiple distribution points concurrently. Although you can schedule when the distribution points are refreshed, the initial copy takes place at the time you create the package and identify the distribution points.

Also, keep in mind that when a client accesses a distribution point to run a program, the installation might also generate a significant amount of traffic between the distribution point and the client. The more clients accessing the distribution point at the same time, the more traffic generated and the greater the performance hit taken by the distribution point. This can be particularly significant if the distribution is a branch distribution point that is running on a high-end desktop in a remote location. In general, if you're targeting large numbers of clients, you should consider distributing the package load across several distribution points, perhaps local to the clients in question. This is where a branch distribution point can come in handy.

If a program fails, start your troubleshooting with the status message system or the log files. Often, simply retracing your steps will be sufficient to spot the problem. Check the package and program parameters. Test the package yourself. Check the clients' system time to be sure that they're receiving the advertisements when you think they should. Check the Advertised Programs Client Agent polling cycle to be sure that the client agent is checking for new advertisements in a timely fashion. Check that the client has a management point available. Remember, too, to monitor the client download cache and modify it appropriately as well.

Summary

This chapter covered one of the most significant functions of Configuration Manager—distributing and advertising packages and programs to clients. This function facilitates remote installation, updating, and maintenance of Configuration Manager client computers. However, think of Configuration Manager as more than a delivery system. As you've seen, it's still your responsibility as the Configuration Manager administrator to create (and script, if necessary) the packages you distribute. Other features of Configuration Manager use the software distribution infrastructure to carry out their tasks. One of the most significant of these is Operating System Deployment, which is discussed in Chapter 12. This feature lets you script the installation of an operating system to facilitate the upgrade of existing computers and installation of new computers. It also includes a feature called task sequences that lets you script other functions as well. On to Chapter 12.

Chapter 12
Deploying Operating Systems

Planning is the key

Task sequences go to work

Client exists now

~ Dan Bernhardt, Technical Writer

One of the more successful add-ons for Systems Management Server 2003 was the Operating System Deployment Feature Pack. This feature pack was designed to facilitate the deployment of operating system upgrades and installations to Advanced Client computers managed by Systems Management Server 2003. It was so successful that the product development team for Systems Center Configuration Manager 2007 reengineered the feature and incorporated it into the product. In fact, operating system deployment was a major development pillar for Configuration Manager.

The operating system deployment feature provides a tool for images that can be deployed to computers managed by Configuration Manager 2007 and to unmanaged computers using bootable media such as CD sets, DVD, or USB. The image, stored as a Windows Image Format (WIM) file, contains the desired version of a Microsoft Windows operating system. However, it could also include any line-of-business applications that need to be installed on the computer, service packs, or security upgrades, and so on.

Operating system deployment introduces task sequences as a means of scripting and customizing your deployment, although you can use task sequences independently of operating system deployment.

There are enough nuances wrapped around and within this feature to merit its own book—as the Configuration Manager Documentation Library found at *http://technet.microsoft.com /en-us/library/bb680651.aspx* clearly shows. That content provides a great deal of detailed information about the various scenarios in which you can use operating system deployment. This chapter is aimed at the new user and focuses on a specific common scenario: upgrading an operating system.

Understanding the Working Components of Operating System Deployment

All operating system deployments share common elements and components. You begin with an image to deploy. As stated earlier, this image is created and stored as a WIM file. The image might be supplied to you, perhaps by a manufacturer such as Microsoft or Dell, or you might create the image yourself by capturing it from an existing computer that has been configured to your specifications. This computer is generally referred to as the reference computer.

You then identify the target computers that should receive and install the image. Target computers are usually Configuration Manager clients, but could also be nonmanaged computers configured to boot automatically through network cards that support the Preboot Execution Environment (PxE) boot method.

The image to be deployed is treated similarly to other packages you can create and deploy using Configuration Manager. So the next obvious step is to advertise the image to the target computers. You do this using a task sequence. Task sequences consist of one or more task steps that run in a specific order and carry out tasks specific to the deployment process you create or customize. They are basically used with operating system deployment to build reference computers, capture an image, migrate user or computer settings, advertise the image to target computers, and run a specific sequence of steps. They can also be used to deploy existing Configuration Manager packages, apply software updates, modify registry settings, and otherwise customize the target computer. Task sequences are a powerful scripting tool, and they are looked at in more detail next.

Understanding Task Sequences

Because task sequences represent a basic building block for all operating system deployment actions, they are looked at first. A task sequence is composed of one or more task steps. These task steps can be grouped into task sequence groups that can function as a block and can be made dependent on previous task steps or task groups. Each task step consists of either a built-in action or a command-line string called a custom action that you provide. The configuration parameters available for each built-in action are specific to that action. As you use these actions in this chapter, you'll explore the configuration parameters specific to that action. Each task step and task group can be further customized through a set of conditions that can be applied, and that determines whether the action should or should not be processed.

You create a new task sequence by running the New Task Sequence Wizard. Follow these steps:

1. Navigate to the Task Sequences node under Operating System Deployment in the Configuration Manager console, as shown in Figure 12-1.

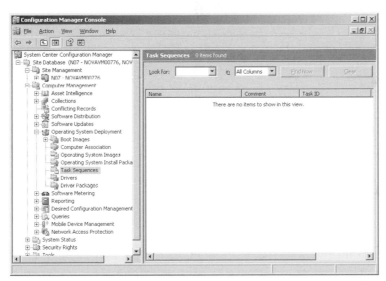

Figure 12-1   A representative Configuration Manager console displaying the Operating System Deployment node with the Task Sequences node highlighted

2. Right-click Task Sequences, choose New from the context menu, and then choose Task Sequence to start the New Task Sequence Wizard, as shown in Figure 12-2.

3. There are three kinds of task sequences that you can build using the New Task Sequence Wizard. Select the Install An Existing Image Package option if you already have an operating system image that you want to deploy to one or more target computers. Select the Build And Capture A Reference Operating System Image option if you create an image by building and capturing it from a reference computer. Select the Create A New Custom Task Sequence option to build and customize a task sequence. For this example, select this third option and click Next.

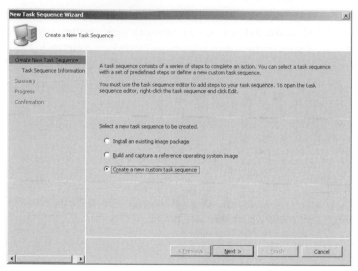

Figure 12-2   The New Task Sequence Wizard

4. On the Task Sequence Information page, shown in Figure 12-3, type a name for the task sequence and a descriptive comment. Optionally, you can select a boot image if you are creating a task sequence that will capture an image from a reference computer.

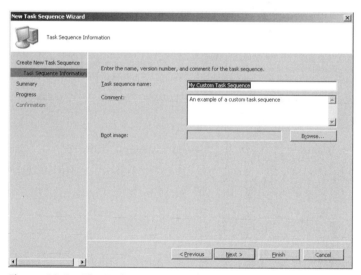

Figure 12-3   The Task Sequence Information page of the New Task Sequence Wizard

5. Click Next or Finish to display the Summary page. Click Next to create the new task sequence, and then click Close to exit the wizard. The new task sequence is displayed in the results pane of the Task Sequences node.

To edit and customize the new task sequence, right-click the task sequence in the results pane and select Edit from the context menu to open the task sequence in the Task Sequence Editor. Figure 12-4 shows the result of creating a new custom task sequence—basically an empty task sequence to which you can add task steps and task groups.

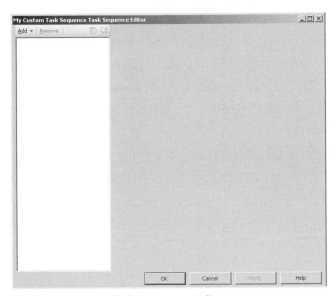

Figure 12-4   The Task Sequence Editor

Click Add to display the different task steps that you can add to the task sequence, as shown in Figure 12-5.

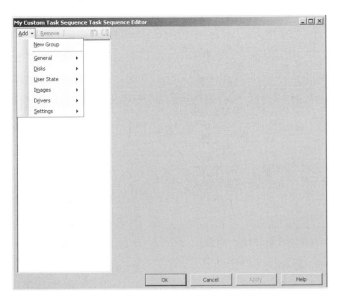

Figure 12-5   The Task Sequence Editor Add options

Task steps are categorized into six areas:

- General: A list of seven task steps that can be added to any task sequence
  - ❑ Run Command Line
  - ❑ Install Software
  - ❑ Install Software Update
  - ❑ Join Domain Or Workgroup
  - ❑ Connect To Network Folder
  - ❑ Reboot To Windows PE Or Hard Disk
  - ❑ Set Task Sequence Variable
- Disks: A list of four task steps that are specific to an operating system deployment and are used to customize disk configuration on a target computer
  - ❑ Format And Partition Disk
  - ❑ Convert Disk To Dynamic
  - ❑ Enable BitLocker
  - ❑ Disable BitLocker
- User State: A list of four task steps that are specific to an operating system deployment and are used to facilitate migrating user state from before to after the deployment
  - ❑ Request State Store
  - ❑ Release State Store
  - ❑ Capture User State
  - ❑ Restore User State
- Images: A list of seven task steps that are specific to building an operating system image for deployment and are used to create and customize the image for capture
  - ❑ Apply Operating System
  - ❑ Apply Data Image
  - ❑ Setup Windows And ConfigMgr
  - ❑ Install Deployment Tools
  - ❑ Prepare ConfigMgr Client For Capture
  - ❑ Prepare Windows For Capture
  - ❑ Capture Operating System Image

■ Drivers: A list of two task steps that are specific to building an operating system image for deployment and are used to add supporting device drivers to the image

❑ Auto Apply Drivers

❑ Apply Driver Package

■ Settings: A list of four task steps that are specific to building an operating system image for deployment and are used to facilitate migrating network and Windows settings from before to after the deployment

❑ Capture Network Settings

❑ Capture Windows Settings

❑ Apply Network Settings

❑ Apply Windows Settings

The catch-all task step is the General task step Run Command Line. The properties of a Run Command Line task are displayed in Figure 12-6. The Type field is read-only for all task steps. Type a Name and a Description for the command if you want. The important field is the Command Line field. This is a required field and represents the action you want the task step to run on the target computer. You should include file extensions. If you don't, the task step will try .com, .exe, and .bat to run the command.

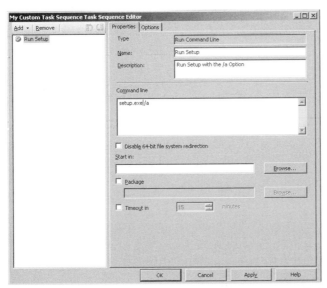

Figure 12-6   The Task Sequence Editor Run Command Line options

Important   If you want to specify a command such as Copy or Print, you must precede the command with cmd.exe /c to run successfully, as in this example: *cmd.exe /c copy z:\files*.dat c:\files*.dat*

You can optionally specify a Start In folder. You can also select the Package option and type the name of a Configuration Manager package that contains source files that you might want to copy to the target computer as well as a timeout value for the task step to complete.

Every Task Step and Task Group contains an Options tab, similar to that shown in Figure 12-7. The settings on the Options tab are used to configure conditions that the task step or group needs to evaluate before running the action. Table 12-1 defines these settings.

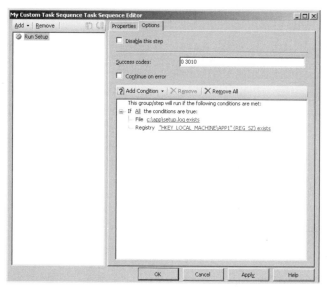

Figure 12-7   The Task Sequence Editor Run Command Line options

Table 12-1   Task Step and Task Group Option Settings

Options setting	Description
Disable This Step	Prevents the step or group from running under any condition.
Success Codes	Unique to the Run Command Line task step, this is an administrator-defined number that the task step will return when it runs successfully and can be used to determine and report status of the step.

Table 12-1   Task Step and Task Group Option Settings

Options setting	Description
Continue On Error	Determines what to do if the step or group does not complete successfully. For a task step, if this option *is* selected and the task step fails, the error is ignored, and the next step is processed. If this option *is not* selected and the task step fails, any remaining task sequence steps in the group or subgroup that the task step is a member of will be skipped. If the task step is not a member of a group or subgroup, the task sequence itself ends with an error.
	For a task group, if this option *is* selected and the task group fails, the error is ignored, and the next step in the task sequence is processed. If this option *is not* selected and the task group fails, any remaining task sequence steps in the group or subgroup that the task group is a member of will be skipped. If the task group is not a member of another group, the task sequence itself ends with an error.
Add Condition	Used to add one or more conditional statements to the step or group for evaluation before running the step or group. The conditional statements must evaluate to "true" for the step or group to run.
If Statement	Used to combine two or more of the seven available conditional statements.
Task Sequence Variable	Checks for the existence of a task sequence variable to compare the value of that variable to the value entered in the condition.
Operating System Version	Evaluates whether the target computer is running a specified processor architecture, operating system, and version.
File Properties	Verifies that a specific file exists on a destination computer. The following parameters can be configured for this condition: path, version, timestamp.
Folder Properties	Verifies that a specific folder exists on a destination computer. The following parameters can be configured for this condition: path and timestamp
Registry Setting	Verifies that the specified Windows registry key exists and/or has the specified values on a destination computer. The following parameters can be configured for this condition: root key, key, value type, value name value.
Query WMI	Lets you run a WMI query on the destination computer. This condition is evaluated as true if the WMI query returns at least one record.
Installed Software	Evaluates whether the specified software is installed on the destination computer. You can only evaluate software that was installed using a Windows Installer file (.msi).

After you create, customize, and save your task sequence, you can use it with other task sequences, or advertise it to one or more target computers. You'll learn more about how task sequences integrate with operating system deployment throughout the remainder of this chapter.

Creating an Image for Deployment

You begin the process of deploying an operating system by either obtaining an image to deploy or creating one yourself. In fact, you are most likely to create or customize your own images. At its essence, an image is a collection of files and folders that duplicates the original file and folder structure of an existing computer, including the file and folder structure of the operating system, or that is a file-based replica of a hard disk. There are two kinds of images: boot images and operating system images.

Understanding Boot Images

Boot images are used as part of the deployment process. Boot images contain the appropriate version of Windows Preinstallation Environment (Windows PE). Windows PE is a Windows operating system with limited services built on the full operating system platform that you are deploying. It is used during deployment to boot the target computer into a temporary operating system so that the new image (with operating system) can be applied and installed. Boot images are generally supplied to you by an external source such as Microsoft or Dell. Configuration Manager 2007 includes two boot images built on Windows PE 2.0 that support the x86 and x64 Windows Vista platforms. They are located in their respective <InstallationPath>\SMS\OSD\Boot\i386 and <InstallationPath>\SMS\OSD\Boot\x64 folders on the site server. You can—and should—update your boot images with the appropriate drivers needed by the target computer. If you feel adventurous, you can also build your own boot images using Windows PE.

> **More Info**   You can find detailed information about Windows PE on the Windows Preinstallation Web page at *http://www.microsoft.com/whdc/system/winpreinst/default.mspx*. For detailed steps describing how to update a boot image with additional drivers, see the topic "How to Update Boot Images" in the Configuration Manager Documentation Library at *http://technet.microsoft.com/en-us/library/bb680651.aspx*.

To add a new boot image to use with Configuration Manager's operating system deployment feature, follow these steps:

1. Navigate to the Boot Images node under Operating System Deployment in the Configuration Manager console.

2. Right-click Boot Images and select Add Boot Image from the context menu to display the Add Boot Image Package Wizard Data Source page, as shown in Figure 12-8. Type a path to the location of the WIM file to use, and then select a Boot Image contained in the WIM file to use.

> **Note**   A WIM file can contain more than one boot image, especially if obtained from an external source.

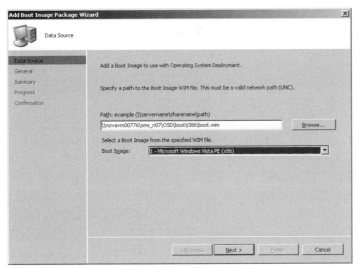

Figure 12-8   The Add Boot Image Package Wizard Data Source page

3. Click Next to display the General page, as shown in Figure 12-9. Type a name, and optionally, a version and descriptive comment.

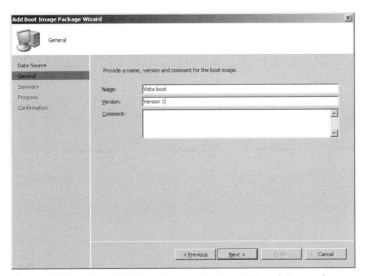

Figure 12-9   The Add Boot Image Package Wizard General page

4. Click Next or Finish to display the Summary page and review your selections. Click Next again to add the boot image, and then click Close to exit the wizard.

Keep in mind that a boot image is also considered to be a package. As such, in order to use it successfully when advertising the task sequence that references it, you must distribute the boot image to all appropriate distribution points. When you expand the boot image entry in the Configuration Manager console, you'll see a Distribution Points folder just as you would for any other package. Right-click that folder to copy or update the image to distribution points you've selected.

Understanding Operating System Images

The operating system image can contain all the files necessary to install the desired operating system on a target computer, including all supported drivers, updates, and any other packages needed. You could also supply these support files as separate packages to keep your image more generic. The image creation can be automated by using a task sequence, or you can manually configure a reference computer and capture the image yourself.

Keep in mind that as the image contains the entire operating system, and potentially other files as well, the image itself is very large—often 2 GB or larger. Images are deployed much like other Configuration Manager packages. They are distributed to distribution points and downloaded to target computers. So be sure to consider the bandwidth that your network can support and the disk space needed to store the image.

In addition, be sure to check the client cache size and modify it to accommodate the image if necessary. Recall from Chapter 11, "Distributing Software Packages," that the cache is used to store packages that are downloaded from a distribution point. Configuration Manager manages the cache by deleting the oldest packages from the cache. However, the default cache size will likely not be able to accommodate the size of an operating system deployment image.

As noted earlier, there are several deployment scenarios supported by operating system deployment. You'll focus on upgrading an existing computer to a new operating system (Windows XP to Windows Vista) and migrating existing computer and user settings as part of the upgrade.

Configuring a Reference Computer

The operating system image is captured from a reference computer. The basic process involves configuring a computer to look the way you want it to look—the appropriate operating system, service packs, software updates, support drivers, and any additional software packages. You'll also need to have packages for the appropriate version of Sysprep (which is used to facilitate the migration of computer settings), the appropriate version of the User State Migration Tool (USMT) (which is used to migrate user files and settings), and for any other support scripts you might need to run to support your specific deployment scenario. The key here is to create Configuration Manager packages for everything you need to successfully set up the target computer. You'll then create a task sequence to bundle these together and run them in the proper order.

You can set up the reference computer manually and install everything you need on the computer yourself. The obvious downside is that it takes time, but you will know that you have the right configuration. On one hand, you can automate any or all of the reference computer setup. The downside here is that it takes some time to get the task sequence right. On the other hand, once you create the task sequence, you can reuse it and tweak it as needed, making future deployments much simpler. The following focuses on the automated method.

To build and configure a reference computer using a task sequence, follow these steps:

1. Navigate to the Task Sequences node under Operating System Deployment in the Configuration Manager Console as was shown in Figure 12-1.

2. Right-click Task Sequences, choose New from the context menu, and then Task Sequence to start the New Task Sequence Wizard, as was shown in Figure 12-2. Select the Build And Capture A Reference Operating System Image option and click Next.

3. On the Task Sequence Information page shown in Figure 12-10, type a name in the Task Sequence Name field and a description in the Comment field. In this scenario, you must select a boot image because you are creating a task sequence that will capture an image from a reference computer. Click Browse to display the list of boot images included with Configuration Manager and that you might have added from other external sources. In this example, the Vista Boot image file is selected.

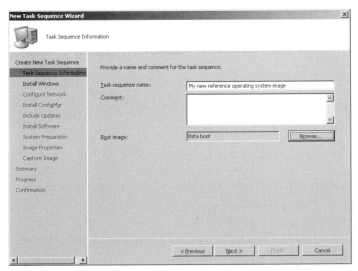

Figure 12-10   The New Task Sequence Wizard Task Sequence Information page

4. Click Next to display the Install The Windows Operating System page, as shown in Figure 12-11. Specify the Package that contains the operating system source files. Click Browse to display the list of Operating System Installation Packages you added through the Configuration Manager console. Specify the appropriate Edition to use if the package contains multiple editions. Type the Product Key to use and the Server Licensing Mode. By default, Disable Local Administrator Account is selected. This disables the local administrator account. If you need to enable the local administrator account, remove the default. If you do this, you will be able to specify a password for the local administrator account that Configuration Manager will assign for all installations of the operating system.

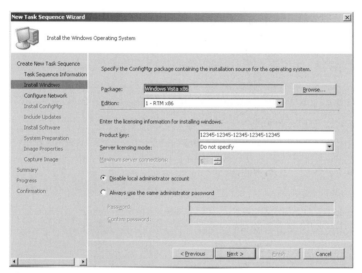

Figure 12-11   The New Task Sequence Wizard Install The Windows Operating System page

5. Click Next to display the Configure The Network page, as shown in Figure 12-12. On this page, specify whether the reference computer should be a member of a workgroup or domain and supply the appropriate connection information for each, including the account that has permissions to join the specified domain.

6. Click Next to display the Install The ConfigMgr Client page, as shown in Figure 12-13. Click Browse to display a list of Configuration Manager packages. Select the package that contains the Configuration Manager 2007 client installation source files. By default, the client will be assigned to the Configuration Manager site that is advertising the task sequence. However, you can also specify other installation properties associated with the CCMSetup.exe command. In this example, the command

CCMSetup.exe /mp:SMSMP01 instructs the task sequence to download installation files from a specific management point named SMSMP01.

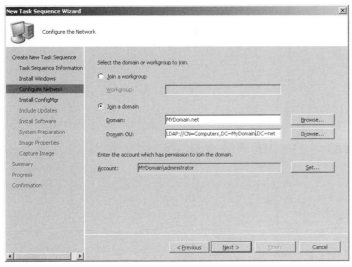

Figure 12-12   The New Task Sequence Wizard Configure The Network page

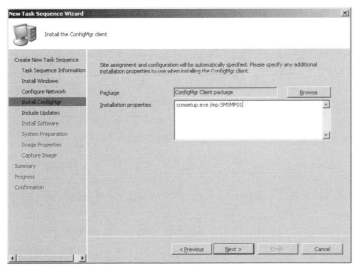

Figure 12-13   The New Task Sequence Wizard Install The ConfigMgr Client page

7. Click Next to display the Include Updates In Image page, as shown in Figure 12-14. On this page you can select the Mandatory Software Updates option to install all

software updates configured as mandatory for the target computers, the All Software Updates option to install all software updates advertised for the target computers, or the Don't Install Any Software Updates option, the default, to skip this step.

Important   For software updates to be installed, the target computer must be a member of a collection where software updates are available. This option would not apply, for example, to a bare-metal installation on a computer that is not yet a member of a Configuration Manager site.

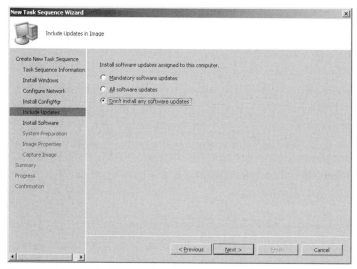

Figure 12-14   The New Task Sequence Wizard Include Updates In Image page

8. Click Next to display the Install Software Packages page, as shown in Figure 12-15. You can include software packages created with Configuration Manager. Click the New button to display a browse window from which you can select from a list of packages created for that site.

Note   You cannot include packages that are configured to run with the option Only When A User Is Logged On, or the option Run With User Rights. Programs that are configured to run another program first also cannot be included.

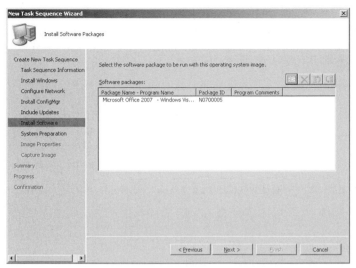

Figure 12-15 The New Task Sequence Wizard Install Software Packages page

9. Click Next to display the System Preparation page, as shown in Figure 12-16. On this page, you need to specify the Configuration Manager package that contains the appropriate version of Sysprep to use to capture reference computer settings. If the operating system you are installing is Windows Vista, Sysprep is already installed on the computer, and the option on this page will be grayed out.

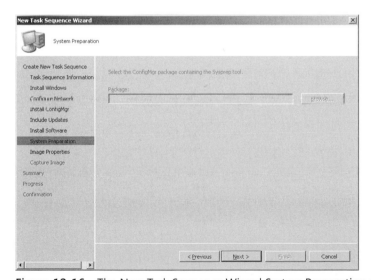

Figure 12-16 The New Task Sequence Wizard System Preparation page

10. Click Next to display the Image Properties page, as shown in Figure 12-17. Here you can identify who created the image, its version, and include a descriptive comment.

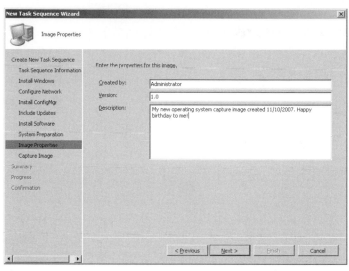

Figure 12-17   The New Task Sequence Wizard Image Properties page

11. Click Next to display the Capture Image Settings page, as shown in Figure 12-18. On this page, you need to specify a network location to save the image to. You can also supply the name of an account that has access to the network location.

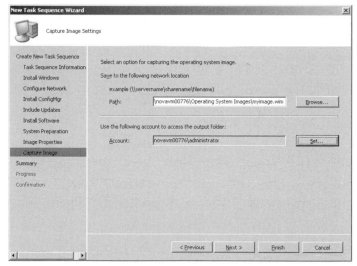

Figure 12-18   The New Task Sequence Wizard Capture Image Settings page

12. Click Next or Finish to display the Summary page, as shown in Figure 12-19, and review your configuration settings. Click Next to create the task sequence and then Close to exit the wizard.

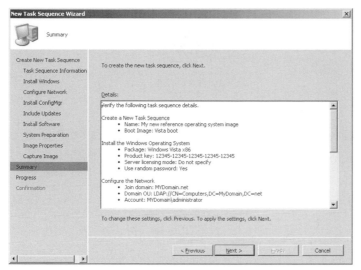

Figure 12-19   The New Task Sequence Wizard Summary page

The task sequence that you just created is an end-to-end set of steps that builds the reference computer according to the parameters that you specified and that also captures and stores an operating system image based on the configuration of the reference computer. However, you can modify the task sequence to carry out only those specific tasks that you want.

Editing the Reference Computer Task Sequence

The next step is to review the task sequence in the Task Sequence Editor. You can do this by right-clicking the task sequence in the Configuration Manager console and selecting Edit from the context menu. Figure 12-20 displays the task sequence you just created.

Using the Task Sequence Editor, you can see the task steps relating to the wizard pages you configured earlier categorized into two task groups: Build The Reference Machine and Capture The Reference Machine. Notice on the corresponding Properties tab as you click each task step that the text displayed in the Type field represents one of the actions discussed earlier. Notice, too, that the text displayed in the Name field is an arbitrary task step name that Configuration Manager assigned. Both the Name and the Description fields are editable, and it is recommended that you annotate each step in detail so that you understand what each step is doing and that any other administrator could easily understand the task steps as well.

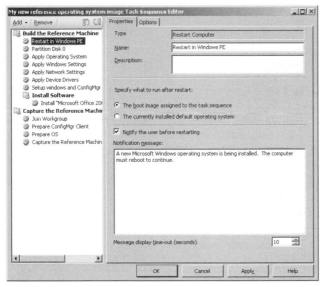

Figure 12-20   The new task sequence displayed in the Task Sequence Editor

You'll also see other task steps that Configuration Manager added for you to facilitate the process. For example, you can see that the task sequence begins by restarting the reference computer into the Windows Preinstallation Environment (Windows PE). On the Properties tab of the Restart in Windows PE task step, you can use either the boot image you supplied, or you can use the operating system already installed on the reference computer as the basis for the image. You can also customize or disable a notification message to the user of the computer.

Another example of a task step added to the resulting task sequence that you did not configure during the wizard is the Partition Disk 0 task step shown in Figure 12-21. Because in building the reference computer, you might also be installing a new operating system, Configuration Manager adds the step that reformats the hard disk. On the Properties tab you can identify which Disk Number and Disk Type to use. If you click the New button above the Volume list box, the Partition Properties dialog box is displayed, as shown in Figure 12-22. Here you can get much more detailed in the settings you choose.

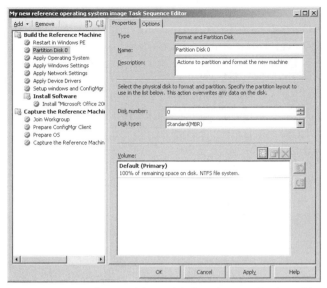

Figure 12-21   The Partition Disk 0 task step displayed in the Task Sequence Editor

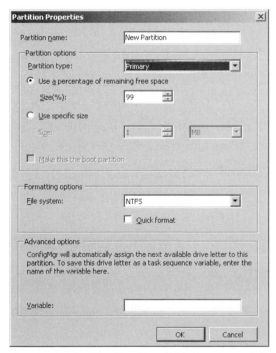

Figure 12-22   The Partition Disk 0 task step's Partition Properties dialog box

Select each task step and view its properties to see how you can customize the task sequence. Most task step properties will match the settings you configured using the New Task Sequence Wizard. However, often you can configure to a more granular level as shown with the Partition Disk 0 task step. For example, on the New Task Sequence Wizard's Install The Windows Operating System page, you identified the operating system source file package to use, the product key, the server licensing mode, and whether to disable the local administrator account. But something inside you probably said that there should be much more to configure than just that, and you are correct. In fact, that one wizard page is supported by two task steps in the resulting task sequence: Apply Operating System, shown in Figure 12-23, and Apply Windows Settings, shown in Figure 12-24.

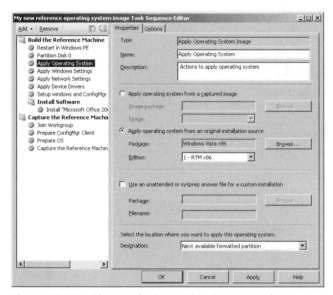

Figure 12-23   The Apply Operating System task step

Notice that on the Apply Operating System task step you can stick with the package you identified in the wizard, or alternatively use an operating system from another captured image file. You can also reference an unattended sysprep file and modify the location where the operating system files should be applied.

The Apply Windows Settings has the other wizard page settings that you can modify, but also includes fields for specifying a User Name and Organization Name, as well as the Time Zone setting.

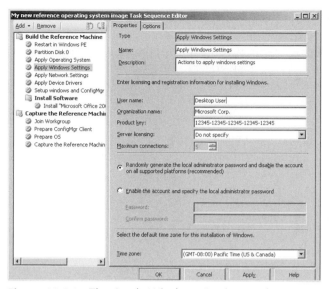

Figure 12-24   The Apply Windows Settings task step

You can add and remove task steps as required. For example, perhaps you need to run a custom script that modifies a registry setting after you run the Install Microsoft Office 2007–Windows Vista Setup task step. To add a new task step (or task group), follow these steps:

1.   In the Task Sequence Editor, select the task step or task group that the new step should follow.

2.   Click Add, and then locate the task step you want to add. In this example, choose Add, General, Run Command Line.

3.   Modify the Properties of the task step as required.

4.   Click Apply to save your changes.

In this example, the result is a new task step called Modify the Office registry that runs an appropriate script, as shown in Figure 12-25.

After you make all the modifications you need, click OK to save and close the task sequence.

Note   Unlike other Configuration Manager packages, task sequences are policy-based. This means that when you modify a task sequence, the change is included in a policy update rather than you having to refresh a package on a distribution point.

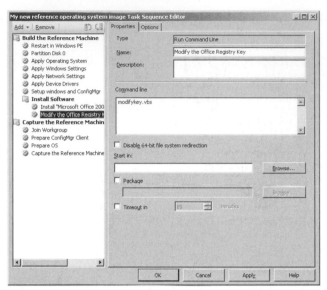

Figure 12-25   The Task Sequence Editor with the new task step displayed

Advertising the Task Sequence to the Reference Computer

Now you're ready to advertise the task sequence to the reference computer so that it can be configured and the new operating system image captured. You should create a collection that contains the Configuration Manager client that will act as the reference computer. With few exceptions, this wizard runs the same as the New Advertisement Wizard, which is used to advertise other Configuration Manager packages and discussed in Chapter 11.

To advertise the task sequence, follow these steps:

1. Navigate to the task sequence that you want to advertise.

2. Right-click the task sequence and select Advertise from the context menu to run the New Advertisement Wizard.

3. On the General page shown in Figure 12-26, specify the collection that contains the reference computer in the Collection field. Optionally, you can choose to make the advertisement available to target computers that are using Boot Media or PxE to deploy the image.

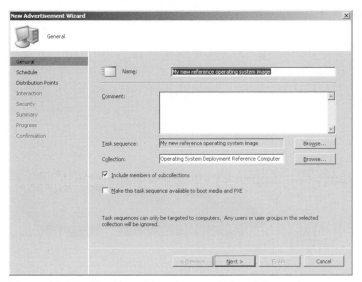

Figure 12-26 The New Advertisement Wizard General page

4. Click Next to display the Schedule page. Configure the advertisement schedule settings as you would for any other advertisement.

5. Click Next to display the Distribution Points page, as shown in Figure 12-27. This page differs somewhat from its counterpart for other Configuration Manager advertisements. For one thing, it is fairly well detailed and descriptive. The default option is Download Content Locally When Needed By Running Task Sequence. This option optimizes the download process by only downloading the files needed for each task step in the task sequence as needed. This helps to mitigate bandwidth issues and helps manage the download cache on the target computer.

6. Click Next to display the Interaction page, as shown in Figure 12-28. This page lets you choose whether users can run the task sequence independently of assigned times, whether to display client reminders, or whether to modify the custom countdown notification setting. Optionally, you can display the progress of the task sequence on the computer as each task step completes.

7. Complete the wizard by reviewing your settings on the Summary page, creating the advertisement, and then closing the wizard.

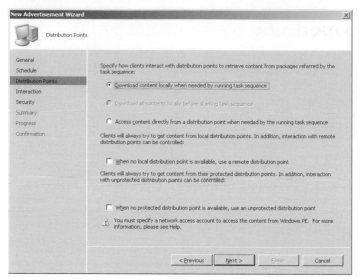

Figure 12-27   The New Advertisement Wizard Distribution Points page

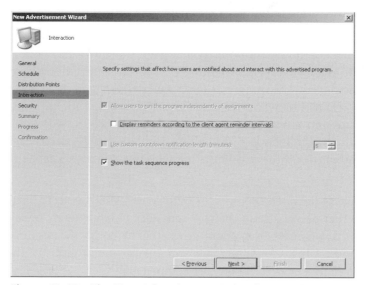

Figure 12-28   The New Advertisement Wizard Interaction page

The task sequence runs on the target reference computer according to the settings and schedule you configured. The next step is to customize and deploy the new operating system image.

Deploying the Operating System Image

When you ran the task sequence that built your reference computer, it also captured and saved the resulting operating system image. To deploy this image to a set of target computers, you need to add the new operating system image to the Operating System Images node in the Configuration Manager console and customize it. Then you can distribute it to appropriate distribution points and advertise it to the target computers.

To add the operating system image to the Configuration Manager console, follow these steps:

1. Navigate to the Operating System Images node in the Configuration Manager console.

2. Right-click the node and select Add Operating System Image Package to run the Add Operating System Image Wizard.

3. On the Data Source page shown in Figure 12-29, click Browse to locate the UNC path to the location of the operating system image you created earlier.

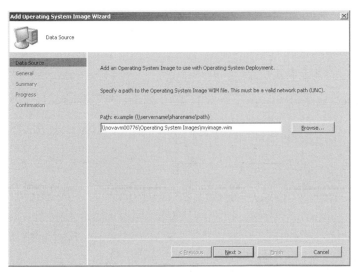

Figure 12-29   The Add Operating System Image Wizard Data Source page

4. Click Next to display the General page, as shown in Figure 12-30, and type a descriptive Name, Version, and Comment for the Operating System Image package you are creating.

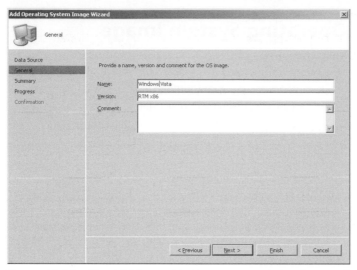

Figure 12-30   The Add Operating System Image Wizard General page

5. Click Next to review the settings you configured. Click Next to create the package and Close to exit the wizard.

You'll see the new operating system image package listed in the results pane of the Operating System Images node, as shown in Figure 12-31.

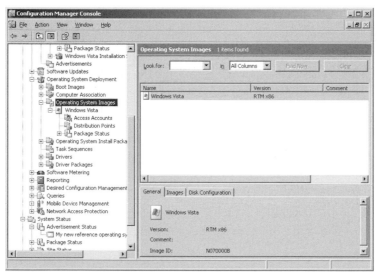

Figure 12-31   The operating system image displayed in the results pane of the Operating System Images node

Distribute the Operating System Image

When you added the new operating system image to the Operating System Images node in the Configuration Manager console, you in effect created an operating system image package. Before you can advertise and deploy the new image to target computers—which is your final goal—you must put the image package source files on the appropriate distribution points as you would any other Configuration Manager package.

To distribute the operating system image, follow these steps:

1. Navigate to the Operating System Images node in the Configuration Manager console and expand it.

2. Locate the entry for the image you want to distribute and expand that entry.

3. Right-click Distribution Points and select New Distribution Points from the context menu. You'll run the same New Distribution Points Wizard that you run for other Configuration Manager packages as discussed in Chapter 11.

4. Select the distribution point(s) to which you want the image to be copied. When you are finished, exit the wizard.

Just as you would with any other Configuration Manager package, if you modify or update the image, you should also update the image on any distribution points to which you've copied the image.

Deploying the Operating System Image to Target Computers

Now you can advertise the image to the set of target computers you wanted to upgrade at the beginning of this chapter, right? Well, not quite, but you're almost there. You first need to create a task sequence. Remember that the task sequence acts as the image package's "program" and lists the steps that need to be run and in what order. So you'll create a task sequence first that you can customize and then advertise to a collection of target computers.

Create the Deployment Task Sequence

To create the task sequence that you can use to advertise the operating system image to a collection of target computers, follow these steps:

1. Start the New Task Sequence Wizard.

2. On the Create A New Task Sequence page, shown in Figure 12-32, select the Install An Existing Image Package option.

3. Click Next to display the Task Sequence Information page, as shown in Figure 12-33. Type a name and descriptive comment and select an appropriate boot image as you did before.

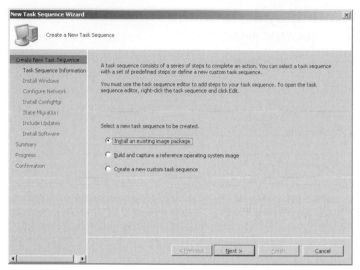

Figure 12-32   The New Task Sequence Wizard Create A New Task Sequence page

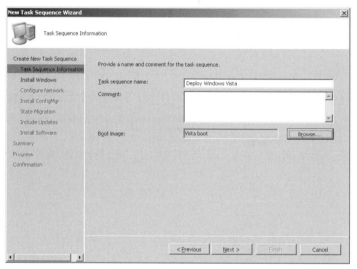

Figure 12-33   The New Task Sequence Wizard Task Sequence Information page

4. Click Next to display the Install The Windows Operating System page, as shown in Figure 12-34. Click Browse to display a list of operating system image packages and select the image you want to deploy. Leave Partition And Format The Target Computer Before Installing The Operating System selected unless you prefer not to repartition the target computer hard drive. Type the product key to use and the server licensing mode and determine whether to leave the local administrator account disabled or to enable it and provide a password to assign. The same password will be

used on all the target computers if you select the Always Use The Same Administrator Password option and might not be as secure.

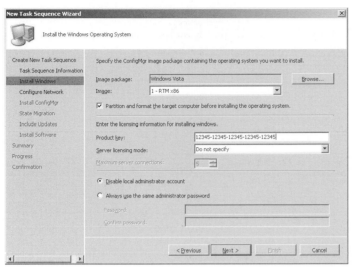

Figure 12-34   The New Task Sequence Wizard Install The Windows Operating System page

5. Click Next to display the Configure The Network page, as shown in Figure 12-35. On this page, specify whether the reference computer should be a member of a workgroup or domain and supply the appropriate connection information for each, including the account that has permissions to join the specified domain.

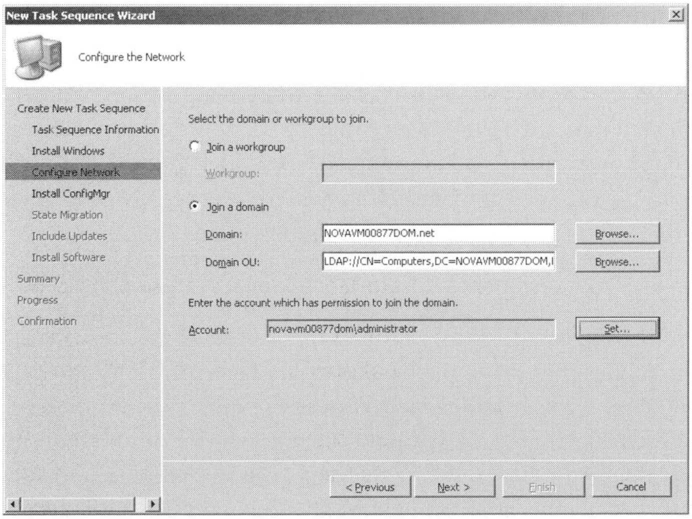

Figure 12-35   The New Task Sequence Wizard Configure The Network page

6. Click Next to display the Install The ConfigMgr Client page, as shown in Figure 12-36. Click Browse to display a list of Configuration Manager packages. Select the package that contains the Configuration Manager 2007 client installation source files. By default, the client will be assigned to the Configuration Manager site that is advertising the task sequence. However, you can also specify other installation properties associated with the CCMSetup.exe command, the SMSSITECODE command excepted.

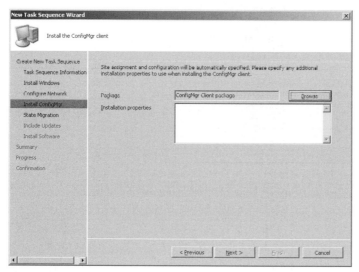

Figure 12-36   The New Task Sequence Wizard Install ConfigMgr Client page

7. Click Next to display the Configure State Migration page, as shown in Figure 12-37. If you are upgrading an existing computer to a new operating system as you are in this example, then you might also want to migrate the user's settings as well as the computer's network and Windows settings. The three main options on this page are enabled by default to do just that. Notice that you can disable any or all of them to control how many or whether you migrate any settings. If you select the Capture User Settings option, you need to use the most current version of the User State Migration Tool (USMT 3.0). As with other task steps, the USMT already must be included as a separate Configuration Manager package that you will specify in the USMT Package browse field. Notice that you can select one of two options referencing where to save the migrated settings. The Save User Settings On A State Migration Point option implies that you must have identified a server as a state migration point. There will be more discussion about that in the next section. If you did not choose to partition and format the disk on the Install The Windows Operating System page, you can alternately select the Save User Settings Locally option and bypass the need for a state migration point. Because you might have no way of know-

ing whether enough free space is available locally to store the user and computer settings, saving the settings on a state migration point might be the safer choice.

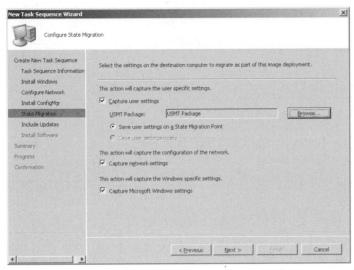

Figure 12-37   The New Task Sequence Wizard Configure State Migration page

8. Click Next to display the Include Updates In Image page, as shown in Figure 12-38. On this page, you can select the Mandatory Software Updates option to install all software updates configured as mandatory for the target computers, the All Software Updates option to install all software updates advertised for the target computers, or the Don't Install Any Software Updates option, the default, to skip this step.

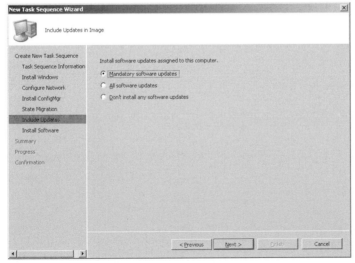

Figure 12-38   The New Task Sequence Wizard Include Updates In Image page

9. Click Next to display the Install Software Packages page, as shown in Figure 12-39. You can include any software packages created with Configuration Manager. Click the New button to display a browse window from which you can select from a list of packages created for that site.

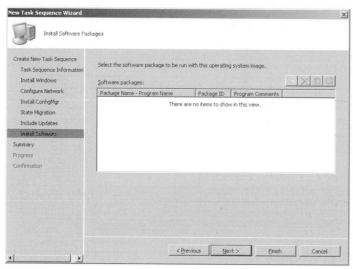

Figure 12-39   The New Task Sequence Wizard Install Software Packages page

10. Click Next to display the Summary page, as shown in Figure 12-40 and review your configuration settings. Click Next to create the task sequence, and then click Close to exit the wizard.

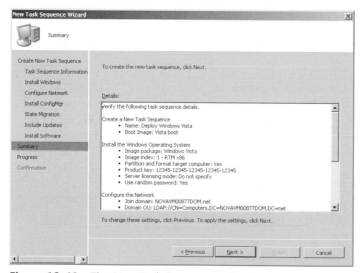

Figure 12-40   The New Task Sequence Wizard Summary page

Real World   About State Migration

A common scenario you'll face when deploying operating system upgrades will be the migration of settings from the current environment to the new environment. Operating System Deployment does this using two components: the User State Migration Tool (USMT) and the state migration point.

Operating System Deployment uses USMT 3.0 to migrate user state and settings. It captures user settings, called the scan state, from computers running Windows operating systems, and restores those settings, called the load state, to computers running the Windows 2000 Service Pack 4 operating system or later. When you obtain USMT 3.0, you create a Configuration Manager package for it using the methods described in Chapter 11.

> **More Info**   For more information about USMT, refer to the User State Migration Tool 3.0 documentation located on the Windows Vista Tech-Center at *http://technet2.microsoft.com/WindowsVista/en/library /91f62fc4-621f-4537-b311-1307df0105611033.mspx?mfr=true*. You can read more about how to migrate user and computer state in the topic "Planning for Operating System Deployment" in the Configuration Manager 2007 Documentation Library at *http://technet.microsoft.com/en-us/library /bb680651.aspx*.

The state migration point is used to store migrated settings during the capture phase of the deployment task sequence. A state migration point is a Configuration Manager site system role that you can assign to a server. To assign the state migration point role, follow these steps:

1. In the Configuration Manager console navigate to the Site Settings\Site Systems folder.

2. Select an existing site system in the results pane, right-click it, and select New Roles from the context menu to run the New Site Role Wizard or right-click Site Systems and select New, and then Server to run the New Site System Wizard.

3. On the System Role Selection page, select the State Migration Point option.

4. On the State Migration Point page, shown in Figure 12-41, you can specify how the migrated data should be managed. Specify a folder on the server that has enough available disk space to store the aggregate amount of data you'll be migrating. Select the Deletion Policy option, also known as the retention policy. During capture, the

settings are collected and saved to the state migration point for the Configuration Manager site of which the target computer is a client. During the restore process, the data is written to the target computer and then released by the task step Release State Store. At this step, a data retention timer begins. If you choose Immediately, the captured data is not saved, but deleted immediately. If you choose Delete After and specify a specific retention value, the captured data will be retained for the specified interval.

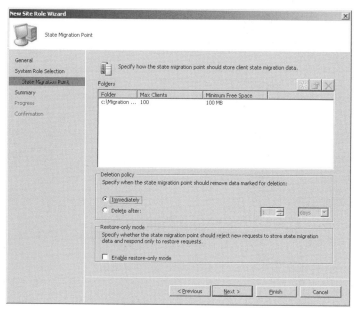

Figure 12-41   The New Site Role Wizard State Migration Point page

5. Click Next to review your selection; click Next again to assign the new role. Click Close to exit the wizard.

Editing the Deployment Task Sequence

The next step for you is to review this task sequence in the Task Sequence Editor just as you reviewed the reference computer task sequence earlier. You can do this by right-clicking the task sequence in the Configuration Manager console and selecting Edit from the context menu. Figure 12-42 displays the deployment task sequence you just created.

Using the Task Sequence Editor, you can see the task steps relating to the wizard pages you configured earlier categorized into three task groups: Capture Files And Settings, Install Operating System, and Setup Operating System. Notice on the corresponding

Properties tab as you click each task step that the text displayed in the Type field represents one of the actions discussed earlier. Notice, too, that the text displayed in the Name field is an arbitrary task step name that Configuration Manager assigned. Both the Name and the Description fields are editable, and it is recommended that you annotate each step in detail so that you understand what each step is doing and that any other administrator could easily understand the task steps as well.

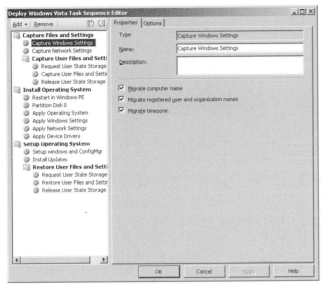

Figure 12-42   The new deployment task sequence displayed in the Task Sequence Editor

As before, you can see other task steps that Configuration Manager added for you to facilitate the process, and as before, you can edit and customize each task step to a greater level of granularity, as well as add and remove task steps and task groups.

Notice the task groups named Capture User Files And Settings and Restore User Files And Settings. These two task groups are complementary and facilitate the capture and migration of user settings. Each task group has three task steps that match the actions required when capturing and when restoring the user settings. Figure 12-43 shows the Request User State Storage task step from the Capture User Files And Settings task group, and Figure 12-44 shows the same task as configured in the Restore User Files And Settings task group. This task step is used to locate the network location you specified for the captured files and settings to be stored. The only difference is that the first uses that location to capture user state, while the second uses that location to restore user state.

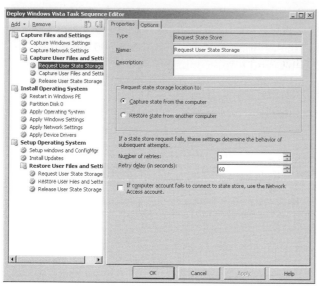

Figure 12-43   The Request User State Storage task step from the Capture User Files And Settings task group

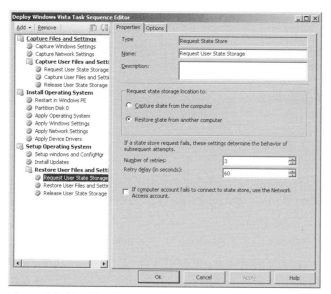

Figure 12-44   The Request User State Storage task step from the Restore User Files And Settings task group

Figure 12-45 shows the Capture User Files And Settings task step from the Capture User Files And Settings task group, and Figure 12-46 shows the Restore User Files And Settings task step as configured in the Restore User Files And Settings task group. These task steps carry out the capture and restore actions. Both reference the USMT package required to capture and restore user settings, and both allow you to determine how user profiles are handled. One difference is the Restore Local Computer User Profiles option in the Restore User Files And Settings task step. This option restores local user profiles. However, because the corresponding user account password cannot be migrated, you'll need to provide a single password that will be used for all local profiles that are restored.

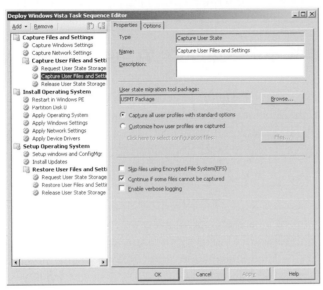

Figure 12-45   The Capture User Files And Settings task step from the Capture User Files And Settings task group

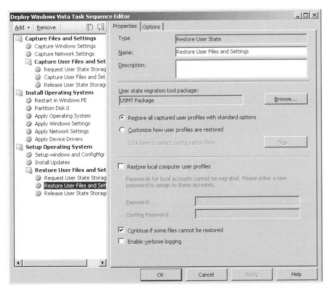

Figure 12-46   The Restore User Files And Settings task step as configured in the Restore User Files And Settings task group

The Release User State Storage task step is the same for both task groups and has no configurable settings. As described earlier, this task step triggers the Retention Policy you set when configuring the state migration point. During capture, the settings are collected and saved to the state migration point for the Configuration Manager site of which the target computer is a client. During the restore process, the data is written to the target computer and then released by the task step Release State Store. At this step, the data retention timer begins.

Advertising the Deployment Task Sequence to the Target Computers

Now you're ready to advertise the task sequence to the target computers that you want to upgrade to the new operating system. As before, create a collection that contains the Configuration Manager clients that will be the target computers. Then follow the same steps you did in the section "Advertising the Task Sequence to the Reference Computer."

Monitoring Status

You can monitor the status of the task sequences you advertised in much the same way that you would monitor status for any other advertisement. However, as you've seen with several of the new features of Configuration Manager, operating system deployment includes a home page that provides detailed information about advertisements that are specific to task sequences. You can view the home page in the results pane when you select the Operating System Deployment node in the Configuration Manager console. An example of this home page is displayed in Figure 12-47.

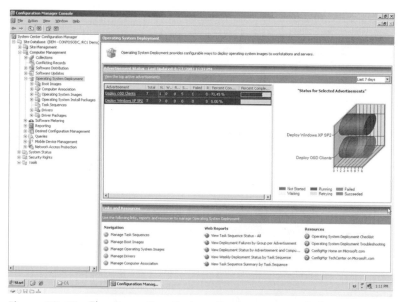

Figure 12-47   The Operating System Deployment node home page

You can see the list of advertisements that were created and can view the status of each one. If you select an advertisement from the list, you can run a Web report that provides greater detail, as shown in Figure 12-48. Notice that at the bottom of the home page there are links to several other Web reports that you can use to help you assess the status of your task sequences and operating system deployments.

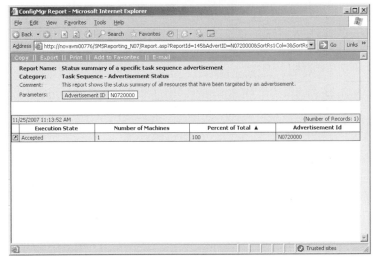

Figure 12-48   An example of a Web report generated for an advertised task sequence

Real World   Deploying Servers with Task Sequences

Generally, when you think about Configuration Manager, or Systems Management Server in the past, you think primarily about managing the desktop computers within your organization. Typically, you don't think about provisioning or managing server computers. However, with this version of operating system deployment, provisioning and managing your server computers becomes a very real scenario.

Often, organizations have very specific requirements for deploying servers, including security software, Flash Bios settings, drivers, supporting software, and so on. Change management for these servers is very controlled. Now think about what task sequences offer you. Task sequences carry out a set of deployment tasks in a specified order, return status, and provide you with a way to monitor and report on server deployment, just as it does for client deployments.

Figure 12-49 displays an example of a task sequence designed to deploy a baseline server image. Notice the groups that install firmware, partition the drive, install drivers, and install support programs such as Data Protection Manager, Operations Manager Management Pack, and ForeFront Client. Notice also, that you can configure Windows Server Roles as well. So consider Configuration Manager and task sequences as a viable server deployment and management tool.

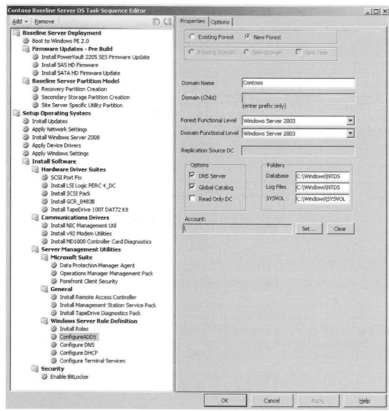

Figure 12-49   An example of a task sequence designed to deploy a baseline server image

Manual Deployment Methods

If you need to manually deploy the operating system image task sequence, operating system deployment provides a way to create stand-alone or bootable media that you can use. Configuration Manager supports the use of CD, DVD, or USB media for this purpose.

To create stand-alone media, follow these steps:

1. Navigate to the Task Sequences node.

2. Right-click the deployment task sequence for which you want to create the media. Select Create Task Sequence Media from the context menu to run the Task Sequence Media Wizard.

3. On the Select Media Type page, as shown in Figure 12-50, select the Stand-Alone Media option.

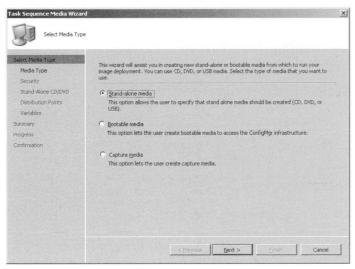

Figure 12-50   The Task Sequence Media Wizard Select Media Type page

4. Click Next to display the Media Type page, as shown in Figure 12-51. Select either USB Flash Drive and then enter the drive letter associated with the USB media or select CD/DVD Set. Specify the size of the media file. In the Media File field, specify the path to and the name of the file where the content will be copied.

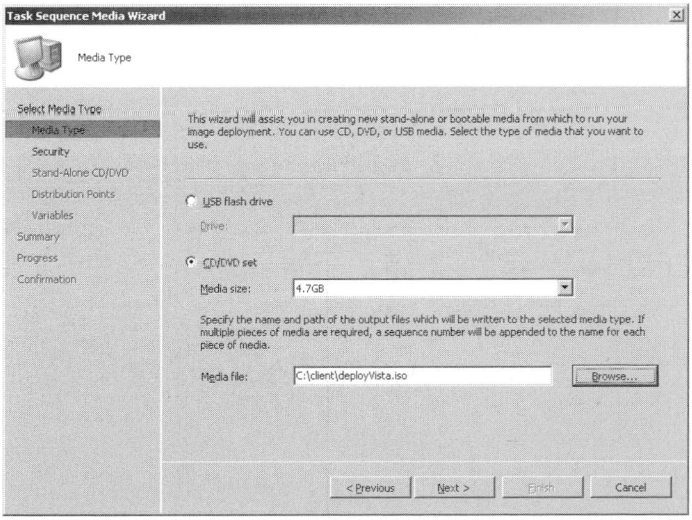

Figure 12-51   The Task Sequence Media Wizard Media Type page

5. Click Next to display the Security page, as shown in Figure 12-52. Select the Protect Media With A Password option if you want that added level of security, and then type and confirm a password. This password will be required when you use the media to run the task sequence.

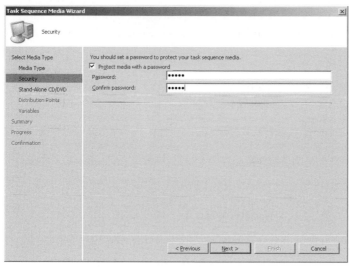

Figure 12-52   The Task Sequence Media Wizard Security page

6. Click Next to display the Stand-Alone CD/DVD page, as shown in Figure 12-53. The task sequence you selected is displayed along with all the packages referenced by that task sequence. If you initiated this wizard from the Task Sequence node, you can browse for and select the appropriate task sequence.

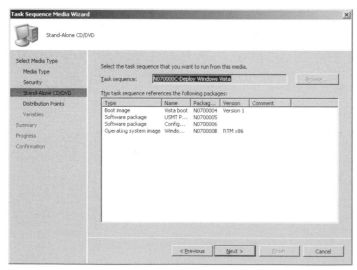

Figure 12-53   The Task Sequence Media Wizard Stand-Alone CD/DVD page

7. Click Next to display the Distribution Points page, as shown in Figure 12-54. Select the distribution points that contain the packages referenced by the task sequence from the list displayed in the Available Distribution Points Containing Packages Required By The Task Sequence list box, as shown in Figure 12-54. The list will indicate how many of the required packages are available on each distribution point. Click Add to add them to the Selected Distribution Points Containing Packages Required By The Task Sequence list box, as shown in Figure 12-55.

> **Important**   All the packages referenced in the task sequence must already be present on one or more distribution points, or the wizard will fail when you click Next.

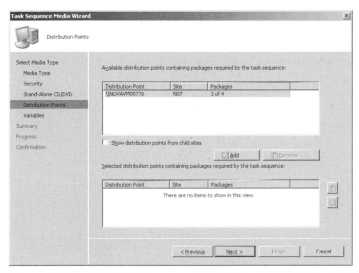

Figure 12-54   The Task Sequence Media Wizard Distribution Points page

8. Click Next to display the Add Variables page, as shown in Figure 12-56. Specify the task sequence variables that should be added to the stand-alone media.

> **More Info**   This chapter does not cover task sequence variables. You can find detailed information about task sequence variables in the topic "About Task Sequence Variables" in the Configuration Manager Documentation Library at *http://technet.microsoft.com/en-us/library/bb680651.aspx*.

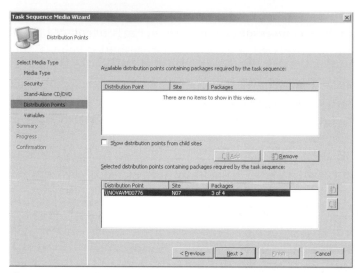

Figure 12-55   The Task Sequence Media Wizard Distribution Points page after selecting Distribution Points and clicking Add

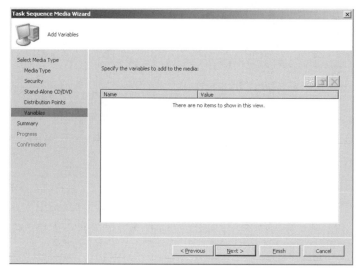

Figure 12-56   The Task Sequence Media Wizard Add Variables page

9. Click Next to review your selections; click Next again to create the media file. After the media file is created and copied to the specified media, click Close to exit the wizard.

10. If you chose CD or DVD as your media type, use a CD/DVD writing program to burn the .iso file to the media before you use it in the target computer.

To create boot media, follow these steps:

1. Navigate to the Task Sequences node.

2. Right-click the deployment task sequence for which you want to create the media. Select Create Task Sequence Media from the context menu to run the Task Sequence Media Wizard.

3. On the Select Media Type page, as shown in Figure 12-57, select the Bootable Media option.

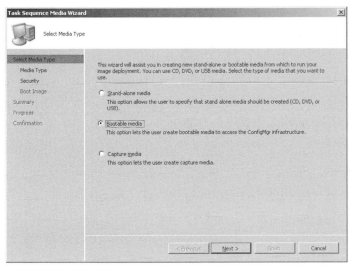

Figure 12-57   The Task Sequence Media Wizard Select Media Type page

4. Click Next to display the Media Type page, as shown in Figure 12-58. Select either USB Flash Drive and then enter the drive letter associated with the USB media, or select CD/DVD Set. Specify the size of the media file. In the Media File field, specify the path to and the name of the file where the content will be copied.

Note   Booting from USB is supported only on Windows Vista computers. Check that the USB drive you are using supports bootable media.

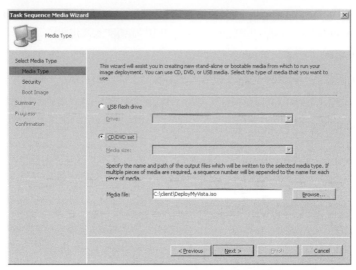

Figure 12-58   The Task Sequence Media Wizard Media Type page

5.   Click Next to display the Security page, as shown in Figure 12-59. Select the Protect Media With A Password option if you want that added level of security, and then type and confirm a password. This password will be required when you use the media to run the task sequence. You can have the task sequence create a self-signed certificate for the media to use, which is the default, or you can select Import Certificate and click Browse to find a certificate to use.

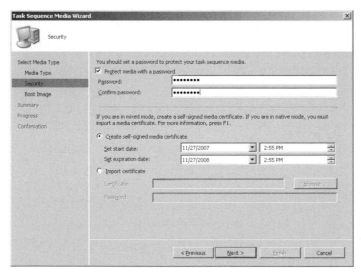

Figure 12-59   The Task Sequence Media Wizard Security page

6. Click Next to display the Boot Image page, as shown in Figure 12-60. Select the boot image that will run from the media you are creating. Select the distribution point that has the boot image package from the Distribution Point drop-down list.

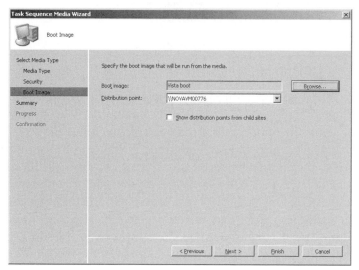

Figure 12-60   The Task Sequence Media Wizard Boot Image page

7. Click Next to review your selections; click Next again to create the media file. After the media file is created and copied to the specified media, click Close to exit the wizard.

8. If you chose CD or DVD as your media type, use a CD/DVD writing program to burn the .iso file to the physical media before you use it in the target computer.

Important   This really bears repeating: If you chose CD or DVD as your media type, remember that you need to use a CD/DVD writing program to burn the .iso file to the physical media before you can use it in the target computer.

After you create the media, you can run it at each target computer to which you want to deploy the task sequence.

Checkpoints

Operating system deployment has many facets and components, most of which are configurable and, therefore, subject to human error. This chapter focused on a common deployment scenario to get you started quickly with this feature. However, it is strongly recommended that you take the time to read the supporting documentation Microsoft provides for operating system deployment before exploring other deployment scenarios. You can find this content under the topic "Operating System Deployment for Configuration Manager" in the online Configuration Manager Documentation Library at *http://technet.microsoft.com/en-us/library/bb632767.aspx*.

Summary

This chapter discussed how to use operating system deployment to upgrade the operating system on one or more target computers in your Configuration Manager site. You explored the various components of operating system deployment including the boot and operating system images, the reference computer, and most importantly task sequences. You saw how to use task sequences to automate the various tasks that needed to be carried out in order to build a reference computer, capture an image from the reference computer, deploy the operating system to a target computer, and create custom task sequences. You saw how task sequences and operating system deployment fit into the software distribution process. You saw, too, that there is more to operating system deployment than this chapter or this book has room to cover. In the next chapter, you learn about another key pillar of Configuration Manager 2007: software updates.

Chapter 13

Deploying Software Updates

State messages sent

Software updates are deployed!

In danger no more

~Doug Eby, Senior Technical Writer, Configuration Manager

This chapter explains how you can use the software updates feature in Configuration Manager 2007 along with the Microsoft-recommended software updates management process to provide an effective system for updating software in your environment.

Much of this chapter's content is drawn from the software updates management best practices documented by *Microsoft Solutions for Management (MSM) 2.5* and the *Microsoft Operations Framework (MOF)*, which provides operational guidance covering reliability, availability, supportability, and manageability of Microsoft products and technologies. For more information about MSM and MOF, see Microsoft Management and Operations at *http://www.microsoft.com/technet/solutionaccelerators/cits/mo/default.mspx* and Microsoft

Operations Framework at *http://www.microsoft.com/technet/solutionaccelerators/cits/mo/mof/default.mspx.*

The Need for Effective Software Updates Management

Today's computer systems and networks are under an unprecedented level of threat, ranging from viruses and worms to malicious insiders. Software updates management, when properly implemented as part of a defensive strategy, can help organizations adopt a security posture and mitigate vulnerability in their systems. Consequently, software updates management has become an increasingly important topic for management, who is anxious to demonstrate corporate responsibility to shareholders, and for the IT manager, whose job it is to maintain and keep running secure systems.

According to the joint 2005 Computer Security Institute/Federal Bureau of Investigation Computer Crime and Security Survey, nearly 84 percent of respondents detected an attack related to a virus, which was defined as a virus, a Trojan horse, or a worm. While the percentage of reported virus attacks remains high, the average reported loss due to virus activity has continued to drop over the last few years from nearly $200,000 in 2003 to just over $65,000 in 2005. This decrease in overall damages from virus activity can be largely attributed to the growing awareness for the need of an effective software updates management strategy in the enterprise.

When the SQL Slammer worm swept the Internet in January 2003, a fix was available from Microsoft 184 days earlier. Today, you no longer have the luxury of time when an exploit is discovered in the wild. The trend has continued to move toward zero-day exploits, where an exploit is discovered on the same day that Microsoft releases an update to remove the vulnerability. In fact, there have been several recent exploits released within days of Microsoft's bulletin describing the vulnerability. The diminishing window between update and exploit is perhaps one of the more compelling arguments for an organization to implement a software updates management process that is capable of deploying software updates quickly, reliably, and efficiently.

Introduction to the Software Updates Management Process

The remaining sections in this chapter describe a software updates management process as recommended by Microsoft. This process, introduced in MSM 2.5, uses a four-phase approach of Identify, Evaluate & Plan, and Deploy and was based on several MOF functions. Also discussed is the implementation of Windows Server Update Services (WSUS) and software updates infrastructure, along with instructions on responding to software update emergencies and accelerated timelines.

The Microsoft Operations Framework

There are many approaches to planning and implementing software updates management solutions. The preferred approach is to base a solution upon an existing operations framework, such as MOF. MOF was designed to provide prescriptive guidance to organizations about how to manage their IT operations. MOF consists of three models:

- Process
- Team
- Risk

Of specific interest to software updates management, the MOF *process model* is a functional model of the processes performed by operations teams when managing and maintaining IT services. It's based upon the Office of Government Commerce's IT Infrastructure Library (ITIL), a widely accepted body of practice for operations management. The *team model* and *risk model* might also be of interest, as they provide guidance on the formation of software updates management teams, including duties and responsibilities, and a structured approach to managing risk, which is useful when evaluating alerts of vulnerability and software updates and determining the best course of action.

More Info   For more information about the Office of Government Commerce's ITIL, visit its Web site at *http://www.itil.co.uk*.

The MOF process model defines four quadrants of management, as shown in Figure 13-1. The quadrants are Changing, Operating, Supporting, and Optimizing. Each quadrant has a mission of service. In the Changing quadrant, the mission is to introduce new service solutions, technologies, systems, applications, and processes. The mission of the Operating quadrant is to perform and manage the daily tasks associated with running IT Services. As the name suggests, the Supporting quadrant's mission is to resolve incidents, problems, and inquiries as they arise. Last, the Optimizing quadrant's mission is to examine the environment the IT services run in and drive changes to optimize cost, performance, capacity, and availability.

Within each quadrant are major management review processes. These are necessary checkpoints used to guarantee success of the management processes. The reviews are split into two categories: time-based and release-based. The Release Readiness Review and Release Approved Review are release-based reviews and take place before and after a release into the computing environment. The Operations Review and SLA (Service Level Agreement) Review, both time-based reviews, should occur at regular intervals to assess the performance of the internal operations and the agreed-upon customer service levels.

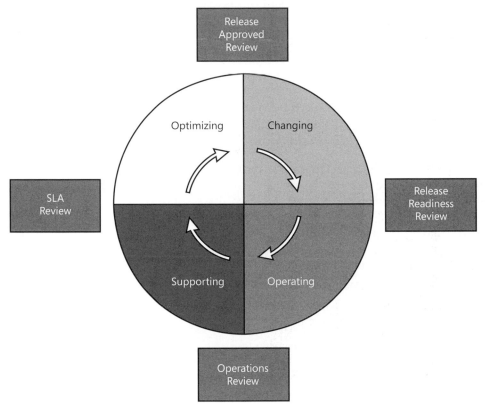

Figure 13-1   The MOF process model

Any comprehensive software updates management solution will touch on all four quadrants of the MOF process model—for example, an organization is focused on auditing systems for software updates compliance and monitoring alerts for vulnerability and software updates in the Operating quadrant, on assessing and planning response to alerts and downloading and evaluating any software updates in the Supporting quadrant, packaging and testing updates in the Optimizing quadrant, and deploying and installing updates as well as auditing and rolling back the update, if required, in the Changing quadrant.

The Microsoft-Recommended Software Updates Management Process

Introduced in Microsoft Solutions for Management 2.5 and based on the MOF Change Management, Release Management, and Configuration Management service management functions, the Microsoft–recommended software updates management process is a four-phase approach to managing updates to software. The four phases are Assess, Identify, Evaluate & Plan, and Deploy. The process and its four phases are shown in Figure 13-2.

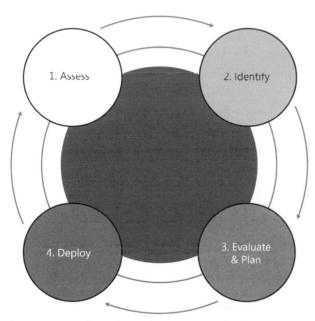

Figure 13-2 The Microsoft-recommended four-phase software updates management process

Defined events trigger movement through the phases of the process. Beginning with the Assess phase, the triggering event that causes a move to the Identify phase is notification that a software update exists. The event that causes a move from the Identify phase to the Evaluate & Plan phase is the submission of a formal Request for Change

(RFC). The triggering event for a move to the Deploy phase from the Evaluate & Plan phase is receipt of approval to deploy the software update into the production environment. Finally, the move from the Deploy phase to the Assess phase and the beginning of the process cycle again is triggered by completion of the release of the software update.

Within each phase there are discreet steps that together implement the software updates management process. These steps, and the phase they belong to, are described in Table 13-1.

Table 13-1   Steps in the Four-Phase Software Updates Management Process

Phase	Steps
Assess	Inventory/discover existing computing assets.
	Assess security threats and vulnerabilities.
	Determine the best source for information about new software updates.
	Assess the existing software distribution infrastructure.
	Assess operational effectiveness.
Identify	Discover new software updates in a reliable way.
	Determine whether software updates are relevant.
	Obtain and verify software update source files.
	Determine nature of software update and submit RFC.
Evaluate & Plan	Determine the appropriate response.
	Plan the release of the software update.
	Build the release.
	Conduct acceptance testing of the release.
Deploy	Deployment preparation.
	Deployment of the software update to targeted computers.
	Post-implementation review.

Although no technology solution can automate the entire software updates management process, they can help somewhat, and Configuration Manager 2007 integrates well into software updates management processes.

Preparing for Software Updates Management

Before an organization can implement a software updates management process, it needs to prepare for it. Although the four-phase model has an Assess phase, with steps that would appear to cover the initial preparation for software updates management, the phase is part of an established and running software updates management process. Without careful preparation, a software updates management solution is extremely likely to fail. Preparing for software updates management is a project in itself, with the defined goal of getting the organization to the point where it can enter the Assess phase of the four-phase model. Among the tasks that need to be accomplished during the preparation project are identifying, inventorying, and bringing the IT assets that will fall under the solution to a known configuration, deployment of the software updates management infrastructure, and establishment and training of the software updates management team.

Necessary tasks in the project of preparing for software updates management are the identification of assets that will fall under the software updates management process, inventorying them, and configuring them so that they conform to a secure baseline. Not all the IT assets within an organization might qualify for inclusion in a software updates management process. Examples of such systems might be legacy systems due for retirement, development and test systems, and systems leased from a vendor with which there's a support agreement including upgrade maintenance in place. The goal of identifying and inventorying assets is to quantify the number of systems that the software updates management process needs to cover, their physical and logical positions within the enterprise, and their hardware and software profiles. You use this information in two ways: to categorize the systems and to determine what the secure configuration or baseline should be in each category and to design the software updates management infrastructure to support the software updates management process.

Identifying IT Assets

There are ways to identify IT assets, which can be divided into two categories: manual and automated. In medium and large organizations, manual identification of assets might not be feasible, and an automated approach might be favored. Configuration Manager is able to discover assets using a variety of mechanisms, including searching Active Directory or performing network-based discovery. The quandary here is that you can't deploy Configuration Manager 2007 to support the software updates management solution effectively without the information that's derived from this task. But with Configuration Manager 2007 in place, you can perform this task, and subsequent tasks, more efficiently. One strategy is to deploy a minimal Configuration Manager infrastructure that's used solely to gather this information and which is reconfigured when building out the software updates management infrastructure.

Inventorying IT Assets

After you identify IT assets, you must inventory them. The goal is to determine what the hardware profile of the system is and what software is installed on each. Without this information it won't be possible to determine which systems need to be brought to a secure baseline configuration. A comprehensive software updates management solution will need to cope for variations in hardware and software, but it's not possible or desirable for most organizations to manage a large number of combinations. Instead, the organization should categorize IT assets—either by function, such as server, desktop, or by hardware or software configuration. You can use Configuration Manager 2007 to help with the inventory process. It will accurately report the operating system, configured services, and any programs or updates that registered themselves with Add/Remove Programs on clients. You can use the Configuration Manager 2007 Software Inventory Client Agent to scan Configuration Manager client computers for all installed executables, which is useful for inventorying those applications that didn't register themselves. You can examine information about installed applications on any Configuration Manager-managed client using the Resource Explorer, and it's contained under both Hardware and Software nodes in the Microsoft Management Console (MMC)–based view.

Before you can inventory systems using Configuration Manager, the Configuration Manager Client must be installed on them. Configuration Manager provides several methods for installing clients. As mentioned previously, clients can be installed and assigned to a site in a minimal Configuration Manager infrastructure that's used solely to inventory IT assets. Once the software updates management infrastructure is built out, clients can be assigned to Configuration Manager sites other than the one in which the Configuration Manager client was initially assigned.

Configuring IT Assets

After assets are identified, inventory has been performed, and each has been categorized, you need to configure the assets and bring them to a secure baseline. Each category will have its own configuration, and you should be careful when determining what that configuration should be. The secure baseline should address both the hardware and software configuration for IT assets. As a rule of thumb, each system should be configured for the task to which it is applied, with no extraneous hardware or software and with all appropriate updates applied. Once a secure baseline configuration is identified for a category, all new systems deployed in that category should conform to the baseline. During the software updates management process, as updates to software are deployed, the secure baseline configuration will change.

Until a system is brought to the secure baseline for the category within which it's placed, it can't be included in the software updates management process. As with identifying and inventorying IT assets, you can use Configuration Manager 2007 to bring systems to a secure baseline configuration in preparation for a software updates management process. Of concern to most organizations is ensuring that the software updates necessary to bring a system to a secure baseline configuration are applied. Automating this process with Configuration Manager 2007 is discussed in detail in the "Deploying Software Updates" section later in this chapter.

Building the Configuration Manager Software Updates Infrastructure

Building out a software updates management infrastructure can be a daunting task. A poorly designed infrastructure can have a serious impact on the performance of the software updates management process and might result in updates not being applied to systems in a timely fashion. With Configuration Manager, organizations have the ability to reconfigure and optimize their software updates management infrastructure once it's deployed, but this shouldn't be relied on in place of a good initial design and implementation. The goal of the implementation should be to build an infrastructure that you can rely on to deploy software updates to systems in a timely fashion.

As discussed earlier, you should use the information gathered during the identification and inventorying of IT assets to design the software updates management infrastructure. When planning the Configuration Manager site hierarchy, take into consideration the categories of assets that will be in each site. For example, Configuration Manager sites are comprised of IPv4 or IPv6 subnets, and network design best practices recommend placing servers on different subnets from workstations, so it might make sense to create Configuration Manager sites designed to achieve the different software updates management needs of each category of system on each subnet. An example of a Configuration Manager infrastructure that has several sites, each for a specific category of IT asset, is shown in Figure 13-3.

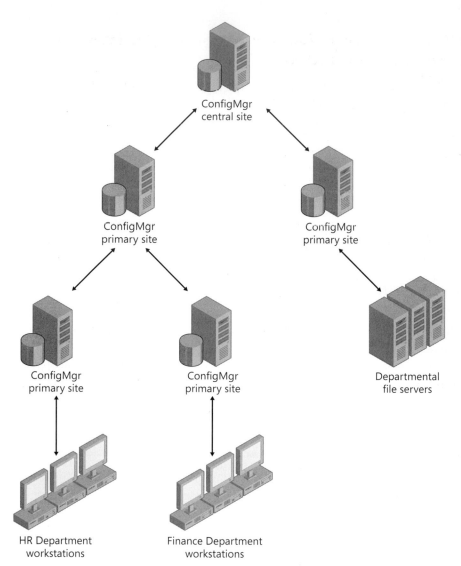

Figure 13-3   A Configuration Manager infrastructure designed to support software updates management

> ### Real World   Considerations for the Software Updates Management Infrastructure
>
> Keep in mind how critical each category of system is when considering the software updates management infrastructure. Sites with line-of-business systems, such as servers and workstations that are required for the organization to function, should be placed higher up in the Configuration Manager site hierarchy. To guarantee that critical updates can be deployed to them as soon as required, intersite links to these sites from the Configuration Manager central site shouldn't be configured with bandwidth restrictions. Sites containing noncritical systems can be placed further down in the hierarchy and the intersite links bandwidth restricted as needed. Where a site has multiple categories of assets with a large number of systems in each, it might be desirable to deploy multiple Configuration Manager site servers in the site and assign one or more categories to each in order to balance the load against software updates management requirements.

Establishing and Training the Software Updates Management Team

When preparing for software updates management, you need to make an effort to establish the software updates management team. The software updates management team will be responsible for monitoring for alerts of updates to software. When an alert is received, the team needs to assess the impact on the production environment protected by the software updates management process. If, as a consequence of an alert, a software update or configuration change needs to be applied to part of or to the entire production environment, the software updates management team will be responsible for building, testing, and deploying the update or change.

The makeup of the software updates management team will vary from organization to organization and will depend on many factors, including the organization's size, the number of categories of IT assets, the number of systems, and the complexity of the production environment. In larger organizations many people might fulfill a role, while in smaller organizations team members might hold more than one role. The MOF team model white paper, which is available at *http://www.microsoft.com/technet/solutionaccelerators/cits/mo/mof/moftml.mspx*, is a useful reference and provides guidance when building operations teams for organizations of all sizes.

The software updates management team will need to undergo training on the software updates management process and on how to use the software updates management infrastructure and associated tools. This training should be tailored to the production environment protected by the software updates management process.

The Four-Phase Software Updates Management Process

As detailed earlier, the Microsoft-recommended software updates management process is a four-phase process: Assess, Identify, Evaluate & Plan, and Deploy. The process is a continuous cycle, reflecting the reality of operations management. As the result of an alert of a software update, the organization shifts from the Assess phase to the Identify phase and begins its journey through the process cycle. It's important to realize that movement through the phases of the process is update-specific. This means that if an organization is in the Evaluate & Plan phase in response to one update when an alert is received for another, the organization will move to the Identify phase for the second update and be in two phases of the process simultaneously. This can pose both logistical and technical challenges to the organization, especially if the alerts are somewhat related or dependencies exist in the updates, and care should be taken.

The Assess Phase

The Assess phase is the first phase in the software updates management process. In the Assess phase the organization is concerned primarily with the ongoing assessment of its production environment covered by the software updates management process and with monitoring for alerts of software updates. Although many of the steps and tasks in the Assess phase are similar to the tasks undertaken during preparation for the implementation of a software updates management process, they're instead focused on optimizing and improving the existing software updates management process

Inventorying and Discovering Existing Computing Assets

As part of the operations of any production environment, IT assets will be added, updated, or retired. This task in the Assess phase is concerned solely with ensuring that the record of IT assets is accurate. As assets are added to the production environment, they should be inventoried and evaluated for inclusion into the software updates management process. Assets that are retired should be removed from the record and from the software updates management process. Existing assets should continuously be inventoried to ensure that their configuration hasn't changed without a formal change management process or the software updates management process. You can automate these tasks somewhat by using Configuration Manager's Active Directory and network-based discovery techniques, which is especially useful for discovering unmanaged or rogue systems that were deployed outside a management process.

Assessing Security Threats and Vulnerabilities

Although the IT assets within an organization might have the latest software updates applied to them, there might still be risk from security threats and vulnerabilities introduced by the addition, configuration, or removal of hardware or software components. The organization needs to remain vigilant and frequently check for vulnerabilities by reviewing software updates compliance for clients, which is discussed later in this chapter, or by reviewing the compliance for configuration baselines, which is discussed in Chapter 14, "Implementing Desired Configuration Management." When a vulnerability is discovered, you need to undertake a risk analysis to determine the best course of action. Typically, you'll take steps to mitigate the vulnerability through a configuration change or software update deployment.

Determining the Best Source for Information about Software Updates

The software updates management team needs to remain informed about new software updates for IT assets under control of the software updates management process. The team can remain informed by subscribing to e-mail notifications, visiting vendor Web sites, and through regular contact with representatives of software vendors.

Microsoft's authoritative Web site for technical bulletins, advisories, updates, tools, and other security-related information for IT professionals is *http://www.microsoft.com/technet /security*, where users can also sign up for technical security notifications and the *Microsoft Security Newsletter.*

Assessing the Existing Software Updates Infrastructure

Although careful planning and implementation might yield a versatile software updates management infrastructure that meets the needs of the organization at implementation time, it might not suffice as the organization changes. The software updates management team needs to assess the software updates management infrastructure continuously to ensure that it continues to meet the organization's needs. Configuration Manager 2007 is an extremely flexible management solution and can be reconfigured as needed to support the addition, change in configuration, or removal of categories of IT assets or sites.

If the Assess phase was entered after the completion of the last phase in the software updates management process, the Deploy phase, the organization should evaluate how successful the deployment of software updates was. If problems were encountered, the infrastructure should be examined for problems.

Assessing Operational Effectiveness

Last, in the Assess phase, the software updates management team needs to validate the entire software updates management process. It needs to ask questions such as the following:

- Does the software updates management team have the necessary resources?

- Do key security stakeholders have the necessary training and understanding of the software updates management process?

- Are formal processes in place for day-to-day operations that have an impact on security?

You can find the Microsoft Operations Framework Self-Assessment Tool 2.0, designed to gauge an organization's operational excellence, at *http://www.microsoft.com/technet /solutionaccelerators/cits/mo/mof/moftool.mspx*.

As with assessing the software updates infrastructure for problems after a deployment, the software updates management team should assess the operational effectiveness of the process, including its own performance. Lessons learned in this assessment should be applied in order to improve operational excellence for future software updates.

Leaving the Assess Phase and Moving to the Identify Phase

When the software updates management team receives notification of a software update that affects the production environment, the software updates management process moves into the Identify phase.

The Identify Phase

During the Identify phase of the four-phase software updates management process, the organization is focused on gathering information about the software update that triggered entry into the Identify phase, whether or not the update is relevant to the production environment; obtaining the software update itself; and categorizing the update as either an emergency update or one that can be dealt with routinely within the time frame set by the organization for software updates.

Discovering New Software Updates Reliably

When an organization receives a technical security notification from Microsoft about a software update, the alert contains links to the TechNet Security Center Web site at *http://www.microsoft.com/technet/security*, where more detailed information is made available. Organizations might choose to subscribe to other sources of information about software updates or receive e-mail messages from account representatives or other Microsoft employees. Regardless of where the alert came from, the software updates management team needs to verify its authenticity. For alerts detailing software updates to Microsoft products, the authoritative source of information is the TechNet Security Center Web site, which the team should visit. Of special note, Microsoft never releases software updates as attachments to e-mail messages. If the team receives an e-mail message with an attachment purporting to come from Microsoft and containing a software update, the safest course of action is to delete the message. Similarly, rather than clicking on links contained in e-mail messages that appear to take the reader to a Microsoft Web site, the reader should copy and paste the URL into his or her browser, as the true Web site that the user will be taken to can be hidden in the formatting of the e-mail message.

Software updates in Configuration Manager 2007, when configured, will automatically synchronize with the Microsoft Update Web site, retrieving information about software updates in the products that it's aware of. Using the Configuration Manager information, you can view just about every applicable software update for the production environment, as well as detailed information about software updates compliance on clients. Figure 13-4 shows a screenshot of software updates listed in the Configuration Manager console and the different levels of compliance. You can find details on how to configure software updates to show this information later in this chapter.

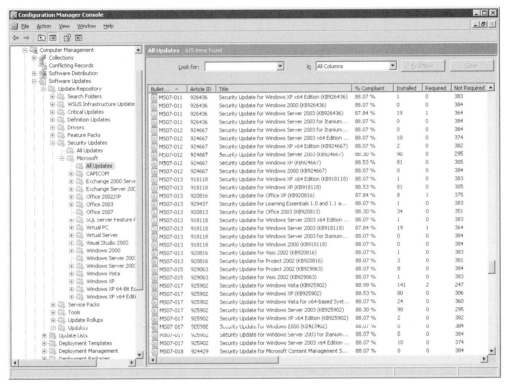

Figure 13-4 Software updates compliance information displayed in the Configuration Manager console

Determining Whether Software Updates Are Relevant

Benjamin Franklin wrote, "In this world nothing is certain but death and taxes." Although this was written long before software was invented, today he would no doubt feel compelled to add software updates to the list of certainties faced in life. The fact is that software releases are made on a continual basis and can come from a variety of sources, such as operating systems and application vendors, independent software vendors (ISVs), original equipment manufacturers (OEMs), and hardware manufacturers. Not every released software update will necessarily apply to an organization's production environment, even when it touches a software product in use. The software updates management team will need to evaluate and determine whether or not updates are relevant to the production environment covered by the software updates management process. For example, a software update to a word-processing package that's deployed within the organization might apply only to a feature that isn't installed or used, or perhaps the risk from not installing the update is considered so low that it can be safely ignored. A good starting point for evaluating the relevance of a software update issued by Microsoft is the detailed bulletin, which can be found on the Security Bulletin Search Web site at *http://www.microsoft.com/technet/security/current.aspx*. The bulletin will contain details of the vulnerability addressed by the update, any mitigating factors that might affect the requirement to update a system, and any workarounds if available.

Each software update should be assessed from a risk management perspective, with the organization making a determination about whether or not the update should be applied to its affected IT assets. When considering the risk from not installing an update, the organization must balance it against the risk from installing the update. Risk from installation includes incompatibilities with already-installed applications, system instability, and loss of functionality.

As described earlier, software updates in Configuration Manager are configured to synchronize with the Microsoft Update Web site to retrieve the information for available software updates and list them in the Configuration Manager console. Only software updates for the configured products and classifications are listed. You can find full details on configuring software updates in Configuration Manager, and details on how the software updates feature works, later in this chapter.

Obtaining and Verifying Software Update Source Files

When assessing the relevance of a software update, it's often desirable to have the source files for the update at hand. The software updates management team should take care when obtaining software updates to ensure that they come from legitimate sources only. Every software update that Microsoft releases is digitally signed, and you can verify its authenticity by examining the signature. Although you can do this manually, you can also do it using Configuration Manager. You can download software updates in Configuration Manager by using the Download Updates Wizard. When the wizard downloads the software updates, it checks the signature to verify that each is legitimate. If you decide to download the software update manually, you can verify the software update's digital signature through its properties using Windows Explorer. Figure 13-5 shows the dialog box of a software update's digital signature, accessible through Windows Explorer.

Until a software update identified in an alert has been successfully downloaded and verified, the software updates management process can't leave the Identify phase.

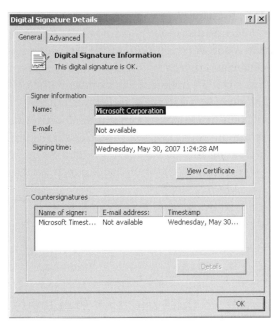

Figure 13-5   A digital signature dialog box, accessible through Windows Explorer

Determining the Nature of the Software Update and Submitting a Request for Change

Every software update released by Microsoft is assigned a severity rating. The purpose of the ratings is to provide guidance to administrators and software updates management teams about the urgency with which the update should be handled. These ratings, and their meanings, are listed in Table 13-2. You can find full details of the ratings used by Microsoft on the TechNet Security Center Web site at *http://www.microsoft.com /technet/security/bulletin/rating.mspx.*

Table 13-2   Software Updates Severity Ratings

Rating	Definition
Critical	A vulnerability whose exploitation could allow the propagation of an Internet worm without user action.
Important	A vulnerability whose exploitation could result in compromise of the confidentiality, integrity, or availability of users' data or of the integrity or availability of processing resources.
Moderate	Exploitability is mitigated to a significant degree by factors such as default configuration, auditing, or difficulty of exploitation.
Low	A vulnerability whose exploitation is extremely difficult or whose impact is minimal.

The software updates management team should take its severity rating into account when determining the nature of an update. Software updates with a low rating might be safely ignored until a predefined refresh cycle is begun, whereas an update rated as critical might need to be deployed as soon as possible. Mitigating factors should also be taken into consideration when determining the nature of an update. For example, with sufficient perimeter defenses and a secure VPN in place, a software updates management team might consider not rushing an update for a newly discovered vulnerability that a worm is exploiting if the port used by the worm to propagate itself is blocked at the firewall and not allowed over a VPN connection.

Other considerations that the software updates management team should examine are the impact of the update on the production environment. For example, does the update require systems to be restarted after installation and can it be rolled back if it's determined that the update has a negative effect on the production environment?

After the software updates management team determines the nature of the software update, it should submit an RFC to the Change Management Board.

Leaving the Identify Phase and Moving to the Evaluate & Plan Phase

The events that trigger leaving the Identify phase and the handover to the Evaluate & Plan phase are the successful acquisition of the software update and the submission of the RFC.

The Evaluate & Plan Phase

The Evaluate & Plan phase of the software updates management process is where the organization needs to examine how it will respond to a software update, how it will release the update, how it will build the update, and how it will conduct acceptance testing for the release.

Determining the Appropriate Response

When an RFC is created, the initiator assigns an initial priority and category to the request. The software updates management team should review the RFC and agree to, or change, the priority and category. The finally determined values will have an impact on the remainder of the software updates management process, including how and when the software update is released. When the team reviews the initial priority attached to an RFC, it should consider what assets are impacted by the vulnerability the update addresses and whether these are critical systems, whether controls are in place (or can be put in place) to mitigate the vulnerability, and whether the update needs to be applied to as many systems as first thought. It's recommended that the organization define priorities for release of software updates and time frames consistent with their needs, such as those in Table 13-3.

Table 13-3   Release Priorities and Time Frames

Priority	Recommended Time Frame	Maximum Recommended Time Frame
Emergency	Within 24 hours.	Within two weeks.
High	Within one month.	Within two months.
Medium	Depending on availability, deploy a new service pack or update rollup that includes a fix for this vulnerability within four months.	Deploy the software update within six months.
Low	Depending on availability, deploy a new service pack or update rollup that includes a fix for this vulnerability within one year.	Deploy the software update within one year, or you might choose not to deploy at all.

The organization might want to consider formalizing the criteria used when determining whether or not to adjust a release's priority. You can find an example of formalized criteria in the form of environmental and organizational factors and the corresponding priority adjustments in Table 13-4.

Table 13-4   Release Priorities Adjustment Criteria

Environmental/Organizational Factor	Priority Adjustment
High-value or high-exposure assets impacted	Raise
Assets historically targeted by attackers	Raise
Mitigating factors in place, such as countermeasures that minimize the threat	Lower
Low-value or low-exposure assets impacted	Lower

Emergency change requests, where vulnerability is being exploited within the production environment or system instability is affecting line-of-business applications, need to be handled expeditiously. These requests might cause other requests with lower priorities to be delayed or halted if already in deployment in order to free the necessary resources required to process them. You can find more information on emergency response later in the chapter.

Not all software updates are the same, and each might have a different effect when applied to a system. Some updates might require a system to be restarted while others do not. It's possible that some updates will rely on other updates, perhaps a service pack, and can't be installed without them. Also, some software updates, once applied, can't be removed from a system. The software updates management team members need to assess the impact that a software update will have on the environment in order to plan for it. This is called categorizing the update.

Once the release priority and category of the software update have been determined, the release needs to be reviewed and authorized for deployment. Before authorization is granted, the software updates management team will need to consider various factors, such as what is currently happening in the production environment, the release's projected cost, the best means of deploying the release, the resources required to manage the release, and any dependencies the release requires. After authorization has been granted, a member of the team should take ownership of the release. The release owner is responsible for assembling the necessary resources to guarantee the building of the release, its testing, and its eventual deployment.

Planning the Release

Once the release has been approved, detailed planning should take place to guarantee the deployment's success. Although considered previously in the Identify phase and when determining the appropriate response in this phase, the IT assets that need to receive the software update need to be identified and recorded. The software updates component of Configuration Manager can help identify assets that need updating, but if Configuration Manager can't discover the vulnerability that the update addresses, the software updates management team might need to resort to mining through the information recorded by the Configuration Manager client hardware and software inventory agents.

The software updates management team will need to determine when to release the software update and whether to allow users to influence the release process. The team might decide, for example, to allow users a seven-day grace period during which they can choose to install the update contained within the release before it becomes mandatory. The team will also have to take into account the release's impact on the production environment. For many organizations it might be easier to release updates over the weekend instead of during the week. The team will need to factor in the size of the update, as larger updates will take longer to download to clients, especially those that connect over slow links.

The team might also want to consider a staged release, where some systems receive the update before others. For example, if the update is determined to be a high priority and is applicable to the software updates management infrastructure servers as well as other IT assets, the team might decide to apply the update to the servers first to guarantee their availability while deploying the update even if an exploit has been discovered.

The team will also want to draw up a timetable for the release life cycle. As part of the preparation for software updates management, the organization might want to consider developing templates of release timetables, one for each combination of category of asset and priority level.

Building the Release

After the release has been approved, the software updates management team needs to determine what components are required for the release. There are several components that will be used to build the release, each of which will be discussed in more detail later in this chapter. The software updates should be added to an update list and the update files downloaded to a deployment package using the Update List Wizard. When creating the deployment package you must assign at least one distribution point. A deployment template should be created using the Deployment Template Wizard, or a previously created template should be identified, that provides the deployment properties appropriate for the current deployment scenario. The test deployment and production deployment will both use the update list, deployment package, and deployment template components. The test deployment is created by using the update list and deployment template to open the Deploy Software Updates Wizard, and then selecting the target test collection and configuring the schedule in the wizard. As you go through the process of creating the release components and creating the test deployment, you should document the steps taken and the configuration settings for each component. This is especially true when you build the release in a test environment because the components will need to be re-created in the production environment, and you should follow the same steps and configure the components using the same settings.

Conducting Acceptance Testing

When the test deployment has been created, it must be tested to ensure that no problems will result in the production environment from the installation of the updates in the deployment. The goal of testing should be to test the deployment process within an environment that's representative of the production environment. At a minimum, the following tests should be conducted:

- The software updates can be deployed successfully to assets within the production environment, including over slow links, such as those connecting remote sites and portable computers.

- The computer restarts correctly, if required, after the software updates are installed.

- The software updates are installed within the configured maintenance window associated with the target collection.

- The software updates do not prevent business-critical and infrastructure systems from functioning normally after the software updates have successfully installed.

Most organizations will want to conduct more than these minimum tests to ensure that line-of-business applications continue to function normally. The number, range, and detail of the tests will depend on the categories of IT assets in the production environment and the software installed on them.

Before beginning testing, the software updates management team should build test plans, which define what should be tested and what the desired results should be. As with release timelines, these test plans might be developed while preparing for software updates management.

Building a software updates test environment that mimics the production environment, complete with software updates management infrastructure, can be expensive. An alternative to a test environment is to designate certain computers in the production environment as test computers that will receive the deployment prior to the rest of the production environment. If the assignment policy for the deployment is received by the clients and the software updates install on the client computers successfully, a new deployment that uses the release components can be created that targets computers in the production environment. This testing strategy needs to be managed carefully, as end users will become the testers and might require additional training. This strategy is also likely to result in acceptance of a software update without the rigorous testing that would be achieved in a test lab.

Leaving the Evaluate & Plan Phase and Moving to the Deploy Phase

The build of the release components and the success of the acceptance testing for the software update deployment are the triggers for the change to the Deploy Phase.

The Deploy Phase

The last phase of the Microsoft-recommended four-phase software updates management process is the Deploy phase, which the software updates management team prepares to deploy the software updates that were tested in the Evaluate & Plan phase into the production environment. If problems develop during, or as a result of, the deployment, the team might have to roll back or manually apply the update on affected systems. After the software updates have been deployed, and perhaps rolled back, the team will want to conduct a review of the experience to look for ways to improve future deployments of software updates.

Preparing the Deployment

After the release components and test deployment successfully pass acceptance testing in the Evaluate & Plan phase and the organization moves into the Deploy phase, the software updates management infrastructure and the organization needs to prepare for deployment. Among the steps that need to be taken to prepare the organization are communicating the rollout schedule to affected parties and configuring the software updates management infrastructure to prepare for the deployment.

Communicating information about impending updates to stakeholders such as system administrators and end users is extremely important. A simple and effective communication tool is e-mail. By informing the organization that a software update is pending or in progress, the team can accomplish many things, including reducing the number of calls to the help desk from users wondering what's happening to their systems and giving users the opportunity to install an update when it suits them before forcing a mandatory update on them.

The steps that the software updates management team will take to prepare the software updates management infrastructure for the update will depend largely on the work done in the Evaluate & Plan phase, as well as the technology used and the software updates management infrastructure. The update list, deployment package, and deployment template components must be available in the production environment before the deployment can be created. When a test environment was used during the Evaluate & Plan phase to test the release, the components must be re-created in the production environment. It is extremely important to create the components using the same configuration settings that were used in the test environment. Use the document that was created during the Evaluate & Plan phase that details the steps taken and settings used for each component to help ensure that the release will work as expected when creating the deployment in the product environment. When testing in the Evaluate & Plan phase was performed to a collection of test computers in the production environment, the existing release components can be reused for the new deployment.

The software updates management team will need to assign distribution points to the deployment package and provision the software updates on the distribution points. Whether using an existing deployment package or creating a new one, it is important that you verify that the distribution points assigned to the package are appropriate for the release.

More Info   For more information about distribution points, see the Configuration Manager Documentation Library at *http://technet.microsoft.com/en-us/library /bb680614.aspx*.

Deploying the Software Update to Targeted Computers

As with the preparation, the steps taken to deploy the software updates will depend largely on the work done in the Evaluate & Plan phase, as well as the technology used and the software updates management infrastructure. The relative priority of the release and the options chosen when building the deployment will also figure into the deployment of updates. Essentially, there are three steps to deploying software updates: making clients aware of the update's availability, monitoring the deployment, and recovering from failed deployments.

The deployment contains information about how the software updates will be presented to end users and how the software updates are installed on clients. For example, a deployment containing a relatively low priority update might allow the end user to choose whether or not to install the update on the user's system, whereas a deployment with a high-priority update might be mandatory and leave the user with no choice but to have the update installed. The organization might also want to create multiple deployments for the same set of updates, each configured appropriately and targeting different categories of IT assets to reflect different priorities across each.

During the deployment, the software updates management team needs to monitor the production environment for problems that might arise on the systems to which the deployment is being delivered or within the software updates management infrastructure itself. Configuration Manager clients create state messages for a variety of operations, including the evaluation of deployments, the installation of software updates, and the overall compliance for a deployment. The software updates reports use these state messages to provide administrators with detailed information, such as how many clients have received the deployment, the overall compliance levels for a deployment, the installation states for the updates in a deployment, and drill-downs from each report that allow administrators to retrieve all clients in a specific state or specific information for a client computer. If during the deployment's monitoring the software updates management team sees a number of systems receive the deployment but fail to install the software updates, they should begin an investigation into why.

In most deployments there will always be a few systems that can't be updated using the software updates feature of Configuration Manager, either because of their configuration or because they aren't managed by the software updates management infrastructure. In these cases the team will likely have to visit each system and apply the update manually. Care should be taken when deploying an update in this fashion to ensure that the correct installation options are used to guarantee the updated system's integrity.

The worst-case scenario for the software updates management team is a successful deployment only to find that an update in the deployment needs to be rolled back due to unforeseen circumstances, such as application incompatibility that wasn't identified during testing. Rolling back software updates is discussed in more detail in the section "Responding to Emergencies" later in this chapter. Complicating factors might be that the update performs as expected on some machines but not on others. If there are no initial reports that the update causes problems to systems and the software updates management process leaves the Deploy phase, the subsequent actions that need to be taken to remedy the problem can be considered a software update in their own right and require movement through the four-phase software updates management process.

Reviewing the Implementation

The goal of the review process is to gather information and lessons learned from the deployment that can be used in future applications of the software updates management process. Typically held a short time after it has been determined that the software updates were successfully deployed, the review should focus on ensuring that the IT assets in the production environment have been categorized correctly, that the vulnerability that was mitigated by the software updates has been removed, that the update will form part of the secure baseline configuration for new systems deployed into the production environment. The review should also examine the software updates management team's performance.

Leaving the Deploy Phase

Once the Post-Implementation Review has been completed, the organization leaves the Deploy phase of the software updates management process and reenters the Assess phase.

Integrating Configuration Manager 2007 into the Software Updates Management Process

Although no technology solution can automate a software updates management process completely, a well-rounded software updates management infrastructure can certainly help the software updates management team by automating many of the routine tasks. Configuration Manager is an extremely flexible tool, and you can easily integrate it into software updates management processes, including the Microsoft-recommended four-phase software updates management process described earlier in this chapter.

Careful planning and preparation is necessary to create a healthy Configuration Manager software updates infrastructure. First, the general requirements that must be in place before installing the software updates components and using the software updates feature are explained, and then you'll learn about how to install each component that makes up the software updates infrastructure.

> **Important** The rest of this chapter provides details about configuring your infrastructure in a basic Configuration Manager environment and software updates management infrastructure, suitable for most small to midsized organizations. When the Configuration Manager site is in native mode or when the software updates management infrastructure is complex, there are many other considerations that require careful planning and testing. For more information about planning for software updates in a more complex environment or software updates management infrastructure, see the Configuration Manager Documentation Library at *http://technet.microsoft.com/en-us/library/bb694244.aspx*.

Software Updates General Requirements

Before configuring and using the software updates feature, there are several requirements that your computer must meet. The software updates client components should be installed automatically and will only require intervention from the software updates management team if the installation fails for some reason. When Configuration Manager 2007 client is installed on assigned computers, the Software Updates Client Agent is also installed by default. As part of the software updates client installation, the most recent version of the Windows Update Agent (WUA) is also installed or upgraded on the client, if necessary.

Important   When the WUA is in use on the client during an upgrade attempt, the upgrade will fail, and another upgrade attempt will not occur. Clients that have an earlier version of the WUA will not be able to scan for software updates compliance. For more information about identifying computers that do not meet the WUA minimum requirements, see the Configuration Manager Documentation Library at *http://technet.microsoft.com/en-us/library/bb680319.aspx*.

The software update point for the site requires that WSUS 3.0 is installed and running on the server that will be configured for the software update point site system role. When the software update point is installed on a remote site system, the WSUS 3.0 Administration console or WSUS 3.0 must be installed on the site server. This allows the site server to communicate with WSUS running on the remote site system.

Software Updates Client Agent Settings

The Software Updates Client Agent is the client-side software updates component. The agent is enabled by default and configured with default settings so configuring these settings is optional, but you should get to know the client agent settings to see whether the defaults are appropriate for clients in the production environment. The client agent is installed with other client agents and can be viewed and configured through the Configuration Manager console. Figure 13-6 shows the list of client agents.

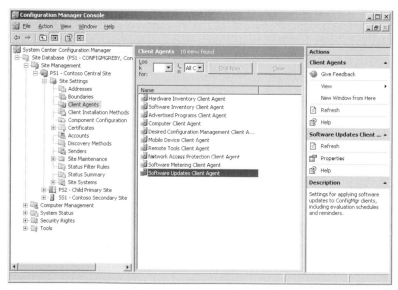

Figure 13-6   A list of client agents available on the site server

To configure the Software Updates Client, follow these steps:

1. In the Configuration Manager console, navigate to the Site Settings node and expand it, and then select the Client Agents folder to display the list of client agents, as shown in Figure 13-6.

2. Right-click Software Updates Client Agent and choose Properties from the context menu to display the Software Updates Client Agent Properties dialog box, as shown in Figure 13-7.

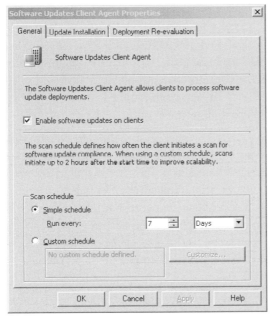

Figure 13-7   The Software Updates Client Agent Properties dialog box

3. On the General tab, verify that Enable Software Updates On Clients is selected. The Software Updates Client Agent is enabled by default when you install Configuration Manager.

    You can also configure the scan schedule that specifies how often client computers will initiate a scan for software updates compliance. The custom schedule provides the ability to set the specific start time as well as the recurrence. For example, you can schedule client computers to run the scan for software updates compliance every Saturday at 3 A.M. When a computer is offline at the scheduled scan time, the scan will initiate shortly after the computer is back online.

4. On the Update Installation tab, you can configure the Enforce All Mandatory Deployments setting. When this setting is enabled, the software updates in a mandatory

deployment install at the configured deadline, as well as the software updates in all other mandatory deployments that have a deadline within the specified time frame. This setting is particularly nice when you have a lot of mandatory deployments and you want to reduce the number of display notifications that pop up on client computers and provide for a single installation experience for end users.

You can also enable the Hide All Deployments From End Users setting. This setting essentially creates a silent software update installation experience on client computers, where display notifications, software updates notification area icons, and the Available Software Updates and Installation Progress dialog boxes are hidden. When a restart is required after the software update installation, the System Restart Required dialog box and notification area icon are displayed. When the Hide All Deployments From End Users setting is enabled, the software updates in a mandatory deployment are installed at the configured deadline. Because deployments are hidden, users won't have the ability to display or manually install software updates from the Available Software Updates dialog box.

5. On the Deployment Reevaluation tab, you can configure the schedule for when client computers scan for software updates and evaluate the software update installation status. When software updates that were previously installed are no longer found and still required on a client computer, the software update is automatically reinstalled. The default schedule is seven days, but you should adjust this schedule based on your policy for software updates compliance.

The Software Update Point

Software updates in Configuration Manager integrate with WSUS by using the software update point site system role. Each primary site must have an active software update point that interacts with the WSUS services to configure the update settings, to request synchronization to upstream update servers, and from the central site, to synchronize the software updates metadata from the WSUS database to the Configuration Manager database. The software updates management team must consider several configuration settings when planning for and implementing the software update point at each site in the Configuration Manager hierarchy. This section describes the software updates management infrastructure for a simple configuration. In more advanced infrastructures, such as running a site in native mode, configuring an Internet-based software update point, and configuring the software update point to use network load balancing (NLB), read the software updates planning documentation in the Configuration Manager Documentation Library at *http://technet.microsoft.com/en-us/library/bb694244.aspx*.

More Info   For detailed information about the software update point, see the Configuration Manager Documentation Library at *http://technet.microsoft.com /en-us/library/bb632674.aspx*.

Choosing the Software Update Point Computer

The software update point site system server role can be installed on the site server or a remote site system server. As stated earlier, the software update point must be installed on a computer running WSUS 3.0, and there are several other things that you should consider before choosing the computer that will be configured with the software update point site server role. Here are some things to consider.

- **Client Connections**   Client computers connect to WSUS running on the software update point site system server when they scan for software updates compliance. The more clients that connect to WSUS the more it will impact server resources and network bandwidth. When there will be a lot of computers assigned to your site, consider using a remote server for the software update point to reduce the impact on the site server.

- **Internet Information Services (IIS)**   Both the Configuration Manager site server and WSUS use IIS for communication. When WSUS is installed on the site server, consider using a custom Web site for WSUS to prevent conflicts with virtual directory settings or security.

- **SQL Server 2005**   When WSUS is installed on the site server, you can choose to use the SQL Server 2005 installation that is also used by the site server. When sharing the SQL Server, it is recommended that you configure WSUS to use a different SQL Server instance. This allows you to monitor the two databases independently.

More Info   For more information about determining the software update point infrastructure, see the Configuration Manager Documentation Library at *http://technet.microsoft.com/en-us/library/bb633245.aspx*.

WSUS 3.0 Installation

Once the computer has been selected for the software update point site system role, WSUS 3.0 must be installed on it. An existing WSUS server can be used for the active software update point, but if it's possible, it is recommended that you perform a fresh installation of WSUS to prevent unexpected software updates metadata from showing up in the Configuration Manager database. If that's not an option, you might consider deleting the software updates metadata from the WSUS server before configuring it as the active software update point. Remember, WSUS is used only for the synchronization of software updates metadata and for clients to retrieve the software updates metadata that will be scanned for compliance. Existing computer groups, deployments, and so on, that have been configured in the WSUS console will not be used by the Configuration Manager software updates process.

To install WSUS 3.0, follow these steps:

1. Download the WSUS installer file from the Microsoft Windows Server Update Services Web page at *http://technet.microsoft.com/en-us/wsus/default.aspx* and save it to a location accessible to the server that will be configured with the software update point site system role.

2. From the site system computer, double click the WSUS installation file and click Next.

3. Select Full Server Installation Including Administration Console and click Next.

4. Review and accept the terms of the license agreement and click Next.

5. Select the Store Updates Locally option, as shown in Figure 13-8, specify the location to store the software update source files, and click Next.

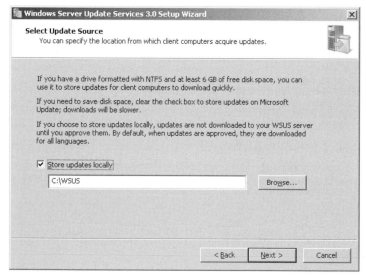

Figure 13-8   The Select Update Source page of the Windows Server Update Services 3.0 Setup Wizard

When Store Updates Locally is selected in WSUS, the license terms for software update that have associated license terms, such as service packs, are downloaded to the WSUS content share during WSUS synchronization. During Configuration Manager synchronization, WSUS Synchronization Manager on the site server looks for the license terms for associated software updates in the WSUS content share. When the license terms are not available for a software update, the software update is not synchronized. When clients scan for software updates compliance, they must have access to the license terms for applicable updates or the scan for those updates will fail. Storing the license terms locally is highly recommended so clients can quickly and reliably access them. Selecting the Store Updates Locally option will not result in update files being downloaded to the WSUS content share because Configuration Manager handles the deployment of software updates and does not approve the updates in WSUS. Only approved software updates are downloaded to the WSUS content share.

6. Specify the software used to manage the WSUS 3.0 database and click Next.

   You can choose an existing installation of SQL Server 2005 or have WSUS install the Windows Internal Database (Microsoft SQL Server 2005 Embedded Edition) on the local computer. The Windows Internal Database is provided as part of the free WSUS download and doesn't require a license to use it.

   Note   For WSUS to be configured as a network load-balancing cluster, you must use Microsoft SQL Server 2005.

   When you choose a local Microsoft SQL Server 2005 installation, select the SQL instance from the drop-down list. You can also choose to use a remote installation of Microsoft SQL Server 2005 by specifying the server name and SQL instance. Setup tests the connection to the SQL server and instance before proceeding.

7. Specify whether to use the existing Internet Information Services (IIS) Default Web site or to create a custom WSUS 3.0 Web site and click Next.

   When there are other Configuration Manager site system roles configured or when other applications are using IIS on the computer, you should consider using the custom WSUS Web site to avoid a possible conflict in Web site settings.

   Important   Write down the port settings that are configured for the Web site. You will need to provide these settings when configuring the active software update point.

   ---

8. Review the settings, click Next, and when the wizard completes, click Finish.

   Important   When Setup completes, the WSUS 3.0 Configuration Wizard automatically starts. Exit the WSUS Configuration Wizard and close the WSUS console. Configuration Manager will connect to the WSUS server and configure the settings after you install the active software update point in the next section.

After the Web site used by WSUS has been installed, the Web site displays under the Web Sites node in the Internet Information Services (IIS) Manager, and the Web site settings can be displayed and configured in the properties for the Web site, as shown in Figure 13-9.

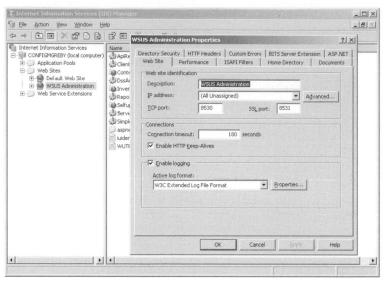

Figure 13-9   The WSUS Administration custom Web site displayed in the Internet Information Services (IIS) Manager and the WSUS Administration Properties dialog box

When the software update point is remote from the site server, the WSUS Administration Console must be installed on the site server. The installation makes the WSUS application programming interface (API) files available for the site server to use when connecting to WSUS running on the remote software update point to configure the WSUS settings and request WSUS synchronization.

To install WSUS 3.0 Administration Console, follow these steps:

1. Download the WSUS installer file from the Microsoft Windows Server Update Services Web page at *http://technet.microsoft.com/en-us/wsus/default.aspx* and save it to a location accessible to the site server.

2. From the site server, double-click the WSUS installation file and click Next.

3. Select Administration Console only and click Next.

4. Review and accept the terms of the license agreement and click Next.

5. The Required Components To Use Administration UI page will display if the computer doesn't have Microsoft Report Viewer 2005 installed. If this page displays, click Next. The WSUS 3.0 Administration Console installation continues.

    During normal Configuration Manager operations you will not likely need to open the WSUS Administration Console, but it is recommended that the Microsoft Report Viewer 2005 still be installed. There might be times when opening the

WSUS Administration Console will be helpful when verifying and troubleshooting connectivity to WSUS running on a remote software update point.

6. When the wizard completes, click Finish.

Software Update Point Site System Role

Now that you have installed WSUS 3.0, you are ready to install and configure the active software update point for the site. The software update point is installed as one of the Configuration Manager site system server roles and can be viewed and configured through the Configuration Manager console.

To install and configure the active software update point site system role, follow these steps:

1. In the Configuration Manager console, navigate to the Site Settings node and expand it, and then select the Site Systems folder to display the current site systems.

2. The software update point site system role can be installed on an existing site system server or a new site system server can be created. Follow the associated step:

    ❑ Add software update point site system server role to a new site system server: Right-click the Site Systems folder, click New, and then click Server to open the New Site System Server Wizard.

    ❑ Add software update point site system server role to an existing site system server: Right-click the site system server name and click New Roles to open the New Site Role Wizard.

3. On the General page, configure the general site system settings for the site system server and click Next. It is important that the fully qualified domain name (FQDN) for the site system server is entered correctly, or the connection to the software update point will likely fail.

    Note   When an existing site server is selected, these settings should already be populated.

    ---

4. On the System Role Selection page, select Software Update Point and click Next.

5. On the Software Update Point page, select whether to use a proxy server when synchronizing software updates and click Next. When enabled, you must provide the proxy server name, port, and whether to use specific credentials when connecting to the proxy server.

    Configuration Manager configures WSUS to use these proxy settings, which are used by WSUS when it connects to Microsoft Update (central site) or WSUS running on the active software update point on the parent site (child sites) when synchronizing software updates metadata.

6. On the Active Software Update Point Settings page, select Use This Server As The Active Software Update Point, specify the port settings that you wrote down earlier when for the Web site used by WSUS, and click Next. You will see five additional wizard pages when the Use This Server As The Active Software Update Point is selected, as shown in Figure 13-10.

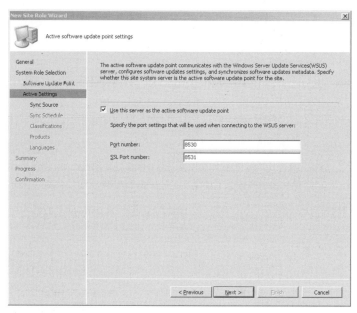

Figure 13-10   The Active Settings page of the New Site System Server Wizard or New Site Role Wizard

The port settings on this page are used when the site server connects to WSUS running on the software update point site system server to configure the WSUS settings and to request software updates synchronization. Oftentimes, when Configuration Manager fails to connect to the WSUS server, incorrect port settings have been specified on this page. Typically, ports 80 (HTTP) and 443 (HTTPS) are configured when WSUS uses the default Web site, and ports 8530 (HTTP) and 8531 (HTTPS) are configured when a custom WSUS Web site is used.

7. On the Synchronization Source page, the settings should be correctly configured automatically. Verify that Synchronize From Microsoft Update is selected if you are configuring the software update point on the central site and Synchronize From An Upstream Update Server if you are configuring any other software update point in the Configuration Manager hierarchy. Configuration Manager does not use WSUS reporting events. Verify that Do Not Create WSUS Reporting Events is selected and click Next.

8. On the Synchronization Schedule page, software updates synchronization is scheduled for every 7 days by default on the central site, as shown in Figure 13-11. Determine how often you want to synchronize software updates, and click Next.

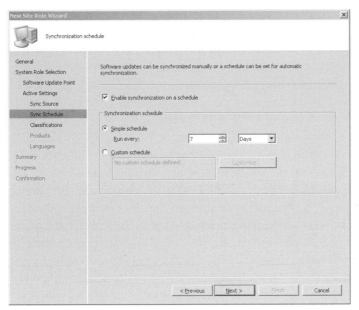

Figure 13-11 The Synchronization Schedule page of the New Site System Server Wizard or New Site Role Wizard

The synchronization schedule can be configured only on the active software update point for the central site. Synchronization is initiated on child sites when they receive a synchronization request from their parent site. On the central site, Configuration Manager will start the synchronization process as soon as the software update point site server role installation completes when a simple schedule is selected. If you want synchronization to be scheduled, but start at a specified time, you can configure a custom schedule. Using the custom schedule to start the synchronization after hours or on the weekend might be preferred because the synchronization process can take quite a long time to run the first time. When you do not configure a schedule, you still can initiate a manual synchronization from the Update Repository node in the Configuration Manager console.

9. On the Update Classifications page, select the classifications for which you want software updates to be synchronized and click Next.

> **Note** The classifications can be configured only on the active software update point for the central site.

10. On the Products page, select the products for which you want software updates to be synchronized and click Next.

> **Note** The products can be configured only on the active software update point for the central site.

11. On the Languages page, select the languages in which software update files should be downloaded for synchronized software updates and software updates summary details that should be included in the metadata for synchronized software updates and click Next.

Note   The summary details language settings can be configured only on the active software update point for the central site.

It is important to select all of the languages for the summary details before synchronizing the first time. You can add summary details languages later, but the summary details in the new languages will be included only in the software updates metadata for new software updates or software updates that change and not the existing software updates. When the summary details for additional languages are needed after the initial synchronization, the active software update point site role on the central site must be removed, which disassociates the software updates from the software update point. The software update point site role can then be added back to the site system server and all software updates metadata will be updated during the next software updates synchronization process.

More Info   When selecting languages in the Update files column, a separate software update file is downloaded for each language to the deployment package. When a client receives a deployment for the software update, it will download the update file in the language of the operating system running on the computer, if it is available. When the update file is not available in the required language, the update is not downloaded, and the deployment will fail to run until the appropriate update file is available to the client computer.

When selecting the languages in the Summary details column, the software updates metadata, such as title and description, are synchronized into the Configuration Manager database. The Configuration Manager console will display the software updates in the language of the operating system running on the computer, if it is available. When the summary details for the operating system language are not available, the software updates metadata is displayed in English.

---

12. On the Summary page, review the configuration settings, and then click Next to create the active software update point. When the Confirmation page displays, verify that the software update point site role was created successfully, and then click Close to exit the wizard. You can verify that the software update point was installed by reviewing the SUPSetup.log file in *<ConfigMgrInstallationPath>*\Logs. Look for the following log entry: Installation Was Successful, as shown in Figure 13-12.

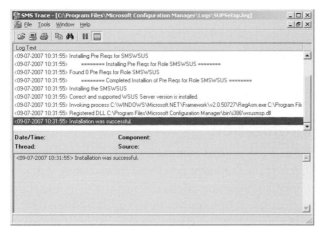

Figure 13-12   Trace of the SUPSetup.log showing that the software update point installed successfully

After the software update point site role has been installed, you can review or modify the settings in the properties for the Software Update Point Component, as shown in Figure 13-13.

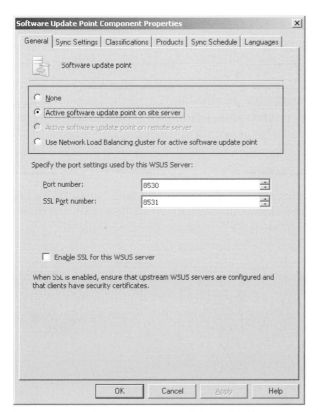

Figure 13-13   The Software Update Point Component Properties dialog box

To open the Software Update Point Component properties, follow these steps:

1. In the Configuration Manager console, navigate to the Site Settings node and expand it, and then select the Component Configuration folder to display the components.

2. Right-click Software Update Point Component, and then click Properties.

Software Updates Synchronization

Software updates synchronization is the process of retrieving software updates metadata from Microsoft Update and inserting the metadata into the Configuration Manager database on the central site. The metadata then is replicated down the Configuration Manager hierarchy so that all the sites have the same software updates metadata. When synchronization completes on the central site, a synchronization request is sent to child sites. The child sites will request that WSUS running on the active software updates point synchronize with WSUS running on the active software update point for the parent site. This process results in the same software updates metadata in the WSUS databases in the Configuration Manager hierarchy. As each site completes synchronization, a synchronization request is sent to any child sites, and the process repeats.

You can initiate software updates synchronization from only the central site by configuring the synchronization schedule, which was discussed previously as one of the software update point settings, and by manually initiating synchronization by using the Run Synchronization action from the Updates Repository node of the Configuration Manager console. When you configure the synchronization schedule during the software update point installation, software updates synchronization will initiate as soon as the software update point installation completes. You can monitor the synchronization progress by reviewing the entries in the wsyncmgr.log file or display the status messages for the SMS_WSUS_SYNC_MANAGER component.

Depending on how many classifications, products, and languages are configured for the active software update point, and the bandwidth to Microsoft Update, will determine how long it takes to complete the synchronization process on the central site. You should expect that the first synchronization will take one or more hours to complete. After the first synchronization, only new or updated software updates are synchronized, which usually results in a fairly quick synchronization. When synchronization completes, you will receive a status message ID 6702 on the site server and see a log entry in wsyncmgr.log similar to Done Synchronizing SMS With WSUS Server <FQDN>. When synchronization completes, the software updates will be displayed in the Configuration Manager console.

More Info   For more information about software updates synchronization, see the Configuration Manager Documentation Library at *http://technet.microsoft.com /en-us/library/bb632485.aspx*.

Scanning for Software Updates Compliance

After your site completes software updates synchronization and after the client receives its next machine policy, the Software Updates Client Agent on client computers enables the Specify Intranet Microsoft Update Service Location local group policy setting. Both the Set The Intranet Update Services For Detecting Updates and Set The Intranet Statistics Server settings are configured for the URL to the WSUS Web site running on the active software update point. The client agent then will initiate a scan to check the compliance for the software updates that meet the configured classifications and products, and then sends a state message with the current compliance state for each software update to the management point, which in turn sends the state messages to the site server. Using state messages to report compliance provides for a very accurate and detailed compliance reporting experience.

There are three possible states reported when a client computer scans for software updates compliance.

- **Required**   The software update is applicable to and required on the client computer.

- **Installed**   The software update is installed on the client computer and therefore not required.

- **Not Required**   The software update was previously required, but is no longer required on the client computer. An example would be a client computer that has Office 2003 installed. The client was scanned for compliance and an update for Office 2003 was required. Say you upgrade to Office 2007 on that computer. On the next scan for software updates compliance, the client would report the Not Required status for the Office 2003 update. This state is different than the Not Required state set by the site server representing a software update that is not required on the client.

There are two additional states that are set by the site server:

- **Unknown**   After software updates have been synchronized on a site, but before the site server has received the compliance state messages from a client computer, the site server will list all new software updates for the client as Unknown.

- **Not Required**   After a client computer sends the compliance state messages from a scan for software updates compliance, the site server will assume that any software updates that weren't reported with the Required or Installed state are not applicable and, therefore, sets the state for the software updates as Not Required on the client.

You can verify the scan state for client computers by running the Scan 1 – Last Scan State By Collection or Scan 2 – Last Scan States By Site Software Updates report. These reports provide the scan states for all clients in a collection or site and can be extremely helpful when troubleshooting scan failures on client computers. For example, say you run Scan 2 – Last Scan States By Site report and have a group of computers that reported a scan state of Scan Failed. You can use the drill-down in the first column to open the Scan 4 – Clients Of A Site Reporting A Specific State <Secondary> report. This report provides information such as the WUA version, the last error code, and the scan package location, which should be the URL for the WSUS server. When you suspect scan errors, the best way to troubleshoot them is to run the Troubleshooting 1 – Scan Errors report that provides a grouping for all errors with the count of computers for each. As the compliance state messages are received at a site, the Configuration Manager console and the software updates compliance reports will display the current compliance state for software updates. Figure 13-14 shows the compliance information for clients on the Software Updates home page.

Note   On the Software Updates home page, you might need to initiate the Run Home Page Summarization action and within the Updates Repository node you might need to run the Refresh action before the current software updates information is displayed.

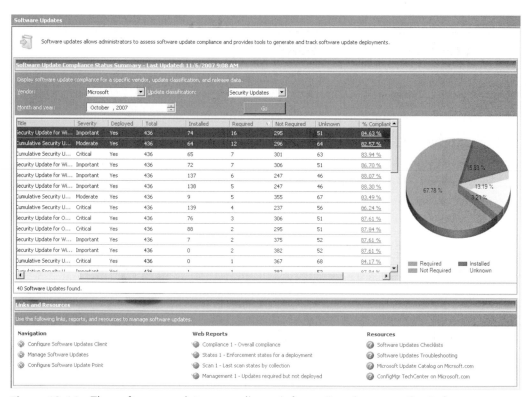

Figure 13-14   The software updates compliance information shown on the Software Updates home page

Completing the Software Updates Infrastructure

In this section, you have learned how to prepare the software updates infrastructure for a basic Configuration Manager environment. When the Configuration Manager site is in native mode or when the software updates management infrastructure is complex, there are many other considerations that will require careful planning and testing. For example, when the site server is in native mode and the software updates infrastructure must handle connections from Internet-based clients, a decision must be made whether or not to install and configure an active Internet-based software update point in addition to the active software update point. Another example is when the number of clients that will be connecting to the WSUS server is expected to be over the maximum number allowed, which is around 25,000 clients when the WSUS server is remote from the site server; the WSUS server might need to be configured as a network load balancing (NLB) cluster.

> **More Info**   For additional information about planning for more complex environments and advanced configurations, it is strongly recommend that you read the software updates planning information found in the Configuration Manager Documentation Library at *http://technet.microsoft.com/en-us/library/bb694244.aspx.*

Software Updates Fundamentals

Now that the software updates infrastructure is installed and configured, you can move on and learn about how to prepare for a deployment, create the deployment, learn how to publish custom software updates, and take a look at the software updates reports.

Preparing for the Deployment

When preparing for a software update deployment, you should precreate and test several objects. These objects were discussed earlier when talking about the four-phase software updates management process, and this section goes into more detail about how to create and configure these objects.

Deployment Templates

The deployment template is a software updates object that stores predefined deployment settings. Different deployment templates should be created for the typical deployment scenarios in the production environment. When a deployment is created using a deployment template, the settings specified in the deployment template are used for the deployment. This simplifies the deployment creation process and provides a level of consistency for each deployment scenario. In most deployment templates, you probably will want to leave the collection property blank so you can specify the collection when creating the deployment. This allows you to use the template for multiple deployments that target a different set of target computers.

More Info   For more information about deployment templates, see the Configuration Manager Documentation Library at *http://technet.microsoft.com /en-us/library/bb632940.aspx*.

Real World   Scenarios for Deployment Templates

There are many different scenarios that warrant the use of a deployment template, but consider the following deployment scenarios:

Every month two deployments are created for the software updates that have been approved by the software updates management team—one that targets desktops and the other that targets servers. It is extremely important to you that the servers do not perform a system restart after a software update installation. You create a deployment template with the default settings, except that it suppresses the system restart on servers after the software updates in the deployment complete the installation. You also want desktop computers to download the deployed software updates and install them regardless of the network bandwidth. You create a deployment template with the default settings, except that it is configured to download software updates from the distribution point and install whether or not the computer is connected within a slow or unreliable network boundary. When you create each deployment, you drag the update list, which contains the approved updates for the month, to the appropriate deployment template, and the deployment settings are prepopulated with the settings configured in the deployment template.

A deployment template is created in the Configuration Manager console from the Deployment Template Wizard. There is no limit to the number of deployment templates that can be created, just that the name for each template is unique.

To create a deployment template, follow these steps:

1. In the Configuration Manager console, expand the Computer Management node, expand the Software Updates node, right-click the Deployment Templates node, and then click New Deployment Template to open the Deployment Template Wizard.

2. On the Template Name page, provide a name and description for the deployment template, and then click Next to continue. The deployment template name must be unique and should help to describe the scenario that the deployment template addresses, as shown in Figure 13-15.

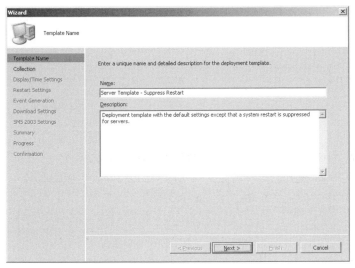

Figure 13-15   The Template Name page in the Deployment Template Wizard

3. On the Collection page, choose whether to specify a collection or leave the setting blank, and then click Next to continue. You will most likely want to leave the collection setting blank. This gives you the option to use the deployment template in multiple deployments that will target different clients. When the collection setting is not specified in the deployment template, it will be specified when creating the deployment. If this template will be used for deployments that always target the same set of clients, then choose the collection.

4. On the Display/Time Settings page, choose whether display notifications should be displayed on clients for applicable software updates in a mandatory deployment. Display notifications remind end users that there are mandatory software updates available for installation and that the deadline for installing the mandatory software updates is approaching.

> **More Info**   The intervals for displaying the reminders to clients is configured on the Reminders tab of the Computer Client Agent Properties dialog box.

5. Next, choose whether the deployment schedules should be evaluated using the local time on the client or using Universal Coordinated Time (UTC). Finally, configure the duration setting that is used to set the default schedule for the deadline in deployments that use the deployment template. For example, if the Duration value is set to 2 weeks, when you create a deployment using the deployment template, the default setting for the deadline in the deployment will be the configured start time plus 2 weeks. Configure this value to the time span that you would typically have

between making the software updates in the deployment available to end users and enforcing the installation of the software updates. Click Next to continue.

6. On the Restart Settings page, choose whether to suppress system restarts on servers or workstations and whether to allow a system restart outside of any configured maintenance windows, as shown in Figure 13-16. Suppressing system restarts can be useful in server environments or when you don't want desktop computers to restart automatically when it's required after software updates install. Some installations won't fully complete until the system restarts, and until then the systems might be in an insecure or unstable state. Allowing a system restart outside of the configured maintenance windows is especially useful when an emergency release has been built and the updates must be deployed to high-value or high-exposure computers in the environment. In this scenario, you will probably not want to suppress the system restart and consider having the system restart as soon as the installation is complete whether or not there is a maintenance window. Click Next to continue.

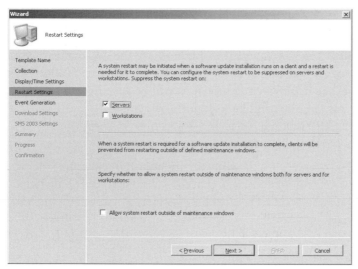

Figure 13-16   The Restart Settings page in the Deployment Template Wizard

7. On the Event Generation page, specify whether to disable Operations Manager alerts during software update installation and whether alerts will be created when a software update installation fails. Click Next to continue.

8. On the Download Settings page, you specify the installation behavior if a client is connected to a slow network boundary. In the first section, you specify whether clients will install the software updates in the deployment if they are in boundaries that have been specified as slow or unreliable. Before selecting Download Software

Updates From Distribution Point And Install consider what type of updates are in the deployment and whether there is a branch distribution point installed local to the clients. When there are large updates in the deployment, such as a service pack, and the connection to the closest distribution point is slow, you probably will want to configure Do Not Install Software Updates. The software updates management team should have a strategy in place to update clients that are in a slow or unreliable boundary when deploying the updates is not an option.

9. In the next section on this page, specify whether clients that are within the boundaries of one or more protected distribution points should download the updates in the deployment when no protected distribution points have the updates available. Click Next to continue.

10. When there are SMS 2003 clients in the Configuration Manager 2007 hierarchy, you can select Deploy Software Updates To SMS 2003 Clients to create the package, program, and advertisement that are used to deploy software updates to SMS 2003 clients. There are additional requirements that must be taken into consideration when selecting this setting in a deployment template; for example, you can deploy software updates to SMS 2003 clients only after the Inventory Tool for Microsoft Updates has been installed and synchronized on the Configuration Manager 2007 central site. Click Next to continue.

> **More Info**   When you have SMS 2003 clients in the Configuration Manager 2007 hierarchy, it is strongly recommended that you read the planning information available in the Configuration Manager 2007 Documentation Library at *http://technet.microsoft.com/en-us/library/bb680931.aspx.*

11. On the Summary page, review the configuration settings and click Next to create the deployment template. When the Confirmation page displays, verify that the deployment template was created successfully. Click Close to exit the wizard. To see the new deployment template in the Configuration Manager console, you might need to use the Refresh action on the Deployment Template node.

Deployment Package

The deployment package is an object used to store downloaded software update files and to deliver them to the package share on distribution points. It is recommended as part of the software updates management process that software update files are downloaded to a deployment package and provisioned on distribution points prior to creating a deployment. The software updates can be downloaded by selecting the updates in the Configuration Manager console and using the Download Software Updates action to open the Download Updates Wizard, or by selecting the Download The Files Associated With The

Selected Software Updates setting when you are in the Update List Wizard. Enabling this setting essentially adds the Download Updates Wizard pages to the Update List Wizard. Either method for downloading software update files to a deployment package works well, but in this section you learn how to use the Update List Wizard to download software updates. Alternatively, the software updates can be downloaded to a deployment package and copied to distribution points from the Deploy Software Updates Wizard when creating the deployment.

More Info   For more information about deployment packages, see the Configuration Manager Documentation Library at *http://technet.microsoft.com /en-us/library/bb693754.aspx.*

Strategies for Managing Deployment Packages

There are several strategies for managing deployment packages in Configuration Manager. For example, you can have one deployment package for the year, and each month you would add the new software updates approved by the software updates management team to the deployment package. When clients receive the assignment policy for the deployment, they will determine what software updates are applicable, and then download only the applicable updates. This new software updates feature is called selective download and provides for much more flexibility when creating your deployment package strategy.

Important   Only Configuration Manager 2007 clients utilize the selective download technology. Use caution when creating deployments that target both Configuration Manager 2007 and Systems Management Server (SMS) 2003 clients. When SMS 2003 clients are configured to download and install software updates deployed from a Configuration Manager site, they will download the entire contents of the package share on the distribution point. When there are large updates, such as service packs, or a large number of files, you should configure the SMS 2003 clients to run the installation from the distribution point. For more information about deploying software updates to SMS 2003 clients, see the Configuration Manager Documentation Library at *http://technet.microsoft.com /en-us/library/bb694063.aspx.*

Alternatively, a more focused deployment package can be created for different priority levels, different applications, and so on. The maximum recommended software update files contained in a single deployment package is about 500, which should be taken into consideration when the software updates management team determines what the best deployment package strategy is for the environment.

> **More Info**   When a client computer downloads a software update file that is applicable, it looks for the update files on any distribution point from any deployment package that contains the update file, whether or not the deployment package was defined in the deployment. For more information about deployment packages, see the Configuration Manager Documentation Library at *http://technet.microsoft.com/en-us/library/bb693754.aspx*.

Preparing the Package Source Folders

Before creating the deployment package, you must create and share the package source folder that will be used for the deployment package. Package source folders will contain the downloaded update files that will be copied to the distribution points for the deployment package, as shown in Figure 13-17, and eventually deployed to Configuration Manager clients. For this reason, their integrity should be strictly maintained. The Access Control List (ACL) on a package folder should be set so the SMS Provider computer account and the logged-on user both have Write access. No other user or group should have access to the package source folders. Instead of specifying permissions each time a folder is created, you can consider creating a folder hierarchy exclusively for use in storing package sources, securing the top folder, and ensuring that permissions are inherited to all subfolders as they're created.

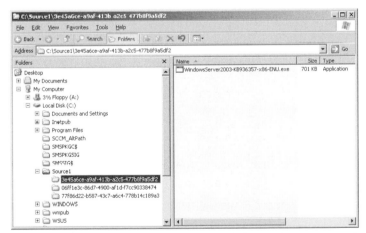

Figure 13-17   Windows Explorer view of the package source shared folder that contains downloaded software updates

The Update List

The update list is simply a software updates object that contains a list of software updates. Adding software updates to an update list, and then using the update list to create deployments provides the ability to delegate the deployment responsibility. Another important benefit of using an update list is the ability to use the software updates reports specific to an update list that provide detailed information about the updates defined in the update list. Using an update list also provides a simple way to create multiple deployments with the same set of updates.

> **More Info**   For more information about update lists, see the Configuration Manager Documentation Library at *http://technet.microsoft.com/en-us/library /bb693591.aspx*.

Creating the Update List

There are several advantages of using an update list in the deployment process. As described earlier, the update list provides the ability to delegate deployment administration and provides better compliance reporting. Two of the most useful reports in software updates are Compliance 1 – Overall Compliance, which returns the compliance states for the software updates in a specific update list, and Compliance 3 – Update list (per update), which returns the compliance states for each update in the update list. When software updates are deployed without using an update list, you can retrieve the compliance for the software updates in a deployment, but typically there are multiple deployments for the same set of updates each targeting a different set of computers, and you would have to run multiple reports to retrieve the overall compliance for the set of updates. By using an update list to create the deployments, the overall compliance for the updates can be easily reported.

Before creating the update list, you must select at least one software update in the Configuration Manager console. An easy way to do this is to use a search folder to find a specific set of updates; for example, the Security updates that were released in the last 30 days, as shown in Figure 13-18.

From the results of the search folder, you can choose all of the software updates or a subset of them that meet your criteria and add the updates to the update list. The recommendation in this chapter is to download the update files to a deployment package, if required, when in the Update List Wizard.

> **More Info**   For more information about using search folders in software updates, see the Configuration Manager Documentation Library at *http://technet.microsoft.com/en-us/library/bb693850.aspx*.

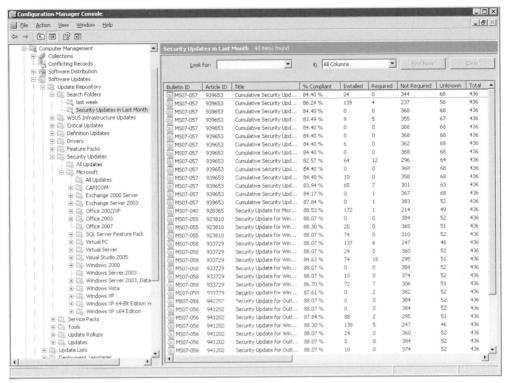

Figure 13-18 The software updates that meet the search folder criteria

To add software updates to a new update list and download the associated update files to a deployment package, follow these steps:

1. In the Configuration Manager console, select the software updates that you want to add to the new update list, and then click Update List to open the Update List Wizard.

2. On the Update List page, select Create A New Update List and provide a unique name that describes the update list, as well as a brief description. You have the option to download the update files to a deployment package in the wizard, and as part of the recommended process, select the Download The Files Associated With The Selected Software Updates option. Three additional pages are displayed in the wizard to facilitate the software updates download process, as shown in Figure 13-19. Click Next to continue.

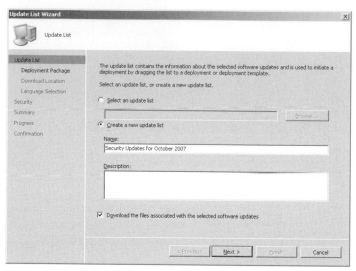

Figure 13-19   The Update List page in the Update List Wizard

3.   On the Deployment Package page, select Create A New Deployment Package. For the purposes of this procedure, it is assumed that this is the first set of software updates downloaded to a deployment package. Depending on the deployment package strategy, you will probably most often select an existing deployment package when downloading software updates. Provide a name and description for the deployment package that will help identify what types of updates are downloaded to it, as displayed in Figure 13-20. Specify the package source for the deployment package. The package source must be created before completing the wizard, or the download process will fail. Take care to secure the folder using the guidelines described earlier. Set the appropriate sending priority (Low, Medium, or High) and choose whether to Enable Binary Differential Replication. Click Next to continue.

> **More Info**   For more information about binary differential replication, see the Configuration Manager Documentation Library at *http://technet.microsoft.com/en-us/library/bb693953.aspx*.

4.   On the Distribution Points page, click Browse to select the distribution points for the deployment package and click OK. Click Next to continue.

5.   On the Download Location page, specify whether the wizard will download the update files automatically from the Internet or download them manually from a location on the local network. Click Next to continue.

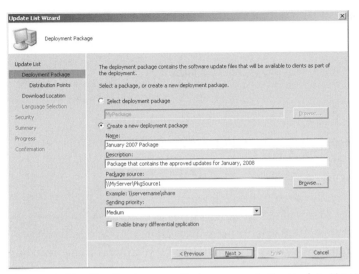

Figure 13-20   The Deployment Package page in the Update List Wizard

> **More Info**   For more information about how to manually download a software update file to a local network location, see the Configuration Manager Documentation Library at *http://technet.microsoft.com/en-us /library/bb694047.aspx.*

6. On the Language Selection page, select the languages in which the update file will be downloaded, and then click Next to continue.

7. On the Security page, specify the user accounts that should have security rights to the update list object. Remember, one advantage of using an update list is that it provides the ability to delegate deployment responsibility. When other administrators will be using this update list to deploy software updates or to add updates to the update list, add the appropriate security rights for the user account. Click Next to continue.

8. On the Summary page, review the configuration settings, and click Next to create the update list. When the Confirmation page appears, verify that the update list was created successfully, and then click Close to exit the wizard. To see the new update list in the Configuration Manager console, you might need to select Refresh on the Update Lists node.

Deploying Software Updates

The software update deployment is a software updates object that stores the configuration settings for the deployment and the settings that affect the installation behavior on clients. The deployment is delivered to clients using machine policy, where clients evaluate whether the software updates in the deployment are applicable and required.

> **More Info**   For more information about deployments, see the Configuration Manager Documentation Library at *http://technet.microsoft.com/en-us/library/bb680906.aspx.*

Creating the Software Update Deployment

When deployment templates have been created for your typical deployment scenarios, software updates added to an update list, and the update files downloaded to a deployment package, you are ready to begin the deployment process. There are several methods for which you can open the Deploy Software Updates Wizard to create the deployment, and depending on which method you choose will result in a lot of wizard pages with settings that must be configured, or very few. Continuing with the recommended approach to deploying updates, you will use a precreated deployment template, an update list for a set of updates, and assume that the update files have been downloaded to a deployment package. This approach results in the fewest wizard pages with the least number of settings to configure.

To deploy software updates, follow these steps:

1. In the Configuration Manager console, expand the Computer Management node, expand the Software Updates node, and expand the Deployment Templates node making the deployment template that is appropriate for this deployment scenario visible in the console.

2. Under the Software Updates node, expand the Update Lists node, and select the update list for the set of updates to deploy.

3. Drag and drop the update list to the appropriate deployment template, as shown in Figure 13-21. The Deploy Software Updates Wizard opens with only four pages to complete before the deployment is created.

   Alternatively, you can highlight the update list and run the Deploy Software Updates action. This opens the Deploy Software Updates Wizard, and from the wizard you can select the appropriate deployment template.

4. On the General Page, provide the name and description for the deployment. The deployment name must be unique and the combined information on this page should provide administrators with a clear understanding about the nature of the deployment. Click Next to continue.

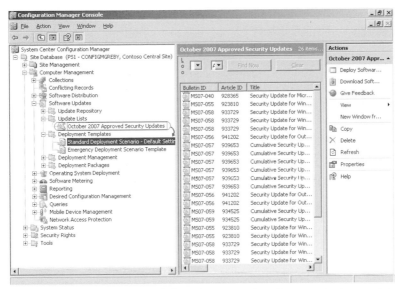

Figure 13-21   Dragging and dropping an update list on a deployment template in the Configuration Manager console

5. On the Collection page, which is displayed if the collection wasn't specified as part of the deployment template, choose the target collection for the deployment and whether members of subcollections will be included. Click Next to continue.

6. On the Schedule page, specify the start time for the deployment and the deadline, as shown in Figure 13-22. When the As Soon As Possible option is selected for the start time, the deployment assignment policy is created as soon as the components are able to process the request. The clients will receive the policy during their next machine policy cycle, and the software updates in the deployment will be available for installation. When a custom start time is specified, the deployment assignment policy will not be created until after the specified date and time.

   Next, specify whether the software updates in the deployment will automatically install on clients at a deadline or whether the updates are optional. When the Set A Deadline For Software Update Installation option is selected, specify the date and time for the installation to automatically initiate on clients. You will notice that the default deadline is set to the start time plus the Duration setting that was specified in the deployment template. When a deadline is configured, specify whether to send wake-up packets to computers that require at least one update in the deployment. Computers that support Wake On LAN will power on approximately 3 minutes prior to the deadline to provide enough time for the computer to power up, and then install the required software updates. The computer is not returned to a sleep state or shut down after the installation, but power management schemas can be configured to do this.

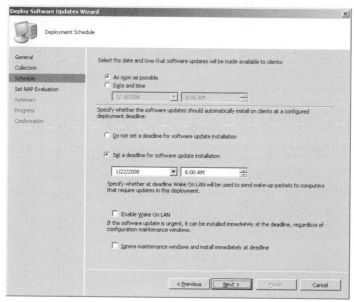

Figure 13-22   The Deployment Schedule page in the Deploy Software Updates Wizard

---

More Info   For more information about using Wake On LAN in Configuration Manager, see the Configuration Manager Documentation Library at *http://technet.microsoft.com/en-us/library/bb693668.aspx.*

You can also choose whether to ignore maintenance windows when the deadline is reached. When this setting is selected, the software update will install on the computer at the deadline regardless of the configured maintenance window. Click Next to continue.

7. On the NAP Evaluation page, select whether the software updates in the deployment will be included in an NAP evaluation. This page is displayed only when Network Access Protection (NAP) is configured for the site. If you are interested in using NAP at your site, read Chapter 15, "Implementing Network Access Protection," for more information about this feature. Click Next to continue.

8. On the Summary page, review the configuration settings and click Next to create the deployment. When the Confirmation page displays, verify that the deployment was created successfully, and then click Close to exit the wizard. To see the new deployment in the Configuration Manager console, you might need to use the Refresh action on the Deployment Management node.

Monitoring the Progress of the Deployment

Monitoring the progress of a software update deployment can easily be accomplished by using the software updates reports. For example, the States 1 – Enforcement States For A Deployment report provides the overall count of computers for each enforcement state that has been reported by clients. You can then use the drill-down for a particular evaluation state to open the States 4 – Computers In A Specific State For A Deployment <Secondary> that returns a list of computers that reported the state, the assigned site for each client, the client version, the error status ID, and so on.

When you detect problems with a deployment, you can use the Troubleshooting 2 – Deployment Errors report to list a grouped listing of the deployment errors at the site with the count of computers within each group. You then can use the drill-down for a particular group to open the Troubleshooting 4 – Computers Failing With A Specific Deployment Error <Secondary> report to see a list of the computers in that group.

Responding to Emergencies

Even with the best planning and resources, the chances are high that at some point, an organization will have to cope with an emergency, such as a software update with an emergency release priority or the realization that a previously applied update is causing systems to fail. An organization can react to problems and resolve them more quickly if it is well prepared for the eventuality.

The software updates management team should attempt to anticipate the types of emergencies that it will have to deal with, and even conduct fire drills. In the event that the entire software updates management team cannot be brought together quickly enough to address an emergency, there should be a core emergency response team that has the authority to handle the problem appropriately. By far, the most common emergencies requiring the participation of the software updates management team are releases with accelerated timelines and the rollback of previously applied updates.

Releases with Accelerated Timelines

There can be many reasons why a release is deemed to be an emergency and the software updates management team needs to accelerate the release timeline. Regardless of the reason, there can be extreme pressure to ignore the software updates management process in place and deploy a software update immediately. By circumventing the process, however, organizations risk the integrity of the production environment. The four-phase software updates management process recommended by Microsoft is designed to cope with emergencies and should be followed when responding to one.

Note   It is important to stress that just because a software update is given a critical rating by Microsoft, it doesn't necessarily translate to an emergency release for the organization. A software update is designated with an initial release priority in the identify phase of the four-phase software updates management process. This initial priority is confirmed or adjusted in the Evaluate & Plan phase. If the priority is confirmed as being an emergency release, the software updates management team needs to make accommodations from that point on in the process to ensure that it is dealt with in a timely fashion.

The greatest difficulty in dealing with releases with accelerated timelines is that of completing the acceptance testing for deployments and the updates contained within them. Often the software updates management team is faced with the prospect of having to deploy software updates that haven't been fully tested in order to meet the accelerated timeline. In such cases, the team should concentrate on testing core functionality to ensure that day-to-day operations are not affected by the deployment and application of the update. The software updates management team may have to continue testing the release through deployment and afterward in order to confirm that deployment was the best course of action and to satisfy themselves that a rollback will not be required in the future.

Configuration Manager 2007 deployments that contain emergency releases should be mandatory (configured with the deadline), forcing clients to install the software updates in the deployment. Deployment templates should already be precreated for the different deployment scenarios, including deployments that contain emergency updates. As described earlier, a deployment template used in an emergency release should consider whether to suppress display notifications, should not suppress system restarts unless it is absolutely necessary but consider allowing a system restart outside of maintenance windows, and consider how clients will handle the installation when they are in a slow network boundary or when a protected distribution point doesn't have the updates in the deployment. For large packages that cannot be feasibly downloaded to clients connecting over slow links, a branch distribution point should be configured at the remote location. If that isn't an option, the software updates management team might want to resort to issuing a call for those systems to be brought in to a local office for updating or some other out-of-band software updates management strategy.

When an emergency release affects the servers hosting the software updates management infrastructure, the software updates management team might choose to update those systems manually or out of band to ensure that any necessary system restarts do not affect the deployment of updates. Another consideration for the software updates management infrastructure is how software updates are deployed between sites. With Configuration Manager 2007, the intersite senders should be configured with all restrictions removed in order to deploy the updates to other sites as quickly as possible.

Halting a Software Update Deployment

Occasionally, a deployment may need to be halted if an update within the deployment is causing problems in the production environment. Doing so can allow an investigation to take place before any additional clients install the updates. There are several methods that can be used to stop the updates in the deployment from installing on clients, such as configuring the start time and deadline to a date and time several months into the future, simply removing the suspected software update from the deployment, or by deleting the deployment all together.

Rolling Back Software Updates

When a previously deployed update is deemed to be causing or be likely to cause problems in the production environment there might be the need to roll back the deployed update. A rollback might not always be an emergency event, and the software updates management team must determine the appropriate priority to place on the event. In all cases, the team should strive to treat a rollback as though it were a software update and follow the established software updates management process. Whether or not the rollback is deemed an emergency, any ongoing deployments of the update in question should be halted as discussed previously.

The mechanism for rolling back an update is update-specific. Not all software updates, especially updates addressing security vulnerabilities or updates to core components of an operating system can be rolled back. For those that can be rolled back, the administrator needs to determine what the command is to initiate the rollback, build a package with a program to invoke it, and use the software distribution feature to deploy it. The Configuration Manager administrator has two options when deploying a rollback package. The first is to have the rollback program determine whether or not the update has been applied to a system before initiating the rollback and advertise the package with the program to the same systems to which the software update was deployed. The second is to attempt to identify the systems that applied the update and target an advertisement for a package with the program that performs a rollback to these systems.

Creating and Publishing Custom Updates

Software updates in Configuration Manager provide the ability to scan for and deploy software updates available on Microsoft Update, but you know that there are many other applications that will occasionally need to be updated in the software updates production environment. System Center Updates Publisher is a stand-alone tool that enables independent software vendors and line-of-business developers to create custom updates for these applications and then publish them to WSUS.

After Updates Publisher has been installed, there are several settings that must be configured so that the custom updates can be created and published, such as the database location that stores the custom update definitions and the update server for which the custom updates will be published. When using Updates Publisher to publish custom updates that will be synchronized into Configuration Manager, the update server setting should initially be configured as the active software update point site system server in the test environment. This allows you to publish the custom updates to the test environment when building the release and performing acceptance testing while in the Evaluate & Plan phase of the Microsoft-recommended software updates management process. After the acceptance testing for the deployment containing the custom update has succeeded, the update server setting should be changed so that the custom update is published to WSUS running on the active software update point for the central site in the production environment.

Catalogs published by non-Microsoft organizations or catalogs created from within your internal organization can be imported automatically or manually, allowing the software updates within the catalogs available for publishing to the configured update server. Software update definitions can be authored in Updates Publisher, allowing you to create your own custom updates for an unlimited number of applications in your environment. Creating the rules associated with the update definition can sometimes be complicated and will require thorough testing before publishing the custom updates to the production environment.

When custom updates are ready to publish to the update server, there are security considerations that must be met on both the server and client side. The following is a list of requirements for custom updates to be published and for clients to scan for software updates compliance for the published updates:

- **Port Settings** The port settings for WSUS must be specified on the Update Server tab of the Settings dialog box in Updates Publisher. When WSUS uses a custom Web site, the default port settings are 8530 (HTTP) and 8531 (HTTPS), and when the default Web is used, the default port settings are 80 (HTTP) and 443 (HTTPS).

- **Certificate Requirements** For a custom update to be published to WSUS, the updates must be signed by a certificate, and the same certificate must be in the appropriate certificate stores on the WSUS server and to the computer running Updates Publisher if it is remote. The client computers also require that the certificate is located in the appropriate certificate stores. Clients will scan the published updates for software updates compliance, but they will fail to install them unless the certificate for the updates is available on the client.

- **Group Policy** Before clients will accept custom updates signed by publishers other than Microsoft, the Allow Signed Content From Intranet Microsoft Update

Service Location must be enabled. When this setting is enabled, the updates are accepted if they are signed in the Trusted Publishers store on the local computer.

Before locally published custom updates will be synchronized, you must configure the active software update point product setting to include locally published updates.

1. To configure the Software Update Point to synchronize locally published updates, follow these steps: In the Configuration Manager console, navigate to the Site Settings node and expand it, and then select the Component Configuration folder to display the components.

2. Right-click Software Update Point Component and then click Properties.

3. Click the Products tab, and in the list of products, select the Local Publisher product group, as shown in Figure 13-23. Click OK to exit the dialog box.

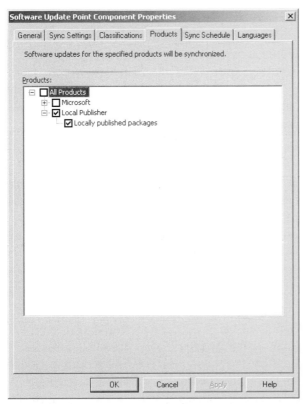

Figure 13-23   The Local Publisher product group selected in the Products tab in the Software Update Point Component Properties dialog box

After selecting the Local Publisher product group, initiate software updates synchronization on the central site to retrieve the metadata for the locally published updates, and the scan for software updates compliance and creating deployments for the updates will be the same as any update from Microsoft Update.

> **More Info**   For detailed information about installing and using System Center Updates Publisher, see the System Center Updates Publisher TechNet Library at *http://technet.microsoft.com/en-us/library/bb531022.aspx*. Updates Publisher Setup is available on the Configuration Manager 2007 DVD in the *<DVD Drive>*:\SCUP folder. A local version of the Updates Publisher help file is also located in this folder.

Checkpoints

As you have learned, to successfully deploy software updates in Configuration Manager you really should have a strong software updates management process in place, such as the Microsoft-recommended four-phase software updates management process. In preparation for the software updates management process, the IT assets should be brought to a known configuration, the software updates management infrastructure should be developed, and the software updates management team should be trained.

There are several components that that must be installed prior to using software updates in Configuration Manager. After the software updates management team decides what computer will host the software update point site system role, WSUS must be installed on the computer, and then the active software update point is installed and configured. Pay close attention to the port settings used by WSUS and the active software update point and make sure they are configured to use the same ports. When the active software update point is remote from the site server, WSUS Administration Console must be installed on the site server. After the active software update point site role has been installed on the central site, synchronization is initiated with Microsoft Update and the software updates metadata replicated down the Configuration Manager hierarchy.

The Software Updates Client Agent is enabled by default and the settings are configured with default values, but it is highly recommended that you become familiar with these settings and make adjustments to them if necessary. The WUA must be upgraded to a version compatible with WSUS 3.0. During the Configuration Manager client installation, WUA on each client is upgraded if required. After the active software update point has installed on a site, and after the client receives its next machine policy, the client will scan for software updates compliance. A state message, containing the compliance state, is created for each software update. When there are scan failures, look at the Troubleshooting

1 – Scan Errors report for specific error messages and the number of computers reporting each error. A typical scan failure might be the result of a failed WUA upgrade on clients during the software updates client installation.

There are several objects used in the recommended deployment process. Deployment templates provide consistency for most of the deployment settings and should be precreated for the typical deployment scenarios in the production environment. The recommended deployment process is to create an update list with the set of approved updates and download the update files to a deployment package using the Update List Wizard. The deployment is created either by dragging and dropping the update list to an appropriate deployment template or by using the Deploy Software Updates action on the update list and then selecting the appropriate deployment template from within the Deploy Software Updates Wizard.

When a release is deemed to be an emergency and the software updates management team needs to accelerate the release timeline, it is important to follow the four-phase software updates management process and not circumventing the process and risk the integrity of the production environment. When software updates must be deployed before being fully tested, it is important to test core functionality at a minimum to ensure that day-to-day operations are not affected by the deployment. Deployments for emergency releases should be mandatory, most likely have an aggressive deadline for installation, and a deployment template precreated for the emergency deployment scenario should be used. The software updates management team should have a documented plan for halting a deployment or rolling back deployed software updates before getting into an emergency situation.

When publishing custom updates from System Center Updates Publisher to WSUS, you must have certificates in the appropriate certificate stores on the Updates Publisher computer, the WSUS server, and the client computers. The port settings for the WSUS server must be configured in the Updates Publisher console, the Allow Signed Content From Intranet Microsoft Update Service Location group policy setting must be enabled, and the Local Publisher product group must be selected in the Software Update Point Component properties dialog box.

Summary

The Microsoft-recommended four-phase patch management process, documented in Microsoft Solutions for Management 2.5, describes a process that can be applied to organizations of all sizes. The four phases, Assess, Identify, Evaluate & Plan, and Deploy, contain prescriptive steps that the organization should follow to ensure successful updates to the configuration of the production environment.

The vulnerability rating for every alert received by an organization's software updates management team should be examined for guidance on the level of attention that the software update should receive. The team should look at mitigating factors and factors inherent to their production priority and assign a release priority to the update. The update then needs to be tested and accepted and a release plan developed before deployment can begin. Deployment templates should be created for typical deployment scenarios before the deployment process is initiated. The recommended deployment process consists of adding approved software updates to an update list, which provides a better reporting experience and allows for delegation, and the update files are downloaded while creating the update list. The update list then is used to create the deployment, and the appropriate deployment template is selected for the deployment scenario. After an update has been successfully applied to systems in the production environment, the organization needs to update the secure baseline configurations for its IT assets and use them when deploying new systems.

Each organization should expect and plan for emergency situations in which a software update has to be deployed in an expedited fashion, or a previously deployed update needs to be rolled back. In both situations, the software updates management team should follow through with its software updates management process to guarantee the integrity of the production environment.

Custom software updates can be created and published to WSUS running on the active software update point on the central site to allow locally published applications, such as line-of-business applications, to be added to the set of updates that are available for the scan for software updates compliance on clients and deployed to clients using the software updates infrastructure.

The Desired Configuration Management feature, discussed in the Chapter 14, "Implementing Desired Configuration Management," provides information about how you can create configuration items and secure baseline configurations, and then report on baseline compliance for computers in the Configuration Manager hierarchy.

Chapter 14

Implementing Desired Configuration Management

Configuration desired

Author and digest in vain

The way forward is import

~ Rob Stack, Technical Writer, Configuration Manager

This chapter looks at one of the key new features in Configuration Manager—desired configuration management. You'll learn how to configure this feature, download best practices configuration data, and evaluate your computers against this data. Then you'll look at how to produce reports showing compliance in your organization and how to remediate any noncompliant computers you find.

The Need for Desired Configuration Management

In modern organizations, hardware and software configuration errors can account for a large proportion of unplanned downtime for servers and workstations. Although there are several tools available to help with the correct and consistent deployment of worksta tions and servers such as the Microsoft Solution Accelerator for Business Desktop Deployment (BDD), these do not address the need to monitor production computers to guarantee that configuration changes made after deployment do not affect the operation of the computer or the network.

In 2005, Microsoft introduced desired configuration monitoring, a solution accelerator for Systems Management Server 2003 that enabled administrators to define required configurations for computers, and then to evaluate these computers for compliance against the configuration. In 2006, version 2 of the solution accelerator was released, which introduced new features and a new user interface.

With the release of Configuration Manager, this feature has been fully integrated into the product and is now called desired configuration management. Some of the key differences between the two products include:

- SMS 2003 desired configuration monitoring uses an external, Web-based interface for authoring configuration data. Desired configuration management's interface is built in to the product.

- SMS 2003 desired configuration monitoring uses a proprietary format for representing configuration data. Desired configuration management is built on the Service Modeling Language (SML), a standard for describing and modeling information technology resources. Although you can author directly in SML and import this into Configuration Manager, desired configuration management also supports DCM Digest, a specialized XML document that helps to abstract some of the complexities associated with SML. For more information about how desired configuration management uses SML and DCM Digest, see "About Authoring Configuration Data for Desired Configuration Management" in the Configuration Manager Documentation Library. For more information about authoring configuration data with DCM Digest, see the Configuration Manager 2007 SDK.

> **Note**   You can learn more about the Service Modeling Language from the Manageability TechCenter: Service Modeling Language Web page at *http://go.microsoft.com/fwlink/?LinkId=78991.*

- Configuration data in SMS 2003 desired configuration monitoring is stored as files. In desired configuration management, configuration baselines and configuration items are stored as configuration manager objects that support versioning and auditing information.

■ Desired configuration monitoring uses a separate scan engine, which has to be deployed to client computers using software distribution. The scan engine in desired configuration management is built right in to the Configuration Manager client.

■ Desired configuration monitoring stores compliance results in WMI where they can be picked up by SMS 2003 hardware inventory. In desired configuration management, these results are reported to the site using state messages.

■ Compliance reporting in SMS 2003 desired configuration monitoring requires the installation of Microsoft SQL Reporting Services (SRS). Desired configuration management uses the reporting feature built in to Configuration Manager and also offers a home page with a summary of compliance information.

Desired configuration management provides tools to detect and help to resolve configuration issues in a proactive manner, which can help to reduce support calls, increase the reliability of computer systems, and save money. The capabilities of the feature include:

■ Comparing the configuration of computers in your enterprise against best practice configurations from Microsoft and other vendors

■ Verifying the configuration of provisioned computers against custom defined configuration baselines before they go into production

■ Identifying computer configurations that are not authorized by change control procedures

■ Prioritizing noncompliance with four levels of severity

■ Reporting compliance with regulatory policies and in-house security policies

■ Identifying security vulnerabilities, as defined by Microsoft and other software vendors, across the enterprise

■ Providing the help desk with the means to detect probable cause for reported incidents and problems by identifying noncompliant configurations

■ Remediating noncompliance with software distribution that targets noncompliant computers with software packages or scripts by using a collection that is automatically populated with computers reporting noncompliance

■ Leveraging management products (such as System Center Operations Manager) that monitor Windows events on computers to take automatic action when a configuration is reported out of compliance

Real World   Planning for Desired Configuration Management

Before you dive in and start downloading best practices configuration data and authoring your own configuration data, take some time to think about what you want to accomplish with desired configuration management and the staff in your organization you might need to work with in order to define the required compliance information. For example, consider the following scenario:

You intend to roll out an upgrade to a payroll software package to computers in your organization. This update requires that a specific version of the software is already installed on computers and has a company-specific configuration text file present.

In this scenario, you would likely work with the payroll team to define the correct settings that the application needs to run, and then author an application configuration item that checks for the correct version of the software package and also contains a file or folder object that checks whether the configuration file is present on the computer and in the correct folder.

Understanding what you are trying to accomplish makes the task of using desired configuration manager considerably easier.

Understanding the Components of Desired Configuration Management

Begin by exploring the basic components that make up desired configuration management.

Configuration Items

Configuration items define units of configuration that you want to evaluate for compliance. They typically contain one or more configurations and the validation they will be evaluated against. For example, you might want to assess the compliance of the value of a particular registry key and report noncompliance if the value is found to be different or missing on client computers. Configuration items can be reused for different scenarios.

There are four configuration item types in Configuration Manager. Each one (with the exception of the Software Updates configuration item) allows you to define configurations related to details such as installed applications, the installed operating system and many other items. The four types of configuration item are:

- **Operating System Configuration Item**   Determines compliance related to the operating system version and its associated configuration.

- **Application Configuration Item**   Determines compliance related to applications and their configuration.

- **General Configuration Item**   Determines compliance for configurations that are not covered by the other types of configuration item.

- **Software Updates Configuration Item**   If you are using the software updates feature in Configuration Manager, software updates are made available as configuration items when they are downloaded using the Configuration Manager software updates feature, and you can use these to evaluate compliance on client computers. Unlike the other configuration item types, however, you cannot modify this type of configuration item.

Configuration items typically contain objects and settings to define the configuration to be evaluated. Objects refer to physical items on the computer such as files, folders, and registry keys. Settings refer to values obtained from the client computer such as values obtained from Active Directory Domain Services through an LDAP query or settings obtained from a server's SQL configuration.

Real World   Tips for Managing Configuration Items

At some point, it is likely that you will want to begin authoring your own configuration data to address business requirements unique to your company. It's important that you take some time to plan the methodology you will use to accomplish this. A single configuration item can contain many objects and settings. You could, for example, author a configuration item that contains the necessary objects and settings to evaluate the compliance of your organization's payroll application, checking that the application is installed, that certain files are present, and that a number of registry keys are set to their correct values. This method has its advantages in that you only have one configuration item to manage that contains all of the necessary objects and settings you need to evaluate compliance of the in-house application.

You should aim to create configuration items that contain all of the objects and settings necessary to perform a specific task, such as evaluating the compliance of the payroll application mentioned previously. Although it might seem like a good idea to have each object and setting defined in its own configuration item and then reuse these for specific configuration baselines, this method can degrade performance on client computers when they have large numbers of configuration items to evaluate.

When you begin to create large numbers of configuration items, there is a possibility that you might begin to create configuration items that contain the same objects and settings multiple times. This could become confusing when deciding which configuration items to reference in configuration baselines. You can use folders and configuration categories to help you more efficiently search and find configuration items and configuration baselines. As a starting point, consider downloading some of the best practice Configuration Packs from the Microsoft System Center Configuration Packs Web page at *http://go.microsoft.com/fwlink/?LinkId=71837* to see how the configuration items in these are constructed.

Configuration Baselines

Configuration baselines are a type of configuration item that is used to define a configuration that will be evaluated for compliance when it is assigned to client computers. Configuration baselines typically contain one or more configuration items and associated rules that control how compliance is evaluated. A configuration baseline can also reference other configuration baselines. This facilitates the easy reuse of authored configuration data for granular administration. For example, you might create a configuration baseline that evaluates the compliance of your organization's antivirus software. Later, your security department asks you to create a configuration baseline that evaluates a wider range of security software. It is not necessary to reauthor the configuration data for your antivirus software; you can simply reference the existing configuration baseline to the new configuration baseline.

The following rules can be applied to configuration items referenced by a configuration baseline:

- One of the following operating system configuration items must be present and properly configured.

- These applications and general configuration items are required and must be properly configured.

- If these optional application configuration items are detected, they must be properly configured.

- These software updates must be present.

- These application configuration items must not be present.

- These configuration baselines must also be validated.

Configuration baselines are assigned to collections of client computers together with a schedule by which they are evaluated for compliance.

> **Note**   It is possible to give multiple configuration baselines or configuration items the same name. Generally this is not a good idea as management of your configuration data will quickly become very difficult if you have duplicate names. However, if multiple configuration baselines or configuration items share the same name, they will have a unique ID number by which you can differentiate them. See the topic "How to Distinguish Configuration Data with the Same Name in Desired Configuration Management" in the Configuration Manager Documentation Library for details on how to access the unique ID.

For more information on creating configuration items and configuration baselines, see the topic "Tasks for Desired Configuration Management" in the Configuration Manager Documentation Library.

> **More Info**   You can download best practices Configuration Packs from the Microsoft System Center Configuration Packs Web page at *http://go.microsoft.com/fwlink/?LinkId=71837*. These contain ready-made configuration baselines and configuration items that cover a number of common scenarios.

Preparing to Use Desired Configuration Management

Desired configuration management requires three prerequisites before you can begin to use it:

- Your site and client computers must be running Configuration Manager. SMS 2003 client computers do not support desired configuration management.

- All client computers on your site must be running version 2.0 of the Microsoft NET framework. This can be downloaded from *http://go.microsoft. com/fwlink/?LinkID=56407*. You can use standard Configuration Manager software distribution to install this software. The Configuration Manager Documentation Library includes the topic "How to Identify Computers that Do Not Have the .NET Framework v2.0 for Desired Configuration Management," which helps you to identify computers that do not have the correct version of the .NET Framework installed. Note that installing the .NET Framework might require you to restart the client computer to complete the installation. Until you do this, the Desired Configuration Management Client Agent will not function correctly.

- The Desired Configuration Management Client Agent must be enabled for your Configuration Manager site.

Enabling Desired Configuration Management

To begin, enable and configure the Desired Configuration Management Client Agent on your client computers. The Desired Configuration Manager Client Agent is enabled by default when a Configuration Manager site is installed, but for the purposes of this example, assume that it has been disabled. Enable the Desired Configuration Management Client Agent through the Configuration Manager console. To do so, follow these steps:

1. Expand the site's Site Settings node, and then click Client Agents.

2. Right-click Desired Configuration Management Client Agent and choose Properties from the context menu to display the Desired Configuration Management Client Agent Properties dialog box, as shown in Figure 14-1.

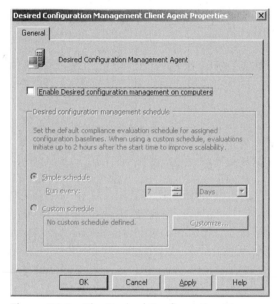

Figure 14-1   The Desired Configuration Management Client Agent Properties dialog box

3. Select the Enable Desired Configuration Management On Computers check box.

4. The default schedule for client computers to evaluate assigned configuration baselines is once every 7 days. With the Simple Schedule option, you can specify that assigned configuration baselines should be evaluated every 1 to 59 minutes, 1 to 23 hours, or 1 to 31 days. You can also select Custom Schedule, and then click Customize to display the Custom Schedule dialog box, as shown in Figure 14-2. In this dialog box, you can specify a more specific start time and recurrence pattern for evaluation.

5. When you have selected your chosen schedule, click OK.

6. Click OK to close the Desired Configuration Management Client Agent Properties dialog box.

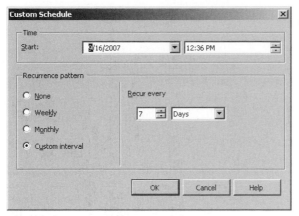

Figure 14-2   The Custom Schedule dialog box

The setting to enable desired configuration management is downloaded by client computers as part of their policy according to the policy polling interval in the Computer Client Agent Properties dialog box (by default every 60 minutes). This also applies to configuration baseline assignments.

Using Desired Configuration Management

In the following example, a sample best practice Configuration Pack is downloaded from the Microsoft System Center Configuration Packs Web page at *http://go.microsoft.com/fwlink/?LinkId=71837*, imported into Configuration Manager, and then assigned to a collection of client computers. If you want to download and test a Configuration Pack other than the example used here, the procedure given works just as well. However, for clarity, this procedure assumes you have downloaded a Configuration Pack named System Center Configuration Manager Configuration Pack (filename: ConfigMgr2007ConfigPack.msi), which contains the following configuration items to detect the compliance of the following Configuration Manager site system roles:

■ **Microsoft System Center Configuration Manager Distribution Point** Evaluates the configuration of a Configuration Manager site distribution point against best practices recommended by Microsoft.

■ **Microsoft System Center Configuration Manager Management Point** Evaluates the configuration of a Configuration Manager site management point against best practices recommended by Microsoft.

■ **Microsoft System Center Configuration Manager Software Update Point** Evaluates the configuration of a Configuration Manager site software update point against best practices recommended by Microsoft.

- **Microsoft System Center Configuration Manager SQL Server** Evaluates the configuration of a Configuration Manager SQL Server installation against best practices recommended by Microsoft.

- **Windows Server Update Services configuration for Microsoft System Center Configuration Manager Software Update Point** Evaluates the configuration of a Windows Server Update Services (WSUS) server against best practices recommended by Microsoft.

To download, import, and assign a configuration baseline, follow these steps:

1. From the Microsoft System Center Configuration Packs Web page at *http://go.microsoft.com/fwlink/?LinkId=71837*, download the Configuration Pack System Center Configuration Manager Configuration Pack and save this on your Configuration Manager site server's hard drive.

2. On the Configuration Manager site server, run the installation file for this Configuration Pack, ConfigMgr2007ConfigPack.msi, which unpacks the Configuration Pack data to your hard drive.

3. In the Configuration Manager console, navigate to the Computer Management node and expand Desired Configuration Management.

4. Right-click the Configuration Baselines node and select Import Configuration Data from the context menu to display the first page of the Import Configuration Data Wizard, as shown in Figure 14-3.

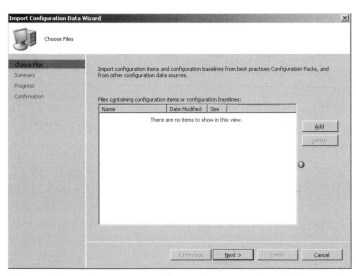

Figure 14-3   The Import Configuration Data Wizard Choose Files page

5. On the Choose Files page of the Import Configuration Data Wizard, click Add, and then navigate to the location where the Configuration Pack you installed was saved. The default location for this is C:\Program Files\System Center Configuration Manager 2007 Configuration Pack. Select the required Configuration Pack (named ConfigMgr2007SiteServerRoles.cab) and click Open.

6. At this point, you might see a security warning dialog box indicating that the publisher of this Configuration Pack could not be verified, as shown in Figure 14-4. If you are sure this Configuration Pack was downloaded from a reliable source (such as Microsoft's Web site), click Run to continue.

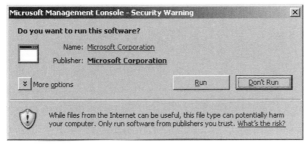

Figure 14-4   The Security Warning dialog box

7. You should now be back at the Choose Files page of the Import Configuration Data Wizard and the Configuration Pack you selected will be displayed in the main window. Click Next to continue.

8. The Summary page of the Import Configuration Data Wizard appears, showing the name of the configuration baseline you are about to import together with the names of all referenced configuration items, as shown in Figure 14-5. Review this list, and then click Next to continue.

9. The Progress page of the Import Configuration Data Wizard will now be displayed after which the Completing The Import Configuration Data Wizard page is displayed, showing the success or failure of each import operation, as shown in Figure 14-6. Click Close to close the Import Configuration Data Wizard.

> **Note**   If you receive any errors importing configuration data, refer to the topic "Import Failures with Desired Configuration Management" in the Configuration Manager Documentation Library.

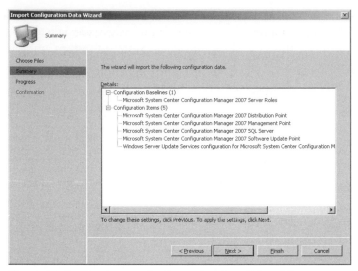

Figure 14-5   The Import Configuration Data Wizard Summary page

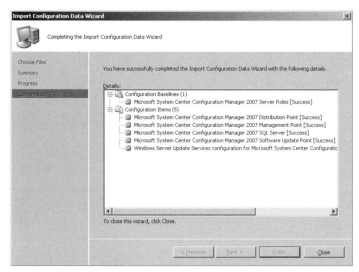

Figure 14-6   The Completing The Import Configuration Data Wizard page

Clicking in the Configuration Baselines or Configuration Items nodes of the Configuration Manager console should now display the various items you have just imported (you might need to refresh the console display to see newly added items). You can right-click any of these items and choose Properties from the context menu to examine the various objects, settings, and rules they contain. If you've done this, then you might have noticed that they are read only (as they are standard best practices items so should not be changed). If you want to modify any of the configuration items you have downloaded, you have two choices:

- Create a duplicate configuration item. If you right-click any configuration item in the Configuration Manager console and select Duplicate from the context menu, a copy of the configuration item is made that you can edit.

- Create a child configuration item. This creates a copy of the original configuration item, but retains a link to it. You can add new objects and settings, but you cannot change any existing values as these are inherited from the parent configuration item. This is a good option to use when you want to retain best practices settings from a Configuration Pack and also add configuration data specific to your organization.

If you expand the Configuration Baselines node and click on the Microsoft System Center Configuration Manager Server Roles configuration baseline and examine its rules in the main console window, as shown in Figure 14-7, you'll see that all of the configuration items referenced by this configuration baseline use the rule If These Optional Application Configuration Items Are Detected, They Must Be Properly Configured. This means that each of the referenced configuration items must be compliant if they are found to be present on the computer to which the configuration baseline has been assigned.

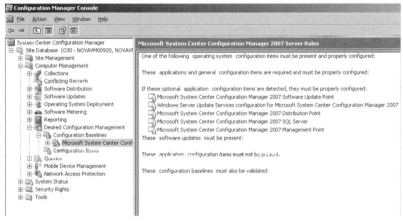

Figure 14-7   The Configuration Manager console showing the Imported Configuration Items

At this point, your configuration baseline is set up and ready to go. The next thing to do is to actually assign this to client computers on your site. The following procedure takes you through this process:

1. In the Configuration Manager console, navigate to Computer Management and expand the Desired Configuration Management node.

2. Expand the Configuration Baselines node and right-click the configuration baseline Microsoft System Center Configuration Manager Server Roles. From the context menu, choose Assign To A Collection to open the Assign Configuration Baseline Wizard as shown in Figure 14-8.

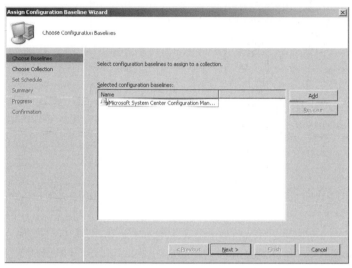

Figure 14-8   The Choose Configuration Baselines page of the Assign Configuration Baseline Wizard

3. In the Choose Configuration Baselines page of the Assign Configuration Baseline Wizard, the configuration baseline that you selected is automatically added to the Selected Configuration Baselines list. You can select further configuration baselines to add by clicking Add. Click Next to continue.

4. In the Choose Collection page of the Assign Configuration Baseline Wizard, specify a Configuration Manager collection to assign the configuration baseline to, as shown in Figure 14-9. Click Browse to open the Browse Collection dialog box from where you can choose a collection, and then click OK. For the purposes of this example, select the built-in All Windows Server Systems collection, though in practice you might want to set up a test collection containing fewer client computers. Because this collection evaluates Configuration Manager server roles, ensure that it contains at least one Configuration Manager server. The Choose Collection page also allows you to specify that you want to include subcollections of the specified collection, also. If you select this option, be sure that you are aware which computers in the subcollection will be targeted by this assignment. Click Next when you are ready to continue.

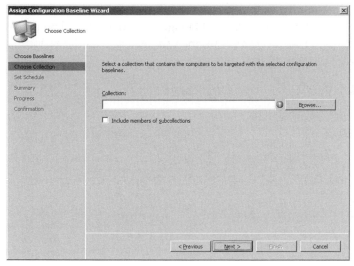

Figure 14-9   The Choose Collection page of the Assign Configuration Baseline Wizard

5. The next page of the Assign Configuration Baseline Wizard is the Set Schedule page, as shown in Figure 14-10. On this page, you can set a schedule by which client computers will evaluate the assigned configuration baseline if you want this to be different than the default schedule (which you learned how to specify in the section "Enabling Desired Configuration Management"). Set a simple or custom schedule if required, and then click Next.

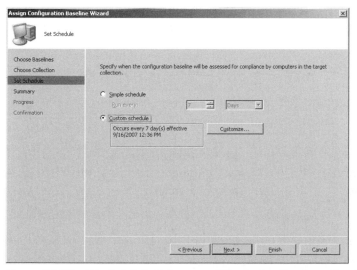

Figure 14-10   The Set Schedule page of the Assign Configuration Baseline Wizard

6. Review the information presented on the Summary page of the Assign Configuration Baseline Wizard. When you finish, click Next. If you want to change anything, you can click Previous and revise any options you have specified.

7. After the Progress page of the Assign Configuration Baseline Wizard is displayed, the final page you will see is the Wizard Completed page, as shown in Figure 14-11. Review the assignment details, and then click Close to finish.

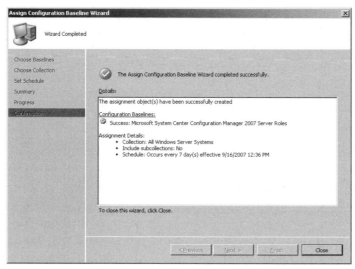

Figure 14-11   The Wizard Completed page of the Assign Configuration Baseline Wizard

Configuration baseline assignments are downloaded by client computers as part of their policy according to the policy polling interval in the Computer Client Agent Properties dialog box (by default every 60 minutes).

Organizing Configuration Data

As you build a library of configuration baselines and configuration items on your site, you will likely start to find that you need a method of filing these to make them easier to find. Desired configuration management provides three methods of organizing your configuration data to make it easier to manage.

Folders

You can create a folder structure under the Configuration Baselines or Configuration Items nodes in the Configuration Manager console to allow you to sort items into convenient "buckets." You can move items around between folders, creating any structure that suits your needs. To create a new folder, right-click either the Configuration Baselines or Configuration Items node, and then select New Folder from the context menu. In the New Folder dialog box, type a name for the folder and click OK.

To move items into a folder, select one or more items, right-click a highlighted item, and then select Move Items. In the Move Items dialog box, select the folder into which you want to place the items, and then click Move.

You can also move an entire folder to another location. To do this, right-click the folder and select Move Folder from the context menu. In the Move Items dialog box, select the location to which you want to move the folder, and then click Move.

> **Note**   Folders created on a Configuration Manager site automatically replicate to child sites.

Search Folders

Another type of folder is the search folder. This folder type offers a more sophisticated method of sorting configuration baselines and configuration items than standard folders. In search folders, you can specify search criteria that will be used when deciding which items to show in the folder. For example, you might want to have a folder showing all configuration items related to Microsoft SQL Server settings. One way of doing this could be to search for the phrase "SQL" in the configuration item name. To set up a search folder for configuration items, follow these steps:

1. Right-click the Configuration Items node of the Configuration Manager console. In the context menu, select New, and then select Search Folder.

2. In the Search Folder Criteria dialog box, select Name in the Select Object Properties To Search section. Notice that there are a number of other properties you can use as criteria for the search folder.

3. Under Edit The Property's Search Criteria, click the underlined text, *<text to find>*.

4. In the Search Text dialog box, you can type a list of words or phrases. If the configuration item contains these words or phrases, then it will appear in the search folder. You can type as many search terms as you want, and these can be as simple or complex as you want. Type a term, in this case SQL, and then click Add to add it to the search list. When you are finished, click OK.

5. You should now be back in the Search Folder Criteria dialog box. Select the Search All Folders Under This Feature check box if required. This searches all folders under desired configuration management, not just the folder in which the search folder resides.

6. Type a descriptive name for the search folder. In this example, SQL Server Search Folder is used. Click OK to close the Search Folder Criteria dialog box.

Notice the new node that appears under the Configuration Items node of the Configuration Manager console. When you select this new node, the search results are automatically displayed in the main window of the Configuration Manager console.

Note   You might need to refresh the Configuration Manager console display before you can see the new search folder. To do this, right-click the Desired Configuration Management node and select Refresh from the context menu.

Configuration Categories

Configuration categories are another way to improve how you can filter or search for configuration items and configuration baselines in your Configuration Manager hierarchy. Assigned categories appear in the main window of the Configuration Manager console when you click the Configuration Baselines or Configuration Items nodes. By clicking on the Categories column heading in this view, you can sort the configuration data list by category. You can also use the Look For and drop-down lists to restrict the display to show only those categories you choose.

Note   If you export a configuration baseline or configuration item to a file, configuration category information is not exported. However, categories created at a parent site are replicated to child sites. You can assign as many categories to an item as you want.

To assign a configuration category to a configuration baseline or a configuration item, follow these steps:

1. Click either the Configuration Baselines or Configuration Items node in the Configuration Manager console to display the list of items.

2. Select one or more configuration baselines or configuration items. Right-click the highlighted objects and select Manage Categories from the context menu.

3. In the Categories dialog box, select one or more categories to assign to this item. You can create new categories by typing the name in the Add A New Category field and then clicking Add. You can also delete categories by selecting the desired category and clicking Delete.

    Note   When you click Delete to remove a configuration category, you are not asked to confirm this action; the selected category is immediately deleted. Configuration baselines and configuration items that have been assigned to this category are not deleted.

4. Click OK when you finish.

To display only items of a specified category in the Configuration Manager console, follow these steps:

1. Click either the Configuration Baselines or Configuration Items node in the Configuration Manager console to display the list of items.

2. In the Look For box, type the name of the configuration category you want to filter on.

3. In the drop-down list, select Categories.

4. Click Find Now to display only items assigned to the category you typed in the Look For box.

5. To reset the display to show all items, click Clear.

Understanding Compliance Evaluation

When a configuration baseline is evaluated for compliance on a client computer, the following steps generally occur:

1. Each configuration item contained in the configuration baseline is individually evaluated for compliance.

2. Each configuration item is then evaluated against the rule to which it has been referenced in the configuration baseline.

3. If any of the configuration items referenced by a configuration baseline report as being noncompliant, then the configuration baseline itself is reported as noncompliant.

4. The compliance state of a computer is evaluated by evaluating the compliance of all configuration baselines assigned to it. If any of these configuration baselines report noncompliance, then the computer itself is reported as noncompliant.

There are essentially three processes that take place when a configuration item is evaluated for compliance in desired configuration manager:

■ **Applicability** When you create an application or general configuration item, you can specify the operating systems to which it is applicable. Operating system configuration items are always considered applicable; therefore no applicability check is performed. For example, a configuration item might specify that it is to only be evaluated on client computers running Windows XP Service Pack 1. If the target client computer is running Windows Vista then the configuration item will report as Not Applicable, and processing stops here. If the configuration item is Applicable, you then move on to detection.

- **Detection** Application and operating system configuration items allow you to specify further information that must be detected on client computers before compliance evaluation can take place. For an application configuration item, you can specify Windows Installer information in the Detection Method page of the Create Application Configuration Item Wizard. For an operating system configuration item, you can specify Windows version information in the Microsoft Windows Version tab of the Create Operating System Configuration Item Wizard. If either of these items is specified but not detected on the client computer, then the configuration item reports as Not Detected, and processing stops here. If the item is detected, you move to compliance.

- **Compliance** The objects and settings contained in the configuration item are now evaluated for compliance. To reach this stage, the configuration item has to be both Applicable and Detected. After the configuration item is evaluated, it generally reports one of two results: Compliant or Noncompliant.

  A further result could be reported: Failed. This can happen if there is corruption in the configuration item, for example, as a result of invalid coding in an externally authored configuration item.

After each configuration item is evaluated for compliance, it reports the result of the evaluation. This result is known as the actual compliance of the configuration item and can be reported as:

- Not Applicable
- Not Detected
- Compliant or Noncompliant
- Failed

In addition, when you create objects and settings in a configuration item, you can also specify the severity level to report if the particular object or setting is found to be noncompliant. This can help you to prioritize which configuration item evaluation failures you will attend to first. The four levels of severity are:

- **Information—no Windows event messages** Computers that are not compliant with one or more of the objects or settings in the configuration item (either not present or present but fail the validation criteria) do not log a Windows application event message. Computers send a state message and status message with the noncompliant severity level of Information.

- **Information** Computers that are not compliant with one or more of the objects or settings in the configuration item (either not present or present but fail the validation criteria) log a Windows application event message of the type Informational.

State messages and status messages sent by the client will have the noncompliant severity level of Information.

- **Warning** Computers that are not compliant with one or more of the objects or settings in the configuration item (either not present or present but fail the validation criteria) log a Windows application event message of the type Warning. State messages and status messages sent by the client will have the noncompliant severity level of Warning.

- **Error** Computers that are not compliant with one or more of the objects or settings in the configuration item (either not present or present but fail the validation criteria) log a Windows application event message of the type Error. State messages and status messages sent by the client will have the noncompliant severity level of Error.

You can use this severity level as a filter in the desired configuration management home page, reports, and queries. Additionally, you can use software such as System Center Operations Manager to notify you, in real time, when a failed evaluation writes a message to the Windows Event Log.

The actual compliance result is then evaluated against the configuration baseline rule to which it is applied, known as the desired configuration. As an example, take the configuration item named Microsoft System Center Configuration Manager SQL Server that you imported previously. If you view the properties of the configuration baseline named Microsoft System Center Configuration Manager Server Roles (by right-clicking the configuration baseline and selecting Properties from the context menu) that references this configuration item and click the Rules tab, you can see that the rule that the configuration item uses is named If These Optional Application Configuration Items Are Detected, They Must Be Properly Configured. This means that your configuration item must be detected and applicable before it is evaluated for compliance. The configuration item detects the existence of SQL Server by using a custom script specified in the Detection Method tab of the Configuration Item Properties dialog box.

As you can see in the example, you have a number of configuration items referenced by your configuration baseline. If any of these are evaluated as noncompliant, then the configuration baseline as a whole is considered noncompliant.

How to View Compliance Results in Desired Configuration Management

After you assign a configuration baseline to a collection of computers, the next thing to do is to find out if it is compliant on those computers. An easy way to do this is to navigate to the desired configuration management home page in the Configuration Manager console.

This section covers using the home page to detect noncompliant computers and using Configuration Manager reports to examine any compliance issues in greater detail.

The Desired Configuration Management Home Page

This page is normally your first port of call when you want an overview of which of your assigned configuration baselines are reporting a noncompliant status. As well as containing a list and pie chart of noncompliant configuration baselines, it also contains handy links to reports that give more detailed information on compliance, and to other useful resources. You can filter this information by the noncompliance severity level and by the category of the configuration baseline. The desired configuration management home page is shown in Figure 14-12. Although this is useful information, it is important to remember that the information is not displayed in real time. The information is retrieved from the database according to the summarization schedule, which is every 2 hours for this home page by default. You can change this schedule by clicking Schedule Home Page Summarization in the Actions pane, and you can request that the data is updated ad hoc with the Run Home Page Summarization in the Actions pane. However, this last request will take some time to complete, and you must refresh the screen to see the latest data. Reference the Last Updated value displayed to know at what time the information displayed was current.

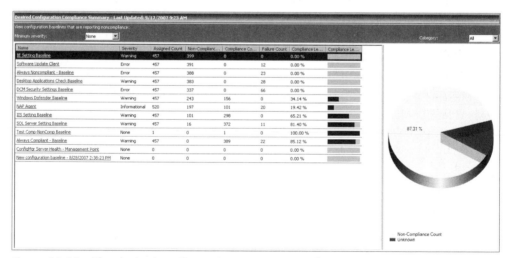

Figure 14-12   The desired configuration management home page

Using Reports to View Compliance

You can also use the built-in reports in Configuration Manager to view a wealth of information about the compliance of configuration baselines and configuration items. You'll look at two examples here: by viewing the compliance of a single computer and by viewing the compliance of a collection of computers. There are a host of other reports you can use, which are listed in full in the topic "About Reports for Desired Configuration Manager" located in the Configuration Manager Documentation Library.

Look first at viewing the compliance of a single computer by running the report Compliance For A Computer By Baseline. You will need a working reporting point on your site before doing this. Instructions on how to enable Configuration Manager reporting can be found in Chapter 19, "Extracting Information Using Queries and Reports."

1. In the Configuration Manager console, navigate to Computer Management and expand the Reporting node.

2. In the Reports node, find and right-click the report Compliance For A Computer By Configuration Baseline, then click Run from the context menu.

> **Note**   To make it easier to find the report you need, click the headings at the top of each column to sort items into order. For example, clicking the Category column will make it easier to find the reports relating to desired configuration management.

3. In the Computer Name text box, type the computer name or click Values to select it from a list. Note that if you have more than one configuration baseline assigned to a computer, you can further refine the report by selecting the required configuration baseline.

4. Click Display to view the report. The list of configuration baselines assigned to this computer will be displayed, along with an indication of whether the computer is compliant or noncompliant with each configuration baseline. For more details about which configuration item was out of compliance, drill down into each configuration baseline to view the report Compliance Details For A Configuration Baseline For A Specified Computer.

5. When you finish, close the report.

Next, try looking at the compliance results for an entire collection. Follow these steps:

1. In the Configuration Manager console, navigate to System Center Configuration Manager / Site Database / Computer Management / Desired Configuration Management.

2. In the section Links and Resources, under Web Report, click Compliance By Collection.

3. Type the required collection ID, or click Values and select it.

4. Click Display. The report Summary Compliance For A Collection By Computer appears. You can drill further into this report to look at detailed compliance for any computer.

Viewing Compliance Directly at the Client Computer

A third way of evaluating compliance is to view it directly from the client computer. If you have administrator privileges on the computer, you can also view a report of the compliance results.

1. Navigate to Configuration Manager in the Control Panel of the client computer, and double-click the icon to open the Configuration Manager Properties dialog box.

2. Click the Configurations tab, and view the list of configuration baselines that are assigned to this client computer, as shown in Figure 14-13.

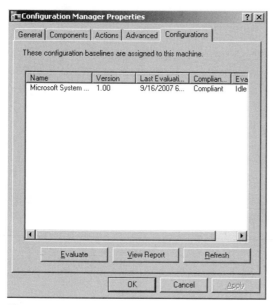

Figure 14-13   The Configurations tab of the Configuration Manager Properties dialog box

3. View the Compliance State column for each assigned configuration baseline. The state could be one of the following:

    ❑   **Compliant** The client computer is in compliance with the assigned configuration baseline.

    ❑   **Noncompliant** The client computer is out of compliance with the assigned configuration baseline.

❑ **Unknown** The client computer has not yet evaluated the assigned configuration baseline. If required, initiate evaluation outside the compliance evaluation schedule by selecting the configuration baselines to evaluate, and then click Evaluate.

4. You can also click View Report to see a detailed compliance report for the selected configuration baseline.

> **Important**   You must have administrator rights on the client computer to view the compliance report.

5. When finished, click OK to close the dialog box.

Remediating Noncompliant Computers

In this version of Configuration Manager, desired configuration management cannot automatically correct noncompliance issues found on your client computers. However, you can use Configuration Manager collections and software distribution to accomplish this task and effectively automate the remediation of noncompliant computers.

The compliance of the client computer against assigned configuration baselines is reported to the Configuration Manager site database using state messages. This means that you can construct a query-based collection that contains only those computers that reported noncompliance for an assigned configuration baseline or any of the configuration items it references.

> **Note**   State messages are a new feature in Configuration Manager that should not be confused with status messages. State messages use a new messaging system that allows client computers to send reports to the site when they change their state (for example, when they change from compliant to noncompliant). For more information, see the topic "About State Messages" in the Configuration Manager Documentation Library.

The following is an example using the configuration baseline you already created in the previous example. In this example, you will create a collection that contains only computers that have Microsoft SQL Server loaded and reported noncompliance for the configuration item named Microsoft System Center Configuration Manager SQL Server. You can then deploy a script to this collection of computers that implements the recommended settings for SQL Server.

Creating a Collection of Noncompliant Computers

Although an example query for noncompliant client computers appears in the Configuration Manager Documentation Library, for this example, you'll construct the collection manually. Follow these steps:

1. In the Configuration Manager console, navigate to Computer Management and expand the node.

2. Right-click the Collections node, and select New Collection from the context menu.

3. On the General Page of the New Collection Wizard, type a descriptive name for the collection such as Computers Failing Compliance For SQL Server and a comment, if desired. Click Next to continue.

4. On the Membership Rules page of the New Collection Wizard, click the New Query Rule button, as shown in Figure 14-14.

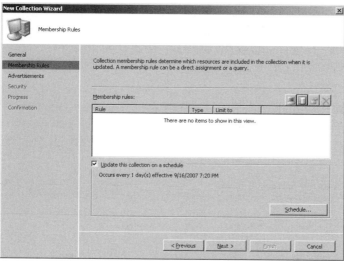

Figure 14-14   The Membership Rules page of the New Collection Wizard

5. In the Query Rule Properties dialog box, type a name for the query such as Computers Failing Compliance For SQL Server. Click the Edit Query Statement button.

6. You should be looking at a dialog box named Computers Failing Compliance For SQL Server Query Statement Properties. Because this is a collection, you cannot change any values on the General tab, so click the Criteria tab to continue.

7. On the Criteria tab, click the New Criterion button, as shown in Figure 14-15.

8. In the Criterion Properties dialog box, make sure that Criterion Type is set to Simple Value, and then click the Select button.

Figure 14-15   The Query Statement Properties dialog box

9. In the Select Attribute dialog box, set the following values:

    ❑ **Attribute Class** Configuration Item Compliance State

    ❑ **Alias As** Leave this field blank

    ❑ **Attribute** Localized Display Name

10. Click OK when you are done.

11. Back in the Criterion Properties dialog box, select Is Equal To as the Operator, and then click the Value button.

12. In the Values dialog box, look down the list for your configuration item, which is Microsoft System Center Configuration Manager SQL Server, and select it. Click OK.

13. In the Criterion Properties dialog box, click OK to close it.

What you have accomplished so far is to create a collection that lists all computers that have evaluated a configuration baseline named Microsoft System Center Configuration Manager SQL Server; they will be listed in the collection no matter what compliance state is reported. You now need to refine this collection showing only those computers that have reported a state of noncompliance. To do this, follow these steps:

1. In the Computers Failing Compliance For SQL Server Query Statement Properties dialog box, click the Criteria tab if it is not already selected.

2. On the Criteria tab, click the New Criterion button.

3. In the Criterion Properties dialog box, make sure that Criterion Type is set to Simple Value, and then click the Select button.

4. In the Select Attribute dialog box, set the following values:

    ❑   **Attribute Class** Configuration Item Compliance State

    ❑   **Alias As** Leave this field blank

    ❑   **Attribute** Compliance State Name

5. Click OK.

6. In the Criterion Properties dialog box, make sure Operator is set to Is Equal To, and then click the Value button.

7. In the Values dialog box, look down the list for the state Non-compliant and select it. Click OK.

> **Note**   If you have not run compliance evaluations before on your site then this list might be blank. You can type the name Non-compliant into this box; make sure to use the same case as shown in this note.

8. In the Criterion Properties dialog box, click OK to close it.

9. In the Computers Failing Compliance For SQL Server Query Statement Properties dialog box, make sure the operator is set as shown in Figure 14-16. Click OK.

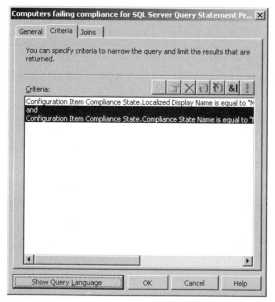

Figure 14-16   The Query Statement Properties dialog box showing the completed query

10. In the Query Rule Properties dialog box, select Limit To Collection, and then click Browse to select a collection. Alternatively, type the name of the collection for which you want to limit results. This is typically the same collection to which you assigned the configuration baseline, which in this example is All Windows Server Systems. Click OK.

11. Back on the Membership Rules page of the New Collection Wizard, click Next.

12. On the Advertisements page of the New Collection Wizard, click Next.

13. On the Security page of the New Collection Wizard, click Next.

14. After viewing the Progress page of the wizard, you should now be looking at the Confirmation page. Review the actions you have just taken and click Close to close the wizard.

You now have a Configuration Manager collection containing only those computers that reported a noncompliant state for the configuration item Microsoft System Center Configuration Manager SQL Server. You can now use standard methods of software distribution to distribute a software package containing a script or program that remediates any incorrect settings. For more information about Configuration Manager software distribution, refer to Chapter 11, "Distributing Software Packages."

Note You can make this query-based collection more complex by adding attributes such as the severity level of any noncompliance. For more information on how to do this, refer to the Configuration Manager Documentation Library.

Checkpoints for Using Desired Configuration Management

First, make sure you have the correct prerequisites in place before using desired configuration management. All client computers must be using version 2.0 of the Microsoft .NET Framework. Desired configuration management only works on Configuration Management 2007 client computers; it will not work on SMS 2003 clients.

When you download configuration data from an external source, remember that it will be read only. You can modify this data by duplicating configuration items, or you can add to this data and retain the original settings by creating child configuration items. The section "Planning for Desired Configuration Management" in the Configuration Manager Documentation Library contains more detailed information to help you decide which type of configuration item to create.

If you are using reports to view compliance of your assigned configuration items and the status of Unknown appears, it's likely that the computer to which you have assigned the configuration baseline has not yet performed a compliance evaluation. This could be because the time specified in the assignments schedule has not yet been reached. In this case, you can either wait until the schedule permits the evaluation to run, or manually initiate the compliance evaluation directly from the client computer.

Remember that configuration baselines and configurations can have duplicate names. This is not a recommended practice, but if you are importing configuration data from external sources, then it is a situation that might arise. In this case, you can use the CI Unique ID value of the configuration baseline or configuration item to differentiate them For more details, refer to the topic "How to Distinguish Configuration Data with the Same Name in Desired Configuration Management" in the Configuration Manager Documentation Library.

Take time to plan the process that you will use to create configuration data. For example, performance will be improved if you create configuration items with multiple objects and settings instead of using only one setting or object for each one. Make sure to specify useful names and descriptions for configuration data so that other administrators can use them without having to interpret their contents. If you are using wildcard characters in configuration item objects and settings, these might cause high processor usage when they are evaluated on client computers if they trigger an extensive search.

Summary

In this chapter, you covered one of the most significant new features of Configuration Manager and learned how you can use it to begin managing desired configurations in your organization. You also explored how to use Configuration Manager reporting to view the compliance of collections of computers in your Configuration Manager site and how to drill into these reports to isolate noncompliance issues on individual computers. Finally, you learned how to create collections of noncompliant computers that can be targeted with Configuration Manager software packages to remediate the problem causing noncompliance.

In Chapter 15, you will look at another new feature of Configuration Manager 2007—Network Access Protection.

Chapter 15

Implementing Network Access Protection

Tomorrow's gatekeeper

Prevents dangerous talking!

NAP it to be safe.

~ Carol Bailey, Technical Writer, Configuration Manager

This chapter lifts the lid on Network Access Protection (NAP), one of the exciting improvements Microsoft includes with newer operating systems. It is another step closer to developing self healing systems. Network Access Protection is a natural complement to System Center Configuration Manager in that it extends central management of software updates with compliance enforcement, and it can be used in concert with enforcing other components and applications on computers that you require for compliance.

In the long term, implementing Network Access Protection can help to protect your network assets. However, it should be considered one of many security strategies and does not replace other security tools or negate existing security practices. In addition, because of the potential for caching and inherent latency, Network Access Protection in Configuration Manager should not be considered a real-time security mitigation for noncompliant computers.

Understanding Network Access Protection

Most people think of Network Access Protection as a means of keeping noncompliant computers from accessing the network, where they could infect other computers with viruses. Network Access Protection can do this, but it is in fact far more sophisticated in its design and potential. This sophistication requires a learning curve for administrators, a significant investment in the underlying infrastructure, and buy-in from management. Network Access Protection offers a tangible step toward the goal of self-healing systems, but its requirements, risks, and limitations must also be thoroughly understood before implementation if it is to fulfill the requirements of adding business value by decreasing the total cost of ownership.

So, before diving into how to configure Network Access Protection with Configuration Manager, take a step back and peel away some of the layers that make up the underlying Network Access Protection architecture. This will allow you to better understand how Configuration Manager fits into the Network Access Protection equation and also better understand the Network Access Protection configuration options in Configuration Manager.

The Many Layers of Network Access Protection

Network Access Protection uses the concept of "health" to define which elements and components should be configured or installed on computers. In the context of Configuration Manager, this relates to any software update that you can deploy through the software updates feature in Configuration Manager, including security updates, service packs, hardware vendor updates, and custom updates. In the context of the Windows Security Center, it could be basic Windows security checks such as whether the firewall is enabled, Windows Update is configured, and antivirus software is installed. As an open and extensible architecture, it allows other vendors to offer their own solutions that contribute toward the health of computers, such as a specific anti-spyware application that is installed and has the latest signature files.

For every health state that is checked in this way, you need a separate client component and a corresponding server component. On the client, a system health agent is responsible for assessing the health of a computer. On the server, a system health validator receives this information and validates it. These two components (system health agent and system health validator) are often abbreviated to just SHA and SHV. In Configuration Manager, the Configuration Manager System Health Agent is enabled when the Network Access Protection client agent is enabled, and the Configuration Manager System Health Validator is enabled when the System Health Validator point is installed.

Multiple system health agents on a single computer run under the direction of the Windows Network Access Protection agent. On computers running Windows Vista and Windows Server 2008, the Windows Network Access Protection agent is built into the operating system. For computers running Windows XP Professional with one of the latest service packs, you can install a Network Access Protection client that provides this functionality. One layer further down, each computer needs a Network Access Protection enforcement mechanism enabled that provides the networking layer that carries the packets related to Network Access Protection.

Network Access Protection enforcement mechanisms include DHCP, VPN, IPsec, 802.1X, and Terminal Services Gateway. You can use one or many enforcement mechanisms, depending on your business requirements. Each requires different setup and configuration, so it makes sense to choose selectively. For example, you might decide to configure DHCP enforcement only in a test lab as an initial proof of concept, with the view of configuring IPsec and 802.1X later on the production network. Or you might decide that Network Access Protection enforcement is required only for computers connecting over the VPN, but decide to test with DHCP first. Because Network Access Protection uses a layered architecture, the Network Access Protection processes of restricting network access and automatically remediating should be independent from the underlying Network Access Protection enforcement mechanisms. You can find step-by-step guides for the individual Network Access Protection enforcement mechanisms on the Network Access Protection Web site at *http://go.microsoft.com/fwlink/?LinkId=59125*.

The information that the system health agent sends to the system health validator is called the statement of health, which you will often see abbreviated to SoH. The system health validator validates this information and determines whether the client is compliant, noncompliant, or an error condition occurred that prevents the determination of the compliance status. The result of its validation is a statement of health response (SoHR). Statement of health responses from all system health validators are collected for a client so that a decision can be made about the client's network access. The decision is sent back to the client so that it knows whether it is deemed compliant or noncompliant and its resulting network access.

The Network Policy Server

The server that runs the system health validators and performs the role of a gatekeeper to the network is a computer running Windows Server 2008 that has installed on it the server role of Network Policy Server. It has policies configured that determine the network access that is allowed depending on whether the computer is compliant or noncompliant or whether an error condition occurred.

Although most people think of Network Access Protection as restricting network access for noncompliant computers, it can also give full network access but report the noncompliant status (known as reporting mode), and it can give full network access for a limited time (also known as deferred enforcement). This latter configuration provides a grace period until a set date that you configure. When this date is reached, a computer that remains noncompliant will have restricted network access.

Note This date is a set date for all computers and is not relative to the time that the client is found to be noncompliant. So you can't, for example, specify that all noncompliant computers have a week's grace to get compliant from the

time that they are found to be noncompliant. You can specify a date a week
ahead, at which time all noncompliant computers will have restricted network
access, even if they have been offline for six days.

For this configuration to work, you need a combination of policies configured on the Network Policy Server:

- **Connection request policy**   This allows network access with at least one condition (such as the time and day condition, even if configured for 7 days and 24
hours) and can identify the type of Network Access Protection enforcement server
you want to use.

- **Health policy**   This identifies which system health validators are being used to
determine the health of computers, and you will usually configure two health policies for each system health validator: one health policy in which health checks pass
(indicating a compliant status) and another for when health checks fails (indicating
a noncompliant status). After installing the system health validator point in Configuration Manager, you will be able to select the Configuration Manager System
Health Validator in the Network Policy Server as one of the available system health
validators when you configure health policies.

- **Network policy**   This determines the network access that a computer will be given
based on a number of factors that can include selected health policies—for example,
giving a noncompliant computer restricted network access and a compliant computer full network access. Additionally, there is a separate option to invoke automatic remediation for noncompliant computers. However, Network Access
Protection in Configuration Manager will always invoke remediation for noncompliant computers unless the reporting mode is selected. When the reporting mode
is selected, Network Access Protection in Configuration Manager will never invoke
remediation, even if the option to automatically update noncompliant computers is
selected in the policy. In this scenario, use the standard software updates feature in
Configuration Manager to install software updates on computers that require them.

When the Network Policy Server is being used with Network Access Protection, it is
referred to as an NAP health policy server.

Real World   The Balance of Power for Enforcing Compliance and Controlling Network Access

It is important to realize that it's the configuration of the policies on the Network
Policy Server that ultimately determines whether noncompliant computers are
remediated and whether they have full or restricted network access. Configuring

Network Access Protection in Configuration Manager does not provide this level of administrative control. Instead, the Configuration Manager administrator controls the definition of compliance with respect to software updates, which is then used by the health policies and network policies on the NAP health policy server. Of course, if you're the administrator for both Configuration Manager and the NAP health policy server, this division of control is not important. But if you have a different administrator for the NAP health policy server, plan a strategy for how you're going to work together and define the policies that collectively meet your business requirements.

Remediating Noncompliant Configuration Manager Clients

While it's undoubtedly satisfying to identify noncompliant computers and potentially prevent them from communicating with other computers on the main network, the key benefit in Network Access Protection is to automatically remediate them. After all, if the first priority for keeping them off the network is to ensure business continuity for existing network resources, the second priority should be to restore business continuity to the noncompliant computer quickly and without administrator or user intervention. Cue auto-remediation.

The means by which noncompliant Configuration Manager clients are remediated are exactly the same as when using the software updates feature in Configuration Manager. Clients still require access to their management point, software update point, and distribution points. These site systems are all considered potential remediation servers for Network Access Protection in Configuration Manager. The only difference during the remediation process for Configuration Manager is that software updates are installed with a high priority – before any software distribution packages or software updates that are not NAP-enabled. And, when remediation is complete, the client reassesses its health state and sends another statement of health.

If you are using IPsec as your Network Access Protection enforcement mechanism, configure software update points, distribution points, and management points as boundary servers. In Network Access Protection IPSec enforcement, boundary servers have the ability to communicate with both compliant and noncompliant Network Access Protection clients. Configuring these site system servers as boundary servers ensures that noncompliant Configuration Manager clients can access the remediation services they need. If you are using DHCP or VPN as your Network Access Protection enforcement mechanism, noncompliant Configuration Manager clients are given direct routes to the Configuration Manager remediation servers they need to access. There is no need to add these servers into a Remediation Servers Group on the Network Policy server, although you must add infrastructure servers such as global catalog servers, DNS servers, and WINS servers into a Remediation Servers Group so that clients can complete the underlying server communications when required, such as management point location, name resolution, and authentication.

Planning for Network Access Protection in Configuration Manager

Now that you have a better understanding of the underlying processes involved when using Network Access Protection in Configuration Manager, you can move on to what needs to be in place before beginning to install and configure it.

Confirm the Windows Network Access Protection Infrastructure

At the time of this writing, Windows Server 2008 has not been released but has been working with Configuration Manager Network Access Protection since the beta 2 release of Windows Server 2008 (when it was still code named "Longhorn"). Configuration Manager Network Access Protection has been deployed in production on the Microsoft network with very successful results. For the latest information on how to deploy the Windows Network Access Protection infrastructure, refer to the Windows Network Access Protection Web site at *http://go.microsoft.com/fwlink/?LinkId=59125*.

The Windows Network Access Protection infrastructure needs to be in place and confirmed working before you attempt to add Configuration Manager into the equation. Use the step-by-step guides from the Windows Network Access Protection Web site to confirm a simple test using the default Windows Security Health Validator, such as checking that the firewall is enabled. This also requires that you have the correct operating system platforms on the client and server: either Windows Vista on the client, which has native Network Access Protection support, or the Network Access Protection Client for Windows XP; and Windows Server 2008 configured as an NAP health policy server.

Extend the Active Directory Schema

To use Network Access Protection in Configuration Manager, you must first extend the Active Directory schema for Configuration Manager 2007 and ensure that all sites that you want to enable for Network Access Protection are publishing to Active Directory Domain Services. This is the first feature in the history of the product that has required that the Active Directory schema is extended, and there are no workarounds. It is needed because when you mark a software update for Network Access Protection evaluation in

Configuration Manager, the site server writes a health state reference to Active Directory Domain Services, which is then retrieved by the System Health Validator point and used during the validation process. To store the health state reference, the Active Directory schema must be extended for Configuration Manager 2007, and the site must be published to Active Directory Domain Services.

Note   The Active Directory attribute that Configuration Manager Network Access Protection uses is called smSSMSHealthState, which resides in the site's object in the System Management container. You can confirm that the site can support Network Access Protection by the presence of this attribute.

Additionally, the log file %systemdrive%\SMSSHV\SMS_SHV\Logs \SmsSHVADCacheClient.log on the System Health Validator point records "AD Schema is EXTENDED for SMSv4 Network Access Protection" when the System Health Validator point is installed and started.

Extending the Active Directory schema can be a big deal for many companies, so this needs careful planning and organizing beforehand. However, there is an additional factor here. You don't have to extend the site server's Active Directory forest but can extend and use another Active Directory forest to store and retrieve the health state reference. This involves additional configuration, but once set up, the behavior is the same, so it's worth considering whether extending the site server's Active Directory forest is problematic. You don't even need a trust relationship between the two forests, but if a trust doesn't exist, you will need to specify an account with credentials in the other forest.

Decide on Server Placement for the System Health Validator Points

With the ability to use another Active Directory forest to store and retrieve the health state reference comes another design consideration. You can place the System Health Validator points in a different Active Directory forest to the site server's forest. The System Health Validator point is one of the few site systems that are supported across forests, but note that they must still reside in an Active Directory domain. Although installation will still succeed on a workgroup computer, the System Health Validator point is not supported in this environment.

If you are installing the System Health Validator points in a different Active Directory forest to the rest of the Configuration Manager hierarchy, you must specify which Active Directory forest will store the health state reference. By default, the site server will write the health state reference to its own Active Directory forest, and the System Health Validator points will retrieve the health state reference from its own Active Directory forest. So you can see that if they don't use the same Active Directory forest, you must specify a single Active Directory forest that will be used by both the site server and System Health Validator points. You'll come to the configuration part later of how to specify the Active Directory forest that will store the health state reference, but in the planning stages it's important to identify which Active Directory forest will be used and extend the schema for Configuration Manager if necessary.

Identify and Configure Firewalls

When you determine the design of where the System Health Validator points will be installed and which Active Directory forest will be used to store the health state references, check whether firewalls or other network perimeter devices are placed in between them and clients. This is particularly important if you are installing the System Health Validator points in a different Active Directory forest, because the forest represents a security boundary that is often protected by firewalls. If there will be intervening firewalls, identify which ports will need to be open to allow the traffic associated with Network Access Protection and ensure that these ports are open by the time you come to implement your solution. For a list of the ports you might need to configure, see the topic "Determine the Ports Required by Firewalls to Support Network Access Protection" in the Configuration Manager Documentation Library (*http://technet.microsoft.com/en-us/library/bb694170.aspx*).

Confirm Software Updates Operation

Enforcing compliance with software updates is an enhancement to and not a replacement for the standard software updates feature. Once hooked into the Windows Network Access Protection infrastructure, scanning and installing software updates uses the same processes as those used with the Configuration Manager software updates feature. If clients cannot successfully install software updates outside the Network Access Protection infrastructure, they will not be able to do so with Network Access Protection, with the potential consequence that they cannot access the network.

Note   It pays to do thorough testing with the Configuration Manager software updates feature outside the Network Access Protection environment before implementing Network Access Protection!

Engage Other Business Groups

Network Access Protection is one of those features that crosses many administrative boundaries (and political ones!), and you will have to do your own homework here in determining who else needs to be involved when implementing Network Access Protection. For example, do you have a security team that advises which software updates are critical enough to risk a temporary loss of network connectivity for noncompliant computers? Do you have service level agreements (SLAs) that might be affected by users having limited network access for a specified period of time that might influence how many software updates are selected for Network Access Protection in a single month?

And don't forget your help desk will need warning and training for how to deal with customer calls if noncompliant computers will have limited network access until remediation is successful. Help desk staff will require information on which software updates are included in Network Access Protection and the expected amount of time it takes for remediation to complete.

Additionally, plan whether you are going to make use of the in-house Network Access Protection troubleshooting Web site that users can be redirected to if remediation fails and they click the More Information button in the Network Access Protection dialog box. This could present users with useful data such as information about Network Access Protection and contact information for the help desk, links to download the software updates if remediation is failing, and other files that might be needed for compliance if automatic remediation fails. For more information about the troubleshooting Web site, see the Network Access Protection product information or the topic "Configuring the Remediation User Experience for Configuration Manager Network Access Protection" in the Configuration Manager Documentation Library (*http://technet.microsoft.com/en-us/library/bb680466.aspx*).

Educate Your Users

The process of educating users about changes to computer management might be handled by the help desk, but it's important enough to call it out separately here. Particularly if you are going to implement Network Access Protection with limited network access for noncompliant computers, you must warn and educate users in advance. Explain to users the business benefits in protecting the network from noncompliant computers and then provide them with appropriate information about what they should do if they find themselves with limited network access.

The information provided to users will vary from company to company and depend on how tech savvy the users are. In an ideal environment, provide users with the details of the software updates that will be included in Network Access Protection and the date the updates will be enforced so that users can proactively install them. In a nonurgent scenario, use software update deployments with a deadline that is at least a few days ahead of when those updates will be included with Network Access Protection and encourage users to install the software updates or risk having limited network access.

On the other hand, if you operate with minimum user interaction, the advice might be to wait a specified period of time before calling the help desk if users experience problems accessing resources and see the Network Access Protection icon in the notification area.

Decide on the user experience and processes that will be used ahead of time and make sure that the help desk is included in these decisions.

Identify Users and Computers That Need Exemptions

When you create a software update deployment in Configuration Manager, you identify which computers will receive the software update through collection targeting. However, Network Access Protection in Configuration Manager doesn't use collection targeting. A software update marked for Network Access Protection will automatically be targeted to computers assigned to the site, and this configuration flows down the hierarchy with the following consequences:

- If a Configuration Manager client is installed but not yet assigned to a site, the Configuration Manager client will not evaluate the software update for Network Access Protection compliance because at this point it does not know whether the Configuration Manager Network Access Protection client agent should be enabled or disabled. In this scenario, the client sends a special statement of health to the System Health Validator point to indicate that it hasn't yet received its client policy. The System Health Validator point gives the client a compliant health status so that it can find its assigned site and download its client policy.

- If the Network Access Protection client agent is not enabled and the computer is capable of supporting Network Access Protection (it is NAP-capable), the Configuration Manager client will not evaluate the software update for Network Access Protection compliance. However, it will still send a statement of health, and the System Health Validator point gives the client a compliant health status.

- If the Network Access Protection client agent is enabled, but the computer is not capable of supporting Network Access Protection, perhaps because it is running Windows XP Service Pack 1 (it is NAP-ineligible), the Configuration Manager client will not evaluate the software update for Network Access Protection compliance. In this scenario, no statement of health can be sent, and network policies on the NAP health policy server determine whether these computers have full network access or limited network access. However, Network Access Protection remediation is not possible.

- If the Network Access Protection client agent is enabled and the computer can support Network Access Protection (for example, it is running Windows Vista), the software update will be automatically evaluated for Network Access Protection compliance. The only way to exclude Configuration Manager clients from evaluating software updates marked for Network Access Protection is to disable the Configuration Manager Network Access Protection client agent, or ensure that they are not running an operating system capable of supporting Network Access Protection, or disable the Windows Network Access Protection Agent service on an NAP-capable computer.

Instead of relying on these exceptions, use policy exemptions when configuring the network policies on the NAP health policy server. This is particularly important if you have computers that do not have the Configuration Manager client installed. In this scenario, an NAP-capable computer will still send a statement of health, but it will not contain any information from the Configuration Manager System Health Agent. If the NAP health policy server is expecting a compliant or noncompliant health state for Configuration Manager, this scenario will result in an error condition. By default, error conditions are mapped to noncompliant. If noncompliant computers are configured for limited network access, this computer will have limited network access and report an error message of "SHA Not Present" with unsuccessful remediation. Automatic remediation is not possible in this scenario because remediation in Configuration Manager is restricted to software updates. Configuration Manager Network Access Protection cannot automatically install the Configuration Manager if there is a problem with the client installation or the client is not installed.

If you have computers that do not have the Configuration Manager client installed, and should have in order to manage them, you can use this process to enforce the installation of the Configuration Manager client. However, you will have to make sure that users (or help desk engineers) can manually install the Configuration Manager client when the computer has restricted network access. This can be achieved, for example, if you are using the troubleshooting Web site and configure a link to install the client. For optimal user experience, ensure that the installation is as streamlined as possible to keep to a minimum the delay in getting the computer back onto the full network. This is particularly important if you are using VPN Network Access Protection enforcement and users have to download the client source files over a slow, remote network.

However, in many cases there will be genuine reasons why a computer should not have the Configuration Manager client installed. These computers must be identified and included in an exemption policy that does not expect compliance information from the Configuration Manager System Health Validator.

You might need other exemption policies for computers that do have the Configuration Manager client installed but should be treated differently. For example, even if they are noncompliant, they should have unlimited network access or full network access for a limited time. Another possibility is to create exemption policies that do not restrict network access outside the hours that the help desk is open.

Identify these exemptions ahead of time, agree to them with stakeholders, and document them so that this information can be shared with the help desk and the NAP health policy server administrator. And don't forget to test that they work as expected before you go live on a production network!

For more information about configuring exemption policies for Network Access Protection, see the Network Access Protection product documentation.

Checkpoints for Identifying Which Clients Can Support Network Access Protection

The Network Access Protection client status in Configuration Manager is one of the following: NAP-capable (the client can support Network Access Protection, either natively or after installing the Network Access Protection client); NAP-upgradable (the client doesn't natively support Network Access Protection but could be upgraded to support Network Access Protection with the Network Access Protection client); or NAP-ineligible (the client cannot support Network Access Protection).

Note   You can use the Network Access Protection report "List of NAP-capable and NAP-upgradable computers" to identify the NAP-capable and NAP-upgradable computers, and use the following SQL query to identify how many NAP-capable clients you have: *Select NapEnabledCount from v_Network Access ProtectionSystemInfo*.

Implementing Network Access Protection in Configuration Manager

When you've completed your planning for Network Access Protection, you're ready to start implementing and configuring Network Access Protection in Configuration Manager.

Important   More than for any other feature in Configuration Manager, make sure that you plan for Network Access Protection before you begin implementing it. When other features are misconfigured or lack a planning step, they most likely result in an error or no action. However, when Network Access Protection is misconfigured or lacks a planning step, it could result in a massive denial of service with all computers on the network having indefinite restricted network access.

Creating and Configuring the System Health Validator Point

The decision process involved with installing the System Health Validator point is slightly different from installing other site system roles in Configuration Manager. First, it must be installed on a computer running Windows Server 2008 that has the role of Network Policy Server installed on it. Second, there is no direct correlation between Configuration Manager clients in a site and a System Health Validator point. Network Access

Protection clients are directed to the System Health Validator point through the Windows Network Access Protection infrastructure, not through the Configuration Manager infrastructure.

Generally, the decision as to where and how many System Health Validator points to install is not the Configuration Manager administrator's choice, but the Windows Network Access Protection administrator's decision. Wherever a Network Policy Server is installed and configured for Network Access Protection, you should install a Configuration Manager System Health Validator point. This might be a single server or multiple servers. It might mean that all System Health Validator points reside in one Configuration Manager site—not necessarily the central site in the hierarchy—or that they are installed in multiple Configuration Manager sites. The Configuration Manager site does not have to be enabled for Network Access Protection in order to install a System Health Validator point.

When you have multiple System Health Validator points, bear in mind that they share a common configuration within a site. If, for some reason, you need different settings for System Health Validator points, your only choice is to install them in different sites. However, wherever possible, use the same configuration for all System Health Validator points in the hierarchy to ease administration and troubleshooting. When all System Health Validator points share a common configuration, the behavior of clients using them will be consistent, which is especially important when NAP-capable clients roam between Configuration Manager sites.

Installing a System Health Validator Point

The process for installing a System Health Validator point is no different from installing any other site system role. Remember, however, that it must be installed on a computer running Windows Server 2008 that is configured with the server role of Network Policy Server. Configuration Manager will not prevent you from installing it if these requirements are not met, but the installation will not be successful.

To create a site system on the computer that is configured for an NAP health policy server and install the Configuration Manager System Health Validator point, follow these steps:

1. In the Configuration Manager Administrator Console, expand the site's Site Settings node and then right-click Site Systems.

2. Click New and choose Server from the context menu to launch the New Site System Server Wizard.

3. In the General page of the wizard, provide the following information:

    ❑ **Name:** Type the short name of the NAP health policy server.

❑ **Specify A Fully Qualified Domain Name (FQDN) For This Site Server On The Intranet:** Type the FQDN of the NAP health policy server.

❑ **Specify An Internet-Based Fully Qualified Domain Name For This Site System:** Leave this field blank. The System Health Validator point is not supported with Internet-based client management.

❑ **Use The Site Server's Computer Account To Install This Site System:** Leave this selected if the site server's computer account can be authenticated on the computer running Windows Server 2008.

❑ **Use Another Account For Installing This Site System:** Select this option only if you are installing the System Health Validator point in a different Active Directory forest, and there is no trust relationship that will allow the site server's computer account to be authenticated on the computer running Windows Server 2008. Then click Set, and in the Windows User Account dialog box, specify a user account and credentials that have local administrator permissions on the computer running Windows Server 2008.

❑ **Enable This Site System As A Protected Site System:** Do not select this option. It is not applicable for a System Health Validator point.

❑ **Allow Only Site Server Initiated Data Transfers From This Site System:** Do not select this option. It is not supported for a System Health Validator point.

4. Click Next to display the System Role Selection page in the wizard.

5. Select System Health Validator Point and then click Next to display the System Health Validator page.

6. Read the information relating to the System Health Validator point, which includes the following points:

   ❑ Remember that this site system role must be installed on a computer running Windows Server 2008 and configured for Network Access Protection policies.

   ❑ The System Health Validator point configuration is on the System Health Validator Point Component Properties page.

   ❑ If you are configuring the System Health Validator point in a different Active Directory forest, you might have additional configuration for the storage and retrieval of the health state reference.

7. Configuring the System Health Validator points is covered in the next section, so click Next.

8. On the Summary page of the wizard, click Next, and if you are happy with your configuration, click Next, and then click Close.

9.   In the results pane, you should now see the additional site system, with the roles displayed as ConfigMgr Component Server, ConfigMgr Site System, ConfigMgr System Health Validator Point.

10.   If you have additional System Health Validator points to install, repeat steps 1 through 9.

Configuring the System Health Validator Points

For most installations, you will not need to change the default settings for the System Health Validator points. However, if you have installed a System Health Validator point in a different Active Directory forest, or if you want to store and retrieve the health state references from a different Active Directory forest, additional configuration is required.

To configure System Health Validator points, follow these steps:

1.   In the Configuration Manager Administrator Console, expand the site's Site Settings node and click Component Configuration. In the results pane, double-click System Health Validator Point Component.

You will see that the System Health Validator Point Component Properties dialog box has two tabs, the General tab and the Health State Reference tab, as shown in Figure 15-1.

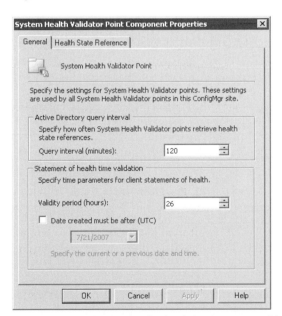

Figure 15-1   The General tab of the System Health Validator Point Component Properties dialog box

2. In the General tab, the Query Interval is how often the System Health Validator points retrieve the health state reference from Active Directory Domain Services. The default is every 2 hours from startup of the System Health Validator service. If this value is set too high, the compliance of clients might be based on out-of-date information, which could result in clients that haven't downloaded their latest Configuration Manager client policy having full network access when they should not. However, if this value is set too low, it can result in clients being found noncompliant, not because they need software updates, but because their compliance assessment is out of date. A recommended value is twice the value specified for the policy polling interval in the Computer client agent properties (by default, set once an hour). Change the Query Interval (Minutes) value if the default of 120 minutes is not suitable for your environment.

3. Also on the General tab is the Validity Period (Hours). The default value is every 26 hours. A computer will cache its statement of health and can present this to the System Health Validator point to increase performance. Not using a cached statement of health will delay connecting to the network and incur additional processing on the client. This setting configures how old the cached statement of health can be before the System Health Validator point considers it out of date. If the cached statement of health is older than the configured validity date, the client will be considered noncompliant. In this scenario, remediation is invoked for the client to reevaluate its compliance and produce a new statement of health. A recommended value is to ensure that this setting is higher than the Network Access Protection evaluation schedule, which is configured on the Network Access Protection client agent properties (and by default, configured for once every 24 hours). Change the Validity Period (Hours) value if the default of 26 hours is not suitable for your environment.

4. Finally on the General tab is the Date Created Must Be After (UTC) option. Do not use this setting as a day-to-day configuration. It is designed specifically for a zero-day exploit scenario, where you have just configured a software update for Network Access Protection and it is imperative that clients immediately include this software update in their Network Access Protection compliance assessment rather than wait for them to next download their client policy. In the situation where you have just deployed the critical software update, you would then select this option and set the current date and time. Any client presenting a statement of health that was not as current as this value would be deemed noncompliant. Remediation in this scenario involves the client downloading the latest Configuration Manager Network Access Protection policies, reevaluating Network Access Protection compliance, and resending a current statement of health. Configure this option only if you have just configured a Network Access Protection policy for an urgent evaluation.

5. The Health State Reference tab, as shown in Figure 15-2, is where you specify whether you want to use a different Active Directory forest, and if so, the additional configuration that this requires.

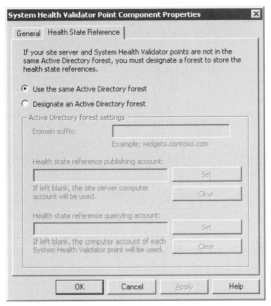

Figure 15-2   The Health State Reference tab of the System Health Validator Point Component Properties dialog box

6. If you are using just one Active Directory forest, there is nothing to configure on this tab. Keep the default selection of Use The Same Active Directory Forest.

7. If you are using a different Active Directory forest, select the Designate An Active Directory Forest option and then specify the domain suffix in the Domain Suffix field.

8. If there is a trust relationship between the site server and the designed Active Directory forest such that the site server's computer account can be authenticated, there is no need to specify the Health State Reference Publishing Account. Where this is not the case, click Set and specify in the Windows User Account dialog box a user account and credentials that will be authenticated in the designed Active Directory forest. Then click OK.

9. If there is a trust relationship between the System Health Validator point site system servers and the designed Active Directory forest such that the site system servers' computer account can be authenticated, there is no need to specify the Health State Reference Querying Account. Where this is not the case, click Set and specify in the Windows User Account dialog box a user account and credentials that will be authenticated in the designed Active Directory forest. Then click OK.

10. Click OK to close the System Health Validator Point Component Properties dialog box. Any new System Health Validator points added to the site will be automatically configured with these settings.

Enabling and Configuring Network Access Protection Client Settings

You will need to enable the Network Access Protection client agent, because this client agent is not enabled by default on new sites or sites that have been upgraded from SMS 2003. Additionally, you might want to change the default client agent settings, which include how often the client evaluates its Network Access Protection compliance and whether a fresh scan will be forced for each evaluation.

Checkpoints for Enabling Network Access Protection in Configuration Manager

Before you enable Network Access Protection in Configuration Manager, make sure that the Windows Network Access Protection Agent service is running—and set to start automatically—and that the Network Access Protection enforcement client is enabled. In addition to starting these manually, Group Policy can be used to configure these on both Windows Vista and Windows XP with the Network Access Protection client installed. See the Windows Network Access Protection documentation for more information about configuring these underlying components.

If the Windows Network Access Protection service is not started before enabling the Configuration Manager Network Access Protection client agent, the computer will behave as if it is NAP-ineligible and will not send a statement of health. Network policies on the NAP health policy server determine whether NAP-ineligible computers have full network access or limited network access, and Network Access Protection remediation is not possible.

If the Windows Network Access Protection service is mistakenly not started before enabling the Configuration Manager Network Access Protection client agent, start the service and then restart the Configuration Manager client. Alternatively, if restarting all clients is not practical, disable the Configuration Manager Network Access Protection client agent, wait a full policy cycle (by default, set to 60 minutes), and then enable it again.

Additionally, if you are deploying an operating system in a Network Access Protection environment by using the operating system deployment feature in Configuration Manager, make sure that either the reference computer is fully configured for Windows Network Access Protection before installing the Configuration Manager client, or that additional steps are added to the task sequence, which includes a restart before installing the Configuration Manager client.

> **More Info**   See the topic "Planning for Operating System Deployment in a Network Access Protection-Enabled Environment" at *http://technet.microsoft.com /en-us/library/bb892794.aspx* in the Configuration Manager Documentation library for more information.

To enable the Network Access Protection Client Agent and configure Network Access Protection client settings, follow these steps:

1. In the Configuration Manager Administrator Console, expand the site's Site Settings node and click Client Agents. In the results pane, double-click Network Access Protection Client Agent.

2. The General tab has the single setting Enable Network Access Protection On Clients, as shown in Figure 15-3. Select this option.

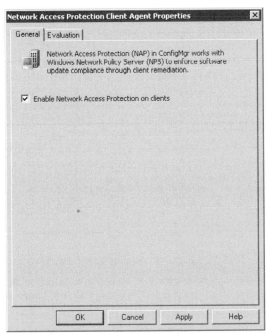

Figure 15-3   The General Tab of the Network Access Protection Client Agent Properties dialog box

3. On the Evaluation tab, the configuration options relate to how often and when a client evaluates its Network Access Protection compliance for Configuration Manager. This tab is shown in Figure 15-4.

4. By default, the Network Access Protection evaluation schedule is in universal coordinated time rather than local time. If you want a client to evaluate compliance using local time, clear the UTC (Coordinated Universal Time) check box.

5. By default, the Force A Fresh Scan For Each Evaluation check box is not selected. This allows the client to use a cached statement of health to speed up connectivity times and reduce processing usage on the client. If you are particularly security conscious and want to ensure that a new statement of health is produced every time, select this option. This option can mean a few minutes wait without full network access while the client reevaluates compliance and produces a new statement of health.

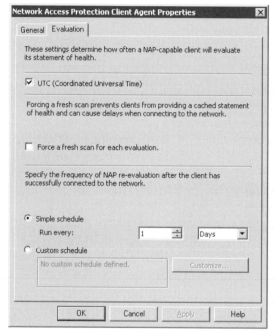

Figure 15-4   The Evaluation tab of the Network Access Protection Client Agent Properties dialog box

6. By default, Network Access Protection evaluation occurs once a day, using the Simple Schedule. As with any schedule in Configuration Manager, you can change this by using the Simple Schedule drop-down boxes or select the Custom Schedule option, click Customize, and configure your choice of schedule.

These settings affect all clients assigned to the site that are capable of supporting Network Access Protection. If the client cannot support Network Access Protection, the settings are ignored.

Note Even if the Network Access Protection client agent is disabled, clients that are capable of supporting Network Access Protection will still send a statement of health. However, the statement of health contains information that tells the System Health Validator point that the client agent is disabled, which results in the System Health Validator point giving the client a compliant health state.

Creating and Managing Network Access Protection Policies

After enabling the Network Access Protection client agent, you can select software updates for Network Access Protection evaluation. Click the Network Access Protection node in the Configuration Manager console and then press F5 to refresh the display. A new child node called Policies appears under Network Access Protection.

Click the Policies node, and the results pane shows columns that are shared with the software updates feature—all except one unique column called Effective Date. The Effective Date is when the software update will be included in Network Access Protection evaluation. Until that date, the software update that is selected for Network Access Protection lies dormant, which gives users a chance to install the software update themselves and provides adequate time for the software update package to replicate to all distribution points. Figure 15-5 shows sample Network Access Protection policies with their effective date configured for August 15, 2007, together with their current compliance status.

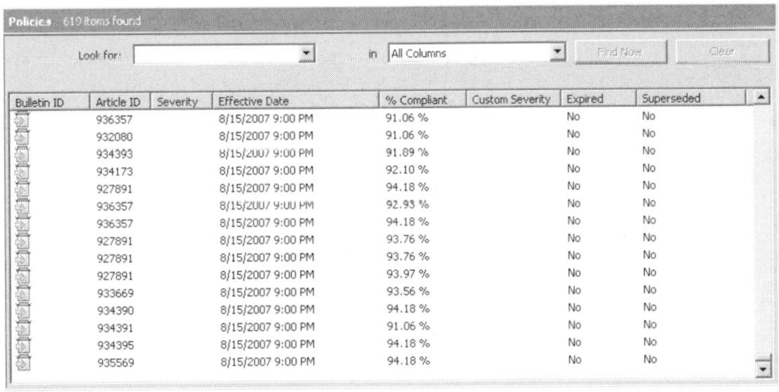

Bulletin ID	Article ID	Severity	Effective Date	% Compliant	Custom Severity	Expired	Superseded
	936357		8/15/2007 9:00 PM	91.06 %		No	No
	932080		8/15/2007 9:00 PM	91.06 %		No	No
	934393		8/15/2007 9:00 PM	91.89 %		No	No
	934173		8/15/2007 9:00 PM	92.10 %		No	No
	927891		8/15/2007 9:00 PM	94.18 %		No	No
	936357		8/15/2007 9:00 PM	92.93 %		No	No
	936357		8/15/2007 9:00 PM	94.18 %		No	No
	927891		8/15/2007 9:00 PM	93.76 %		No	No
	927891		8/15/2007 9:00 PM	93.76 %		No	No
	927891		8/15/2007 9:00 PM	93.97 %		No	No
	933669		8/15/2007 9:00 PM	93.56 %		No	No
	934390		8/15/2007 9:00 PM	94.18 %		No	No
	934391		8/15/2007 9:00 PM	91.06 %		No	No
	934395		8/15/2007 9:00 PM	94.18 %		No	No
	935569		8/15/2007 9:00 PM	94.18 %		No	No

Figure 15-5 Sample Network Access Protection Policies displayed in the Policies home page

When you select a software update to be included in Network Access Protection evaluation, it appears as a Network Access Protection policy, as shown in Figure 15-5, that you can easily monitor and edit from this Policies node. Each Network Access Protection policy results in writing to the health state reference in Active Directory Domain Services so that the System Health Validator point knows that a change was made to Configuration

Manager Network Access Protection policies. Although each software update selected for Network Access Protection evaluation is displayed as a separate Network Access Protection policy, in reality all Network Access Protection policies for the site are stored in a single Network Access Protection policy for the site. It is this single Network Access Protection policy that creates the health state reference in Active Directory Domain Services.

There are actually a number of ways to select software updates for Network Access Protection evaluation, but one of the easiest is to use the New Policies Wizard from the Policies node. To create Network Access Protection policies using the New Policies Wizard, follow these steps:

1.   In the Configuration Manager Administrator Console, right-click the Policies node and then select New Policies to launch the New Policies Wizard.

2.   In the Select Software Updates for Network Access Protection page of the wizard, a list of software updates that have been downloaded and are stored as software update packages in Configuration Manager are displayed. See Figure 15-6 for an example. If the software update you want to include in Network Access Protection evaluation is not displayed, it is most likely not downloaded, and you will have to download it using standard software update operation (for example, using the Download Updates Wizard). If this is not the first time you have run the New Policies Wizard, another explanation for a missing software update is that it has already been selected for Network Access Protection evaluation.

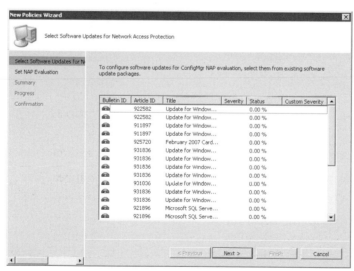

Figure 15-6   The Select Software Updates for Network Access Protection page of the New Policies Wizard where you select the software updates to include in Network Access Protection evaluation

3. Select one or more software updates displayed and click Next.

4. On the Set NAP Evaluation page of the wizard, as shown in Figure 15-7, specify the date when you want the software update to be included in Network Access Protection evaluation by the client. Select either the As Soon As Possible option (appropriate for an urgent update, such as a zero-day exploit) or select the Date And Time option to specify the exact date and time.

Note   If you specify As Soon As Possible and the software update package has not yet replicated to all distribution points, a noncompliant client might have to request the software update over slow WAN links because it is not yet locally available. This can result in network saturation, long remediation times, and even timeout errors.

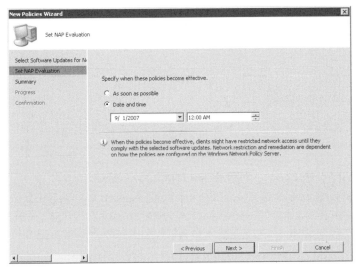

Figure 15-7   The Set NAP Evaluation page of the New Policies Wizard where you select the date to start Network Access Protection evaluation

5. Click Next, review the summary information, click Next again, and then click Close.

6. View the software updates you selected in the results pane. Each appears as a separate Network Access Protection policy with the same Effective Date, similar to Figure 15-5.

If you want to modify the Effective Date of one or more Network Access Protection policies, select them, right-click, and then select Properties. Make the modification and click OK. Figure 15-8 shows the Properties dialog box of a sample Network Access Protection policy.

To stop a software update from being included in Network Access Protection evaluation, simply select it and then press Delete. This action doesn't remove the software update from Configuration Manager or affect existing software update deployments that reference the software update. It simply means the software update will no longer be included in Network Access Protection evaluation.

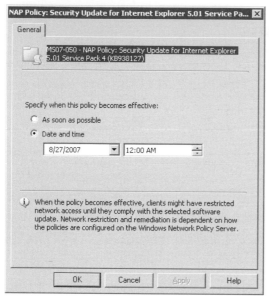

Figure 15-8   The Network Access Protection Policy Properties dialog box

The Network Access Protection policy that you see when using the Policies node is actually an attribute of the downloaded software update. This becomes more obvious if you view the properties of a software update in Update Repository under the Software Updates node. When the Network Access Protection client agent is enabled, a new tab called NAP Evaluation appears for each downloaded software update. Figure 15-9 shows an example of a software update's Properties dialog box with this NAP Evaluation tab.

As an alternative to creating Network Access Protection policies using the Policies node, you can use this tab to select the option NAP Evaluation and then configure the Effective Date. And similarly, if you created a Network Access Protection policy using the New Policies Wizard, you could delete the policy by clearing the Enable NAP Evaluation option on the software update's NAP Evaluation tab. Refreshing the Policies node will reflect your changes.

The NAP Evaluation tab also appears as a property of a software update deployment and of a software update package.

Additionally, the software updates wizards also include an NAP Evaluation page when the Network Access Protection client agent is enabled. This means that you can download a software update with the Deploy Software Update Wizard or create a software update deployment with the Deploy Software Update Wizard, and at the same time, mark the software updates for NAP evaluation.

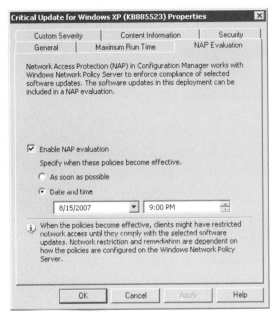

Figure 15-9   The NAP Evaluation tab of a downloaded software update

There really is no right or wrong way to mark a software update to be included in Network Access Protection evaluation. All rivers lead to the same sea. Choose the method that best suits your working practices.

Monitoring Network Access Protection

On a computer that supports Network Access Protection, the Windows client Network Access Protection notification displays when a computer has limited network access because it is noncompliant. As shown in Figure 15-10, the Network Access Protection shield displays yellow with a warning exclamation, and the network adapter icon also has a warning symbol against it to denote a network connectivity issue. In comparison, Figure 15-11 shows the Windows Network Access Protection notification a user sees when their computer is noncompliant, but does not have limited network access, and instead remediates on the full network. In this scenario, the computer has full network access for a limited time, and so the network adapter still displays the warning symbol because network connectivity is in doubt if the computer remains noncompliant after the specified time.

Figure 15-10   The Windows client Network Access Protection notification of a noncompliant computer with limited network access

Figure 15-11   The Windows client Network Access Protection notification of a noncompliant computer with full network access for a limited time, automatically remediating

Figure 15-12 shows the Network Access Protection notification after remediation has successfully completed. The Network Access Protection shield has changed to green with a tick, and the network adapter no longer has the warning symbol.

Figure 15-12   The Windows client Network Access Protection notification when a noncompliant computer has been successfully remediated

If a user clicks the Network Access Protection notification, the Windows client Network Access Protection dialog box shows the active system health agents and their current status. As with the Windows client Network Access Protection notification, this dialog box is called by Windows Network Access Protection and is not part of the Configuration Manager interface, although it displays information from the Configuration Manager System Health Agent.

The Windows Network Access Protection dialog box can be branded with your choice of title, description, and image using Group Policy. Figure 15-13 shows an example Windows Vista Network Access Protection dialog box on the client, which is not branded. The example shows the Configuration Manager System Health Agent, with the client undergoing remediation for software updates.

If remediation fails, this dialog box can provide useful troubleshooting information for the help desk, because it will show which system health agent experienced the error with related error information. Some errors result in two new buttons displayed in this dialog box: a Try Again button and a More Information button. If users click More Information, their default Web browsers connect to the troubleshooting Web site configured in the network policy. The Try Again button generates a new statement of health and is only available to users with administrator rights. This might be applicable if automatic remediation fails and the user manually remediates on the restricted network and then needs to update the health status to move onto the unlimited network. A user without administrator rights can achieve the same result by restarting the computer after the completion of the manual remediation.

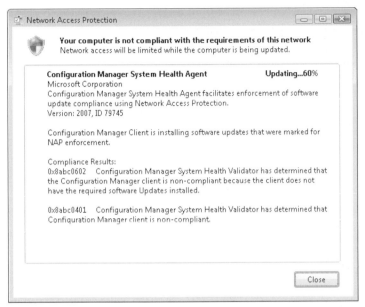

Figure 15-13   The Client Network Access Protection dialog box displaying a noncompliant computer undergoing remediation for Configuration Manager Network Access Protection

Figure 15-14 shows an example of the Network Access Protection dialog box when remediation is successful, and Figure 15-15 shows an example of unsuccessful remediation. The unsuccessful remediation in Figure 15-15 is the result of the Configuration Manager client not being installed, which was covered earlier in the section "Identify Users and Computers That Need Exemptions." When the Configuration Manager client is not installed but the NAP health policy server is expecting a statement of health from Configuration Manager, the Windows Network Access Protection dialog box is unable to map the required system health agent to a friendly name. Instead, it displays the system health agent ID that is sent from the NAP health policy server. In the case of the Configuration Manager System Health Agent, this ID is 79745.

Note   The error condition shown in Figure 15-15 is one of the most commonly reported scenarios for failed Network Access Protection remediation on a network running Configuration Manager. If a user reports a "SHA Not Present" error message with ID 79745, you must either install the Configuration Manager client on their computer, or reconfigure policies on the NAP health policy server so that their computer is exempt from Configuration Manager Network Access Protection evaluation.

Figure 15-14   The Client Network Access Protection dialog box displaying a successfully remediated computer

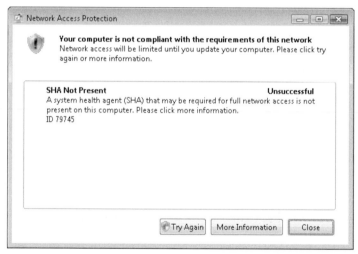

Figure 15-15   The Client Network Access Protection dialog box displaying an unsuccessfully remediated computer

More detailed client information about Network Access Protection can be obtained by running the following command from a command prompt: `netsh nap client show state.`

This provides a lot of information that you might want to redirect to a file so that you can search through it more easily. The output includes the following information:

- Network Access Protection status (for example, enabled) and restriction state (for example, not restricted)

- Enforcement client states, listing each enforcement client by ID and vendor, and whether it is initialized

- System health agent states, listing the details of each including the ID (the Configuration Manager System Health Agent has ID 79745), remediation state and percentage complete (if in remediation), and compliance results

The following shows an extract of this command's output for the Configuration Manager System Health Agent section.

```
Id                     = 79745
Name                   = Configuration Manager System Health Agent
Description            = Configuration Manager System Health Agent facilitates
enforcement of software update compliance using Network Access Protection.
Version                = 2007
Vendor name            = Microsoft Corporation
Registration date      = 8/17/2007 4:03:22 PM
Initialized            = Yes
Failure category       = None
Remediation state      = Success
Remediation percentage = 100
Fixup Message          = (90701) The Configuration Manager System Health Agent is
 compliant with the required software updates.
Compliance results     = (0x00000000) - (null)

Remediation results    = (0x00000000) - (null)
```

If you have administrator rights, you can run this command at any time on an NAP-capable client. Together with the client notification and Network Access Protection dialog box, these are useful informational and troubleshooting tools to find out how Network Access Protection is operating on individual computers. However, you need a different method to centrally monitor Network Access Protection activity for multiple Configuration Manager clients.

Using the Network Access Protection Home Page to Monitor Network Access Protection

One of the easiest ways to centrally monitor Network Access Protection activity is to use the Network Access Protection home page from the Network Access Protection node. Figure 15-16 shows an example home page with Network Access Protection activity.

One of the slightly disconcerting things about this home page is that it does not offer confirmation that Network Access Protection is working when all the clients are compliant.

It only lists "bad news" information in that it provides a count of how many computers were in remediation (on the restriction network or unlimited network), the most frequently requested software updates needed for remediation, and the most frequently occurring remediation errors.

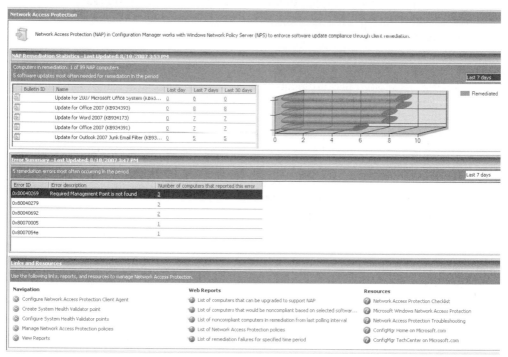

Figure 15-16   The Network Access Protection home page showing sample activity

While this snapshot information is very useful, it is important to remember that it is not real time. The information is retrieved from the database with the summarization schedule, which by default is every 30 minutes for this home page. You can change this schedule by clicking the Schedule home page summarization in the actions pane, and you can request that the data is updated ad hoc with the Run Home Page Summarization in the actions pane. However, this last request will take some time to complete, and you must refresh the screen to see the latest data. Reference the last updated value displayed to know at what time the information displayed was current. In addition, the count of Network Access Protection computers displayed in the Network Access Protection Remediation Statistics is taken from the latest hardware inventory information. This is useful in displaying how many computers assigned to the site are capable of supporting Network Access Protection without having to reference the reports.

The one unusual characteristic about this home page that is different from other home pages in Configuration Manager is that the count of computers in remediation is not restricted to Configuration Manager remediation. If you are using other system health agents (for example, the Windows System Health Agent and System Health Validator) and Configuration Manager clients are remediated because they are noncompliant with their policies (for example, the client is not configured with an antivirus software), this will be registered in the count of computers in remediation. Do not assume that the count of computers in remediation equates to computers being remediated for Configuration Manager.

Using Reports to Monitor Network Access Protection

The following Network Access Protection reports offer more detailed information to help you to monitor Network Access Protection usage for the site:

- List of software updates installed through remediation
- Comparison of software updates installed by software update deployments and Network Access Protection remediation
- List of computers that installed a specific software update through remediation during a specified period
- List of noncompliant computers in remediation from last polling interval
- List of noncompliant computers in remediation within a specified period
- Summary of noncompliant computers in remediation from last polling interval
- Summary of noncompliant computers in remediation within a specified period
- Frequency a computer has been in remediation within a specified period

Additionally, use the following report to help you identify any failures that occur during remediation:

- List of remediation failures for specified time period

You can also use the following reports for planning, to help you identify which clients in the site can support Network Access Protection and which could be upgraded with the Network Access Protection client for Windows XP:

- List of computers that can be upgraded to support Network Access Protection
- List of NAP-capable and NAP-upgradable computers

You can use the following report as a "what if" mechanism to find out how many computers would be liable to remediation based on selected software updates:

- List of computers that would be noncompliant based on selected software updates

And to help you record and identify which software updates are selected for Network Access Protection (particularly if you are creating Network Access Protection policies using the software update wizards), use the following report:

- List of Network Access Protection policies

Using Performance Counters and Event Logs to Monitor Network Access Protection

Installing the System Health Validator point automatically installs some Windows performance counters for the object Configuration Manager System Health Validator. Use this for each System Health Validator point to monitor validation activity. For example, by monitoring the counter SoH Requests Total, you can confirm that the Configuration Manager Network Access Protection infrastructure is working. Configuration Manager clients that are capable of supporting Network Access Protection will send a statement of health (SoH) even if the Configuration Manager Network Access Protection client agent is disabled, and even if no software updates are marked for Network Access Protection. So this counter provides a useful confirmation that the System Health Validator point is working.

Other useful counters include SoH Response: Compliant and SoH Response: Noncompliant to monitor the number of compliant and noncompliant clients. Also, remembering that noncompliant doesn't necessarily mean that software updates were missing, reference the counter Software Updates Not Installed to determine how often clients were remediated with software updates. You can reference the full list of performance counters and a description of each in the topic "How to Monitor the System Health Validator Point with Performance Counters for Network Access Protection" from the Configuration Manager documentation library.

Additionally, entries for the SMS_SYSTEM_HEALTH_VALIDATOR appear in the Windows Application log on the NAP health policy server.

Using Log Files to Monitor Network Access Protection

If you need more nitty-gritty details (for example, to confirm each component is working or to troubleshoot a problem), log files on clients and the Network Access Protection policy server provide this level of detail. For a list of log files related to Network Access Protection, see the topic "Log Files for Network Access Protection" in the Configuration Manager 2007 documentation library. Additionally, to find which log file and the entries to search for to verify Network Access Protection components, see "How to Verify Network Access Protection Components."

Checkpoints for Phasing in Network Access Protection

In addition to testing in a lab environment, it pays to be cautious when implementing Network Access Protection on a production network. Consider baby steps before jumping in and enabling Network Access Protection on all sites with limited access for noncompliant computers.

You should always implement Network Access Protection in Configuration Manager in a top-down approach, enabling it first on your central site or wherever you synchronize your software update point with the Microsoft Windows Update site. However, enable it carefully one site at a time, noting the number of NAP-capable clients in each as a measure of its potential reach.

Second, although Network Access Protection in Configuration Manager cannot remediate in reporting mode, consider this configuration as a pilot and confirm that the Network Access Protection components are working as expected. Then enable the option for full network access for a limited time, specifying a date and time comfortably in the future so that there is no chance of noncompliant computers having restricted network access. This tests remediation on the full network, and although users will not see the Network Access Protection notification, you can use the Configuration Manager reports and Network Access Protection home page to monitor remediation activity.

Because remediating on the full network for a limited time brings about compliance without loss of network connectivity, some customers might find this mode of Network Access Protection operation more productive and less risky than enforcing compliance with limited network access. However, it does not help to prevent noncompliant computers from accessing network resources, so you need to balance this risk with the risk of loss of business continuity from anything from a few minutes to indefinitely (for example, the client's management point is not operational, or there is a network failure between the client and distribution points needed for remediation).

Finally, when you have proved that noncompliant computers are successfully remediated within an acceptable time frame, and all the help desk processes are in place to deal with calls from users who do not have network access, enable restriction of noncompliant computers with the option of limited network access.

Note If you ever need an emergency Off button for Configuration Manager Network Access Protection because computers indefinitely fail to gain full network access (for example, all computers experience an unrecoverable Network Access Protection failure), the most expedient method is not to disable Network Access Protection in Configuration Manager, but to change the network policies on the NAP health policy server such that they no longer include health policies for the Configuration Manager System Health Validator. Then restart the computers that cannot get full network access.

Summary

This chapter introduced you to the underlying architecture that Network Access Protection in Configuration Manager depends upon to enforce compliance of software updates for clients that can support Network Access Protection. It took you through the careful planning that must go into a deployment of Network Access Protection, how to install and configure the System Health Validator point on the NAP health policy server, and how to configure the Network Access Protection client agent for NAP-enabled sites. You looked at the different ways in which you can create Network Access Protection policies in Configuration Manager and how to monitor them and Network Access Protection activity for the site.

For detailed information about how to implement Network Access Protection on Windows Server 2008, see the Windows Network Access Protection Web site for current documentation and information, as well as the book titled *Windows Server 2008 Networking and Network Access Protection (Network Access Protection)* (Microsoft Press, 2008).

Chapter 16

Managing Clients Across the Internet

Cozy Starbucks calls

Internet client management

Inventory to go

~ Carol Bailey, Technical Writer, Configuration Manager

This chapter explains how you can use System Center Configuration Manager 2007 to manage clients when they are not connected to the corporate network but have a standard Internet connection. This management solution is suitable for road warriors, home workers, remote branches, and any other situation where you can install a Configuration Manager client that has a standard Internet connection. Using this method of computer management rather than a VPN solution can save implementation and support costs, and can be more reliable from the administrator's point of view because it doesn't rely on user interaction. However, there will still be occasions when you might need your VPN service, so read on to understand exactly what you can and cannot do with Internet-based client management in Configuration Manager, the management scenarios that it supports, and its requirements.

Understanding Internet-Based Client Management

When a client is configured to be managed across the Internet, it can send inventory data, status information and state messages to its assigned site, and it can receive client policy that instructs it to install software updates, install software distribution packages, and assess its compliance with desired configuration baselines. It can do all this even if the user is not logged in, as long as the computer or device has an Internet connection.

However, there are some Configuration Manager features that are not supported when the client is on the Internet. These mostly require access to Active Directory Domain Services or require high bandwidth usage that is not appropriate for Internet connectivity. The

Configuration Manager features that are not supported when the client is on the Internet are the following:

- Network Access Protection (NAP)
- Wake On LAN
- Operating system deployment
- Remote control

There are also some additional limitations with software distribution, including the following:

- Clients on the Internet cannot install software distribution advertisements when it is targeted to users (either directly or through Microsoft Windows security groups).
- Clients on the Internet cannot be configured as a branch distribution point (and a branch distribution point cannot support clients over the Internet).

Client installation and site assignment for a site that supports Internet-based client management also has the following limitations:

- You cannot install clients from the Internet-based site (for example, using the source files from the Internet-based management point or using the software update point). They must either be installed on the intranet (for example, over a VPN connection) or using independent media (such as a CD-ROM that is given to the user) with all the source files and an installation script.
- You cannot use auto-site assignment if you want a client to be managed by a site that supports Internet-based client management. Instead, you must directly assign it to the site. In this assignment scenario, no site checks are made for site assignment so you must take extra care that you are assigning the client to the correct site and that it is not running Windows 2000 Server (which is not supported with native mode).

When workgroup clients and mobile devices are assigned to a site that supports Internet-based client management, they are configured for Internet-only or intranet-only mode. If you want them to be managed on the Internet, configure them for Internet-only mode and even if they connect to the intranet, they still behave as if they are connected to the Internet and will never be able to support the Configuration Manager features that are not supported with Internet-based client management. If you have workgroup clients or mobile devices that do not need to be managed on the Internet, you can still use the Internet-based site to manage intranet clients that will have access to the full feature set. In this scenario, configure them for intranet-only client management.

When nonworkgroup client computers are assigned to a site that supports Internet-based client management, you have more flexibility. You can configure them for Internet-only or intranet-only mode, but they also support a third configuration—Internet or intranet management. This configuration allows the client to automatically detect whether it is on the Internet or on the intranet. When it detects that it is on the Internet, it behaves as an Internet-only client. When it detects that it is on the intranet, it behaves as an intranet-only client. This allows you to manage clients with the Configuration Manager feature set when they are on the intranet, and still manage them with the essential features when they move from the intranet to the Internet.

Checkpoints for Managing Internet-Based Clients

When a client can be configured for Internet-only, intranet-only, or Internet or intranet, how does an administrator or help desk engineer know which configuration a client is using? For example, if a client on the intranet can't install user-targeted software, how can you check that it's not because the client is mistakenly configured for Internet-only configuration?

Fortunately, there's a client property displayed on the General tab of the Configuration Manager Properties dialog box called ConfigMgr Connection Type. If the client has been installed for Internet-only, this value displays Always Internet. If the client cannot support Internet-based client management (for example, it is not in Native mode or it is not assigned to an Internet-based management point), it displays Always Intranet. If it can be managed on both the Internet and the intranet, but detects that it is currently on the Internet, it displays Currently Internet. And similarly, if it can be managed on both the Internet and the intranet, but detects that it is currently on the intranet, it displays Currently Intranet.

Figure 16-1 shows the General tab of a native mode Configuration Manager client that is configured for Internet-based client management and is currently on the Internet.

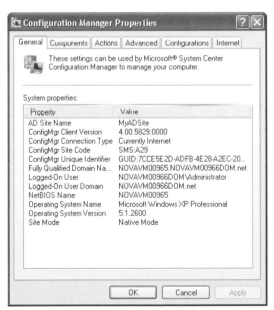

Figure 16-1   The Configuration Manager Properties dialog box displaying the ConfigMgr Connection Type Value of Currently Internet

Real World   Taking Advantage of BITS-Level Resume

One of the neatest features when a client computer moves from the intranet to the Internet and back to the intranet, is taking advantage of BITS-level resume on distribution points. For example, if the client is in the middle of downloading a large software package (for example, a service pack or Microsoft Office upgrade) and the download is interrupted because the user disconnects from the intranet, the download automatically resumes where it left off when it has an Internet connection, providing that the package is also hosted on the Internet-based distribution points. Similarly, if a large download starts when the client is on the Internet and the user comes into the office, as soon as the computer detects it is now connected to the intranet it will resume its download with an intranet distribution point, taking full advantage of the faster network connectivity.

Planning for Internet-Based Client Management

Although the configuration for Internet-based client management is relatively straightforward, there is a considerable amount of planning work that needs to be completed before it becomes operational.

First, look at the requirements:

- The site must be a primary site in native mode. This means that the site and clients must be configured for specific PKI certificates. Refer to Chapter 2, "Planning for and Deploying Configuration Manager Sites," for more information about the PKI certificates. Additionally, a native mode site cannot have a parent site in mixed mode, and a secondary site cannot support Internet-based client management. This requirement might mean that you must migrate your central site to native mode before you can implement a new native mode child site that supports Internet-based client management.

- Site systems that will support Internet-based client management must have connectivity to the Internet. This requirement might sound obvious, but in reality it often proves to be one of the biggest stumbling blocks to implementing Internet-based client management because it raises security issues and firewall reconfiguration requirements to allow Internet traffic to servers and potentially into the intranet.

- Site systems that will support Internet-based client management must be configured with an Internet fully qualified domain name (FQDN), and these FQDNs must be registered on Internet DNS servers so that clients can resolve them when they are on the Internet. Additionally, these same Internet FQDNs must be in the PKI certificates used by these site systems, in either the Subject Name field or the Subject Alternative Name field.

■ Site systems that will support Internet-based client management must be configured to accept connections from Internet clients. When a site is in native mode and site systems are configured with an Internet FQDN, client connections can be configured for intranet-only, Internet-only, or Internet and intranet. The option you select depends on your choice of server placement.

■ Clients must be running the Configuration Manager client in native mode, directly assigned to the site, and directly assigned to the site's Internet-based management point. If proxy server details are required, these must be specified on each client.

The site systems that can support Internet-based client management are the management point, distribution points, software update point, and fallback status point (if you are using a fallback status point for Internet-based clients). The interesting thing about these site systems is that they don't have to be the same servers that fulfill these roles on the intranet. In fact, it is a positive security advantage if you can designate different servers for these roles, so that if they are compromised by Internet traffic, it doesn't affect your intranet management.

Additionally, the Internet-based site systems do not have to be in the same Active Directory forest. They can reside in a different Active Directory forest that has no trust relationship with the Active Directory forest used by the intranet site systems. This makes them suitable to be placed in a perimeter network (sometimes known as a screened subnet, or a DMZ).

Configuration Manager supports a number of different scenarios and server placements for Internet-based client management that range from the site being in the perimeter network to the whole site being in the intranet, and having the site split between the perimeter network and intranet.

More Info   For more information about the possible scenarios, see the topic "Supported Scenarios for Internet-Based Client Management" and related network diagrams in the Configuration Manager Documentation Library at *http://technet.microsoft.com/en-us/library/bb693824.aspx*. To help you decide server placement, the related topic "Determine Server Placement for Internet-Based Client Management" (*http://technet.microsoft.com/en-us/library/bb632871.aspx*) contains a table of pros and cons for each supported server placement for each scenario. Use this to decide the best design for your Internet-based client management site and what additional network infrastructure changes would be needed to support it (such as firewall reconfiguration).

Security Suitable for the Internet

Implementing the PKI certificates required for native mode on the intranet might seem too heavy a burden for most companies. But native mode comes into its own with Internet-based client management. After all, if you're allowing connections from the Internet into your Configuration Manager hierarchy, you wouldn't want any Jane Doe to be able to access your package source files, read inventory data from other clients, modify client policy, or subvert connections to a rogue management point.

Let's have a quick look at how the PKI certificates provide security that's suitable for the Internet:

- The client certificates allow the Internet-based site systems to authenticate clients before they connect to the site systems. They allow connections only from computers that have certificates with client authentication capability that chains to a trusted root certification authority (CA).

- The Internet-based site systems have Web server certificates that allow the clients to authenticate the server and encrypt all data that passes between them using SSL.

- The site server signing certificate means that clients know that their client policy comes from a site server in their assigned site and that it has not been altered since it left the site server. Even if the Internet-based management were to become compromised, false policies or modified policies would not be accepted by Internet-based clients because they would not be signed by their site server (or the hash would fail).

For additional security, use a certificate revocation list (CRL) and an IIS Certificate Trust List (CTL). The CRL allows Internet client computers and Internet-based site servers to verify that certificates used as the basis for secured connections are still valid (for example, the issuing certificate authority is not revoked because it is compromised). An IIS Certificate Trust List allows you to limit the number of certification authorities trusted by the Internet-based site systems, so that you can restrict the list to just the root certification authorities used by Internet clients assigned to the site. Although both of these mechanisms are recommended to increase your security, they also come at the cost of additional administrative overheads. And in the case of the CRL, the risk is that if clients or servers cannot locate it, connections will fail. For more details about the pros and cons of implementing CRL checking and an IIS CTL, see the following topics in the Configuration Manager Documentation Library:

- Determine If You Need to Enable Certificate Revocation Checking (CRL) On Clients (Native Mode)

- Determine If You Need to Configure a Certificate Trust List (CTL) with IIS (Native Mode)

Implementing Internet-Based Client Management

After all the planning requirements are in place, configuring a site for Internet-based client management requires the following configuration:

- The site systems that will support Internet-based connections must be placed appropriately such that they have Internet connectivity and connectivity with other site systems. They must also be able to contact a CRL distribution point if your PKI uses a CRL.

- If the site systems that will support Internet connections are in a different Active Directory forest, they must be configured with an installation account and with the option to accept data retrieval from the site server.

- The site systems that will support Internet connections must be configured with an Internet FQDN.

- The site system roles that will support Internet connections must be configured to allow connections from the Internet (either Allow Internet-Only Client Connections or Allow Both Intranet And Internet Client Connections, depending on your design and server placement).

> **Note** Unlike the other Internet-based site system roles, the fallback status point does not use a PKI certificate, accepts unauthenticated connections, and sends all data unencrypted. This is necessary to its operation so that it can accept state messages from the clients that fail to connect to their Internet-based site systems because of certificate issues. However, because it cannot be secured using PKI controls, you cannot configure it within Configuration Manager for intranet-only connection, or Internet-only connections. Instead, you will see the Allow Both Intranet And Internet Client Connection option, which cannot be changed.

Note   Because of the lack of security controls to help protect this site system role, it should be installed on a dedicated server and not on a site system that has other site system roles installed.

■ The distribution points that will support Internet connections must be configured with the Allow Clients To Transfer Content From This Distribution Point Using BITS, HTTP, And HTTPS option (required for device clients and Internet-based clients).

Figure 16-2 shows a site system configured for an Internet FQDN and an installation account, and configured to accept data retrieval from the site server.

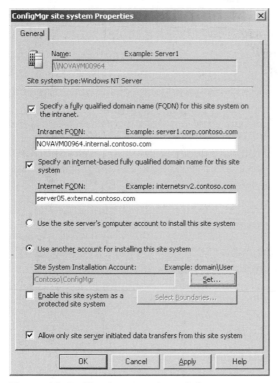

Figure 16-2   The Internet-based site system configured for an Internet FQDN and placement in another Active Directory forest

Figures 16-3, 16-4, and 16-5 show a management point, a distribution point, and an active software update point configured for Internet-based client management with the configuration to support both intranet and Internet client connections.

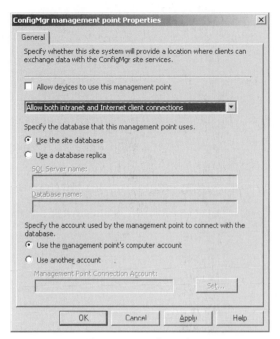

Figure 16-3   The Internet-based management point configured for client connections from both the intranet and the Internet

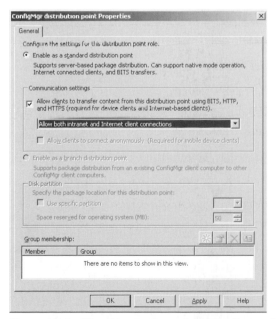

Figure 16-4   The Internet-based distribution point configured for client connections from both the intranet and the Internet

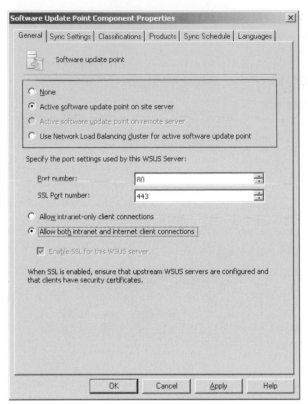

Figure 16-5   The Internet-based software update point configured for client connections from both the intranet and the Internet

> **More Info**   For more detailed information with links to procedural topics, see the topic "Administrator Checklist: Configuring a Site for Internet-Based Client Management" in the Configuration Manager Documentation Library.

Configuring clients for Internet-based client management requires the following configuration:

- If not already completed, install clients for native mode with their PKI certificate.

- Manually assign clients to the site and to their Internet-based management point and Internet-based fallback status point.

- If client computers need to specify proxy server details and credentials, specify this on the Internet tab of the Configuration Manager Properties dialog box from the client's Control Panel.

Figure 16-6 shows the Internet tab of the Configuration Manager Properties dialog box in the client's Control Panel where you can specify the Internet-based management point, and proxy server details with credentials. The site code can be specified on the Advanced tab if it is not set during client installation, but the Internet FQDN of the Internet-based fall-back status point must be specified using CCMSetup client.msi command-line properties.

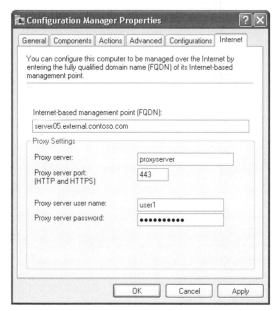

Figure 16-6   The Internet tab of the Configuration Manager Properties dialog box show-ing Internet-based site configurations

> **More Info**   For more detailed information with links to procedural steps, see the topics "Administrator Checklist: Configuring Client Computers for a Site that Supports Internet-Based Client Management" at *http://technet.microsoft.com/en-us/library/bb694139.aspx* and "Administrator Checklist: Configuring Mobile Devices for a Site that Supports Internet-Based Client Management" at *http://technet.microsoft.com/en-us/library/bb632873.aspx* in the Configuration Manager Documentation Library.

Real World   Specifying Custom FQDNs in a Web Server Certificate

The Configuration Manager Documentation Library contains a step-by-step exam-ple of how you can deploy and install the PKI certificates for a basic native mode site if you are using a Microsoft enterprise certification authority (CA) ("Step-By-Step Example Deployment of the PKI Certificates Required for Configuration Man-ager Native Mode" at *http://technet.microsoft.com/en-us/library/bb694035.aspx*), but the Web server certificates in this example are automatically created with the internal (private) DNS FQDN. When deploying a native mode site for Internet-based client management, the Internet-based site systems must have in the Subject Name field (or Subject Alternative Name) the external (public) DNS FQDN. Furthermore, if your design is such that your Internet-based site systems support both Internet-based client management and clients on the intranet, it must have both FQDNs in the certificate. How is this done?

Using the same Microsoft enterprise certification authority solution with a Web Server template, an external FQDN can be configured in the certificate's Subject Name field with the Web Enrollment page and requested from each Internet-based site system. The procedure is very similar to creating the site server signing certificate in the step-by-step guide, with the following key requirements:

- Make sure that the Web Server certificate template has selected the Supplied In The Request option in the Subject Name tab (enabled by default on the Web Server certificate template).

- Request the certificate by logging in as a domain administrator from the Internet-based site system rather than using Group Policy automatic certificate enrollment, and load a Web browser with the command http://<CA_*servername*>/certsrv.

- Choose to request a certificate, select the Advanced Certificate Request option, select the Create And Submit A Request To This CA option, choose the Web Server certificate template from the drop-down menu, and under the Identifying Information For Offline Template section, type the public FQDN of your Internet-based site system in the Name text box. Finally, ensure that the Store Certificate In The Local Computer Store option is selected before you submit your request.

The process is a little more complex if you need to supply multiple FQDNs. You could use the same technique and specify multiple FQDNs in the Subject Name tab, separated by the ampersand (&) symbol. There is nothing in the PKI rules that say you cannot do this. However, the standard procedure for specifying multiple FQDNs in a certificate is to use the Subject Alternative Name (SAN) attribute of the certificate. Because this is the standard and accepted procedure, it is recommended that you follow it. However, the Subject Alternative Name attribute is not supported by default on a Windows Server 2003 CA. So the first step is to enable this, using the following procedure:

On the server running the Windows Server 2003 CA, from a command prompt, run the following commands:

```
Certutil -setreq policy\EditFlags +EDITF_ATTRIBUTESUBECTALTNAME2
Net stop certsvc Net start certsvc
```

Now you can supply values for the Subject Alternative Name (SAN) attribute when requesting a certificate. You can do this using the Certreq.exe utility and a text file, but again, the easiest way is to request the certificate using the Web Enrollment pages. Follow the same process as before using the Web Server template and requesting it with an advanced request, with the following additional steps:

1. In the Advanced Options section, ensure that the request format selected is CMC.

2. In the Attributes box, type your multiple FQDNS using this format: **san:dns=<first.dns.name.com>&dns=<second.dns.name.com>**. So in the example of using server05.external.contoso.com as your Internet FQDN, and novavm00964.internal.contoso.com as your intranet FQDN, the entry would look like this: san:dns=server05.external.contoso.com&dns=novavm 00964.internal.contoso.com. The order in which the FQDNs are specified does not matter.

Figure 16-7 shows the portion of the Web Enrollment page where the Subject Alternative Name attribute is specified, and Figure 16-8 shows the resulting certificate details when it is installed.

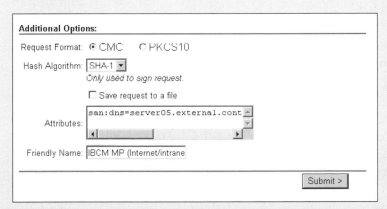

Figure 16-7 Requesting multiple FQDNs on the Web Enrollment page

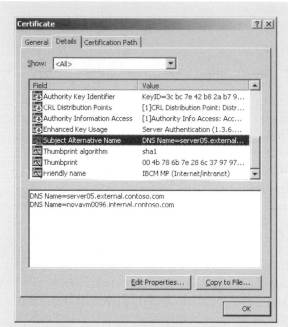

Figure 16-8   The resulting Web Server certificate with multiple FQDNs specified in the Subject Alternative Name (SAN) attribute

For more information about specifying multiple FQDNs using the Subject Alternative Name field (including example text files for the Certreq.exe utility), see the Knowledge Base article "How to add a Subject Alternative Name to a Secure LDAP Certificate" at *http://go.microsoft.com/fwlink/?LinkID=93692*.

If you are not using a Microsoft PKI solution, consult your particular PKI documentation for information about specifying Subject Alternative Name attributes in a certificate.

Checkpoints for Using Internet-Based Client Management

The underlying infrastructure requirements are your biggest enemy when trying to implement Internet-based client management. By definition, you don't have control over all the elements that make up the Internet. For this reason, it pays to implement Internet-based client management in controlled stages so that if you do experience problems, you will be better able to identify breakpoints and focus your troubleshooting efforts.

For example, make sure the site is operating successfully on the intranet in native mode first, before extending it to support Internet-based site systems. If native mode clients on the intranet can't receive policy and install software as expected, clients on the Internet will not be able to do so, either.

As a proof of concept, set up an Internet scenario in a lab environment with two disjointed networks that represent the Internet and the intranet. You will need to make sure that you have two DNS systems on each network that successfully resolve external and internal FQDNs to represent your intranet DNS and Internet DNS. Specifying the FQDNs correctly so that they match—for example, the Internet FQDN configured in the Internet-based management point must be specified on the Web server certificate and on the client—is critical to a successful implementation of Internet-based client management. The onus is on the administrator to ensure that the FQDNs are specified correctly on all components in addition to ensuring that they successfully resolve to the correct IP address.

Get this proof of concept working initially without firewalls, and then, if possible, introduce the same firewall configuration that your company uses. Reconfiguring the firewall is one of the key elements in a successful implementation of Internet-based client management, so if you can prove that the solution works without the firewall and fails with the introduction of the firewall, you know where to concentrate your efforts.

Note Unfortunately, when the solution goes into production you won't have control over all the intervening devices on the Internet, so you must be prepared that in some scenarios, Internet-based client management traffic is going to be blocked between the client and its Internet-based site.

These scenarios are difficult to diagnose because of lack of errors reported by the client or site systems. From their perspective, everything is functional and simply waiting on a reply from the other computer, which will never happen because an intervening device is blocking the traffic. The best you can do when this happens is to troubleshoot using the process of elimination, which is why it is so important to have a working baseline with known components that you control.

With so many different firewalls and possible configurations, there is no single size that fits all when it comes to reconfiguring firewalls and similar network devices. However, to identify the ports you will need to open, use the network diagrams associated with your Internet-based design in the Configuration Manager Documentation Library, together with the topic "Determine the Ports Required for Internet-Based Client Management." Additionally, if your firewall filters at the application level, you might have to allow certain verbs and headers. See the details for "Intervening firewalls or proxy servers between the client and the Internet-based systems" in the topic "Prerequisites for Internet-Based Client Management" for more information.

Finally, if you are using a Web proxy server to publish your Internet-based site systems, see the topic "Determine Requirements for Proxy Web Servers to Use With Internet-Based Client Management" in the Configuration Manager Documentation Library at *http://technet.microsoft.com/en-us/library/bb680995.aspx.*

Summary

This chapter explained the benefits of using Internet-based client management, how it is implemented in Configuration Manager 2007, its requirements and limitations, the planning considerations, and the necessary configuration for site systems and clients.

Chapter 17
Managing Clients Remotely

Don't touch the machine

Unseen hands guide the cursor

Go and drink coffee

~Robert Stack, Technical Writer

As most of you know from experience, many computer-related problems can be solved only through a hands-on approach. You have to see the error message displayed, re-create the scenario that caused a crash, or watch the user perform a task. So it's no surprise that being able to remotely control client systems appeals to the typical administrator. Tools that provide remote access and diagnostic abilities have actually been around for a while. Some are built into the operating system, such as Remote Assistance in Windows Vista. Some tools are separate applications that provide a broader scope of functionality.

Remote control has long been a key feature of Microsoft Systems Management Server (SMS) and has been enhanced in Configuration Manager. Performance and security has been improved, and a new remote tools agent included that supports the Remote Desktop Protocol (RDP) used by Remote Desktop and Remote Assistance on computers running Windows XP, Windows Vista, and Windows Server 2003. Also, a modified version of the SMS 2003 remote client agent is included to support computers running Windows 2000 Server.

Veteran users of remote tools will note that the following functions of remote control have been removed from Configuration Manager:

- Reboot
- Chat
- File transfer
- Remote execute
- Windows 98 diagnostics
- Ping

This is consistent with the change in emphasis from a purely Configuration Manager–based remote control function to the standard Remote Desktop and Remote Assistance functionality included with later operating systems.

In this chapter, you learn about the remote tools available with Configuration Manager and how to use them. You look at the configuration of remote tools for the client, including system requirements, protocol considerations, and configuring the remote options at the client system. Then you look at the remote tools installation process itself and how to monitor status of the remote client and network performance.

Configuring a Client for Remote Control

Configuration Manager remote tools enables you to deliver help desk support from the Configuration Manager administrator's desktop to all supported Configuration Manager clients. As with other Configuration Manager components, you begin by configuring the client agent component through the Configuration Manager console. Keep in mind that, like other client agent settings, the Remote Tools Client Agent settings are configured and effective on a sitewide basis.

If you enable remote tools for a site, the Remote Tools Client Agent is enabled and installed on all Configuration Manager clients that belong to that Configuration Manager site—with no exceptions. If you require users to give permission for an administrator to initiate a remote tools session, permission is required on all Configuration Manager clients that belong to that site. This is the nature of all Configuration Manager client agents.

The discussion of configuration begins by looking at the client system requirements, including network connection considerations, followed by a look at the configuration of the Remote Tools Client Agent and the remote options.

Client System Requirements

Clients must meet the following general requirements to use remote tools for monitoring and control:

- The client must be installed as a Configuration Manager client. This allows the client to receive and run the Remote Tools Client Agent.

- The Remote Tools Client Agent must be enabled on the client computer.

- Access to the client must be allowed. The level of remote access to the client must be defined, including who has the ability to initiate a session.

- The Configuration Manager console computer and the client must use a common protocol and that protocol is Remote Desktop Protocol (RDP) for computers running Windows XP, Windows Vista, or Windows Server 2003 or later, and Transmission Control Protocol/Internet Protocol (TCP/IP) for computers running Windows 2000 Server.

- If you have configured a firewall for your clients, you must allow TCP ports 2701 and 2702 to successfully use remote control, and TCP port 3389 to successfully use Remote Assistance (RDP and RTC).

If your clients meet these requirements, you can proceed with enabling and configuring the Remote Tools Client Agent, as you see in the next section.

Configuring the Remote Tools Client Agent

The Remote Tools Client Agent is the only component that needs to be configured to enable remote control functionality for your site. This agent is installed with the other client agents and can be viewed and configured through the Configuration Manager console. Figure 17-1 shows the list of client agents.

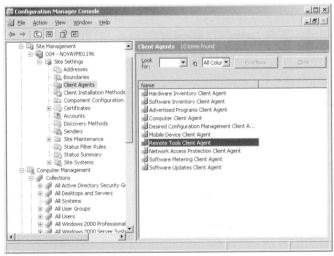

Figure 17-1   A list of client agents installed on the site server

To enable and configure the Remote Tools Client Agent, follow these steps:

1. In the Configuration Manager console, navigate to the Site Settings node and expand it. Select the Client Agents folder to display the list of client agents (see Figure 17-1).

2. Right-click Remote Tools Client Agent and choose Properties from the context menu to display the Remote Tools Client Agent Properties dialog box, as shown in Figure 17-2.

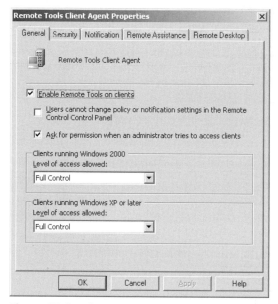

Figure 17-2   The Remote Tools Client Agent Properties dialog box

3. On the General tab, select the Enable Remote Tools On Clients check box.

   In Configuration Manager, you have the ability to "lock" your configuration of Remote Tools so that users can't arbitrarily change your settings. If you want to enable this feature, select the Users Cannot Change Policy Or Notification Settings In The Remote Control Control Panel check box.

   You can indicate whether you want the user to give permission for the remote tools session to be initiated. If you select Ask For Permission When An Administrator Tries To Access Clients, the user must respond Yes or No in a pop-up message box on the computer before the session can begin. This option might be required in organizations that must comply with C2-level security guidelines.

   You can also select the level of access to allow. These are fairly self-explanatory. For computers running Windows 2000 Server, you can allow either full control or no access to the client. For computers running Windows XP or later, you can allow full control, view only, or no access.

4. On the Security tab, shown in Figure 17-3, you can configure the Permitted Viewers list. This list defines which users or user groups are allowed to perform remote functions on Windows clients. Before a remote tools session can be established on a Windows client, the client agent evaluates this list to determine whether the administrator initiating the session is a valid member.

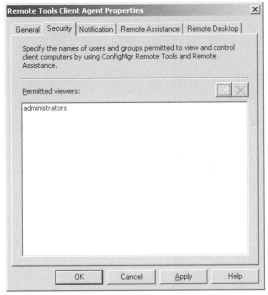

Figure 17-3   The Remote Tools Client Agent Properties dialog box Security tab

To add users or user groups to this list, click the New button (the yellow star) to display the New Viewer dialog box and type the name of the Windows user or security group. Although it's recommended that you manage this list using security groups, you can use user accounts when necessary.

Note   In order to run remote tools on a client computer, the Configuration Manager administrator must either be a local Administrator on the client computer or appear in the permitted viewers list explicitly or as a member of a group.

5. Settings on the Notification tab, shown in Figure 17-4, let you specify how the client will be notified that a remote tools session has been established.

By default, both a visual and an audible indicator will be enabled on the client. The visual indicator can be either a taskbar status icon (the Show Status Icon On Taskbar option) or a high-security icon (the Show Indicator On Desktop option) that appears in the top-right corner of the user's desktop and can't be hidden. The indicators display when a session is active. Audible indicator choices include playing a sound when the session begins and ends or repeatedly throughout the session (the default).

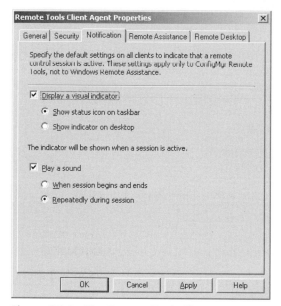

Figure 17-4   The Remote Tools Client Agent Properties dialog box Notification tab

Note   The settings in the Notification tab apply only to Configuration Manager remote tools and not to Remote Assistance.

6. The Remote Assistance tab, shown in Figure 17-5, allows you to manage Remote Assistance settings when they are initiated from the Configuration Manager console. Unlike remote control for which you can specify whether the user needs to provide permission for the session, user permission is always required when using Remote Assistance.

    Select Configure Unsolicited Remote Assistance Settings to allow Configuration Manager to manage Remote Assistance sessions that are not initiated by the user at a client computer. Select Configure Solicited Remote Assistance Settings to allow Configuration Manager to manage Remote Assistance sessions that are requested by the user at a client computer. Like remote control, you can specify one of three levels of access: Full Control, Remote Viewing, and None.

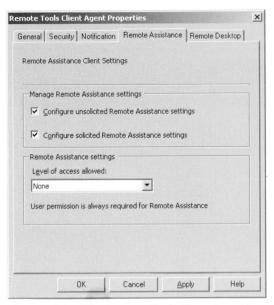

Figure 17-5   The Remote Tools Client Agent Properties dialog box Remote Assistance tab

7. The Remote Desktop tab, shown in Figure 17-6, allows you to manage Remote Desktop settings when they are initiated from the Configuration Manager console.

    Select Configure Remote Desktop Settings to allow Configuration Manager to manage Remote Desktop sessions that are initiated through the Configuration Manager console. Selecting Allow Permitted Viewers To Connect Using Remote Desktop Connection allows any user listed in the Permitted Viewers list on the Security tab to initiate a Remote Desktop session through the Configuration Manager console. Optionally, you can also select Require Network Level Authentication on computers running Windows Vista by the user at a client computer. This option provides a more secure level of authentication before the session can be established. You can select Disable Remote Desktop Connection if you want to disallow the use of Remote Desktop from the Configuration Manager console altogether.

    > **More Info**   For more information about Network Level Authentication and other Remote Desktop connection settings as they apply to Windows Vista, refer to the Windows Vista help topic "What types of Desktop Connections should I allow?"

8. Click OK to begin the site update process.

As usual, the Remote Tools Client Agent is enabled on Configuration Manager clients during the next update cycle on the client or when the client forces an update through the Configuration Manager program in the Control Panel. At this point, a Configuration

Manager administrator can initiate a remote tools session according to the options you configure for the agent.

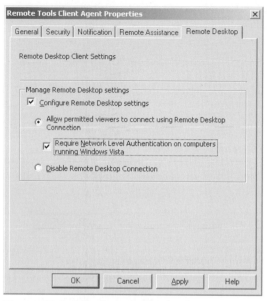

Figure 17-6   The Remote Tools Client Agent Properties dialog box Remote Desktop tab

Like the other client agents, remote tools is installed but not enabled on Configuration Manager client computers. When you enable remote tools in the Configuration Manager console, a client policy is generated and applied to the client at the client's next policy update interval (once an hour by default). Remote control activity on the client is recorded in the %systemroot%\system32\ccm\logs\RemoteControl.log file, an example of which is shown in Figure 17-7.

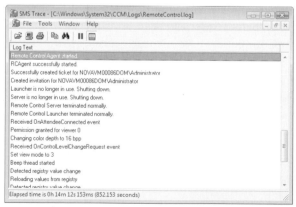

Figure 17-7   Sample RemoteControl.log file from the Configuration Manager client

Setting Remote Options at the Client System

If the Configuration Manager administrator doesn't enable the Clients Cannot Change Policy Or Notification Settings option in the General tab of the Remote Tools Client Agent Properties dialog box, the user at the client computer can choose some site settings for the remote tools session. For example, the user can specify the level of access to allow, whether permission for the remote tools session must be granted first, and how the remote tools session is announced on the client system. The user can modify the remote control options on the client from the remote control program in Control Panel, which is added when the Remote Tools Client Agent is installed, as shown in Figure 17-8. The client's remote control settings take precedence over the site's default settings. You must determine whether allowing the user such latitude is practical or desirable.

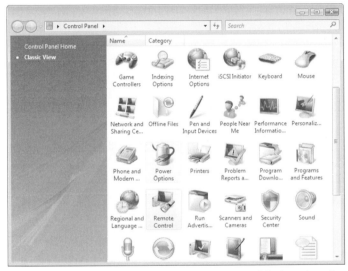

Figure 17-8 The Remote Control program added to the client's Control Panel

To configure the remote tools options on a client, follow these steps:

1. From the client's Control Panel, double-click the Remote Control program to display the Remote Control Properties dialog box. The General tab is shown in Figure 17-9, and the Notification tab is shown in Figure 17-10.

   The settings in the General and Notification tabs reflect those configured in the Configuration Manager console.

2. To make a change, clear the Use Administrator Settings check box at the bottom of either tab and configure the policy and notification settings as described in the previous section.

3. Click OK to save your settings.

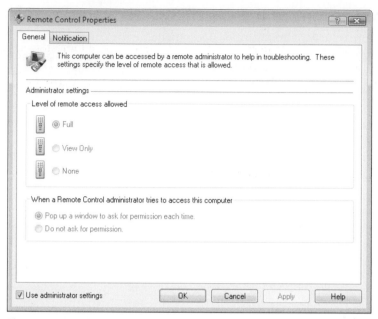

Figure 17-9   The Remote Control Properties dialog box General tab

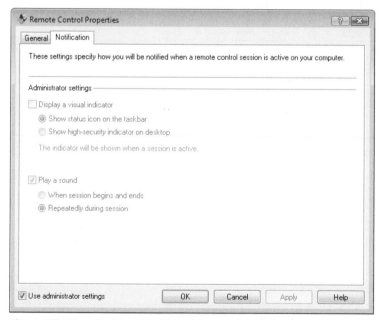

Figure 17-10   The Remote Control Properties dialog box Notification tab

When the Remote Tools Client Agent is correctly configured and installed on your Configuration Manager clients, you should be able to establish remote control sessions. When a session is established, the user can right-click on the visual indicator—for example, the remote control session icon on the taskbar as indicated in Figure 17-11—to close the session or view session status. Figure 17-12 displays the status of a current session on a Windows Vista client.

Figure 17-11   The remote control session icon on the status bar

Figure 17-12   The Remote Control Status dialog box

Exploring Remote Tools Functions

The Configuration Manager administrator is frequently called on to diagnose problems on client computers. Remote tools enables you to run diagnostics on Windows 2000 Server, Windows XP, Windows Vista, and Windows Server 2003 and later clients. You can then use this diagnostic information to help analyze and troubleshoot client hardware and other problems.

Running Diagnostic Tools for Windows Clients

The diagnostic tools for Windows clients are based on the standard System Information utility (WinMsd). This utility provides a static view of the system configuration parameters, services, resources, environment settings, and other system information.

To run the System Information utility, follow these steps:

1. In the Configuration Manager console, navigate to Collections and select the collection that contains the Windows client for which you want to initiate remote diagnostics.

2. Select the client, right-click it, choose Start from the context menu (as shown in Figure 17-13), and then choose Windows Diagnostics.

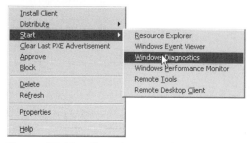

Figure 17-13   Choosing Start from the context menu to access the Windows Diagnostics utility

3. The System Information window appears, as shown in Figure 17-14. This is the same System Information window you see if you log on at the client and execute the utility there. You can view information about the hardware connected to the computer and identify device drivers and services that should start when you start the computer. For more information about using this utility, see the Windows product documentation.

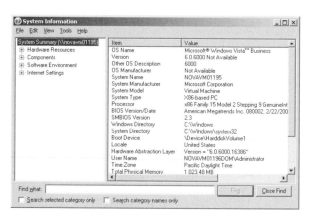

Figure 17-14   The System Information window

4. Close the window when you finish.

> **Note**   As you can see in Figure 17-13, you can also run the Windows Event Viewer and Windows Performance Monitor utilities remotely for Windows clients by choosing Start from the context menu for that client.

In SMS 2003, you had the option of configuring hot keys and other key sequences. Those options are no longer available for Configuration Manager. When you initiate a remote control session, all mouse actions and keystrokes are passed to the remote client computer through the Configuration Manager console except for the following:

- Ctrl+Alt+Delete

- Ctrl+Esc

- Alt+Tab

- Alt+Key

Remote Tools Session Process Flow

Now that you've examined how to configure and run a remote tools session on a Configuration Manager client, take some time to explore the process of initiating a remote tools session. An understanding of this process will enable you to analyze problem situations when you attempt to remotely control a client computer.

When the Configuration Manager administrator starts a remote tools session, a specific sequence of events occurs. This flow of events allows the communication between the Configuration Manager console computer and the remote client computer. This section guides you through the steps that take place in the Configuration Manager console computer and on the primary site server when a remote tools session is initiated with a client computer. It also gives you a fair indication of the network traffic that's generated.

As you know, you initiate a remote tools session by selecting a client in the Collection folder in the Configuration Manager console. So really, the first step that occurs is that Configuration Manager determines whether the Configuration Manager administrator has permission to start a remote tools session through that collection. This permission is different from the Permitted Viewers list that can be configured as part of the remote tools settings; it involves object security set on the collection itself through Configuration Manager security. This type of security allows you to create customized Configuration Manager consoles and delegate specific tasks, such as remote troubleshooting, to specific individuals without having to give them access to everything else. (This aspect of security is discussed in detail in Chapter 20, "Configuration Manager 2007 Security.")

Now when the Configuration Manager administrator begins a remote tools session, RC.exe (remote.exe if the client is running the Windows 2000 operating system) makes a connection through the SMS Provider to the Configuration Manager site database using the resource ID of the client in question. The SMS Provider returns the IP address of the client. This information is passed to LDWMNT.dll, which attempts to connect to the client.

In the meantime, the client agent is "listening," waiting for a connection attempt. When a connection is attempted, the client agent responds, and returns the Permitted Viewers list to RC.exe. The list is evaluated to determine whether it includes the logged-on Configuration Manager administrator. If not, the logged-on Configuration Manager administrator is prompted for the name of a valid user. If user permission is required, the client displays a Remote Control Agent dialog box asking the user for permission. If user permission is granted, the session is established and the Remote Tools window is displayed in the Configuration Manager console. If permission is denied, a message box similar to the one shown in Figure 17-15 is displayed on the Configuration Manager administrator's desktop.

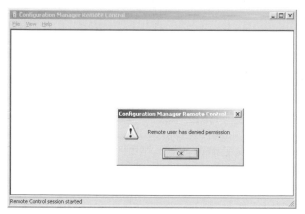

Figure 17-15   Message box notifying the Configuration Manager administrator that user permission has been denied

As you can see, a fair amount of network traffic is involved in establishing the Remote Tools session. In addition, the remote tools session itself can generate a rather significant amount of CPU usage on the client.

Monitoring Status and Flow

As you've seen, when the Remote Tools Client Agent is configured, Configuration Manager status messages are generated at the site server by the site update process—Hierarchy Manager, Site Control Manager, and so on. These status messages help you determine whether the Remote Tools Client Agent is available for installation on the client. Additionally, status messages are generated for each remote tools session between a user at a Configuration Manager console and a client computer. Status messages provide the necessary information for tracking remote tools sessions. Unfortunately, no log files are generated for the remote tools session itself.

Monitoring Configuration

Log activity is also generated at the client computer when the Remote Tools Client Agent is enabled or updated, just as with any other client agent. As you've seen, you can open the remote control log file, RemoteControl.log. You can use this log file to identify the following events that occur during the Remote Tools Client Agent configuration:

- Detection of the operating system on an Intel processor

- Configuration of registry settings, including security and permissions

- Configuration of hardware-specific remote tools settings from the registry
- Start-up of the agent

You can also view the log files CcmExe.log and PolicyAgent.log, searching on Remote Control Session, as shown in Figure 17-16.

Figure 17-16   Sample CcmExec.log file on a Configuration Manager client computer

Monitoring a Remote Tools Session

When the Configuration Manager administrator initiates a remote tools session of any kind with the client, the Remote Tools Client Agent generates status messages. You can, of course, view these messages through the Status Message Viewer. Relying on the Status Message Viewer in this case gives you more useful information.

You can view status messages specific to a remote tools session by executing one of the following status message queries related to remote tools sessions:

- Remote Tools Activity Initiated At A Specific Site
- Remote Tools Activity Initiated By A Specific User
- Remote Tools Activity Initiated From A Specific System
- Remote Tools Activity Targeted At A Specific System

The status messages displayed by these queries are in the range 300xx and provide you with the following details:

- The domain name and user account of the user that's viewing the client
- The computer name of the Configuration Manager console that's being used
- The computer name of the client computer on which remote functions are being carried out
- The types of functions being performed

Figure 17-17 shows an example of the status messages returned by the status message query Remote Tools Activity Targeted At A Specific System. Notice the entries in the Description column for initiating and ending each type of remote function.

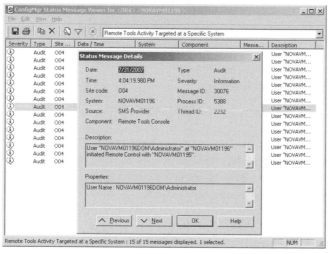

Figure 17-17   Sample status message query results

Remote Assistance and Remote Desktop Support

As mentioned earlier, Configuration Manager supports the Remote Assistance and Remote Desktop features available in the applicable Windows operating systems. Configuration Manager leverages these features by integrating them into the Configuration Manager console. You initiate a remote session using Remote Assistance or Remote Desktop essentially the same way you initiate a remote tools session. Follow these steps:

1. Navigate to the Collections node in the Configuration Manager console.

2. Open the collection that contains the Configuration Manager client with which you want to initiate a remote session.

3. Right-click the client and select Start from the context menu.

4. Select either Remote Assistance or Remote Desktop Client.

The command that you can select from the context menu depends on the operating system running on the client computer. If the client computer and the computer running the Configuration Manager console are both running Windows XP Professional, Windows Vista, or Windows Server 2003 or later, the command Remote Assistance appears on the context menu of the client you've selected in the collection.

However, the command Remote Desktop Client appears if the client computer has Terminal Server client installed and enabled, and it and the Configuration Manager console computer are both running one of these operating systems:

- Windows 2000 Server family

- Windows XP Professional

- Windows Vista

- Windows Server 2003 family

- Windows Server 2008 family

Selecting Remote Assistance initiates a remote session using the Remote Assistance feature. Selecting Remote Desktop Client initiates a Terminal Services session.

Using Remote Control from a Command Line

Configuration Manager gives you the ability to initiate a remote tools session from a command line if necessary. Two command line commands are available. RC.exe supports the Windows XP and later operating systems, and Remote.exe supports Windows 2000 Server.

To launch a remote tools session from the command line on computers running Windows XP and later, run the following command:

```
RC.exe <AddressType> <AddressOrResourceID> [\\Site Server Name\]
```

where either AddressType = 0 and AddressOrResourceID = the SMS Resource ID, or AddressType = 1 and AddressOrResourceID = the IP Address or hostname of the target computer. The command option Site Server Name is needed if the Configuration Manager database resides on a computer other than the one from which you are initiating the remote tools session.

Note   You can find out the resource ID for any Configuration Manager client by locating that client in a collection in the Configuration Manager console, right-clicking it and selecting Properties, then scrolling through the Discovery Data list box to find the entry for Resource ID. You can also create a Configuration Manager query which lists the resource IDs for any or all of the clients.

To launch a remote tools session from the command line on computers running Windows 2000 Server, run the following command:

```
Remote.exe <AddressType> <AddressOrResourceID> [\\Site Server Name\]
```

where either AddressType = 0 and AddressOrResourceID = the SMS Resource ID, or AddressType = 2 and AddressOrResourceID = the IP Address or hostname of the target computer. The command option Site Server Name is needed if the Configuration

Manager database resides on a computer other than the one from which you are initiating the remote tools session.

Checkpoints

Configuring and running remote tools sessions is pretty straightforward using Configuration Manager. There are really just a few things to keep in mind:

- If you have configured a firewall for your clients, you must allow TCP ports 2701 and 2702 to successfully use remote control, and TCP port 3389 to successfully use Remote Assistance (RDP and RTC).

- Be sure to limit the entries in the Permitted Viewers list. Local administrator rights are not required for a user to be able to use remote tools. If the collection and Permitted Viewers list security is met, the remote tools user can use remote tools on the client.

- Remember that when you access a client using remote control or Remote Assistance, you are performing actions on that client using the credentials of the logged on user at that client. That means you might not be able to carry out some actions, especially those which might require local administrator permissions on the client. However, if you are accessing a client using Remote Desktop, you are accessing the client using your own credentials.

- You'll note that you can enter an account into the Permitted Viewers list without specifying a domain for the account. This is by design, as the list is authenticated at the client, and the client might have access to different domains than the site server. However, for an added level of security, it is recommended that you enter accounts in the list using the format domain\account to remove any ambiguity there might be at the client.

- Finally, don't enter local groups into the Permitted Viewers list if they have global groups as members because the global group membership will not be enumerated when the list is checked for authentication. Include global groups explicitly in the list.

Summary

In this chapter, you explored the various remote tools as well as the configuration settings for the Remote Tools Client Agent. You also explored the process for installing and initiating a remote tools session with a client, monitoring the session's status, and troubleshooting potential problems. In Chapter 18 you'll explore how to monitor software usage using the software metering feature of Configuration Manager 2007.

Chapter 18

Monitoring Software Usage with Software Metering

Applications run

How many and how often

The meter spins

~Steve Kaczmarek, Content Manager

In this chapter, you explore the software metering feature of Configuration Manager 2007 and the components that are involved in the software metering process. You look at how to configure the Software Metering Client Agent and at software metering rules. And you explore how to view reports based on metered data and identify some maintenance tasks.

Understanding Software Metering

Software metering gives you the ability to collect and monitor program usage on Configuration Manager client computers, including the users running the program, when the program started, and when it stopped. A program is any executable file that can run in memory on the client computer, especially .exe and .com files. You can use this information to help determine how programs are used within an organization, whether programs are being used, and whether you're in compliance with license agreements for the programs being run. You tell the clients what programs to meter by creating software metering rules that are copied down to each client. You can also enable Configuration Manager to create software metering rules automatically depending on how programs are used in your organization.

Configuration Manager uses Windows Management Instrumentation (WMI) to store software metering rules and collected data. To facilitate viewing and analyzing the metered data, Configuration Manager provides specific software metering reports that can be used with the Configuration Manager Web reporting tool.

Software metering collects the following information about a program:

- Usage information
    - Start time
    - End time
    - Meter data ID
    - Resource ID (computer name)
    - User name
    - Users in Terminal Services sessions
    - Still running
- File information
    - File ID
    - File name
    - File version
    - File description
    - File size (KB)
- Program information
    - Company name
    - Product name
    - Product version
    - Product language

Software Metering Process Flow

This section provides an overview of the software metering process and the components involved in that process. Two main components make up software metering: the Software Metering Client Agent and software metering rules. The rules represent the programs that you want to monitor on each client, and the agent is responsible for keeping the rules up to date on the client and collecting and reporting metered data back to the site.

Software metering rules are stored in the Configuration Manager database and copied to management points. The rules are propagated to the Configuration Manager clients during the client agent's next update cycle. Rules created at a Configuration Manager site higher up in the hierarchy can apply either to only that site or to that site and all its lower-level child sites.

When the program runs, the Software Metering Client Agent collects required information about the program, such as the file name, version, and size, when the program started and when it ended, and the client on which it's running. The agent then uploads the data to the management point on its next update cycle. If the client isn't connected to the network, the data remains on the client and is uploaded the next time the client connects to the network.

After the data is uploaded to the appropriate site server, it's added to the site database, and, if the rule was created at a higher-level parent site, the data is propagated to the higher-level Configuration Manager sites.

Configuring Software Metering

Software metering is configured in two areas of reference: software metering rules and the client agent. Begin by looking at the two elements of software metering that you need to configure: the Software Metering Client Agent and software metering rules. Software metering rules represent the parameters you set for monitoring software usage on a Configuration Manager client. The Software Metering Client Agent runs the rules on the Configuration Manager client, monitors software usage according to the parameters you set in the rules, and reports that usage data back to the Configuration Manager site database.

Configuring the Software Metering Client Agent

Like the other Configuration Manager client-based features you've seen, you enable software metering by configuring a client agent—in this case, the Software Metering Client Agent. And, like the other client agent settings, the options you choose when you configure the agent are considered site-wide options and are propagated to all clients in the site.

To configure the Software Metering Client Agent, follow these steps:

1. In the Configuration Manager console, navigate to the Client Agents node under Site Settings. The client agents are listed in the results pane.

2. Right-click Software Metering Client Agent in the results pane and choose Properties from the context menu to display the Software Metering Client Agent Properties dialog box, as shown in Figure 18-1.

3. On the General tab, select the Enable Software Metering On Clients check box.

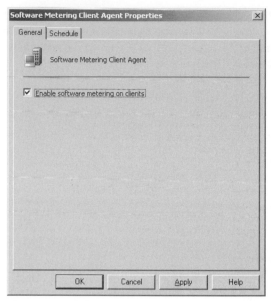

Figure 18-1   The Software Metering Client Agent Properties dialog box

4.   On the Schedule tab, shown in Figure 18-2, click the Schedule buttons to determine how frequently you want to send collected data from the client back to the site system (Data Collection Schedule). The default interval that Configuration Manager uses is seven days.

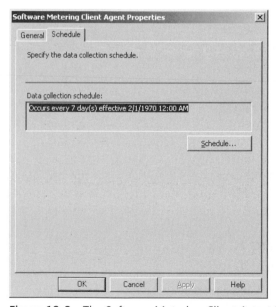

Figure 18-2   The Software Metering Client Agent Properties dialog box Schedule tab

5.   Click OK to save your settings and configure the agent.

Note   Software metering won't collect a data file that's more than 90 days old. If it finds such a file, it generates status message 5614 and moves the data file to its own folder.

All Configuration Manager client agents are automatically installed, but not enabled, when the Configuration Manager client is installed. So, at the Configuration Manager client's next refresh cycle, it receives a new client policy that indicates that the Software Metering Client Agent has been enabled. At that point the agent is configured and started on the client.

After the rules are downloaded to the client, the agent can begin to monitor programs, even if the program is currently running in computer memory.

Configuring Software Metering Rules

Software metering rules identify for the client agent which programs should be monitored and how they should be monitored. Rules can be identified at any Configuration Manager site in your hierarchy and can apply only to that site or, as mentioned earlier, to any lower-level child site below it in the hierarchy. The catch is that any rules created higher up in the hierarchy can be modified only in the site in which they were created. This behavior is consistent with the way package, advertisement, and collection data is handled as well.

The rule configuration information is propagated down the hierarchy to child sites, but maintenance of the rule is affected at the site in which the rule is created. Consequently, it's important that you carefully consider whether the rule you create should be propagated and applied to Configuration Manager clients in child sites.

Software metering is supported on Configuration Manager clients running Terminal Services or Remote Desktop Connection. Program usage in this case is monitored individually—that is, each program run through a Terminal Services session is counted as a distinct usage of that program, even if the same program is being run in each session. However, the programs run in the Terminal Services session are treated as remote connections and are reported with the same computer name. Programs run using Microsoft Windows 2000 Server, Windows XP, or Windows Vista Remote Desktop Connection, however, are treated as local connections and the local computer name is reported.

Creating a Software Metering Rule

To configure a software metering rule, follow these steps:

1.   In the Configuration Manager console, expand the Computer Management node, and then select the Software Metering node.

2. Right-click Software Metering, click New, and then click Software Metering Rule from the context menu to open the New Software Metering Rule Wizard, as shown in Figure 18-3.

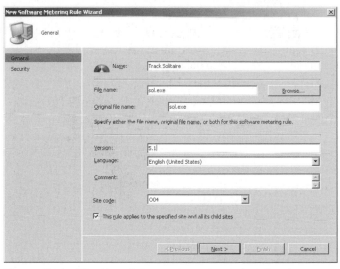

Figure 18-3   The New Software Metering Rule Wizard

3. On the General page, type the appropriate information in each field (all fields are required except Version and Comment):

    ❑   In the Name field, type a descriptive name for the rule itself; it's suggested that you include the program name or file name.

    ❑   In the File Name field, type the file name that launches the program, or click Browse to search for the appropriate executable file. Note that some programs are used as placeholders to launch other programs. Specify the name of the program that ultimately executes the program itself or you might not collect the appropriate tracking information. For example, if you track a command file that launches, say, Solitaire, software metering tracks only the command file and not Solitaire. This field isn't required if you specify an Original File Name.

    ❑   In the Original File Name field, type the file name of the program as it appears in the header information contained in the program's executable file. If the executable file is renamed and you are tracking on the File Name value, software metering no longer recognizes the application as the one to monitor. The value in Original File Name, on the other hand, directs the agent to read the application's name from the header information contained in the application's executable file. Thus, even if the file is renamed, the agent still recognizes the application as the one to monitor. This field isn't required if you specify a File Name.

Important   Not all applications are written to contain the program name in the header information of the executable file. Games, for example, tend not to do this.

❑ In the Version field, type the version of the program if you want software metering to monitor a specific version. Here you can use wildcards to broaden or narrow the entry. Use the default asterisk (*) to match on any version. Use the question mark (?) to substitute for any character. For example, if you want to monitor versions 5.0, 5.1, and 5.2, type 5.? in the Version field.

Important   If you leave this field blank, software metering monitors the program only if the version listed in the header information of the program executable file is also blank.

❑ In the Language field, select the language of the software program from the drop-down list.

❑ In the Comment field, type any additional descriptive information that you think can be useful in identifying how or why this rule is used. It's generally better to err on the side of having more descriptive information than is needed rather than not enough.

❑ In the Site Code field, select the site code that the rule should apply to. If you have only one site, or if the site is the lowest in the hierarchy, this field is dimmed. If the rule should apply to this site and all its child sites, select the This Rule Applies To The Specified Site And All Its Child Sites option.

4. Click Next to display the Security page. Modify the class and instance security on this page as you've seen in previous dialog boxes, and click Finish to save the rule.

Automatically Generating Software Metering Rules

A new feature in Configuration Manager 2007 software metering is the capability to automatically generate software metering rules for frequently used applications in your organization. This feature is enabled by default as long as you have enabled software metering in the Software Metering Client Agent Properties dialog box. There are three options you can configure to automatically generate software metering rules which can be accessed in the Software Metering Properties dialog box as shown in Figure 18-4.

You access this dialog box by right-clicking the Software Metering node in the Configuration Manager 2007 console and then clicking Properties. The items you can configure are as follows:

- The amount of time that recently used metering data will be retained in the Configuration Manager site database

- The percentage of computers that must run a program before a software metering rule is automatically created for that program

- The threshold after which software metering rules will no longer be automatically created

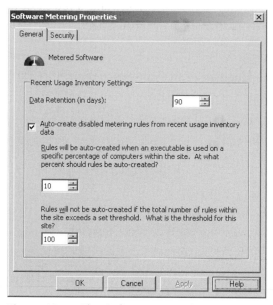

Figure 18-4   The Software Metering Properties dialog box

Important   When software metering rules are automatically created, they are created in a disabled state. You must enable them before they will begin to collect usage data on your site. See the section "Enabling and Disabling a Software Metering Rule" for more information about how to enable these rules.

Real World   Monitoring a Suite of Products

Let's say you want to monitor usage information for the 2007 Microsoft Office system as a suite as opposed to monitoring individual usage of Microsoft Word, Excel, PowerPoint, and so on. It's possible to do this with Configuration Manager software metering.

Software metering supports creating metering rules that have the same name. If you want to monitor a suite of applications, create a rule for each application in the suite (Word, Excel, and so on), but give each rule the same name; for example, Office 2007. Be sure to use the correct version numbers and file names. Configuration Manager reports the usage information for each application aggregately under the name Office 2007.

Enabling and Disabling a Software Metering Rule

After you create a new software metering rule, it's automatically enabled and, if you chose to do so, propagated to child sites. However, you might want to stop monitoring a particular program but still view the data already collected without completely deleting the rule. In this case you can disable the rule and, when you want to run the rule again, enable it again. The client is notified of the change in status of the rule during the next rule update on the client.

To disable a software metering rule, follow these steps:

1. In the Configuration Manager console, expand the Computer Management node, and then select the Software Metering node.

2. In the results pane, right-click the software metering rule you want to disable, and choose Disable from the context menu.

To enable a software metering rule that has been disabled, follow these steps:

1. In the Configuration Manager console, expand the Computer Management node, and then select the Software Metering node.

2. In the results pane, right-click the software metering rule you want to enable, and choose Enable from the context menu.

Summarizing Data

The amount of program usage information that's collected can add up quickly and use a lot of space in the Configuration Manager site database. To keep the information manageable, Configuration Manager periodically summarizes the collected data as well as deletes old data. You can't view collected metering data until the next summarization cycle—once a day by default—is completed.

Data is summarized based on monthly usage and file usage. File usage tracks the approximate total number of concurrent users who have run a specific program during a specific time interval. The Summarize Software Metering File Usage Data maintenance task condenses the individual software metering data records into one record that provides aggregate information about the program—its name, version, language, and number of users. This task runs once a day and summarizes data over 15-minute and 1-hour intervals. Monthly usage tracks the number of times a program is run by a specific user on a specific computer.

Similarly, the Summarize Software Metering Monthly Usage Data maintenance task condenses the individual software metering data records into one record but summarizes the data over monthly periods. This task runs once a day and summarizes data over one-month intervals.

In addition, by default, each day Configuration Manager deletes software metering data records older than five days and summarized data older than 270 days.

Software metering summarization tasks and deletion tasks are configurable maintenance tasks in Configuration Manager 2007. To configure the Delete Aged Software Metering Data task, follow these steps:

1. In the Configuration Manager console, navigate to the Site Maintenance node under Site Settings, expand it, and, under Site Maintenance, select Tasks.

2. In the results pane, right-click the Delete Aged Software Metering Data task and select Properties from the context menu.

3. In the Delete Aged Software Metering Data Task Properties dialog box, shown in Figure 18-5, select the number of days after which data is considered old and the schedule for the task to be executed.

4. Click OK when you finish.

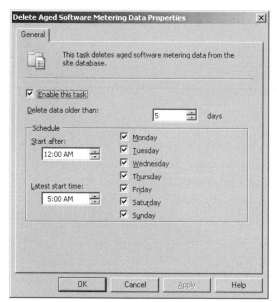

Figure 18-5   The Delete Aged Software Metering Data Properties dialog box

To configure the Delete Aged Software Metering Summary Data task, follow these steps:

1. In the Configuration Manager console, navigate to the Site Maintenance node under Site Settings, expand it, and, under Site Maintenance, select Tasks.

2. In the results pane, right-click the Delete Aged Software Metering Summary Data task and choose Properties from the context menu.

3. In the Delete Aged Software Metering Summary Data Properties dialog box, shown in Figure 18-6, select the number of days after which data is considered old and the schedule for the task to be executed.

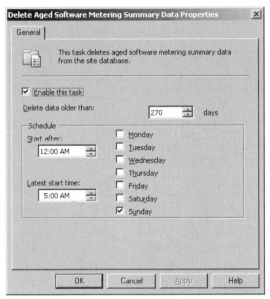

Figure 18-6   The Delete Aged Software Metering Summary Data Properties dialog box

4. Click OK when you finish.

To configure the Summarize Software Metering File Usage Data task, follow these steps:

1. In the Configuration Manager console, navigate to the Site Maintenance node under Site Settings, expand it, and, under Site Maintenance, select Tasks.

2. In the results pane, right-click the Summarize Software Metering File Usage Data task and choose Properties from the context menu.

3. In the Summarize Software Metering File Usage Data Properties dialog box, shown in Figure 18-7, select the schedule for the task to be executed.

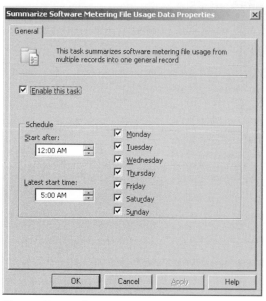

Figure 18-7   The Summarize Software Metering File Usage Data Properties dialog box

4. Click OK when you finish.

To configure the Summarize Software Metering Monthly Usage Data task, follow these steps:

1. In the Configuration Manager console, navigate to the Site Maintenance node under Site Settings, expand it, and, under Site Maintenance, select Tasks.

2. In the results pane, right-click the Summarize Software Metering Monthly Usage Data task and choose Properties from the context menu.

3. In the Summarize Software Metering Monthly Usage Data Properties dialog box, shown in Figure 18-8, select the schedule for the task to be executed.

4. Click OK when you finish.

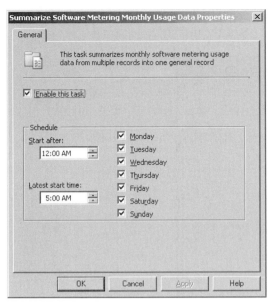

Figure 18-8   The Summarize Software Metering Monthly Usage Data Properties dialog box

Running Software Metering Reports

The Configuration Manager Report Viewer feature of Configuration Manager 2007 provides you with several reports for viewing the collected software metering data. Using reports is discussed in greater detail in Chapter 19, "Extracting Information Using Queries and Reports." However, this section contains a brief overview of how to view these reports.

To launch the reporting tool, follow these steps:

1. In the Configuration Manager console, expand the Computer Management node, and then select the Reporting node. Right-click the Reporting node, and choose Run from the context menu to start the Configuration Manager Report Viewer, as shown in Figure 18-9. In the Reports list on the left side of the viewer, find and expand Software Metering to display a list of all the available Software Metering reports included with Configuration Manager.

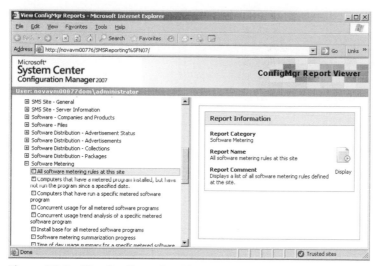

Figure 18-9   The Configuration Manager Report Viewer with Software Metering reports expanded

2. Select the report that you want to run from the list of reports on the left side of the viewer.

3. Type any information required for the report, such as time period or software metering rule name that you're prompted for on the right side of the viewer.

4. Click Display to display the report results.

Figure 18-9 displays a list of the reports available for viewing software metering data. As you select each report, you are prompted for information specific for that report. For example, if you select the report All Software Metering Rules At This Site, as selected in Figure 18-9, all you need to do is click Display to see a list of all the rules configured for this site, as shown in Figure 18-10.

However, if you select the report Total Usage For All Metered Software Programs, you will need to specify the month and the year for which you want to view reported data, as shown in Figure 18-11. Figure 18-12 shows the result of that last report.

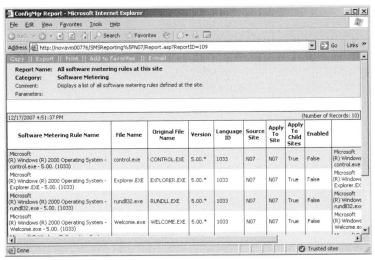

Figure 18-10   Results of running the report All Software Metering Rules At This Site

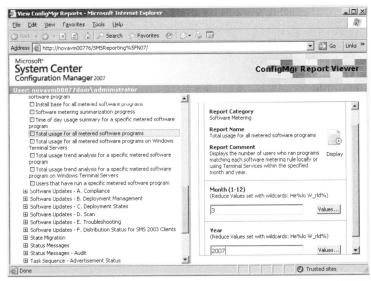

Figure 18-11   The Configuration Manager Report Viewer with Total Usage For All Metered Software Programs selected

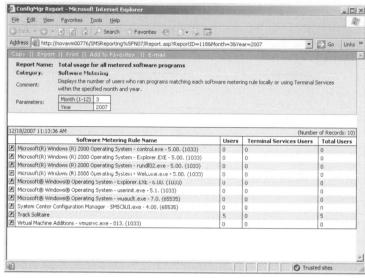

Figure 18-12   Results of running the report Total Usage For All Metered Software Programs

Checkpoints

Remember that after you create a new rule and propagate it to your Configuration Manager clients, you still need to wait for the next collection and summarization cycles to complete before you can view the data. Because the default for collecting data from the client is seven days and summarization takes place once a day, you might wait for up to eight days for the first data to be viewable.

Also, be sure to review your rule properties. Check the program name and especially the version number you're trying to match. It might be a good idea to try out your rules in a test environment to be sure that you're actually monitoring the programs you want to monitor.

Summary

In Configuration Manager 2007, software metering allows you to monitor program usage and then use that information to extrapolate data about how programs are used in your organization, who uses them, how long, and so on. Together with software inventory, you can use software metering to determine whether you're meeting the requirements of your software licenses. Through the Configuration Manager Report Viewer, you can view statistical information about the programs you're monitoring.

More Info   For more information about using and configuring software metering, see the Configuration Manager Documentation Library that is installed when you install the Configuration Manager console, and which is available through the Microsoft Configuration Manager TechCenter site at *http://technet.microsoft.com/en-us/configmgr/default.aspx.*

In this part of the book you've examined various ways to manage client applications. The package distribution process showed you how you can remotely install programs on your Configuration Manager clients and how you can maximize the package distribution process using collections. With the Configuration Manager Installer, you can fully script your packages to require little or no user input during the package's execution. In this chapter, you've seen how to monitor the usage of client applications. Part III explores various ways to retrieve and present information from the Configuration Manager database, as well as site database maintenance.

Part III
Site Database Management

Chapter 19
Extracting Information Using Queries and Reports

Information treasure

Use the queries and reports

Key to all data

~Steve Kaczmarek, Content Manager

The first two parts of this book have covered the primary functions of Microsoft Systems Center Configuration Manager 2007. You've explored the inventory collection process, package distribution and management, software updates, and remote client management. Along the way, a lot of information has made its way into the Configuration Manager database, and you've seen periodic references to using a query or a report to extract information from the Configuration Manager database—for example, you might use a query as a membership rule to populate a collection or to view status messages generated by various client agents, or you can use a report to view collected software metering data. This section of the book focuses on database maintenance tasks, including extracting and analyzing data, setting security, and recovering data.

Queries are an efficient and relatively easy way to retrieve information from the Configuration Manager site database. Configuration Manager also makes its Report Viewer available as a Web tool accessible through the Configuration Manager console. You explore these methods of accessing Configuration Manager database information in this chapter.

Working with Queries

As you know, the premise behind any database query is the return of information based on a set of criteria. In other words, you define what information you're trying to obtain in the form of a query statement. The query engine then searches the database for entries that match your criteria. The query result then displays the data that matches your criteria.

The same is true for Configuration Manager queries. To define a simple Configuration Manager query, you specify a Configuration Manager object to search on, one or more attributes of the object, an operator of some kind, and a value. For example, suppose you're querying for computers with processors greater than 700 MHz. In this case, *computer* is an object, *processor* is an attribute of the object, *greater than* is the relational operator, and *700 MHz* is the value.

You can use Configuration Manager queries for a variety of purposes. Generally, queries are thought of as a means of reporting on data in the database. Indeed, you might use Configuration Manager queries to find all the computers that meet certain memory, disk space, and platform requirements before sending out a package to them. And as you've seen, queries are particularly useful in defining collection memberships. Collections whose members are based on the results of a query can be updated periodically to keep them current. Any programs advertised to a collection are automatically made available to the collection's members. As the query runs and updates the collection, new members automatically receive any advertisements that target the collection, and deleted members no longer receive the advertisements.

You can generate Configuration Manager queries a couple of ways. The easiest way to create and run a query—and the easiest method to learn—is using Configuration Manager Query Builder, which is built into the Configuration Manager console. This interface provides you with a point-and-click method for building your query. You can also write the query statements yourself; however, this method entails learning a query language—specifically, Windows Management Instrumentation (WMI) Query Language (WQL).

Unlike other SQL Server databases, Configuration Manager relies on the WMI layer to expose its database information to the Configuration Manager console and other tools. Therefore, you can't use regular SQL queries or commands to extract data from the Configuration Manager database. Instead, you specify WMI object classes and attributes that the query uses to access and search the Configuration Manager database. For example, most of the queries that you create and use for collection membership are likely to be based on the SMS_R_System discovery class, which contains discovery record properties such as IP Address, OperatingSystemNameandVersion, and Name, and on the SMS_G_System set of inventory classes, such as SMS_G_System_Processor, which includes processor data such as Name and ResourceId, and SMS_G_System_x86_PC_Memory, which includes memory data such as TotalPhysicalMemory.

> **More Info**   For more information about Configuration Manager object classes
> and properties, see the Systems Center Configuration Manager 2007 Software
> Development Kit (SDK) available through the Microsoft Configuration Manager
> TechCenter site *(http://technet.microsoft.com/en-us/configmgr/default.aspx)*
> and through the Microsoft Developer Network (MSDN) program
> *(http://msdn.microsoft.com)*. While you could access the Configuration Manager
> database using regular SQL database queries, this chapter focuses on querying
> through the Configuration Manager console.

Configuration Manager loads 18 predefined queries, as shown in Figure 19-1. As you can
see, these predefined queries are fairly general in scope and are meant to be more globally
oriented, perhaps as the target of an advertisement. However, you can certainly create
your own queries—for example, to assist with certain management tasks, including populating and updating collections and viewing client status messages.

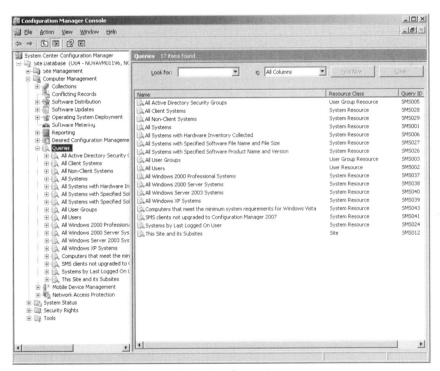

Figure 19-1   Predefined queries in Configuration Manager

Query Elements

Before reviewing the steps for creating a query, look at the individual elements that make up a query. The relationship between these elements is illustrated in Figure 19-2. As mentioned, begin your query definition by selecting a WMI object class to query on. However, when you use the Configuration Manager Query Builder, these objects use friendly names that make it easier to select the correct object and attribute. The discussion is focused on using these friendly object names.

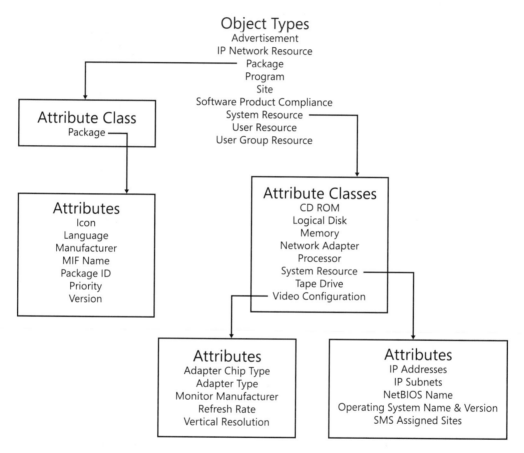

Figure 19-2   The relationship between objects, their attribute classes, and the attributes of each class

Configuration Manager provides several object types for generating queries. An object type has specific attribute classes that describe it. For example, the *System Resource* object type is defined by its memory, environment, logical disk, processor, and network attribute classes, among other elements. An *attribute class* is essentially a category of attributes that contains an attribute list. For example, the System Resource attribute class includes the IP Addresses, IP Subnets, NetBIOS Name, Operating System Name and Version, and Configuration Manager Assigned Sites attributes.

Table 19-1 lists the more frequently used object types, some of their attribute classes, and a short list of key attributes.

Table 19-1   Configuration Manager Objects and Some of Their Attribute Classes and Attributes

Object type	Attribute classes	Attributes
Advertisement	Advertisement	Action in Progress, Advertisement ID, Assigned Schedule, Assignment ID, Collection ID, Name, Package ID, Priority, Program
Package	Package	Action in Progress, Description, Manufacturer, MIF File Name, Name, Package ID, Priority, Stored Package Path, Version
Program	Program	Action in Progress, Command Line, Comment, Device Flags, MSI File Path, MSI Product ID, Name, Package ID, Program Flags, Working Directory
Site	Site	Build Number, Install Directory, Reporting Site Code, Server Name, Site Code, Version
Software Metering Rule	Software Metering Rule	Enabled, File Name, File Version, Original File Name, Rule ID, Site Code
System Resource	Add/Remove Programs	Display Name, Product ID, Publisher, Version
	Collected Files	Collection Date, File Name, File Path, File Size, Resource ID
	Device Certificates	Group ID, Issuer, Store, TimeStamp, ValidFrom
	Device Computer System	ISA, Number of Processors, OEM Info, Platform Type
	Device Network	Bandwidth, IP Address, IP Subnet, MAC
	Extended Software Updates	Authorization Name, Date Posted, ID, Info Path, Language, Q Numbers, Scan Agent, Severity
	Logical Disk	Availability, File System, Free Space, Volume Name
	Memory	Available Virtual Memory, Total Pagefile Space, Total Physical Memory, Total Virtual Memory
	NAP Client	Fix-up URL, NAP Enabled, NAP Protocol Version, Probation Time, System Isolation Stamp

Table 19-1   Configuration Manager Objects and Some of Their Attribute Classes
and Attributes (Continued)

Object type	Attribute classes	Attributes
	Network Adapter	Adapter Type, MAC Address, Manufacturer
	Operating System	Build Number, CSD Version, Manufacturer, Registered User, System Directory, Version
	Patch Status	Agent Install Date, Last State, Last Status Message Severity, Q Numbers, Title, Type
	Processor	Family, Manufacturer, Max Clock Speed, IS64bit, Processor Type
	System Resource	AD Domain Name, Always Internet, Client Type, IP Addresses, IPv6 Addresses, Last Logon User Name, NetBIOS Name, Obsolete, Operating System Name And Version, System Container Name, System Group Name, System OU Name
User Group Resource	User Group Resource	Domain, Name, Resource ID, Resource Type, SID, Unique User Group Name
User Resource	User Resource	Domain, Full User Name, Resource ID, Resource Type, Unique User Name, User Container Name, User Group Name, User OU Name

The *criterion type* defines what you're comparing the attribute with. The six criterion types are listed in Table 19-2.

Table 19-2   Criterion Types

Type	Description
Null Value	Used when the attribute value may or may not be null
Simple Value	Constant value against which the attribute is compared
Prompted Value	Prompts you to enter a value before the query is evaluated
Attribute Reference	Lets you compare the query attribute to another attribute that you identify
Subselected Values	Lets you compare the query attribute to the results of another query that you specify
List Of Values	List of constant values against which the attribute is compared

Along with the criterion type, you will select a relational operator and supply a value to search for. This value can be null, numeric, a string, or a date/time. The list of relational *operators* is pretty much what you would expect: *Is Equal To, Is Not Equal To, Is Greater Than, Is Less Than,* and so on. However, the kinds of operators that are available depend on whether the attribute is null, numeric, string, or date/time. Table 19-3 outlines the subtle differences between these operators.

Table 19-3   Relational Operators

Data type	Relational operators
Null	Is Null, Is Not Null
Numeric	Is Equal To, Is Not Equal To, Is Greater Than, Is Less Than, Is Greater Than Or Equal To, Is Less Than Or Equal To
String	Is Equal To, Is Not Equal To, Is Like, Is Not Like, Is Greater Than, Is Less Than, Is Greater Than Or Equal To, Is Less Than Or Equal To, Is Like, Is Not Like, Lowercase Is Equal To, Lowercase Is Greater Than, Lowercase Is Greater Than or Equal To, Lowercase Is Less Than, Lowercase Is Less Than Or Equal To, Lowercase is Like, Lowercase Is Not Like, Uppercase Is Equal To, Uppercase Is Greater Than, Uppercase Is Greater Than or Equal To, Uppercase Is Less Than, Uppercase Is Less Than Or Equal To, Uppercase is Like, Uppercase Is Not Like
Date/Time	*Unit* Is Equal To, *Unit* Is Not Equal To, *Unit* Is Greater Than, *Unit* Is Less Than, *Unit* Is Greater Than Or Equal To, *Unit* Is Less Than Or Equal To
Date/Time	*Unit* Is Not, *Unit* Is After, *Unit* Is Before, *Unit* Is On Or After, *Unit* Is On Or Before

(*Unit* is a date or time unit—millisecond, second, minute, hour, day, week, month, quarter, or year.)

When string values are used in a query, the exact string must be provided without quotation marks unless the quotation marks are part of the string. If you use either the *Is Like* or *Is Not Like* relational operator, you can use wildcard characters as part of the string. Acceptable wildcard characters include those shown in Table 19-4.

Table 19-4   Wildcard Characters

Symbol	Meaning
% (percent)	Any string of characters
_ (underscore)	Any single character
[ ] (brackets)	Any character within a specified range of characters
^ (caret)	Any character *not* within the specified range of characters

For example, if you want to query the database for all Configuration Manager clients that contain the string FIN in the client name, you might use the value %FIN%. String *operators* are not case sensitive unless the SQL code page you use uses case-sensitive comparisons.

In real life, your queries will probably be more complex and will consist of several query statements. These statements are connected using logical *operators* and are grouped for evaluation using parentheses. The three primary logical *operators* used with Configuration Manager queries are *AND*, *OR*, and *NOT*.

An *AND* operation finds all data that matches two query statements connected by the *AND operator*. *AND operations* generally result in a more restricted search because every expression must be satisfied to generate a result.

An *OR* operation finds all the data that matches any portion of the two statements connected by the *OR*. As you might expect, *OR* operations generally result in a broader search because any expression may be satisfied to generate a result.

A *NOT* operation finds all the data that doesn't satisfy the statement preceded by the *NOT*. For example, in your sample query you might want to exclude all the computers running a version of Windows earlier than Windows XP for upgrade purposes.

Creating a Query

Now that you've gotten your feet wet, put some of these Configuration Manager query elements to use by creating a query. Your test query will search for all computers running Windows XP that have at least 2 GB of free disk space (perhaps so that you can install Microsoft Office 2007 or upgrade to Windows Vista).

As you've seen in previous chapters, you can create a query from a number of locations—for example, you can create or reference a query when you define the membership of a collection, or you can create a status message query in the Status Message Queries node in the Configuration Manager console. The process is essentially the same wherever the query is created. For this example, you'll create a query from the Queries node in the Configuration Manager console. To do so, follow these steps:

1. In the Configuration Manager console, expand the Computer Management node, and then expand the Queries node to view the existing queries.

2. Right-click the Queries node, choose New from the context menu, and then choose Query to run the New Query Wizard.

3. On the General page, type a name for your query. This name can be up to 127 characters, so it can be quite descriptive, as shown in Figure 19-3. You can also select an existing query to copy and modify by clicking Import Query Statement.

4. Type a more detailed description of the query in the Comment text box if desired.

5. In the Collection Limiting section, you can narrow the query's scope by selecting Limit To Collection and then typing or browsing for the collection name. You can also make the query more interactive and therefore more useful by selecting Prompt For Collection, in which case you need to supply the collection name whenever the query runs. If you leave the default Not Collection Limited option selected, the query runs against the entire database, assuming that the administrator executing the query has access to the entire database.

> **Note**   As described in Chapter 17, "Managing Clients Remotely," and Chapter 20, "Configuration Manager 2007 Security," you can create Configuration Manager security rights so that administrators have access to various objects in the database, including specific collections. If an administrator can't access a collection, the query won't run.

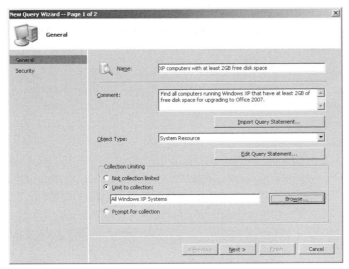

Figure 19-3   The New Query Wizard General page, showing a descriptive query name

6. Select the object type you want to run the query on, and then click Edit Query
    Statement to display the Query Statement Properties dialog box, as shown in
    Figure 19-4. In this case, you'll find the free space logical disk attribute by selecting
    the *System Resource* object.

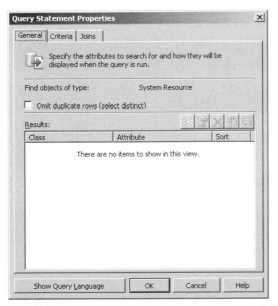

Figure 19-4   The Query Statement Properties dialog box

Part III   Site Database Management

7. On the General tab, you'll define the query results window—that is, the data (the attributes) displayed in the Configuration Manager console when the query is run. To add a class and an attribute, click the New button (the yellow star) to display the Result Properties dialog box, as shown in Figure 19-5.

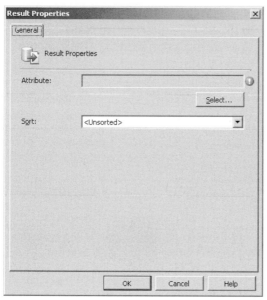

Figure 19-5   The Result Properties dialog box

8. Click Select to display the Select Attribute dialog box, as shown in Figure 19-6, where you define an attribute class and an attribute.

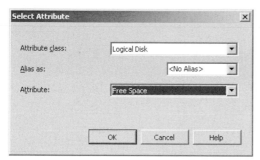

Figure 19-6   The Select Attribute dialog box

9. Type or select an alias if desired. This must be a valid SQL alias. (Refer to your SQL documentation for more information about aliases.) Click OK to save your selections and return to the Result Properties dialog box.

10. Select a sort order if desired, and then click OK to return to the Query Statement Properties dialog box.

11. Repeat steps 7 through 10 to add as many attributes as you want displayed when the query runs. Remember, the query results displayed are based on your query criteria.

12. Click the Criteria tab. In this tab you actually define your query statement. Click the New button to display the Criterion Properties dialog box, as shown in Figure 19-7. Here you will define the specific query elements.

Figure 19-7   The Query Statement Properties dialog box Criterion tab

13. Select a criterion type from the drop-down list. To select an attribute class and an attribute to fill the Where text box, click Select to display the Select Attribute dialog box and choose the appropriate entries from the drop-down lists. In this example, because you're looking for computers with at least 2 GB of free space (2000 MB), your Attribute Class setting is Logical Disk and the Attribute setting is Free Space.

14. Click OK to return to the Criterion Properties dialog box and then select an appropriate operator from the drop-down list. In this case, choose Is Greater Than or Equal To because you want all computers with at least 2 GB of free space.

15. Type a value. If you click Values, Configuration Manager displays the Values dialog box, as shown in Figure 19-8, which lists all the Free Space values currently recorded in the Configuration Manager database. You can select one of these values or type the appropriate value (2000, in this case) in the Value text box and click

OK. Notice that the value is added automatically to the Value text box in the Criterion Properties dialog box.

Note   To keep the values list manageable, Query Builder limits the number of values that are displayed to the first 1000 when you click Values. You can change this default value by making the following registry change on the site server hosting the reporting point role: for the HKEY_Local_Machine_User\Software\Microsoft\SMS\Reporting, create a DWORD value called Values Rowcount. Set Values Rowcount to the number of values you want returned. If you want all values returned, set Values Rowcount to -1 (hexadecimal 0xffffffff). Be aware that modifying this value can cause a decrease in performance on the site server.

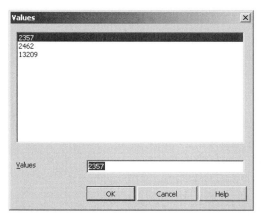

Figure 19-8   The Values dialog box

16. The completed Criterion Properties dialog box is shown in Figure 19-9. Click OK to save your settings and return to the Criteria tab.

17. Repeat steps 12 through 16 to add query statements and use the logical operator buttons listed in the Criteria tab to connect these query statements. The New button, used to add a query statement, creates an *AND* connection by default. Selecting the *AND* operator and clicking the &| button changes the *AND* to an *OR*, and clicking the ! button changes the *AND* to a *NOT*. The two Parentheses buttons are for grouping (or ungrouping) two or more selected statements.

18. Group your statements together using parentheses to define the order of evaluation. For example, Figure 19-10 shows what the query statement would look like if you had not restricted the query to the All Windows XP Systems collection.

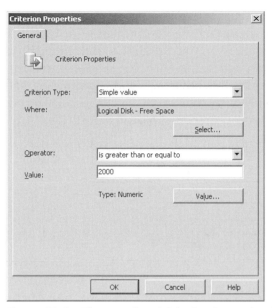

Figure 19-9   The completed Criterion Properties dialog box

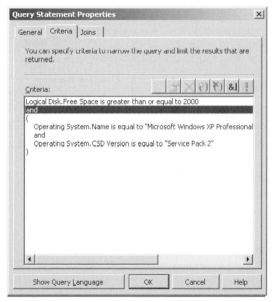

Figure 19-10   A sample query statement using logical operators and parentheses

19. Click OK to close the Query Statement Properties dialog box.

20. Click Next to display the Security page of the New Query Wizard. Use this page to assign the security rights you want specific users and groups to have to all queries, and to this specific query. In Figure 19-11, you can see that while the administrator has full permissions for all queries and for this query, the Helpdesk group only has permissions to Read this query. The Read permission in this case means that members of the Helpdesk can view the query results, but not change the query properties. Chapter 20 discusses the Security properties page in more detail.

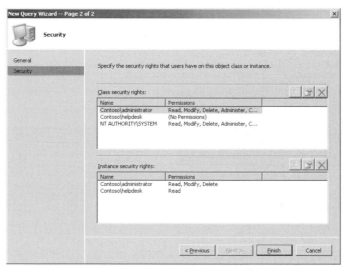

Figure 19-11   The New Query Wizard Security page

Notice that this example also specifies more precisely the service pack version of computers running Windows XP and that the collection is more generic. Notice, too, that the operating system name and service pack are grouped together to ensure that you evaluate clients as those running Windows XP Service Pack 2 instead of clients that are running a version of Windows XP and that might have some other application that has a Service Pack 2 installed.

Modifying a Query

After you create your queries, you might need to make changes to the query to achieve a different set of results. You might also want to create new queries based on existing queries. For example, you might want to create a query like the one you just created for Windows Vista computers.

To modify an existing query, follow these steps:

1. In the Configuration Manager console, expand the Computer Management node, and then expand the Queries node to view the existing queries.

2. Select the query you want to modify in the Queries node.

3. Right-click the query and choose Properties from the context menu to display the properties dialog box, as shown in Figure 19-12. The settings on the General and Security tabs are the same as in the New Query Wizard.

Figure 19-12   The query properties page

4. Make your changes, and then click OK to save the modified query.

To create a new query from an existing query, follow these steps:

1. In the Configuration Manager console, expand the Computer Management node, and then expand the Queries node to view the existing queries.

2. Right-click the Queries node, choose New from the context menu, and then choose Query to run the New Query Wizard.

3. On the General page, type a name for your query. Type a more detailed description of the query in the Comment text box if desired.

4. Click Import Query Statement to display a list of available queries, as shown in Figure 19-13. Select the query whose properties you want to copy, and click OK.

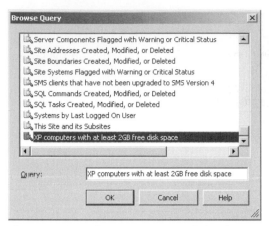

Figure 19-13   The Browse Query dialog box

5.   It will not look like anything has happened when you view the New Query Wizard's General page, as shown in Figure 19-14. However, when you click Edit Query Statement, you see that the properties of the query you chose to import are displayed in the Query Properties dialog box. You can now modify the properties as you need to. For example, as shown in Figure 19-15, the operating system is changed to Windows Vista, and the service pack entry is deleted.

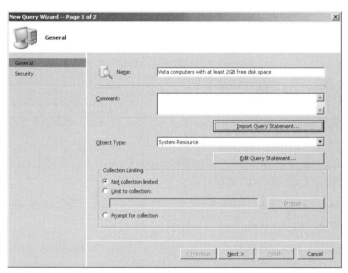

Figure 19-14   The New Query Wizard General page

Figure 19-15   The Criteria tab of the Query Statement dialog box

6. After you make your changes, click OK to close the Query Statement dialog box and return to the New Query Wizard.

7. Click Next to modify the security settings if you need to, and click Finish to save the query.

Combining Attributes

The Joins tab of the Query Statement Properties dialog box, as shown in Figure 19-16, displays the links made between the attribute classes. For the most part, this linking is done automatically by Configuration Manager as you select attributes from different attribute classes. Sometimes, however, because of the nature of the query, you might need to create joins between different attribute classes manually.

To create your own joins to different attribute classes, follow these steps:

1. Click the Joins tab, and click the New button to display the Attribute Class Join Properties dialog box, as shown in Figure 19-17.

2. In the Type drop-down list, select the join type. Four types of attribute class joins exist in Configuration Manager:

   ❑ *Inner*—Displays only matching results

   ❑ *Left*—Displays all results for the base attribute and matching results for the join attribute

❑ *Right*—Displays all results for the join attribute and matching results for the base attribute

❑ *Full*—Displays all results for both the base and the join attributes

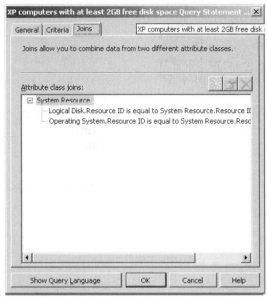

Figure 19-16   The Joins tab

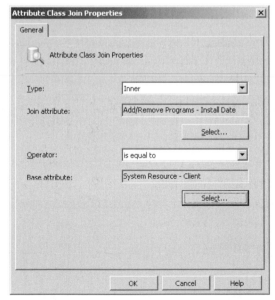

Figure 19-17   The Attribute Class Join Properties dialog box

3. To select an attribute class and attribute for the Join Attribute text box, click Select to display the Select Attribute dialog box, where you can select appropriate entries from the drop-down lists. The attribute you specify will be connected to the base attribute and become a child of the base attribute.

4. Choose an appropriate relational operator from the Operator drop-down list.

5. To fill in the Base Attribute text box, click Select to display the Select Attribute dialog box and choose the appropriate base attribute. The base attribute class is an existing attribute class on which you base the query. Notice that you can't change the base attribute class; you can change only the base attribute.

6. Click OK to close and save your query configuration.

7. Click OK again to save the query.

More Info   Working with joins requires a better-than-good understanding of Configuration Manager attribute classes and attributes. For a complete discussion of WQL, refer to the Configuration Manager 2007 SDK, as mentioned earlier in this chapter.

Viewing the Query Language

Figure 19-18 shows your sample query using WQL. You can display the WQL version of any query by clicking Show Query Language in the General, Criteria, or Join tab of the Query Statement Properties dialog box. As you can see, writing a Configuration Manager query using WQL is not trivial.

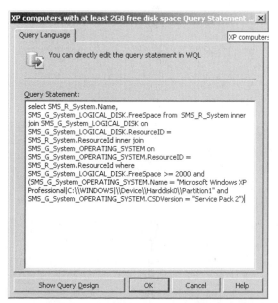

Figure 19-18   The WQL version of your sample query

Creating Prompted Queries

The query you just created will satisfy your immediate quest for information from the Configuration Manager database. However, it's static in the sense that it always checks the database for the same information—that is, all computers running Windows XP that have at least 2 GB of free disk space.

A more useful query would be one that prompts us for value information as the query is being evaluated. For example, instead of hard-coding the value *2000*, it might be more useful to have the query prompt you for the *Size* value. This way, you can use the query repeatedly to find computers with different amounts of free space for different packages and purposes.

To change your query to a prompted query, you need to open it and modify it. You can modify any query by right-clicking it in the Configuration Manager console and choosing Properties from the context menu to display the Query Properties dialog box. Click Edit Query Statement to return to the Query Statement Properties dialog box, click the Criteria tab, and then double-click the element you want to modify to display the Criterion Properties dialog box. In the example in Figure 19-19, you're modifying the Logical Disk:Free Space statement. The criterion type has been changed from Simple Value to Prompted Value.

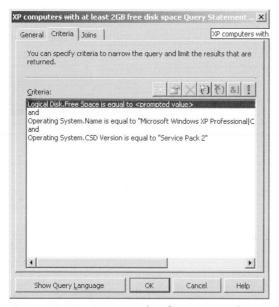

Figure 19-19   An example of a prompted query

Compare this figure with Figure 19-9; the Value field changes to indicate a prompted value. When this query is executed, it first asks you to provide the value for Logical Disk-Free Space.

Executing Queries

Now that you've seen how to create a query, it's time to explore how to run a query. All Configuration Manager queries run through the Configuration Manager console. The results of the queries are also displayed in the Configuration Manager console. To execute your sample query, follow these steps:

1. In the Configuration Manager console, expand the Computer Management node, and then expand the Queries node to view the existing queries.

2. Select the query you want to run in the Queries node.

3. If the query contains any prompts, the Input Query Value dialog box appears, as shown in Figure 19-20. Type the appropriate value and click OK.

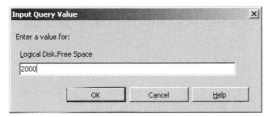

Figure 19-20   The Input Query Value dialog box

4. You can view the results of the query in the results pane of the Configuration Manager console interface, as shown in Figure 19-21. You might need to scroll to the right to see all the result fields you chose to display.

As with other Configuration Manager–managed objects, such as collections, packages, and advertisements, only users who have access to the database objects can run the query. The user must have rights to execute the Configuration Manager console, rights to access the Queries node, and rights to access data in the Configuration Manager database. This permission is assigned by applying object security through the Configuration Manager console or sometimes through the WMI itself. Configuration Manager security is discussed in more detail in Chapter 20.

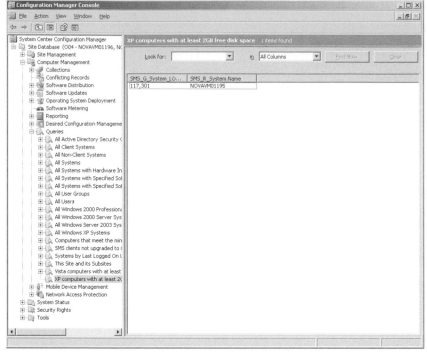

Figure 19-21   The query results

Working with Reports

Configuration Manager contains the same fully integrated reporting tool called the Report Viewer that was introduced with SMS 2003. This tool is accessible through the Configuration Manager console and uses your Web browser as a report viewer. Another companion feature for reporting, first introduced in SMS 2003, is the dashboard. Dashboards are sets of reports that display in grid fashion in a single window.

Configuration Manager provides nearly 300 predefined reports in the following categories:

- Asset Management
- Client Framework
- Desired Configuration Management
- Device Management
- Driver Management

- Hardware

- Network

- Network Access Protection

- Operating System

- SMS Site

- Software

- Software Distribution

- Software Metering

- Software Updates

- SSL Configuration

- Status Messages

- Task Sequence

- Upgrade Assessment

- Users

- Wake On LAN

You can view the list of available reports through the Configuration Manager console or through the Report Viewer. The Report Viewer has a slight advantage in usability as it groups the reports by their categories. However, unlike with SMS 2003, you can filter the console to display the kinds of reports you want to see.

To view the list of available reports through the Configuration Manager console, follow these steps:

1. In the Configuration Manager console, expand the Computer Management node, and navigate to the Reporting node.

2. Expand the Reporting node and select Reports. The complete list of reports available is displayed in the results pane, as shown in Figure 19-22.

3. By default, reports are listed alphabetically. If you want to see the reports grouped by category, click the Category column header in the results pane. The reports are then displayed grouped by category, as shown in Figure 19-23.

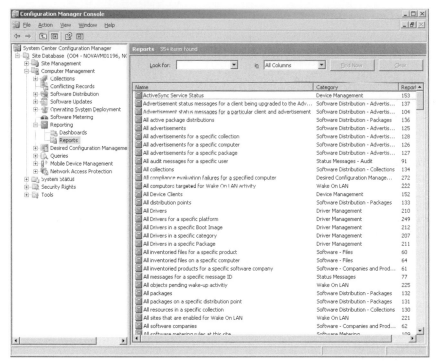

Figure 19-22   The list of reports displayed in the results pane

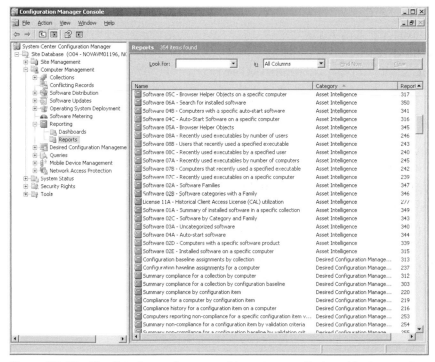

Figure 19-23   The list of reports grouped by category displayed in the results pane

To view the list of available reports through the Reports Viewer, follow these steps:

1. In the Configuration Manager console, expand the Computer Management node, and then expand the Reporting node.

2. Right-click Reporting, and select Run from the context menu. The Report Viewer is displayed in a browser window, as shown in Figure 19-24. Notice that the reports are already nicely grouped by category. To view the reports in any given category, select and expand that category in the Report Viewer.

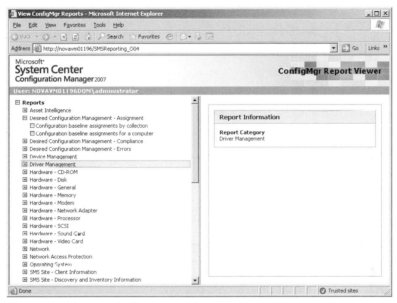

Figure 19-24   The Configuration Manager Report Viewer

You can create your own custom reports either from scratch or by copying and modifying an existing report. The principal element of a Configuration Manager report is an SQL statement that defines the data to be gathered and how the results should be displayed. If you're going to create or modify reports effectively, you need a good working knowledge of SQL. Unfortunately, a discussion of SQL statements and syntax is beyond the scope of this book. However, the Configuration Manager Documentation Library provides several examples of the use of SQL statements in reports.

As with queries, you can use report prompts to make a report more flexible. Reports can also include links to additional sources of data to make them more effective, such as other reports, the Computer Details and Status Message Details pages of the Report Viewer, and a URL that points to any file supported by HTTP.

You can also make reports created outside of Configuration Manager available for viewing. These are called supplemental reports, and although they're primarily Active Server Pages (ASP), they can be any file that can be displayed using Microsoft Internet Explorer 5.0 or later.

> **Note**   Configuration Manager uses the reporting point site system to enable reporting at a site. Chapter 3, "Configuring Site Server Properties and Deploying Site Systems," discusses how to define and configure Configuration Manager site systems. Reports are run against the database of the site in which they were created. However, because of the way Configuration Manager propagates data from child sites to parent sites, you might want to set up reporting points based on where the data resides and on the reporting needs of the administrators at each site. For example, site administrators might want to be able to run reports against the data in their respective sites' databases, but company managers might want more generic reports that run against the collected data at the central site.

Using Reports

As stated earlier, creating or modifying a report requires a good working knowledge of SQL, and that's beyond the scope of this book. However, here are some common elements necessary for every report for you to keep in mind:

- Every new report requires a category. You can choose an existing category or create a new category.

- Report names must be unique within each category.

- Configuration Manager assigns each report a unique ID.

You can configure each report to refresh results automatically according to an interval. You can also configure some reports to display their data as a chart.

> **Note**   To display data as a chart, you must have a licensed copy of Microsoft Office 2000 SP2 Web Components, Microsoft Office XP Web Components, or Microsoft Office 2003 Web Components installed on the reporting point. You can install the Microsoft Office Web Components from the Microsoft Office installation CD.

Creating and Modifying a Report

To create or modify a report, follow these steps:

1. In the Configuration Manager console, expand the Computer Management node, and then expand the Reporting node.

2. Right-click Reports and choose New, then Report, from the context menu to run the New Report Wizard and create a new report. Right-click a specific report and

select Properties to display the report's Properties dialog box and modify that report. For ease of discussion, Figure 19-25 shows the properties of an existing report. The tabs referred to here display the same properties as the wizard pages of the same name.

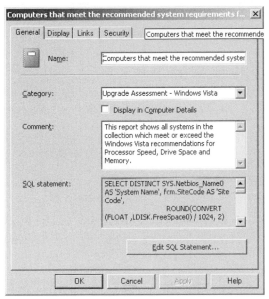

Figure 19-25   The Report Properties dialog box

3. On the General tab, type the name of the report, select a category, and type a descriptive comment. Select the Display In Computer Details option if you want the report to be accessible through the Computer Details page of the Report Viewer.

4. Click Edit SQL Statement to display the Report SQL Statement dialog box, as shown in Figure 19-26. The Views and Columns lists display the available SQL views and columns from the Configuration Manager database that you can select to insert into your SQL statement. Select a view or column and click Insert to add it to your SQL statement. Select a column entry and click Values to see the values associated with that column entry. Type or modify the SQL statement for this report in the SQL Statement text box. Click Prompts to view, add, or modify any prompts included as part of the report.

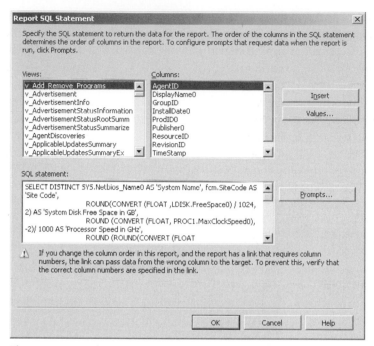

Figure 19-26   The Report SQL Statement dialog box

5. In the Display tab, shown in Figure 19-27, you can specify whether the report results should refresh automatically, the desired refresh interval, and whether you want to display a chart for the report.

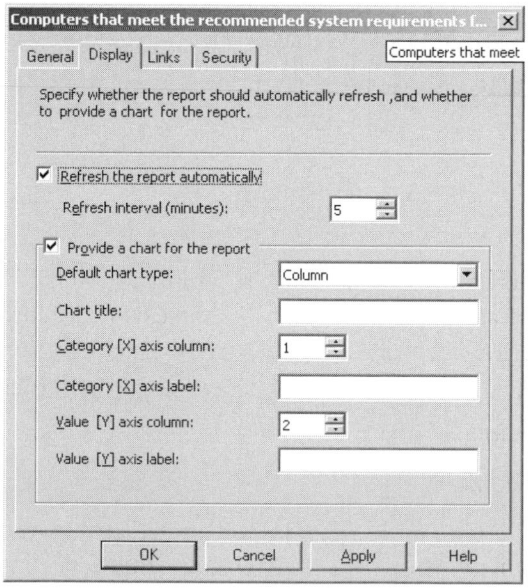

Figure 19-27   The Display tab of the Report Properties dialog box

6. In the Links tab, specify whether you want this report to link to another target (another report, the Computer Details page or Status Messages page in the Report Viewer, or a URL) and the appropriate target information. The target information changes based on your choice of link type and is fairly self-explanatory. The example shown in Figure 19-28 is linking to another report. You select the target report by clicking Select, selecting the report you want from the list, and clicking OK. The selected report is displayed in the Report text box. The Prompts list box displays any prompts associated with the target report and the column in this report that contains the data for each prompt. Click the Properties button (the icon just above the Prompts list box) to specify the appropriate column.

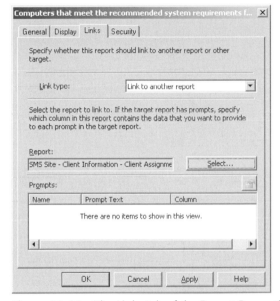

Figure 19-28   The Links tab of the Report Properties dialog box

7. Click OK to save the report.

Copying an Existing Report

If you modify an existing report, there's really no easy way to return the report to its former state. You probably wouldn't want to directly modify the preexisting reports anyway. The better practice is to make a copy of a report that you want to modify and work with the copy instead of the original.

To make a copy of an existing report, follow these steps:

1. In the Configuration Manager console, expand the Computer Management node, then expand the Reporting node, and then navigate to Reports.

2. Right-click the report you want to copy and select Clone from the All Tasks context menu.

3. Type a name for the new report when prompted and click OK.

Importing and Exporting Reports

Configuration Manager gives you the ability to import into your Configuration Manager database report objects that were created in another Configuration Manager site and to export report objects from your site. You can export all your reports or a specific report. Report objects are exported to a Managed Object Format (MOF) file, which is a text-based file. Only report object definitions are exported. This means that when you import the report at another site, the report runs against the other site's database and returns results based on the data contained in that site's database. The exported report doesn't contain any information from the source site's database.

If you export a report that includes links, only links to URLs are preserved. Links to other objects, such as other reports, must be manually reconfigured. When you import reports from another Configuration Manager site, it's recommended that you use a text editor to review the MOF file entries for any report names that might duplicate reports you already have in your site. If you import a report that has the same name in the same category as an existing report in your site, you'll overwrite the existing report with the imported report, so be careful.

To export a report, follow these steps:

1. In the Configuration Manager console, expand the Computer Management node, then expand the Reporting node, and then navigate to Reports.

2. Right-click Reports to export all report objects, or the specific report you want to export, and select Export Objects from the All Tasks context menu.

3. Complete the wizard and click Finish.

To import a report, follow these steps:

1. In the Configuration Manager console, expand the Computer Management node, then expand the Reporting node, and then navigate to Reports.

2. Right-click Reports and select Import Objects from the All Tasks context menu.

3. Complete the wizard and click Finish.

Scheduling a Report

Each report and dashboard that you create has a unique URL associated with it that contains the report ID and the variable names you used to run the report. You can use this URL to schedule a report or dashboard to run at a specified interval. You can see what the URL is by running a Web report and then copying the URL that displays in the Address box of your Web browser, as shown in Figure 19-29. If you use a prompted report, you must provide all the prompt information in order to run the report. Thereafter, the scheduled report always runs using the same prompt values that you provided.

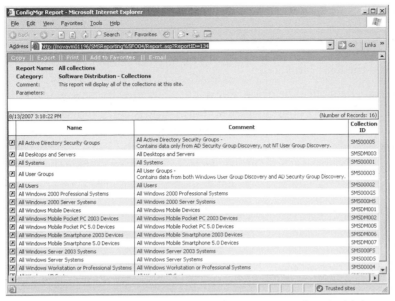

Figure 19-29 A report showing the unique URL associated with it

Schedule the report to run using the Scheduled Tasks feature of your operating system. For example, on a Windows XP computer, follow these steps:

1. Start Scheduled Tasks from the Control Panel.

2. Double-click Add Scheduled Task and click Next.

3. Select Internet Explorer from the Application list and click Next. If it's not listed in the Application list, click Browse, navigate to it, and click Open.

4. Type a task name, select a time interval, and click Next.

5. If prompted, select the time and day you want the task to run and click Next.

6. Type a user name and password that has permission to run the report, and click Next.

7. Select the Open Advanced Properties For This Task When I Click Finish option and click Finish.

8. In the Properties dialog box, insert a space after the entry in the Run text box and type or paste the URL for the report.

9. Click OK to save the new scheduled report.

Note You can use the report URL in several ways to facilitate the viewing of specific reports. For example, you can send the URL as a link in an e-mail or add it to a manager's Web browser as a favorite. The important thing to remember is that whoever launches the link must have at least Read permission for the report.

Running a Report

After all that, running a report is easy. To run a report, follow these steps:

1. In the Configuration Manager console, expand the Computer Management node, and then expand the Reporting node.

2. In the results pane, right-click the report you want to run and choose Run from the context menu. In the Report Information section of the Report Viewer, type any required information. In Figure 19-30, the selected report requires that you specify the computer name. You can type the name or click Values to display a list of computer names in the database. Click Display when you finish to display the report results in your Web browser.

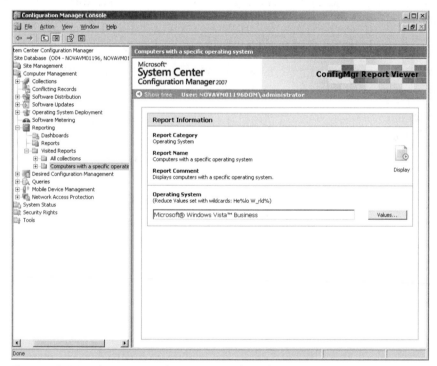

Figure 19-30   The Report Information section of the Report Viewer

---

Note   Although it looks like you can use wildcards, the wildcards you type are used only to reduce the number of values displayed when you click Values. You can't use wildcards to alter the results of the report.

Similarly, if you are viewing the list of reports through the Report Viewer, you can select the report you want to run, type any required report information and click Display to display the results.

Real World   Using Filters to Find a Report

As you saw, Configuration Manager gives you hundreds of reports to choose from. They are grouped by category, but let's face it—you might not know exactly what category the report you want is in. When you create new reports, you can help yourself out quite a lot by creating custom categories that are descriptive. However, don't forget that the new Configuration Manager console makes it easy to search through the objects in the results pane and find something in particular. You can narrow down the list of reports to choose from by using the filter feature in the results pane.

Let's say, for example, that you want to run a report that displays driver information, but you're not quite sure if the report you want exists in the hardware category or, perhaps, in the Task Sequence category. You can type driver in the Look For text box at the top of the results pane, select Category in the In field, and then click Find Now. The results pane, as demonstrated in Figure 19-31, shows a significantly reduced list of reports that you can continue to filter until you find the report you want to run or perhaps clone to meet your specific reporting needs.

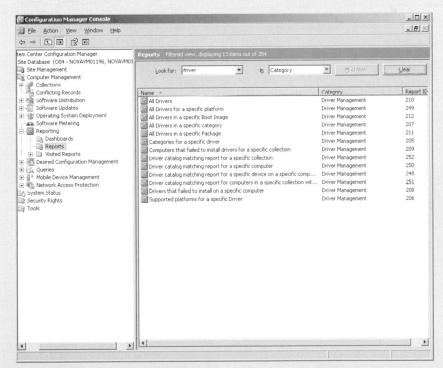

Figure 19-31   A filtered results pane

718 **Part III** Site Database Management

Using Dashboards

A dashboard is a set of reports that you can display in a grid format to facilitate the quick review of one or more specific or related reports. Dashboards can display any report except those that require prompted values. You can view available dashboards through the Configuration Manager console or the Report Viewer in much the same way as you view reports. Configuration Manager creates a unique ID and URL for each dashboard, so you can schedule them, send them out as links, or set them up as a Web browser favorite much the same as you do for reports. However, Configuration Manager doesn't provide any default or predefined dashboards, so you have to set them up first.

Creating a Dashboard

To create a new dashboard, follow these steps:

1. In the Configuration Manager console, expand the Computer Management node, and then expand the Reporting node.

2. Right-click Dashboards, and choose New Dashboard from the context menu to display the New Dashboard Wizard, as shown in Figure 19-32.

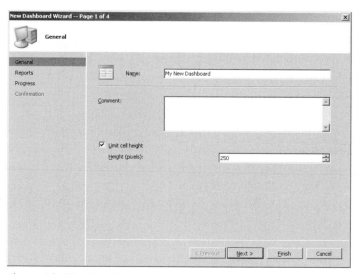

Figure 19-32 The New Dashboard Wizard

3. On the General page, type a name for the dashboard and a descriptive comment. Select the Limit Cell Height option (possibly for larger reports), and type the maximum height in pixels you want for the report.

4. On the Reports page, shown in Figure 19-33, type the number of rows and columns to display in the dashboard and click Set. For example, if you want to display four reports, you might select 2 rows and 2 columns, or 4 rows and 1 column, or 1 row and 4 columns.

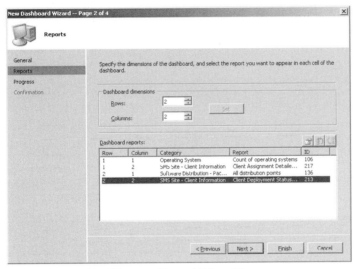

Figure 19-33   The New Dashboard Wizard Reports page

5. In the Dashboard Reports section on the Reports page, identify the report that you want to display in each cell of the dashboard. Select an entry from the Dashboard Reports list, and click the Properties icon (the first of the three icons immediately above the Dashboard Reports section) to display the list of available reports that you can select. You will see only reports to which you have read access and that do not require prompted values.

6. When you select all the reports, click OK.

Running a Dashboard

To run a dashboard from the Configuration Manager console, follow these steps:

1. In the Configuration Manager console, expand the Computer Management node, and then expand the Reporting node.

2. Select Dashboards and select the dashboard you want to run from the list of dashboards in the results pane.

3. Right-click the dashboard and choose Run from the All Tasks context menu. The dashboard appears in your Web browser similar to that shown in Figure 19-34.

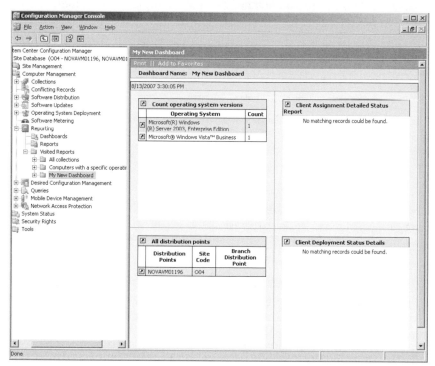

Figure 19-34 The dashboard displayed in a Web browser

To run a dashboard from the Report Viewer, follow these steps:

1. In the Configuration Manager console, expand the Computer Management node, and then expand the Reporting node.

2. Right-click Reporting, and choose Run from the All Tasks context menu to display the Report Viewer.

3. Select and expand Dashboards to see the list of available dashboards, as shown in Figure 19-35.

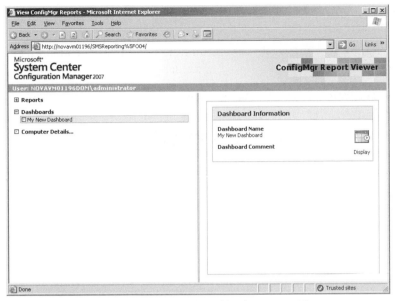

Figure 19-35   The dashboards displayed in the Report Viewer

4. Select the dashboard you want to run and click Display.

Checkpoints for Using Queries and Reports

The main issues you would encounter when running a query or report, aside from creating the wrong query statement, involve security. It's important to remember that for someone to run a query or report, that person must have read access permission to the Configuration Manager console, the node containing the query or report (such as the Queries, Reporting, or Status Message Queries node), and the database information the query is searching for; otherwise, the request will fail. As mentioned, you learn more about security in Chapter 20.

Summary

As you can see, there are several ways to extract and use the data collected and stored in the Configuration Manager database. Throughout this book, you've looked at examples of queries and reports to view information stored in the Configuration Manager database, and now you should have a better understanding of how to create—and improve—them and how to generate queries and reports of your own to view status messages, populate collections, and otherwise search for data based on your specific criteria. Chapter 20 focuses on another database management issue—security.

Chapter 20

Configuration Manager 2007 Security

The secure network

The most secure network is

The one that is down

~*Cathy Moya, Technical Writer, Configuration Manager*

Network management is the janitor of the network operations world. No matter how top secret your company is, you still need to give someone the master keys to come in and empty the wastebaskets. No matter how high the security level in your environment, you still need some way to manage routine change and configuration management, which usually involves handing out admin rights to somebody. If you're reading this, you probably have admin rights. Maybe several people in your organization have admin rights; maybe you even have little groups of admins, each with a specific task. Or maybe it's just you. Whatever your administrative model, you'll have to share those admin rights with System Center Configuration Manager, because it is your janitor. Hand out those rights wisely and carefully. Think about it for a minute—Configuration Manager has the ability to push any program or script to every computer and mobile device in your site, and all child sites, and make it run with administrative rights. That program could be an antivirus, or a virus, a mission-critical finance application, or a back door for an attacker. Failing to adequately secure Configuration Manager is like letting your janitors prop the doors open and invite their friends in to help themselves to your stuff.

This chapter begins with a review of some basic security principals and then looks at your options for Configuration Manager security. The benefits and drawbacks of native and standard security are discussed, including the major certificate infrastructure you might need. Then the focus shifts to the nuts and bolts of Configuration Manager security—WMI security, DCOM security, file and registry permissions, and object security. A section about the types of user accounts that you might need to configure is included. A discussion about how to create custom consoles so you can limit what some of your co-administrators can do in the Configuration Manager console concludes the chapter.

Security Planning and Considerations

The good news about security in Configuration Manager is that even if you didn't think about your security plan before you installed, it's not too late. There are no irrevocable security decisions in Configuration Manager, although there are some that are very inconvenient to change later. It's always best to think about security as you plan your Configuration Manager environment. It's even better to think about your entire network security before you bring in a powerful "janitor" like Configuration Manager.

Basic Security Configurations

If you click all the right buttons and configure Configuration Manager perfectly but forget about the security basics, you are still leaving yourself open for attack. It would be like hiring former NSA workers as your janitors, but neglecting to put locks on the front door. There are many sources for good security fundamentals and many top ten lists about security. Here are the top five things to remember about Configuration Manager:

- **Your administrators are your weakest link.**   Hopefully you already know this. But stop and think for a minute about what a disgruntled administrator can do with Configuration Manager. Configuration Manager makes it easier and faster to manage your Windows computers, or to distribute something nasty to all your computers. Sure, if attackers get access to an account in Domain Admins, there are many nasty things they can do. If they wanted to distribute a root kit to every client, they could create a Group Policy object (if they have the root kit in the handy Windows Installer format.) With Configuration Manager, your disgruntled coworker with right to distribute software can distribute a root kit script to every Configuration Manager client without ever being a member of Domain Admins or even being a local administrator on the client computers. Conduct background checks. Audit what your coadministrators are up to. If you have to fire an administrator, immediately walk him or her out of the building and then go over everything he or she did in the Configuration Manager console. (Later, you'll learn how to check the Configuration Manager audit messages.)

■ **If they can touch it, they can own it.**   In security terms, "to own" a device is to have admin rights and be able to do anything you want to it. If someone can get physical access to your site server, there are all sorts of creative things that can be done to get administrative access—for example, installing keystroke loggers to capture your passwords. If evil-doers can get administrative rights on your site server or database server, it's game over. Anything can be sent to any client in your site. If someone can get administrative rights on any site system role, there are things that could potentially be done to exploit those rights. If you configured your site properly, you can mitigate a lot of the damage that can be done, but the best mitigation is to keep the servers locked up in the first place.

■ **Update, update, update.**   New exploits are being discovered all the time. As you are reading this, someone somewhere is figuring out a way to crack into some system in your environment. Fortunately, new software updates are being written almost as quickly, but they are useless unless you apply them. The good news? You have a janitor that can deploy just about any update to any computer in your organization. Read Chapter 17, "Managing Clients Remotely," for more information about how to use the software updates feature. If you want to tack on an extra layer of security, read Chapter 11, "Distributing Software Packages," about how to use Network Access Protection with Configuration Manager to prevent clients from getting on the network if they don't have critical security updates. You can also read Chapter 10, "Collecting Inventory," about how to get reports about clients that aren't compliant with your security update requirements.

■ **Check out the stuff you import.**   There are a few handy wizards in the Configuration Manager console that let you export your various settings and then import them on the same site or a different site. What happens if you leave one of those files lying around? Attackers can substitute their own settings for the ones that are supposed to be there. When you export something, especially task sequences, set the permissions so everyone can't go in and modify the files. Better yet, keep them on removable media and lock them up.

If someone in the community offers to help you out by writing you a query or exporting a collection definition for you, say thank you and then check out the file before you import it, just to make sure you know what you are getting before you install it.

When you create packages that have source files, Configuration Manager needs to copy those source files from somewhere. If that somewhere can be accessed by someone other than a trusted administrator (and your trusty janitor), that zombie script can be swapped for the real application, and it's game over. Configuration Manager sets access control lists (ACLs) on the files when they are on distribution points, but securing the source location for software distribution, operating system deployment, and software updates is up to you.

- **Don't give out more rights than you absolutely have to.**   This is also known as "the principle of least privilege," giving the minimum required rights to do the job. In Configuration Manager, most of the heavy janitorial work is done by the computer accounts such as the site server computer account. The biggest advantage of using computer accounts is you don't have to manage them. They maintain their own passwords, and no one can watch them type those passwords on a keyboard. You still have to be smart about the accounts. Don't add the site server computer account to the Domain Admins group, even though it would make using Client Push Installation so very convenient. You also have to use accounts to install Configuration Manager and then run the console – do they have to be administrators? The account you use to install Configuration Manager must be a local administrator and a domain user, but not a Domain Admin. The account you use to run the console does not have to be a local administrator (though if it isn't, you have to create your own MMC snap-in instead of using the one that installs with the product). There are a bunch of optional accounts you might need for various features and functions. Don't use one super powerful account for everything. Use passwords for everything. Yes, there are still environments where everybody runs as administrator and no one has passwords. If you take that approach with Configuration Manager, you may as well put the office keys under the front mat.

Real World   Security and Branch Distribution Points

Let's say you have a remote office without any server in it. You think, "Great! I can use Rick's computer as a branch distribution point, and it can serve packages to the other five users in that office!" Sure you can. But if Rick can touch it, then everyone else in the office can probably touch it, too. Are you putting yourself at risk? Not necessarily. Whenever a client downloads a package from a distribution point, before it runs the package, it checks the digital signature on that package. If even one bit has changed, the client will not run the package. That helps prevent Rick from substituting a zombie script for your new word processing program. If you run the package from the distribution point, the client doesn't check the signature. The moral of the story is this: Downloading is the better security choice, especially on branch distribution points. There are a few other things you can do to help make branch distribution points more secure. If possible, don't make Rick's account an administrator on that branch distribution point. If he runs as an ordinary user, it's harder for him to get in and mess with any Configuration Manager components, either accidentally or on purpose. Make sure Rick doesn't turn off his computer when he goes home, and don't let it fall into hibernation. It would be bad if a new software update came out but the people in that office can't install it because Rick was trying to conserve power. Even if you don't have a server in the branch office, consider buying a separate client computer to be the branch distribution point and locking it in a server closet somewhere. There is no substitute for limiting physical access to a computer.

Security Planning

You have two major security questions to answer when you plan for Configuration Manage security:

- Will you use native mode or mixed mode?
- Will you publish to Active Directory Domain Services?

After you answer those major questions, you have two additional security considerations:

- Do you need to configure additional accounts?
- What should your administration model look like?

Native Mode versus Mixed Mode

Native mode uses HTTPS for most (but not all) communication between the Configuration Manager clients and most (but not all) site systems.

Note   Native mode does nothing to secure the communication channel between the site server and site systems, or between the various site systems. If you need to secure those channels, you should implement Internet Protocol security (IPsec).

Native mode uses a Public Key Infrastructure (PKI) to issue certificates from what is assumed to be a secure, trustworthy central authority. Or if not actually a central authority, the clients must in some way be able to trust the certificates presented by the site systems, and vice versa, before they will talk to each other. (If you don't want to get into some of the subtle PKI concepts like rooted trust models and cross-certification, you might want to just nod your head and go with mixed mode for now.) The final major benefit of native mode is that the policies sent down to clients are signed by a special site server signing certificate, which makes it nearly impossible for a bad guy to create his own policy and slip it to your management point.

This is not to imply that mixed mode is not secure. Mixed mode does have some signing going on, but it's a bit more simplistic and uses mostly self-signed certificates, instead of PKI certificates. Some client information is signed in mixed mode. For a side-by-side comparison of native and mixed mode, see "Benefits of Using Native Mode" at *http://technet.microsoft.com/en-us/library/bb632573.aspx.*

Important   Native mode is required if you need to support Internet-based clients. For more information, see Chapter 16, "Managing Clients Across the Internet."

Native mode is definitely the more secure mode, so why would you even consider using mixed mode? For one thing, if you have Windows 2000 clients, they can't do native mode. Regardless of your client base, unless you have an excellent understanding of what PKIs are, and unless you really understand their care and feeding, you probably just don't want to go there. Really. If you don't already have a PKI in your environment, you will have to spend some time and money to set them up properly. And woe to you if you do not set them up properly, because they can leave you even less secure than you would be in mixed mode. For example, if the bad guys can get hold of your root certification authority (CA), then they can just make their own certificates for everything, and Configuration Manager will happily trust them, completely defeating the purpose of the certificates. From a business standpoint, if you don't plan for all of your current and future certificate needs, you might design a PKI that works great for Configuration Manager but won't work for your wireless and 802.1x and your encrypted file system and your code signing. You might even have to rip it all out and start over again, which would be very messy for Configuration Manager. A very practical Configuration Manager consideration is that before you can even complete Setup in native mode, you must create and install a site server signing certificate. You should also really install all of your client and site system certificates before running Setup. If you don't have everything in place, without stepping on a crack, you could wind up with a bunch of clients that can't talk to the site.

Best Practices   If you can't easily create the site server signing certificate and deploy the rest of the required certificates, you really shouldn't choose native mode. Start with standard and go crack some PKI books. You can always change your mode later.

If you start with native mode, can you change back? Yes, but it's not an easy changeover. If you do it wrong, you can leave all of your clients in an unmanaged state. Do not plan to revert from native to mixed mode unless you really need to and have done some very thorough planning. If you still don't believe that it's complicated, see *http://technet.microsoft.com/en-us/library/bb693556.aspx.*

Publishing to Active Directory Domain Services

Should you publish to Active Directory Domain Services? Yes. When you enable publishing, your life as an administrator is easier, and your network is more secure. Some features, such as Network Access Protection, actually require Active Directory publishing. Configuration Manager puts a bunch of information in the Global Catalog, such as where to find trusted management points and what parameters to use for Client Push Installation. If you don't publish to Active Directory, you will have to type in a bunch of parameters for Client Push Installation. Configuration Manager uses a rather interesting system called the trusted root key to figure out which management points are probably trustworthy, assuming the client gets a copy of the trusted root key when you actually install the client components. If your clients can query the global catalog, you don't need to read about the trusted root key or worry about preprovisioning it and managing it.

The main reason you might not publish to Active Directory Domain Services is because it involves extending the schema of the forest where Configuration Manager is installed. In some organizations, the Keepers of the Schema are a cagey bunch who require much process and discussion before they even think about talking to you about maybe perhaps extending the schema two years from next Tuesday.

The other possible reason for not publishing is if the clients can't read the information anyway. Configuration Manager information is published only to the one forest. There is no replication mechanism across forests, so if your site systems are in forest A but all of your clients are in forests B, C, and D, you can publish all you want and the clients will never be able to see it in the global catalog. Also, if you have workgroup clients, they cannot query the global catalog.

For more information, see "Decide If You Should Extend the Active Directory Schema" at *http://technet.microsoft.com/en-us/library/bb694066.aspx.*

Configuring Additional Accounts

Do you have to configure additional accounts? Like most things in Configuration Manager, it depends. The only absolutely required account is the site server computer account, represented as Local System if the computer is talking to itself and as computername$ if it is talking to a resource on the network.

Note   Local System is required to run the Configuration Manager services. Changing the service configuration is not supported.

As for the rest of the accounts, they are required only for specific circumstances. For example, you need a Client Push Installation account only if you are using Client Push Installation—maybe. You can also use the site system computer account instead of creating a separate user account.

There is more discussion later in the chapter about the accounts and when you might need them. You should refer to that section and, if you need additional accounts, plan for them before deploying the features that require them. Also plan for password management of the accounts. For example, if your security policy requires you to change all account passwords every 45 days, you must have a plan to change the service accounts, or Configuration Manager operations will fail.

Administration Models

Who else needs access to the Configuration Manager console? In a smaller environment, you might be the only administrator, but even then you should have someone to back you up when you go on vacation. (And if you are the only administrator, you probably need a vacation!) How will you assign rights to your backup? If you are in a larger organization, each administrator might have different responsibilities. For example, one admin might do all of the packaging, while another handles software updates, and a totally different person does the operating system deployment. Do you have more than one site? Will one person or team administer all of the sites, or will there be regional administrators? It's best to plan for an administrative model that supports your business practices, and then figure out how to set the permissions and rights in Configuration Manager to support that model. The rights and permissions you have available to restrict access to the Configuration Manager console are discussed later in the chapter.

Privacy Planning

Privacy planning is something you should care about. How much you care may depend on where and what you plan to do with Configuration Manager. Some countries take privacy very seriously. If you collect any kind of personally identifiable information at all, you'd better know what that information is, how long you plan to keep it, how to safely get rid of it, and how you plan to protect it.

Does Configuration Manager collect personally identifiable information? It depends. Discovery collects IP addresses in the Data Discovery Record, but maybe you didn't turn on discovery. Besides, is that IP address personally identifiable? It depends. If you remotely control a client, do you have to notify that client first? Maybe. What sort of information are you collecting in inventory and what might be considered personally identifiable?

This book is no substitute for a lawyer with a good understanding of privacy law in your jurisdiction. If you have a legal expert in your company, talk to that person. Then read the Configuration Manager Documentation Library (*http://technet.microsoft.com /en-us/library/bb694249.aspx*) and note the privacy considerations for each feature. Lawyers really like to have a chance to think about these things before a lawsuit or law enforcement arrives, so do your homework.

Real World   Who's Watching?

A major defense contractor was in the middle of deploying a network management product. Somewhere along the way, the Human Resources department realized that the product included the ability to remotely control computers. HR was so concerned about workers viewing employees working on secret projects that the project was stopped completely for several weeks while the problem was analyzed. In the end, HR allowed the deployment to continue, but all administrators had to have security clearance. The moral of the story is, involve HR and legal early on in the planning phase. They don't like surprises, and you won't like the consequences of surprising them.

Certificates and PKI Security

If you want to use Configuration Manager native mode, you must use certificates issued by a PKI. Configuration Manager doesn't care what kind of PKI you use, or how you issue the certificates, or what your revocation policy is, if any. Configuration Manager is a consumer of the PKI services but does not dictate anything about the PKI implementation. Most of the certificates that Configuration Manager uses are based on standard templates that should be easily available. The exception is the site server signing certificate, which has some very specific requirements.

Providing a total solution to your PKI implementation to support Configuration Manager native mode is outside the scope of this book. In fact, it's outside the scope of the Configuration Manager Documentation Library. In the Configuration Manager Documentation Library you will find a topic called "Step-by-Step Example Deployment of the PKI Certificates Required for Configuration Manager Native Mode" at *http://technet.microsoft.com/en-us/library/bb694035.aspx*. If you want to play with native mode in a lab, and if you have a copy of Windows Server 2003 Enterprise Edition along with a spare member server and client, you can use the step-by-step to walk you through a proof of concept. The step-by-step is not intended to be used as your actual production PKI solution. There are many variables about doing a proper PKI implementation, and a proof of concept in a lab doesn't help you with those variables. For some configurations, there are no shortcuts. Either take the time to really learn about PKIs and deploy one properly, hire a consultant to do it for you, or don't plan on using native mode.

Assuming you already understand the basics of PKIs, this chapter gives you an overview of the certificates required by Configuration Manager. For the recipe to create these certificates, see "Certificate Requirements for Native Mode" at *http://technet.microsoft.com /en-us/library/bb680733.aspx*, but be aware that this topic assumes you know enough about your particular brand of PKI to create your own certificates.

Site Server Signing Certificate

In Native mode, to provide an extra level of protection, the site server signs policies before it sends them to the management point. When the client requests a policy from the management point, it validates the signature using the public key copy of the certificate that you have somehow deployed to the clients. (For more information, see "Decide How to Deploy the Site Server Signing Certificate to Clients (Native Mode)" at *http://technet.microsoft.com/en-us/library/bb694140.aspx*.) If an attacker has tampered with the policy, the signature won't match and the client discards the policy. Even if attackers manage to create a bogus management point and somehow manage to get your client to trust it, they would still have to compromise your PKI to create a site server signing certificate to sign the policies. There are probably much easier ways to attack your network that don't involve hacking the PKI and then figuring out how to create a site server signing certificate.

The site server signing certificate is used for document signing, and the Enhanced Key Usage value must contain Document Signing (1.3.6.1.4.1.311.10.3.12). But wait, there's more. The Subject Name field of the certificate must be The site code of this site server is <XXX>. XXX is the three-character site code for the site server. You must type the string exactly. Even if you are configuring a non-English site server, you must type the string in English.

For the other certificates you need for native mode, if you are using a Microsoft PKI, you can start with a template. With the site server signing certificate, there is no default template for document signing. If your PKI is installed on Windows Server 2003 Enterprise Edition, you can use any version 2 template, add document signing, and remove anything else. If your PKI is not installed on Windows Server 2003 Enterprise Edition, Configuration Manager doesn't really care how you get the certificate, so it's up to you to figure out how to make a certificate that fits the requirements.

If you are running Setup and choose native mode, Configuration Manager validates the site server signing certificate before completing Setup. If you don't have a valid site server signing certificate, you must install in mixed mode and then change later. You can change from mixed to native mode at any time, as long as you have the site server signing certificate ready to be validated.

Important   The site server signing certificate is the only certificate validated by Configuration Manager before changing to native mode. You should deploy the other certificates before changing, but if you don't, Configuration Manager won't stop you.

Client and Site System Certificates

One of the main features of native mode is the ability for clients to authenticate their site systems, and site systems to authenticate the clients before conducting Configuration Manager business, so all of your clients and most of your site systems require certificates for authentication.

Client Certificates

Your client certificates are fairly simple. If you have a Microsoft PKI, you can use either the Computer or Workstation template. If you use some other flavor of PKI, make sure the Enhanced Key Usage value contains Client Authentication (1.3.6.1.5.5.7.3.2). If your clients already have a certificate for authentication, Configuration Manager can probably use your existing certificate.

Note If you have more than one client authentication certificate, Configuration Manager can easily become confused. On the site properties where you configure native mode, you can provide the criteria you want Configuration Manager to use when choosing between multiple client authentication certificates, but if multiple certificates meet the criteria, you have to tell Configuration Manager what to do. By default, Configuration Manager doesn't pick any certificate, which means your clients will be unmanaged until you make it so just one certificate matches. If you change the default, Configuration Manager will randomly pick one certificate that matches. If all of the possible client authentication certificates will authenticate the client to the management point, everything will be fine. If, however, your client has two certificates issued by different CAs, and the management point trusts only one of those CAs, you have to hope that Configuration Manager picks the certificate that the management point trusts, or your client cannot be managed.

Best Practices If you are in mixed mode and planning to change to native mode, you should run the Configuration Manager Native Mode Readiness Tool first to see whether your clients are ready. For more information, see the article "How to Determine if Client Computers are Ready for Native Mode" at *http://technet.microsoft.com/en-us/library/bb680986.aspx*.

Certificates are supposed to uniquely identify the clients. Duplicating certificates is bad. If you use imaging software, remove the client authentication certificates first, or Configuration Manager will be very confused trying to deal with multiple iterations of the same client.

By the way, your management point and state migration point must have client authentication certificates, even if you never plan to install the Configuration Manager client on them.

Site System Certificates

The client has to verify that it is talking to a valid site system, and then the client and site system establish an encrypted communication channel over Secure Socket Layer (SSL) for most of their communication. SSL? The same protocol you use for things like Internet banking? Yes. So an easy way to (mostly) remember which site systems need Web server certificates for SSL is to remember which site systems need IIS. Here is the list of site systems that need Web server certificates.

- Management point

- Proxy management point

- Distribution point

- Software update point

- State migration point

The enhanced key usage must contain Server Authentication (1.3.6.1.5.5.7.3.1). You must put this certificate in the personal store in the computer certificate store.

The thing that can be a bit tricky about your site system certificates is the name. If you are using this site system to support Internet-based clients, you might have specific requirements to make the Subject Name or Subject Alternative Name the Internet or intranet Fully Qualified Domain Name (FQDN.) For more information, see Chapter 16, "Managing Clients Across the Internet."

Real World   Is Everything Encrypted in Native Mode?

Even if you configure native mode, some communication is never encrypted. When a client communicates with a fallback status point, the communication is never encrypted because the whole point of a fallback status point is to let native mode clients send status messages when their certificates aren't working. (Fallback status points are also useful for mixed mode, but they were primarily designed to help native mode clients.)

When clients communicate with the server locator point, the communication is never encrypted. Clients always access the server locator point anonymously, although for native mode clients you have to specifically enable the Allow HTTP Communication For Roaming And Site Assignment option to allow the unencrypted communication. The server locator point doesn't care about authentication clients because it is just handing them pointers to Configuration Manager services. If you are concerned about clients talking to unauthenticated server locator points, you should extend Active Directory Domain Services so clients have a more secure

735 Chapter 20 Configuration Manager 2007 Security 735

way to find Configuration Manager services. For more information, see "Determine If You Need a Server Locator Point for Configuration Manager Clients" at *http://technet.microsoft.com/en-us/library/bb693467.aspx*.

Clients might also communicate with a distribution point without encryption. If you configure an advertisement to run from the distribution point, the connection is never encrypted. If the distribution point is a branch distribution point, the connection is never encrypted, even though you always download packages before running them. If you enabled the distribution point for BITS, it is possible that the client will make an encrypted connection using HTTPS, but it is not guaranteed. This is because when you enable a distribution point for BITS in native mode, you have one virtual directory that requires certificate authentication, but you have a fallback virtual directory that uses Windows authentication, not certificates. When the client requests a distribution point, the cert and the nocert virtual directories are returned as though they are separate distribution points and so the client picks randomly between them. If the client picks the cert directory, and if the certificates are all validated, then communication is encrypted. If the client picks the nocert directory, or if the certificate validation fails for some reason, the client can still download the package over HTTP and BITS, but the connection is not encrypted.

If a client from a native mode site roams to a Mixed mode site, you have to decide whether you want the roaming client to communicate without encryption when contacting the management point and distribution point in the resident site. It's less secure but can save you network bandwidth. If you do not enable Allow HTTP Communication For Roaming And Site Assignment, the client will have to go back to the assigned site for content location requests and to access packages.

Mobile Device Clients

Mobile device clients can use native mode, just like client computers. Also just like client computers, the mobile device client must have a copy of the site server signing certificate to validate policy signatures.

Unlike client computers, however, you don't issue a computer authentication certificate to the mobile device because the device doesn't really have a security context. Instead, for mobile device clients, you issue a mobile device user certificate and set the Enhanced Key Usage for User Authentication.

Like client computers, mobile device clients must have some way to validate the certificate chain, but on mobile devices, you install the intermediate and root CAs on the client.

For more information, see "About Native Mode Certificates for Mobile Device Clients" at *http://technet.microsoft.com/en-us/library/bb693603.aspx*.

Operating System Deployment Certificates

Operating system deployment presents an interesting challenge in native mode. According to the rules of native mode, most site systems won't talk to a client unless it has a valid client authentication certificate. If your computer is booting from the network adapter and has no operating system, how can it have a certificate? Or if the computers are booting from task sequence media, how can they present uniquely identifiable certificates? They can't. However, Configuration Manager has a workaround in native mode to support these clients. When the developers created the workaround, they called it "rent-a-cert" and that actually helps describe the concept.

When you create a PXE service point in native mode, you have to create a special client authentication certificate that has a private key in it and import that certificate on the PXE service point. The PXE service point rents, well, freely loans, the same certificate to every client. When you create bootable task sequence media in native mode, you import that client authentication certificate (with the private key) when you create the bootable media. Every computer that boots from that bootable media uses the same certificate. In both scenarios, you can and should apply a password so that only authorized users can complete the operating system deployment. You also need to secure the PXE service point and the bootable media because if attackers get hold of them, they can pretend to be a valid client, and management points will trust them. If you find out that these special client authentication certificates are compromised, you should block the certificate to prevent it from being used again.

For more information about creating the certificates for operating system deployment, see "How to Manage Native Mode Certificates and Operating System Deployment" at *http://technet.microsoft.com/en-us/library/bb633147.aspx*. For more information about blocking certificates, see "How to Block Configuration Manager Clients" at *http://technet.microsoft.com/en-us/library/bb694107.aspx*.

Note   When a client doesn't have an operating system yet, it can't figure out which root CAs to trust, so you set the trusted root CA on the site server properties in native mode and Configuration Manager tells the clients which CAs to trust.

Deploying the Certificates

If you don't know much about PKI, this is probably where you get very frustrated. Configuration Manager doesn't care how you deploy the certificates. If you have a Microsoft PKI and an Enterprise CA, you can leverage Active Directory Domain Services to do some automatic enrollment, but that is outside the scope of this book. With other PKI scenarios, you might do Web enrollment or some sort of manual enrollment. You have to figure out how to get the right certificates to the right places, and then you can flip the switch to start native mode.

Security Controls in Configuration Manager

Defense in depth is always an important part of security. In addition to having a firewall to protect the perimeter of your network, run antivirus software, antispyware, and possibly other types of intrusion detection software. Configuration Manager also benefits from a defense in-depth approach.

Network Security Controls

All of your basic network fortifications help protect Configuration Manager, such as Active Directory authentication, Group Policy, DCOM, and IPsec. Next, Configuration Manager uses access controls like the NTFS file permissions and the registry permissions to help protect your Configuration Manager deployment. Configuration Manager relies on security granted to the Windows Management Instrumentation (WMI) layer to access the Systems Management Server (SMS) Provider. Finally, you must have permissions granted to Configuration Manager objects in the site database before you can manage them.

Firewalls

You should be running some sort of firewall, either a hardware device or a software-based firewall such as Microsoft Internet Security and Acceleration (ISA). Of course, just having a firewall isn't enough—you have to know how to configure it properly. Usually with firewalls you deny all traffic except for specific ports. Configuring your firewall is especially important if you plan to use the Internet-based client feature of Configuration Manager because you need to allow some traffic through to support the Configuration Manager site roles. For more information about supporting Internet-based clients, see Chapter 16, "Managing Clients Across the Internet." For more information about the ports required for Configuration Manager, see "Ports Used by Configuration Manager" at *http://technet.microsoft.com/en-us/library/bb632618.aspx.*

IPsec

Whether you use Configuration Manager native mode or mixed mode, Configuration Manager does not encrypt any traffic between the site server and site systems, or between two sites in a hierarchy. You should use IPsec to encrypt and sign those communications. Configuration Manager has no specific requirements for how to use IPsec to help secure the connection. For some recommendations, see "Implementing IPsec in Configuration Manager 2007" at *http://technet.microsoft.com/en-us/library/bb632851.aspx.*

DCOM

Distributed Component Object Model (DCOM) is technology that supports communication among objects on different computers. Most of the time, DCOM is something you care about only if you are a programmer and want to create a distributed application. However, as the Configuration Manager administrator, you need to know a few basic things about DCOM. (If you are actually a programmer, you can skip this part because this will be very oversimplified.)

The Component Object Model (COM) gives you one way to access the chunks of code tucked away in the dynamic link libraries (files with .dll extensions). For example, maybe you want to open a file. If you know the chunk of code in the library, you can ask for it. If you don't know, you can use COM to tell you which chunks of code are available. This is all well and good on the same computer, but when you are running something on computer A and need to run a chunk of code in a DLL on Computer B, it's a good idea to have some security controlling what you can actually do on that remote computer.

Starting with Windows XP Service Pack 2 and continuing to Windows Server 2003 Service Pack 1, the security on running DCOM was made more granular so it could be more restrictive. By default, Everyone can have Local Launch and Local Activation, but only Administrators can have Remote Launch and Remote Activation. If you are running the Configuration Manager console on the computer where the SMS Provider is installed, you are local and everything runs with no problem. When you want to run the Configuration Manager console somewhere other than the computer where the SMS Provider is installed, you are remote. If you are an administrator on the SMS Provider computer, the console will work, but you should not go around making all the admins in your organization local administrators on the SMS Provider, because they don't need all those rights. Instead, you grant Remote Activation permissions to the user running the console. The best way to do this is to grant Remote Activation to the SMS Admins group because they should have rights to run the console anyway. You must do this on the site server, and if you installed the SMS Provider anywhere except the site server, you have to do it on the SMS Provider computer, too. For more information, see "How to Configure DCOM Permissions for Configuration Manager Console Connections" at *http://technet.microsoft.com/en-us/library/bb633148.aspx.*

Is there risk in opening these DCOM permissions? Well, yes. If you grant SMS Admins the Remote Activation permission, they can launch DCOM attacks against the SMS Provide computer. But this goes back to the first rule in basic security considerations: Your administrators are your weakest link. Either trust them enough to give them access to the console (and check them out first) or send them off to dust the server racks. Granting them Remote Activation is much better than making them full administrators on the SMS Provider computer.

WMI Security

Windows Management Instrumentation (WMI) is Microsoft's version of Web Based Enterprise Management (WBEM), an industry-standard way to capture and use management information about devices. If you know even a little bit about scripting, WMI gives you an easy way to access lots of information. If you actually know something about WMI, skip to the last paragraph in this section.

If you have absolutely no clue about what WMI does but want an analogy, think for a minute about that cultural phenomenon, *Star Trek*. It portrayed a piece of fiction called the universal translator that makes it possible for every species to talk to every other species. Convenient, right? Well, so is WMI, except instead of being a fictional point-to-point translator, WMI gives you a common place to store information (the WMI repository) and a common way to pull that information out again when you need it. Providers put information into the repository and pull it out again, but you don't have to know how to write or use a provider. You just use one of several common scripting languages to access all of that data. The providers are sort of translating all of that in the background.

You've probably been using WMI data from WMI providers without knowing it for years. If you use the Windows Event Log or performance counters, the Event Log Provider and the Performance Counter Provider were putting information in the WMI repository and pulling it out again when an application or script requested it. If you want to, you can write a script that can retrieve information from the WMI repository. Go see the WMI Scripting Primer at *http://www.microsoft.com/technet/scriptcenter/guide/sas_wmi_overview.mspx?mfr=true*.

Configuration Manager has a provider called the SMS Provider. (It's still SMS because changing it might have broken a lot of scripts people had already written.) The SMS Provider goes through WMI to access the site database. There is security on WMI, so administrators can ask WMI to hand over information, but not just anybody else can. If you don't want to make everyone in your organization an administrator, you can just give each person a few WMI permissions, and he or she will have what is needed to run the Configuration Manager console (though object rights, as described later, are still needed).

The two WMI permissions required to access the SMS Provider are Enable Account and Remote Enable. Enable Account is basically read access to the WMI namespace. Remote Enable lets you access WMI from a remote computer. Just like DCOM, when you want to run the console on a computer that isn't running the SMS Provider, you need some additional permissions—in this case, Remote Enable. Enable Account and Remote Enable permissions are automatically granted to the SMS Admins group. (If you really don't like that group, you could try making your own group and granting it Enable Account and Remote Enable, but using SMS Admins is much, much simpler.)

Group Policy

Group Policy provides centralized management of many computer settings. You can use Group Policy to lock down computers, such as deciding who can access a computer from the network and which services are permitted to run. While Group Policy is an important part of hardening operating systems to help provide greater security, some security settings will prevent Configuration Manager from running. Remember, Configuration Manager is your janitor. If you don't let the janitor in, the trash cans start overflowing. If you prevent users from accessing distribution points from the network, then they won't be able to download packages.

Real World   So Secure It Doesn't Work

In the previous version of Configuration Manager, SMS, all administrative functions were performed by a special user account that ran the SMS Executive service. At one company, the domain administrators didn't have a good working relationship with the SMS administrators. The domain administrators were concerned about SMS having so much power in the network so they restricted its access to just the site server computer. SMS broke, and it took the SMS administrators a while to figure it out.

Well-meaning security auditors might try to restrict the access that Configuration Manager has in your environment. Windows Server has a Security Configuration Wizard (SCW) that configures services, ports, registry settings, and some security policy settings to help reduce the attack surface on the server. If you run SCW on your Configuration Manager site systems, use the Configuration Manager template in the Configuration Manager Toolkit. The Configuration Manager template has been designed to look for the site system roles required by Configuration Manager and to enable settings required by the site system role that might have been disabled by other templates in SCW. However, if you make additional security configuration changes outside of SCW, for example, preventing the site server computer account from accessing site systems across the network, Configuration Manager might fail. Test your security configuration changes in a lab before deploying them in production. If Configuration Manager stops working, think about the security required for the failed operation and think about any recent security changes you might have made.

Windows auditing can be a helpful troubleshooting tool. Audit for failed security access to see whether your changes have prevented Configuration Manager components from completing their tasks.

Access Control Lists

You are probably already familiar with Access Control Lists (ACLs) used to assign permissions to file folders on NTFS partitions and to registry keys. Configuration Manager requires NTFS partitions for most site operations, and even though a few components could be installed on FAT32, such as the site server database, you shouldn't ever think about using FAT32 for one minute.

When you install Configuration Manager from scratch, Setup creates the installation directory, assigns the NTFS permissions to all of the files and folders, creates the registry keys, and assigns registry permissions. If you do a site reset of a site that was set up from scratch, Configuration Manager also resets all of the permissions back to the installation defaults. However, if you upgrade a Configuration Manager site, Setup doesn't touch your existing permissions because it has no way of knowing what you did and doesn't want to mess them up. When you reset a site that was upgraded from a previous version, the site reset does not reset the permissions to the installation default. This can be both good and bad: If you made a conscious change and everything is working properly, it's good not to have Configuration Manager mess up your work. If you made some bad permission changes, a site reset won't get you out of them.

When you install a site system role, Configuration Manager also sets the ACLs on the folders, files, and registry keys for the site system role. For example, when you install the management point role, Configuration Manager automatically creates the SMS_CCM directory and the CCM registry key and assigns all of the permissions. If you remove the role and then reassign it to the same site system, Configuration Manager sets the permissions back to the default permissions.

If you look at the default installation permissions, usually just Administrator and Local System have access to most files and registry keys. The Site System to Site Server connection group also has permissions in several places to allow Configuration Manager to transfer data from the site system back to the site server. Ordinary users sometimes have permissions because they or their computers transfer data to site systems such as inventory and status messages.

Important   Like all Microsoft products these days, Configuration Manager had a pretty thorough security review before it was released. Even if you think it's a little odd to give users permissions in some places, it really is required for Configuration Manager to function, and it wasn't determined to be a security risk. If you're concerned, you can try to restrict who has the client components installed. And hey, one of the best ways to make sure you have only trustworthy clients in your site is to use native mode. Of course, that assumes that you have trustworthy PKI installed and know how to issue certificates only to trustworthy clients. Whether you are in native mode or mixed mode, you probably don't want to be changing the default permissions to make them more or less restrictive. Making them less restrictive could open you to attacks. Making them more restrictive might stop Configuration Manager from running and is not supported.

Auditing

Trust but verify. Sure, there is no way to protect against a disgruntled administrator, but you can sure as heck watch what he or she is up to. Auditing is the way to keep tabs on what the other administrators are doing in the Configuration Manager console.

There are two precreated queries for viewing all audit messages under the Status Message Queries node: All Audit Status Messages for a Specific User and All Audit Status Messages from a Specific Site. You can also create your own query for audit messages using the following criteria:

- Attribute class is Status message.
- Attribute is Message type.
- Message type = 768.

Audit messages show when objects are created, deleted, or modified; when configurations are changed; when security rights are changed; and when remote tools activity is initiated. To see specific types of audit status messages, you might find the following reports to be helpful:

- Advertisements Created, Modified, or Deleted
- Packages Created, Modified, or Deleted
- Programs Created, Modified, or Deleted
- Client Component Configuration Changes
- Remote Tools Activity
- Security Rights Created, Modified, or Deleted
- Server Component Configuration Changes
- SQL Commands Created, Modified, or Deleted

> **Important**   By default, the user that runs Setup has the right to delete status messages, including audit messages. You should remove the right to delete from all console users and then check periodically to make sure no one has delete rights. Even if users grant themselves the right to delete status messages, delete messages to cover their tracks, and then remove the delete right, it leaves a status message that they cannot delete after they remove their rights.

Configuration Manager Object Security

Anything created in the Configuration Manager console is an object, such as packages, software update deployments, task sequences, and status messages. If you have rights, you can do things to objects, like read them, modify them, and delete them.

> **Important**   Granting object security rights is not enough. You must also make sure the user has WMI and DCOM permissions, as described earlier in this chapter.

Configuration Manager object rights are assigned in the Configuration Manager console under the Security Rights node. You can view the assigned rights in two ways: by user or by security rights. You see the same information in both views, but if you have lots and lots of objects and you want to see what rights Ben has, for example, it's easier to look at the Users node, as shown in Figure 20-1.

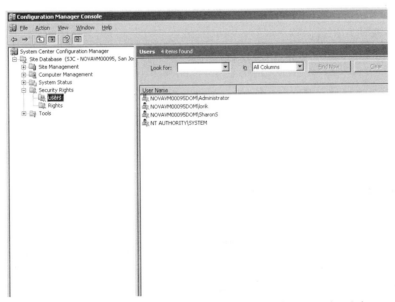

Figure 20-1   The Users node for setting and viewing security rights

On the other hand, if you want to see all of the classes and instances, you can click the Rights node, as shown in Figure 20-2. You can sort by clicking the column headings or use the Look For filter at the top of the page.

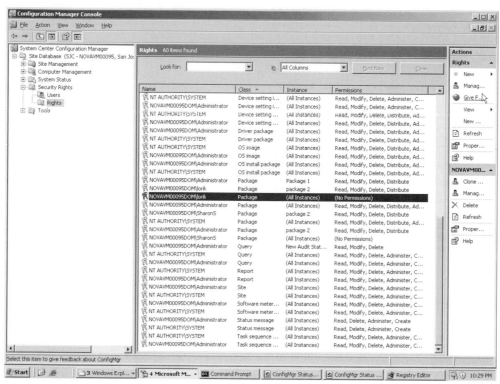

Figure 20-2   The Rights node for setting and viewing security rights

Classes and Instances

When referring to types of objects, we call them classes. If you have Modify rights to the package class, then you can modify any package created in that site. Each package in the site is called an instance. You might have the Modify right for the Word 2007 package but not the Excel 2007 package.

When you assign rights to a class for a user, the user automatically gets all rights to all instances in that class. You can go back and remove rights from a particular instance, but if any new instances are created, the user inherits the class rights on the instance. If you want a user to have rights only to specific instances, assign the rights instance by instance. If you do this, the user will appear in the console as having no permission on the class, but that's how it is supposed to look when you have rights only to instances and not the whole class.

Common Object Rights

There are eight common rights that apply to several classes and instances, as described in Table 20-1.

Table 20-1   Common Configuration Manager Object Rights

Right	Description
Administer	Lets you grant or remove rights on the object. This is similar to the NTFS Change Permissions. Just like Change Permissions in NTFS, Administer just gives someone the right to change the permissions but does not automatically give them all of the permissions.
	When you grant the Administer right, the ConfigMgr User Wizard automatically grants Delete, Modify, and Read to the class.
Create	Lets you create an instance. For example, if you have Create rights to the package class, you can create a new package.
Delegate	If you have Administer rights, you can grant any right to an object, even if you don't have that right. With Delegate, if you don't already have the right, you can't pass it along. For example, if you have Modify and Delegate on the Word 2007 package, you can give your friends Modify and Delegate rights on that package, too. Just remember that Modify and Delegate won't help them if they don't have the WMI and DCOM permission they need to use a remote console.
Delete	Pretty obvious; however, there is one twist: If you want to delete an advertisement, you must have a bunch of rights in addition to Delete. If you want to delete the Word 2007 advertisement for the Word 2007 package that goes to the Bldg 44 collection, to delete the Word 2007 advertisement, you must have Advertise rights on the Bldg 44 collection, Read rights on the Word 2007 package, and Delete rights on the Word 2007 advertisement.
Distribute	Lets you put the object on a distribution point. This right applies only to objects that can be sent to distribution points, such as packages and configuration items, but not to objects like queries or reports. You must also have Read and Modify rights to distribute a package.
Manage Folders	Folders are not treated as objects unto themselves. Instead, having a folder is an organizing tool included with some objects. If you have Manage Folders, you can create, modify, and delete the folders under the node.
Modify	Lets you change an object. There are two objects that cannot be modified for security reasons: status messages and computer associations used in operating system deployment with a state migration point. If you could modify status messages, you could change auditing information. If you could change computer associations, you could redirect one user's saved user state to a different computer.
Read	Lets you view an object. Read is required for most other rights because if you can't see it, you probably can't do anything else to it.

Special Object Rights

There are a few rights that apply only to specific objects. Collections and site objects are slightly unusual objects and have very specific rights. Operating system deployment requires some extra granularity of rights to help protect sensitive data. You also need a special right to apply network access protection policy to a configuration item.

Special Rights on Collection Objects

Collections have several special object rights. If you have Delete rights on the Collection class, you can delete any collection, but if you want to delete a member of a collection, you need to have Delete Resource on either the class or the instance. If you have Modify on the Collection class or instance, you can change the membership rules for the query or how often it is refreshed.

If you want to change the maintenance windows, the collection variables, the collection-specific restart settings, and collection-specific policy polling intervals, you must have the right to Modify Collection Setting. You probably don't want to grant that right to just anyone because those particular collection settings have significant impact in how clients process policy.

There are four special object rights to help you manage resources in a collection: Modify Resource, Read Resource, View Collected Files, and Use Remote Tools. Finally, collection objects have a special right called Advertise. If you don't have Advertise to a Collection class or instance, you can't send them packages.

Special Rights on Site Objects

The site object is interesting because if you have child sites, you can manage the site object rights for a single site or for all site instances, meaning all child sites. This is not the same as saying that Sharon has the rights to distribute packages at a child site, because that involves different rights on different objects. The site object is really just the site. Can you create a site? Can you delete a site? Can you meter a site? Yes, if you have the rights. And yes, applying software metering rules is something you have to do at the site level and requires the meter right on the site.

Status filters allow you to change how Configuration Manager processes the status message you receive. One of the things you can do with the status filters is have Configuration Manager run a program, *any* program, when it gets a certain status message, so you don't want just anyone able to change the status filters. Yes, a disgruntled administrator could launch a command to wipe the hard drive when you get a particular status message. It's already been said that there is no defense against a disgruntled administrator. The best that you can do is to restrict who has the rights to create, modify, or delete status filters; you must have both the special Manage Status Filters right and the standard Modify right on the site object.

Creating SQL commands is another interesting thing for administrators to do. A happy administrator can make Configuration Manager run any stored procedure on a recurring schedule. A disgruntled administrator can also run any stored procedure on a recurring schedule, maybe one that deletes all of your data. You must have both the Modify right and the Manage SQL Commands right on the site object to create, modify, and delete SQL Commands. If you want to delete an SQL command, you must also have the Administer right on the site object.

There are two special rights on the site object that relate to operating system deployment tasks. Allowing computers to use the PXE boot process for operating system deployment is restricted to users with the Import Computer Entry right on the site object. The Manage OSD and ISV Proxy Certificates right allows you to manage that special, powerful client certificate discussed in the section "Operating System Deployment Certificates" earlier in this chapter.

Special Rights for Operating System Deployment Objects

There are two special rights that apply to operating system deployments. One right applies to task sequence media and one right applies to state migration.

Create Task Sequence Media is a right that applies only to the Task Sequence Package class. Having Create rights on the Task Sequence Package class would give you rights to create a new task sequence package, but creating task sequence media is a special right because the task sequence might contain sensitive data such as licensing information and credentials.

When you want to upgrade a user, you can save all of the user state to a state migration point and then bring that user state data back down to either an existing computer or a new computer. The user state data might contain very sensitive information such as private keys and stored credentials, so you have to be very careful about protecting this information. The information is encrypted, and you create a computer association between the computer putting the data on the state migration point and the computer pulling the information down from the state migration point. The association gives the destination computer the key to decrypt the user state data. What happens if the destination computer dies and no longer has the decryption key? A user with the right View Recovery Information can access the information and associate it with a new computer.

Special Rights on Configuration Items

If you want to apply Network Access Protection (NAP) to a configuration item, you must have the Network Access right on the Configuration Item object class or instance.

Delegating Object Rights

If you are the only Configuration Manager administrator, you probably don't need to configure any object security. Just log on with the account you used to install Configuration

Manager and you have all of the rights to everything. Create objects, delete objects, and modify objects as much as you like. As long as you are never sick or on vacation, the Configuration Manager tasks will always get done. Although you could take your laptop with you to the beach, it's probably better to configure at least one person to be your backup administrator, and maybe even several administrators to own different pieces of Configuration Manager administration.

There are several ways to manage object security in the Configuration Manager console. You can use the ConfigMgr User Wizard as a central place to manage all object rights. You can also manage rights individually on the Security tab for object classes and instances or under the Users node. For specific procedures, see "How to Assign Rights for Objects to Users and Groups" at *http://technet.microsoft.com/en-us/library/bb680648.aspx.*

Using the ConfigMgr User Wizard

One cool feature of using the ConfigMgr User Wizard to assign object rights is that if the SMS Provider is on the site server, the ConfigMgr User Wizard automatically adds the user account to the SMS Admins group. Assuming you have also assigned the DCOM permissions to the SMS Admins group, that user will have everything he or she needs to run the Configuration Manager console on a remote console. To run the ConfigMgr User Wizard, follow these steps:

1. Expand the Security Rights node.

2. Right-click Security Rights and click Manage ConfigMgr Users.

3. Click Next to pass the Welcome page. The User Name page is displayed, as shown in Figure 20-3.

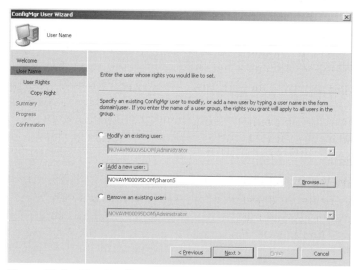

Figure 20-3   The ConfigMgr User Wizard User Name page

Granting Rights to Security Groups

The name ConfigMgr User Wizard is a bit misleading. You can also use the wizard to assign rights to a group. Usually the best practice is to assign rights to a group instead of an individual user. Then when you want another user to have the same rights, you add that user to the group, and he or she has everything needed. This works with Configuration Manager, but you should review the rules for which types of groups can be nested in other types of groups. For more information, see the information at *http://technet2.microsoft.com/windowsserver/en/library/79d93e46-ecab-4165-8001-7adc3c9f804e1033.mspx?mfr=true.*

Remember that you need those WMI permissions and you usually get them by membership in the SMS Admins group, which is a local group (or if you installed Configuration Manager on a domain controller, which is not recommended, the SMS Admins group is a domain local group). Say you create a local group called Local ConfigMgr Package Administrators on the site server. Because the usual Windows best practice is to add users to a global group, you also create Global ConfigMgr Package Administrators and add Sharon, Lori, and Ben to that group. You add Global ConfigMgr Package Administrators to Local ConfigMgr Package Administrators. Then you use the ConfigMgr User Wizard to assign various package rights to the Local ConfigMgr Package Administrators local group. ConfigMgr User Wizard will try to add Local ConfigMgr Package Administrators to the SMS Admins group, but because you can't nest a local group (Local ConfigMgr Package Administrators) in a local group (SMS Admins), it will fail. What happens when Sharon, Lori, and Ben try to use the console? They fail.

What can you do? You can tweak the rules and assign the Configuration Manager rights directly to the Global ConfigMgr Package Administrators group, and then if the SMS Provider is on the site server, the ConfigMgr User Wizard can add Global ConfigMgr Package Administrators to SMS Admins (because you can nest a global in a local group). If the SMS Provider is on a different computer, you can manually add the Global ConfigMgr Package Administrators to SMS Admins on the SMS Provider computer. If you don't want to assign the object rights directly to the global group, you could also assign the WMI permissions Enable Account and Remote Enable to the Local ConfigMgr Package Administrators group. If you plan on using remote Configuration Manager consoles, you should also grant Remote Activation DCOM permissions to the Local ConfigMgr Package Administrators group.

Granting Rights Using the Object Properties

If an object has security rights, the object properties will have a Security tab. For example, folders are not security objects, and they do not have properties or a security tab. Packages are security objects. You can see the class security rights on the Packages node, as shown in Figure 20-4.

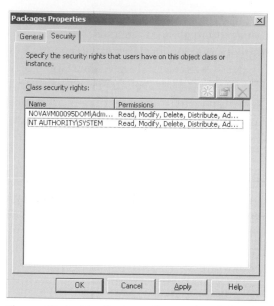

Figure 20-4   The Package Properties dialog box

If you right-click one package and then click Properties, you can see both the class rights that you saw on the class object and the instance rights for that particular package, as shown in Figure 20-5.

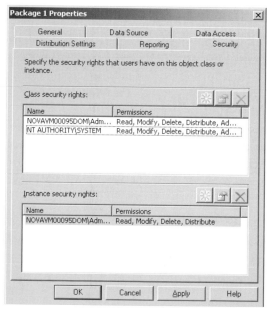

Figure 20-5   The Package Name Properties dialog box

Notice that even though this is one instance of a package, you can set both the class object rights and the instance object rights from the same tab. When you create a new object using a wizard, the Security tab is usually included in the wizard, making it convenient to add new instance rights when you create the instance. However, when you add new object rights using the Security tab, Configuration Manager does not try to add the user or group to the SMS Admins group. If you do not manually add the users or groups to SMS Admins, the users can't get past the WMI (and probably the DCOM) permission requirements and won't be able to use the lovely rights you just gave them.

Cloning Users

There are two ways to create a copy of an existing user. Your first option is to run the ConfigMgr User Wizard and copy the rights from an existing ConfigMgr user or user group, as shown in Figure 20-6.

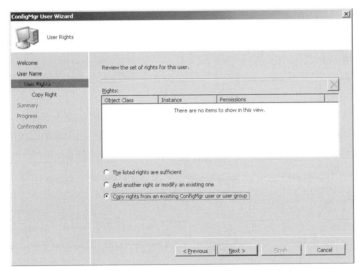

Figure 20-6   The ConfigMgr User Wizard User Rights page

For example, the account you used to run Setup already has all rights to all objects. Run the ConfigMgr User Wizard and copy all of the rights from that Setup account to your coadministrator and voila! You're done. (Well, assuming you have the WMI and DCOM permissions.)

Option 2 is to right-click any user in the Users node under Security Rights and then click Clone ConfigMgr User, as shown in Figure 20-7.

Figure 20-7   The Clone ConfigMgr User dialog box

However, if you use this method you must manually add the user to the SMS Admins group and assign the DCOM permissions.

Role-Based Access Control

If you have multiple administrators, each with a specific scope of administration, you can assign permissions more granularly to administrators.

A common way to restrict administration scope is to use collections. Say you want separate administrative scopes for sales and marketing, engineering, and IT. You create a collection for each administrative scope and assign Sharon the instance rights to manage the sales and marketing collection, Lori the rights to manage the engineering collection, and Ben the rights to manage the IT collection.

Another way to restrict administration is along functional lines. For example, you might want a help desk role that can use remote tools and view resources in a collection, but not distribute packages or have any rights to the site object. You would have to decide whether you want the help desk worker to read status message or not. There is no hard and fast rule, just what works best for your processes.

You might want to have one person or group responsible for creating packages and a different group responsible for distributing packages. By creating this role separation, you can reduce the chance that one disgruntled administrator can push out a package that would do bad things to your clients. The people responsible for creating the packages probably need Read, Create, Distribute, and Modify rights on the package class for the type of package. Deployment packages, software distribution packages, task sequence packages, operating system installation packages, and boot image packages are all treated as separate objects with separate object rights. You might want to grant the package administrator the right to create and manage folders for his or her package classes, or you might not. The people responsible for actually assigning packages to client computers need the Read and Advertise rights to the collection class or to a specific collection instance and Read rights to the Advertisement.

Account Security

Configuration Manager requires that the site server and all site systems be members of an Active Directory domain. Configuration Manager relies on accounts, especially computer accounts, to perform background operations. For example, even if your whole office is gone for the holidays, the Configuration Manager site server account will still be checking the configuration of your site systems. If that site system isn't functioning properly, the site server account will try to reinstall it. If there are parent and child sites, the site server computer account will copy inventory up to the parent or copy packages down to the child. Even client computers use their computer accounts to copy data such as inventory and status messages to the management point.

Depending on your configuration, the only Configuration Manager accounts you might need are the computer accounts for your site server, site systems, and client computers. Computer accounts are generally more secure because they manage themselves without messy human intervention. They never use their dog's name as a password, they change their own passwords in Active Directory Domain Services, and attackers can't watch them type their passwords at the keyboards when they log on to the domain.

You might need to create and configure some special user accounts in the following scenarios:

- You have a multi-forest environment.

- You need to use task sequence steps that require a user context.

- You want to use Client Push Installation but don't want to use the site server computer account.

- You need credentials to access a proxy server for Internet access.

Most of the accounts that you can configure in the Configuration Manager console appear in the Accounts node under Site Settings, as seen in Figure 20-8.

From the Accounts node, you can view the accounts you have configured in the site settings and you can modify the password of the account, but you can't change anything else about the account. If you decommission an account it still appears in the list, in case Configuration Manager has been configured to use the account for a different purpose.

For a complete list of the accounts in Configuration Manager, see "Accounts and Groups in Configuration Manager" at *http://technet.microsoft.com/en-us/library/bb693732.aspx*.

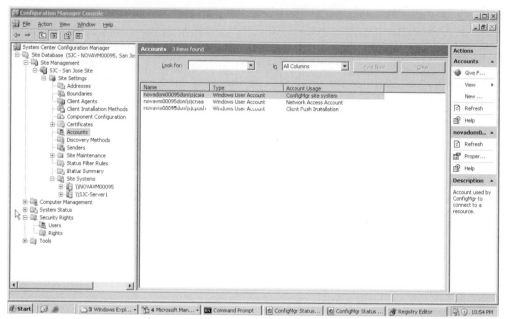

Figure 20-8   The Accounts node

Accounts in Sites with Multiple Forests

When all of the site systems and site server are in the same forest, it's easy to grant the permissions you need among the domains in the forest. In this scenario, you can do most of your account management using only computer accounts. You add the site server computer account to the local administrators group of every site system, and your site system computer accounts (except for the reporting points, server locator points, and distribution points) to the Site System to Site Server Connection Group so they can transfer their data back to the site server. The reporting points, server locator points, and distribution points should not be in the group because they don't need to push information back to the site server.

Note   Site systems can be in domains other than the site server except for the site database server, which must be in the same domain as the site server.

Also, if the management point is accessing a site database or a replica of the site database in a different domain, you must configure a Management Point Database Connection account and add it to the smsdbrole_MP role in the Configuration Manager site database.

Even when all of your site systems and site server are in the same forest, you can still have clients in different forests or even in workgroups; however, it introduces several complexities.

For example, clients can't query Active Directory Domain Services for site information such as which management points to trust or what parameters to use for Client Push Installation. If you have trusts between the forests, you either have to remember to grant permissions for the users in the other forest to access the distribution points in the site server forest, or configure a Network Access Account. If you do not have a trust between the forests, you must configure a Network Access Account, or clients won't be able to reach the distribution point at all.

There are a few supported scenarios in which you can have a site system in a different forest than the site server.

Site Systems Supporting Internet-Based Clients

If you are supporting Internet-based clients, it is supported to have the following site systems in a separate forest in your perimeter network:

- Management point
- Distribution point
- Software update point
- Fallback status point

If these site systems are not in the perimeter network and are not supporting Internet-based clients, they must be in the same forest as the site server.

Network Policy Servers for Network Access Protection

If you are using Network Access Protection, you might have the Network Policy Server in a completely separate forest from the Configuration Manager site server. Some companies have several different forests, but they still want the Configuration Manager System Health Validator points to receive the correct health state reference information, so Configuration Manager is designed to let you pick one forest to hold the health state reference information. This scenario does not require Internet-based clients to be supported. If the designated forest is in a different domain than the site server and there is no trust between the forests, you create and configure an account with permissions to publish the Health State Reference to Active Directory Domain Services. Then you also have to configure an account for the other forests that has permissions to read the Health State Reference from Active Directory Domain Services.

Other Site Systems

If you are using PXE service points for operating system deployment, having the PXE service point in a different forest than the site server is supported, but it is not the most secure configuration.

The server locator point can be located in any forest because clients don't need a user context to look up Configuration Manager services; clients query the Web services on server locator points with anonymous access.

Maintaining Site Systems in Other Forests

If you have site systems in a different forest than the site server, and if you happen to have a trust relationship between those forests, you add the site system computer account to the Site System to Site Server Connection Group and add the site server computer account to the local administrators group on the site systems. However, if you don't have a trust between the forests, you do not have to create a trust for Configuration Manager to work. When you create a site system, you have the option to create a Site System Installation account and tell Configuration Manager to use the Site System Installation account instead of the site server computer account when installing and maintaining the site system. The Site System Installation account installs and maintains all site roles on the site system.

> **Note**   Even though the account is called the Site System Installation account, it does more than just install the site system. It handles most of the routine maintenance and data transfers necessary for that site system role, including uninstalling that site role if necessary. The exceptions are for software update points and System Health Validator points. If you can't use the site server computer account to install the software update point, you must also configure a Software Update Point Connection account to request synchronizations and manage settings on the WSUS server. Also, the Site System Installation account will not publish or query Active Directory Domain Services, so you need to configure a Health State Reference Publishing account or a Health State Reference Querying account.

In addition to using the Site System Installation account to access the site system, you must also configure the site systems to Allow Only Site System Initiated Data Transfers From This Site System, which means the site server will pull information from the site system using the Site System Installation account instead of using the site system computer account to push information. If there is no trust relationship between the forests, you can't add the site system computer account to the Site System to Site Server Connection Group so the site system won't have the rights to push information.

Accounts Used for Task Sequences

There are three accounts that you can configure in task sequences:

- Capture Operating System Image Account
- Task Sequence Editor Domain Joining Account
- Task Sequence Editor Network Folder Connection Account

You can create one domain user account to perform all three functions in task sequences.

Client Push Installation

There are several methods to install the Configuration Manager client components. If you choose to use Client Push Installation, Configuration Manager must have an account that has administrative rights on the computers where the client will be installed. If your site server computer account has the necessary administrative rights, Configuration Manager can use it for Client Push Installation.

Important   Do not add the site server computer account to the Domain Admins group. Even though it makes using Client Push Installation very easy, you are giving way too many permissions to the site server computer account.

If your site server computer account doesn't have the necessary administrative rights, you should create one or more Client Push Installation accounts. You can create several Client Push Installation accounts; Configuration Manager keeps trying the list until it finds one that works; if that fails, it tries the site server computer account.

If you create just one Client Push Installation Account and add it to the Domain Admins group, you are concentrating a lot of power in one account. Anyone who can compromise that account has admin rights to every computer in your organization. To help mitigate this risk, you might create several accounts, each with a smaller administrative scope. For example, you could create one Client Push Installation account for each building or each division. You can use Group Policy to automatically add the Client Push Installation account to the local administrators groups in the corresponding scope. For example, you could use Group Policy restricted groups on the Building 44 organizational unit to add the Building 44 Client Push Installation account to the administrators group.

Proxy Accounts

If you are using the software updates feature, you must have at least one software update point that can access the Internet to download the software update catalog. If your organization requires authenticated access to a proxy server, you can set the software update point to use whatever credentials you want.

If you have Internet-based clients, they might require authenticated access to a proxy server. You can configure the proxy server used by clients by using the Configuration Manager Control Panel.

Configuration Manager Groups

When you install Configuration Manager, it automatically creates the groups shown in Table 20-2.

Table 20-2   Configuration Manager Groups

Group name	Purpose	Where created
Reporting Users Group	To grant access to reports to users	On reporting points
Site System to Site Server Connection Group	To allow site systems to connect back to the site server. (This group should contain site systems except the distribution point, reporting points, and server locator points because they never copy data back to the site server.)	On the site server
Site to Site Connection Group	To grant NTFS permission to the account used to transfer data between two sites	On the site server
SMS Admins Group	To grant WMI permissions to the SMS Provider	On the site server and on the computer running the SMS Provider

If you are using remote tools for computers running Windows XP, Windows Server 2003, and Windows Vista, then Configuration Manager also creates a group called the Config-Mgr Remote Control Users Group to grant DCOM permissions to the users in the Permitted Viewers list on the Remote Tools Client Agent properties. This group is created on the supported Configuration Manager client computers when the client receives a policy enabling remote tools.

Database Roles

SQL Server has something called roles that perform the same function as Active Directory groups, but are not Active Directory groups. The good news is you don't have to do much with the roles created by Configuration Manager because it does most of the management. In fact, modifying the roles and the default permissions is not supported. However, if you need to use a user account instead of the site server computer account to connect to the site database, you have to create that user account and then add the account to the corresponding role. For example, by default the server locator point uses the site server computer account to access the site database, but if you need to use a different account, you have to create a user account to be the Server Locator Point Database Connection account, and then add it to the smsdbrole_SLP role in the site database so it has the rights and permissions it needs to retrieve service location information. The other two site system roles that have database connections accounts are the PXE service point and the management point, and if you use those connection accounts you must add them to the smsdbrole_PSP role or the smsdbrole_MP role, respectively.

Accounts Used by Humans

All of the accounts configured in the Configuration Manager console are used by Configuration Manager to access resources behind the scenes, and they don't need any help from you. In fact, the accounts you configure in the console like the Network Access Account shouldn't require interactive logon rights, meaning no one should ever be sitting down at a keyboard to log on as Fred if Fred is the name you assigned to your Network Access Account. However, there are two very important interactive logon accounts that you need—the user who runs Setup and the users who will run the Configuration Manager console.

When you run Setup, your account must be a domain user account, or Setup will look like it worked but really fails. The account must also be a local administrator on the site server, on the database server, and the SMS Provider computer; however, the account does not need to be a domain administrator. The account must be a member of sysadmins on the SQL Server. During Setup, the account is automatically added to the SMS Admins group on the SMS Provider computer so it has all of the WMI permissions it needs to access the Configuration Manager console. Setup also grants it all rights to all Configuration Manager objects so the Setup account can do anything in the console immediately after installation.

After you finish running Setup, you can always log on with that account to run the Configuration Manager console, but it's a good idea to have at least one backup account just in case. If you have multiple people in your organization helping to administer Configuration Manager, you must assign them WMI permissions, DCOM permissions, and object rights in the console so they can do their jobs. Assuming you already assigned the DCOM permissions to the SMS Admins group as described in "How to Configure DCOM Permissions for Configuration Manager Console Connections," add your fellow administrators to the SMS Admins group to give them the required DCOM and WMI permissions. Then grant them object rights, as described earlier in this chapter.

Note   When you run Setup, the Configuration Manager console is automatically installed on the site server. You can run Setup on other computers to install additional consoles. You must be a local administrator to run Setup, even to install the console. However, the account used to run the Configuration Manager console does not have to be an administrator on the additional console computer unless you are planning to create task sequence media. For example, say Bob is a member of the local Administrators group and installs the console on ComputerA. Barbara wants to use that console but she is not an administrator on ComputerA. If she tries to run the console from the Start menu, she gets an error. What she has to do is run MMC first and then add the Configuration Manager 2007 Snap-in to create a new console session. After Barbara saves that MMC, she should use that console to access the Configuration Manager console.

Checkpoints for Configuring Accounts Correctly

Verify that the computer accounts for the following site systems are added to the Site System to Site Server Connection group if they are in same forest as the site server:

- Fallback status points
- Management points
- PXE service points
- Site database server (if on a remote computer)
- SMS Provider computer
- Software update points
- State migration points
- System Health Validator points

If you have a site system that is supported to be in a different forest than the site server, verify that you have configured Allow Only Site Server Initiated Data Transfers From This Site System on the General tab of the site system properties and have configured a Site System Installation account for the site system.

Verify that the site server computer account is added to the local Administrators group for the following site system roles if they are in same forest as the site server:

- Distribution points
- Fallback status points
- Management points
- PXE service points
- Reporting points
- Server locator points
- Site database server
- SMS Provider computer
- Software update points
- State migration points
- System Health Validator points

If you have a site system that is supported to be in a different forest than the site server, verify that you have configured a Site System Installation account for the site system.

If you have more than one site, verify that you have an account for site-to-site communications between all child and grandchild sites. If you have sites in different forests, configure a Site Address account, even if you have a trust between the two forests. If you have sites in the same forest, use the site server computer account when you configure the address between the sites. Verify that the account you use for site-to-site communications is a member of the Site to Site Connection group on the destination server.

Verify that all users who will use the Configuration Manager console are either in the SMS Admins group on the SMS Provider computer or have been assigned the WMI permissions Enable Account and Remote Enable.

Verify that all users who will use the Configuration Manager console on any computer except the SMS Provider have the DCOM Remote Activation permission on the SMS Provider computer and the site server.

Custom Configuration Manager Consoles

Creating a customized version of the Configuration Manager console is not really a security control, but it can make it harder for unauthorized users to do things they shouldn't do.

If you have run Setup to install the Configuration Manager console, when you run MMC to create a custom console, you can add the Snap-in System Center Configuration Manager. As soon as you add the Snap-in, it starts the Database Connection Wizard, as shown in Figure 20-9.

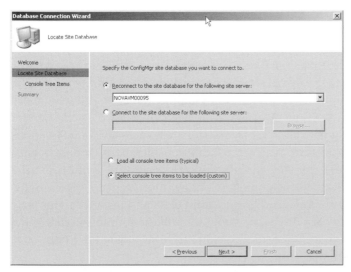

Figure 20-9   The Database Connection Wizard Locate Site Database page

If you click Select Console Tree Items To Be Loaded (Custom), you can decide which nodes will be displayed in the MMC session, as shown in Figure 20-10.

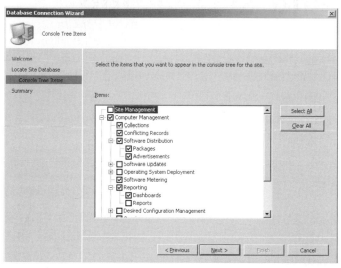

Figure 20-10   The Database Connection Wizard Console Tree Items page

You have to use object security rights together with custom consoles to achieve your desired results. For example, if a user still has object rights to Desired Configuration Management, there is nothing stopping that user from creating a different custom console that displays the node for Desired Configuration Management. On the other hand, if you create a console that displays the Software Distribution node, but do not give the users class or instance rights to any packages or advertisements, the users will see an empty Software Distribution node when they open the console.

Summary

This chapter described some of the typical security concerns and how they relate to Configuration Manager. Key planning decisions for Configuration Manager security and privacy were discussed. There was a brief overview of the types of certificates required for native mode, but probably not enough to satisfy someone who actually wants to implement native mode because there are too many certificate considerations that are outside the scope of Configuration Manager. Also discussed were the security controls in Windows and networking and how they might impact Configuration Manager. How Configuration Manager object security works and how to grant class and instance rights were described. The chapter ended with a discussion about some of the accounts used by Configuration Manager and how to create custom consoles in MMC if you have users who need a more limited administrative scope.

## Chapter 21

Backing Up and Recovering the Site

To back up, recover

Use the maintenance tasks

But wait for RTM

~ Jeff Gilbert, Technical Writer

Disaster recovery! No one wants to experience it, right? But all systems administrators need to be prepared for the possibility. By the end of this chapter, you'll learn what you need to know about maintaining, backing up, and recovering your Systems Center Configuration Manager site.

The key to a successful disaster recovery effort is, of course, a sound backup strategy and keeping complete and up-to-date documentation on the state of your site. This includes site system settings, software distribution packages, and advertisements you've created for them, as well as custom collection settings among other things. The focus of this chapter is just that—the establishment of a useful backup strategy and strategies for recovering your Configuration Manager database server, site server, and site systems. This chapter and Chapter 22, "Maintaining the Configuration Manager Database through Microsoft SQL Server," which focuses on database maintenance strategies, provide you with the resources you need to be amply prepared for disaster recovery, but more importantly, teach you how to avoid disaster in the first place.

You begin by establishing sound site database maintenance practices, including a regular backup process, and then you'll learn how to recover or move the Configuration Manager database server, recover or move the Configuration Manager site server, and restore Configuration Manager site systems.

Database Maintenance

Perhaps the most obvious way to keep your Configuration Manager site systems from experiencing failure is to keep them running in top form, much like you might develop an exercise and diet program for yourself or regularly change the oil in your car. In addition to developing a backup and recovery strategy, you can do several things for your Configuration Manager servers on a regular basis both to keep them running well and to spot problems before they cause damage. For the most part, these maintenance tasks can be broken down into four groups: general, daily, weekly, and monthly maintenance tasks.

> **More Info**   For more recommendations about database maintenance tasks, see "Maintaining Configuration Manager 2007" in the Configuration Manager 2007 Documentation Library at *http://technet.microsoft.com/en-us/library/bb693882.aspx*.

General Maintenance Tasks

Probably the most important general task you can perform for any Microsoft Windows system is to develop a backup plan for your servers. At a minimum, you want to develop a backup strategy for your Configuration Manager site server and Configuration Manager database server, as these are your key systems. Much has been written about backup strategies—full versus differential, daily versus weekly, and so on.

For example, one backup strategy might be that you perform a full, or complete, backup of your database once a week, say on Friday nights, while you perform a differential backup of the database Mondays through Thursdays. Different backup types can take longer to run the backup process and take longer to restore as well. For example, a full backup backs up all the data each time and so will necessarily take longer to back up and restore. A *differential backup*, in contrast, backs up only data that has changed since the last full backup and will result in reduced backup time and less backup space used.

It all comes down to this ultimate question: How important is it that you recover your data, and how current must that data be?

Most general maintenance tasks might more properly be called troubleshooting assistance tasks, such as configuring the Status Message Viewer, configuring the Performance Monitor and SQL Server alerts, performing a database and site backup, and monitoring the performance of the site systems. You've looked at some of these tasks in previous chapters, such as the following:

- **Configure the Status Message Viewer to view status messages**   Recall from Chapter 6, "Analysis and Troubleshooting Tools," that the status message system is your first and often best source of information regarding the state of your Configuration Manager site systems. You can configure the display interval for status messages, set filters, have programs such as pager alerts executed based on message events, and so on. Take some time to determine how the Status Message Viewer might figure into your overall maintenance—and ultimately disaster recovery—strategy.

- **Configure Performance Monitor alerts for key events**   You can set up alerts for the events, such as low disk space, overutilization of the processor and memory, excessive pagefile access, and so on.

- **Configure SQL Server alerts**   You can set up the alerts in the SQL Server Management Studio to monitor database space usage, user locks, and connections. (For more information about setting up SQL Server alerts, refer to the SQL Server product documentation.)

- **Determine a fault tolerance strategy**   If your server supports a fault tolerance method such as redundant array of independent disks (RAID) 1 (disk mirroring) or RAID 5 (disk striping with parity) either through a hardware method or through Windows, consider configuring one of these fault tolerance methods. Maintaining data redundancy is a hallmark of disaster recovery.

You will undoubtedly think of many other troubleshooting assistance tasks to add to this list. Be as creative—and redundant—as you like. In the following sections, you'll explore some specific daily, weekly, and monthly tasks you can perform as a Configuration Manager site administrator.

Daily Maintenance Tasks

As the Configuration Manager administrator, you decide when various maintenance tasks should be performed within your organization and with what frequency. No single blueprint will provide a perfect fit for every Configuration Manager site or site structure. Microsoft recommends that you perform the following tasks daily to protect your Configuration Manager servers. You can modify this list to suit your needs.

- **Perform a site backup**   Only Configuration Manager site backups created by the Backup ConfigMgr Site Server maintenance task can be used with the Site Repair Wizard to recover a site. Regularly scheduling this task ensures that you will have the ability to recover the site should it fail using the Site Repair Wizard.

- **Review status messages**   This is especially important if Configuration Manager generates a status message alert indicating a potential problem with a component.

By default, the Status Message Viewer displays only messages generated since the previous midnight. If you skip a couple of days, you might miss significant status messages. Consider changing the display interval or setting up custom filters so that you will be alerted about serious events. You should review site server and site system status messages every day. However, Configuration Manager clients also generate status messages. Although it might be unrealistic to review client status messages on a daily basis, perhaps because of the number of clients you might have installed, consider reviewing them on a weekly or monthly basis.

- **Monitor the Windows Event logs and SQL Server logs**   Check for errors or warnings that might be indicative of an impending failure of your Configuration Manager site. You can view the SQL Server logs in the Management node of the SQL Server Management Studio.

- **Monitor system health and performance through the Performance Monitor and Configuration Manager Service Manager tools**   Check for performance-related events, such as low disk space, overutilization of the processor and memory, excessive pagefile access, and so on, to help determine when your server isn't running at optimum performance levels and what processes might be affecting performance.

- **Monitor network utilization using a network traffic analysis tool such as Network Monitor**   This task is especially important if package distribution or intersite communication appears to be poor in order to determine when and where traffic congestion is occurring.

- **Monitor Configuration Manager system folders for file backlogs**   The appearance of a large or growing number of files in the Configuration Manager system folders might indicate that the site server is unable to process requests for information. Check status messages and Configuration Manager services for errors.

Weekly Maintenance Tasks

Microsoft recommends that you perform the following tasks weekly. Again, you can modify this list to fit your needs.

- **Monitor the size and percentage of database growth of the Configuration Manager site database**   SQL Server 2005 automatically monitors the size of the Configuration Manager database and makes adjustments appropriately. Of course, this doesn't absolve you from monitoring the database on a regular basis to determine how fast the database is growing and especially whether you might run out of disk space. However, you might not need to look at the database so frequently, and you can set an SQL Server alert to let you know when and how much the database grows.

- **Monitor the amount of free disk space on the Configuration Manager database server, the site server, and the site systems—especially distribution points** Remember, with few exceptions, Configuration Manager components will just stop working if they run out of disk space.

- **Purge data that's no longer needed or relevant** Remove bad Management Information Format (MIF) files, duplicate computer records, aged inventory records, and so on.

- **Perform regular disk cleanup tasks** This cleanup would include your weekly full virus check or disk optimization routine or monitoring for unused or old Temp files. Check the Configuration Manager directories as well for folders that have an unusually high number of files, such as a BadMIFs folder or an inbox with files that aren't being processed, and cross-check these folders with status messages and logs for the specific components involved.

Monthly Maintenance Tasks

Here are some of the recommended maintenance tasks that you might perform on a monthly or an as-needed basis:

- Verify and test your ability to restore the database or the site server.

- Modify Configuration Manager accounts and passwords for those accounts you have control over. Refer to Chapter 20, "Configuration Manager 2007 Security," for a discussion of Configuration Manager accounts.

- Review Configuration Manager object permissions.

- Review Configuration Manager boundaries and component configuration.

- Review your maintenance plans.

You can protect your Configuration Manager site by scheduling and performing these maintenance tasks regularly. In the following section, you'll look at how to schedule these tasks.

Scheduling Maintenance Tasks

You can schedule several of the maintenance tasks just mentioned to run on your timetable through the Configuration Manager console. You can find these tasks in the Site Maintenance node under Site Settings. Two types of database maintenance objects can be configured: SQL commands and tasks.

Scheduling SQL Commands

No predefined SQL commands are available for you to schedule; you must configure these commands yourself. For example, among the recommended weekly tasks is a database size check. You can view database size using the SQL Server Management Studio, of course, but you can also determine it by executing the SQL stored procedure SP_SPACEUSED.

Important   Before running any SQL stored procedure, be sure to consult the SQL Server documentation for correct syntax and usage.

You can configure this SQL stored procedure to run according to your defined schedule and generate a report based on its results. To do so, follow these steps:

1. Navigate to the SQL Commands node under Site Management\Site Settings in the Configuration Manager console and select it.

2. Right-click the folder, choose New from the context menu, and then choose New SQL Commands to display the New SQL Command dialog box, as shown in Figure 21-1.

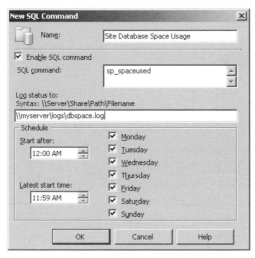

Figure 21-1   The New SQL Command dialog box

3. Type a descriptive name for the command.

4. Verify that Enable SQL Command is selected. Type the command in the SQL Command text box. Be sure to use the appropriate syntax, or the command will fail when it is run. Configuration Manager will not verify the syntax of the command you create.

5. In the Log Status To text box, enter the path and filename of the text file to which you want the command results written. This must be an existing share.

6. Define your schedule and click OK.

The SQL command you created will now be listed in the Configuration Manager console when you select the SQL Commands node. You might consider scheduling other SQL maintenance commands, such as DBCC CHECKDB, DBCC CHECKALLOC, DBCC CHECKCATALOG, and DBCC UPDATEUSAGE. For example, if you recently reindexed the database, you might want to run the DBCC UPDATEUSAGE command to reset space usage reporting so that SP_SPACEUSED returns accurate data. You could schedule this command to run with SP_SPACEUSED or separately, under its own schedule.

When the SQL command is run, it writes the results of its execution to the log file you specified. Figure 21-2 shows the results of the SQL command created in the previous example.

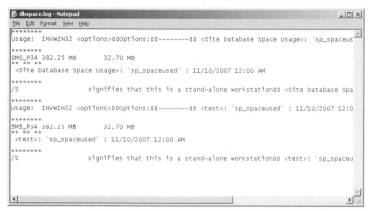

Figure 21-2   Results of running the SP_SPACEUSED SQL stored procedure as an SQL command

The first line of data (beginning with *SMS_P34*) indicates the total database size and the available free space.

Scheduling Tasks

The other type of database maintenance objects you can schedule, tasks, is found in the Tasks node in the Configuration Manager console. The Tasks folder contains 18 predefined tasks; you can't add tasks to this list. Table 21-1 describes these predefined tasks.

Notice that 12 of these tasks are already enabled by default to ensure that vital tasks such as rebuilding SQL Server database table indexes are carried out on a regular schedule. All the deletion tasks are designed to keep the database from becoming too large and unwieldy. You can, of course, modify the schedule and disable or enable any of these tasks as you choose. (To enable or disable a task in the Tasks folder, right-click the task and choose Properties from the context menu. In the Task Properties dialog box, select or clear the Enable This Task option.) For example, you could enable the Backup Config-Mgr Site Server task to schedule a regular backup of the Configuration Manager database and site server components without having to do so in SQL Server. In fact, this is the recommended method for backing up your site server because only backups created by this maintenance task can be used with the Site Repair Wizard to recover a failed site. While SQL Server database backups alone can not be used to recover a failed site, they can be used to recover a failed site database or move the site database to a new SQL Server instance.

Table 21-1   Database Maintenance Tasks

Task	Description
Backup ConfigMgr Site Server	Performs a comprehensive backup of the Configuration Manager site including the site database, files, registry keys, and system configuration information. This task isn't enabled by default.
Rebuild Indexes	Rebuilds indexes created on database tables that are used to more efficiently retrieve data. Enabled by default to run every Saturday.
Monitor Keys	Monitors the integrity of primary keys used to uniquely identify all Configuration Manager database tables. Enabled by default to run every Saturday.
Delete Aged Inventory History	Deletes all hardware inventory that hasn't been updated within a specified period of days (by default, 90 days). By default, this task is enabled and runs every Saturday.
Delete Aged Status Messages	Deletes status messages older than seven days by default and runs every day. Enabled by default.
Delete Aged Discovery Data	Deletes all discovery data records (DDRs) that haven't been updated within a specified period of days (by default, 90 days). By default, this task is enabled and runs every Saturday.
Delete Aged Collected Files	Deletes all collected files that haven't been updated within a specified period of days (90 days, by default). By default, this task is enabled and runs every Saturday.
Delete Aged Software Metering Data	Deletes metered software data that's older than five days to conserve space in the Configuration Manager database. This task is enabled by default to run daily.
Delete Aged Software Metering Summary Data	Deletes metered software summary data that's older than 270 days to conserve space in the Configuration Manager database. This task is enabled by default.
Summarize Software Metering File Usage	Enables summarization of collected software metering data to conserve space in the Configuration Manager database. This task is enabled by default to run daily.
Summarize Software Metering Monthly Usage Data	Enables summarization of collected monthly software metering data to conserve space in the Configuration Manager database. This task is enabled by default to run daily.

Table 21-1   Database Maintenance Tasks

Task	Description
Clear Install Flag	Directs Configuration Manager to clear the install flag for clients that have been uninstalled. The install flag identifies to Configuration Manager those clients that have been installed as Configuration Manager clients. When the client is uninstalled, the install flag isn't automatically removed, and the client can't be successfully reinstalled. This task clears the flag so that a client can be reinstalled using the client push installation method. This task isn't enabled by default.
Delete Inactive Client Discovery Data	Deletes all client records that haven't received an updated DDR within the specified number of days—for example, through Heartbeat Discovery. This task is useful when you're using Active Directory Discovery to create DDRs for computers. When you delete a computer in Active Directory Domain Services, its Active Directory record might remain for some time before being purged. As a result, Configuration Manager Active Directory Discovery would continue to report the computer as a valid client, even though the computer is no longer physically present on the network.
	This task isn't enabled by default.
Delete Obsolete Client Discovery Data	Deletes client records marked as obsolete from the site database that hasn't been updated within a specified period of days (7 days, by default). This task isn't enabled by default.
Delete Aged Configuration Management Data	Deletes configuration item definitions and any associated configuration item compliance history data that hasn't been updated within a specified period of days (90 days, by default). By default, this task is enabled and runs every Saturday.
Delete Aged Client Access License Data	Deletes all Client Access License (CAL) data that hasn't been updated within a specified period of days (180 days, by default). This task isn't enabled by default.
Summarize Client Access License Weekly Usage Data	Summarizes CAL usage and creates a weekly data point for long-term trending. This task isn't enabled by default.
Delete Aged Computer Association Data	Deletes all Operating System Deployment computer association data that hasn't been updated within a specified period of days (30 days, by default). By default, this task is enabled and runs every Saturday.

The most powerful of these tasks is Backup Configuration Manager Site Server site maintenance task. This is by far the most comprehensive backup routine available for Configuration Manager. It backs up not only the Configuration Manager site database, but also the full Configuration Manager directory structure on the site server, site configuration information stored in the site control file, and the Configuration Manager registry keys in the Windows registry on the site server—all necessary to fully recover a failed site server.

This task is discussed in more detail in the section "Backing Up the Site Server" later in this chapter.

Backing Up the Site Through Configuration Manager

You can back up the site database using a number of techniques. You could use SQL Server's BACKUP command through the SQL Server Management Studio. This process is described in Chapter 22. You could use your favorite third-party backup system that includes add-ons that back up SQL Server databases. (Review your backup product's documentation to learn how.) However, these methods are not recommended to be used as a replacement for the Backup ConfigMgr Site Server maintenance task because they cannot be used by the Configuration Manager Site Repair Wizard to completely restore a failed site. However, these database backup methods can be used when you need to recover a failed site database or move the site database to another SQL Server computer or instance.

The recommended backup method is the Backup ConfigMgr Site Server maintenance task available through the Configuration Manager console.

Backing Up the Site Server

The Backup ConfigMgr Site Server maintenance task essentially performs all the required backups outlined earlier in this chapter—the site database, essential registry keys, data files, and site configuration information.

The SMS_Site_Backup service executes the Configuration Manager backup maintenance task. This service runs according to the backup schedule you configure. Like other Configuration Manager service components, this service comes with a log file (Smsbkup.log) that is created the first time the service is run. You can later configure the backup logging options through ConfigMgr Service Manager (see Chapter 3, "Configuring Site Server Properties and Deploying Site Systems," for more information). The site backup log maintains a record of the site backup process. When you restore a site, you can use the log (included in the backed up files) to verify that you're restoring from a valid backup. Like other logs, as this log reaches its maximum size (2 MB by default), it's written to Smsbkup.lo_, and a new Smsbkup.log file is created. Figure 21-3 shows a portion of an Smsbkup.log file created after the Backup ConfigMgr Site Server task is run.

It's not necessary to predefine a backup device when you enable the Backup ConfigMgr Site Server task. You must, however, provide the name of a backup folder location where the SMS_Site_Backup service will write the backed-up data. This location can actually serve as the main backup location for several site servers because when the task is run, the SMS_Site_Backup service creates a subdirectory named by the site code, and all backup data is written there.

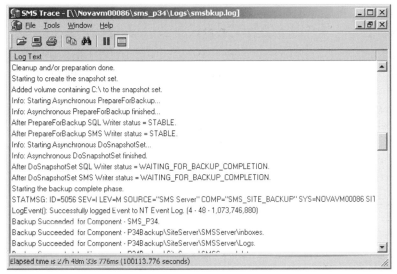

Figure 21-3   Sample Smsbkup.log file

It should be of no little significance, then, that the location of the backup folder must be on a partition with adequate disk space to accommodate the data being written there. It's recommended that you have enough space to accommodate not only the Configuration Manager database, but the entire Configuration Manager system folder structure as well. You can determine a more accurate accounting of the space required by considering the following factors:

- Amount of disk space used by the entire Configuration Manager directory structure

- Amount of space used by the following SQL Server databases: master, msdb, and site server

- At least 10 MB of additional space for miscellaneous files such as saved registry keys

Because Configuration Manager backups are created using the Volume Shadow Copy Service (VSS), in addition to the size of the files to be backed up, the size of the VSS temporary backup snapshot created during the backup process should be considered when planning the backup location. Configuration Manager 2007 does not consider the VSS storage associations for volumes containing site data or the SQL Server site database during the site backup process. The VSS Admin tool can be used to check the Volume Shadow Copy (VSS) storage associations for the drives containing Configuration Manager data and ensure that they are configured to use a volume with free space equivalent

774 Part III Site Database Management

to at least 50% of the size of the Configuration Manager data to be backed up. To use the vssadmin tool, open a command prompt, type **vssadmin**, and press enter. The backup destination specified in the Backup ConfigMgr Site Server maintenance task should refer to a different volume than the source volume.

At each subsequent scheduled backup, the SMS_Site_Backup service first removes the old backed up data before writing the new data. It also records each backup event in the Smsbkup.log file, which is viewable using any text editor. To maintain an archive of previous backup snapshots, a simple batch file named *afterbackup.bat* can be written and used to copy the backup snapshot to an archive location after it is created by the backup site maintenance task. The afterbackup.bat file is automatically run at the end of the backup process if one has been created. By default, there is no afterbackup.bat file present in Configuration Manager installations.

The Backup Control File

The entire Backup ConfigMgr Site Server task is actually governed by a backup control file named Smsbkup.ctl, as shown in Figure 21-4, which is stored in the <InstallationPath> \Inboxes\SMSbkup.box folder. This file outlines exactly what will be backed up and where. Smsbkup.ctl is a text file, and, as such, it's fully customizable. It's also well annotated, which will assist you in reading and understanding its flow, as well as in customizing it.

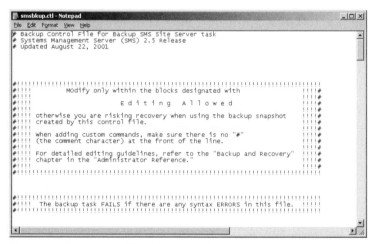

Figure 21-4 Sample Smsbkup.ctl file

This file contains the names of the files, registry keys, and databases that need to be backed up. It also contains commands that run during the backup operation to gather configuration information. You can customize this file to include additional files, directories, registry keys, and so on. However, it isn't recommended that you remove or modify any of the default entries in this file unless you've tested that, by doing so, you haven't compromised your backup's integrity.

Appendix B, "Backup Control File," presents the code for the backup control file for your reference.

Configuring Backup ConfigMgr Site Server

To configure the Backup ConfigMgr Site Server maintenance task, follow these steps:

1. In the Configuration Manager console, navigate to the Site Maintenance node under Site Settings and expand it.

2. Select the Tasks node, select Backup ConfigMgr Site Server, right-click it, and choose Properties to display the Backup ConfigMgr Site Server Properties dialog box, as shown in Figure 21-5.

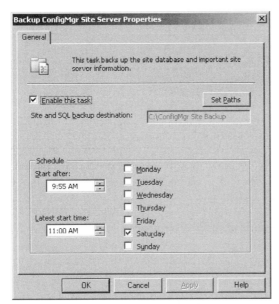

Figure 21-5   The Backup ConfigMgr Site Server Properties dialog box

3. Select the Enable This Task check box.

4. Click Set Paths to define the backup snapshot storage location to use. If the site database is installed on the site server computer, you can use a local drive on the site server to store both the site database backup and site server backup files to the same location. If the database server is remote to the site server, you can select to use a shared network folder to store the files all in one place, or you can define local drive locations to store the backup files. If local backup destinations are used, when

the database server is remote from the site server, the site databases will be stored on the remote computer at the location you specify. Be sure that the destination location has enough disk space available before specifying it as the backup destination.

5.   Specify a schedule for the backup. For active databases, a daily backup is recommended.

6.   Click OK to save your configuration and enable the backup task.

At the scheduled time, the SMS_Site_Backup service finds or creates the backup destination folders, stops appropriate Configuration Manager site server services, and performs the backup. After the backup is complete, you can view the backup folder's contents using Windows Explorer. Figure 21-6 shows the contents of a sample backup folder.

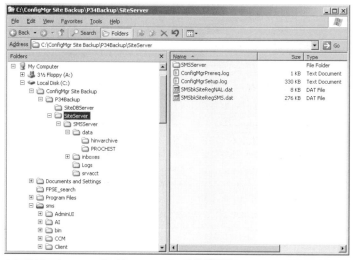

Figure 21-6   Sample backup folder contents

Notice that the SMS_Site_Backup service created a subfolder called Backup, prepended with the site code. Within this subfolder are other subfolders containing information relating to the site database server (SiteDBServer), and the Configuration Manager site server (SiteServer), which itself contains the entire site directory structure, registry entries, and site control information. The following registry keys are backed up from the Windows Registry on the Configuration Manager site server:

■   HKEY_LOCAL_MACHINE\Software\Microsoft\NAL

■   HKEY_LOCAL_MACHINE\Software\Microsoft\SMS

The SiteDBServer directory is shown in Figure 21-7. Notice that this directory contains the backup of the Configuration Manager site database (SMS_P34.mdf) as well as the transaction log file (SMS_P34_log.LDF).

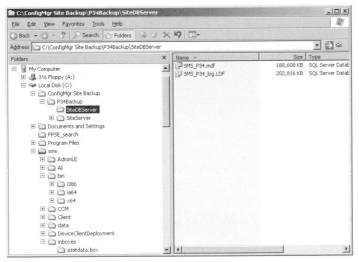

Figure 21-7   The SiteDBServer directory

As you can see, this backup routine is quite comprehensive and should be more than adequate to act as your Configuration Manager backup routine.

> **More Info**   You can change the scheduled time for the Backup ConfigMgr Site Server task to whenever you want, but the SMS_Site_Backup service is engineered to check the schedule only once per day. If you need to execute this maintenance task immediately, configure the task and then start the SMS_Site_Backup service by running Services in the Control Panel on the site server or typing **net start SMS_Site_Backup** from a command prompt on the site server computer.

Recovering Configuration Manager Sites

Recovery of a Configuration Manager site generally falls into two categories: recovering the site database and recovering the site server. If the Configuration Manager database fails for some reason, you can restore it from its backup using SQL Server Management Studio. You need to have access to a current backup, of course, as well as to the SQL Server Management Studio console. There's no restore function in Configuration Manager because, presumably, if you need to restore the site in some fashion, you probably can't open the Configuration Manager console.

Recovering the Site Database

Recovering the Configuration Manager database itself is a fairly straightforward task—which isn't to imply that it's a mundane or trivial matter, but rather that it's cut and dried.

You recover the site database by restoring it from a current backup. For example, if you need to move the Configuration Manager database to another server running SQL Server for some reason, you would follow these steps:

1. Close all Configuration Manager related tools, such as all Configuration Manager consoles, that are accessing the current database, as well as the SMS Executive (SMS_Executive) and SMS Site Component Manager (SMS_Site_Component_Manager) site server services. You don't want anything trying to connect to or update the database while you're managing it.

2. Locate a new system running SQL Server, ensuring that the same database sort order has been used as on the original server running SQL, as well as the same version of SQL Server and hardware platform.

3. Create database and log devices or files (depending on the SQL Server version) that are at least as large as the backed-up database.

4. Use either a recent site database backup created using SQL Server's backup task, or the site database .mdf and .ldf files created by the Configuration Manager site database backup task (much larger than the compressed SQL Server backup would be), to restore the backed-up Configuration Manager database to the new SQL Server computer.

5. Start Configuration Manager Setup and use the Modify or reset the current installation option to point the site server to the location of the new system running SQL Server containing the database.

6. Open the Configuration Manager console and delete the existing database connection. It will probably not be working anyway because it will think the site database is somewhere else. Use the Site Database Connection Wizard (right-click the top node in the console and select All Tasks\Connect to Site Database) to connect to the new site database location.

You follow similar steps if the database needs to be restored for any other reason, although if you are restoring to the same system running SQL Server, you might not need to perform steps 5 or 6.

Recovering the Site Server

If you encounter a situation in which the Configuration Manager site server itself needs to be recovered—perhaps it crashed or it had be moved to a different physical system—the steps for recovery are somewhat more involved. First of all, your situation would probably be hopeless if you had not already created a current site backup using the Backup Config-Mgr Site Server maintenance task so assume that you've been backing it up regularly.

As you've seen, other significant elements of the site server in addition to the Configuration Manager database need to be backed up in order to completely restore the site server to its previous state. These elements include the SMS and NAL registry keys, the site control file (<InstallationPath>\Inboxes\Sitectrl.box\Sitectrl.ct0), and the Configuration Manager directory structure and files.

The recovery process begins with the restoration of the Configuration Manager site database. However, it also involves the restoration of the backed-up elements from the site server itself. For example, if you need to reinstall Configuration Manager on the site server or install it on a new computer, you'll restore the previous site by copying the backed-up Configuration Manager directory and site control file over to the new installation or over to the reinstallation. Similarly, you can restore the Configuration Manager-related registry keys by using the Windows Registry Editor to replace the existing registry keys (created when you reinstalled Configuration Manager or installed it to a new server) with the backed-up versions of those keys.

In some cases, you could restore just the database itself and let the Configuration Manager site server rebuild itself—which it will do eventually as long as the site server name, site code and description are the same as the failed site. However, any changes you made that were written to the registry but not yet updated to the database will probably be lost so you'll lose all of the preconfigured site settings. Restoring the Configuration Manager site server completely, as described here, will ensure that all elements of the site server are properly synchronized and recovered properly.

Sounds like a lot of work, doesn't it? Fortunately, you do not have to do these steps manually to recover the site. Configuration Manager includes a utility called the Site Repair Wizard that carries out the site recovery process for you and performs these necessary key steps as well as others that would be impossible for you to do using only backup files.

Real World   Using Preinst.exe

Included on the Configuration Manager product DVD and installed into the <InstallationPath>\Bin\i386\\<language code> (00000409 is for English) folder on the site server is the hierarchy maintenance tool tool (Preinst.exe). This tool is installed on site servers and is used to interact programmatically with the hierarchy manager service to help diagnose problems, repair the site control file, delete incorrectly removed sites, or stop Configuration Manager site server services, among other things.

Look at three of this tool's command-line options here that can be of particular use in the Configuration Manager site server recovery and maintenance process: /DUMP, /DELSITE, and /DELJOB. You can run this tool from a command prompt by changing the path to the appropriate directory from the command prompt and executing the tool.

Figure 21 8 displays the command switches available for PREINST. Executing the PREINST /DUMP command causes a new site control image to be written to the root of the partition on which Configuration Manager was installed. An *image* is a binary representation of the site control file. This image is based on the current site control data stored in the Configuration Manager database and is named SMS_sitecode.scf. This file then can be copied to the Site Control Manager's inbox (<InstallationPath>\Inboxes\Sitectrl.box) and renamed Sitectrl.ct0 to rebuild the site's properties. This function is useful if the site control file becomes corrupted or if you don't have a current backup of it.

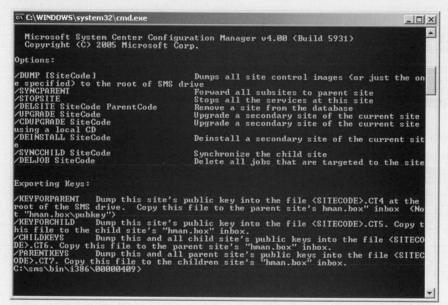

Figure 21-8   PREINST switches

You can use PREINST /DELSITE to remove a "phantom" child site. When a child site is to be removed from a parent site, the correct process is to break the parent-child relationship through the child site's properties, wait for the parent and child sites to update their respective databases, and then remove the addresses. A *phantom* child site occurs if the child site is removed from the parent site before the relationship has been broken or before the databases can be correctly updated, and references to the deleted child site may remain at the parent. This issue most commonly happens when a secondary site is deleted instead of uninstalled using the Delete Secondary Site Wizard, but still appears in higher level sites.

To delete the removed site from the parent site, execute PREINST /DELSITE: {childsitecode, parentsitecode}, where *childsitecode* represents the site code of the site that needs to be deleted and *parentsitecode* represents the parent's site code for the site that needs to be deleted.

Last, PREINST /DELJOB is designed to remove jobs or commands targeted to a specific site. You can use this command to remove jobs, such as software package distribution replication, that might still be in the queue for the removed site but keep trying to be sent or executed, resulting in error status messages. Executing PREINST /DELJOB:sitecode will delete all commands that are targeting the specified site code.

Using the Configuration Manager Site Repair Wizard

The Configuration Manager Site Repair Wizard is automatically installed on your Configuration Manager site server during site setup and on any computer running the Configuration Manager console. The Configuration Manager Site Repair Wizard doesn't need to be run on the site that's being recovered, but in many cases it can be more efficient and faster than executing steps across the network. This wizard automates many recovery tasks and is useful in repairing as well as recovering a Configuration Manager site server. Here's an example.

When a Configuration Manager site server is a member of a site hierarchy, it receives management and configuration information about packages, collections, and advertisements (among other things) from its parent site, sends that kind of information to its own child sites, and sends its client database information such as collected inventory and status messages to its parent site. Sites participating in a hierarchy keep track of what needs to be sent back and forth by using a series of version stamps. There are version stamps for various objects in the Configuration Manager database, and version information is stored in many places—in the registry on the site server, the site control file, and in the database itself. If the version stamps get out of sync for some reason, your site might not receive or accept any new information or send information of its own because it can't ascertain whether the information is valid any longer. The Configuration Manager Site Repair Wizard helps to put your site server back in sync by resetting the version values.

Another way the Configuration Manager Site Repair Wizard can help recover a site is through the use of a reference site. This would be a parent or child site that the wizard can contact to read the last data set that the failed site sent in an effort to restore your site's configuration and reset its version information.

Here is a complete list of the tasks carried out by the Configuration Manager Site Repair Wizard:

- Save the Svracct folder
- Stop and disable site services on the site server
- Restore the site database
- Restore Configuration Manager files
- Restore SMS registry key
- Restore NAL registry key
- Restore the Svracct folder
- Increment the Transaction ID
- Increment the DDM serial number
- Synchronize client policy with the site database
- Increment serial numbers in the site database
- Reset status messages
- Insert the most current site control file
- Start and enable the Windows Management Instrumentation (WMI) service on the site database server
- Reconfigure child sites
- Reconfigure senders
- Reconfigure site systems
- Re-create other configuration changes
- Return the site server to service
- Restart the site server and check Configuration Manager services
- Reset the ACL objects on the Configuration Manager folders and the registry
- Reset the site again
- Resynchronize the parent and child site servers
- Create addresses for other sites
- Change the site's parent assignment
- Synchronize with other sites

- Delete phantom child sites

- Regenerate orphaned collections, advertisements, and packages that were created after the backup used to restore the site was made

This tool can help facilitate the recovery and repair of your Configuration Manager site. What can go wrong, then? Well, the recovery is going to be only as good as the work you put into thoroughly documenting your site—its configuration, packages, collections, and so on—and the frequency with which you back up your site. For a detailed discussion about the recovery process, please read the topic "Recovering Configuration Manager Sites" in the Configuration Manager Documentation Library online at *http://technet.microsoft.com/en-us/library/bb680651.aspx*.

To run the Configuration Manager Site Repair Wizard, follow these steps:

1. From the Microsoft System Center\Configuration Manager 2007 Start menu program group, click ConfigMgr Site Repair Wizard to display the Welcome page shown in Figure 21-9.

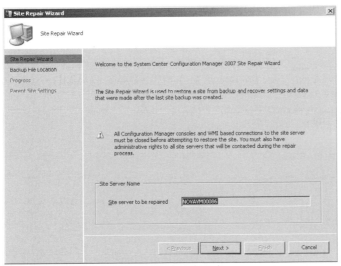

Figure 21-9   The Site Repair Wizard Welcome page

2. Click Next to display the Backup File Location page, as shown in Figure 21-10. Click Browse to locate and select the backup folder that contains the last successful site backup you scheduled using the Backup ConfigMgr Site Server maintenance task. You can choose to restore site settings only by selecting the Do Not Restore Database option. This can be useful if the database resides on another server and has not failed. Select the Repair Or Reconfigure A Site option if you do not have a

recent successful backup of the site server. This option will not restore site server files of the site database.

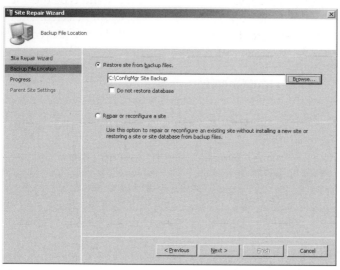

Figure 21-10   The Site Repair Wizard Backup File Location page

3. Click Next to display the Progress page, as shown in Figure 21-11. On this page you can follow each main step of the recovery process. If you selected Repair Or Reconfigure A Site on the previous page, you'll need to select the approximate date of the last site backup before proceeding to the Progress page.

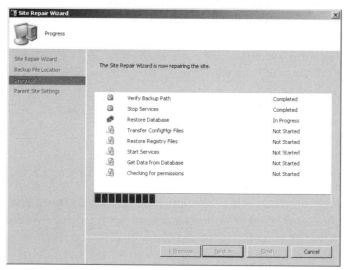

Figure 21-11   The Site Repair Wizard Progress page

4. When the Site Repair Wizard completes its tasks, you can click Next to display the Parent Site Settings page, as shown in Figure 21-12. If the site you are recovering is a child site of another site, select This Site Is A Child Site Of and type the parent site code. Otherwise leave the default option This Is A Central Site selected. The remaining wizard pages that are selected depend on whether the site you are recovering is a child site or a central site. If you selected the default, click Next and proceed to step 6.

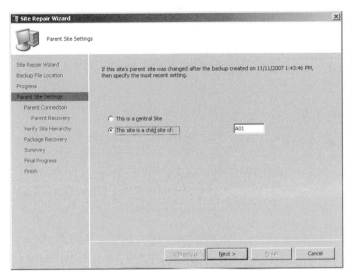

Figure 21-12   The Site Repair Wizard Parent Site Settings page

5. If the site is a child site, then it might be possible for the Site Repair Wizard to recover settings that were changed since the last site backup from the parent site. If you select This Site Is A Child Site Of, then when you click Next, the Parent Connection page, shown in Figure 21-13, is displayed, prompting you for the appropriate sender address for the parent site. By default, the Recover Data From Parent Site option is selected. Clicking Next displays the Parent Recovery page, as shown in Figure 21-14. Click Next when the steps are displayed as completed.

> **Note**   Depending on the options you select, you might be prompted to provide additional information such as the name of a site that can act as a reference site, and any additional objects such as advertisements and collections you might have created since the last site server backup. For detailed information about these pages, and a discussion about reference sites, please refer to the topics included in the Configuration Manager Documentation Library at *http://technet.microsoft.com/en-us/library/bb680651.aspx*.

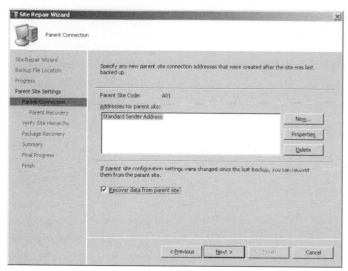

Figure 21-13   The Site Repair Wizard Parent Connection page

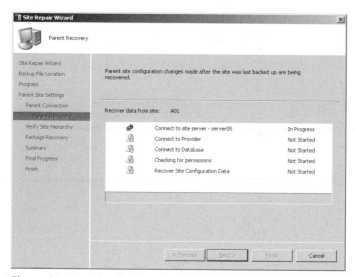

Figure 21-14   The Site Repair Wizard Parent Recovery page

6. On the Verify Site Hierarchy page, shown in Figure 21-15, confirm that the site hierarchy displayed represents the site hierarchy that can be retrieved from the site server backup. If you added or deleted child sites since the last backup, click Add to include them in the recovery process. In the Addresses For Selected Site section, add any new site connection addresses that were added since the last backup.

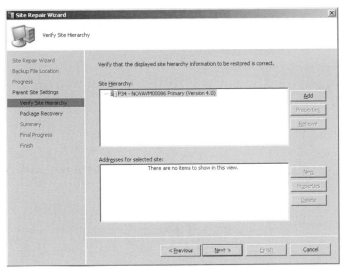

Figure 21-15   The Site Repair Wizard Verify Site Hierarchy page

7. Click Next to display the Package Recovery page, as shown in Figure 21-16. The default option Verify That All Package Source Files Are Accessible determines whether software distribution source files can be accessed by the site you are recovering. You can optionally select Update The Distribution Point On This Site Server option to ensure that if the site server is acting as a distribution point, any changes to package source files since the last backup are included and restored.

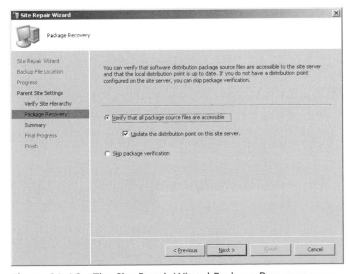

Figure 21-16   The Site Repair Wizard Package Recovery page

8. Click Next to display the Summary page, as shown in Figure 21-17, which displays a list of the recovery actions that will take place.

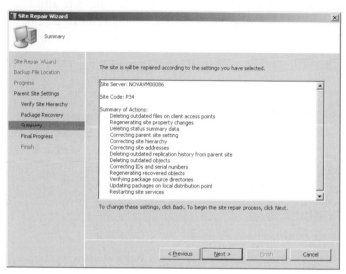

Figure 21-17   The Site Repair Wizard Summary page

9. Click Next to display the Final Progress page, as shown in Figure 21-18, which displays a summary of all the tasks that were carried out and their relevant status. Click Next to complete, and then click Close to end the wizard.

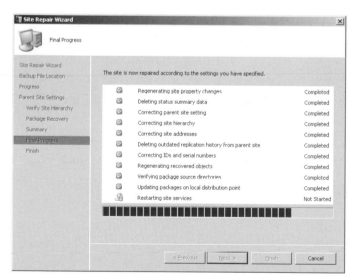

Figure 21-18   The Site Repair Wizard Final Progress page

After you have repaired or recovered your site server, verify that site data has been correctly recovered. Check site addresses, monitor site processes, and check or reconfigure site settings. If you have done a great job documenting your site and managing change control for your site, then this final verification task should be easy. If not, well, you'll likely do a better job documenting your site and managing change control going forward.

Restoring Site Systems

Compared to recovering a site server, restoring a Configuration Manager site system such as a management point or distribution point, and so on, is rather elemental. Recall from Chapter 3 that the Configuration Manager site server builds Configuration Manager site systems. You identify the site systems and assign their roles through the Configuration Manager console. Consequently, if a site system should need to be rebuilt or replaced, it's merely a matter of reassigning that server through the site server.

For example, suppose that a site system such as a management point fails and needs to be replaced. When you bring the failed server back on line, Configuration Manager will simply restore the appropriate files and components to that site system. If the site system itself needs to be replaced and its computer name has changed, you would remove the old server as a site system from the site server and then add the new server to the Configuration Manager site as a site system and assign it the appropriate role.

In a similar fashion, distribution points actually assume their role as packages are distributed and refreshed to these distribution points. Consequently, replacing or recovering a distribution point is simply a matter of refreshing the packages for that distribution point. To do that, follow these steps:

1. In the Packages node of the Configuration Manager console, select the package you need to redistribute, right click it, and choose Manage Distribution Points to launch the Manage Distribution Points Wizard, as shown in Figure 21-19.

2. Click Next to display the Select Destination Distribution Point page, as shown in Figure 21-20. Select the Refresh The Package On Selected Distribution Points option.

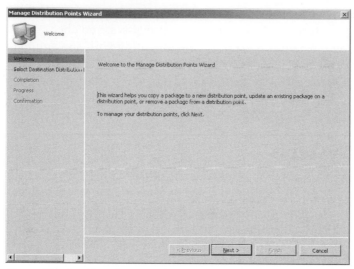

Figure 21-19   The Manage Distribution Points Wizard Welcome page

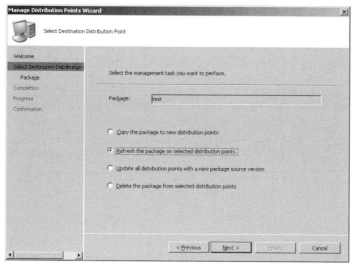

Figure 21-20   The Select Destination Distribution Point page of the Manage Distribution Points Wizard

3. Click Next to display the Package page, as shown in Figure 21-21. In the Distribution Points list, find the distribution point you just recovered and select it.

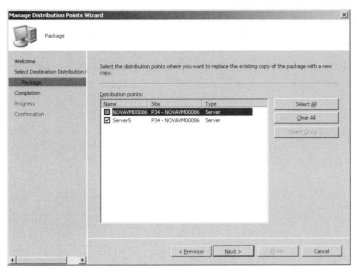

Figure 21-21   The Package page of the Manage Distribution Points Wizard

4.   Click Next to display the Completing The Manage Distribution Points Wizard page and click Finish to begin the update process.

Important   If you're recovering a distribution point that has gone down, the packages must be redistributed to the same drive and directory on which they were originally configured. For example, if you created your own shared folders to which the package was originally distributed, re-create the shares before redistributing the packages.

You can recover other site systems by reassigning them through the Configuration Manager console.

More Info   If the system running SQL Server or the site server fails, Configuration Manager components running on site systems will continue to function correctly, although status messages and data updates won't be forwarded to the site server until it's restored. This means that Configuration Manager clients will continue to report inventory data, run advertised programs, and meter software.

Summary

At this point you have developed sound strategies for maintaining, backing up, and restoring Configuration Manager within your site. You have configured the database maintenance tasks and scheduled these tasks within appropriate time periods—daily, weekly, or monthly. You have established a regular backup plan that includes backing up not only the Configuration Manager database, but also the strategic files, folders, and registry keys contained on the site server. You have outlined and practiced recovery procedures to be followed in the event the Configuration Manager database server or site server fails or needs to be moved or a site system needs to be replaced.

Chapter 22 takes you a step further, as you explore maintenance and configuration from the point of view of SQL Server. Together, these two chapters provide the groundwork necessary to keep your Configuration Manager site optimized and well prepared should you ever encounter a recovery event.

Chapter 22

Maintaining the Configuration Manager Database through SQL Server

Prevent disaster

Keep the database humming

Make SQL happy!

~ Steve Kaczmarek, Content Publishing Manager

Chapter 2, "Planning for and Deploying Configuration Manager Sites," outlined the prerequisites for a computer running Microsoft SQL Server to host the System Center Configuration Manager 2007 site database successfully. Those requirements are recapped here. Recall that Configuration Manager primary sites require an SQL Server 2005 (Service Pack 2 or later) database to store site information. Either SQL Server 2005 Standard or Enterprise Editions can be used to host the site database. However, it is not supported to use SQL Server 2005 Express Edition to host the site database. You can install SQL Server either on its own server or on the same system as the site server. The decision as to which location is more appropriate depends on many factors, not the least of which is the performance capabilities of the server itself. You can also install the site database using an SQL Server–named instance or even a clustered SQL Server virtual server instance name.

The same decision also affects the way in which the Configuration Manager installation will proceed. If SQL Server is installed on the same server as Configuration Manager, the Configuration Manager Setup program can create the necessary database devices and files for you. Unlike Systems Management Server 2003, Configuration Manager Setup can also install the database if SQL Server is installed on a server other than the site server. In this scenario, Configuration Manager Setup will use the database defaults set on the SQL Server when it creates the database. However, if you want a more customized installation, for example, with specific log file directories or database installation volumes, you can precreate the database and then specify it when you run Configuration Manager Setup. Several SQL parameters affect the way SQL Server handles the Configuration Manager database. Some of those parameters, such as the number of open connections and the amount of memory allocated, were discussed in Chapter 2. Other parameters are discussed in this chapter.

This chapter focuses on some specific tasks and terms, beginning with the SQL Server components used by the Configuration Manager database. Then it looks at the management tools available in SQL Server and discusses how to maintain the Configuration Manager database using SQL Server 2005. Last, you explore how to modify SQL Server parameters and how to solve the problems that might occur with your SQL Server system. This chapter's intent is not to teach you all there is to know about SQL Server. Plenty of good books and courses on SQL Server are available to provide you with that information. Here, however, you explore how to maintain the Configuration Manager database through SQL Server.

Note   It's possible to install and use Configuration Manager without a working knowledge of SQL Server, but in the long run you'll need to master at least SQL Server administration tasks. Configuration Manager is not itself a database server; instead, it acts as a front end to the Configuration Manager database maintained in SQL Server. Therefore, you'll need to initiate many database maintenance tasks through SQL Server. Consider taking a class about SQL Server administration, such as Microsoft Official Curriculum (MOC) 2789, "Administering and Automating Microsoft SQL Server 2005 Databases and Servers," or the Microsoft E-Learning class 2937, "Administering and Monitoring Microsoft SQL Server 2005." *Microsoft SQL Server 2005 Administrator's Pocket Consultant* and *Microsoft SQL Server 2005*

Administrator's Companion (both published by Microsoft Press) are also good sources of information regarding the execution of administrative tasks and optimizing server performance, respectively.

SQL Server Components

In this section, you review some basic terminology and see how it relates to the Configuration Manager database. Every entity that is called a database actually consists of two components: the database and its transaction log. SQL Server 2005 maintains the database and transaction logs in their own files. The *database* is a collection of data records, object tables, and indexes organized in a specific structure designed to facilitate the displaying, sorting, updating, and analysis of the information it contains. The *transaction log* is used to record each action performed on the database, such as adding a new record or updating or deleting an existing record.

If you install Configuration Manager on the same computer as SQL Server, Configuration Manager not only creates the database for you, but also tunes SQL Server for use with Configuration Manager. This feature doesn't, of course, relieve you of all responsibility in the maintenance of the server running SQL, but it does ease some of the setup concerns regarding SQL Server, especially if you've had little experience with it. SQL Server needs to be installed before running Configuration Manager Setup. Keep the following considerations in mind when installing SQL Server 2005:

- The only SQL Server component required to host the Configuration Manager 2007 site database is SQL Server Database Services. Installing the optional SQL Server Workstation components allows the SQL Server instance to be managed from the site database server computer. These components are not necessary if the site database will be managed from a different computer with the Workstation components installed.

- You can install either a default instance or named instance during SQL Server Setup to host the site database.

- If you configure a domain user account to run the SQL Server service instead of the local system account (SQL Server best practice), a Service Principal Name (SPN) must be configured for the domain user account in Active Directory Domain Services. For more information about configuring an SQL Server service account SPN in Active Directory Domain Services, see the topic "How to Configure an SPN for SQL Server

Site Database Servers" in the System Center Configuration Manager Documentation Library online at *http://technet.microsoft.com/en-us/library/bb735860.aspx.*

- SQL Server Windows Authentication Mode (default) is required.

- Dictionary order, case-insensitive, for use with 1252 Character Set (default) should be selected as the SQL Server collation.

Configuration Manager Setup automatically creates the site database, using SQL Server defaults, on the SQL Server computer and instance specified during setup. If the configured SQL Server default settings are not sufficient to manage your site database, it is recommended that you precreate the database and set the required settings. If you are using a remote SQL Server to host the site database, you should ensure that the site server's computer account has sufficient privileges on the SQL Server computer to create the site database before beginning the installation process. Also, ensure that the user account running Configuration Manager Setup is in the sysadmin SQL Server role on the SQL Server computer specified for site database installation. By default, the local administrators group is added to the sysadmin role, but an SQL Server best practice is to remove the local administrators group from the sysadmin SQL Server role. The SQL Server Management Studio (installed with SQL Server client tools) can be used to determine the members of the sysadmin role on the SQL Server computer.

You can accomplish most of the actions you'll need to perform on the server running SQL through the SQL Server Management Studio console. Through this console, you can create databases and transaction logs, set security, back up and restore the database, perform routine database maintenance tasks, and optimize SQL Server parameters for the Configuration Manager database. The following sections explore the process of creating databases using SQL Server 2005.

Creating a Database in SQL Server 2005

The SQL Server Management Studio console, shown in Figure 22-1, is run from the SQL Server 2005 Program Files folder. It groups its managed objects into six main categories:

- Databases
- Security
- Server Objects
- Replication
- Management
- Notification Services

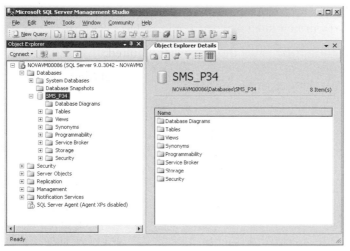

Figure 22-1   SQL Server Management Studio console

Configuration Manager Setup will create the database file for you during setup. However, if you need to create the database file before running Configuration Manager Setup, you can follow these basic steps:

1. In SQL Server Management Studio console, navigate to the Databases folder, right-click it, and choose New Database from the context menu to display the New Database Properties dialog box, as shown in Figure 22-2.

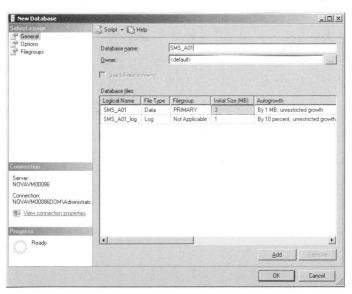

Figure 22-2   The New Database Properties dialog box

2. In the General tab, type a name for the database, such as SMS_xxx, where *xxx* represents the site code for your new site.

3. The database file name will appear in the Database Files list. You can modify the initial size of the database by typing the desired data and log file sizes in the Initial Size column. You can click the ellipsis (Browse) button (found in the Path column) to display the Locate Folder dialog box, where you can modify the location of the file.

4. The Autogrowth option is enabled by default. This option ensures that SQL Server monitors the size of your database and expands it as necessary according to the File Growth parameter you specify. You can allow the growth to be unrestricted or set a maximum size. You can enable or disable Autogrowth and modify its settings by clicking the ellipsis button in the Autogrowth column to display the Change Autogrowth dialog box, as shown in Figure 22-3.

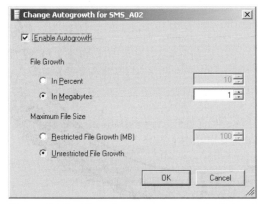

Figure 22-3   The Change Autogrowth dialog box

5. Click OK to create the database.

Configuration Manager Database Components

The Configuration Manager database contains data objects and their attributes arranged in an organized fashion. Each database consists of seven main elements, as follows:

- Tables
- Views
- Synonyms
- Programmability
- Service Broker
- Storage
- Security

Of these, you are most concerned with tables and their elements.

A *table* is a database object that contains data in the database organized as a collection of rows and columns. Each row in the table represents a data record, and each column represents an associated field for that record. Generally, each table defines one or more columns (fields) as a key entry that can be used to link tables for the purpose of sorting, searching, and reporting on data in the database. Configuration Manager contains more than 400 predefined tables.

Each table contains an index. An *index* can be thought of as a companion object to a table. Separate from the table, an index functions much like an index in a book, providing a quick way to search and locate data. If an index is available for a table, your queries will exhibit better performance. If no index is available, the entire table must be searched. The two index types, clustered index and nonclustered index, determine how the data records are searched. The nonclustered index is similar to a book index—each entry contains a bookmark that tells the database where to find the data that corresponds to the key in the index. For example, when you look up an entry such as "site-server" in a book index, you might be directed to several locations in the book. The index doesn't represent the order in which the data is stored in the book. The clustered index is similar to a telephone directory—it contains the data itself, not just the index keys. The clustered indexes are usually based on a primary key defined in each table. Each index entry corresponds to the order in which the data is stored in the book. Like looking up a name in the phone book, when you find the name, you also find the address and phone number.

When you execute a query, you're searching tables for a specific value based on the criteria you enter, using indexes whenever possible. The query result represents the records or data values obtained from records contained in one or more tables.

A *trigger* is a Transact-SQL statement that's executed whenever a specific event occurs in a given table. Most tables include one or more triggers. The Transact-SQL language is used for communication between applications and SQL Server. It's an enhancement to SQL and provides a comprehensive language for defining tables, maintaining tables, and controlling access to data in the tables. If data is added, deleted, or modified within a specific table, an event trigger will be executed. Configuration Manager uses event triggers to notify its components that an event has occurred that a particular component needs to attend to. Event triggers cause components to "wake up" in response to an event rather than waiting for a specific polling cycle to occur. Obviously, this translates to better performance for the site server. For example, when you change a site setting, an event trigger causes SQL Monitor to write a wake-up file in the Hierarchy Manager inbox (see Chapter 3, "Configuring Site Server Properties and Deploying Site Systems," for more information).

A *stored procedure* is a group of Transact-SQL statements that have been compiled into a single executable routine. You could think of a stored procedure as a kind of batch file for

SQL Server. When an SQL Server event activates a trigger, a corresponding stored procedure is executed that writes the wake-up file into the appropriate Configuration Manager component's inbox on the site server. Two common stored procedures that you might execute are SP_SPACEUSED, which displays the amount of reserved and actual disk space used by a table in the database or by the entire database, and SP_WHO, which identifies SQL Server connections (users and processes) currently in use. Both are included with SQL's master database. There are more than 300 stored procedures specific to Configuration Manager. You can view them in the Stored Procedures folder under Programmability in the Microsoft SQL Server Management Studio.

SQL Server Management Tools

A quick scan of the SQL Server program group reveals that many tools are installed to assist the SQL Server administrator in maintaining the server running SQL. Unless you're the SQL Server administrator as well as the Configuration Manager administrator or you get the necessary education to fully understand and appreciate the product, you'll probably use only two or three of these tools. The three tools you are most likely to use are described in Table 22-1.

More Info For a complete description of all SQL Server tools, including directions for use, please refer to the SQL Server 2005 Books Online located on the SQL Server TechCenter at *http://technet.microsoft.com/en-us/library/ms130214.aspx.*

Table 22-1   SQL Server 2005 Program Tools

Tool	Description
Books Online (Optional)	Provides an online version of the documentation set *SQL Server Books Online* with full searching capabilities. You can choose to download this file locally.
SQL Server Configuration Manager	An MMC snap-in tool used to manage the services associated with SQL Server, to configure the network protocols used by SQL Server, and to manage the network connectivity configuration from SQL Server client computers. The SQL Server Configuration Manager combines the functionality of the following SQL Server 2000 tools: Server Network Utility, Client Network Utility, and Service Manager.
SQL Server Management Studio	A tool that provides an integrated environment for accessing, configuring, managing, administering, and developing all components of SQL Server.
	SQL Server Management Studio combines the functionality of the following SQL Server 2000 tools: Enterprise Manager, Query Analyzer, and Analysis Manager.

Many SQL Server maintenance tasks specific to the Configuration Manager database can be configured and scheduled to run through the Configuration Manager console, including a backup (see Chapter 21, "Backing Up and Recovering the Site," for more information). You can also affect database backups by using a third-party backup program capable of including SQL Server databases as part of its backup routine. Consequently, as a Configuration Manager administrator, you're most likely to use the SQL Server Management Studio to perform any additional or advanced maintenance tasks. Through this interface you can create database devices, manage space usage, configure the server, schedule events, back up and restore the database, and so on. You can also use the SQL Server Query Analyzer to execute maintenance tasks such as those described in Chapter 21.

When you install SQL Server, several performance objects and counters are included to assist you in evaluating the ongoing performance and resource use of your server running SQL as well as to facilitate the troubleshooting of specific performance-related problems. To view the available SQL Server performance objects and counters, you can start the Windows System Monitor utility, accessible through the Performance Console. For example, the SQL Server:Database object has a counter called Data File(s) Size (KB) that will help you monitor the cumulative size of your databases, such as Tempdb.

Database Maintenance

As you've seen, some database maintenance tasks should be carried out on a regular basis—daily, weekly, or monthly. For example, every day you might execute a database backup and review status messages and system performance. Once a week, you might monitor database size usage and purge old data from the database. Once a month, you might verify the integrity of the database backup by testing a restore of the database. Once a month, you might also review security and make appropriate adjustments such as resetting account passwords.

Most of these tasks can be performed or configured and scheduled to run through the Configuration Manager console. However, you can perform many of these same tasks, and database backup and restores, through SQL Server. In this section, you review the commands used for performing the essential maintenance tasks and how to perform these tasks.

Commands Used for Performing Essential Maintenance Tasks

Some of the database integrity checking and space monitoring commands you might consider running on a weekly or monthly basis appear in the following list. These database consistency checker (DBCC) commands are certainly not the only ones available, but they're among the commands that Microsoft most often recommends.

- **DBCC CHECKALLOC**   Checks the specified database to verify that all pages have been correctly allocated and used; reports the space allocation and usage.

- **DBCC CHECKDB**   Checks every database table and index to verify that they are linked correctly, that their pointers are consistent, and that they are in the proper sort order.

- **DBCC CHECKCATALOG**   Checks consistency between tables and reports on defined segments.

- **DBCC UPDATEUSAGE**   Used with a recently reindexed database to reset space usage reporting so that SP_SPACEUSED returns accurate data. You could schedule this command to run with SP_SPACEUSED or to run separately under its own schedule.

Note   To obtain a complete list and explanation of all Transact-SQL statements and stored procedures, including the DBCC commands, query the online help for SQL Server 2005.

Before you run any DBCC command, remember to set SQL Server to Single-user mode. You look at how to start SQL Server in Single-user mode in the section "Backing Up and Restoring the Database" later in this chapter. The following sections discuss how to run these commands.

Executing a Maintenance Command Using SQL Server 2005

To execute a database maintenance command in SQL Server 2005 follow these steps:

1. Run the SQL Server Management Studio. Click New Query on the toolbar to display the query entry window, as shown in Figure 22-4.

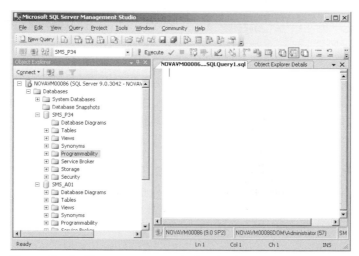

Figure 22-4   The query entry window in the SQL Server Management Studio

2. Type the command that you want to execute—in this case, **DBCC CHECKDB**—in the query entry window, as shown in Figure 22-5. Be sure that you've selected the correct database to run the command against.

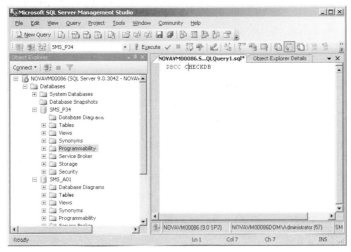

Figure 22-5   The query entry window in the SQL Server Management Studio with the database command entered

3. Choose Execute from the Query menu or click the Execute Query button (the red exclamation point) on the toolbar. The results of the query are displayed on the bottom half of the Query window, as shown in Figure 22-6.

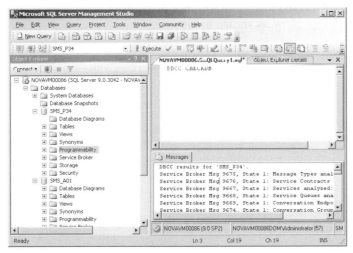

Figure 22-6   The query entry results window

Note   Each of the DBCC commands and stored procedures might have additional syntax options that will affect how the command is executed. Refer to your SQL Server documentation for a complete description of each command and its syntax.

Real World   Using Site Maintenance Commands to Tune SQL Server

In Chapter 21, we explored the site maintenance commands provided in the Configuration Manager console. These commands can be used to your advantage as an administrator for optimizing SQL Server database performance. Here are a couple tips for consideration.

Periodically rebuilding indexes can help to speed up database operations for Configuration Manager. You can schedule this using the predefined site maintenance task Rebuild Indexes.

If you find yourself running specific stored procedures as part of your regular maintenance tasks, you can schedule these to run on a regular basis using the Custom site maintenance task.

Plan to back up the site database regularly using the Backup ConfigMgr Site Server site maintenance task. This is the only backup method supported when running the Configuration Manager Site Repair Wizard. When you back up the site using this maintenance task, you can use Simple Recovery mode for recovering the site database. This also keeps the SQL Server tempdb from becoming too large between SQL Server backups.

Backing Up and Restoring the Database

The discussion of backing up and restoring the database began in Chapter 21, when you explored some of the built-in database maintenance routines configurable through the Configuration Manager console. In this section, you'll review the procedure for backing up and restoring the database directly through SQL Server.

Important   An SQL Server–based database backup is not sufficient to restore a failed Configuration Manager site. Complete site backups using the Backup ConfigMgr Site Server site maintenance task contain much more data than just the site database itself. Also, only backups run using the Backup ConfigMgr Site Server site maintenance task are supported when running the Recovery Wizard for a failed site.

You can back up the contents of the database and transaction log to a device such as a tape drive or to another file location on the server. The frequency of the backup is up to you, the Configuration Manager administrator. Generally, you'll back up the Configuration Manager database as frequently as necessary to ensure a current and accurate restoration of the data. A common database strategy involves performing a complete backup of the database once a week, with incremental backups of the data that has changed each day between full backups.

Note   As you've seen throughout this book, Configuration Manager components have frequent communication with the Configuration Manager database. Before implementing a production site, develop and test a backup and restore strategy that will adequately protect your data.

Real World   Backing Up Using Third-Party Utilities

Several third-party backup programs include modules designed specifically for backing up SQL Server databases. If you have access to such a product, you can have it perform the backup as part of its systemwide backup routine, eliminating the need to configure a backup redundantly through SQL Server or through the Configuration Manager console. To preserve the data's integrity, it's important that no Configuration Manager components try to access the Configuration Manager database when the backup or restore is taking place. Be sure that no Configuration Manager consoles are running and that all Configuration Manager components on the site server have been stopped. In addition, when you're restoring the database be sure to set the database to Single-user mode. This is set as a property of the database. Note that you won't be able to set the Single-user mode option if any open connections exist to the database.

However, while backups performed this way are useful for backing up the site database itself, and are especially useful and recommended when planning to move the database server, keep in mind that these backups are not valid for restoring the site using the Configuration Manager Repair wizard. Only backups run using the Backup ConfigMgr Site Server site maintenance task can be used to restore a site.

Backing Up and Restoring Using SQL Server 2005

If you need SQL Server to back up and restore the Configuration Manager site database, you can do so using the SQL Server Management Studio.

To back up the Configuration Manager database using SQL Server 2005, follow these steps:

1. In SQL Server Management Studio, navigate to the Databases folder and expand it.

2. Select the Configuration Manager database you want to back up, right-click it, choose Tasks, and then choose Backup to display the Back Up Database dialog box, as shown in Figure 22-7.

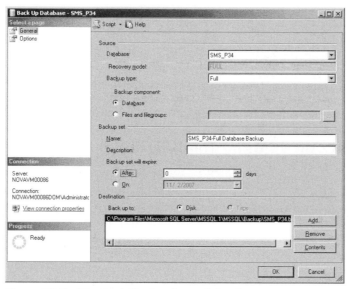

Figure 22-7   The Back Up Database dialog box

3. On the General page, confirm that your Configuration Manager database is selected as the source. Select the Backup Type to use. The default is Full, but you can choose Differential if you want, or choose to back up only the transaction log. By default, the entire database you selected is backed up.

4. Modify the name of the backup if you want and verify that the Database - Complete option has been selected. You can also specify when the backup set should expire.

5. Finally, you can use the default backup destination or add a new destination.

> **Note**   If you want or need to set additional SQL backup options such as appending to an existing backup set, verifying the backup, or truncating the transaction log, you can do so on the Options page.

6. Click OK to begin the backup process.

7. When the backup is complete, a message to that effect is displayed. Click OK.

To restore the database, follow these steps:

1. In SQL Server Management Studio, navigate to the Databases folder and expand it.

2. Select your Configuration Manager site database, right-click it, choose Tasks from the context menu, choose Restore, and then choose Database to display the Restore Database dialog box, as shown in Figure 22-8.

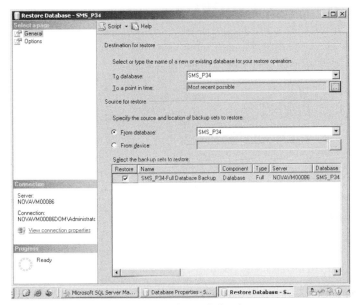

Figure 22-8   The Restore Database dialog box

3. On the General page, verify that the correct database is selected as the To Database. By default the To A Point In Time value is set to Most Recent Possible. However, by clicking the ellipsis button, you can specify a different date and time to use.

4. Verify or specify the appropriate source and backup set to restore from.

> **Note**   As with the backup command, if you need to set additional restore parameters such as overwriting the database, restricting access to the restored database, or setting the recovery state, you can do so on the Options page.

5. Click OK to begin the restore process.

6. When the restore process has completed successfully, SQL Server displays a message to that effect. Click OK.

In this section, you've looked at the procedures for backing up and restoring Configuration Manager databases using SQL Server. Note that the discussion concerned only essential procedures. You should consult the SQL Server documentation for other configuration options.

Modifying SQL Server Parameters

Several SQL Server parameters can affect how well the Configuration Manager database will be managed. SQL Server self-manages most of these parameters—that is, you shouldn't need to fool around with them. In some scenarios, however, you might choose to manually configure one or more parameters—for example, when trying to optimize the use of server resources on the SQL Server system. In those cases, when you install SQL Server pay particular attention to the following SQL Server configuration parameters and set them appropriately before installing Configuration Manager: User Connections, Open Objects, Memory, Locks, and Tempdb Size. Table 22-2 provides guidelines for setting these parameters for SQL Server 2005.

Table 22-2   SQL Server Configuration Parameters

Parameter	Guidelines
User Connections	Configuration Manager requires a minimum of 40 user connections for the site server and two connections for each Configuration Manager console you plan to install. It also requires five additional user connections for each instance of the Configuration Manager console, if more than five consoles will be running concurrently on your site. You can set Configuration Manager to calculate this number and configure it automatically during setup. Each installation of Configuration Manager requires 20 user connections. In SQL Server, this allocation is made dynamically at the time of the connection, providing more efficient memory management. The default is set to 0, which allows an unlimited number of connections.
Memory	This parameter indicates the amount of RAM that should be used for database caching and management. SQL Server allocates memory dynamically in 8-KB units. You can define a range for SQL Server to use.
Locks	This parameter prevents users from accessing and updating the same data at the same time. Because of the volume of information contained in the database, Microsoft recommends setting this value from 5000 to 10,000 depending on the size of the database and the number of Configuration Manager consoles.
Tempdb Size	This temporary database and log are used to manage queries and sorts. By default, the tempdb database and log information are maintained on the same server running SQL. It's recommended that the tempdb data device size should be at least 20 percent of the Configuration Manager database size. SQL Server, as you have by now surmised, sizes the tempdb database dynamically.

Modifying Parameters for SQL Server 2005

To modify these parameter settings for SQL Server 2005, follow these steps:

1. In SQL Server Management Studio, select your SQL Server entry (the icon of a computer with a white triangle within a green circle), right-click it, and choose Properties from the context menu to display the SQL Server Properties dialog box, as shown in Figure 22-9.

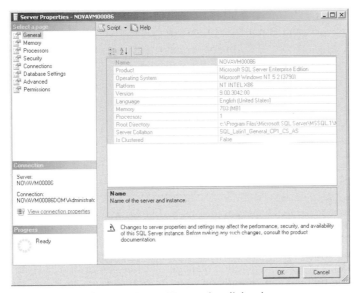

Figure 22-9   The SQL Server Properties dialog box

2. The SQL Server Properties dialog box contains pages for those parameters for which you can modify settings. (Recall from Table 22-2 that SQL Server dynamically manages most Configuration Manager–specific parameters.)

3. Select the Memory page, shown in Figure 22-10. Notice that the Index Creation Memory option is set to dynamic (0) by default, although you can modify the memory range within which SQL Server should manage memory allocation.

4. Select the Connections page, as shown in Figure 22-11. This tab displays the maximum number of user connections that were configured for SQL Server during the Configuration Manager Setup. By default, this value is set to 0, which means that SQL Server will dynamically allocate connections and appropriate resources to support them as required. The allocation of user connections is a value you should monitor, especially if you choose to enter your own maximum value. If you add Configuration Manager consoles or define additional site systems, you might need

to increase the maximum number of connections to accommodate the increased resource demand by modifying this setting.

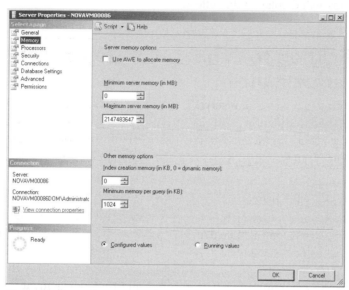

Figure 22-10   The SQL Server Properties dialog box Memory page

5. Navigate to the other pages as needed to modify settings. Refer to the SQL Server documentation for information about making changes to default settings.

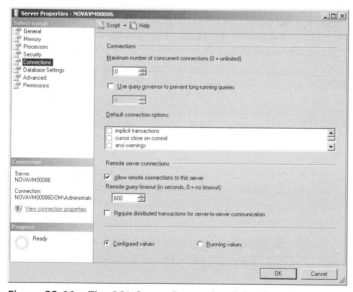

Figure 22-11   The SQL Server Properties dialog box Connections page

6. When you finish making your changes, click OK to save them. You might need to stop and then restart SQL Server to implement your changes. If this step is necessary, a message box will display to that effect.

Using SQL Replication to Enhance Configuration Manager Site Performance

Management points, and to a lesser extent server locator points, can access the Configuration Manager site database frequently to service requests made by Configuration Manager clients. This can place a significant strain on server resources on the computer hosting the Configuration Manager site database as well as generate a significant amount of network traffic.

You can mitigate these issues by installing a separate instance of SQL Server on another computer in your network and replicating the client policy tables from the Configuration Manager site database to the second instance of SQL Server. SQL Server database replication will then keep the replicated client policy database synchronized with the Configuration Manager site database. The replication process is handled entirely by the SQL Server publication and subscription services. Then configure the management point or server locator point to connect to the SQL Server computer that contains the replicated database rather than the Configuration Manager site database server. Refer to Chapter 3 for detailed steps for configuring a management point.

> **More Info**   For a more detailed discussion of how to configure SQL Server replication for Configuration Manager, see the topic "How to Configure SQL Server Site Database Replication" in the Configuration Manager Documentation Library online at the Configuration Manager TechCenter at *http://technet.microsoft.com /en-us/library/bb693697.aspx*.

Summary

After reading Chapter 21 and this chapter, you should be well aware of the importance of creating and following an ongoing maintenance schedule for your Configuration Manager database. Chapter 21 focused on tasks that can be performed directly through the Configuration Manager console. This chapter focused on the server running SQL and the tools and procedures that facilitate the management and maintenance of the server and the Configuration Manager database. You've explored ways to extract and report on data in the database, how to secure that data, and how to recover in the event of a failure of some kind. Ways to maintain the integrity of the Configuration Manager database and optimize the server running SQL that's hosting that database were also discussed.

Part IV
Appendixes

Appendix A
Recommended Web Sites

By now you should have the insight and information you need as you implement and begin managing your network using Microsoft Systems Center Configuration Manager 2007. As you venture forth into the exciting world of systems management using Configuration Manager as your management tool of choice, it will be important for you to stay on top of the product and to continue to develop your knowledge. The following Internet sites can help you in this regard.

- *http://technet.microsoft.com/en-us/configmgr/default.aspx* This site is the new Microsoft TechCenter for System Center Configuration Manager 2007. At this site, you'll find the latest information about Configuration Manager, including updates and service packs, downloadable products, software updates, and so on, as well as links to deployment and technology white papers, and the Configuration Manager Documentation Library referenced throughout this book. You'll notice six tabs on this site including the Home tab. Each provides links to additional resources related to Configuration Manager including the Configuration Manager Documentation Library, training and other learning options, downloads, support resources, and community resources. Besides the Library tab, the Community tab will be a valuable Web site for you to visit frequently. It includes links to the new Configuration Manager Forums, which replace the Systems Management Server newsgroups, a list of blogs run by Microsoft employees and teams, a list of Microsoft Valued Professionals (MVPs) and their blogs, and external resource sites. Altogether, there is a rich source of support for you as an administrator.

- *http://technet.microsoft.com/en-us/library/bb735860.aspx* The Configuration Manager Documentation Library is the online version of the local help file installed on the site server and computers running the Configuration Manager console. This is the complete set of core documentation including conceptual, planning, implementation, and management of the following features:

  - ❑ Deploying operating systems
  - ❑ Deploying software applications
  - ❑ Deploying software updates
  - ❑ Metering software usage
  - ❑ Assessing variation from desired configurations

❑   Taking hardware and software inventory

❑   Remotely administering computers

Configuration Manager 2007 has many features. Some implementations will use every feature while others might use only software updates or operating system deployment. Some administrators will inherit a fully functioning site while others must start from the beginning. The library has been structured to try to eliminate redundancy and help you find just the information you need for the features you plan to use. For example, the main table of contents as well as each new Configuration Manager feature listed under the topic Configuration Manager 2007 features has been arranged to include the following topic areas:

❑   Overview of <*feature name*>

❑   Prerequisites for <*feature name*>

❑   Planning for <*feature name*>

❑   Configuring <*feature name*>

❑   Tasks for <*feature name*>

❑   Troubleshooting <*feature name*>

❑   Security and Privacy Best Practices for <*feature name*>

❑   Technical Reference for <*feature name*>

❑   Conceptual topics that describe a feature or function begin with "About," and procedural step-by-step instructions begin with "How To" to facilitate searching through the content to find what you need. The topic "How to Use the Configuration Manager 2007 Documentation Library," located at *http://technet.microsoft.com/en-us/library/bb693895.aspx*, provides information on how to use the library more efficiently.

■ *http://blogs.technet.com/wemd_ua_-_sms_writing_team/default.aspx*   This link takes you to the Configuration Manager Writing Team blog. While the blog is not intended to provide technical support, it is used by the writing team to keep you informed about the content they are writing, the availability of new documents, updates to documents, and other news. This blog is also intended to collect feedback from you, our customers, about existing content and what you'd like to see in the future and to request your participation in early reviews of content. You can set an RSS feed from this site to keep you apprised to the newest posts.

■ *http://technet.microsoft.com/en-us/sqlserver/default.aspx*   This Microsoft Tech-Center site hosts links to updates and service packs, downloadable products, software updates, and so on, as well as links to deployment and technology white papers, and the SQL Server Books Online supporting Microsoft SQL Server 2005 and 2008 technology. Like the Configuration Manager TechCenter—in fact, like all Microsoft TechCenters—each tab provides links to valuable resources including training, support, and community resources.

■ *http://www.myitforum.com* MyITforum.com, in my opinion, continues to be the Internet's premier knowledge and information forum for IT professionals focusing on Configuration Manager and Windows management. This Web site gives IT administrators the opportunity to gain better insight about what they do by learning from and sharing information with other IT experts throughout the world. The centerpiece of myITforum.com is a collection of member forums, e-mail lists, and technical articles where IT professionals actively exchange technical tips, share their expertise, and download utilities that help them better manage their Windows environments.

myITforum.com, Inc. is owned and managed by Rod Trent, author of the best-selling books *Microsoft SMS Installer, Admin911: SMS,* and *IIS 5.0: A Beginner's Guide.* He has also written thousands of articles on topics related to the management of Microsoft Windows installations. Rod is a leading authority on Microsoft SMS and a regular speaker at the Microsoft Management Summit. Rod is also a member of a select group of Microsoft "Most Valuable Professionals" (MVPs), an honor accorded by Microsoft to "standouts in technical communities who share a passion for technology and the spirit of community."

Please visit *http://www.myitforum.com/aboutus/portfolio.asp* for a complete discussion of the value and benefits *myITforum.com* can bring to you and your organization.

Backup Control File

This appendix presents the code for the backup control file (*<Installation-Path>*\Inboxes\SMSbkup.box\SMSbkup.ctl) used by the SMS_Site_Backup service when performing a site server backup scheduled through the Backup ConfigMgr Site Server database maintenance task. This task can be enabled through the Configuration Manager console and is discussed at length in Chapter 21, "Backing Up and Recovering the Site."

```
# Backup Control File for Backup SMS Site Server task
# Systems Management Server (SMS) 2.5 Release  # Updated August 22, 2001
#!!!!!!!!!!!!!!!!!!!!!!!!!!!!!!!!!!!!!!!!!!!!!!!!!!!!!!!!!!!!!!!!!!!!!!!!!!!!!!!!!!!!
#!!!!          Modify only within the blocks designated with              !!!!#
#!!!!                                                                      !!!!#
#!!!!                  E d i t i n g   A l l o w e d                       !!!!#
#!!!!                                                                      !!!!#
#!!!! otherwise you are risking recovery when using the backup snapshot    !!!!#

#!!!! created by this control file.                                        !!!!#
#!!!!                                                                      !!!!#
#!!!! When adding custom commands, make sure there is no "#"               !!!!#
#!!!! (the comment character) at the front of the line.                    !!!!#
#!!!!                                                                      !!!!#
#!!!! For detailed editing guidelines, refer to the "Backup and Recovery"  !!!!#
#!!!! chapter in the "Administrator Reference."
#!!!!                          !!!!#
#!!!!                                                                      !!!!#
#!!!!!!!!!!!!!!!!!!!!!!!!!!!!!!!!!!!!!!!!!!!!!!!!!!!!!!!!!!!!!!!!!!!!!!!!!!!!!!!!!!!!
#!!!!!!!!!!!!!!!!!!!!!!!!!!!!!!!!!!!!!!!!!!!!!!!!!!!!!!!!!!!!!!!!!!!!!!!!!!!!!!!!!!!!
#!!!!  The backup task FAILS if there are any syntax ERRORS in this file.  !!!!!
#!!!!!!!!!!!!!!!!!!!!!!!!!!!!!!!!!!!!!!!!!!!!!!!!!!!!!!!!!!!!!!!!!!!!!!!!!!!!!!!!!!!!
#---------#
[Tokens]
#---------#
#------------------------- Default Tokens -------------------------------#
#                                                                         #
# Default tokens and their values:                                        #
# ----------------------------------------                                #
#  SITE_CODE                (3 character site code)                       #
#  SITE_SERVER              (site server)                                 #
#  SITE_DB_SERVER           (site's site system running SQL server)       #
#  PROVIDER_SERVER          (server hosting SMS provider)                 #
#  SITE_SERVER_ROOT_DIR     (SMS root directory on site server)           #
#  SITE_DB_SERVER_ROOT_DIR  (site database root directory on the site system#
#                            running SQL server)                          #
```

```
#   SITE_DB_NAME                  (site database name)                          #
#   SITE_BACKUP_DESTINATION    (BackUP Destination\<SITE_CODE>Backup)           #
#     (Backup Destination = "Backup Destination" value                         #
#                               from the "Backup SMS Site Server Proprties"    #
#                               dialog box in the Administrator console)        #
#                                                                              #
#                                                                              #
# Default destination tokens:                                                  #
#                                                                              #
SITE_SERVER_DEST     =  %SITE_BACKUP_DESTINATION%\SiteServer
SITE_DB_SERVER_DEST =   %SITE_BACKUP_DESTINATION%\SiteDBServer
PROVIDER_SERVER_DEST=   %SITE_BACKUP_DESTINATION%\ProviderServer
#-----------------------------------------------------------------------------#
#*****************************************************************************
#                                                                             *
#*-*-*-*-*-*-*-*-*-*-*-* E d i t i n g    A l l o w e d *-*-*-*-*-*-*-*-*-*-*-*
#                                                                             *
# Custom tokens syntax:                                                       *
#   <Token>=<Token Value>                                                     *
#                                                                             *
# Example:                                                                    *
#   MyToken=FOO                                                               *
#   Where MyToken is the token variable and FOO is its value                  *
#                                                                             *
#                                                                             *
# Add custom Tokens here:                                                     *
#*-*-*-*-*-*-*-*-*-*-*-*-*-*-*-*-*-*-*-*-*-*-*-*-*-*-*-*-*-*-*-*-*-*-*-*-*-*-*-*
#                                                                             *
#*****************************************************************************
#--------#
[Stop]
#--------#
#------------------------- Default Services    ------------------------#
#                                                                             #
# The following basic services are stopped by default                         #
#                                                                             #
# service      \\%SITE_SERVER%\SMS_SITE_COMPONENT_MANAGER                      #
# service      \\%SITE_SERVER%\SMS_EXECUTIVE                                   #
#-----------------------------------------------------------------------------#
#*****************************************************************************
#                                                                             *
#*-*-*-*-*-*-*-*-*-*-*-* E d i t i n g    A l l o w e d *-*-*-*-*-*-*-*-*-*-*-*
#                                                                             *
# Commands syntax :                                                           *
#   service <service name>                                                    *
#   exec <executable name>                                                    *
#   sleep <seconds>                                                           *
#                                                                             *
# Examples:                                                                   *
#   service \\%SITE_SERVER%\SMS_SQL_MONITOR                                    *
#   exec runme.exe                                                            *
```

```
#                                                                        *
# Add custome commands here :                                            *
#                                                                        *
#                                                                        *
#                                                                        *
#*-*-*-*-*-*-*-*-*-*-*-*-*-*-*-*-*-*-*-*-*-*-*-*-*-*-*-*-*-*-*-*-*-*-*-*   *
#                                                                        *
#*********************************************************************************
#--------#
[Tasks]
#--------#
# DO NOT MODIFY - Default File backup tasks - DO NOT MODIFY:#
#-----------------------------------------------------------------
file   %SITE_SERVER_ROOT_DIR%\bin            %SITE_SERVER_DEST%\SMSServer\bin
file   %SITE_SERVER_ROOT_DIR%\inboxes        %SITE_SERVER_DEST%\SMSServer\inboxes
file   %SITE_SERVER_ROOT_DIR%\Logs           %SITE_SERVER_DEST%\SMSServer\Logs
file   %SITE_SERVER_ROOT_DIR%\data           %SITE_SERVER_DEST%\SMSServer\data
file   %SITE_SERVER_ROOT_DIR%\srvacct        %SITE_SERVER_DEST%\SMSServer\srvacct
#*********************************************************************************
#                                                                        *
#*-*-*-*-*-*-*-*-*-*-* E d i t i n g   A l l o w e d *-*-*-*-*-*-*-*-*-*-*
#                                                                        *
# Command syntax :                                                       *
#                                                                        *
#   file <source> <destination>                                         *
#                                                                        *
# For examples, see default backup tasks.                               *
#                                                                        *
# Add files to back up here:                                            *
#                                                                        *
#*-*-*-*-*-*-*-*-*-*-*-*-*-*-*-*-*-*-*-*-*-*-*-*-*-*-*-*-*-*-*-*-*-*-*-*   *
#                                                                        *
#*********************************************************************************
# DO NOT MODIFY - Default Registry backup tasks - DO NOT MODIFY:#
#-----------------------------------------------------------------
# Site Server
reg \\%SITE_SERVER%\HKEY_LOCAL_MACHINE\Software\Microsoft\NAL
%SITE_SERVER_DEST%\SMSbkSiteRegNAL.dat
reg \\%SITE_SERVER%\HKEY_LOCAL_MACHINE\Software\Microsoft\SMS
%SITE_SERVER_DEST%\SMSbkSiteRegSMS.dat
#*********************************************************************************
#                                                                        *
#*-*-*-*-*-*-*-*-*-*-* E d i t i n g   A l l o w e d *-*-*-*-*-*-*-*-*-*-*
#                                                                        *
# Command syntax :                                                       *
#                                                                        *
#   reg <source> <destination>                                          *
#                                                                        *
#                                                                        *
# For examples, see default backup tasks.                               *
#                                                                        *
```

```
# The following are some registry keys that might be of interest        *
#                                                                       *
#reg \\%SITE_SERVER%\HKEY_LOCAL_MACHINE\Software\Microsoft\SNMP_EVENTS
%SITE_SERVER_DEST%\SMSbkSiteRegSNMPEvents.dat
#reg \\%SITE_SERVER%\HKEY_LOCAL_MACHINE\Software\Microsoft\Updates
%SITE_SERVER_DEST%\SMSbkSiteRegAppHotfix.dat
#reg `\\%SITE_SERVER%\HKEY_LOCAL_MACHINE\Software\Microsoft\Windows
NT\CurrentVersion\HotFix`   %SITE_SERVER_DEST%\SMSbkSiteRegOSHotfix.dat
#                                                                       *
#                                                                       *
# Add registry keys to back up here:                                   *
#*-*-*-*-*-*-*-*-*-*-*-*-*-*-*-*-*-*-*-*-*-*-*-*-*-*-*-*-*-*-*-*-*-*-*-*
#                                                                       *
#**********************************************************************************
# DO NOT MODIFY - Default SQL Data backup tasks - DO NOT MODIFY:#
#--------------------------------------------------------------------
sitedbdump  %SITE_DB_NAME%  %SITE_DB_SERVER_DEST%\SMSbkSQLDBsite.dat
#--------#
[Start]
#--------#
#**********************************************************************************
#                                                                       *
#*-*-*-*-*-*-*-*-*-* E d i t i n g   A l l o w e d *-*-*-*-*-*-*-*-*-*
#                                                                       *
# Commands syntax :                                                     *
#                                                                       *
#   service <service name>                                              *
#   exec <executable path and name>                                     *
#   sleep <seconds>                                                     *
#                                                                       *
# Examples:                                                             *
#   service \\%SITE_SERVER%\SMS_SQL_MONITOR                             *
#   exec c:\exec_full_path\runme.exe                                    *
#                                                                       *
# Add custome commands here :                                           *
#                                                                       *
#*-*-*-*-*-*-*-*-*-*-*-*-*-*-*-*-*-*-*-*-*-*-*-*-*-*-*-*-*-*-*-*-*-*-*-*
#                                                                       *
#**********************************************************************************
```

Appendix C
Understanding Windows Management Instrumentation

Windows Management Instrumentation (WMI) is Microsoft's implementation of Web-Based Enterprise Management (WBEM), an industry initiative adopted by the Distributed Management Task Force (DMTF) to implement a common interface between management applications, such as Configuration Manager, and management entities, such as Configuration Manager objects. Configuration Manager objects include discovery data, client computers, packages, advertisements, sites, and site control information. This common interface is called the Common Information Model (CIM) repository. It defines a standard schema for storing and exposing object data. Providers are components that collect object information from managed objects and store them in the CIM repository. A management application can then obtain that information from the CIM repository and make it available for viewing and analysis.

This interface feature is similar to installing a Windows device driver such as a printer driver. The print device manufacturer provides a printer driver that's compatible with Windows. All Windows applications use this same printer driver to generate print jobs on the print device. Using a similar premise, with WMI installed, any management application program can collect and set configuration details for a wide variety of hardware types, operating system components, and application systems because it uses providers to work with those systems. Providers can be written to store and expose data in the CIM repository, and management applications (written with Microsoft Visual Basic, SQL Server, Java, Open Database Connectivity [ODBC], Active Directory Service Interface [ADSI], and so on) can be created to obtain that data from the CIM repository.

To illustrate, a hardware provider on the Configuration Manager client stores Configuration Manager object information such as hardware inventory in the CIM repository. Configuration Manager agents such as the Hardware Inventory Client Agent extract that data from the CIM repository and report it to the Configuration Manager database. The Configuration Manager Provider, which can be installed on the Configuration Manager site server or the SQL Server, accesses the Configuration Manager database to provide the data to the Configuration Manager Administrator Console.

The Configuration Manager site database objects, views, and tables aren't directly accessible or modifiable except through the WMI layer. Configuration Manager provides an open architecture, however, that makes it possible to create tools other than the Configuration Manager Administrator Console that can access and manipulate the Configuration Manager database objects. In essence, you could use any WMI-compliant and ODBC-compliant application to access these objects. So you could view the data with a Web browser using ActiveX controls or Java, through applications written using C++, Visual Basic, or the Component Object Model (COM).

WMI is installed with Windows 2000 Server and later operating systems.

Glossary

Active Directory   The fully extensible and scalable directory service used by Windows Server 2003 to identify all resources on a network and make them available to users and applications. It is designed to make the physical location of the resource transparent to the user or application, thus providing a single point of logon for users and a single point of object administration.

Active Directory system discovery   The Configuration Manager discovery method designed to poll the closest Active Directory domain controller and return system objects that are stored as discovered records in the Configuration Manager site database.

Active Directory system group discovery   The Configuration Manager discovery method designed to poll the closest Active Directory domain controller and return system group objects that are stored as discovered records in the Configuration Manager site database.

Active Directory user discovery   The Configuration Manager discovery method designed to poll the closest Active Directory domain controller and return user objects that are stored as discovered records in the Configuration Manager site database.

active Internet-based software update point   The software update point for a site that accepts communication from only client computers on the Internet. An active Internet-based software update point can only be installed when the site server is configured for native mode and when an active software update point has been configured to handle communication from only clients on the intranet. There can be only one active Internet-based software update point configured for a site.

active software update point   The software update point for a site that communicates with WSUS to configure software updates synchronization settings and initiate synchronization with WSUS. The active software update point can be configured to accept communication from clients from the intranet and Internet. There can be only one active software update point configured for a site.

actual compliance   Defines the compliance as evaluated for a configuration item when it is applied to a selected configuration baseline rule.

address   A property of the Configuration Manager site that defines connection information to other Configuration Manager sites.

advanced client   An SMS 2003 client type supported on Windows 2000 or later operating systems. The advanced client can be assigned to a Configuration Manager 2007 mixed mode site, but cannot support all Configuration Manager features.

Advertised Programs client agent   The Configuration Manager client agent that monitors for available advertised programs that target the client or the user at the client.

advertisement   A Configuration Manager object that makes the program and package available to a specified collection.

applicability   Defines whether a configuration item should be included in the evaluation compliance (for example, an exact Windows platform version).

application configuration item   Determines compliance for an application.

This can include whether the application is installed as well as details about its configuration.

assigned management point   The default management point located by the client for its assigned site.

assigned site   A site to which a Configuration Manager client is currently assigned.

Background Intelligent Transfer Service (BITS)   A Configuration Manager bandwidth throttling tool that enables administrators to control network transfer rates as well as providing a checkpoint restart of a download. For example, if a package download is interrupted or the connection is lost as the result of slow or unreliable network connections, the download can continue at that point rather than restarting from the beginning of the download.

BITS   See *Background Intelligent Transfer Service (BITS)*.

boot image   A WIM image that contains the appropriate version of Windows PE. A boot image used during deployment of the target computer to allow the Task Sequence to lay down the new image on the drive. While running from the boot image, you are able to format and repartition the system drive on the target computer(s).

boundary   An IP subnet, IP address range, IPv6 prefix, or Active Directory site that is used to define the scope of administrative control for a Configuration Manager site. Boundaries are used by the site to determine which distribution points are closest for retrieving content and used by the client to automatically determine to which site it should be assigned. The Configuration Manager 2007 administrator configures each boundary in the site to be either fast or slow, depending on the connection speed. If a client is connected to a fast boundary, such as a 10-Mbps local area network (LAN), it might install software; but if the client is connected to a slow boundary, such as a dial-up network or a wireless network, it might install the software differently, or might not install the software at all.

branch distribution point   A Configuration Manager site system that has the role of storing package source files but is designed to be located in a distributed location with limited network bandwidth or a limited number of clients. As such, it can utilize either a server-class or a desktop-class computer. When used, clients contact a branch distribution point in the same manner as they would a standard distribution point to obtain source files when they run advertised programs.

central site   A Configuration Manager primary site that resides at the top of the Configuration Manager hierarchy. Database information rolls from child to parent and is collected ultimately at the central site's Configuration Manager database. A central site can administer any site below it in the Configuration Manager hierarchy and can send information down to its child sites.

child configuration item   A copy of a configuration item that continues to inherit the properties of the original configuration item.

child site   A site that has a parent site. In a Configuration Manager site hierarchy, every site except the central site is another site's child. Unlike the terms primary site and secondary site, in which a site is one or the other, the terms parent and child are relative; a site can be both.

client agent   Software that runs on Configuration Manager clients and performs client-side functions associated with a specific Configuration Manager feature, such as software metering.

client component   A Configuration Manager thread, service, or application that runs on clients and provides Configuration Manager functionality to the client.

client configured for Internet or intranet management   A Configuration Manager 2007 client that has been installed and configured such that it can be managed either on the intranet or over the Internet.

client configured for Internet-only management   A Configuration Manager 2007 client that has been installed such that it cannot be managed on the intranet and can be managed only over the Internet.

client configured for intranet-only management   A Configuration Manager 2007 client that has been installed such that it is currently configured to be managed on the intranet and could be managed over the Internet if configured to do so.

collection   A group of Configuration Manager resources that can consist of computers, Microsoft Windows users and user groups, and any resources discovered through the Network Discovery method or the Active Directory directory service discovery method.

Collection Evaluator   The Configuration Manager thread component that performs collection management tasks such as updating or refreshing collection data

ConfigMgr connection type   A property displayed in the client's Configuration Manager to indicate whether the client is currently being managed on the Internet or the intranet, or can be managed only on the Internet or the intranet.

configuration baseline   Defines a set of configurations that are evaluated for compliance as a group.

configuration baseline assignment   The means by which a configuration baseline is targeted to computers. It contains the configuration baseline, the targeted collection, and the compliance evaluation schedule.

configuration baseline rules   Specifies how the configuration items included in the configuration baseline are to be evaluated for compliance on client computers.

configuration category   A logical grouping in the Configuration Manager console that provides the administrator with a method of sorting and filtering configuration baselines and configuration items.

configuration data   A collective term that includes one or more configuration baselines or configuration items.

configuration item   Contains one or more elements and their validation criteria, and they typically define a unit of configuration to monitor at the level of independent change.

Configuration Manager client   A computer, mobile device, or other type of device running Configuration Manager client components.

Configuration Manager client policy   Instructions for the Configuration Manager clients that clients download from their default or proxy management point.

Configuration Manager console   The primary interface used to administer Configuration Manager. The Configuration Manager console allows you to configure, run, and access ConfigMgr features and tools. The Configuration Manager console is an MMC snap-in.

Configuration Manager health state reference   A reference that is published to Active Directory Domain Services to refer to Configuration Manager NAP policies and stored for the System Health Validator (SHV) to use in determining the compliance of NAP-capable Configuration Manager clients.

Configuration Manager resource   An object (such as a computer, a router, a mobile device, or a user group) that can be discovered and potentially become a Configuration Manager client and be managed by Configuration Manager. Resources and clients are organized into collections.

Configuration Manager site   A collection of clients and Configuration Manager site systems that are bounded by a group of subnets, such as IP subnets or an Active Directory site, and which are specified by a Configuration Manager administrator as a site.

Configuration Manager site hierarchy   The relationship of all the Configuration Manager sites in an organization. A site hierarchy is made up of parent and child sites. The main administrative site at the top of the hierarchy is known as the central site.

Configuration Manager site server   The Windows server on which Configuration Manager has been installed and that manages the Configuration Manager site and all its component attributes and services.

Configuration Manager site system   A Windows server that performs one or more of the nine Configuration Manager roles for a Configuration Manager site.

Configuration Pack   Configuration data published by Microsoft and partners as best practice configurations.

courier sender   A type of Configuration Manager communication mechanism that enables you to create and send package information to another Configuration Manager site through non-network channels.

Dashboard   A set of reports that you can display in a grid format to facilitate the quick review of one or more specific or related reports. Dashboards can display any report except those that require prompted values.

database   A collection of data records, object tables, and indexes organized in a specific structure designed to facilitate the

displaying, sorting, updating, and analysis of the information it contains.

default management point   The active management point for a site. Although additional management points can be configured in a site, clients will not communicate with it unless it is designated as a default management point, part of the designated default NLB management point cluster, or an Internet-based management point.

dependent configuration baseline   A configuration baseline that is included in the compliance of another configuration baseline.

deployment package   The software updates object that is used to store software update files and deliver the update files to distribution points.

deployment template   The software updates object that stores many of the deployment settings and is used as part of the recommended deployment process to automatically populate the settings when creating deployments.

desired configuration management   The ability to define granular computer configurations within an organization and compare and report compliance or non compliance among managed computers.

detection   Defines how to identify an application in an application configuration item, or identifies the Windows version for an operating system configuration item.

device management point   A Configuration Manager site system role that communicates with mobile device clients.

direct membership collection   A collection whose members are explicitly defined and maintained by the Configuration Manager administrator rather than by an automated query.

Discovery Data Manager   The Configuration Manager site server component responsible for receiving and processing discovery records into the Configuration Manager site database. It is also responsible for forwarding appropriate data to parent sites.

Discovery Data Record (DDR)   The record that is created for a resource and included in the Configuration Manager database when a Configuration Manager discovery method discovers that resource.

distribution point   A Configuration Manager site system role that stores the package files, programs, and scripts necessary for a package to execute successfully at a Configuration Manager client computer.

DNS publishing   The use of a service resource record (SRV) in DNS to facilitate the location of a client's default management point.

duplicate configuration baseline   An exact copy of another configuration baseline that does not retain any relationship to the original configuration baseline and can be edited.

duplicate configuration item   An exact copy of another configuration item that does not retain any relationship to the original configuration item and can be edited.

effective date   Date associated with a specific Microsoft software update so that Configuration Manager 2007 clients that can support Network Access Protection and have the Network Access Protection client agent enabled will evaluate their compliance for that software.

fallback status point   A Configuration Manager site system that gathers state messages from clients that cannot install properly, cannot assign to a Configuration Manager 2007 site, or cannot find or communicate with their assigned management point. State messages are also sent to the fallback status point when the client installs and assigns successfully.

general configuration item   Determines compliance for general settings and objects, where their existence does not depend on the operating system, an application, or a software update.

Hardware Inventory   The automated process Configuration Manager uses to gather detailed information about the hardware in use on client computers in your organization.

Hardware Inventory Client Agent   The Configuration Manager client component responsible for collecting and reporting hardware inventory data to a management point based on an administrator-defined frequency.

health   Information about an NAP-capable client computer that Network Access Protection uses to allow or deny unlimited access to a network. Health is defined by a client computer's configuration state. Health information is encapsulated in a statement of health (SoH), which is issued by a system health agent (SHA) on an NAP-capable client computer.

health state reference publishing account   The account used by the Configuration Manager site server to publish the Configuration Manager health state reference to Active Directory Domain Services.

health state reference querying account   The account used by the Configuration Manager System Health Validator point to retrieve the Configuration Manager health state references from Active Directory Domain Services.

Heartbeat Discovery   The Configuration Manager discovery method designed to keep existing Discovery Data Records (DDRs) up to date rather than re-creating new DDRs.

IDMIF file   A customized Management Information Format (MIF) file that creates or updates new or custom architectures in the Configuration Manager database.

image   A collection of files and folders that duplicates the original file and folder structure of an existing computer, including the file and folder structure of the operating system, or that is a file-based replica of a hard disk saved as a WIM format file.

index   A companion object to a table that functions much like an index in a book, providing a quick way to search and locate data.

instance   A copy of SQL Server running on a computer. A computer can run multiple instances of SQL Server 2005.

Internet-based client management   A deployment configuration in Configuration Manager 2007 that allows you to manage computers that have the Configuration Manager 2007 client but do not connect into the network through a VPN or dial-up connection. Internet-based client management requires Configuration Manager 2007 native mode.

Internet-based computer management   The ability to manage Configuration Manager 2007 clients when they are not connected to your company network but have a standard Internet connection.

Internet-based site system   A site system role that allows connections from clients when they are managed over the Internet.

maintenance window   A property of a collection that lets you define a specific period of time within which changes can be made to clients that are members of that collection.

Managed Object Format (MOF) file   A text file that loads schema information into the CIM Object Manager. Using any text editor, you can modify this file to customize the hardware data collected from Configuration Manager clients. The master template for this file is stored on the Configuration Manager site server in

C:\Program.Files\MicrosoftSCCM2007\inboxes\clifiles.src\hinv. It is incorporated into a client policy that is stored on the management point and updated at each client at the next client update interval.

Management Information Format (MIF)   A standard file format designed by the Desktop Management Task Force for defining the way data is viewed and added to a database. In Configuration Manager, additional inventory information from a client is reported using an MIF file. MIF files can be ASCII text or binary (formerly called a Delta MIF file), and either type can be a full MIF file or an update (formerly called a partial MIF file). Configuration Manager services use MIF files to add information to the Configuration Manager site database.

management point   The Configuration Manager site system role that serves as the primary point of contact between clients and the Configuration Manager site server.

Microsoft System Center Configuration Manager 2007 Configuration Packs   Configuration data published by Microsoft and partners as best practice configurations.

mixed mode   An operational mode of Configuration Manager 2007 that provides backward compatibility with SMS 2003 sites and provides a basic level of security for organizations that cannot meet the PKI requirements for native mode.

mobile device management   The ability to manage Configuration Manager 2007 Windows Mobile and Windows CE mobile devices similar to the way that Configuration Manager 2007 manages desktop computers, including hardware and software inventory, software distribution and updates, file collection, and Windows Mobile Settings.

NAP agent   The Windows NAP agent is a client-side service that collects and manages health information. The NAP agent mediates communication of client health status between installed system health agents and enabled NAP enforcement clients.

NAP-capable computer   Windows-based clients that support Network Access Protection, either natively or after installing a Network Access Protection client. Examples are Windows Vista, Windows Server 2008, and Windows XP Professional Service Pack 2 with Network Access Protection Client for Windows XP Service Pack 2.

NAP enforcement client   An NAP client software component that integrates with network access or communication technologies, such as DHCP, VPN, 802.1X, IPsec, and Terminal Services gateway. The NAP enforcement client requests access to a network, communicates the NAP client's health status to the NAP enforcement point that is providing the network access, and communicates the restricted status of the client computer to other components of the NAP client architecture.

NAP enforcement method   Types of network access or communication that can use NAP to enforce restricted network access or communication for noncompliant clients. The enforcement methods included with Windows Vista and Windows Server 2008 are Internet Protocol security (IPsec)-protected traffic, 802.1X-authenticated connections, remote access virtual private network (VPN) connections, Dynamic Host Control Protocol (DHCP) address configurations, and Terminal Server Gateway connections.

NAP evaluation   Means by which Configuration Manager 2007 NAP clients evaluate compliance with Configuration Manager NAP policies.

NAP health policy server   A Network Policy Server that is acting in the role of an NAP health evaluation server. The NAP health policy server has health policies and network policies that are used to evaluate compliance of NAP client computers.

NAP-ineligible computer   Clients that are not capable of supporting Network Access Protection either natively or by installing a Network Access Protection client. Examples are Windows 2000 Professional, Windows XP Professional Service Pack 1, and Windows Server 2003.

NAP-upgradable computer   An operating system that does not ship with NAP client bits, although NAP client bits shipped out-of-band can be installed on the operating system. By using Configuration Manager, these machines can be upgraded by distributing NAP client bundle. Example: XP SP2.

native mode   A security-based operational mode setting in Configuration Manager 2007, where the site server signs all policies and where site systems require mutually authenticated SSL connections to client computers.

Network Access Protection (NAP)   A policy enforcement platform built into Microsoft Windows Vista and Windows Server 2008 that allows you to better protect your private network by enforcing compliance with computer health requirements.

Network Access Protection (NAP) for Configuration Manager   The ability to leverage Windows server NAP to identify and remediate managed clients using Configuration Manager features such as software updates.

network discovery   The Configuration Manager discovery method designed to provide the Configuration Manager administrator with the means of discovering any network resources that are IP addressable.

NOIDMIF file A customized Management Information Format (MIF) file that can be used to extend hardware inventory collected at the Configuration Manager client. NOIDMIFs can be created by the administrator or supplied by third-party developers or products.

noncompliance severity level A property of a configuration item that allows the administration to rate the severity of the noncompliance status to prioritize attention and the need to take remedial action.

operating system configuration item Determines compliance for settings relating to the operating system version and configuration.

operating system deployment The ability to create and manage images that can be deployed to computers managed by Configuration Manager 2007 and to unmanaged computers using bootable media such as CD set or DVD.

operating system image A WIM image that contains all the files necessary to install the desired operating system on a target computer, and any other packages needed.

package Generally represents a software application that needs to be installed on a Configuration Manager client computer, but might also contain update programs or software patches, single files such as a virus update file, or no files at all—just a command to execute a program already resident on the client.

package definition file A predefined file that contains all the package and program information required for Configuration Manager to successfully distribute the package and, usually, to deploy it.

parent site A Configuration Manager site that has one or more child sites. Parent sites are always primary sites. The parent site at the top of a Configuration Manager hierarchy is called the central site.

perimeter network A computer host or small network inserted as a neutral or boundary network between a private network and a public network such as the Internet. Firewalls isolate perimeter networks both from the Internet and from the private network. A perimeter network is also known as a demilitarized zone (DMZ) or screened subnet.

primary site A site that has its own Configuration Manager site database to store information for itself and its child sites. Primary sites can report to other primary sites and can have both primary and secondary sites report to them.

program Identifies what should occur on the client when the package is received, such as an installation command or script file.

Program Download Monitor A Configuration Manager application that is installed on Configuration Manager clients and provides audit information about programs that are pending to run on the client.

proxy management point A Configuration Manager site system role that clients can use in place of their default management point when it is installed in a secondary site that is attached to their assigned site.

PXE service point A Configuration Manager site system role that is configured to respond to PXE requests from computers that have been imported into Configuration Manager.

query A set of criteria used to find objects in a Configuration Manager site database. When run, a query searches the Configuration Manager site database for objects that match the query's criteria.

query attribute An object contained within an attribute class such as the IP Addresses, IP Subnets, NetBIOS Name, Operating System Name and Version, and Configuration Manager Assigned Sites attributes contained in the System Resource attribute class.

query attribute class   A category of attributes that contains an attribute list. For example, the System Resource attribute class includes the IP Addresses, IP Subnets, NetBIOS Name, Operating System Name and Version, and Configuration Manager Assigned Sites attributes.

query-based collection   A collection whose members are defined by running a Configuration Manager query and that can be configured to automatically update its membership by specifying the query to run on a predefined schedule.

query criteria   The set of criteria used to search for objects.

query expression   A statement that uses an operator (such as "is equal to" or "is like") to compare a specific value against a specific attribute. An expression is made up of an attribute, an operator, and a value.

query group   A set of expressions that are explicitly grouped by parentheses. By making a set of expressions a group, you ensure that the group's expressions are treated as a single entity. Groups have a higher operator precedence than the logical operators (AND, OR, and NOT).

query relational operator   Part of an expression (such as "is equal to" or "is like") that defines how a specified attribute should be compared with a value.

query result format   The format used to display the results of a query. You use a query result format to select which attributes to display for the list of objects returned in the Details pane. A format is specific to a single architecture. For example, you cannot use a query format defined for an Employee object type to display computers that have a Systems object type.

read-only configuration data   A configuration baseline or configuration item that has been imported or inherited from a parent site and cannot be edited.

remediation server   A server used to bring a noncompliant computer back into compliance.

reference computer   An existing computer configured with the appropriate operating system and other settings and programs from which you create an operating system deployment operating system image.

Remote Assistance   A feature of Windows XP and later operating systems that allows you to ask for or accept help from someone using a different computer by creating an encrypted connection between the two computers over the network or Internet.

Remote Control   A subfeature of remote tools that can be used to view or operate a computer, troubleshoot hardware and software configuration problems on remote client computers, and to provide remote help desk support when access to the user's computer is necessary anywhere in the Configuration Manager 2007 site hierarchy.

Remote Desktop   A feature of Windows XP and later operating systems that allows you to connect to a computer at a different location from your own and have access to all the programs, files, and network resources available on that computer. While connected to a system by remote desktop, the display on the remote system indicates that the system is locked, preventing the remote user(s) from viewing your actions.

Remote Desktop Protocol (RDP)   The networking protocol used by Remote Desktop and Remote Assistance on computers running Windows XP, Windows Vista, and Windows Server 2003.

Remote Tools   A Configuration Manager feature that allows you to remotely access and operate client computers in the Configuration Manager site.

Remote Tools client agent   One of the client components that is installed when a computer becomes a Configuration Manager client. This agent is enabled and configured through the Configuration Manager console and defines how remote sessions are handled and initiated through Configuration Manager.

reporting point   A Configuration Manager site system role that stores the report files used for the Web-based reporting feature in Configuration Manager

resource   An object (such as a computer, a router, a mobile device, or a user group) that can be discovered and potentially become a Configuration Manager client and be managed by Configuration Manager.

restricted network access   Specifies the type of access that a noncompliant computer has to a network. Usually, a computer with restricted network access can access only remediation servers.

results pane   The middle pane in Microsoft Management Console (MMC) that displays details for the selected item in the console tree. The details can be a list of items or they can be administrative properties, services, and events that are acted on by a snap-in.

Run Advertised Programs   A Configuration Manager application that is installed on Configuration Manager clients and is used to display available advertisements, select advertisements to run, and view the properties of advertisements.

secondary site   A child of a primary Configuration Manager site that does not have its own site database to store information. Secondary sites propagate data to its primary site's site database and cannot support child sites of their own.

selective download   The process where Configuration Manager clients retrieve only the update files that are applicable and required from a deployment package.

sender   Any of the six Configuration Manager communication mechanisms used to transmit data and control bandwidth usage and fault tolerance between sites.

server locator point   A Configuration Manager site system that completes site assignment and can locate management points for Configuration Manager clients when clients cannot retrieve that information from Active Directory Domain Services or other mechanisms.

service location   The means by which clients can automatically discover and select a network service—for example, through Active Directory publishing or DNS SRV resource records.

Service Manager   A tool in the Configuration Manager console that is used to configure and enable browsing for Configuration Manager components. It also provides an at-a-glance view of Configuration Manager components and services running on the site server and on each site.

site assignment   The process of including selected resources in a Configuration Manager site.

site assignment rules   The conditions by which a Configuration Manager client can belong to a site, and includes boundaries, client version, and site mode.

site boundary   Used to assign Configuration Manager clients to a Configuration Manager site based on their IP subnet, IPv6 prefix, the IP address range they belong to, or an Active Directory site association.

site code   A three-character code that Configuration Manager uses to uniquely identify a

Configuration Manager site. The site code is specified during the site installation and cannot be changed after installation.

site control file An ASCII text file that contains the settings of a Configuration Manager site

site database server A Configuration Manager site system role assigned to the computer that hosts the Configuration Manager site database (a SQL Server database). The computer might or might not be the site server.

Software Inventory The automated process Configuration Manager uses to gather detailed information about the software installed on client computers in your organization.

Software Inventory Client Agent The Configuration Manager client component responsible for collecting and reporting software inventory data to a management point based on an administrator-defined frequency.

Software Metering A Configuration Manager feature that gives you the ability to collect and monitor program usage on Configuration Manager client computers, including the users running the program, when the program started, and when it stopped.

Software Metering Rule A software metering instruction that identifies for the client agent which programs should be monitored and how they should be monitored.

software update file The software update file is the actual file that the client downloads and installs as part of a deployment. Update files can be executables (.exe), Windows Installer (.msi) files, Windows Installer patches (.msp), or update package (.msu) files.

software update point A site role installed on a computer running Windows Server Update Services 3.0. There can be multiple software update point site system servers in a site, but only one active software update point and one active Internet-based software update point can be configured. For more information, see Active software update point and Active Internet-based software update point.

software update point A Configuration Manager site system role required for the software updates feature that is configured on a computer running Windows Server Update Services 3.0.

Software Updates Client Agent The client agent for the software updates feature that is made up of several subcomponents that handle the scan for software updates compliance, takes action on deployment policies received, and handles the download and installation of software updates. The Software Updates Client Agent is enabled by default and is a required component of software updates.

software updates configuration item Determines compliance of software updates using the software updates feature in Configuration Manager.

software updates metadata The software updates metadata is received on the central site when synchronizing with Microsoft Update and then replicated down the Configuration Manager hierarchy. The metadata includes information about each software update, such as name, description, installation information, applicability rules, relationship to other updates, and revision number.

software updates synchronization Software updates synchronization is the process of retrieving software updates metadata from the configured upstream update server. The active software update point on the central site synchronizes with Microsoft Update. The active software update point child sites in the hierarchy synchronize with the active software update point configured for the parent site.

standard sender   A type of Configuration Manager communication mechanism that enables you to create and send package information to another Configuration Manager site over standard network channels.

state migration point   A Configuration Manager site system role used to store migrated settings during the capture phase of the deployment task sequence.

Statement of Health (SoH)   A declaration from a System Health Agent (SHA) on an NAP-capable client computer that asserts its health status. SHAs create SoHs and send them to a corresponding System Health Validator (SHV) on an NAP health policy server.

status filter rule   Configuration Manager rule that controls how status messages are reported and viewed.

status message   A message generated by Configuration Manager components and services that represents the flow of process activity for each site system and client.

status message threshold   A limit that defines when the summary status for a Configuration Manager component or site system should indicate OK, Warning, or Critical status.

status message summarizer   A Configuration Manager component that consolidates the data generated by Configuration Manager status messages into a succinct view of the status of a component, a server, a package, or an advertisement.

status message viewer   A tool in the Configuration Manager console that is used to browse the status messages in the Configuration Manager site database.

stored procedure   A group of Transact-SQL statements that have been compiled into a single executable routine.

subcollection   In Configuration Manager, subcollections are collections that have been linked to other collections. These might simply be existing collections that have been linked to another collection, or a collection specifically created as dependent on a parent collection. Subcollections do not inherit the attributes of the parent collection and are not considered to be members of the containing collection. Each subcollection has its own identity and membership rules, and the query that creates a collection is completely separate from the query that creates the subcollection.

Subject Alternative Name (SAN)   Also known as the Subject Alternate Name extension. An optional attribute of a PKI certificate that allows you to specify multiple FQDNs, which is required with Internet-based client management if the Internet-based site systems allow clients to connect from both the Internet and from the intranet.

System Health Validator (SHV)   Server software that validates the output from a Microsoft policy client to determine whether or not the statement of health (SoH) submitted by an individual System Health Agent is policy-compliant.

System Health Validator point   The Configuration Manager site system role assigned to the Network Policy Server(s) for a Configuration Manager 2007 site that validates the output from a non-Microsoft policy client to determine whether or not the Statement of Health (SoH) submitted by an individual System Health Agent is policy-compliant.

table   A database object that contains data in the database organized as a collection of rows and columns.

target computer   Configuration Manager client computers that receive a Configuration Manager advertisement such as a software distribution package program or a task sequence.

task group   A collection of one or more task steps within a task sequence that functions as a related set of tasks.

task sequence   A collection of one or more task steps that run in a specific order and carry out tasks specific to the deployment process you create or customize. They are used with operating system deployment to build reference computers, capture an image, migrate user or computer settings, advertise the image to target computers, and run a specific sequence of steps.

task step   A configurable action that carries out a specific task within a task sequence.

transaction log   A portion of the database used to record each action performed on the database, such as adding a new record or updating or deleting an existing record.

trigger   A Transact-SQL statement that's executed whenever a specific event occurs in a given table.

unlimited network access   The access that a compliant or exempted computer has to a network (does not have any location or time-based constraints).

unmanaged client   A client that is not communicating with its assigned site in the Configuration Manager hierarchy, and so, for example, cannot receive policy or upload inventory data.

update list   The server that WSUS running on the active software update point or active Internet-based software update

point connects to when synchronizing software updates metadata. For the active software update point on the central site, the upstream update server is Microsoft Update. For the active software update point on child sites, the upstream update server is the active software update point for the parent site. For active Internet-based software update points, the upstream update server is the active software update point for the same site.

upstream update server   The software updates object that is simply a list of software updates. Using the update list is part of the recommended deployment process.

Windows Management Instrumentation (WMI)   The Microsoft implementation of Web-Based Enterprise Management (WBEM), one of the Desktop Management Task Force (DMTF) standards for identifying and manipulating managed objects.

Wake On Lan (WOL)   A feature of Configuration Manager that can send wake-up transmissions prior to the configured deadline for a software update deployment or at the configured schedule of a mandatory advertisement (which can be for software distribution or a task sequence).

Windows Preinstallation Environment (Windows PE)   Windows PE is a Windows operating system with limited services built on the full operating system platform that you are deploying.

Index

About the Author

Steven D. Kaczmarek, MCP, MCT, MCSE, is a content publishing manager in the Management Solutions Division – User Assistance (MSD UA) at Microsoft in Redmond, Washington. He and his team are responsible for generating customer-ready documentation for System Center Configuration Manager 2007 and its related products and Microsoft Application Virtualization based in Cambridge, Massachusetts. Prior to this role, Steve was a senior technical writer on the same team and the project lead for Systems Management Server (SMS) 2003 core documentation. He is the author of the *Microsoft Systems Management Server 2003 Administrator's Companion* published by Microsoft Press, which won a Merit Award from the Puget Sound Chapter of the Society for Technical Communication (STC) in 2005. Prior to joining Microsoft, Steve enjoyed success as a professional trainer, writer, and consultant specializing in SMS and contributes as a speaker at the annual Microsoft Management Summits. Outside of Microsoft, Steve enjoys tending his garden and traveling about the Puget Sound area with his partner, Bill, and their dog, Scruffy.

Steve has a master of science degree from Loyola University in Chicago, Illinois, with a specialization in computational mathematics.

2007 Microsoft® Office System Resources for Developers and Administrators

Microsoft Office SharePoint® Server 2007 Administrator's Companion

Bill English with the Microsoft SharePoint Community Experts
ISBN 9780735622821

Get your mission-critical collaboration and information management systems up and running. This comprehensive, single-volume reference details features and capabilities of SharePoint Server 2007. It delivers easy-to-follow procedures, practical workarounds, and key troubleshooting tactics—for on-the-job results.

Microsoft Windows SharePoint Services Version 3.0 Inside Out

Jim Buyens
ISBN 9780735623231

Conquer Microsoft Windows SharePoint Services— from the inside out! This ultimate, in-depth reference packs hundreds of time-saving solutions, troubleshooting tips, and workarounds. You're beyond the basics, so now learn how the experts tackle information sharing and team collaboration— and challenge yourself to new levels of mastery!

Microsoft SharePoint Products and Technologies Administrator's Pocket Consultant

Ben Curry
ISBN 9780735623828

Portable and precise, this pocket-sized guide delivers immediate answers for the day-to-day administration of Sharepoint Products and Technologies. Featuring easy-to-scan tables, step-by-step instructions, and handy lists, this book offers the straightforward information you need to get the job done—whether you're at your desk or in the field!

Inside Microsoft Windows® SharePoint Services Version 3

Ted Pattison and Daniel Larson
ISBN 9780735623200

Get in-depth insights on Microsoft Windows SharePoint Services with this hands-on guide. You get a bottom-up view of the platform architecture, code samples, and task-oriented guidance for developing custom applications with Microsoft Visual Studio® 2005 and Collaborative Application Markup Language (CAML).

Inside Microsoft Office SharePoint Server 2007

Patrick Tisseghem
ISBN 9780735623682

Dig deep—and master the intricacies of Office SharePoint Server 2007. A bottom-up view of the platform architecture shows you how to manage and customize key components and how to integrate with Office programs—helping you create custom enterprise content management solutions.

Microsoft Office Communications Server 2007 Resource Kit

Microsoft Office Communications Server Team
ISBN 9780735624061

Your definitive reference to Office Communications Server 2007—direct from the experts who know the technology best. This comprehensive guide offers in-depth technical information and best practices for planning, designing, deploying, managing, and optimizing your systems. Includes a toolkit of valuable resources on CD.

Programming Applications for Microsoft Office Outlook® 2007

Randy Byrne and Ryan Gregg
ISBN 9780735622494

Microsoft Office Visio® 2007 Programming Step by Step

David A. Edson
ISBN 9780735623798

See more resources at **microsoft.com/mspress**
and **microsoft.com/learning**

Microsoft Press® products are available worldwide wherever quality computer books are sold. For more information, contact your bookseller, computer retailer, software reseller, or local Microsoft Sales Office, or visit our Web site at **microsoft.com/mspress**. To locate a source near you, or to order directly, call 1-800-MSPRESS in the United States. (In Canada, call **1-800-268-2222**.)

Windows Vista™ Resources for Administrators

Windows Vista Administrator's Pocket Consultant
William Stanek
ISBN 9780735622968

Portable and precise, this pocket-sized guide delivers immediate answers for the day-to-day administration of Windows Vista. Featuring easy-to-scan tables, step-by-step instructions, and handy lists, this book offers the straightforward information you need to solve problems and get the job done—whether you're at your desk or in the field!

Windows Vista Resource Kit
Mitch Tulloch, Tony Northrup, Jerry Honeycutt, Ed Wilson, Ralph Ramos, and the Windows Vista Team
ISBN 9780735622838

Get the definitive reference for deploying, configuring, and supporting Windows Vista—from the experts who know the technology best. This guide offers in-depth, comprehensive technical guidance on automating deployment; implementing security enhancements; administering group policy, files folders, and programs; and troubleshooting. Includes an essential toolkit of resources on DVD.

MCTS Self-Paced Training Kit (Exam 70-620): Configuring Windows Vista Client
Ian McLean and Orin Thomas
ISBN 9780735623903

Get in-depth preparation plus practice for Exam 70-620, the required exam for the new Microsoft Certified Technology Specialist (MCTS): Windows Vista Client certification. This 2-in-1 kit focuses on installing client software and configuring system settings, security features, network connectivity, media applications, and mobile devices. Ace your exam prep—and build real-world job skills—with lessons, practice tests, evaluation software, and more.

MCITP Self-Paced Training Kit (Exam 70-622): Installing, Maintaining, Supporting, and Troubleshooting Applications on the Windows Vista Client – Enterprise
Tony Northrup and J.C. Mackin
ISBN 9780735624085

Maximize your performance on Exam 70-622, the required exam for the new Microsoft® Certified IT Professional (MCITP): Enterprise Support Technician certification. Comprehensive and in-depth, this 2-in-1 kit covers managing security, configuring networking, and optimizing performance for Windows Vista clients in an enterprise environment. Ace your exam prep—and build real-world job skills—with lessons, practice tests, evaluation software, and more.

MCITP Self-Paced Training Kit (Exam 70-623): Installing, Maintaining, Supporting, and Troubleshooting Applications on the Windows Vista Client – Consumer
Anil Desai with Chris McCain of GrandMasters
ISBN 9780735624238

Get the 2-in-1 training kit for Exam 70-623, the required exam for the new Microsoft Certified IT Professional (MCITP): Consumer Support Technician certification. This comprehensive kit focuses on supporting Windows Vista clients for consumer PCs and devices, including configuring security settings, networking, troubleshooting, and removing malware. Ace your exam prep—and build real-world job skills—with lessons, practice tests, evaluation software, and more.

See more resources at **microsoft.com/mspress**
and **microsoft.com/learning**

Windows Server 2008— Resources for Administrators

Windows Server® 2008 Administrator's Companion

Charlie Russel and Sharon Crawford
ISBN 9780735625051

Your comprehensive, one-volume guide to deployment, administration, and support. Delve into core system capabilities and administration topics, including Active Directory®, security issues, disaster planning/recovery, interoperability, IIS 7.0, virtualization, clustering, and performance tuning.

Windows Server 2008 Administrator's Pocket Consultant

William R. Stanek
ISBN 9780735624375

Portable and precise—with the focused information you need for administering server roles, Active Directory, user/group accounts, rights and permissions, file-system management, TCP/IP, DHCP, DNS, printers, network performance, backup, and restoration.

Windows Server 2008 Resource Kit

Microsoft MVPs with Windows Server Team
ISBN 9780735623613

Six volumes! Your definitive resource for deployment and operations—from the experts who know the technology best. Get in-depth technical information on Active Directory, Windows PowerShell™ scripting, advanced administration, networking and network access protection, security administration, IIS, and more—plus an essential toolkit of resources on CD.

Internet Information Services (IIS) 7.0 Administrator's Pocket Consultant

William R. Stanek
ISBN 9780735623644

This pocket-sized guide delivers immediate answers for administering IIS 7.0. Topics include customizing installation; configuration and XML schema; application management; user access and security; Web sites, directories, and content; and performance, backup, and recovery.

Windows PowerShell Step by Step

Ed Wilson
ISBN 9780735623958

Teach yourself the fundamentals of the Windows PowerShell command-line interface and scripting language—one step at a time. Learn to use *cmdlets* and write scripts to manage users, groups, and computers; configure network components; administer Microsoft® Exchange Server 2007; and more. Includes 100+ sample scripts.

Additional Resources for IT Professionals

Windows Server 2008 Virtualization Resource Kit
Robert Larson and Janique Carbone
ISBN 9780735625174

Internet Information Services (IIS) 7.0 Resource Kit
Mike Volodarsky et al. with Microsoft IIS Team
ISBN 9780735624412

Windows® Administration Resource Kit: Productivity Solutions for IT Professionals
Dan Holme
ISBN 9780735624313

Windows Server 2008 Security Resource Kit
Jesper M. Johansson, MVPs, Microsoft Security Team
ISBN 9780735625044

See our complete line of books at: **microsoft.com/mspress**

What do you think of this book?

We want to hear from you!

Do you have a few minutes to participate in a brief online survey?

Microsoft is interested in hearing your feedback so we can continually improve our books and learning resources for you.

To participate in our survey, please visit:

www.microsoft.com/learning/booksurvey/

...and enter this book's ISBN-10 or ISBN-13 number (located above barcode on back cover*). As a thank-you to survey participants in the United States and Canada, each month we'll randomly select five respondents to win one of five $100 gift certificates from a leading online merchant. At the conclusion of the survey, you can enter the drawing by providing your e-mail address, which will be used for prize notification only.

Thanks in advance for your input. Your opinion counts!

* Where to find the ISBN on back cover

ISBN-13: 000-0-0000-0000-0
ISBN-10: 0-0000-0000-0

0 000000 000000

Example only. Each book has unique ISBN.

Microsoft®
Press

No purchase necessary. Void where prohibited. Open only to residents of the 50 United States (includes District of Columbia) and Canada (void in Quebec). For official rules and entry dates see:

www.microsoft.com/learning/booksurvey/